PEARSON CUSTOM
BUSINESS RESOURCES

PEARSON

This special edition published in cooperation with Pearson Learning Solutions.

Printed in the United States of America.
V092
Please visit our website at *www.pearsonlearningsolutions.com*.

Attention bookstores: For permission to return any unsold stock, contact us at *pe-uscustomreturns@pearson.com*.

Pearson Learning Solutions, 501 Boylston Street, Suite 900, Boston, MA 02116
A Pearson Education Company
www.pearsoned.com

ISBN 10: 1-269-23962-7
ISBN 13: 978-1-269-23962-2

PEARSON ·

Table of Contents

Managers and Management

Managers and Management

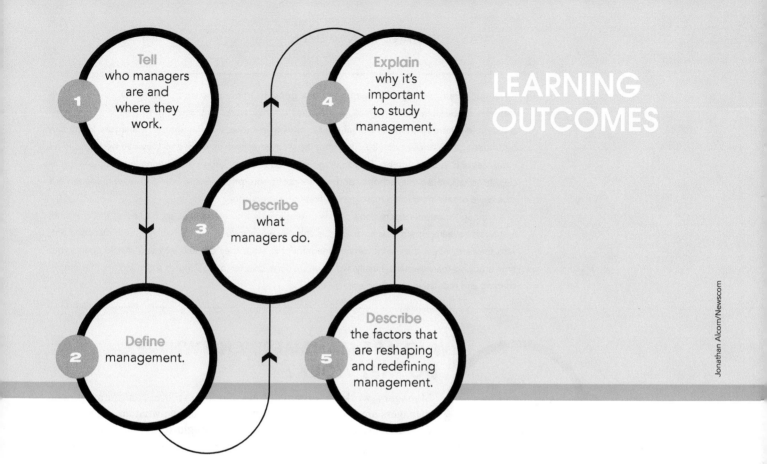

1. **Tell** who managers are and where they work.

2. **Define** management.

3. **Describe** what managers do.

4. **Explain** why it's important to study management.

5. **Describe** the factors that are reshaping and redefining management.

Saving the World

"Imagine what life would be like if your product were never finished, if your work were never done, if your market shifted 30 times a day."[1] Sounds pretty crazy, doesn't it? However, the computer-virus hunters at Symantec Corporation don't have to imagine . . . that's the reality of their daily work. At the company's well-obscured Dublin facility (one of three around the globe), operations manager Patrick Fitzgerald must keep his engineers and researchers focused 24/7 on identifying and combating what the bad guys are throwing out there. Right now, they're trying to stay ahead of the biggest virus threat, Stuxnet, which targets computer systems running the environmental controls in industrial facilities, such as temperature in power plants, pressure in pipelines, automated timing, and so forth. The consequences of someone intent on doing evil getting control over such critical functions could be disastrous. That's why the virus hunters' work is never done. And it's why those who manage the virus hunters have such a challenging job.

Symantec's Patrick Fitzgerald seems to be a good example of a successful manager—that is, a manager successfully guiding employees as they do their work—in today's world. The key word here is example. There's no one universal model of what a successful manager is. Managers today can be under age 18 or over age 80. They may be women as well as men, and they can be found in all industries and in all countries. They manage small businesses, large corporations, government agencies, hospitals, museums, schools, and not-for-profit enterprises. Some hold top-level management jobs while others are middle managers or first-line supervisors.

Although most managers don't deal with employees who could, indeed, be saving the world, all managers have important jobs to do. In this chapter, we introduce you to managers and management: who they are, where they work, what management is, what they do, and why you should spend your time studying management. Finally, we'll wrap up the chapter by looking at some factors that are reshaping and redefining management.

WHO ARE MANAGERS AND WHERE DO THEY WORK?

Tell who managers are and where they work.

1

Managers work in organizations. So before we can identify who managers are and what they do, we need to define what an **organization** is: a deliberate arrangement of people brought together to accomplish some specific purpose. Your college or university is an organization. So are the United Way, your neighborhood convenience store, the Dallas Cowboys football team, fraternities and sororities, the Cleveland Clinic, and global companies such as Nestlé, Nokia, and Nissan. These organizations share three common characteristics. (See Exhibit 1.)

What Three Characteristics Do All Organizations Share?

The first characteristic of an organization is that it has a distinct purpose, which is typically expressed in terms of a goal or set of goals. For example, Bob Iger, Disney's president and CEO, has said his company's goal is to "focus on what creates the most value for our shareholders by delivering high-quality creative content and experiences, balancing respect for our legacy with the demand to be innovative, and maintaining the integrity of our people and products."[2] That purpose or goal can only be achieved with people, which is the second common characteristic of organizations. An organization's people make decisions and engage in work activities to make the goal(s) a reality. Finally, the third characteristic is that all organizations develop a deliberate and systematic structure that defines and limits the behavior of its members. Within that structure, rules and regulations might guide what people can or cannot do, some members will

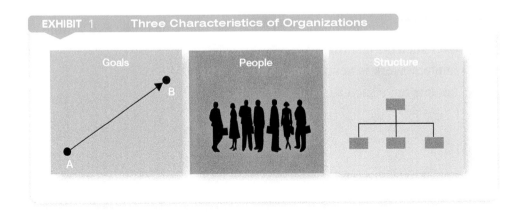

EXHIBIT 1   Three Characteristics of Organizations

Goals   People   Structure

supervise other members, work teams might be formed, or job descriptions might be created so organizational members know what they're supposed to do.

How Are Managers Different from Nonmanagerial Employees?

Although managers work in organizations, not everyone who works in an organization is a manager. For simplicity's sake, we'll divide organizational members into two categories: nonmanagerial employees and managers. Nonmanagerial employees are people who work directly on a job or task and have no responsibility for overseeing the work of others. The employees who ring up your sale at Home Depot, make your burrito at Chipotle, or process your course registration in your college's registrar's office are all nonmanagerial employees. These nonmanagerial employees may be referred to by names such as associates, team members, contributors, or even employee partners. Managers, on the other hand, are individuals in an organization who direct and oversee the activities of other people in the organization. This distinction doesn't mean, however, that managers don't ever work directly on tasks. Some managers do have work duties not directly related to overseeing the activities of others. For example, regional sales managers for Motorola also have responsibilities in servicing some customer accounts in addition to overseeing the activities of the other sales associates in their territories.

What Titles Do Managers Have?

Identifying exactly who the managers are in an organization isn't difficult, but be aware that they can have a variety of titles. Managers are usually classified as top, middle, or first-line. (See Exhibit 2.) Top managers are those at or near the top of an organization. For instance, as the CEO of Kraft Foods Inc., Irene Rosenfeld is responsible for making decisions about the direction of the organization and establishing policies and philosophies that affect all organizational members. Top managers typically have titles such as vice president, president, chancellor, managing director, chief operating officer, chief executive officer, or chairperson of the board. Middle managers are those managers found between the lowest and top levels of the organization. For example, the plant manager at the Kraft manufacturing facility in Springfield, Missouri, is a middle manager. These individuals often manage other managers and maybe some nonmanagerial employees and are typically responsible for translating the goals set by top managers into specific details that lower-level managers will

RIGHT ? OR WRONG

Managers at all levels have to deal with ethical dilemmas and those ethical dilemmas are found in all kinds of circumstances. For instance, New York Yankees shortstop Derek Jeter, who is regarded as an upstanding and outstanding player in Major League Baseball, admitted that in a September 2010 game against the Tampa Bay Devil Rays he faked being hit by a pitch in order to get on base.[3] According to game rules, a hit batter automatically moves to first base. In this case, the ball actually hit the knob of Jeter's bat, but he acted as if the pitch had actually struck him. Jeter later scored a run, although the Yankees ultimately lost the game. Such ethical dilemmas are part and parcel of being a manager and although they're not easy, you'll learn how to recognize such dilemmas and appropriate ways of responding.

Think About:

- What do you think? Were Jeter's actions acceptable (i.e., ethical)?

- Does the fact that theatrics are part of all sports competitions make it acceptable?

- Was it the umpire's "fault" for missing the call?

- Did the team manager have any responsibility to respond to Jeter's action?

- What if the Yankees had actually won the game by one run? Would that make a difference in how you feel about this?

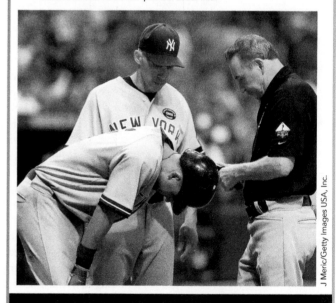

J Meric/Getty Images USA, Inc.

---

organization
A systematic arrangement of people brought together to accomplish some specific purpose

nonmanagerial employees
People who work directly on a job or task and have no responsibility for overseeing the work of others

managers
Individuals in an organization who direct the activities of others

top managers
Individuals who are responsible for making decisions about the direction of the organization and establishing policies that affect all organizational members

middle managers
Individuals who are typically responsible for translating goals set by top managers into specific details that lower-level managers will see get done

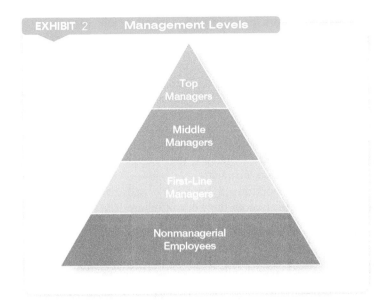

EXHIBIT 2   Management Levels

Top Managers

Middle Managers

First-Line Managers

Nonmanagerial Employees

see get done. Middle managers may have such titles as department or agency head, project leader, unit chief, district manager, division manager, or store manager. **First-line managers** are those individuals responsible for directing the day-to-day activities of nonmanagerial employees. For example, the third-shift manager at the Kraft manufacturing facility in Springfield is a first-line manager. First-line managers are often called supervisors, team leaders, coaches, shift managers, or unit coordinators.

WHAT IS MANAGEMENT?

2 Define management.

Simply speaking, management is what managers do. But that simple statement doesn't tell us much. A better explanation is that **management** is the process of getting things done, effectively and efficiently, with and through other people. We need to look closer at some key words in this definition.

A *process* refers to a set of ongoing and interrelated activities. In our definition of management, it refers to the primary activities or functions that managers perform. We'll explore these functions more in the next section.

Efficiency and effectiveness have to do with the work being done and how it's being done. **Efficiency** means doing a task correctly ("doing things right") and getting the most output from the least amount of inputs. Because managers deal with scarce inputs—including resources such as people, money, and equipment—they're concerned with the efficient use of those resources. Managers want to minimize resource usage and thus resource costs.

It's not enough, however, just to be efficient. Managers are also concerned with completing activities. In management terms, we call this **effectiveness**. Effectiveness means "doing the right things" by doing those work tasks that help the organization reach its goals. Whereas efficiency is concerned with the *means* of getting things done, effectiveness is concerned with the *ends*, or attainment of organizational goals. (See Exhibit 3.)

Although *efficiency* and *effectiveness* are different, they are interrelated. For instance, it's easier to be effective if you ignore efficiency. If Hewlett-Packard disregarded labor and material input costs, it could produce more sophisticated and longer-lasting toner cartridges for its laser printers. Similarly, some government agencies have been regularly criticized for being reasonably effective but extremely inefficient. Our conclusion: Poor management is most often due to both inefficiency and ineffectiveness or to effectiveness achieved without regard for efficiency. Good management is concerned with both attaining goals (effectiveness) and doing so as efficiently as possible.

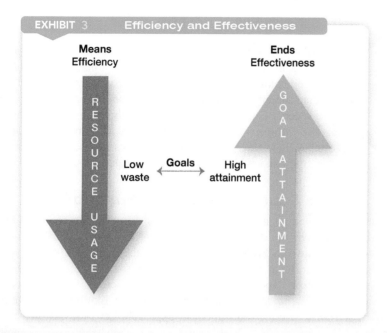

EXHIBIT 3   Efficiency and Effectiveness

Means
Efficiency

Ends
Effectiveness

RESOURCE USAGE

GOAL ATTAINMENT

Low waste ←→ **Goals** ←→ High attainment

From the Past to the Present

Where did the terms *management* or *manager* originate?[4] The terms are actually centuries old. One source says that the word *manager* originated in 1588 to describe one who manages. The specific use of the word as "one who conducts a house of business or public institution" is said to have originated in 1705. Another source says that the origin (1555–1565) is from the word *maneggiare*, which meant to handle or train horses, and was a derivative of the word *mano*, which is from the Latin word for hand, *manus*. That origin arose from the way that horses were guided, controlled, or directed where to go—that is, through using one's hand. As used in the way we've defined it in terms of overseeing and directing organizational members, however, the words *management* and *manager* are more appropriate to the early-twentieth-century time period. Peter Drucker, the late management writer, studied and wrote about management for more than 50 years. He said, "When the first business schools in the United States opened around the turn of the twentieth century, they did not offer a single course in management. At about that same time, the word 'management' was first popularized by Frederick Winslow Taylor." Let's look at what Taylor contributed to what we know about management today.

In 1911, Taylor's book *Principles of Scientific Management* was published. Its contents were widely embraced by managers around the world. The book described the theory of scientific management: the use of scientific methods to define the "one best way" for a job to be done. Taylor worked at the Midvale and Bethlehem Steel Companies in Pennsylvania. As a mechanical engineer with a Quaker and Puritan background, he was continually appalled by workers' inefficiencies. Employees used vastly different techniques to do the same job. They often "took it easy" on the job,

and Taylor believed that worker output was only about one-third of what was possible. Virtually no work standards existed. Workers were placed in jobs with little or no concern for matching their abilities and aptitudes with the tasks they were required to do. Taylor set out to remedy that by applying the scientific method to shop-floor jobs. He spent more than two decades passionately pursuing the "one best way" for such jobs to be done. Based on his groundbreaking studies of manual workers using scientific principles, Taylor became known as the "father" of scientific management. His ideas spread in the United States and to other countries and inspired others to study and develop methods of scientific management. These early management writers paved the way for our study of management, an endeavor that continues today.

Think About:

- How do the origins of the words *manager* and *management* relate to what we know about managers and management today?
- What kind of workplace do you think Taylor would create?
- How have Taylor's views contributed to how management is practiced today?
- Could scientific management principles help you be more efficient? Choose a task you do regularly (such as laundry, grocery shopping, studying for exams, etc.). Analyze it by writing down the steps involved in completing that task. See if there are activities that could be combined or eliminated. Find the "one best way" to do this task. And the next time you have to do this task, try the scientifically managed way! See if you become more efficient—keeping in mind that changing habits isn't easy to do.

---

first-line managers
Supervisors responsible for directing the day-to-day activities of nonmanagerial employees

management
The process of getting things done, effectively and efficiently, through and with other people

efficiency
Doing things right, or getting the most output from the least amount of inputs

effectiveness
Doing the right things, or completing activities so that organizational goals are attained

scientific management
The use of scientific methods to define the "one best way" for a job to be done

3 Describe what managers do.

Describing what managers do isn't easy because, just as no organizations are alike, neither are managers' jobs. Despite that fact, managers do share some common job elements, whether the manager is a head nurse in the cardiac surgery unit of the Cleveland Clinic overseeing a staff of critical care specialists or the president of O'Reilly Automotive establishing goals for the company's more than 44,000 team members. Management researchers have developed three approaches to describe what managers do: functions, roles, and skills/competencies. Let's look at each.

What Are the Four Management Functions?

According to the functions approach, managers perform certain activities or functions as they direct and oversee others' work. What are these functions? In the early part of the twentieth century, a French industrialist by the name of Henri Fayol proposed that all managers perform five management activities: plan, organize, command, coordinate, and control.[5] Today, these management functions have been condensed to four: planning, organizing, leading, and controlling. (See Exhibit 4.) Most management textbooks continue to use the four functions approach. Let's look briefly at each function.

Because organizations exist to achieve some purpose, someone has to define that purpose and find ways to achieve it. A manager is that someone and does this by planning. **Planning** includes defining goals, establishing strategy, and developing plans to

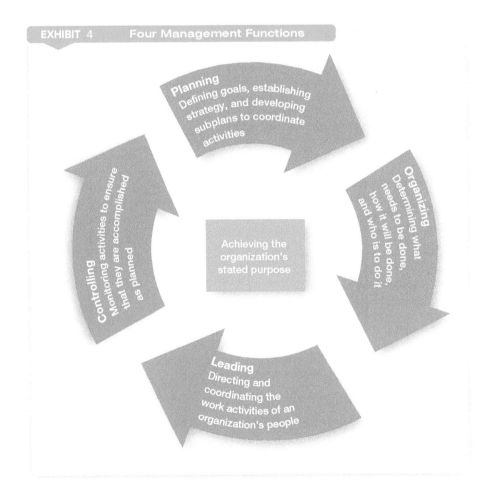

EXHIBIT 4   Four Management Functions

Planning — Defining goals, establishing strategy, and developing subplans to coordinate activities

Organizing — Determining what needs to be done, how it will be done, and who is to do it

Leading — Directing and coordinating the work activities of an organization's people

Controlling — Monitoring activities to ensure that they are accomplished as planned

Achieving the organization's stated purpose

coordinate activities. Setting goals, establishing strategy, and developing plans ensures that the work to be done is kept in proper focus and helps organizational members keep their attention on what is most important.

Managers are also responsible for arranging and structuring work to accomplish the organization's goals. This function is called organizing. Organizing includes determining what tasks are to be done and by whom, how tasks are to be grouped, who reports to whom, and who will make decisions.

We know that every organization has people. And it's part of a manager's job to direct and coordinate the work activities of those people. This is the leading function. When managers motivate employees, direct the activities of others, select the most effective communication channel, or resolve conflicts among members, they're leading.

The fourth and final management function is controlling, which involves monitoring, comparing, and correcting work performance. After the goals are set, the plans formulated, the structural arrangements determined, and the people hired, trained, and motivated, there has to be some evaluation to see if things are going as planned. Any significant deviations will require that the manager get work back on track.

Just how well does the functions approach describe what managers do? Is it an accurate description of what managers actually do? Some have argued that it isn't.[6] So, let's look at another perspective on describing what managers do.

What Are Management Roles?

Fayol's original description of management functions wasn't derived from careful surveys of managers in organizations. Rather, it simply represented his observations and experiences in the French mining industry. In the late 1960s, Henry Mintzberg did an empirical study of five chief executives at work.[7] What he discovered challenged long-held notions about the manager's job. For instance, in contrast to the predominant view that managers were reflective thinkers who carefully and systematically processed information before making decisions, Mintzberg found that the managers he studied engaged in a number of varied, unpatterned, and short-duration activities. These managers had little time for reflective thinking because they encountered constant interruptions and their activities often lasted less than nine minutes. In addition to these insights, Mintzberg provided a categorization scheme for defining what managers do based on the managerial roles they use at work. These managerial roles referred to specific categories of managerial actions or behaviors expected of a manager. (To help you better understand this concept, think of the different roles you play—such as student, employee, volunteer, bowling team member, sibling, and so forth—and the different things you're expected to do in those roles.)

As president and CEO of the Johnny Rockets restaurant chain, John Fuller develops plans to achieve the company's widespread expansion strategy. Fuller's vision is to extend the chain's focus of providing customers with an entertaining dining experience and classic American food such as burgers, fries, and shakes. Fuller plans to increase the chain's market penetration by launching new store concepts and by entering new domestic and international markets such as India and South Korea. Concepts for new restaurants include sports lounges, mobile kitchens, and a model that offers a streamlined menu and a create-your-own-burger option. Fuller is shown here with Johnny Rockets restaurant servers who are known for dancing on the job.

o44/Newscom

---

planning
Includes defining goals, establishing strategy, and developing plans to coordinate activities

organizing
Includes determining what tasks are to be done, who is to do them, how the tasks are to be grouped, who reports to whom, and who will make decisions

leading
Includes motivating employees, directing the activities of others, selecting the most effective communication channel, and resolving conflicts

controlling
Includes monitoring performance, comparing it with goals, and correcting any significant deviations

managerial roles
Specific categories of managerial behavior; often grouped around interpersonal relationships, information transfer, and decision making

Mintzberg concluded that managers perform 10 different but interrelated roles. These 10 roles, as shown in Exhibit 5, are grouped around interpersonal relationships, the transfer of information, and decision making. The interpersonal roles are ones that involve people (subordinates and persons outside the organization) and other duties that are ceremonial and symbolic in nature. The three interpersonal roles are figurehead, leader, and liaison. The informational roles involve collecting, receiving, and disseminating information. The three information roles include monitor, disseminator, and spokesperson. Finally, the decisional roles entail making decisions or choices. The four decisional roles are entrepreneur, disturbance handler, resource allocator, and negotiator.

Recently, Mintzberg completed another intensive study of managers at work and concluded that, "Basically, managing is about influencing action. It's about helping organizations and units to get things done, which means action."[8] Based on his observations, Mintzberg said managers do this in three ways: (1) by managing actions directly (for instance, negotiating contracts, managing projects, etc.), (2) by managing people who take action (for example, motivating them, building teams, enhancing the organization's culture, etc.), or (3) by managing information that propels people to take action (using budgets, goals, task delegation, etc.). According to Mintzberg, a manager has two roles—framing, which defines how a manager approaches his or her job; and scheduling, which "brings the frame to life" through the distinct tasks the manager does. A manager "performs" these roles while managing actions directly, managing people who take action, or managing information. Mintzberg's newest study gives us additional insights on the manager's job, adding to our understanding of what it is that managers do.

So which approach is better—functions or roles? Although each does a good job of describing what managers do, the functions approach still seems to be the generally accepted way of describing the manager's job. Its continued popularity is a tribute to its clarity and simplicity. "The classical functions provide clear and discrete methods of classifying the thousands of activities that managers carry out and the techniques they use in terms of the functions they perform for the achievement of goals."[9] However, Mintzberg's initial roles approach and newly developed model of managing do offer us other insights into what managers do.

| EXHIBIT 5 | Mintzberg's Managerial Roles |

INTERPERSONAL ROLES

- Figurehead
- Leader
- Liaison

INFORMATIONAL ROLES

- Monitor
- Disseminator
- Spokesperson

DECISIONAL ROLES

- Entrepreneur
- Disturbance handler
- Resource allocator
- Negotiator

Source: Based on Mintzberg, Henry, *The Nature of Managerial Work*, 1st edition, © 1973.

What Skills and Competencies Do Managers Need?

The final approach we're going to look at for describing what managers do is by looking at the skills and competencies they need in managing. Dell Inc. is a company that understands the importance of management skills.[10] Its first-line managers go through an intensive five-day offsite skills training program. One of the company's directors of learning and development thought this was the best way to develop "leaders who can build that strong relationship with their front-line employees." What have the supervisors learned from the skills training? Some things mentioned included how to communicate more effectively and how to refrain from jumping to conclusions when discussing a problem with a worker. Management researcher Robert L. Katz and others have proposed that managers must possess and use four critical management skills in managing.[11]

Conceptual skills are the skills managers use to analyze and diagnose complex situations. They help managers see how things fit together and facilitate making good decisions. Interpersonal skills are those skills involved with working well with other people both individually and in groups. Because managers get things done with and through other people, they must have good interpersonal skills to communicate, motivate, mentor, and delegate. Additionally, all managers need technical skills, which are the job-specific knowledge and techniques needed to perform work tasks. These abilities are based on specialized knowledge or expertise. For top-level managers, these abilities tend to be related to knowledge of the industry and a general understanding of the organization's processes and products. For middle- and lower-level managers, these abilities are related to the specialized knowledge required in the areas where they work—finance, human resources, marketing, computer systems, manufacturing, information technology, and so forth. Finally, managers need and use political skills to build a power base and establish the right connections. Organizations are political arenas in which people compete for resources. Managers who have and know how to use political skills tend to be better at getting resources for their groups.

More recent studies have focused on the competencies managers need in their positions as important contributors to organizational success. One such study identified nine managerial competencies including: *traditional functions* (encompassing tasks such as decision making, short-term planning, goal setting, monitoring, team building, etc.); *task orientation* (including elements such as urgency, decisiveness, initiative, etc.); *personal orientation* (including things such as compassion, assertiveness, politeness, customer focus, etc.); *dependability* (involving aspects such as personal responsibility, trustworthiness, loyalty, professionalism, etc.); *open-mindedness* (encompassing elements such as tolerance, adaptability, creative thinking, etc.); *emotional control*, which included both resilience and stress management; *communication* (including aspects such as listening, oral communication, public presentation, etc.); *developing self and others* (including tasks such as performance assessment, self-development, providing developmental feedback, etc.); and *occupational acumen and concerns* (involving aspects such as technical proficiency, being concerned with quality and quantity, financial concern, etc.).[12] As you can see from this list of competencies, "what" a manager does is quite broad and varied.

---

interpersonal roles
Involving people (subordinates and persons outside the organization) and other duties that are ceremonial and symbolic in nature

informational roles
Involving collecting, receiving, and disseminating information

decisional roles
Entailing making decisions or choices

conceptual skills
A manager's ability to analyze and diagnose complex situations

interpersonal skills
A manager's ability to work with, understand, mentor, and motivate others, both individually and in groups

technical skills
Job-specific knowledge and techniques needed to perform work tasks

political skills
A manager's ability to build a power base and establish the right connections

Finally, a recent study that examined the work of some 8,600 managers found that what these managers did could be put into three categories of competencies: conceptual, interpersonal, and technical/administrative.[13] As you can see, these research findings agree with the list of management skills identified by Katz and others.

Is the Manager's Job Universal?

So far, we've discussed the manager's job as if it were a generic activity. That is, a manager is a manager regardless of where he or she manages. If management is truly a generic discipline, then what a manager does should be essentially the same whether he or she is a top-level executive or a first-line supervisor, in a business firm or a government agency; in a large corporation or a small business; or located in Paris, Texas, or Paris, France. Is that the case? Let's take a closer look at the generic issue.

LEVEL IN THE ORGANIZATION. Although a supervisor in a claims department at Aetna may not do exactly the same things that the president of Aetna does, it doesn't mean that their jobs are inherently different. The differences are of degree and emphasis but not of activity.

As managers move up in the organization, they do more planning and less direct overseeing of others. (See Exhibit 6.) All managers, regardless of level, make decisions. They do planning, organizing, leading, and controlling activities, but the amount of time they give to each activity is not necessarily constant. In addition, the content of the managerial activities changes with the manager's level. For example, top managers are concerned with designing the overall organization's structure, whereas lower-level managers focus on designing the jobs of individuals and work groups.

PROFIT VERSUS NOT-FOR-PROFIT. Does a manager who works for the U.S. Postal Service, the Memorial Sloan-Kettering Cancer Center, or the Red Cross do the same things that a manager at Amazon or Symantec does? That is, is the manager's job the same in both profit and not-for-profit organizations? The answer, for the most part, is yes. All managers make decisions, set goals, create workable organization structures, hire and motivate employees, secure legitimacy for their organization's existence, and

---

TECHNOLOGY AND THE MANAGER'S JOB

IS IT STILL MANAGING WHEN WHAT YOU'RE MANAGING ARE ROBOTS?

"The office of tomorrow is likely to include workers that are faster, smarter, more responsible—and happen to be robots."[14] Are you at all surprised by this statement? Although robots have been used in factory and industrial settings for a long time, it's becoming more common to find robots in the office and it's bringing about new ways of looking at how work is done and at what and how managers manage. So what *would* the manager's job be like managing robots? And even more intriguing is how these "workers" might affect how human coworkers interact with them.

As machines have become smarter and smarter—did any of you watch Watson take on the human *Jeopardy* challengers—researchers have been looking at human-machine interaction and "how people relate to the increasingly smart devices that surround them." One conclusion is that people find it easy to bond with a robot,

even one that doesn't look or sound anything like a real person. "All a robot had to do was move around in a purposeful way, and people thought of it, in some ways, as a coworker." People will give their robots names and even can describe the robot's moods and tendencies. As telepresence robots become more common, the humanness becomes even more evident. For example, when Erwin Deininger, the electrical engineer at Reimers Electra Steam, a small company in Clear Brook, Virginia, moved to the Dominican Republic when his wife's job transferred her there, he was able to still be "present" at the company via his VGo robot. Now Deininger "wheels easily from desk to desk and around the shop floor, answering questions and inspecting designs." The company's president was "pleasantly surprised at how useful the robot has proven" and even more surprised at how he acts around it. "He finds it hard to not think of the robot as, in a very

real sense, Deininger himself. After a while, he says, it's not a robot anymore."

There's no doubt that robot technology will continue to be incorporated into organizational settings. The manager's job will become even more exciting and challenging as humans and machines work together to accomplish the organization's goals.

Think About:

· Look back at our definitions of manager and management. Do they fit the organizational office setting described here? Explain.

· Do some research on telepresence and telepresence robots. How might this technology change how workers and managers work together?

· What's your response to the title of this box: *Is it still managing when what you're managing are robots?* Discuss.

· If you had to "manage" people and robots, how do you think your job as manager might be different than what the chapter describes? (Think in terms of functions, roles, and skills/competencies.)

EXHIBIT 6 Management Activities by Organizational Level

First-Level Managers
- Organizing 24%
- Planning 15%
- Controlling 10%
- Leading 51%

Middle Managers
- Organizing 33%
- Planning 18%
- Controlling 13%
- Leading 36%

Top Managers
- Planning 28%
- Organizing 36%
- Controlling 14%
- Leading 22%

Source: Based on T. A. Mahoney, T. H. Jerdee, and S. J. Carroll, "The Job(s) of Management," *Industrial Relations*, 4, no. 2 (1965), p. 103.

develop internal political support in order to implement programs. Of course, the most important difference between the two is how performance is measured. Profit, or the "bottom line," is an unambiguous measure of a business organization's effectiveness. Not-for-profit organizations don't have such a universal measure, making performance measurement more difficult. But don't interpret this difference to mean that managers in those organizations can ignore the financial side of their operations. Even not-for-profit organizations need to make money to continue operating. It's just that in not-for-profit organizations, "making a profit" for the "owners" is not the primary focus.

SIZE OF ORGANIZATION. Would you expect the job of a manager in a local print shop that employs 12 people to be different from that of a manager who runs a 1,200-person printing facility for the *Washington Times*? This question is best answered by looking at the jobs of managers in small businesses and comparing them with our previous discussion of managerial roles. First, however, let's define a small business.

No commonly agreed-upon definition of a small business is available because different criteria are used to define *small*. For example, an organization can be classified as a small business using such criteria as number of employees, annual sales, or total assets. For our purposes, we'll describe a small business as an independent business having fewer than 500 employees that doesn't necessarily engage in any new or innovative practices and has relatively little impact on its industry.[15] So, is the job of managing a small business different from that of managing a large one? Some differences appear to exist. As Exhibit 7 shows, the small business manager's

Like many small business managers, Jessica and Emily Leung spend much of their time in the entrepreneurial activities of searching for new opportunities and stimulating change. The twin sisters launched their e-commerce business Hey Lady Shoes, a designer shoe company to market footwear that is stylish yet comfortable, or, as they put it, "to have a killer shoe that isn't a killer shoe." In looking for new business opportunities, the Hey Lady founders are shown here at a two-day technical business conference where they joined hundreds of other small business owners to learn how to apply new technology such as social media and other online tools to grow their business.

w49/Newscom

small business
An independent business having fewer than 500 employees that doesn't necessarily engage in any new or innovative practices and has relatively little impact on its industry

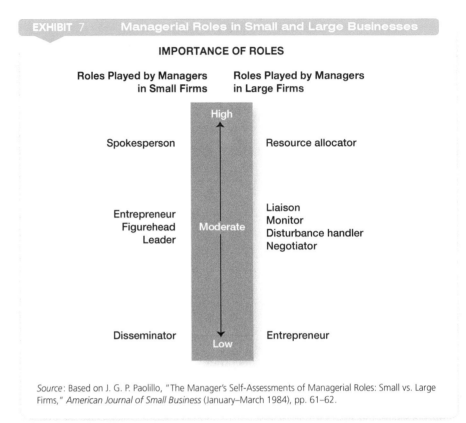

EXHIBIT 7 Managerial Roles in Small and Large Businesses

IMPORTANCE OF ROLES

Source: Based on J. G. P. Paolillo, "The Manager's Self-Assessments of Managerial Roles: Small vs. Large Firms," *American Journal of Small Business* (January–March 1984), pp. 61–62.

most important role is that of spokesperson. He or she spends a great deal of time performing outwardly directed actions such as meeting with customers, arranging financing with bankers, searching for new opportunities, and stimulating change. In contrast, the most important concerns of a manager in a large organization are directed internally—deciding which organizational units get what available resources and how much of them. Accordingly, the entrepreneurial role—looking for business opportunities and planning activities for performance improvement—appears to be least important to managers in large firms, especially among first-level and middle managers.

Compared with a manager in a large organization, a small business manager is more likely to be a generalist. His or her job will combine the activities of a large corporation's chief executive with many of the day-to-day activities undertaken by a first-line supervisor. Moreover, the structure and formality that characterize a manager's job in a large organization tend to give way to informality in small firms. Planning is less likely to be a carefully orchestrated ritual. The organization's design will be less complex and structured, and control in the small business will rely more on direct observation than on sophisticated, computerized monitoring systems. Again, as with organizational level, we see differences in degree and emphasis but not in the activities that managers do. Managers in both small and large organizations perform essentially the same activities, but how they go about those activities and the proportion of time they spend on each are different.

MANAGEMENT CONCEPTS AND NATIONAL BORDERS. The last generic issue concerns whether management concepts are transferable across national borders. If managerial concepts were completely generic, they would also apply universally in any country in the world, regardless of economic, social, political, or cultural differences. Studies that have compared managerial practices between countries have not generally supported the universality of management concepts. At this point, it's important for you to understand that most of the concepts discussed apply primarily to the United States, Canada, Great Britain, Australia, and other English-speaking countries. Managers likely will have to modify these concepts if they want to apply them in India, China, Chile, or other countries whose economic, political, social, or cultural environments differ from that of the so-called free-market democracies.

WHY STUDY MANAGEMENT?

At this point in the chapter, you may be wondering why you need to take a management class. Maybe you're majoring in accounting or marketing or information technology and may not understand how studying management is going to help you in your career. Let's look at some reasons why you may want to understand more about management.

Explain why it's important to study management.

4

First, all of us have a vested interest in improving the way organizations are managed. Why? Because we interact with them every day of our lives and an understanding of management offers insights into many organizational aspects. When you renew your driver's license, are you frustrated that a seemingly simple task takes so long? Were you surprised when well-known businesses you thought would never fail went bankrupt or were you angry when entire industries had to rely on government bailout money to survive changing economic conditions? Are you annoyed when you call an airline three times and its representatives quote three different prices for the same trip? Such problems are mostly the result of managers doing a poor job of managing.

Organizations that are well managed—such as Walmart, Apple, Tata, Starbucks, McDonald's, Singapore Airlines, and Google—develop a loyal following and find ways to prosper even in economically challenging times. Poorly managed organizations may find themselves with a declining customer base and reduced revenues and may even have to file for bankruptcy protection. For instance, Gimbel's, W. T. Grant, Hollywood Video, Dave & Barry's, Circuit City, Eastern Airlines, and Enron were once thriving corporations. They employed tens of thousands of people and provided goods and services on a daily basis to hundreds of thousands of customers. Today those companies no longer exist. Poor management did them in. You can begin to recognize poor management and know what good managers should be doing by studying management.

The second reason for studying management is the reality that for most of you, once you graduate from college and begin your career, you will either manage or be managed. For those who plan to be managers, an understanding of management forms the foundation on which to build your management skills and abilities. For those of you who don't see yourself managing, you're still likely to have to work with managers. Also, assuming that you'll have to work for a living and recognizing that you're likely to work in an organization, you'll probably have some managerial responsibilities even if you're not a manager. Our experience tells us that you can gain a great deal of insight into the way your boss (and fellow employees) behave and how organizations function by studying management. Our point is that you don't have to aspire to be a manager to gain valuable information from a course in management.

In this photo, Starbucks managers and employees cheer their fellow workers as they compete in the Ambassador's Cup contest at company headquarters in Seattle to determine which employees are the best coffee experts. The study of management is important because it provides insights into successful organizations like Starbucks that are well-managed and have developed a loyal customer base as well as unsuccessful organizations that are poorly managed and lose customers. For students pursuing a career in management and for those who will be managed, the study of management provides knowledge about manager skills and responsibilities, how organizations function, and how people behave in the workplace.

Erika Schultz/Newscom

Describe the factors that are reshaping and redefining management.

5

WHAT FACTORS ARE RESHAPING AND REDEFINING MANAGEMENT?

"At Best Buy's headquarters, more than 60 percent of employees are now judged only on tasks or results. Salaried people put in as much time as it takes to do their work. Those employees report better relationships with family and friends, more company loyalty, and more focus and energy. Productivity has increased by 35 percent. Employees say they don't know whether they work fewer hours—they've stopped counting. Perhaps more important, they're finding new ways to become efficient."[17] Welcome to the new world of management!

In today's world, managers are dealing with changing workplaces, ethical and trust issues, global economic and political uncertainties, and changing technology. For example, although people still need to purchase food during tough economic times, grocery stores have struggled to retain their customer base and to keep costs down. At Publix Super Markets, the large grocery chain in the southeastern United States, everyone, including managers, is looking for ways to better serve customers. The company's president, Todd Jones, who started his career bagging groceries at a Publix in New Smyrna Beach, Florida, is guiding the company through these challenges by keeping everyone's focus— from baggers to checkers to stockers—on exceptional customer service.[18] Or consider the management challenges faced by Roger Oglesby, the then-publisher and editor of the *Seattle Post-Intelligencer* (P-I). The P-I, like many other newspapers, had struggled to find a way to be successful in an industry that was losing readers and revenues at an alarming rate. The decision was made to go all-digital and in early 2009, the P-I became an Internet-only news source. Difficult actions followed as the news staff was reduced from 165 to about 20 people. In its new "life" as a digital news source, the organization faces other challenges—challenges for Michelle Nicolosi, now the manager who needs to plan, organize, lead, and control in this changed environment.[19]

Managers everywhere are likely to have to manage in changing circumstances, and the fact is that *how* managers manage is changing. Throughout the rest of this book, we'll be discussing these changes and how they're affecting the way managers plan, organize, lead, and control. We want to highlight two of these changes: the increasing importance of customers and innovation.

The success of Trader Joe's specialty retail chain is built on outstanding customer service. Understanding that employee attitudes and behaviors play a big role in customer satisfaction, the company hires people who are warm, friendly, energetic, enthusiastic, and fun-loving. New hires receive customer service training in product knowledge, communication skills, teamwork, and leadership. The employees shown here beginning their day with stretching exercises in preparation of a new store opening embody the attitudes and behaviors focused on listening to customers and responding to their requests. As frontline employees, they are the driving force behind Trader Joe's high customer satisfaction ratings.

Why Are Customers Important to the Manager's Job?

John Chambers, CEO of Cisco Systems, likes to listen to voice mails forwarded to him from dissatisfied customers. He said, "E-mail would be more efficient, but I want to hear the emotion, I want to hear the frustration, I want to hear the caller's level of comfort with the strategy we're employing. I can't get that through e-mail."[20] This is a manager who understands the importance of customers. Organizations need customers. Without them, most organizations would cease to exist. Yet, focusing on the customer has long been thought to be the responsibility of marketing people. "Let the marketers worry about the customers" is how many managers felt. We're discovering, however, that employee attitudes and behaviors play a big role in customer satisfaction. Think of the times you've been treated poorly (or superbly) by an employee during a service encounter and how that affected the way you felt about the situation.

Managers are recognizing that delivering consistent high-quality customer service is essential for survival and success in today's competitive environment and that employees are an important part of that equation.[21] The implication is clear—they must create a customer-responsive organization where employees are friendly and courteous, accessible, knowledgeable, prompt in responding to customer needs, and willing to do what's necessary to please the customer.[22]

Why Is Innovation Important to the Manager's Job?

"Nothing is more risky than not innovating."[23] Innovation means doing things differently, exploring new territory, and taking risks. And innovation isn't just for high-tech or other technologically sophisticated organizations; innovative efforts are needed in all types of organizations. You'd expect companies like Apple, Facebook, Google, and Nike to be on a list of the world's 50 most innovative companies.[24] But what about the likes of ESPN, the sports programming channel? It has been a leader in integrating new technology with products like ESPN 3D, the first 3-D channel on cable; live streaming on-demand video on Microsoft's Xbox Live; and use of virtual technology to highlight various sports events, people, and feats. Or what about donorschoose.org, an online way to connect kids who need school supplies with donors who want to help. In 2010, the number of donors on the Web site grew to 250,000, who gave away some $30 million to support 60,000 classroom projects. In today's challenging environment, innovation *is* critical and managers need to understand what, when, where, how, and why innovation can be fostered and encouraged throughout an organization. For example, during a presentation by the manager in charge of Walmart's global business, he explained his recipe for success (personal and organizational) as continually looking for new ways to do his job better; that is, to be innovative. Managers not only need to be innovative personally, but encourage their employees to be innovative.

As you can see, being a manager is both challenging and exciting. One thing we feel strongly about is that managers do matter to organizations. The Gallup Organization, which has polled millions of employees and tens of thousands of managers, has found that the single most important variable in employee productivity and loyalty isn't pay or benefits or workplace environment; it's the quality of the relationship between employees and their direct supervisors. Gallup also found that relationship with their manager is the largest factor in employee engagement—which is when employees are connected to, satisfied with, and enthusiastic about their jobs—accounting for at least 70 percent of an employee's level of engagement.[25] Recently, however, one factor that has affected how employees view their manager is the lingering global recession. For instance, a report from Towers Watson, a global consulting firm, found that "relationship with supervisor/manager" was the top-ranked reason *employers* gave for why employees leave an organization. However, the manager relationship wasn't even in the top five reasons given by *employees,* who cited factors such as stress levels and base pay.[26] Since the economic downturn has threatened the very survival of organizations, employees may be more concerned with that and less concerned with their managers. However, Towers Watson also found that the way a company manages its people can significantly affect its financial performance.[27] What can we conclude from such reports? That managers *do* matter and will continue to matter to organizations!

employee engagement
When employees are connected to, satisfied with, and enthusiastic about their jobs

Review

1 **Tell who managers are and where they work.** Managers are individuals who work in an organization directing and overseeing the activities of other people. Managers are usually classified as top, middle, or first-line. Organizations, which are where managers work, have three characteristics: goals, people, and a deliberate structure.

2 **Define management.** Management is the process of getting things done, effectively and efficiently, with and through other people. Efficiency means doing a task correctly ("doing things right") and getting the most output from the least amount of inputs. Effectiveness means "doing the right things" by doing those work tasks that help the organization reach its goals.

3 **Describe what managers do.** What managers do can be described using three approaches: functions, roles, and skills/competencies. The functions approach says that managers perform four functions: planning, organizing, leading, and controlling. Mintzberg's roles approach says that what managers do is based on the 10 roles they use at work, which are grouped around interpersonal relationships, the transfer of information, and decision making. The skills/competencies approach looks at what managers do in terms of the skills and competencies they need and use. Four

critical management skills are conceptual, interpersonal, technical, and political. Additional managerial competencies include aspects such as dependability, personal orientation, emotional control, communication, and so forth. All managers plan, organize, lead, and control although how they do these activities and how often they do them may vary according to level in the organization, whether the organization is profit or not-for-profit, the size of the organization, and the geographic location of the organization.

4 **Explain why it's important to study management.** One reason it's important to study management is that all of us interact with organizations daily so we have a vested interest in seeing that organizations are well managed. Another reason is the reality that in your career you will either manage or be managed. By studying management you can gain insights into the way your boss and fellow employees behave and how organizations function.

5 **Describe the factors that are reshaping and redefining management.** In today's world, managers are dealing with changing workplaces, ethical and trust issues, global economic and political uncertainties, and changing technology. Two areas of critical importance to managers are delivering high-quality customer service and encouraging innovative efforts.

MyManagementLab   For more resources, please visit **www.mymanagementlab.com**

UNDERSTANDING THE CHAPTER

1. What is an organization and why are managers important to an organization's success?

2. How do managers differ from nonmanagerial employees?

3. In today's environment, which is more important to organizations—efficiency or effectiveness? Explain your choice.

4. Using any of the popular business periodicals (such as *BusinessWeek, Fortune, Wall Street Journal, Fast Company*), find examples of managers doing each of

the four management functions. Write up a description and explain how these are examples of that function.

5. Is your course instructor a manager? Discuss in terms of planning, organizing, leading, and controlling. Also discuss using Mintzberg's managerial roles approach.

6. Is there one best "style" of management? Why or why not?

7. Is business management a profession? Why or why not? Do some external research in answering this question.

8. Are managers important to organizations? Does what they do "matter?" Discuss and be specific in explaining your answer.

9. Using current business periodicals, find five examples of managers you would describe as *master managers.* Write a paper describing these individuals as managers and why you think they deserve this title.

10. An article by Gary Hamel in the February 2009 issue of *Harvard Business Review* addresses how management must be reinvented to be more relevant to today's world. Get a copy of that article. Choose one of the 25 grand challenges identified. Discuss what it is and what it means for the way that organizations are managed.

Endnotes

1. Based on D. Waller, "The Virus Hunters," *Management Today,* December 2010, p. 98; A. Ricadela, "Symantec Forecast Tops Estimates on Business Spending," *Businessweek.com,* October 28, 2010; J. Brandon, "Doing Battle with Online Threats," *Inc.,* October 2010, p. 46; "Hackers Seeking Trade Secrets," *Information Management,* May–June 2010, p. 9; and S. Kirsner, "Sweating in the Hot Zone," *Fast Company,* October 2005, pp. 60–65.

2. The Walt Disney Company, Letter to Shareholders, *2010 Annual Report,* pp. 1–3; and *2008 Annual Report,* pp. 2–3.

3. Right or Wrong box based on C. Hausman, "Top Sports News of Week Revolves Around Ethics," *Ethics Newsline,* www.globalethics.org/newsline (September 20, 2010); P. Rogers, "Was It OK for Jeter to Fake Getting Hit by Pitch?" *Chicago Tribune Online,* September 16, 2010; and G. Shelton, "Derek Jeter's Dramatics in Faking Being Hit by Pitch Were Over the Line," *St. Petersburg Times Online,* September 16, 2010.

4. From the Past to the Present box based on Dictionary.com Unabridged, based on the Random House Dictionary, © Random House, Inc. 2009, http://dictionary.reference.com/browse/manage; Online Etymology Dictionary, www.etymonline.com (June 5, 2009); P. F. Drucker, *Management: Revised Edition* (New York: HarperCollins Publishers, 2008); and F. W. Taylor, *Principles of Scientific Management* (New York: Harper, 1911), p. 44. For other information on Taylor, see S. Wagner-Tsukamoto, "An Institutional Economic Reconstruction of Scientific Management: On the Lost Theoretical Logic of Taylorism," *Academy of Management Review,* January 2007, pp. 105–117; R. Kanigel, *The One Best Way: Frederick Winslow Taylor and the Enigma of Efficiency* (New York: Viking, 1997); and M. Banta, *Taylored Lives: Narrative Productions in the Age of Taylor, Veblen, and Ford* (Chicago: University of Chicago Press, 1993).

5. H. Fayol, *Industrial and General Administration* (Paris: Dunod, 1916).

6. For a comprehensive review of this question, see C. P. Hales, "What Do Managers Do? A Critical Review of the Evidence," *Journal of Management* (January 1986), pp. 88–115.

7. H. Mintzberg, *The Nature of Managerial Work* (New York: Harper & Row, 1973).

8. "What Managers Really Do," *Wall Street Journal,* August 17, 2009, p. R2; and H. Mintzberg, *Managing* (San Francisco: Berrett Koehler), 2009.

9. S. J. Carroll and D. A. Gillen, "Are the Classical Management Functions Useful in Describing Managerial Work?" *Academy of Management Review,* January 1987, p. 48.

10. E. White, "Firms Step Up Training for Front-Line Managers," *Wall Street Journal,* August 27, 2007, p. B3.

11. See, for example, J. G. Harris, D. W. DeLong, and A. Donnellon, "Do You Have What It Takes to Be an E-Manager?" *Strategy and Leadership* (August 2001), pp. 10–14; C. Fletcher and C. Baldry, "A Study of Individual Differences and Self-Awareness in the Context of Multi-Source Feedback," *Journal of Occupational and Organizational Psychology* (September 2000), pp. 303–319; and R. L. Katz, "Skills of an Effective Administrator," *Harvard Business Review,* September–October 1974, pp. 90–102.

12. R. P. Tett, H. A. Guterman, A. Bleier, and P. J. Murphy, "Development and Content Validation of a 'Hyperdimensional' Taxonomy of Managerial Competence," *Human Performance,* vol. 13, no. 3 (2000), pp. 205–251.

13. E. C. Dierdorff, R. S. Rubin, and F. P. Morgeson, "The Milieu of Managerial Work: An Integrative Framework Linking Work Context to Role Requirements," *Journal of Applied Psychology* (July 2009), pp. 972–988.

14. Technology and the Manager's Job box based on D. Bennett, "I'll Have My Robots Talk to Your Robots," *Bloomberg BusinessWeek* (February 21–27, 2011), pp. 52–62; E. Spitznagel, "The Robot Revolution Is Coming," *Bloomberg BusinessWeek,* January 17–23, 2011, pp. 69–71; G. A. Fowler, "Holiday Hiring Call: People vs. Robots," *Wall Street Journal,* December 20, 2010, pp. B1+; A. Schwartz, "Bring Your Robot to Work Day," *Fast Company.com* (November 2010), pp. 72–74; and P. J. Hinds, T. L. Roberts, and H. Jones, "Whose Job Is It Anyway? A Study of Human- Robot Interaction in a Collaborative Task," *Human-Computer Interaction* (March 2004), pp. 151–181.

15. "Frequently Asked Questions," *U.S. Small Business Administration,* www.sba.gov/advo (September 2008); T. L. Hatten, *Small Business: Entrepreneurship and Beyond* (Upper Saddle River, NJ: Prentice Hall, 1997), p. 5; L. W. Busenitz, "Research on Entrepreneurial Alertness," *Journal of Small Business Management* (October 1996), pp. 35–44; and J. W. Carland, F. Hoy, W. R. Boulton, and J. C. Carland, "Differentiating Entrepreneurs from Small Business Owners: A Conceptualization," *Academy of Management Review,* vol. 9, no. 2 (1984), pp. 354–359.

16. And the Survey Says box based on C. Kincaid, "On the Front Lines," *Training* (June 2009), pp. 48–49; "Dear Workforce," *Workforce Management Online* (July 1, 2010); J. Yang and A. Gonzalez, "Boss as a Friend?" *USA Today,* November 2, 2010, p. 1B; "Who's Your TV Boss?" *Training* (November–December 2010), p. 8; "Generation Gap: On Their Bosses, Millennials Happier Than Boomers," *Wall Street Journal,* November 15, 2010, p. B6; J. Light, "Bosses Overestimate Their Managing Skills," *Wall Street Journal,* November 1, 2010, p. B10; and J. MacIntyre, "Leadership Perspectives," *Springfield Business Journal,* February 14–20, 2011, p. 11.

17. T. Shelton, "Best Buy's New ROLE," *Training* (June 2009), pp. 24–28; and T. J. Erickson, "Task, Not Time: Profile of a Gen Y Job," *Harvard Business Review,* February 2008, p. 19.

18. T. W. Martin, "May I Help You?" *Wall Street Journal,* April 23, 2009, p. R4.

19. Hearst Seattle Media Staff Directory, www.seattlepi.com/facts/pistaff.shtml (February 23, 2011); and W. Yardley and R. Perez-Peña, "Seattle Paper Shifts Entirely to the Web," *New York Times Online* (March 17, 2009).

20. F. F. Reichheld, "Lead for Loyalty," *Harvard Business Review,* July–August 2001, p. 76.

21. See, for instance, H. Ernst, W. D. Hoyer, M. Krafft, and K. Krieger, "Customer Relationship Management and Company Performance—The Mediating Role of New Product Performance," *Journal of the Academy of Marketing Science* (April 2011), pp. 290–306; J. P. Dotson and G. M. Allenby, "Investigating the Strategic Influence of Customer and Employee Satisfaction on Firm Financial Performance," *Marketing Science* (September–October 2010), pp. 895–908; R. Grewal, M. Chandrashekaran, and A. V. Citrin, "Customer Satisfaction Heterogeneity and Shareholder Value," *Journal of Marketing Research* (August 2010), pp. 612–626; M. Riemann, O. Schilke, and J. S. Thomas, "Customer Relationship Management and Firm Performance: The Mediating Role of Business Strategy," *Journal of the Academy of Marketing Science* (Summer 2010), pp. 326–346; and K. A. Eddleston, D. L. Kidder, and B. E. Litzky, "Who's the Boss? Contending with Competing Expectations from Customers and Management," *Academy of Management Executive* (November 2002), pp. 85–95.

22. See, for instance, C. B. Blocker, D. J. Flint, M. B. Myers, and S. F. Slater, "Proactive Customer Orientation and Its Role for Creating Customer Value in Global Markets," *Journal of the Academy of Marketing Science* (April 2011), pp. 216–233; G. A. Gorry and R. A. Westbrook, "Once More, With Feeling: Empathy and Technology in Customer Care," *Business Horizons* (March–April 2011), pp. 125–134; M. Dixon, K. Freeman, and N. Toman, "Stop Trying to Delight Your Customers," *Harvard Business Review,* July–August 2010, pp. 116–122; D. M. Mayer, M. G. Ehrhart, and B. Schneider, "Service Attribute Boundary Conditions of the Service Climate-Customer Satisfaction Link," *Academy of Management Journal* (October 2009), pp. 1034–1050; B. A. Gutek, M. Groth, and B. Cherry, "Achieving Service Success Through Relationships and Enhanced Encounters," *Academy of Management Executive* (November 2002), pp. 132–144; Eddleston, Kidder, and Litzky, "Who's the Boss? Contending With Competing Expectations From Customers and Management"; S. D. Pugh, J. Dietz, J. W. Wiley, and S. M. Brooks, "Driving Service Effectiveness Through Employee-Customer Linkages," *Academy of Management Executive* (November 2002), pp. 73–84; S. D. Pugh, "Service with a Smile: Emotional Contagion in the Service Encounter," *Academy of Management Journal* (October 2001), pp. 1018–1027; W. C. Tsai, "Determinants and Consequences of Employee Displayed Positive Emotions," *Journal of Management,* vol. 27, no. 4 (2001), pp. 497–512; Naumann and Jackson, Jr., "One More Time: How Do You Satisfy Customers?"; and M. D. Hartline and O. C. Ferrell, "The Management of Customer-Contact Service Employees: An Empirical Investigation," *Journal of Marketing* (October 1996), pp. 52–70.

23. R. A. Hattori and J. Wycoff, "Innovation DNA," *Training and Development* (January 2002), p. 24.

24. *Fast Company* Staff, "World's 50 Most Innovative Companies," *Fast Company,* March 2011, pp. 66+.

25. E. Frauenheim, "Managers Don't Matter," *Workforce Management Online* (April 6, 2010); and K. A. Tucker and V. Allman, "Don't Be a Cat-and-Mouse Manager," The Gallup Organization, www.brain.gallup.com (September 9, 2004).

26. Frauenheim, 2010.

27. "WorkUSA® 2004/2005: Effective Employees Drive Financial Results," Watson Wyatt Worldwide, Washington, DC.

Skill Development: Becoming Politically Adept

Anyone who has had much work experience knows that politics exists in every organization. That is, people try to influence the distribution of advantages and disadvantages within the organization in their favor. Those who understand organizational politics typically thrive. Those who don't, regardless of how good their actual job skills are, often suffer by receiving less positive performance reviews, fewer promotions, and smaller salary increases. If you want to succeed as a manager, it helps to be politically adept.

Personal Insights: How Good Am I at Playing Politics?

Using the following 7-point scale, indicate the response that best describes how much you agree or disagree with each of the 18 statements.

> **1** = Strongly disagree
> **2** = Disagree
> **3** = Slightly disagree
> **4** = Neutral
> **5** = Slightly agree
> **6** = Agree
> **7** = Strongly agree

1. I spend a lot of time and effort making connections, working relationships, and networking with others.   1 2 3 4 5 6 7

2. I am able to make most people feel comfortable and at ease around me.   1 2 3 4 5 6 7

3. I am able to communicate easily and effectively with others.   1 2 3 4 5 6 7

4. It is easy for me to develop good rapport with most people.   1 2 3 4 5 6 7

5. I understand people very well.   1 2 3 4 5 6 7

6. I am good at building relationships with influential people at work.   1 2 3 4 5 6 7

7. I am particularly good at sensing the motivations and hidden agendas of others.   1 2 3 4 5 6 7

8. When communicating with others, it is important that they believe I am genuine and sincere in what I say and do.   1 2 3 4 5 6 7

9. I have developed a large network of colleagues and associates at work whom I can call on for support when I really need to get things done.   1 2 3 4 5 6 7

10. I know a lot of important people and am well connected at work.   1 2 3 4 5 6 7

11. I spend a lot of time at work developing connections and networking with others.   1 2 3 4 5 6 7

12. I am good at getting people to like me.   1 2 3 4 5 6 7

13. It is important that I make people believe I am genuine and sincere in what I say and do.   1 2 3 4 5 6 7

14. I try to show a genuine interest in other people.   1 2 3 4 5 6 7

15. I am good at using my connections and network to make things happen at work. 1 2 3 4 5 6 7

16. I have good intuition or "savvy" about how to present myself to others. 1 2 3 4 5 6 7

17. I always seem to instinctively know the right things to say or do to influence others. 1 2 3 4 5 6 7

18. I pay close attention to people's facial expressions. 1 2 3 4 5 6 7

Source: G. R. Ferris, R. W. Kolodinsky, R. W. Hochwarter, and D. D. Frink, "Conceptualization, Measurement, and Validation of the Political Skill Construct," paper presented at the 61st National Academy of Management Conference, Washington, DC, August 2001.

Analysis and Interpretation

The authors of this instrument define political skill as "an interpersonal style construct that combines social perceptiveness or astuteness with the capacity to adjust one's behavior to different and changing situational demands in a manner that inspires trust, confidence, and genuineness, and effectively influences and controls the responses of others." They have broken this down into four dimensions: *Self- and social astuteness* is the ability to astutely observe others and to be keenly attuned to diverse social situations. *Interpersonal influence/control* is the ability to exert a powerful influence on others. *Network building/social capital* means being adept at developing and using diverse networks of people. And *genuineness/sincerity* is the ability to appear to others as having high integrity, authenticity, and sincerity. The 18 items in this instrument tap into these four dimensions.

To calculate your score, add up your answers for the 18 items. Your score will range between 18 and 126. The higher your score, the better your political skills. That is, the better you are at not only knowing precisely what to do in different social situations at work but exactly how to do it in a sincere, engaging manner that disguises any ulterior, self-serving motives. The authors don't provide any specific cut-off scores, but we suggest that scores below 72 indicate that you are a bit politically naïve and may have difficulty furthering your self-interests in an organization. Scores above 100 suggest you are quite effective in gaining the support and trust of others and using that to advance your agenda.

Skill Basics

Forget, for a moment, the ethics of politicking and any negative impressions you might have of people who engage in organizational politics. If you want to be more politically adept in your organization, follow these eight suggestions:

1. *Frame arguments in terms of organizational goals.* Effective politicking requires camouflaging your self-interest. No matter that your objective is self-serving; all the arguments you marshal in support of it must be framed in terms of the benefits that will accrue to the organization. People whose actions appear to blatantly further their own interests at the expense of the organization are almost universally denounced, are likely to lose influence, and often suffer the ultimate penalty of being expelled from the organization.

2. *Develop the right image.* If you know your organization's culture, you understand what the organization wants and values from its employees—in terms of dress, associates to cultivate and those to avoid, whether to appear to be a risk taker or risk-aversive, the preferred leadership style, the importance placed on getting along well with others, and so forth. Then you are equipped to project the appropriate image. Because the assessment of your performance isn't always a fully objective process, you need to pay attention to style as well as substance. In addition, studies consistently show that people who can successfully project sincerity are perceived in a positive image.

3. *Gain control of organizational resources.* The control of organizational resources that are scarce and important is a source of power. Knowledge and expertise are particularly effective resources to control. They make you more valuable to the organization and, therefore, more likely to gain security, advancement, and a receptive audience for your ideas.

4. *Make yourself appear indispensable.* Because we're dealing with appearances rather than objective facts, you can enhance your power by appearing to be indispensable. You don't really have *to be* indispensable as long as key people in the organization believe that you are. If the organization's prime decision makers believe there is no ready substitute for what you are giving the organization, they are likely to go to great lengths to ensure that your desires are satisfied.

5. *Be visible.* If you have a job that brings your accomplishments to the attention of others, that's great. However, if you don't have such a job, you'll want to find ways to let others in the organization know what you're doing by highlighting successes in routine reports, having satisfied customers relay their appreciation to senior executives, being seen at social functions, being active in your professional associations, and developing powerful allies who speak positively about your accomplishments. Of course, the skilled politician actively and successfully lobbies to get the projects that will increase his or her visibility.

6. *Develop powerful allies.* It helps to have powerful people on your side. Network by cultivating contacts with potentially influential people above you, at your own level, and in the lower ranks. These allies often can provide you with information that's otherwise not readily available. In addition, decisions are sometimes made in favor of those with the greatest support. Having powerful allies can provide you with a coalition of support if and when you need it.

7. *Avoid "tainted" members.* In almost every organization, there are fringe members whose status is questionable. Their performance and/or loyalty is suspect. Keep your distance

from such individuals. Given the reality that effectiveness has a large subjective component, your own effectiveness might be called into question if you're perceived as being too closely associated with tainted members.

8. *Support your boss.* Your immediate future is in the hands of your current boss. Because that person evaluates your performance, you'll typically want to do whatever is necessary to have your boss on your side. You should make every effort to help your boss succeed, make her look good, support him if he is under siege, and spend the time to find out the criteria she will use to assess your effectiveness. Don't undermine your boss. And don't speak negatively of him to others.

Based on S. P. Robbins and P. L. Hunsaker, *Training in Interpersonal Skills: TIPS for Managing People at Work*, 6th ed. (Upper Saddle River, NJ: Prentice Hall, 2011), pp. 181–203; J. Marques, "Organizational Politics: Problem or Opportunity? Strategies for Success in the Workplace," *Human Resource Management International Digest*, 17, no. 6 (2009), pp. 38–41; and G. R. Ferris, S. L. Davidson, and P. L. Perrewe, *Political Skill at Work: Impact on Work Effectiveness* (Mountain View, CA: Davies-Black Publishing, 2005).

Skill Application

You used to be the star marketing manager for Hilton Electronics Corporation. But for the past year, you've been outpaced again and again by Jason, a new manager in the design department, who has been accomplishing everything expected of him and more. Meanwhile your best efforts to do your job well have been sabotaged and undercut by Maria—your and Jason's manager. For example, prior to last year's international consumer electronics show, Maria moved $60,000 from your budget to Jason's. Despite your best efforts, your marketing team couldn't complete all the marketing materials normally developed to showcase all of your organization's new products at this important industry show. And Maria has chipped away at your staff and budget ever since. Although you've been able to meet most of your goals with less staff and budget, Maria has continued to slice away resources from your group. Just last week, she eliminated two positions in your team of eight marketing specialists to make room for a new designer and some extra equipment for Jason. Maria is clearly taking away your resources while giving Jason whatever he wants and more. You think it's time to do something or soon you won't have any team or resources left.

Skill Practice

1. Make an appointment to interview a manager. Try to select someone who has at least three years of management experience. Ask this manager to describe a political situation he or she has confronted. How well-equipped was he or she to handle the situation? What was the outcome? What, if anything, would that person do differently today? What has that person learned about "organizational politics" since he or she left school?

2. Keep a one-week journal of your behavior and describe incidences of when you tried to influence others around you. Assess each incident by asking: Were you successful at these attempts to influence them? Why or why not? What could you have done differently?

For Your Immediate Action

FYIA

Heartland's Traditional Fragrances

To: Eric Kim, Training Coordinator
From: Helen Merkin, Human Resources Director
Re: Supervisory Training and Management Certification Program

The good news: our sales numbers continue to grow. The bad news: it's putting a strain on our manufacturing supervisors. They're finding it difficult to keep our line employees motivated. We need to get some training in place to help them deal with this demanding pace or our line employees are likely to get even more stressed and we may see product quality go down.

I need you to look into two issues for me. One is a training program that focuses on important supervisory skills. Do some research and put together a list of the skills you think are most important for our supervisors to have, together with a justification for why you think these skills are important.

The second issue is how we could help our supervisors achieve certification that verifies their skills, knowledge, and professionalism. Two certification programs that I'm aware of are the Certified Manager and the Certified Business Manager. Please research each of these programs and prepare a bulleted list of what each involves.

Keep your report to one page typed. Also, I'd like both sets of information as soon as possible. Thnx!

This fictionalized company and message were created for educational purposes only, and not meant to reflect positively or negatively on management practices by any company that may share this name.

Bringing the Real World to Life

Case Application:
Saving the World: Part 2

Symantec, which designs content and network security software for both consumers and businesses, reflects the realities facing many organizations today: quickly shifting customer expectations and continuously emerging global competitors that have drastically shortened product life cycles. Managing talented people in such an environment can be quite challenging as well.

Symantec's virus hunters around the world deal with some 20,000 virus samples each month, not all of which are unique, stand-alone viruses. To make the hunters' jobs even more interesting is that computer attacks are increasingly being spread by criminals around the world wanting to steal information, whether corporate data or personal user account information that can be used in fraud. Dealing with these critical and time-sensitive issues requires special talents. The response-center team is a diverse group whose members weren't easy to find. "It's not as if colleges are creating thousands of anti-malware or security experts every year that we can hire. If you find them in any part of the world, you just go after them." The response center team's makeup reflects that. For instance, one senior researcher is from Hungary; another is from Iceland; and another works out of her home in Melbourne, Florida. But they all share something in common: They're all motivated by solving problems.

The launch of the Blaster-B worm, a particularly nasty virus, in late summer 2003 changed the company's approach to dealing with viruses. The domino effect of Blaster-B and other viruses spawned by it meant that frontline software analysts were working around the clock for almost two weeks. The "employee burnout" potential made the company realize that its virus-hunting team would now have to be much deeper talent-wise. Now, the response center's team numbers in the hundreds and managers can rotate people from the front lines, where they're responsible for responding to new security threats that crop up, into groups where they can help with new-product development. Others write internal research papers. Still others are assigned to develop new tools that will help their colleagues battle the next wave of threats. There's even an individual who tries to figure out what makes the virus writers tick—and the day never ends for these virus hunters. When Dublin's team finishes its day, colleagues in Santa Monica take over. When the U.S. team finishes its day, it hands off to the team in Tokyo, who then hands back to

Dublin for the new day. It's a frenetic, chaotic, challenging work environment that spans the entire globe. But the goals for managing the virus hunters are to "try to take the chaos out, to make the exciting boring," to have a predictable and well-defined process for dealing with the virus threats, and to spread work evenly to the company's facilities around the world. It's a managerial challenge that company managers have embraced.

DISCUSSION QUESTIONS

1. Keeping professionals excited about work that is routine and standardized *and* chaotic is a major challenge for Symantec's managers. How could they use technical, human, and conceptual skills to maintain an environment that encourages innovation and professionalism among the virus hunters? What managerial competencies might be important for these managers? Why?

2. What management roles would operations manager Patrick Fitzgerald be playing as he (a) had weekly security briefing conference calls with coworkers around the globe, (b) assessed the feasibility of adding a new network security consulting service, (c) kept employees focused on the company's commitments to customers?

3. Go to Symantec's Web site (www.symantec.com) and look up information about the company. What can you tell about its emphasis on customer service and innovation? In what ways does the organization support its employees in servicing customers and in being innovative?

4. What could other managers learn from Patrick Fitzgerald and Symantec's approach?

A BRIEF HISTORY OF MANAGEMENT'S ROOTS

Henry Ford once said, "History is more or less bunk." Well . . . he was wrong! History is important because it can put current activities in perspective. We propose that you need to know management history because it can help you understand what today's managers do. In this module, you'll find an annotated timeline that discusses key milestones in management theory. Then, in each chapter's "From the Past to the Present" box feature, we highlight a key person and his or her contributions or a key historical factor and its effect on contemporary management concepts. We believe this approach will help you better understand the origins of many contemporary management concepts.

○ Early Management

Management has been practiced a long time. Organized endeavors directed by people responsible for planning, organizing, leading, and controlling activities have existed for thousands of years. Regardless of what these individuals were called, someone had to perform those functions.

3000 – 2500 B.C.E.

The Egyptian pyramids are proof that projects of tremendous scope, employing tens of thousands of people were completed in ancient times.[1] It took more than 100,000 workers some 20 years to construct a single pyramid. Someone had to plan what was to be done, organize people and materials to do it, make sure those workers got the work done, and impose some controls to ensure that everything was done as planned. That someone was managers.

Stephen Sudd/Getty Images USA, Inc.

1400s

At the arsenal of Venice, warships were floated along the canals, and at each stop, materials and riggings were added to the ship.[2] Sounds a lot like a car "floating" along an assembly line, doesn't it? In addition, the Venetians used warehouse and inventory systems to keep track of materials, human resource management functions to manage the labor force (including wine breaks), and an accounting system to keep track of revenues and costs.

Antonio Natale/Bridgeman Art Library (US)

1780s – Mid 1800s

The **Industrial Revolution** may be the most important pre-twentieth-century influence on management. Why? Because with the industrial age came the birth of the corporation. With large, efficient factories pumping out products, someone needed to forecast demand, make sure adequate supplies of materials were available, assign tasks to workers, and so forth. Again, that someone was managers! It was indeed a historical event for two reasons: (1) because of all the organizational aspects (hierarchy, control, job specialization, and so forth) that became a part of the way work was done, and (2) because management had become a necessary component to ensure the success of the enterprise.

Getty Images USA, Inc.

1776

Getty Images USA, Inc.

Although this is an important date in U.S. history, it's also important because it's the year Adam Smith's *Wealth of Nations* was published. In it, he argued the economic advantages of the **division of labor** (or **job specialization**)—that is, breaking down jobs into narrow, repetitive tasks. Using division of labor, individual productivity could be increased dramatically. Job specialization continues to be a popular way to determine how work gets done in organizations.

Classical Approaches

Beginning around the turn of the twentieth century, the discipline of management began to evolve as a unified body of knowledge. Rules and principles were developed that could be taught and used in a variety of settings. These early management proponents were called classical theorists.

Corbis Images

1911

That's the year Frederick W. Taylor's *Principles of Scientific Management* was published. His groundbreaking book described a theory of **scientific management**—the use of scientific methods to determine the "one best way" for a job to be done. His theories were widely accepted and used by managers around the world and Taylor became known as the "father" of scientific management.[3] Other major contributors to scientific management were Frank and Lillian Gilbreth (early proponents of time-and-motion studies and parents of the large family described in the original book *Cheaper by the Dozen*) and Henry Gantt (whose work on scheduling charts was the foundation for today's project management).

Getty Images USA, Inc.

1916 – 1947

Unlike Taylor who focused on an individual production worker's job, Henri Fayol and Max Weber looked at organizational practices by focusing on what managers do and what constituted good management. This approach is known as **general administrative theory.** Fayol was the person who first identified five management functions. He also identified 14 **principles of management**— fundamental rules of management that could be applied to all organizations.[4] (See Exhibit HM–1 for a list of these 14 principles.) Weber is known for his description and analysis of bureaucracy, which he believed was an ideal, rational form of organization structure, especially for large organizations.

EXHIBIT 1   Fayol's Fourteen Principles of Management

1 **Division of Work.** This principle is the same as Adam Smith's "division of labor." Specialization increases output by making employees more efficient.

2 **Authority.** Managers must be able to give orders. Authority gives them this right. Along with authority, however, goes responsibility. Whenever authority is exercised, responsibility arises.

3 **Discipline.** Employees must obey and respect the rules that govern the organization. Good discipline is the result of effective leadership, a clear understanding between management and workers regarding the organization's rules, and the judicious use of penalties for infractions of the rules.

4 **Unity of Command.** Every employee should receive orders from only one superior.

5 **Unity of Direction.** Each group of organizational activities that have the same objective should be directed by one manager using one plan.

6 **Subordination of Individual Interests to the General Interest.** The interests of any one employee or group of employees should not take precedence over the interests of the organization as a whole.

7 **Remuneration.** Workers must be paid a fair wage for their services.

8 **Centralization.** Centralization refers to the degree to which subordinates are involved in decision making. Whether decision making is centralized (to management) or decentralized (to subordinates) is a question of proper proportion. The task is to find the optimum degree of centralization for each situation.

9 **Scalar Chain.** The line of authority from top management to the lowest ranks represents the scalar chain. Communications should follow this chain. However, if following the chain creates delays, cross-communications can be allowed if agreed to by all parties and if superiors are kept informed. Also called chain of command.

10 **Order.** People and materials should be in the right place at the right time.

11 **Equity.** Managers should be kind and fair to their subordinates.

12 **Stability of Tenure of Personnel.** High employee turnover is inefficient. Management should provide orderly personnel planning and ensure that replacements are available to fill vacancies.

13 **Initiative.** Employees who are allowed to originate and carry out plans will exert high levels of effort.

14 **Esprit de Corps.** Promoting team spirit will build harmony and unity within the organization.

• 3000 BC – 1776 •	1911 – 1947	Late 1700s – 1950s •	1940s – 1950s	1960s – present
Early Management	Classical Approaches	Behavioral Approach	Quantitative Approach	Contemporary Approaches

Behavioral Approach ○

The behavioral approach to management focused on the actions of workers. How do you motivate and lead employees in order to get high levels of performance?

Late 1700s – Early 1900s

Managers get things done by working with people. Several early management writers recognized how important people are to an organization's success.[5] For instance, Robert Owen, who was concerned about deplorable working conditions, proposed an idealistic workplace. Hugo Munsterberg, a pioneer in the field of industrial psychology, suggested using psychological tests for employee selection, learning theory concepts for employee training, and studies of human behavior for employee motivation. Mary Parker Follett was one of the first to recognize that organizations could be viewed from both individual *and* group behavior. She thought that organizations should be based on a group ethic rather than on individualism.

1960s – Today

An organization's people continue to be an important focus of management research. The field of study that researches the actions (behaviors) of people at work is called **organizational behavior (OB).** OB researchers do empirical research on human behavior in organizations. Much of what managers do today when managing people—motivating, leading, building trust, working with a team, managing conflict, and so forth—has come out of OB research.

1924 – Mid-1930s

The **Hawthorne studies,** a series of studies that provided new insights into individual and group behavior, were without question the most important contribution to the behavioral approach to management.[6] Conducted at the Hawthorne (Cicero, Illinois) Works of the Western Electric Company, the studies were initially designed as a scientific management experiment. Company engineers wanted to see the effect of various lighting levels on worker productivity. Using control and experimental groups of workers, they expected to find that individual output in the experimental group would be directly related to the intensity of the light. However, much to their surprise, they found that productivity in both groups varied with the level of lighting. Not able to explain it, the engineers called in Harvard professor Elton Mayo. Thus began a relationship that lasted until 1932 and encompassed numerous experiments in the behavior of people at work. What were some of their conclusions? Group pressures can significantly affect individual productivity, and people behave differently when they're being observed. Scholars generally agree that the Hawthorne studies had a dramatic impact on management beliefs about the role of people in organizations and led to a new emphasis on the human behavior factor in managing organizations.

1930s – 1950s

The human relations movement is important to management history because its supporters never wavered from their commitment to making management practices more humane. Proponents of this movement uniformly believed in the importance of employee satisfaction—a satisfied worker was believed to be a productive worker.[7] So they offered suggestions like employee participation, praise, and being nice to people to increase employee satisfaction. For instance, Abraham Maslow, a humanistic psychologist, who's best known for his description of a hierarchy of five needs (a well-known theory of employee motivation), said that once a need was substantially satisfied, it no longer served to motivate behavior. Douglas McGregor developed Theory X and Theory Y assumptions, which related to a manager's beliefs about an employee's motivation to work. Even though both Maslow's and McGregor's theories were never fully supported by research, they're important because they represent the foundation from which contemporary motivation theories were developed.

Quantitative Approach

The quantitative approach, which focuses on the application of statistics, optimization models, information models, computer simulations, and other quantitative techniques to management activities, provided tools for managers to make their jobs easier.

1940s

The **quantitative approach** to management—which is the use of quantitative techniques to improve decision making—evolved from mathematical and statistical solutions developed for military problems during World War II. After the war was over, many of these techniques used for military problems were applied to busi-nesses.[8] For instance, one group of military officers, dubbed the "Whiz Kids," joined Ford Motor Company in the mid-1940s and immediately began using statistical methods to improve decision making at Ford.

1950s

After World War II, Japanese organi-zations enthusiastically embraced the concepts espoused by a small group of quality experts, the most famous being W. Edwards Deming (photo below) and Joseph M. Duran. As these Japanese manu-facturers began beating U.S. com-petitors in quality comparisons, Western managers soon took a more serious look at Deming's and Juran's ideas.[9] Their ideas became the basis for **total quality management (TQM),** which is a management philosophy devoted to continual improvement and responding to customer needs and expectations.

Bert Hardy/Getty Images USA, Inc.

AP Images

3000 BC – 1776	1911 – 1947	Late 1700s – 1950s	1940s – 1950s	1960s – present
Early Management	Classical Approaches	Behaviorist Approach	Quantitative Approach	Contemporary Approaches

Contemporary Approaches ⦵

Most of the early approaches to management focused on managers' concerns inside the organization. Starting in the 1960s, management researchers began to look at what was happening in the external environment outside the organization.

1960s

Although Chester Barnard, a telephone company executive, wrote in his 1938 book *The Functions of the Executive* that an organization functioned as a cooperative system, it wasn't until the 1960s that management researchers began to look more carefully at systems theory and how it related to organizations.[10] The idea of a system is a basic concept in the physical sciences. As related to organizations, the **systems approach** views systems as a set of interrelated and interdependent parts arranged in a manner that produces a unified whole. Organizations function as **open systems**, which means they are influenced by and interact with their environment. Exhibit illustrates an organization as an open system. A manager has to efficiently and effectively manage all parts of the system in order to achieve established goals.

Frederick Brown/Newscom

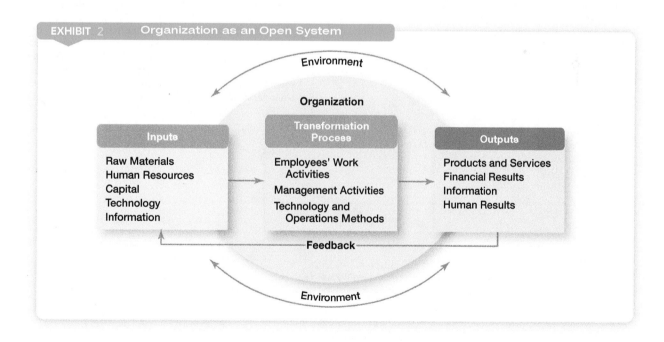

EXHIBIT 2 — Organization as an Open System

Environment

Organization

Inputs	Transformation Process	Outputs
Raw Materials Human Resources Capital Technology Information	Employees' Work Activities Management Activities Technology and Operations Methods	Products and Services Financial Results Information Human Results

Feedback

Environment

○ Contemporary Approaches

Newscom

1960s

Early management theorists proposed manage-ment principles that they generally assumed to be universally applicable. Later research found exceptions to many of these principles. The **contingency approach** (or situational approach) says that organizations, employees, and situations are different and require different ways of managing. A good way to describe contingency is "if . . . then." *If* this is the way my situation is, *then* this is the best way for me to manage in this situation. One of the earliest contingency studies was done by Fred Fiedler and looked at what style of leadership was most effective in what situation.[11] Popular contingency variables have been found to include organization size, the routineness of task technology, environmental uncertainty, and individual differences.

1980s – Present

Although the dawn of the information age is said to have begun with Samuel Morse's telegraph in 1837, the most dramatic changes in information technology have occurred in the latter part of the twentieth century and have directly affected the manager's job.[12] Managers now may manage employees who are working from home or working halfway around the world. An organization's computing resources used to be mainframe computers locked away in temperature-controlled rooms and only accessed by the experts. Now, practically everyone in an organization is connected—wired or wireless—with devices no larger than the palm of the hand. Just like the impact of the Industrial Revolution in the 1700s on the emergence of management, the information age has brought dramatic changes that continue to influence the way organizations are managed. The impact of information technology on how managers do their work is so profound that we've included in several chapters a boxed feature on "Technology and the Manager's Job."

Industrial Revolution
The advent of machine power, mass production, and efficient transportation begun in the late eighteenth century in Great Britain

division of labor (or job specialization)
The breakdown of jobs into narrow repetitive tasks

scientific management
The use of the scientific method to define the one best way for a job to be done

general administrative theory
Descriptions of what managers do and what constitutes good management practice

principles of management
Fayol's fundamental or universal principles of management practice

Hawthorne studies
Research done in the late 1920s and early 1930s devised by Western Electric industrial engineers to examine the effect of different work environment changes on worker productivity, which led to a new emphasis on the human factor in the functioning of organizations and the attainment of their goals

organizational behavior (OB)
The field of study that researches the actions (behaviors) of people at work

quantitative approach
The use of quantitative techniques to improve decision making

total quality management (TQM)
A managerial philosophy devoted to continual improvement and responding to customer needs and expectations

systems approach
An approach to management that views an organization as a system, which is a set of interrelated and interdependent parts arranged in a manner that produces a unified whole

open systems
Systems that dynamically interact with their environment

contingency approach (or situational approach)
An approach to management that says that individual organizations, employees, and situations are different and require different ways of managing

Endnotes

1. C. S. George, Jr., *The History of Management Thought,* 2d ed. (Upper Saddle River, NJ: Prentice Hall, 1972), p. 4.

2. Ibid., pp. 35–41.

3. F. W. Taylor, *Principles of Scientific Management* (New York: Harper, 1911), p. 44. For other information on Taylor, see S. Wagner-Tsukamoto, "An Institutional Economic Reconstruction of Scientific Management: On the Lost Theoretical Logic of Taylorism," *Academy of Management Review*, January 2007, pp. 105–117; R. Kanigel, *The One Best Way: Frederick Winslow Taylor and the Enigma of Efficiency* (New York: Viking, 1997); and M. Banta, *Taylored Lives: Narrative Productions in the Age of Taylor, Veblen, and Ford* (Chicago: University of Chicago Press, 1993).

4. H. Fayol, *Industrial and General Administration* (Paris: Dunod, 1916); M. Weber, *The Theory of Social and Economic Organizations*, ed. T. Parsons, trans. A. M. Henderson and T. Parsons (New York: Free Press, 1947); and M. Lounsbury and E. J. Carberry, "From King to Court Jester? Weber's Fall from Grace in Organizational Theory," *Organization Studies*, vol. 26, no. 4 (2005), pp. 501–525.

5. R. A. Owen, *A New View of Society* (New York: E. Bliss and White, 1825); H. Munsterberg, *Psychology and Industrial Efficiency* (Boston: Houghton Mifflin, 1913); and M. P. Follett, *The New State: Group Organization the Solution of Popular Government* (London: Longmans, Green, 1918).

6. E. Mayo, *The Human Problems of an Industrial Civilization* (New York: Macmillan, 1933); and F. J. Roethlisberger and W. J. Dickson, *Management and the Worker* (Cambridge, MA: Harvard University Press, 1939). Also see G. W. Yunker, "An Explanation of Positive and Negative Hawthorne Effects: Evidence from the Relay Assembly Test Room and Bank Wiring Observation Room Studies," paper presented, Academy of Management Annual Meeting, August 1993, Atlanta, Georgia; S. R. Jones, "Was There a Hawthorne Effect?" *American Sociological Review*, November 1992, pp. 451–468; and S. R. G. Jones, "Worker Interdependence and Output: The Hawthorne Studies Reevaluated," *American Sociological Review*, April 1990, pp. 176–190; J. A. Sonnenfeld, "Shedding Light on the Hawthorne Studies,"

Journal of Occupational Behavior (April 1985), pp. 111–130; B. Rice, "The Hawthorne Defect: Persistence of a Flawed Theory," *Psychology Today*, February 1982, pp. 70–74; R. H. Franke and J. Kaul, "The Hawthorne Experiments: First Statistical Interpretations," *American Sociological Review*, October 1978, pp. 623–643; and A. Carey, "The Hawthorne Studies: A Radical Criticism," *American Sociological Review*, June 1967, pp. 403–416.

7. A. Maslow, "A Theory of Human Motivation," *Psychological Review,* July 1943, pp. 370–396; see also A. Maslow, *Motivation and Personality* (New York: Harper & Row, 1954); and D. McGregor, *The Human Side of Enterprise* (New York: McGraw-Hill, 1960).

8. P. Rosenzweig, "Robert S. McNamara and the Evolution of Management," *Harvard Business Review,* December 2010, pp. 86–93; and C. C. Holt, "Learning How to Plan Production, Inventories, and Work Force," *Operations Research,* January–February 2002, pp. 96–99.

9. T. A. Stewart, "A Conversation with Joseph Juran," *Fortune,* January 11, 1999, pp. 168–170; J. R. Hackman and R. Wageman, "Total Quality Management: Empirical, Conceptual, and Practical Issues," *Administrative Science Quarterly*, June 1995, pp. 309–342; B. Krone, "Total Quality Management: An American Odyssey," *The Bureaucrat*, Fall 1990, pp. 35–38; and A. Gabor, *The Man Who Discovered Quality* (New York: Random House, 1990).

10. C. I. Barnard, *The Functions of the Executive* (Cambridge: Harvard University Press, 1938); and K. B. DeGreene, *Sociotechnical Systems: Factors in Analysis, Design, and Management* (Upper Saddle River, NJ: Prentice Hall, 1973), p. 13.

11. F. E. Fiedler, *A Theory of Leadership Effectiveness* (New York: McGraw-Hill, 1967).

12. "Information Age: People, Information & Technology—An Exhibition at the National Museum of American History," *Smithsonian Institution,* http://photo2.si.edu/infoage/infoage.html (June 11, 2009); and P. F. Drucker, *Management, Revised Edition* (New York: HarperCollins Publishers, 2008).

The Management Environment

From Chapter 2 of *Fundamentals of Management,* Eighth Edition. Stephen P. Robbins, David A. De Cenzo, Mary Coulter. Copyright © 2013 by Pearson Education, Inc. All rights reserved.

The
Management
Environment

Zappos
.com
the web's most popular shoe store!®

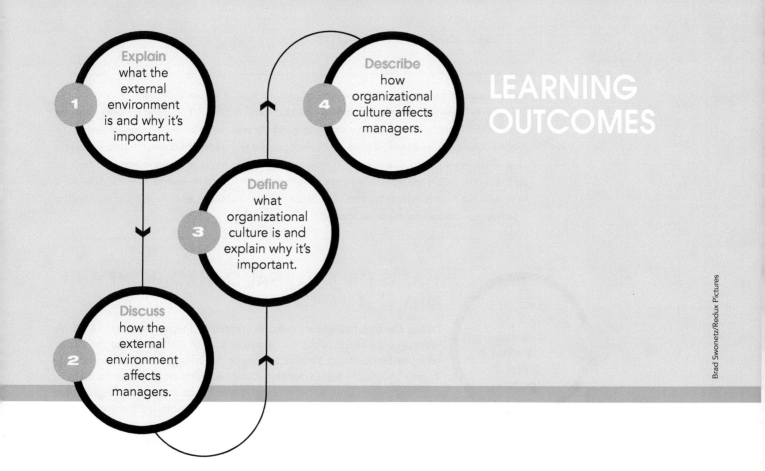

1 Explain what the external environment is and why it's important.

2 Discuss how the external environment affects managers.

3 Define what organizational culture is and explain why it's important.

4 Describe how organizational culture affects managers.

Going to Extremes

No. 1 best e-retailer. For those of you who have shopped on Zappos.com, that number one ranking probably isn't a surprise.[1] For those of you who haven't shopped on Zappos.com, it wouldn't take long for you to see why Zappos deserves that accolade. And it's more than the fact that Zappos has a great selection of products, super-fast shipping, and free returns. The real secret to its success is its people who make the Zappos shopping experience truly unique and outstanding. The company, which began selling shoes and other products online in 1999, has put "extraordinary effort into building a desirable organizational culture, which has provided a sure path to business success." As part of its culture, Zappos espouses 10 corporate values. At the top of that list is "Deliver WOW through service." And do they ever deliver the WOW! Even through the recent economic challenges, Zappos has continued to thrive—a sure sign its emphasis on organizational culture is paying off.

No successful organization, or its managers, can operate without understanding and dealing with the dynamic environment—external and internal—that surrounds it. One of the biggest mistakes managers make today is failing to adapt to the changing world. As one executive said recently, regarding the economic crisis, "I have learned more about management and leadership during the past six months than I had in the previous ten years."[2] Organizations that are too bound by tradition and don't (or refuse to) change are less and less likely to survive the turbulence in today's world. To better understand this issue, we need to look at the important forces in the management environment that are affecting the way organizations are managed today.

WHAT IS THE EXTERNAL ENVIRONMENT AND WHY IS IT IMPORTANT?

1 Explain what the external environment is and why it's important.

When the Eyjafjallajökull volcano erupted in Iceland on April 14, 2010, who would have thought that it would lead to a shutdown at the BMW plant in Spartanburg, South Carolina or the Nissan Motor auto assembly facility in Japan?[3] Yet, in our globalized and interconnected world, such an occurrence shouldn't be surprising at all. When volcanic ash grounded planes across Europe, supplies of tire-pressure sensors from a company in Ireland couldn't be delivered on time to the BMW plant or to the Nissan plant. Because we live in a "connected" world, managers need to be aware of the impact of the external environment on their organization.

The term external environment refers to factors, forces, situations, and events outside the organization that affect its performance. As shown in Exhibit 1, it includes several different components. The economic component encompasses factors such as interest rates, inflation, changes in disposable income, stock market fluctuations, and business cycle stages. The demographic component is concerned with trends in population characteristics such as age, race, gender, education level, geographic location, income, and family composition. The technological component is concerned with scientific or industrial innovations. The sociocultural component is concerned with societal and cultural factors such as values, attitudes, trends, traditions, lifestyles, beliefs, tastes, and patterns of behavior. The

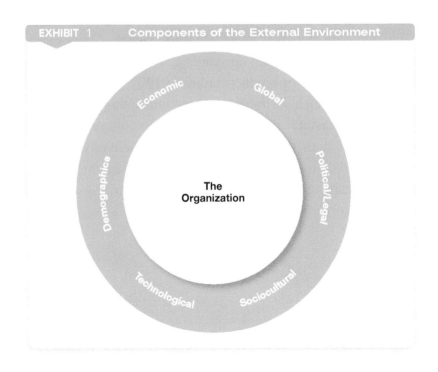

EXHIBIT 1   Components of the External Environment

Economic · Global · Political/Legal · Sociocultural · Technological · Demographic

The Organization

political/legal component looks at federal, state, and local laws, as well as laws of other countries and global laws. It also includes a country's political conditions and stability. And the global component encompasses those issues (like a volcano eruption) associated with globalization and a world economy. Although all these components potentially constrain managers' decisions and actions, we're going to look closely at only two of the components—economic and demographic.

How Has the Economy Changed?

You knew the economic context had changed when a blue-ribbon company like General Motors went bankrupt, the Organization for Economic Cooperation and Development predicted some 25 million unemployed individuals globally, the U.S. unemployment rate hovered around 9 percent, and an economic vocabulary included terminology like *toxic assets, collateralized debt obligations, TARP, bailouts, underwater homeowners, economic stabilization, wraparound mortgages,* and *stress tests*.[4] The recent economic crisis—called the "Great Recession" by some analysts—began with turmoil in home mortgage markets in the United States as many homeowners found themselves unable to make their payments. The problems also soon affected businesses as credit markets collapsed. All of a sudden, credit was no longer readily available to fund business activities. Due to our globally connected world, it didn't take long for economic troubles in the United States to spread to other countries.

What led to the massive problems? Experts cited a long list of factors including excessively low interest rates for a long period of time, fundamental flaws in the U.S. housing market, and massive global liquidity. All these factors led businesses and consumers to become highly leveraged, which wasn't an issue when credit was easily available.[5] However, as liquidity dried up, the worldwide economic system sputtered and nearly collapsed. With trillions lost in home value, millions of home foreclosures, a huge public debt burden in many countries, and widespread social problems due to job losses, it's clear that the U.S. and global economic environments have changed.

In the U.S. economic system, which is based mostly on capitalistic principles, trade and industry are controlled privately rather than by the government. But as we've seen time and time again in such a system, people sometimes make bad, even disastrous, decisions. The esteemed economist John Maynard Keynes once said, "Capitalism is the astounding belief that the most wickedest of men will do the most wickedest of things for the greatest good of everyone."[6] Despite this cynical view, modern capitalism has created "unprecedented wealth in our lifetime, shown its power to lift people out of poverty, and spread a culture of competitive genius."[7] It's also been called the "most productive economic engine invented."[8] Since the early 1900s, the U.S. approach has been the most important model for organizing business activities. It brought the world the corporate model of ownership and organization, large-scale operations based on mass production techniques, open markets, formal organization structures with hierarchies and multiple business divisions, and labor-management collective bargaining. Business organizations in many countries have patterned themselves after this model. However, as the economic problems of the past few years have shown, it's by no means perfect.

Experts believe that as the U.S. economy emerges from recession, the way businesses operate will not be the way it's always been. As the U.S. Secretary of the Treasury said, "Capitalism will be different."[9] The biggest change is likely to be in the role of government, especially in financial markets and in consumer protection. Also, government spending as a share of the U.S. economy is likely to remain at levels not seen since World War II. Beyond that, more government intervention is likely to mean more regulations or at the least, increased enforcement and oversight of regulations already in place. However, some believe

external environment
Factors, forces, situations, and events outside the organization that affect its performance

From the Past to the Present

In February 2010, when Ford Motor Company surpassed General Motors in sales for the first time in at least 50 years, GM announced an overhaul in its top management ranks. GM's North American president said that "he could see clear as day that the mix and the structure of people weren't right and that these changes were necessary for GM to move faster and win."[10] Just how much difference *does* a manager make in how an organization performs? Management theory proposes two perspectives in answering this question: the omnipotent view and the symbolic view.

We have stressed how important managers are to organizations. The dominant view in management theory is that managers are directly responsible for an organization's success or failure. This perspective is called the **omnipotent view of management**. Differences in an organization's performance are assumed to be due to decisions and actions of its managers. Good managers anticipate change, exploit opportunities, correct poor performance, and lead their organizations. When profits are up, managers take the credit and are rewarded with bonuses, stock options, and the like. When profits are down, top managers are often fired in the belief that "new blood" will bring improved results. In this view, someone has to be held accountable when organizations perform poorly regardless of the reasons, and that "someone" is the manager. Of course, when things go well, managers also get the credit—even if they had little to do with achieving the positive outcomes. And this view isn't limited to business organizations. It also explains turnover among college and professional sports coaches, who are considered the "managers" of their teams. Coaches who lose more games than they win are usually fired and replaced by new coaches who are expected to correct the poor performance.

In contrast, others have argued that much of an organization's success or failure is due to external forces outside managers' control. This perspective is called the **symbolic view of management**. The symbolic view says that a manager's ability to affect performance outcomes is influenced and constrained by external factors. According to this view, it's unreasonable to expect managers to significantly affect an organization's performance. Instead, performance is influenced by factors over which managers have little control such as the economy, customers, governmental policies, competitors' actions, industry conditions, and decisions made by previous managers. This view is labeled "symbolic" because it's based on the belief that managers symbolize control and influence. How? By developing plans, making decisions, and engaging in other managerial activities to make sense out of random, confusing, and ambiguous situations. However, the actual part that managers play in organizational success or failure is limited.

In reality, managers are neither all-powerful nor helpless. But their decisions and actions are constrained. External constraints come from the organization's external environment and internal constraints come from the organization's culture.

Think About:

- Why do you think these two perspectives on management are important?

- How are the omnipotent and the symbolic views of management similar? Different?

The home mortgage problems that began in the United States and affected businesses as credit markets collapsed had an enormous economic impact that nearly collapsed the global economic system. During the recent global recession, millions of jobs were eliminated, unemployment rates rose to levels not seen in many years, and unemployed individuals reached 25 million worldwide. This photo shows unemployed Japanese people searching through job vacancies at an employment bureau in Tokyo, where the unemployment rate soared. In our globalized and interconnected world, managers need to stay informed about the economy because it poses constraints and challenges for them in the areas of jobs and employment.

Kazuhiro Nogi/Newscom

that more governmental oversight isn't the answer. For example, social scientist Amitai Etzioni said, "The world economy consists of billions of transactions every day. There can never be enough inspectors, accountants, customs officers, and police to ensure that all or even most of these transactions are properly carried out. Moreover, those charged with enforcing regulations are themselves not immune to corruption, and hence, they too must be supervised and held accountable to others—who also have to be somehow regulated. The upshot is that regulation cannot be the linchpin of attempts to reform our economy. What is needed is something far more sweeping: for people to internalize a different sense of how one ought to behave, and act on it because they believe it is right."[11] We've also seen a shift in public opinion as more people have expressed concerns about the growing budget deficit and increased government intervention in the economy. In a poll by the *Wall Street Journal*, some 49 percent of the respondents said they had a great deal of concern about a greater government role in the economy and business.[12] Keep in mind that over time, this "new" normal will no longer be new—it will have become "the norm."[13] What's important for managers is to stay informed about what's happening not only in the economic component but in the other external environmental components as well. In fact, there is one other important external component we need to look at: demographics.

What Role Do Demographics Play?

Have you ever heard the phrase "demography is destiny"? What this phrase means is that the size and characteristics of a country's population can have a significant effect on what it's able to achieve. For instance, experts say that by 2050, "emerging economies led by India and China will collectively be larger than the developed economies."[14] Small European nations with low birth rates, such as Austria, Belgium, Denmark, Norway, and Sweden, will drop off the list of the 30 biggest economies. Demographics, the characteristics of a population used for purposes of social studies, can and do have a significant impact on how managers manage. Those population characteristics include things such as

TECHNOLOGY AND THE MANAGER'S JOB — CHANGING AND IMPROVING THE WAY MANAGERS MANAGE

One positive aspect of this changed economy comes from the vast possibilities associated with continuing advancements in technology.[15] **Technology** includes any equipment, tools, or operating methods that are designed to make work more efficient. One area where technology has had an impact is in the process where inputs (labor, raw materials, and the like) are transformed into outputs (goods and services to be sold). In years past, this transformation was usually performed by human labor. With technology, however, human labor has been replaced with electronic and computer equipment. From robots in offices to online banking systems to social networks where employees interact with customers, technology has made the work of creating and delivering goods and services more efficient and effective.

Another area where technology has had a major impact is in information. Information technology (IT) has created the ability to circumvent the physical confines of working only in a specified organizational location. With notebook and desktop computers, fax machines, smartphones, organizational intranets, and other IT tools, organizational members who work mainly with information can do that work from any place at any time.

Finally, technology is also changing the way managers manage, especially in terms of how they interact with employees who may be working anywhere and anytime. Effectively communicating with individuals in remote locations and ensuring that work goals are being met are challenges that managers must address. Throughout the rest of the book, we'll look at how managers are meeting those challenges in the ways they plan, organize, lead, and control.

Think About:

· Is management easier or harder with all the available technology? What do you think?

· What benefits does technology provide and what problems does technology pose for (a) employees and (b) managers?

· Which technologies have been most useful to you personally thus far? Why? Do you think they will remain useful to you as you begin your career? Why or why not?

omnipotent view of management
The view that managers are directly responsible for an organization's success or failure

symbolic view of management
The view that much of an organization's success or failure is due to external forces outside managers' control

demographics
The characteristics of a population used for purposes of social studies

technology
Any equipment, tools, or operating methods that are designed to make work more efficient

Al Diaz/Newscom

Age is an important demographic for Michelle Zubizarreta (center), chief administrative officer of Zubi Advertising, a Hispanic agency in Coral Gables, Florida. Surrounded by some of the Gen Y employees whom she manages, Zubizarreta values the enthusiasm and the contributions of her young workers. With the economic recession creating the need for new ways to generate revenue, Zubizarreta asked her tech-savvy, multitasking young staffers for their creative input. She allowed them to use Facebook to conduct consumer surveys, and she formed innovation groups by setting up teams to develop advertising-related iPhone apps and to generate other money-making ideas.

age, income, sex, race, education level, ethnic makeup, employment status, geographic location, and so forth—pretty much the types of information collected on governmental census surveys.

Age is a particularly important demographic for managers since the workplace often has different age groups all working together. *Baby Boomers. Gen X. Gen Y. Post-Millennials.* Maybe you've heard or seen these terms before. They're names given by population researchers to four well-known age groups found in the U.S. population. Baby Boomers are those individuals born between 1946 and 1964. You've heard so much about "boomers" because there are so many of them. The sheer numbers of people in that cohort means they've had a significant impact on every aspect of the external environment (from the educational system to entertainment/lifestyle choices to the Social Security system and so forth) as they've gone through various life cycle stages. Gen X is used to describe those individuals born between 1965 and 1977. This age group has been called the baby bust generation since it followed the baby boom and is one of the smaller age cohorts. Gen Y (or the "Millennials") is an age group typically considered to encompass those individuals born between 1978 and 1994. As the children of the Baby Boomers, this age group is also large in number and making its imprint on external environmental conditions as well. From technology to clothing styles to work attitudes, Gen Y is impacting organizational workplaces. Then, there are the Post-Millennials—the youngest identified age group, basically teens and middle-schoolers.[16] This group also has been called the iGeneration, primarily because they've grown up with technology that customizes everything to the individual. Another name given to this age group is Generation C, since it's a group that's always been digitally connected. One thing that characterizes this group is that "many of their social interactions take place on the Internet, where they feel free to express their opinions and attitudes." It's the first group to have "never known any reality other than that defined and enabled by the Internet, mobile devices, and social networking."[17] Population experts say it's too early to tell whether elementary school-aged children and younger are part of this demographic group or whether the world they live in will be so different that they'll comprise a different demographic cohort.

Demographic age cohorts are important to our study of management because large numbers of people at certain stages in the life cycle can constrain decisions and actions taken by businesses, governments, educational institutions, and other organizations. Studying demographics doesn't only involve current statistics, but also looks to the future. For instance, recent analysis of birth rates shows that more than 80 percent of babies being born worldwide are from Africa and Asia.[18] And here's an interesting fact: India has one of the world's youngest populations with more males under the age of 5 than the entire population of France. And by 2050, it's predicted that China will have more people age 65 and older than the rest of the world combined.[19] Just imagine the impact of these population trends on global organizations.

HOW DOES THE EXTERNAL ENVIRONMENT AFFECT MANAGERS?

Discuss how the external environment affects managers.

2

Knowing *what* the various components of the external environment are and examining certain aspects of that environment are important for managers. However, understanding *how* the environment affects managers is equally as important. We're going to look at three ways the external environment constrains and challenges managers—first, through its impact on jobs and employment; next, through the environmental uncertainty that is present; and finally, through the various stakeholder relationships that exist between an organization and its external constituencies.

JOBS AND EMPLOYMENT.   As any or all of the external environmental conditions change, one of the most powerful constraints managers face is the impact of such changes on jobs and employment—both in poor conditions and in good conditions. The power of this constraint became painfully obvious during the recent global recession as millions of jobs were eliminated and unemployment rates rose to levels not seen in many years. Economists now predict that about a quarter of the 8.4 million jobs eliminated in the United States during this most recent economic downturn won't come back and will instead be replaced by other types of work in growing industries.[20] Other countries face the same issues. Although such readjustments aren't bad in and of themselves, they do create challenges for managers who must balance work demands and having enough people with the right skills to do the organization's work.

Not only do changes in external conditions affect the types of jobs that are available, they affect how those jobs are created and managed. For instance, many employers are using flexible work arrangements with work tasks done by freelancers hired to work on an as-needed basis or by temporary workers who work full-time but are not permanent employees or by individuals who share jobs.[21] Keep in mind that these approaches are being used because of the constraints from the external environment. As a manager, you'll need to recognize how such work arrangements affect the way you plan, organize, lead, and control. Flexible work arrangements have become so prevalent that we'll discuss them in other chapters as well.

ASSESSING ENVIRONMENTAL UNCERTAINTY.   Another constraint posed by external environments is the amount of uncertainty found in that environment, which can affect organizational outcomes. Environmental uncertainty refers to the degree of change and complexity in an organization's environment. The matrix in Exhibit 2 shows these two aspects.

EXHIBIT 2	Environmental Uncertainty Matrix	
	Degree of Change	
	Stable	**Dynamic**
Simple	**Cell 1** Stable and predictable environment Few components in environment Components are somewhat similar and remain basically the same Minimal need for sophisticated knowledge of components	**Cell 2** Dynamic and unpredictable environment Few components in environment Components are somewhat similar but are continually changing Minimal need for sophisticated knowledge of components
Complex	**Cell 3** Stable and predictable environment Many components in environment Components are not similar to one another and remain basically the same High need for sophisticated knowledge of components	**Cell 4** Dynamic and unpredictable environment Many components in environment Components are not similar to one another and are continually changing High need for sophisticated knowledge of components

(Left axis label: **Degree of Complexity**)

environmental uncertainty
The degree of change and complexity in an organization's environment

RIGHT ?OR WRONG

For the second time in two years, Apple's CEO Steve Jobs has taken a medical leave a year and a half after his return following a liver transplant. "The leave raises questions about both his long-term prognosis and the leadership of the world's most valuable technology company." Jobs has said he would remain chief executive and that he hoped to return to Apple as soon as he could. During his first absence, Jobs remained in almost daily telephone contact with other top executives as he monitored the progress of both the iPhone 4 and the iPad. An analyst with a financial firm has said that "regardless of whether Mr. Jobs returned to Apple, the company would probably continue doing well for the foreseeable future, although its long-term prospects were more uncertain." Jobs did return briefly to introduce the iPad2. However, many feel that because Jobs is so closely linked with the firm's creative vision, the company (and Steve Jobs) should be required to release more medical information.[27]

Note: Steve Jobs, who resigned his CEO position in August 2011, passed away on October 5, 2011.

Think About:

- What do you think about this?

- Do the heads of publicly traded firms have a right to medical privacy? Why or why not?

- What stakeholders do you think are most important in this situation?

- What responsibilities do organizations have to stakeholders in situations like this?

- What ethical implications might arise in such a situation?

Jim Wilson/Redux Pictures

The first dimension of uncertainty is the degree of unpredictable change. If the components in an organization's environment change frequently, it's a *dynamic* environment. If change is minimal, it's a *stable* one. A stable environment might be one in which there are no new competitors, few technological breakthroughs by current competitors, little activity by pressure groups to influence the organization, and so forth. For instance, Zippo Manufacturing, best known for its Zippo lighters, faces a relatively stable environment.[22] There are few competitors and little technological change. The main external concern for the company is probably the declining trend in tobacco usage. In contrast, the recorded music industry faces a dynamic (highly uncertain and unpredictable) environment. Digital formats, apps, and music-downloading sites have turned the industry upside down and brought high levels of uncertainty.

The other dimension of uncertainty describes the degree of **environmental complexity**, which looks at the number of components in an organization's environment and the extent of the knowledge that the organization has about those components. An organization that has few competitors, customers, suppliers, or government agencies to deal with, or that needs little information about its environment, has a less complex and thus less uncertain environment.

How does the concept of environmental uncertainty influence managers? Looking again at Exhibit 2, each of the four cells represents different combinations of degree of complexity and degree of change. Cell 1 (stable-simple environment) represents the lowest level of environmental uncertainty and cell 4 (dynamic and complex environment) the highest. Not surprisingly, managers have the greatest influence on organizational outcomes in cell 1 and the least in cell 4. Because uncertainty is a threat to an organization's effectiveness, managers try to minimize it. Given a choice, managers would prefer to operate in the least uncertain environments, but they rarely control that choice. In addition, the nature of the external environment today is that most industries are facing more dynamic change, making their environments more uncertain.

MANAGING STAKEHOLDER RELATIONSHIPS. What has made MTV a popular cable channel for young adults year after year? One reason is that it understands the importance of building relationships with its various stakeholders: viewers, reality show participants, music celebrities, advertisers, affiliate TV stations, public service groups, and others. The nature of stakeholder relationships is another way in which the environment influences managers. The more obvious and secure these relationships, the more influence managers will have over organizational outcomes.

Stakeholders are any constituencies in an organization's environment that are affected by that organization's decisions and actions. These groups have a stake in or are significantly influenced by what the organization does. In turn, these groups can influence the organization. For example, think of the groups that might be affected by the decisions and actions of Starbucks—coffee bean farmers, employees, specialty coffee competitors, local communities, and so forth. Some of these stakeholders also, in turn, may impact decisions and actions of Starbucks' managers. The idea that organizations have stakeholders is now widely accepted by both management academics and practicing managers.[23]

Exhibit 3 identifies the most common stakeholders that an organization might have to deal with. Note that these stakeholders do include internal and external groups. Why? Because both can affect what an organization does and how it operates.

Why should managers even care about managing stakeholder relationships?[24] For one thing, it can lead to desirable organizational outcomes such as improved predictability of environmental changes, more successful innovations, greater degree of trust among stakeholders, and greater organizational flexibility to reduce the impact of change. For instance, social media company Facebook is spending more on lobbying and meeting with governmental officials as lawmakers and regulators look at sweeping changes to online privacy law. The company is "working to shape its image on Capitol Hill and avert measures potentially damaging to its information-sharing business."[25]

Can stakeholder management affect organizational performance? The answer is yes! Management researchers who have looked at this issue are finding that managers of high-performing companies tend to consider the interests of all major stakeholder groups as they make decisions.[26]

Another reason for managing external stakeholder relationships is that it's the "right" thing to do. Because an organization depends on these external groups as sources of inputs (resources) and as outlets for outputs (goods and services), managers should consider the interests of stakeholders as they make decisions. We'll address this issue in more detail in the next chapter when we look at corporate social responsibility.

Some 5,000 employees congregating at a Boston Scientific Corporation meeting were thanked by patients treated with the firm's medical devices they helped produce. Speaking in person and projected on two huge video screens, the patients and their family members expressed gratitude to the employees for products and procedures that either saved their lives or improved the quality of their lives. Along with hospitals and physicians, these patients are stakeholders who are influenced by what the medical technology company does. Hearing the stories of patients also benefits Boston Scientific. Knowing that their work helps other people and saves lives is a key motivating factor for employees.

EXHIBIT 3   Organizational Stakeholders

Employees
Customers
Unions
Social and Political Action Groups
Shareholders
Competitors
Organization
Communities
Trade and Industry Associations
Suppliers
Governments
Media

---

environmental complexity
The number of components in an organization's environment and the extent of knowledge that the organization has about those components

stakeholders
Any constituencies in an organization's environment that are affected by that organization's decisions and actions

As we've tried to make clear throughout this section, it's not going to be "business as usual" for organizations or for managers. Managers will have hard decisions to make about how they do business and about their people. It's important that you understand how changes in the external environment will affect your organizational and management experiences. Now, we need to switch gears and look at the internal aspects of the organization, specifically, its culture.

WHAT IS ORGANIZATIONAL CULTURE AND WHY IS IT IMPORTANT?

3 Define what organizational culture is and explain why it's important.

Each of us has a unique personality—traits and characteristics that influence the way we act and interact with others. When we describe someone as warm, open, relaxed, shy, or aggressive, we're describing personality traits. An organization, too, has a personality, which we call its *culture.*

At Vanguard Group Inc., CEO William McNabb recently received an e-mail from one of his sales reps that a longtime client wanted to have lunch with him.[28] "At the end of the e-mail was a simple request: Please do not suit up." The client specifically asked that the CEO not wear a suit because it made the client feel uncomfortable. Despite being more than 100 miles from the formalities of Wall Street, Vanguard had always required its employees worldwide to dress in business attire—jacket and tie for men and professional dress for women. Not anymore. McNabb announced on his blog that Vanguard was going "business appropriate," meaning that employees would no longer need to suit up unless they were meeting with clients. And employees have embraced the new dress code. Expectations of appropriate work dress are one of the more visible elements of an organization's culture.

What Is Organizational Culture?

Organizational culture has been described as the shared values, principles, traditions, and ways of doing things that influence the way organizational members act. In most organizations, these shared values and practices have evolved over time and determine, to a large extent, how "things are done around here."[29]

Our definition of culture implies three things. First, culture is a *perception.* It's not something that can be physically touched or seen, but employees perceive it on the basis of what they experience within the organization. Second, organizational culture is *descriptive.* It's concerned with how members perceive or describe the culture, not with whether they like it. Finally, even though individuals may have different backgrounds or work at different organizational levels, they tend to describe the organization's culture in similar terms. That's the *shared* aspect of culture.

How Can Culture Be Assessed?

Research suggests that seven dimensions describe an organization's culture.[30] These dimensions (shown in Exhibit 4) range from low to high, meaning it's not typical of the culture (low) or is especially typical of the culture (high). Describing an organization using these seven dimensions gives a composite picture of the organization's culture. In many organizations, one cultural dimension often is emphasized more than the others and essentially shapes the organization's personality and the way organizational members work. For instance, at Sony Corporation the focus is product innovation (innovation

A culture of youthfulness describes the personality of the YOHO brand of e-commerce, online interactive community, and fashion magazine ventures founded by Liang Chao, CEO of New Power Corporation. Chao created a casual, fun-loving, and fast-paced environment for his young college graduate staffers who share similar lifestyles and the belief that "being young is an attitude." Focusing on the fashions of youth, highly energetic and imaginative employees are committed to YOHO's goal of becoming the biggest portal for Chinese young people and are the key factors in attracting young readers and customers. Shown here are staffers holding an online ordering meeting for YOHO's e-commerce Web site at company offices in Nanjing, China.

Chen Qi/Newscom

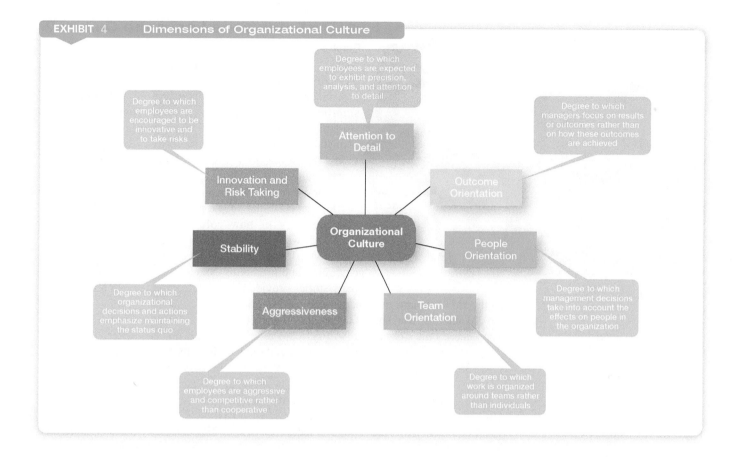

EXHIBIT 4 · Dimensions of Organizational Culture

Degree to which employees are encouraged to be innovative and to take risks

Degree to which employees are expected to exhibit precision, analysis, and attention to detail

Degree to which managers focus on results or outcomes rather than on how these outcomes are achieved

Innovation and Risk Taking

Attention to Detail

Outcome Orientation

Organizational Culture

Stability

People Orientation

Degree to which organizational decisions and actions emphasize maintaining the status quo

Aggressiveness

Team Orientation

Degree to which management decisions take into account the effects on people in the organization

Degree to which employees are aggressive and competitive rather than cooperative

Degree to which work is organized around teams rather than individuals

and risk taking). The company "lives and breathes" new product development and employees' work behaviors support that goal. In contrast, Southwest Airlines has made its employees a central part of its culture (people orientation) and shows this through the way it treats them.

Where Does an Organization's Culture Come From?

An organization's culture usually reflects the vision or mission of the organization's founders. Because the founders had the original idea, they also had biases on how to carry out the idea. They were not constrained by previous customs or ideologies. The founders established the early culture by projecting an image of what the organization should be and what its values were. The small size of most new organizations also helped the founders impose their vision on all organization members. An organization's culture, then, results from the interaction between (1) the founders' biases and assumptions, and (2) what the first employees learn subsequently from their own experiences. For example, the founder of IBM, Thomas Watson, established a culture based on "pursuing excellence, providing the best customer service, and respect for employees." Ironically, some 85 years later, in an effort to revitalize the ailing IBM, CEO Louis Gerstner enhanced that culture with his strong, "customer-oriented sensibility," recognizing the urgency the marketplace imposes on having customers' expectations met. And at Southwest Airlines, former CEO Herb Kelleher reinforced the company's "people culture" by implementing certain practices—such as compensation and benefits above industry averages—to make employees happy.

organizational culture
The shared values, principles, traditions, and ways of doing things that influence the way organizational members act

Dressed up as Woody, the pull-string doll from *Toy Story*, Southwest Airlines chairman and chief executive Gary Kelly (right) enjoys a skit during the company's annual Halloween festivities at corporate headquarters. The party is a ritual that celebrates Southwest's energized and exuberant employees and free-wheeling culture. It reinforces the airline's mission of "dedication to the highest quality of customer service delivered with a sense of warmth, friendliness, individual pride, and company spirit." The Halloween party is one of eight annual corporate events that bring employees together and help keep the company's fun-loving culture alive.

AND THE SURVEY SAYS... [40]

 67 percent of corporate leaders surveyed say that resilience is important in keeping your job during uncertain times.

 57 percent of workers surveyed said that the additional job responsibilities they've assumed in the current economy are a burden.

 63 percent of Americans polled said that what they were most angry about was the economy.

 32 percent of workers surveyed said that acclimating to a different corporate culture could pose the greatest challenge when reentering the workforce.

67 percent of men never wear a tie to work.

 61 percent of senior managers surveyed said their organization was somewhat prepared to deal with a sudden loss of a key senior manager.

 35 percent of CEOs said their biggest challenge during a recession is retaining employee talent.

How Do Employees Learn the Culture?

Employees "learn" an organization's culture in a number of ways. The most common are stories, rituals, material symbols, and language.

Organizational *"stories"* typically contain a narrative of significant events or people including such things as the organization's founders, rule breaking, reactions to past mistakes, and so forth.[31] For instance, managers at Nike feel that stories told about the company's past help shape the future. Whenever possible, corporate "storytellers" (senior executives) explain the company's heritage and tell stories that celebrate people getting things done. When they tell the story of how cofounder Bill Bowerman (now deceased) went to his workshop and poured rubber into his wife's waffle iron to create a better running shoe, they're celebrating and promoting Nike's spirit of innovation. These company stories provide examples that people can learn from.[32] At the 3M Company, the product innovation stories are legendary. There's the story about the 3M scientist who spilled chemicals on her tennis shoe and came up with Scotchgard. Then, there's the story about Art Fry, a 3M researcher, who wanted a better way to mark the pages of his church hymnal and invented the Post-it Note. These stories reflect what made 3M great and what it will take to continue that success.[33] To help employees learn the culture, organizational stories anchor the present in the past, provide explanations and legitimacy for current practices, exemplify what is important to the organization, and provide compelling pictures of an organization's goals.[34]

Corporate *rituals* are repetitive sequences of activities that express and reinforce the important values and goals of the organization.[35] For example, the "Passing of the Pillars" is an important ritual at Boston Scientific's facility near Minneapolis. When someone has a challenging assignment, they're "awarded" a small two-foot high plaster-of-Paris pillar to show that they've got support from all their colleagues.[36]

When you walk into different businesses, do you get a "feel" for what type of work environment it is—formal, casual, fun, serious, and so forth? These reactions demonstrate the power of *material symbols* or *artifacts* in creating an organization's personality.[37] The layout of an organization's facilities, how employees dress, the types of automobiles provided to top executives, and the availability of corporate aircraft are examples of material symbols. Others include the size of offices, the elegance of furnishings, executive "perks" (extra benefits provided to managers, such as health club memberships, use of company-owned facilities, and so forth), employee fitness centers or on-site dining facilities, and reserved parking spaces for certain employees. At WorldNow, an important material symbol is an old dented drill that the founders purchased for $2 at a thrift store. The drill symbolizes the company's culture of "drilling down to solve problems." When an employee is presented with the drill in recognition of outstanding work, he or she is expected to personalize the drill in some way and devise a new rule for caring for it. One employee installed a Bart Simpson trigger; another made the drill wireless by adding an antenna. The company's "icon" carries on the culture even as the organization evolves and changes.[38] Material symbols convey to employees who is important and the kinds of behavior (for example, risk taking, conservative, authoritarian, participative, individualistic, and so forth) that are expected, appropriate, and rewarded.

Many organizations and units within organizations use *language* as a way to identify and unite members of a culture. By learning this language, members attest to their acceptance of the culture and their willingness to help preserve it. At Cranium, a Seattle board game company, "chiff" is used to remind employees of the need to be incessantly innovative in everything they do. "Chiff" stands for "clever, high-quality, innovative, friendly, fun."[39] Over time, organizations often develop unique terms to describe equipment, key personnel, suppliers, customers, processes, or products related to its business. New employees are frequently overwhelmed with acronyms and jargon that, after a short period of time, become a natural part of their language. Once learned, this language acts as a common denominator that bonds members.

HOW DOES ORGANIZATIONAL CULTURE AFFECT MANAGERS?

Describe how organizational culture affects managers.

4

Marjorie Kaplan, president of the Animal Planet and Science networks, understands the power of organizational culture and how it affects her as a manager. She says that one of her company's stated goals is "to make it the place where, when you come to work you feel like you have the opportunity to bring your best self and you're also challenged to bring your best self."[41] And she's trying to create and maintain a culture that does just that for her employees and for herself.

The two main ways that an organization's culture affects managers are (1) its effect on what employees do and how they behave, and (2) its effect on what managers do.

How Does Culture Affect What Employees Do?

An organization's culture has an effect on what employees do, depending on how strong, or weak, the culture is. **Strong cultures**—those in which the key values are deeply held and widely shared—have a greater influence on employees than do weaker cultures. The more employees accept the organization's key values and the greater their commitment to those values, the stronger the culture is. Most organizations have moderate to strong cultures; that is, there is relatively high agreement on what's important, what defines "good" employee behavior, what it takes to get ahead, and so forth. The stronger a culture becomes, the more it affects what employees do and the way managers plan, organize, lead, and control.[42]

Also, in organizations with a strong culture, that culture can substitute for the rules and regulations that formally guide employees. In essence, strong cultures can create predictability, orderliness, and consistency without the need for written documentation. Therefore, the stronger an organization's culture, the less managers need to be concerned with developing formal rules and regulations. Instead, those guides will be internalized in employees when they accept the organization's culture. If, on the other hand, an organization's culture is weak—if no dominant shared values are present—its effect on employee behavior is less clear.

How Does Culture Affect What Managers Do?

Houston-based Apache Corp. has become one of the best performers in the independent oil drilling business because it has fashioned a culture that values risk taking and quick decision making. Potential hires are judged on how much initiative they've shown in getting projects done at other companies. And company employees are handsomely rewarded if they meet profit and production goals.[43] Because an organization's culture constrains what they can and cannot do and how they manage, it's particularly relevant to managers. Such constraints are rarely explicit. They're not written down. It's unlikely they'll even be spoken. But they're there, and all managers quickly learn what to do and not do in their organization. For instance, you won't find the following values written down, but each comes from a real organization.

strong cultures
Cultures in which the key values are deeply held and widely shared

The strong culture of Honest Tea Company is all about honesty. Seth Goldman, cofounder and "TeaEO" of Honest Tea, started the company with a mission to create truly healthy, organic beverages. In growing his company, Goldman used the same authenticity, integrity, and purity in crafting his products as he did in conducting his business and creating relationships with employees, suppliers, and customers. Key values of Honest Tea include communicating with openness and trust, engaging employees in all aspects of the business, focusing on corporate social responsibility, and committing to high environmental standards. Goldman is shown here holding a tea tasting of new products with employees and a supplier at company headquarters.

◆ Look busy even if you're not.

◆ If you take risks and fail around here, you'll pay dearly for it.

◆ Before you make a decision, run it by your boss so that he or she is never surprised.

◆ We make our product only as good as the competition forces us to.

◆ What made us successful in the past will make us successful in the future.

◆ If you want to get to the top here, you have to be a team player.

The link between values such as these and managerial behavior is fairly straightforward. Take, for example, a so-called "ready-aim-fire" culture. In such an organization, managers will study and analyze proposed projects endlessly before committing to them. However, in a "ready-fire-aim" culture, managers take action and then analyze what has been done. Or, say an organization's culture supports the belief that profits can be increased by cost cutting and that the company's best interests are served by achieving slow but steady increases in quarterly earnings. Managers are unlikely to pursue programs that are innovative, risky, long term, or expansionary. In an organization whose culture conveys a basic distrust of employees, managers are more likely to use an authoritarian leadership style than a democratic one. Why? The culture establishes for managers appropriate and expected behavior. For example, Banco Santander, whose headquarters are located 20 kilometers from downtown Madrid, has been described as a "risk-control freak." The company's managers adhered to "banking's stodgiest virtues—conservatism and patience." However, it's those values that triggered the company's growth from the sixth largest bank in Spain to the largest bank in the euro zone.[44]

As shown in Exhibit 5, a manager's decisions are influenced by the culture in which he or she operates. An organization's culture, especially a strong one, influences and constrains the way managers plan, organize, lead, and control.

EXHIBIT 5   Managerial Decisions Affected by Culture

PLANNING

- The degree of risk that plans should contain
- Whether plans should be developed by individuals or teams
- The degree of environmental scanning in which management will engage

ORGANIZING

- How much autonomy should be designed into employees' jobs
- Whether tasks should be done by individuals or in teams
- The degree to which department managers interact with each other

LEADING

- The degree to which managers are concerned with increasing employee job satisfaction
- What leadership styles are appropriate
- Whether all disagreements—even constructive ones—should be eliminated

CONTROLLING

- Whether to impose external controls or to allow employees to control their own actions
- What criteria should be emphasized in employee performance evaluations
- What repercussions will occur from exceeding one's budget

Review

1 **Explain what the external environment is and why it's important.** The external environment refers to factors, forces, situations, and events outside the organization that affects its performance. It includes economic, demographic, political/legal, sociocultural, technological, and global components. The external environment is important because it poses constraints and challenges to managers.

2 **Discuss how the external environment affects managers.** There are three ways that the external environment affects managers: its impact on jobs and employment, the amount of environmental

uncertainty, and the nature of stakeholder relationships.

3 **Define what organizational culture is and explain why it's important.** Organizational culture is the shared values, principles, traditions, and ways of doing things that influence the way organizational members act. It's important because of the impact it has on decisions, behaviors, and actions of organizational employees.

4 **Describe how organizational culture affects managers.** Organizational culture affects managers in two ways: through its effect on what employees do and how they behave, and through its effect on what managers do as they plan, organize, lead, and control.

MyManagementLab   For more resources, please visit www.mymanagementlab.com

UNDERSTANDING THE CHAPTER

1. How much impact do managers actually have on an organization's success or failure?

2. Describe the six external environment components. Why is it important for managers to understand these components?

3. How has the changed economy affected what managers do? Find two or three examples in current business periodicals of activities and practices that organizations are using. Discuss them in light of the changed environment.

4. Why is it important for managers to pay attention to demographic trends and shifts?

5. What is environmental uncertainty? What impact does it have on managers and organizations? Find two examples in current business periodicals that

illustrate how environmental uncertainty affects organizations.

6. "Businesses are built on relationships." What do you think this statement means? What are the implications for managing the external environment?

7. Is organizational culture an asset to an organization? Explain. Can it ever be a liability? Explain.

8. How is an organization's culture formed and maintained?

9. Discuss the impact of a strong culture on organizations and managers.

10. Pick two organizations that you interact with frequently (as an employee or as a customer) and assess their culture according to the dimensions shown in Exhibit 4.

Endnotes

1. "100 Best Companies to Work For," *Fortune,* February 7, 2011, pp. 91+; V. Nayar, "Employee Happiness: Zappos vs. HCL," *Businessweek.com,* January 5, 2011; D. Richards, "At Zappos, Culture Pays," *Strategy+Business Online,* Autumn 2010; T. Hseih, "Zappos's CEO on Going to Extremes for Customers," *Harvard Business Review,* July–August 2010, pp. 41–45; A. Perschel, "Work-Life Flow: How Individuals, Zappos, and Other Innovative Companies Achieve High Engagement," *Global Business & Organizational Excellence,* July 2010, pp. 17–30; T. Hseih, "Why I Sold Zappos," *Inc.,* June 2010, pp. 100–104; T. Hseih, "Happy Feet," *Newsweek,* June 21, 2010, p. 10; M. Betts, "Zappos Earns No. 1 Ranking for E-retailing," *Computerworld,* June 7, 2010, p. 4; S. Elliott, "Tireless Employees Get Their Tribute, Even If It's in Felt and Polyester," *New York Times Online,* March 4, 2010; C. Palmeri, "Now for Sale, Zappos Culture," *Bloomberg BusinessWeek,* January 11, 2010, p. 57; and E. Frauenheim, "Can Zappos Culture Survive the Amazon Jungle?" *Workforce Management Online,* September 14, 2009.

2. J. Robison, "What Leaders Must Do Next," *The Gallup Management Journal Online,* http://gmj.com/ (June 11, 2009).

3. C. Matlack, "The Growing Peril of a Connected World," *Bloomberg BusinessWeek,* December 6–12, 2010, pp. 63–64.

4. C. Rampell, "Big Jump in Private Jobs Bolsters Recovery Hopes," *New York Times Online,* March 4, 2011; D. Das, Gaea News Network, "Men Lost More Jobs Than Women Worldwide: Accenture," *Reuters,* March 9, 2010; P. Izzo, "Economists Expect Shifting Work Force," *Wall Street Journal Online,* February 11, 2010; and BBC News, "Recession May See 25m Jobs Lost," *BBC News Online,* September 16, 2009.

5. S. Reddy, M. Walker, and A. Batson, "Factories Revive Economy," *Wall Street Journal,* April 2, 2010, pp. A1+; and S. Shinn, "Banking on Customers," *BizEd,* March–April 2010, pp. 16–21.

6. N. Gibbs, "25 People to Blame," *BusinessWeek,* February 23, 2009, p. 20.

7. Ibid.

8. F. Zakaria, "Greed Is Good (To a Point)," *Newsweek,* June 22, 2009, pp. 41–47.

9. M. E. Porter and M. R. Kramer, "Shared Value," *Harvard Business Review,* January–February 2011, pp. 63–77; and Zakaria, 2009.

10. From the Past to the Present box based on S. Terlep and N. E. Boudette, "Feeling Heat from Ford, GM Reshuffles Managers," *Wall Street Journal Online,* March 3, 2010; "Why CEO Churn Is Healthy," *BusinessWeek,* November 13, 2000, p. 230; T. M. Hout, "Are Managers Obsolete?" *Harvard Business Review,* March–April 1999, pp. 161–168; S. M. Puffer and J. B. Weintrop, "Corporate Performance and CEO Turnover: The Role of Performance Expectations," *Administrative Science Quarterly,* March 1991, pp. 1–19; C. R. Schwenk, "Illusions of Management Control? Effects of Self-Serving Attributions on Resource Commitments and Confidence in Management," *Human Relations,* April 1990, pp. 333–347; J. R. Meindl and S. B. Ehrlich, "The Romance of Leadership and the Evaluation of Organizational Performance," *Academy of Management Journal* (March 1987), pp. 91–109; J. A. Byrne, "The Limits of Power," *BusinessWeek,* October 23, 1987, pp. 33–35; D. C. Hambrick and S. Finkelstein, "Managerial Discretion: A Bridge between Polar Views of Organizational Outcomes," in L. L. Cummings and B. M. Staw (eds.), *Research in Organizational Behavior,* vol. 9 (Greenwich, CT: JAI Press, 1987), pp. 369–406; and J. Pfeffer, "Management as Symbolic Action: The Creation and Maintenance of Organizational Paradigms," in L. L. Cummings and B. M. Staw (eds.), *Research in Organizational Behavior,* vol. 3 (Greenwich, CT: JAI Press, 1981), pp. 1–52.

11. R. M. Kidder, "Cleaning Up Damage of Economic Collapse Must Be Rooted in Values, Argues Sociologist," *Ethics Newsline,* www.globalethics.org/newsline (June 15, 2009).

12. N. F. Koehn, "How to Stop Trading Away the Future," *New York Times Online,* March 5, 2011; and L. Meckler, "Public Wary of Deficit, Economic Intervention," *Wall Street Journal,* June 18, 2009, pp. A1+.

13. C. Rampell, "The 'New Normal' Is Actually Pretty Old," *New York Times Online,* January 11, 2011; R. Farzad, "Normal," *Bloomberg BusinessWeek,* December 20, 2010–January 2, 2011, pp. 15–18; and N. H. Tseng, "Five 'New Normals' That Really Will Stick," *CNNMoney.com,* August 20, 2010.

14. P. Coy, "If Demography Is Destiny, Then India Has the Edge," *Bloomberg BusinessWeek,* January 17–23, 2011, pp. 9–10.

15. Managing Technology box based on R. M. Kesner, "Running Information Services as a Business: Managing IS Commitments within the Enterprise," *Information Strategy,* Summer 2002, pp. 15–35.

16. M. Richtel, "Growing Up Digital, Wired for Distraction," *New York Times Online,* November 21, 2010; S. Jayson, "iGeneration Has No Off Switch," *USA Today,* February 10, 2010, pp. 1D+; and L. Rosen, *Rewired: Understanding the iGeneration and the Way They Learn* (Palgrave-McMillan), 2010.

17. R. Friedrich, M. Peterson, and A. Koster, "The Rise of Generation C," *Strategy+Business,* Spring 2011, pp. 1–8.

18. S. Cardwell, "Where Do Babies Come From?" *Newsweek,* October 19, 2009, p. 56.

19. Y. Hori, J-P. Lehmann, T. Ma Kam Wah, and V. Wang, "Facing Up to the Demographic Dilemma," *Strategy+Business Online,* Spring 2010; and E. E. Gordon, "Job Meltdown or Talent Crunch?" *Training* (January 2010), p. 10.

20. R. Hampson, "The Changing Face of American Jobs," *USA Today,* January 13, 2011, pp. 1A+; P. Izzo, "Economists Expect Shifting Work Force," *Wall Street Journal Online,* February 11, 2010; and J. Lanhart, "Even In a Recovery, Some Jobs Won't Return," *Wall Street Journal,* January 12, 2010, p. A15.

21. E. Frauenheim, "Companies Focus Their Attention on Flexibility," *Workforce Management Online,* February 2011; P. Davidson, "Companies Do More with Fewer Workers," *USA Today,* February 23, 2011, pp. 1B+; K. Bennhold, "Working Part-Time in the 21st Century," *New York Times Online,* December 29, 2010; M. Rich, "Weighing Costs, Companies Favor Temporary Help," *New York Times Online,* December 19, 2010; P. Davidson, "Temporary Workers Reshape Companies, Jobs," *USA Today,* October 13, 2010, pp. 1A+; P. Davidson, "More Temp Workers Are Getting Hired," *USA Today,* March 8, 2010, p. 1B; S. Reddy, "Wary Companies Rely on Temporary Workers," *Wall Street Journal,* March 6–7, 2010, p. A4; P. Davidson, "Cuts in Hours Versus Cuts in Jobs," *USA Today,* February 25, 2010, p. 1B; and S. A. Hewlett, L. Sherbin, and K. Sumberg, "How Gen Y and Boomers Will Reshape Your Agenda," *Harvard Business Review,* July–August, 2009, pp. 71–76.

22. J. R. Hagerty, "Zippos Preps for a Post-Smoker World," *Wall Street Journal,* March 8, 2011, pp. B1+.

23. J. P. Walsh, "Book Review Essay: Taking Stock of Stakeholder Management," *Academy of Management Review,* April 2005, pp. 426–438; R. E. Freeman, A. C. Wicks, and B. Parmar, "Stakeholder Theory and The Corporate Objective Revisited," *Organization Science,* 15 (2004), pp. 364–369; T. Donaldson and L. E. Preston, "The Stakeholder Theory of the Corporation: Concepts, Evidence, and Implications," *Academy of Management Review,* January 1995, pp. 65–91; and R. E. Freeman, *Strategic Management: A Stakeholder Approach* (Boston: Pitman/Ballinger), 1984.

24. J. S. Harrison and C. H. St. John, "Managing and Partnering with External Stakeholders," *Academy of Management Executive,* May 1996, pp. 46–60.

25. J. Swartz, "Facebook Changes Its Status in Washington," *USA Today,* January 13, 2011, p. 1B+.

26. S. L. Berman, R. A. Phillips, and A. C. Wicks, "Resource Dependence, Managerial Discretion, and Stakeholder Performance," *Academy of Management Proceedings* Best Conference Paper, August 2005; A. J. Hillman and G. D. Keim, "Shareholder Value, Stakeholder Management, and Social Issues: What's the Bottom Line?" *Strategic Management Journal* (March 2001), pp. 125–139; J. S. Harrison and R. E. Freeman, "Stakeholders, Social Responsibility, and Performance: Empirical Evidence and Theoretical Perspectives," *Academy of Management Journal* (July 1999), pp. 479–487; and J. Kotter and J. Heskett, *Corporate Culture and Performance* (New York: The Free Press, 1992).

27. Right or Wrong box based on M. Helft, "Jobs Returns to Introduce a New iPad," *New York Times Online,* March 2, 2011; R. Pyrillis, "Apple Won't Say Who Will Eventually Take Jobs' Job," *Workforce Management Online,* February 25, 2011; A. Satariano, "Apple Challenged by Investors on Jobs Succession Planning," *Bloomberg BusinessWeek Online,* February 23, 2011; J. Sonnenfeld, "The Genius Dilemma," *Newsweek,* January 31, 2011, pp. 12–17; C. Hausman, "Ethics Questions After Steve Jobs Takes Medical Leave from Apple," *Ethics Newsline Online,* January 31, 2011; A. Satariano, "The Essence of Apple," *Bloomberg BusinessWeek,* January 24–30, 2011, pp. 6–8;
J. S. Lublin, "Investors Want Right to Know," *Wall Street Journal,* January 24, 2011, p. B7; G. Strauss, J. Swartz, and J. Graham, "As Jobs Steps Away, It's a Test for Apple," *USA Today,* January 18, 2011, pp. 1A+; Y. I. Kane and J. S. Lublin, "Apple Chief to Take Leave," *Wall Street Journal,* January 18, 2011, pp. A1+; B. Weinstein, "How Truthful Must CEO Steve Jobs Be?" *Bloomberg BusinessWeek Online,* January 18, 2011; S. Lohr, "Can Apple Find More Hits Without Its Tastemaker?" *New York Times Online,* January 18, 2011; and M. Helft, "Jobs Takes Sick Leave at Apple Again, Stirring Questions," *New York Times Online,* January 17, 2011.

28. J. Toonkel, "Vanguard CEO to Employees: Let's Lose the Suits," *Workforce Management Online,* December 3, 2010.

29. K. Shadur and M. A. Kienzle, "The Relationship Between Organizational Climate and Employee Perceptions of Involvement," *Group & Organization Management,* December 1999, pp. 479–503; M. J. Hatch, "The Dynamics of Organizational Culture," *Academy of Management Review,* October 1993, pp. 657–693; D. R. Denison, "What Is the Difference between Organizational Culture and Organizational Climate? A Native's Point of View on a Decade of Paradigm

Wars," paper presented at Academy of Management Annual Meeting, 1993, Atlanta, GA; and L. Smircich, "Concepts of Culture and Organizational Analysis," *Administrative Science Quarterly,* September 1983, p. 339.

30. J. A. Chatman and K. A. Jehn, "Assessing the Relationship between Industry Characteristics and Organizational Culture: How Different Can You Be?" *Academy of Management Journal* (June 1994), pp. 522–553; and C. A. O'Reilly III, J. Chatman, and D. F. Caldwell, "People and Organizational Culture: A Profile Comparison Approach to Assessing Person-Organization Fit," *Academy of Management Journal* (September 1991), pp. 487–516.

31. P. Guber, "The Four Truths of the Storyteller," *Harvard Business Review,* December 2007, pp. 53–59; S. Denning, "Telling Tales," *Harvard Business Review,* May 2004, pp. 122–129; T. Terez, "The Business of Storytelling," *Workforce,* May 2002, pp. 22–24; J. Forman, "When Stories Create an Organization's Future," *Strategy & Business,* Second Quarter 1999, pp. 6–9; C. H. Deutsch, "The Parables of Corporate Culture," *New York Times,* October 13, 1991, p. F25; and D. M. Boje, "The Storytelling Organization: A Study of Story Performance in an Office-Supply Firm," *Administrative Science Quarterly,* March 1991, pp. 106–126.

32. E. Ransdell, "The Nike Story? Just Tell It!" *Fast Company,* January–February 2000, pp. 44–46.

33. J. Useem, "Jim McNerney Thinks He Can Turn 3M from a Good Company into a Great One—With a Little Help from His Former Employer, General Electric," *Fortune,* August 12, 2002, pp. 127–132.

34. Denning, 2004; and A. M. Pettigrew, "On Studying Organizational Cultures," *Administrative Science Quarterly,* December 1979, p. 576.

35. M. T. Dacin, K. Munir, and P. Tracey, "Formal Dining at Cambridge Colleges: Linking Ritual Performance and Institutional Maintenance," *Academy of Management Journal* (December 2010), pp. 1393–1418.

36. D. Drickhamer, "Straight to the Heart," *Industry Week,* October 2003, pp. 36–38.

37. E. H. Schein, "Organizational Culture," *American Psychologist,* February 1990, pp. 109–119.

38. M. Zagoski, "Here's the Drill," *Fast Company,* February 2001, p. 58.

39. "Slogans That Work," *Forbes.com Special,* January 7, 2008, p. 99.

40. And the Survey Says box based on "Best Leaders Bounce Back," *Training,* July–August 2010, p. 7; J. Yang and P. Trap, "Burden vs. Opportunity," *USA Today,* October 13, 2010, p. 1B; C. Hausman, "Harris Asks the U.S. Public What It's Angry About," *Ethics Newsline Online,* November 15, 2010; J. MacIntyre, "Hurdles to Re-Entry," *Springfield, Missouri Business Journal,* August 16–22, 2010, p. 16; G. Kranz, "Fit to Be Tied? Recession May Inspire More Formal Work Attire," *Workforce Management Online,* October 18, 2008; J. Light, "Sudden Leader Loss Leaves Firms in Limbo," *Wall Street Journal,* January 24, 2011, p. B7; and J. Yang and A. Gonzalez, "CEO Challenges," *USA Today,* December 23, 2008, p. 1B.

41. A. Bryant, "Chaos and Order: How to Strike the Best Balance," *New York Times Online,* March 5, 2011.

42. E. H. Schein, *Organizational Culture and Leadership* (San Francisco: Jossey-Bass, 1985), pp. 314–315.

43. C. Palmeri, "The Fastest Drill in the West," *BusinessWeek,* October 24, 2005, pp. 86–88.

44. J. Levine, "Dare to Be Boring," *Time,* February 1, 2010, pp. Global Business 1–2.

YOUR TURN TO BE A MANAGER

Skill Development: Reading an Organization's Culture

An organization's culture is a system of shared meaning. When you understand your organization's culture, you know whether it encourages teamwork, rewards innovation, or stifles initiative. When interviewing for a job, the more accurate a manager is at assessing the culture, the more likely he or she is to find a good person-organization fit. And once inside an organization, understanding the culture allows managers to know what behaviors are likely to be rewarded and which are likely to be punished.

Personal Insights: What's the Right Organizational Culture for Me?

For each of the seven statements, indicate your level of agreement or disagreement using the following scale:

1 = Strongly disagree
2 = Disagree
3 = Uncertain
4 = Agree
5 = Strongly agree

1. I like the thrill and excitement from taking risks.   1 2 3 4 5
2. I prefer managers who provide detailed and rational explanations for their decisions.   1 2 3 4 5
3. If a person's job performance is inadequate, it's irrelevant how much effort he or she made.   1 2 3 4 5
4. No person's needs should be compromised in order for a department to achieve its goals.   1 2 3 4 5
5. I like being part of a team and having my performance assessed in terms of my contribution to the team.   1 2 3 4 5
6. I like to work where there isn't a great deal of pressure and where people are essentially easygoing.   1 2 3 4 5
7. I like things to be stable and predictable.   1 2 3 4 5

Source: S.P. Robbins, *Organizational Behavior*, 8th ed. (Upper Saddle River, NJ: Prentice Hall, 1998), p. 617.

Analysis and Interpretation

This instrument taps the seven primary dimensions of an organization's culture: innovation and risk taking, attention to detail, outcome orientation, people orientation, team orientation, aggressiveness, and stability.

To calculate your score, add up your responses but reverse your scores for items 2 and 7. Your total score will range between 7 and 35. Scores of 21 or lower indicate that you're more comfortable in a formal, mechanistic, rule-oriented, and structured culture. This is often associated with large corporations and government agencies. The lower your number, the stronger your preference for this type of culture. Scores above 22 indicate a preference for informal, humanistic, flexible, and innovative cultures, which are more likely to be found in high-tech companies, small businesses, research units, or advertising agencies. The higher your score above 22, the stronger your preference for these humanistic cultures.

Organizational cultures differ. So do individuals. The better you're able to match your personal preferences to an organization's culture, the more likely you are to find satisfaction in your work, the less likely you are to leave, and the greater the probability that you'll receive positive performance evaluations.

Skill Basics

The ability to read an organization's culture can be a valuable skill. For instance, if you're looking for a job, you'll want to choose an employer whose culture is compatible with your values and in which you'll feel comfortable. If you can accurately assess a potential employer's culture before you make your job decision, you may be able to save yourself a lot of grief and reduce the likelihood of making a poor choice. Similarly, you'll undoubtedly have business transactions with numerous organizations during your professional career, such as selling a product or service, negotiating a contract, arranging a joint work project, or merely seeking out who controls certain decisions in an organization. The ability to assess another organization's culture can be a definite plus in successfully performing those pursuits.

You can be more effective at reading an organization's culture if you use the following behaviors. For the sake of simplicity, we're going to look at this skill from the perspective of a job applicant. We'll assume that you're interviewing for a job, although these skills are generalizable to many situations. Here's a list of things you can do to help learn about an organization's culture.

1. *Do background work.* Get the names of former employees from friends or acquaintances, and talk with them. Also talk with members of professional trade associations to which the organization's employees belong and executive recruiters who deal with the organization. Look for clues in stories told in annual reports and other organizational literature, and check out the organization's Web sites for evidence of high turnover or recent management shake-ups.

2. *Observe the physical surroundings.* Pay attention to signs, posters, pictures, photos, style of dress, length of hair, degree of openness between offices, and office furnishings and arrangements.

3. *Make note about those with whom you met.* Whom did you meet? How did they expect to be addressed?

4. *How would you characterize the style of the people you met?* Are they formal? Casual? Serious? Jovial? Open? Reticent about providing information?

5. *Look at the organization's human resources manual.* Are there formal rules and regulations printed there? If so, how detailed are they? What do they cover?

6. *Ask questions of the people with whom you meet.* The most valid and reliable information tends to come from asking the same questions of many people (to see how closely their responses align). Questions that will give you insights into organizational processes and practices might include: What's the background of the founders? What's the background of current senior managers? What are these managers' functional specialties, and were they

promoted from within or hired from outside? How does the organization integrate new employees? Is there a formal orientation program? Are there formal employee training programs and, if so, how are they structured? How does your boss define his or her job success? How would you define fairness in terms of reward allocations? Can you identify some people here who are on the "fast track"? What do you think has put them on the fast track? Can you identify someone in the organization who seems to be considered a deviant and how has the organization responded to this person? Can you describe a decision that someone made that was well received? Can you describe a decision that didn't work out well, and what were the consequences for that decision maker? Could you describe a crisis or critical event that has occurred recently in the organization and how did top management respond?

Based on A. L. Wilkins, "The Culture Audit: A Tool for Understanding Organizations," *Organizational Dynamics*, Autumn 1983, pp. 24–38; H. M. Trice and J. M. Beyer, *The Culture of Work Organizations* (Upper Saddle River, NJ: Prentice Hall, 1993), pp. 358–362; and D. M. Cable, L. Aiman-Smith, P. W. Mulvey, and J. R. Edwards, "The Sources and Accuracy of Job Applicants' Beliefs About Organizational Culture," *Academy of Management Journal* (December 2000), pp. 1076–1085.

Skill Application

After spending your first three years after college graduation as a freelance graphic designer, you're looking at pursuing a job as an account executive at a graphic design firm. You feel that the scope of assignments and potential for technical training far exceed what you'd be able to do on your own, and you're looking to expand your skills and meet a brand-new set of challenges. However, you want to make sure you "fit" into the organization where you're going to be spending more than eight hours every workday. What's the best way for you to find a place where you'll be happy and where your style and personality will be appreciated?

Skill Practice

1. If you're taking more than one course, assess the culture of the various classes in which you're enrolled. How do the classroom cultures differ?

2. Assume you're a newly hired CEO for a 30-person company that designs and makes computer games. Your past experience has been as a programmer, team leader, and operations vice president at a much larger gaming firm. In your new job, you will be replacing the founder who started the business in his garage. But the founder recently discovered he has a very serious illness and needs to give up active management of the firm. From your viewpoint, the company's current culture closely mirrors the characteristics of the founder: brash, risk-taking, assertive, and highly informal. You believe that future success requires the company to become more business-like: It needs more rules and regulations, more professionalism, less wild risk-taking, and more strategic planning. You realize that these changes will be difficult for many of the firm's employees. Nevertheless, they need to be implemented. How would you go about changing your firm's culture? Be specific.

FYIA

Speedy Car Wash Services, Inc.

To: Michelle Bradley, Employee Care Manager
From: Alex Bilyeu, President
Re: Creating a Fun Workplace

Michelle, I saw an article the other day explaining the results of a survey that said only 8 percent of employers use fun to reduce employee stress at work. That same article said that research

has shown that people who have fun at work are more creative, more productive, work better with others, and call in sick less often. I'm sold! So how and where do we start? Get me a bulleted list of ideas on how we can create a workplace here at Speedy that's both fun and yet still focused on work. I'm sure you'll have to do some research on this. And oh . . . have fun with it!

This fictionalized company and message were created for educational purposes only, and not meant to reflect positively or negatively on management practices by any company that may share this name.

Bringing the Real World to Life

Case Application:
Going to Extremes: Part 2

Not only is Zappos the number one e-retailer, but it also is ranked the sixth best company to work for in *Fortune* magazine's annual survey. Okay, so what is it really about Zappos that makes its culture so great? Let's take a closer look.

Zappos began selling shoes and other products online in 1999. Four years later, it was profitable, and it reached more than $1 billion in sales by 2009. Also, in 2009, Zappos was named *BusinessWeek*'s Customer Service Champ and was given an A+ rating by the Better Business Bureau. Also that year, Amazon (yeah . . . that Amazon) purchased Zappos for 10 million Amazon shares, worth almost $928 million at the time. Zappos' employees divided up $40 million in cash and restricted stock and were assured that Zappos management would remain in place.

The person who was determined to "build a culture that applauds such things as weirdness and humility" was Tony Hsieh (pronounced *Shay*) who became CEO of Zappos in 2000. And Tony is the epitome of weirdness and humility. For instance, on April Fools' Day 2010, he issued a press release announcing that "Zappos was suing Walt Disney Company in a class action suit claiming that Disney was misleading the public by saying that Disneyland is 'the happiest place on earth' because clearly" Hsieh argued, Zappos is.

Before joining Zappos, Hsieh had been cofounder of the Internet advertising network LinkExchange and had seen first-hand the "dysfunction that can arise from building a company in which technical skill is all that matters." He was determined to do it differently at Zappos. Hsieh first invited the 300 employees at Zappos to list the core values that the culture should be based upon. That process led to the 10 values that continue to drive the organization, which now employs about 1,400 people.

Another thing that distinguishes the Zappos culture is the recognition that organizational culture is more than a list of written values. The culture has to be "lived." And Zappos does this by maintaining a "complex web of human interactions." At Zappos, social media is used liberally to link employees with one another and with the company's customers. For instance, one recent tweet said, "Hey. Did anyone bring a hairdryer to the office today?" This kind of camaraderie can maintain and sustain employee commitment to the company.

Also, at Zappos, the company's "pulse" or "health" of the culture is surveyed monthly. In these happiness surveys, employees answer such "unlikely questions as whether they believe that the company has a higher purpose than profits, whether their own role has meaning, whether they feel in control of their career path, whether they consider their co-workers to be like family and friends, and whether they are happy in their jobs." Survey results are broken down by department and opportunities for "development" are identified and acted on. For example, when one month's survey showed that a particular department had "veered off course and felt isolated from the rest of the organization," actions were taken to show employees how integral their work was to the rest of the company.

And one other thing about Zappos: Every year, to celebrate its accomplishments, it publishes a *Culture Book,* a testimonial to the power of its culture. "Zappos has a belief that the right culture with the right values will always produce the best organizational performance, and this belief trumps everything else."

DISCUSSION QUESTIONS

1. Find a list of all 10 of Zappos' corporate values. Pick two of the values and explain how you think those values would influence the way employees do their work.

2. Using this list of corporate values and Exhibit 2–4, describe Zappos' organizational culture. In which areas would you say that Zappos' culture is very high (or typical)? Explain.

3. How did Zappos' corporate culture begin?

4. How is Zappos' corporate culture maintained?

5. "The right culture with the right values will always produce the best organizational performance." What do you think of this statement? Do you agree? Why or why not?

6. What could other companies learn from Tony Hsieh and Zappos' experiences?

Integrative Managerial Issues

Integrative Managerial Issues

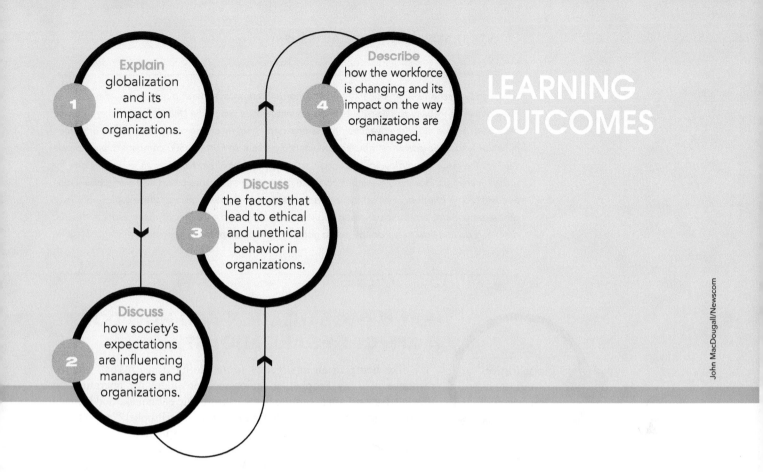

Explain globalization and its impact on organizations. **1**

Describe how the workforce is changing and its impact on the way organizations are managed. **4**

Discuss the factors that lead to ethical and unethical behavior in organizations. **3**

Discuss how society's expectations are influencing managers and organizations. **2**

John MacDougall/Newscom

A Level Playing Field?

Companies across the globe have a problem—a large gender gap in leadership.[1] Men far outnumber women in senior business leadership positions. This sexism exists despite efforts and campaigns to improve equality in the workplace. However, one European company—Deutsche Telekom—is tackling the problem head-on. It says that it intends to "more than double the number of women who are managers within five years." In addition, it plans to increase the number of women in senior and middle management to 30 percent by the end of 2015, up from 12 percent today. With this announcement, the company becomes the first member of the DAX 30 index of blue-chip German companies to introduce a gender quota. Deutsche's chief executive René Obermann said, "Taking on more women in management positions is not about the enforcement of misconstrued egalitarianism. Having a greater number of women at the top will quite simply enable us to operate better."

Although Deutsche Telekom's goal of bringing more women into leadership positions is admirable, it's not alone in its inability to diversify its management ranks. Even in the United States, where women have been graduating with advanced professional degrees in record numbers, the number of women in senior leadership positions remains low—only 3 percent of Fortune 500 companies have female CEOs.[2] The issue of employing and engaging a diverse global workforce is an important one for today's managers. However, managers also face other important issues associated with globalization and with doing business in an ethical and responsible way. Because each of these topics—diversity, globalization, and ethics/social responsibility—are integrated throughout many aspects of what managers do and how they manage, we're going to look closer at these integrative managerial issues in this chapter.

WHAT IS GLOBALIZATION AND HOW DOES IT AFFECT ORGANIZATIONS?

Explain globalization and its impact on organizations.

1

"It's like being in an emergency room, doing triage." That was the response of Tony Prophet, a senior vice president for operations at Hewlett-Packard after learning that a catastrophic earthquake and tsunami had hit Japan. Not long after getting the news, Mr. Prophet "had set up a virtual 'situation room' so managers in Japan, Taiwan, and America could instantly share information." The analogy of an emergency room was very apt, according to experts, because "modern global supply chains mirror complex biological systems. . . . They can be remarkably resilient and self-healing, yet at times quite vulnerable to some specific seemingly small weakness." Normally, the global flow of goods routinely adapts, day in and day out, to all kinds of glitches and setbacks. However, when a major disaster strikes (for instance, an earthquake in Japan or New Zealand, a volcano in Iceland, labor unrest in China, political upheavals in the Middle East, floods in India, or a hurricane in the United States), the fragility of the global supply chain becomes more apparent.[3]

An important issue that managers must deal with is globalization. One important component of the external environment is the global arena. Major events such as catastrophic natural disasters and the global economic meltdown of the past few years have created challenges for managers doing business globally. Despite such challenges, globalization isn't about to disappear. Nations and businesses have been trading with each other for centuries through all kinds of disasters and economic ups and downs. Over the last couple of decades, we've seen an explosion of companies operating almost anywhere in the world. National borders mean little when it comes to doing business. Avon, a so-called American company, gets 79 percent of its annual revenues from sales outside North America. BMW, a German-owned firm, builds cars in South Carolina. McDonald's sells hamburgers in China. Tata, an Indian company, purchased the Jaguar brand—which started as a British company—from Ford Motor Company. Although the world is still a global village—that is, a boundaryless world where goods and services are produced and marketed worldwide—how managers do business in that global village is changing. To be effective in this boundaryless world, managers need to adapt to this changed environment, as well as continue to foster an understanding of cultures, systems, and techniques that are different from their own.

What Does It Mean to Be "Global"?

Organizations are considered global if they exchange goods and services with consumers in other countries. Such marketplace globalization is the most common approach to being global. However, many organizations, especially high-tech organizations, are considered global because they use managerial and technical employee talent from other countries. One factor that affects talent globalization is immigration laws and regulations. Managers must be alert to changes in those laws. Finally, an organization can be considered global if it uses financial sources and resources outside its home country, which is known as financial globalization.[4] As might be expected, the global economic slowdown severely affected the availability of financial resources globally. And even as countries' economies began the slow process of recovery, the impact continued to be felt globally.

What Are the Different Types of Global Organizations?

In the mid-1960s, multinational corporations (MNCs) became commonplace and initiated rapid growth in international trade. MNCs are any type of international company that maintains operations in multiple countries. Today, companies such as Procter & Gamble, Walmart, Exxon, Coca-Cola, and Aflac are among a growing number of U.S.-based firms that earn significant portions of their annual revenues from foreign operations.

One type of MNC is a multidomestic corporation, which decentralizes management and other decisions to the local country in which it is operating. A multidomestic corporation doesn't attempt to replicate its domestic successes by managing foreign operations from its home country. Instead, local employees typically are hired to manage the business and marketing strategies are tailored to that country's unique characteristics. Many consumer product companies organize their global businesses using this approach because they must adapt their products to meet the needs of local markets. For example, Switzerland-based Nestlé operates as a multidomestic corporation. With operations in almost every country on the globe, its managers are responsible for making sure the company's products fit its consumers wherever they are. In parts of Europe, Nestlé sells products that are not available in the United States or Latin America.

Another type of MNC is a global corporation, which centralizes its management and other decisions in the home country. These companies treat the world market as an integrated whole and focus on the need for global efficiency. Although these companies may have considerable global holdings, management decisions with company-wide implications are made from headquarters in the home country. Some examples of global companies include Sony, Deutsche Bank AG, and Merrill Lynch (now a subsidiary of Bank of America).

Other companies use an arrangement that eliminates artificial geographical barriers. This type of MNC is often called a transnational or borderless organization.[5] For example, IBM dropped its organizational structure based on country and reorganized into industry groups. Ford Motor Company is pursuing the One Ford concept as it integrates its global operations. Another company, Thomson SA, which is legally incorporated in France, has eight major locations around the globe. The CEO said, "We don't want people to think we're based anyplace."[6] Managers choose this approach to increase efficiency and effectiveness in a competitive global marketplace.[7]

This young man enjoying a Coke in Copenhagen, Denmark, is consuming one of 1.7 billion servings a day of a beverage brand owned by The Coca-Cola Company. A multinational manufacturer, distributor, and marketer, the company produces more than 400 brands and 3,500 different products, including soft drinks, water, juices and juice drinks, sports and energy drinks, sparkling beverages, and tea and coffee. Based in Atlanta, Georgia, it operates in more than 200 countries and generates almost 80 percent of its revenue from operations outside of the United States. The Coca-Cola Company is a global business that operates on a local scale with hundreds of bottling partners worldwide in achieving its mission "to refresh the world."

Francis Dean/Newscom

---

global village
A boundaryless world where goods and services are produced and marketed worldwide

multinational corporation (MNC)
Any type of international company that maintains operations in multiple countries

multidomestic corporation
An MNC that decentralizes management and other decisions to the local country where it's doing business

global corporation
An MNC that centralizes management and other decisions in the home country.

transnational (borderless) organization
A structural arrangement for global organizations that eliminates artificial geographical barriers

How Do Organizations Go Global?

When organizations do go global, they often use different approaches. (See Exhibit 1.) At first, managers may want to get into a global market with minimal investment. At this stage, they may start with global sourcing (also called global outsourcing), which is purchasing materials or labor from around the world wherever it is cheapest. The goal: take advantage of lower costs in order to be more competitive. For instance, Massachusetts General Hospital uses radiologists in India to interpret CT scans.[8] Although global sourcing may be the first step to going international for many companies, they often continue using this approach because of the competitive advantages it offers. However, as the current economic crisis accelerated, many organizations reconsidered their decisions to source globally. For instance, Dell, Apple, and American Express are just a few that have scaled back some of their offshore customer service operations. One analyst said that companies rethinking their global sourcing decisions are trying to make "choices about the best place to do a given piece of work—be it offshore, onshore, or nearshore. As this transformation occurs, work is being spread throughout the world and companies are globalizing to keep up."[9] When a company wants to take that next step in going global, each successive stage beyond global sourcing requires more investment and thus entails more risk for the organization.

The next step in going global may involve exporting the organization's products to other countries—that is, making products domestically and selling them abroad. In addition, an organization might do importing, which involves acquiring products made abroad and selling them domestically. Both usually entail minimal investment and risk, which is why many small businesses often use these approaches to doing business globally.

Finally, managers might use licensing or franchising, which are similar approaches involving one organization giving another organization the right to use its brand name, technology, or product specifications in return for a lump sum payment or a fee that is usually based on sales. The only difference is that licensing is primarily used by manufacturing organizations that make or sell another company's products, and franchising is primarily used by service organizations that want to use another company's name and operating methods. For example, New Delhi consumers can enjoy Subway sandwiches, Namibians can dine on KFC fried chicken, and Russians can consume Dunkin' Donuts—all because of *franchises* in these countries. On the other hand, Anheuser-Busch InBev *licensed* the right to brew and market its Budweiser beer to brewers such as Labatt in Canada, Modelo in Mexico, and Kirin in Japan.

Once an organization has been doing business internationally for a while and has gained experience in international markets, managers may decide to make more of a direct investment. One way to do this is through a global strategic alliance, which is a partnership between an organization and a foreign company partner or partners in which both

EXHIBIT 1   How Organizations Go Global

Minimal Global Investment ⟷ Significant Global Investment

• Global Sourcing

• Exporting and Importing
• Licensing
• Franchising

• Strategic Alliance
  – Joint Venture
• Foreign Subsidiary

share resources and knowledge in developing new products or building production facilities. For example, Honda Motor and General Electric teamed up to produce a new jet engine. A specific type of strategic alliance in which the partners form a separate, independent organization for some business purpose is called a **joint venture**. For example, Hewlett-Packard has had numerous joint ventures with various suppliers around the globe to develop different components for its computer equipment. These partnerships provide a relatively easy way for companies to compete globally.

Finally, managers may choose to directly invest in a foreign country by setting up a **foreign subsidiary** as a separate and independent facility or office. This subsidiary can be managed as a multidomestic organization (local control) or as a global organization

(centralized control). As you can probably guess, this arrangement involves the greatest commitment of resources and poses the greatest amount of risk. For instance, United Plastics Group of Westmont, Illinois, built three injection-molding facilities in Suzhou, China. The company's executive vice president for business development says that level of investment was necessary because "it fulfilled our mission of being a global supplier to our global accounts."[10]

What Do Managers Need to Know About Managing in a Global Organization?

A global world brings new challenges for managers, especially in managing in a country with a different national culture.[11] A specific challenge comes from the need to recognize the differences that might exist and then find ways to make interactions effective.

U.S. managers once held (and some still do hold) a rather parochial view of the world of business. **Parochialism** is a narrow focus in which managers see things only through their own eyes and from their own perspectives. They don't recognize that people from other countries have different ways of doing things or that they live differently from Americans. This view can't succeed in a global village—nor is it the dominant view held today. Changing such perceptions requires understanding that countries have different cultures and environments.

All countries have different values, morals, customs, political and economic systems, and laws, all of which can affect how a business is managed. For instance, in the United States, laws guard against employers taking action against employees solely on the basis of their age. Similar laws can't be found in all other countries. Thus, managers must be aware of a country's laws when doing business there.

The most important and challenging differences for managers to understand, however, are those related to a country's social context or culture. For example, status is perceived

These young employees pose for a picture at the official opening of Intel's new assembly plant and test facilities in Ho Chi Minh City, Vietnam. While building the complex, Intel's managers faced many challenges in recruiting and training young workers for the new plant due to cultural differences between the United States and Vietnam. For example, the work culture in Vietnam is based on a hierarchical system of power, status, and authority, in contrast to Intel's culture of teamwork. By understanding these differences and knowing that Vietnamese youth love American pop culture, managers used team-building exercises such as Karaoke Fridays to teach the young trainees how to become team players.

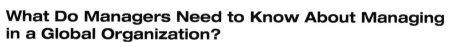

global sourcing
Purchasing materials or labor from around the world, wherever it is cheapest

exporting
Making products domestically and selling them abroad

importing
Acquiring products made abroad and selling them domestically

licensing
An agreement in which an organization gives another the right, for a fee, to make or sell its products, using its technology or product specifications

franchising
An agreement in which an organization gives another organization the right, for a fee, to use its name and operating methods

global strategic alliance
A partnership between an organization and a foreign company partner(s) in which both share resources and knowledge in developing new products or building production facilities

joint venture
A specific type of strategic alliance in which the partners agree to form a separate, independent organization for some business purpose

foreign subsidiary
A direct investment in a foreign country that involves setting up a separate and independent facility or office

parochialism
A narrow focus in which managers see things only through their own eyes and from their own perspective

From the Past to the Present

An illuminating study of the differences in cultural environments was conducted by Geert Hofstede in the 1970s and 1980s.[12] He surveyed more than 116,000 IBM employees in 40 countries about their work-related values. He found that managers and employees vary on five value dimensions of national culture:

- *Power distance.* The degree to which people in a country accept that power in institutions and organizations is distributed unequally. Ranges from relatively low (low power distance) to extremely unequal (high power distance).

- *Individualism versus collectivism.* Individualism is the degree to which people in a country prefer to act as individuals rather than as members of groups. Collectivism is the equivalent of low individualism.

- *Quantity of life versus quality of life.* Quantity of life is the degree to which values such as assertiveness, the acquisition of money and material goods, and competition are important. Quality of life is the degree to which people value relationships and show sensitivity and concern for the welfare of others.

- *Uncertainty avoidance.* This dimension assesses the degree to which people in a country prefer structured over unstructured situations and whether people are willing to take risks.

- *Long-term versus short-term orientation.* People in cultures with long-term orientations look to the future and value thrift and persistence. A short-term orientation values the past and present and emphasizes respect for tradition and fulfilling social obligations.

Here are a few highlights of four of Hofstede's cultural dimensions and how different countries rank on those dimensions:

Think About:

- Look at the ratings for Mexico and the United States. How do you think a team-based rewards program might work in each country?

- Look at the ratings for Italy and the United States. How do you think encouraging employees to take risks and to think "outside the box" might work in each country?

- What does this information tell you about the importance of understanding cultural differences?

COUNTRY	INDIVIDUALISM/ COLLECTIVISM	POWER DISTANCE	UNCERTAINTY AVOIDANCE	ACHIEVEMENT/ NURTURING[a]
Australia	Individual	Small	Moderate	Strong
Canada	Individual	Moderate	Low	Moderate
England	Individual	Small	Moderate	Strong
France	Individual	Large	High	Weak
Greece	Collective	Large	High	Moderate
Italy	Individual	Moderate	High	Strong
Japan	Collective	Moderate	High	Strong
Mexico	Collective	Large	High	Strong
Singapore	Collective	Large	Low	Moderate
Sweden	Individual	Small	Low	Weak
United States	Individual	Small	Low	Strong
Venezuela	Collective	Large	High	Strong

[a]A weak achievement score is equivalent to high nurturing.
Source: Based on G. Hofstede, "Motivation, Leadership, and Organization: Do American Theories Apply Abroad?" *Organizational Dynamics*, Summer 1980, pp. 42–63.

differently in different countries. In France, status is often the result of factors important to the organization, such as seniority, education, and the like. In the United States, status is more a function of what individuals have accomplished personally. Managers need to understand societal issues (such as status) that might affect business operations in another country and recognize that organizational success can come from a variety of managerial practices. Fortunately, managers have help in this regard by turning to the research that has been done on the differences in cultural environments.

HOFSTEDE'S FRAMEWORK. Geert Hofstede's framework is one of the most widely referenced approaches for analyzing cultural variations. His work has had a major impact on what we know about cultural differences among countries and is highlighted in our From the Past to the Present box.

GLOBE FINDINGS. Although Hofstede's work has provided the basic framework for differentiating among national cultures, most of the data are over 30 years old. Another more recent research program, called Global Leadership and Organizational Behavior Effectiveness (GLOBE), is an ongoing cross-cultural investigation of leadership and national culture. Using data from more than 17,000 managers in 62 societies around the world, the GLOBE research team (led by Robert House) has identified nine dimensions on which national cultures differ.[13] For each of these dimensions, we have indicated which countries rated high, which rated moderate, and which rated low.

- *Assertiveness.* The extent to which a society encourages people to be tough, confrontational, assertive, and competitive versus modest and tender. (*High:* Spain, United States, and Greece. *Moderate:* Egypt, Ireland, and Philippines. *Low:* Sweden, New Zealand, and Switzerland.)
- *Future orientation.* The extent to which a society encourages and rewards future-oriented behavior such as planning, investing in the future, and delaying gratification. (*High:* Denmark, Canada, and Netherlands. *Moderate:* Slovenia, Egypt, and Ireland. *Low:* Russia, Argentina, and Poland.)
- *Gender differentiation.* The extent to which a society maximizes gender role differences. (*High:* South Korea, Egypt, and Morocco. *Moderate:* Italy, Brazil, and Argentina. *Low:* Sweden, Denmark, and Slovenia.)
- *Uncertainty avoidance.* As defined in Hofstede's landmark research, the GLOBE team defined this term as a society's reliance on social norms and procedures to alleviate the unpredictability of future events. (*High:* Austria, Denmark, and Germany. *Moderate:* Israel, United States, and Mexico. *Low:* Russia, Hungary, and Bolivia.)
- *Power distance.* As in the original research, the GLOBE team defined this as the degree to which members of a society expect power to be unequally shared. (*High:* Russia, Spain, and Thailand. *Moderate:* England, France, and Brazil. *Low:* Denmark, Netherlands, and South Africa.)
- *Individualism/collectivism.* Again, this term was defined similarly to the original research as the degree to which individuals are encouraged by societal institutions to be integrated into groups within organizations and society. A low score is synonymous with collectivism. (*High:* Greece, Hungary, and Germany. *Moderate:* Hong Kong, United States, and Egypt. *Low:* Denmark, Singapore, and Japan.)
- *In-group collectivism.* In contrast to focusing on societal institutions, this dimension encompasses the extent to which members of a society take pride in membership in small groups such as their family and circle of close friends and the organizations in which they are employed. (*High:* Egypt, China, and Morocco. *Moderate:* Japan, Israel, and Qatar. *Low:* Denmark, Sweden, and New Zealand.)
- *Performance orientation.* This dimension refers to the degree to which a society encourages and rewards group members for performance improvement and excellence. (*High:* United States, Taiwan, and New Zealand. *Moderate:* Sweden, Israel, and Spain. *Low:* Russia, Argentina, and Greece.)
- *Humane orientation.* This cultural aspect is the degree to which a society encourages and rewards individuals for being fair, altruistic, generous, caring, and kind to others. (*High:* Indonesia, Egypt, and Malaysia. *Moderate:* Hong Kong, Sweden, and Taiwan. *Low:* Germany, Spain, and France.)

The GLOBE studies confirm that Hofstede's dimensions are still valid, and extend his research rather than replace it. GLOBE's added dimensions provide an expanded and updated measure of countries' cultural differences. It's likely that cross-cultural studies of human behavior and organizational practices will increasingly use the GLOBE dimensions to assess differences between countries. For instance, GLOBE's research dimensions are being used in creating and assessing international advertising.[14]

GLOBE
The Global Leadership and Organizational Behavior Effectiveness research program, a program that studies cross-cultural leadership behaviors

WHAT DOES SOCIETY EXPECT FROM ORGANIZATIONS AND MANAGERS?

2 **Discuss** how society's expectations are influencing managers and organizations.

It's an incredibly simple but potentially world-changing idea.[15] For each pair of shoes sold, a pair is donated to a child in need. That's the business model followed by TOMS Shoes. During a visit to Argentina in 2006 as a contestant on the CBS reality show *The Amazing Race,* Blake Mycoskie, founder of TOMS, "saw lots of kids with no shoes who were suffering from injuries to their feet." He was so moved by the experience that he wanted to do something. That something is what TOMS Shoes does now by blending charity with commerce. Those shoe donations—now over 1 million pairs—have been central to the success of the TOMS brand. And the brand's popularity is likely to increase as Mary-Kate and Ashley Olsen have partnered with TOMS Shoes in selling a special line of fashionable sandals.

What *does* society expect from organizations and managers? That may seem like a hard question to answer, but not for Blake Mycoskie. He believes that society expects organizations and managers to be respon-sible and ethical. However, as we saw in the publicized stories of notorious financial scandals at Enron, Bernard Madoff Investment Securities, HealthSouth, and others, managers don't always act responsibly or ethically.

How Can Organizations Demonstrate Socially Responsible Actions?

Few terms have been defined in as many different ways as *social responsibility.* Some of the more popular meanings include profit maximization, going beyond profit making, voluntary activities, and concern for the broader social system.[16] On one side is the classical—or purely economic—view that management's only social responsibility is to maximize profits.[17] On the other side is the socioeconomic position, which holds that management's responsibility goes beyond making profits to include protecting and improving society's welfare.[18]

When we talk about **social responsibility** (also known as **corporate social responsibility,** or **CSR**), we mean a business firm's intention, beyond its legal and economic obligations, to do the right things and act in ways that are good for society. Note that this definition assumes that a business obeys the law and pursues economic interests. But also note that this definition views a business as a moral agent. In its effort to do good for society, it must differentiate between right and wrong.

We can understand social responsibility better if we compare it to two similar concepts. **Social obligations** are those activities a business firm engages in to meet certain economic and legal responsibilities. It does the minimum that the law requires and only pursues social goals to the extent that they contribute to its economic goals. **Social responsiveness** is characteristic of the business firm that engages in social actions in response to some popu-lar social need. Managers in these companies are guided by social norms and values and make practical, market-oriented decisions about their actions.[19] A U.S. business that meets federal pollution standards or safe packaging regulations is meeting its social obligation because laws mandate these actions. However, when it provides on-site child-care facilities for employees or packages products using recycled paper, it's being socially respon-sive to working parents and environmentalists who have voiced these social concerns and demanded such actions. For many businesses, their social actions are probably better viewed as being socially responsive rather than socially responsible, at least according to our defini-tions. However, such actions are still good for society. Social responsibility adds an ethical imperative to do those things that make society better and to not do those that could make it worse.

College students surround Blake Mycoskie, the TOMS Shoes founder who believes that management's responsibility goes beyond making profits to include improving society's welfare. TOMS gives shoes to children in need by working with charitable giving partners throughout the world that are already established in countries where TOMS shoes are given. These partners must also meet TOMS criteria for responsible giving. They include giving shoes to the same children on a regular basis as they grow, being considerate of the local economy so giving shoes does not have a negative socioeconomic impact on communities, and incorporating the giving of shoes into their existing health, education, hygiene, and community development programs.

a27/Newscom

EXHIBIT 2	Arguments For and Against Social Responsibility

FOR	AGAINST
Public expectations Public opinion now supports businesses pursuing economic and social goals.	**Violation of profit maximization** Business is being socially responsible only when it pursues its economic interests.
Long-run profits Socially responsible companies tend to have more secure long-run profits.	**Dilution of purpose** Pursuing social goals dilutes business's primary purpose—economic productivity.
Ethical obligation Businesses should be socially responsible because responsible actions are the right thing to do.	**Costs** Many socially responsible actions do not cover their costs and someone must pay those costs.
Public image Businesses can create a favorable public image by pursuing social goals.	**Too much power** Businesses have a lot of power already and if they pursue social goals they will have even more.
Better environment Business involvement can help solve difficult social problems.	**Lack of skills** Business leaders lack the necessary skills to address social issues.
Discouragement of further governmental regulation By becoming socially responsible, businesses can expect less government regulation.	**Lack of accountability** There are no direct lines of accountability for social actions.
Balance of responsibility and power Businesses have a lot of power, and an equally large amount of responsibility is needed to balance against that power.	
Stockholder interests Social responsibility will improve a business's stock price in the long run.	
Possession of resources Businesses have the resources to support public and charitable projects that need assistance.	
Superiority of prevention over cures Businesses should address social problems before they become serious and costly to correct.	

Should Organizations Be Socially Involved?

The importance of corporate social responsibility surfaced in the 1960s when social activists questioned the singular economic objective of business. Even today, good arguments can be made for and against businesses being socially responsible. (See Exhibit 2.) Yet, arguments aside, times have changed. Managers regularly confront decisions that have a dimension of social responsibility: philanthropy, pricing, employee relations, resource conservation, product quality, and doing business in countries with oppressive governments are just a few. To address these issues, managers may reassess packaging design, recyclability of products, environmental safety practices, outsourcing decisions, foreign supplier practices, employee policies, and the like.

Another way to look at this issue is whether social involvement affects a company's economic performance, which numerous studies have done.[20] Although most found a

---

social responsibility (corporate social responsibility, or CSR)
A business firm's intention, beyond its legal and economic obligations, to do the right things and act in ways that are good for society

social obligation
When a business firm engages in social actions because of its obligation to meet certain economic and legal responsibilities

social responsiveness
When a business firm engages in social actions in response to some popular social need

AND THE SURVEY SAYS...[26]

40 percent of employees surveyed who witnessed workplace misconduct said they did not report it.

86 percent of consumers worldwide believe that a business needs to place at least as much weight on society's interests as it does on its own.

52 percent of organizations surveyed do not have a corporate ethics officer.

50 percent: how much more likely ethics books are to be stolen from libraries than other books.

10 times more misconduct is found in companies with weak ethical cultures than in companies with strong ethical cultures.

49 percent of employees surveyed said that if accidentally granted access to a confidential document they would read it.

95 percent of high school students surveyed said that they had cheated in the past year.

57 percent of those high school students said it was morally wrong to cheat.

small positive relationship, no generalizable conclusions can be made because these studies have shown that relationship is affected by various contextual factors such as firm size, industry, economic conditions, and regulatory environment.[21] Other researchers have questioned causation. If a study showed that social involvement and economic performance were positively related, this didn't necessarily mean that social involvement *caused* higher economic performance. It could simply mean that high profits afforded companies the "luxury" of being socially involved.[22] Such concerns can't be taken lightly. In fact, one study found that if the flawed empirical analyses in these studies were "corrected," social responsibility had a neutral impact on a company's financial performance.[23] Another found that participating in social issues not related to the organization's primary stakeholders had a negative effect on shareholder value.[24] Despite all these concerns, after re-analyzing several studies, other researchers have concluded that managers can afford to be (and should be) socially responsible.[25]

What Is Sustainability and Why Is It Important?

It's the world's largest retailer with almost $422 billion in annual sales, 2.1 million employees, and 8,400 stores. Yes, we're talking about Walmart. And considering its size, Walmart is probably the last company that you'd think about in a section describing sustainability. However, Walmart announced in early 2010 that it would "cut some 20 million metric tons of greenhouse gas emissions from its supply chain by the end of 2015—the equivalent of removing more than 3.8 million cars from the road for a year."[27] This corporate action affirms that sustainability has become a mainstream issue for managers.

What's emerging in the twenty-first century is the concept of managing in a sustainable way, which has had the effect of widening corporate responsibility not only to managing in an efficient and effective way, but also to responding strategically to a wide range of environmental and societal challenges.[28] Although "sustainability" means different things to different people, in essence, according to the World Business Council for Sustainable Development (2005), it is concerned with "meeting the needs of people today without compromising the ability of future generations to meet their own needs." From a business perspective, **sustainability** has been defined as a company's ability to achieve its business goals and increase long-term shareholder value by integrating economic, environmental, and social opportunities into its business strategies.[29] Sustainability issues are now moving up the agenda of business leaders and the boards of thousands of companies. Like the managers at Walmart are discovering, running an organization in a more sustainable way will mean that managers have to make informed business decisions based on thorough communication with various stakeholders, understanding their requirements, and factoring economic, environmental, and social aspects into how they pursue their business goals.

The idea of practicing sustainability affects many aspects of business, from the creation of products and services to their use and subsequent disposal by consumers. Following sustainability practices is one way in which organizations can show their commitment to being responsible. In today's world where many individuals have diminishing respect for businesses, few organizations can afford the bad press or potential economic ramifications of being seen as socially irresponsible. Managers also want to be seen as ethical, which is the topic we're going to look at next.

WHAT FACTORS DETERMINE ETHICAL AND UNETHICAL BEHAVIOR?

Discuss the factors that lead to ethical and unethical behavior in organizations.

3

- ◆ Employees at a law firm in Florida that handled foreclosures for Freddie Mac and Fannie Mae changed thousands of documents and hid them in a room when company officials came to conduct audits.
- ◆ A Paris court found Jérôme Kerviel, a former financial trader at French bank Société Générale, guilty of triggering a massive trading scandal

that created severe financial problems for his employer. Mr. Kerviel claims that the company turned a blind eye to his questionable but hugely profitable methods.

♦ According to the NFL Players Association, "352 players were placed on the season-ending injured reserve list in the 2010–11 season. That's 21 percent."[30] Hundreds more players suffered lesser injuries, from concussions to dislocations, keeping them from playing for at least one game.

You might be wondering about the connection among these three unrelated stories. When you read about these decisions, behaviors, and actions, you might be tempted to conclude that businesses just aren't ethical. Although that isn't the case, managers do face ethical issues and dilemmas.

Ethics commonly refers to a set of rules or principles that defines right and wrong conduct.[31] Right or wrong behavior, though, may at times be difficult to determine. Most recognize that something illegal is also unethical. But what about questionable "legal" areas or strict organizational policies? For instance, what if you managed an employee who worked all weekend on a rush project and you told him to take off two days sometime later and mark it down as "sick days" because your company had a clear policy that overtime would not be compensated for any reason?[32] Would that be wrong? As a manager, how will you handle such situations?

In What Ways Can Ethics Be Viewed?

To better understand what's involved with managerial ethics, we need to first look at three different perspectives on how managers make ethical decisions.[33] The utilitarian view of ethics says that ethical decisions are made solely on the basis of their outcomes or consequences. The goal of utilitarianism is to provide the greatest good for the greatest number. In the rights view of ethics, individuals are concerned with respecting and protecting individual liberties and privileges such as the right of free consent, the right to privacy, the right of free speech, and so forth. Making ethical decisions under this view is fairly simple because the goal is to avoid interfering with the rights of others who might be affected by the decision. Finally, under the theory of justice view of ethics, an individual imposes and enforces rules fairly and impartially. For instance, a manager would be using the theory of justice perspective by deciding to pay individuals who are similar in their levels of skills, performance, or responsibility the same and not base that decision on arbitrary differences such as gender, personality, or personal favorites. The goal of this approach is to be equitable, fair, and impartial in making decisions.

Regardless of which view you think is most appropriate, whether a manager (or any employee, for that matter) acts ethically or unethically will depend on several factors. These factors include an individual's morality, values, personality, and experiences; the organization's culture; and the ethical issue being faced.[34] People who lack a strong moral sense are much less likely to do the wrong things if they are constrained by rules, policies, job descriptions, or strong cultural norms that discourage such behaviors. For example, suppose that someone in your class stole the final exam and is selling a copy for $50. You need to do well on the exam or risk failing the course. You suspect that some classmates have bought copies, which could affect any results because your professor grades on a curve. Do you buy a copy because you fear that without it you'll be disadvantaged, do you refuse to buy a copy and

---

sustainability
A company's ability to achieve its business goals and increase long-term shareholder value by integrating economic, environmental, and social opportunities into its business strategies

ethics
A set of rules or principles that defines right and wrong conduct

utilitarian view of ethics
View that says ethical decisions are made solely on the basis of their outcomes or consequences

rights view of ethics
View that says ethical decisions are made in order to respect and protect individual liberties and privileges

theory of justice view of ethics
View that says ethical decisions are made in order to enforce rules fairly and impartially

I17/Newscom

In this photo, employees at a General Mills plant load boxes of cereal onto a community food bank truck as part of the company's commitment to Feeding America, a hunger relief organization. Doing things that make society better is an ethical imperative at General Mills, because it's the right thing to do. Each employee receives a Code of Conduct that outlines ethical expectations and gives examples for how to act with integrity in every decision and action. The company provides ethics training programs, an intranet site for compliance information, and an Ethics Line available 24/7 for help with ethical questions and for reporting violations. General Mills depends on its global workforce to act consistently with local laws and the company's values and ethical policies.

try your best, or do you report your knowledge to your instructor? This example of the final exam illustrates how ambiguity over what is ethical can be a problem for managers.

How Can Managers Encourage Ethical Behavior?

At a Senate hearing exploring the accusations that Wall Street firm Goldman Sachs deceived its clients during the housing-market meltdown, Arizona senator John McCain said, "I don't know if Goldman has done anything illegal, but there's no doubt their behavior was unethical."[35] You have to wonder what the firm's managers were thinking or doing while such ethically questionable decisions and actions were occurring. It's pretty obvious that they weren't encouraging ethical behaviors!

Managers can do a number of things if they're serious about encouraging ethical behaviors—hire employees with high ethical standards, establish codes of ethics, lead by example, link job goals and performance appraisal, provide ethics training, and implement protective mechanisms for employees who face ethical dilemmas. By themselves, such actions won't have much of an impact. But if an organization has a comprehensive ethics program in place, it can potentially improve an organization's ethical climate. The key variable, however, is *potentially*. A well-designed ethics program does not guarantee the desired outcome. Sometimes corporate ethics programs are mostly public relations gestures that do little to influence managers and employees. For instance, even Enron, often thought of as the "poster child" of corporate wrongdoing, outlined values in its final annual report that most would consider ethical—communication, respect, integrity, and excellence. Yet the way top managers behaved didn't reflect those values at all.[36] We want to look at three ways that managers can encourage ethical behavior and create a comprehensive ethics program.

CODES OF ETHICS. Codes of ethics are popular tools for attempting to reduce employee ambiguity about what's ethical and what's not.[37] A code of ethics is a formal document that states an organization's primary values and the ethical rules it expects managers and nonmanagerial employees to follow. Ideally, these codes should be specific enough to guide organizational members in what they're supposed to do yet loose enough to allow for freedom of judgment. Research shows that 97 percent of organizations with more than 10,000 employees have written codes of ethics. Even in smaller organizations, nearly 93 percent have them.[38] And codes of ethics are becoming more popular globally. Research by the Institute for Global Ethics says that shared values such as honesty, fairness, respect, responsibility, and caring are embraced worldwide.[39]

The effectiveness of such codes depends heavily on whether management supports them and ingrains them into the corporate culture, and how individuals who break the codes are treated.[40] If management considers them to be important, regularly reaffirms their content, follows the rules themselves, and publicly reprimands rule breakers, ethics codes can be a strong foundation for an effective corporate ethics program.[41]

ETHICAL LEADERSHIP. In 2007, Peter Löscher was hired as CEO of German company Siemens to clean up a global bribery scandal that cost the company a record-setting $1.34 billion in fines. His approach: "Stick to your principles. Have a clear ethical north. Be trusted and be the role model of your company . . . true leaders have a set of core values they publicly commit to and live by in good times and bad."[42] Doing business ethically requires a commitment from managers. Why? Because they're the ones who uphold the shared values and set the cultural tone. Managers must be good ethical role models both in words *and*, more importantly, in actions. What you *do* is far more important than what you *say* in getting employees to act ethically. For example, if managers take company

---

EXHIBIT 3 **Being an Ethical Leader**

- Be a good role model by being ethical and honest.
- Tell the truth always.
- Don't hide or manipulate information.
- Be willing to admit your failures.
- Share your personal values by regularly communicating them to employees.
- Stress the organization's or team's important shared values.
- Use the reward system to hold everyone accountable to the values.

---

resources for their personal use, inflate their expense accounts, or give favored treatment to friends, they imply that such behavior is acceptable for all employees.

Managers also set the tone by their reward and punishment practices. The choices of whom and what are rewarded with pay increases and promotions send a strong signal to employees. As we said earlier, when an employee is rewarded for achieving impressive results in an ethically questionable manner, it indicates to others that those ways are acceptable. When an employee does something unethical, managers must punish the offender and publicize the fact by making the outcome visible to everyone in the organization. This practice sends a message that doing wrong has a price and it's not in employees' best interests to act unethically!

ETHICS TRAINING.   Yahoo! used an off-the-shelf online ethics training package, but employees said that the scenarios used to demonstrate different concepts didn't resemble those that might come up at Yahoo! and were too middle-American and middle-aged for the global company with a youthful workforce. So the company changed its ethics training! The new ethics training package is more animated and interactive and has more realistic storylines for the industry. The 45-minute training module covers the company's code of conduct and resources available to help employees understand it.[43]

Like Yahoo!, more and more organizations are setting up seminars, workshops, and similar ethics training programs to encourage ethical behavior. Such training programs aren't without controversy as the primary concern is whether ethics can be taught. Critics stress that the effort is pointless because people establish their individual value systems when they're young. Proponents note, however, several studies have shown that values can be learned after early childhood. In addition, they cite evidence that shows that teaching ethical problem solving can make an actual difference in ethical behaviors;[44] that training has increased individuals' level of moral development;[45] and that, if nothing else, ethics training increases awareness of ethical issues in business.[46]

WHAT IS TODAY'S WORKFORCE LIKE AND HOW DOES IT AFFECT THE WAY ORGANIZATIONS ARE MANAGED?

Describe how the workforce is changing and its impact on the way organizations are managed.

4

Walking through the lobby of one of MGM Mirage's hotels, Brenda Thompson, the company's director of diversity and leadership education noted that, "It's amazing all the different languages I can hear. . . . Our guests come from all over the world, and it makes us realize the importance of reflecting that diversity in our workplace." And Thompson has been instrumental in developing a program at MGM that is all "about maximizing 100 percent inclusion of everyone in the organization."[47] Such diversity

---

code of ethics
A formal document that states an organization's primary values and the ethical rules it expects managers and nonmanagerial employees to follow

Michael Bach (right) created an inclusive environment at accounting firm KPMG in Canada by launching a diversity initiative that he heads as the National Director of Diversity, Equity, and Inclusion. Bach introduced programs and formalized policies designed to find, attract, and develop diverse talents that benefit KPMG by engaging its entire workforce. He developed diversity training for employees and formed social clubs, including an international club where members meet regularly to support employees who are new to the country. Among the many employee networks he created are networks for women, for parents with special needs children, and for religious groups, Bach is shown here with members of the firm's Asian network.

can be found in many organizational workplaces domestically and globally, and managers in those workplaces are looking for ways to value and develop that diversity, just as Brenda Thompson is doing.

What Is Workplace Diversity?

Look around your classroom (or your workplace). You're likely to see young/old, male/female, tall/short, blonde/brunette, blue-eyed/brown-eyed any number of races, and any variety of dress styles. You'll see people who speak up in class and others who are content to keep their attention on taking notes or daydreaming. Have you ever noticed your own little world of diversity where you are right now? Many of you may have grown up in an environment that included diverse individuals, while others may have not had that experience. We want to focus on *workplace* diversity, so let's look at what it is.

Diversity has been "one of the most popular business topics over the last two decades. It ranks with modern business disciplines such as quality, leadership, and ethics. Despite this popularity, it's also one of the most controversial and least understood topics."[48] With its basis in civil rights legislation and social justice, the word "diversity" often invokes a variety of attitudes and emotional responses in people. Diversity has traditionally been considered a term used by human resources departments, associated with fair hiring practices, discrimination, and inequality. But diversity today is considered to be so much more.

We're defining **workforce diversity** as the ways in which people in an organization are different from and similar to one another. Notice that our definition not only focuses on the differences, but the similarities of employees, reinforcing our belief that managers and organizations should view employees as having qualities in common as well as differences that separate them. It doesn't mean that those differences are any less important, but that our focus as managers is in finding ways to develop strong relationships with and engage our entire workforce.

What Types of Diversity Are Found in Workplaces?

Diversity is a big issue, and an important issue, in today's workplaces. What types of diversity do we find in those workplaces? Exhibit 4 lists several types of workplace diversity.

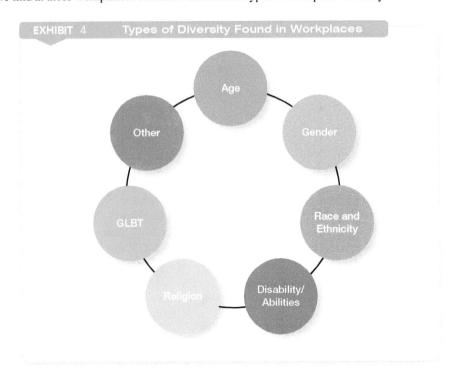

EXHIBIT 4   Types of Diversity Found in Workplaces

AGE. The aging of the population is a major critical shift taking place in the workforce. With many of the nearly 85 million baby boomers still employed and active in the workforce, managers must ensure that those employees are not discriminated against because of age. Both Title VII of the Civil Rights Act of 1964 and the Age Discrimination in Employment Act of 1967 prohibit age discrimination. The Age Discrimination Act also restricts mandatory retirement at specific ages. In addition to complying with these laws, organizations need programs and policies in place that provide for fair and equal treatment of their older employees.

GENDER. Women (49.8%) and men (50.2%) now each make up almost half of the workforce.[49] Yet gender diversity issues are still quite prevalent in organizations. These issues include the gender pay gap, career start and progress, and misconceptions about whether women perform their jobs as well as men do. It's important for managers and organizations to explore the strengths that both women and men bring to an organization and the barriers they face in contributing fully to organizational efforts.

RACE AND ETHNICITY. There's a long and controversial history in the United States and in other parts of the world over race and how people react to and treat others of a different race. Race and ethnicity are important types of diversity in organizations. We're going to define race as the biological heritage (including physical characteristics such as one's skin color and associated traits) that people use to identify themselves. Most people identify themselves as part of a racial group and such racial classifications are an integral part of a country's cultural, social, and legal environments. Ethnicity is related to race, but it refers to social traits—such as one's cultural background or allegiance—that are shared by a human population.

The racial and ethnic diversity of the U.S. population is increasing and at an exponential rate. We're also seeing this same effect in the composition of the workforce. Most of the research on race and ethnicity as they relate to the workplace has looked at hiring decisions, performance evaluations, pay, and workplace discrimination. Managers and organizations need to make race and ethnicity issues a key focus in effectively managing workforce diversity.

DISABILITY/ABILITIES. For persons with disabilities, 1990 was a watershed year—the year the Americans with Disabilities Act (ADA) became law. ADA prohibits discrimination against persons with disabilities and also requires employers to make reasonable accommodations so their workplaces are accessible to people with physical or mental disabilities and enable them to effectively perform their jobs. With the law's enactment, individuals with disabilities became a more representative and integral part of the U.S. workforce.

In August 2009, a viral campaign against McDonald's Web site, 365black.com, began to spread.[50] Anger over the Web site grew as news commentators discovered an additional McDonald's Web site targeting the Asian community, called MyInspirAsian.com. One individual said, "Even if the idea was a good one and truly was promoting Black cultural heritage, it really does come off as manipulation and stereotyping." Check out both Web sites.

Think About:

- What do you think? Do you think these targeted sites are manipulative and stereotypical? Why or why not? Is there anything else the company could or should be doing?

- Go to McDonald's corporate Web site. Find the information on diversity. Make a short list of what McDonald's is doing with respect to diversity programs and actions.

© Directphoto.org/Alamy.

---

workforce diversity
Ways in which people in a workforce are similar and different from one another in terms of gender, age, race, sexual orientation, ethnicity, cultural background, and physical abilities and disabilities

race
The biological heritage (including physical characteristics, such as one's skin color and associated traits) that people use to identify themselves

ethnicity
Social traits, such as one's cultural background or allegiance, that are shared by a human population

In effectively managing a workforce with disabled employees, managers need to create and maintain an environment in which employees feel comfortable disclosing their need for accommodation. Those accommodations, by law, enable individuals with disabilities to perform their jobs but they also need to be perceived as equitable by those not disabled. It's the balancing act that managers face.

RELIGION.   Hani Khan, a college sophomore, had worked for three months as a stock clerk at a Hollister clothing store in San Francisco.[51] One day, she was told by her supervisors to remove the head scarf that she wears in observance of Islam (known as a *hijab*) because it violated the company's "look policy" (which instructs employees on clothing, hair styles, makeup, and accessories they may wear to work). She refused on religious grounds and was fired one week later. Like a number of other Muslim women, she filed a federal job discrimination complaint. A spokesperson for Abercrombie & Fitch (Hollister's parent company) said that, "If any Abercrombie associate identifies a religious conflict with an Abercrombie policy . . . the company will work with the associate in an attempt to find an accommodation."

Title VII of the Civil Rights Act prohibits discrimination on the basis of religion (as well as race/ethnicity, country of origin, and sex). However, you'd probably not be surprised to find out that the number of religious discrimination claims has been growing in the United States.[52] In accommodating religious diversity, managers need to recognize and be aware of different religions and their beliefs, paying special attention to when certain religious holidays fall. Businesses benefit when they can accommodate, if possible, employees who have special needs or requests in a way that other employees don't view it as "special treatment."

GLBT—SEXUAL ORIENTATION AND GENDER IDENTITY.   The acronym GLBT—which refers to gay, lesbian, bisexual, and transgender people—is being used more frequently and relates to the diversity of sexual orientation and gender identity.[53] Sexual orientation has been called the "last acceptable bias."[54] We want to emphasize that we're not condoning this perspective; what this comment refers to is that most people understand that racial and ethnic stereotypes are "off-limits." Unfortunately, it's not unusual to hear derogatory comments about gays or lesbians. U.S. federal law does not prohibit discrimination against employees on the basis of sexual orientation, although many states and municipalities do. However, in Europe, the Employment Equality Directive required all European Union member states to introduce legislation making it unlawful to discriminate on grounds of sexual orientation.[55] Despite the progress that's been made in making workplaces more accommodating of gays and lesbians, obviously much more needs to be done. One study found that more than 40 percent of gay and lesbian employees indicated they had been unfairly treated, denied a promotion, or pushed to quit their job because of their sexual orientation.[56]

As with most of the types of diversity we've discussed in this section, managers need to look at how best to meet the needs of their GLBT employees. They need to respond to employees' concerns while also creating a safe and productive work environment for all.

OTHER TYPES OF DIVERSITY.   As we said earlier, diversity refers to *any* dissimilarities or differences that might be present in a workplace. Other types of workplace diversity that managers might confront and have to deal with include socioeconomic background (social class and income-related factors), team members from different functional areas or organizational units, physical attractiveness, obesity/thinness, job seniority, or intellectual abilities. Each of these types of diversity also can affect how employees are treated in the workplace. Again, managers need to ensure that all employees—no matter the similarities or dissimilarities—are treated fairly and given the opportunity and support to do their jobs to the best of their abilities.

How Are Organizations and Managers Adapting to a Changing Workforce?

Since organizations wouldn't be able to do what they're in business to do without employees, managers have to adapt to the changes taking place in the workforce. They're responding with diversity initiatives such as work-life balance programs, contingent jobs, and recognition of generational differences.

WORK-LIFE BALANCE PROGRAMS. The typical employee in the 1960s or 1970s showed up at the workplace Monday through Friday and did his or her job in eight- or nine-hour chunks of time. The workplace and hours were clearly specified. That's not the case anymore for a large segment of the workforce. Employees are increasingly complaining that the line between work and nonwork time has blurred, creating personal conflicts and stress.[57] Several factors have contributed to this blurring between work and personal life. One is that in a world of global business, work never ends. At any time and on any day, for instance, thousands of Caterpillar employees are working somewhere in the company's facilities. The need to consult with colleagues or customers 8 or 10 time zones away means that many employees of global companies are "on call" 24 hours a day. Another factor is that communication technology allows employees to do their work at home, in their cars, or on the beach in Tahiti. Although this capability allows those in technical and professional jobs to do their work anywhere and at anytime, it also means there's no escaping from work. Another factor is that as organizations have had to lay off employees during the economic downturn, "surviving" employees find themselves working longer hours. It's not unusual for employees to work more than 45 hours a week, and some work more than 50. Finally, fewer families today have a single wage earner. Today's married employee is typically part of a dual-career couple, which makes it increasingly difficult for married employees to find time to fulfill commitments to home, spouse, children, parents, and friends.[58]

More and more, employees recognize that work is squeezing out their personal lives, and they're not happy about it. Today's progressive workplaces must accommodate the varied needs of a diverse workforce. In response, many organizations are offering **family-friendly benefits**, benefits that provide a wide range of scheduling options that allow employees more flexibility at work, accommodating their need for work-life balance. They've introduced programs such as on-site child care, summer day camps, flextime, job sharing, time off for school functions, telecommuting, and part-time employment. Younger people, particularly, put a higher priority on family and a lower priority on jobs and are looking for organizations that give them more work flexibility.[59]

CONTINGENT JOBS. "Companies want a workforce they can switch on and off as needed."[60] Although this quote may shock you, the truth is that the labor force already has begun shifting away from traditional full-time jobs toward a **contingent workforce**—part-time, temporary, and contract workers who are available for

Ernst & Young is a progressive firm that accommodates the needs of its diverse employees by providing family-friendly benefits. Flexible work plans offered by this accounting and tax service firm include telecommuting, reduced work schedules, compressed workweeks, and day-to-day work-hour flexibility. Family-support programs include low-cost backup child and adult care, a college coach program that helps parents and high school students prepare for college, family medical leave, parental leave, and adoption assistance. Young employees, such as the workers at Ernst & Young's Boston office shown here, place a high priority on work-life balance and value organizations that give them flexible work options.

Mary K Merrill/Newscom

---

family-friendly benefits
Benefits that provide a wide range of scheduling options and allow employees more flexibility at work, accommodating their needs for work-life balance

contingent workforce
Part-time, temporary, and contract workers who are available for hire on an as-needed basis

hire on an as-needed basis. In today's economy, many organizations have responded by converting full-time permanent jobs into contingent jobs. It's predicted that by the end of the next decade the number of contingent employees will have grown to about 40 percent of the workforce. (It's at 30 percent today.)[61] In fact, one compensation and benefits expert says that "a growing a number of workers will need to structure their careers around this model," which could likely include you![62]

What are the implications for managers and organizations? Because contingent employees are not "employees" in the traditional sense of the word, managing them has its own set of challenges and expectations. Managers must recognize that because contingent workers lack the stability and security of permanent employees, they may not identify with the organization or be as committed or motivated. Managers may need to treat contingent workers differently in terms of practices and policies. However, with good communication and leadership, an organization's contingent employees can be just as valuable a resource to an organization as permanent employees are. Today's managers must recognize that it will be their responsibility to motivate their entire workforce, full-time and contingent, and to build their commitment to doing good work!

GENERATIONAL DIFFERENCES. Managing generational differences presents some unique challenges, especially for baby boomers and Gen Y. Conflicts and resentment can arise over issues ranging from appearance to technology and management style.

What *is* appropriate office attire? That answer may depend on who you ask, but more importantly, it depends on the type of work being done and the size of the organization. To accommodate generational differences in what is considered appropriate, the key is flexibility. For instance, a guideline might be that when an employee is not interacting with someone outside the organization, more casual wear (with some restrictions) is acceptable.

What about technology? Gen Y has grown up with ATMs, DVDs, cell phones, e-mail, texting, laptops, and the Internet. When they don't have information they need, they just enter a few keystrokes to get it. They're content to meet virtually to solve problems, while baby boomers expect important problems to be solved with in-person meetings. Baby boomers complain about Gen Y's inability to focus on one task, while Gen Y'ers see nothing wrong with multitasking. Again, flexibility and understanding from both is the key in working together effectively and efficiently.

Finally, what about management style? Gen Y employees want bosses who are open-minded; experts in their field, even if they aren't tech savvy; organized; teachers, trainers, and mentors; not authoritarian or paternalistic; respectful of their generation; understanding of their need for work-life balance; providing constant feedback; communicating in vivid and compelling ways; and providing stimulating and novel learning experiences.[63]

Because Gen Y employees have a lot to offer organizations in terms of their knowledge, passion, and abilities, managers have to recognize and understand the behaviors of this group in order to create an environment in which work can be done efficiently, effectively, and without disruptive conflict.

Review

1 **Explain globalization and its impact on organizations.** Organizations are considered global if they exchange goods and services with consumers in other countries, if they use managerial and technical employee talent from other countries, or if they use financial sources and resources outside their home country. Businesses going global are usually referred to as multinational corporations (MNCs). As an MNC, they may operate as a multidomestic corporation, a global corporation, or a transnational or borderless organization. When a business goes global, it may start with global sourcing, move to exporting or importing, use licensing or franchising, pursue a global strategic alliance, or set up a foreign subsidiary. In doing business globally, managers need to be aware of different laws and political and economic systems. But the biggest challenge is in understanding the different country cultures. Two cross-cultural frameworks that managers can use are Hofstede's and GLOBE.

2 **Discuss how society's expectations are influencing managers and organizations.** Society expects organizations and managers to be responsible and ethical. An organization's social involvement can be from the perspective of social obligation, social responsiveness, or social responsibility. After much analysis, researchers have concluded that managers can afford to be (and should be) socially responsible. Sustainability has become an important societal issue for managers and organizations.

3 **Discuss the factors that lead to ethical and unethical behavior in organizations.** Ethics can be viewed from the utilitarian view, the rights view, or the theory of justice view. Whether a manager acts ethically or unethically depends on his or her morality, values, personality, and experiences; the organization's culture; and the ethical issue being faced. Managers can encourage ethical behavior by hiring employees with high ethical standards, establishing a code of ethics, leading by example, linking job goals and performance appraisal, providing ethics training, and implementing protective mechanisms for employees who face ethical dilemmas.

4 **Describe how the workforce is changing and its impact on the way organizations are managed.** The workforce continues to reflect increasing diversity. Types of workforce diversity include age, gender, race and ethnicity, disability/abilities, religion, and sexual orientation and gender identity. Organizations and managers are responding to the changing workforce with work-life balance programs, contingent jobs, and recognition of generational differences.

MyManagementLab   For more resources, please visit www.mymanagementlab.com

UNDERSTANDING THE CHAPTER

1. How does the concept of a global village affect organizations and managers?
2. Describe the different types of global organizations and the ways that organizations can go global.
3. What are the managerial implications of Hofstede's research on cultural environments? The GLOBE study?
4. How are social responsibility, social obligation, and social responsiveness different? Similar?
5. What is sustainability, and how can organizations practice it?
6. Describe how a manager would approach ethical decisions according to each of the three views on ethics.

7. Discuss specific ways managers can encourage ethical behavior.

8. What is workforce diversity, and why is it an important issue for managers?

9. Describe the six types of diversity found in workplaces.

10. Describe and discuss the three ways that organizations and managers are adapting to a changing workforce.

Endnotes

1. C. Skrzypinski, "Study: Employers Fall Short Developing Female Business Leaders," *SHRM Online,* March 15, 2011; L. Stevens and J. Espinoza, "Deutsche Telekom Sets Women-Manager Quota," *Wall Street Journal Online,* March 22, 2010; J. Blaue, "Deutsche Telekom Launches Quota for Top Women Managers," www.german-info.com/business_shownews; N. Clark, "Goal at Deutsche Telekom: More Women as Managers," *New York Times Online,* March 15, 2010; R. Foroohar and S. H. Greenberg, "Working Women Are Poised to Become the Biggest Economic Engine the World Has Ever Known," *Newsweek,* November 2, 2009, pp. B2–B5; News Release, "Women Still Hold Less Than a Quarter of Senior Management Positions in Privately Held Businesses," *Grant Thornton International,* www.gti.org (March 5, 2009); and Catalyst Research Report, *Different Cultures, Similar Perceptions: Stereotyping of Western European Business Leaders,* www.catalyst.org (2006).

2. N. M. Carter and C. Silva, "Pipeline's Broken Promise," *Catalyst,* www.catalyst.org (2010), p. 1; and "Women in Management in the United States, 1950–Present," *Catalyst,* www.catalyst.org (April 2010).

3. S. Lohr, "Stress Test for the Global Supply Chain," *New York Times Online,* March 19, 2011; D. Jolly, "Long Pause for Japanese Industry Raises Concerns About Supply Chain," *New York Times Online,* March 16, 2011; and M. Helft and N. Bunkley, "Disaster in Japan Batters Suppliers," *New York Times Online,* March 14, 2011.

4. E. Beinhocker, I. Davis, and L. Mendonca, "The 10 Trends You Have to Watch," *Harvard Business Review,* July–August 2009, pp. 55–60.

5. P. F. Drucker, "The Global Economy and the Nation-State," *Foreign Affairs,* September–October, 1997, pp. 159–171.

6. P. Dvorak, "Why Multiple Headquarters Multiply," *Wall Street Journal,* November 19, 2007, pp. B1+.

7. D. A. Aaker, *Developing Business Strategies,* 5th ed. (New York: John Wiley & Sons, 1998); and J. A. Byrne et al., "Borderless Management," *BusinessWeek,* May 23, 1994, pp. 24–26.

8. B. Davis, "Migration of Skilled Jobs Abroad Unsettles Global-Economy Fans," *Wall Street Journal,* January 26, 2004, p. A1.

9. A. Pande, "How to Make Onshoring Work," *Harvard Business Review,* March 2011, p. 30; P. Davidson, "Some Manufacturing Heads Back to USA," *USA Today,* August 6, 2010, pp. 1B+; and V. Couto, A. Divakaran, and M. Mani, "Is Backshoring the New Offshoring?" *Strategy & Business,* October 21, 2008, pp. 1–3.

10. J. Teresko, "United Plastics Picks China's Silicon Valley," *Industry Week,* January 2003, p. 58.

11. "Global Business: Getting the Frameworks Right," *Organization for Economic Cooperation and Development,* April 2000, p. 20.

12. From the Past to the Present box based on D. Holtbrügge and A. T. Mohr, "Cultural Determinants of Learning Style Preferences," *Academy of Management Learning & Education,* December 2010, pp. 622–637; G. Hofstede, "The GLOBE Debate: Back to Relevance," *Journal of International Business Studies* (November 2010), pp. 1339–1346; G. A. Gelade, P. Dobson, and K. Auer, "Individualism, Masculinity, and the Sources of Organizational Commitment," *Journal of Cross-Cultural Psychology* (September 2008), pp. 599–617; G. Hofstede, "The Cultural Relativity of Organizational Practices and Theories," *Journal of International Business Studies* (Fall 1983), pp. 75–89; and G. Hofstede, *Culture Consequences: International Differences in Work-Related Values* (Beverly Hills, CA: Sage Publications, 1980), pp. 25–26. For an interesting discussion of collectivism and teams, see C. Gomez, B. L. Kirkman, and D. Shapiro, "The Impact of Collectivism and In-Group Membership on the Evaluation Generosity of Team Members," *Academy of Management Journal* (December 2000), pp. 1097–1106. Hofstede's term for what we've called quantity of life and quality of life was actually "masculinity versus femininity," but we've changed his terms because of their strong sexist connotation.

13. R. J. House, N. R. Quigley, and M. S. deLuque, "Insights from Project GLOBE: Extending Advertising Research Through a Contemporary Framework," *International Journal of Advertising,* 29, no. 1 (2010), pp. 111–139; R. R. McRae, A. Terracciano, A. Realo, and J.Allik, "Interpreting GLOBE Societal Practices Scale," *Journal of Cross-Cultural Psychology* (November 2008), pp. 805–810; J. S. Chhokar, F. C. Brodbeck, and R. J. House, *Culture and Leadership Across the World: The GLOBE Book of In-Depth Studies of 25 Societies* (Philadelphia: Lawrence Erlbaum Associates), 2007; and R. J. House, P. J. Hanges, M. Javidan, P. W. Dorfman, and V. Gupta, *Culture, Leadership, and Organizations: The GLOBE Study of 62 Societies* (Thousand Oaks, CA: Sage Publications), 2004.

14. R. J. House, N. R. Quigley, and M. S. deLuque, 2010.

15. M. Karimzadeh, "Olsens Collaborate with Toms Shoes," *Women's Wear Daily,* February 14, 2011, p. 11b; J. Schechtman, "Good Business," *Newsweek,* October 11, 2010, p. 50; "Toms Shoes to Donate One-Millionth Pair," *Women's Wear Daily,* August 9, 2010, p. 9–10; "Ten Companies With Social Responsibility at the Core," *Advertising Age,* April 19, 2010, p. 88; C. Binkley, "Charity Gives Shoe Brand Extra Shine," *Wall Street Journal,* April 1, 2010, p. D7; J. Shambora, "How I Got Started: Blake Mycoskie, Founder of TOMS Shoes," *Fortune,* March 22, 2010, p. 72; and "Making A Do-Gooder's Business Model Work," *BusinessWeek Online,* January 26, 2009.

16. D. Dearlove and S. Crainer, "Enterprise Goes Social," *Chief Executive,* March 2002, p. 18; and "Bronze Winner: Ben & Jerry's Citizen Cool," *Brandweek,* March 18, 2002, p. R-24.

17. M. Friedman, *Capitalism and Freedom* (Chicago: University of Chicago Press, 1962); and M. Friedman, "The Social Responsibility of Business Is to Increase Profits," *New York Times Magazine,* September 13, 1970, p. 33.

18. See, for instance, N. A. Ibrahim, J. P. Angelidis, and D. P. Howell, "The Corporate Social Responsiveness Orientation of Hospital Directors: Does Occupational Background Make a Difference?" *Health Care Management Review,* Spring 2000, pp. 85–92.

19. See, for example, D. J. Wood, "Corporate Social Performance Revisited," *Academy of Management Review,* October 1991, pp. 703–708; and S. L. Wartick and P. L. Cochran, "The Evolution of the Corporate Social Performance Model," *Academy of Management Review,* October 1985, p. 763.

20. See, for instance, R. Lacy and P. A. Kennett-Hensel, "Longitudinal Effects of Corporate Social Responsibility on Customer Relationships," *Journal of Business Ethics* (December 2010), pp. 581–597; S. Arendt and M. Brettel, "Understanding the Influence of Corporate Social Responsibility on Corporate Identity,

Image, and Firm Performance," *Management Decision,* 48, no. 10 (2010), pp. 1469–1492; J. Peloza, "The Challenge of Measuring Financial Impacts from Investments in Corporate Social Performance," *Journal of Management* (December 2009), pp. 1518–1541; J. D. Margolis and H. Anger Elfenbein, "Do Well by Doing Good? Don't Count on It," *Harvard Business Review,* January 2008, pp. 19–20; M. L. Barnett, "Stakeholder Influence Capacity and the Variability of Financial Returns to Corporate Social Responsibility," 2007; D. O. Neubaum and S. A. Zahra, "Institutional Ownership and Corporate Social Performance: The Moderating Effects of Investment Horizon, Activism, and Coordination," *Journal of Management* (February 2006), pp. 108–131; B. A. Waddock and S. B. Graves, "The Corporate Social Performance–Financial Performance Link," *Strategic Management Journal* (April 1997), pp. 303–319; J. B. McGuire, A. Sundgren, and T. Schneeweis, "Corporate Social Responsibility and Firm Financial Performance," *Academy of Management Journal* (December 1988), pp. 854–872; K. Aupperle, A. B. Carroll, and J. D. Hatfield, "An Empirical Examination of the Relationship Between Corporate Social Responsibility and Profitability," *Academy of Management Journal* (June 1985), pp. 446–463; and P. Cochran and R. A. Wood, "Corporate Social Responsibility and Financial Performance," *Academy of Management Journal* (March 1984), pp. 42–56.

21. Peloza, "The Challenge of Measuring Financial Impacts from Investments in Corporate Social Performance."

22. B. Seifert, S. A. Morris, and B. R. Bartkus, "Having, Giving, and Getting: Slack Resources, Corporate Philanthropy, and Firm Financial Performance," *Business & Society,* June 2004, pp. 135–161; and McGuire, Sundgren, and Schneeweis, "Corporate Social Responsibility and Firm Financial Performance."

23. A. McWilliams and D. Siegel, "Corporate Social Responsibility and Financial Performance: Correlation or Misspecification?" *Strategic Management Journal* (June 2000), pp. 603–609.

24. A. J. Hillman and G. D. Keim, "Shareholder Value, Stakeholder Management, and Social Issues: What's the Bottom Line?" *Strategic Management Journal,* 22 (2001), pp. 125–139.

25. M. Orlitzky, F. L. Schmidt, and S. L. Rynes, "Corporate Social and Financial Performance," *Organization Studies,* 24, no. 3 (2003), pp. 403–441.

26. And the Survey Says box based on *Blowing the Whistle on Workplace Conduct,* Ethics Resource Center, www.ethics.org (December 2010); G. M. Maddock and R. L. Viton, "Co-Creating Planet-Friendly Profits," *Bloomberg Businessweek Online,* December 21, 2010; B. Leonard, "When HR Goes Bad," *HR Magazine,* January 2011, pp. 28–32; C. Hausman, "Ethics Books More Likely Than Other Works To Be Stolen from Libraries," *Global Ethics Newsline Online,* December 20, 2010; "Strong Ethical Culture Helps Bottom Line," *HR Magazine,* December 2010, p. 21; J. Yang and P. Trap, "If Granted Access to a Confidential Document Accidently I'd . . . ," *USA Today,* September 13, 2010, p. 1B; and R. M. Kidder, "Ask Not for Whom the Students Cheat: They Cheat for Thee," *Global Ethics Newsline Online,* February 28, 2011.

27. S. Rosenbloom, "Wal-Mart Unveils Plan to Make Supply Chain Greener," *New York Times Online,* February 26, 2010.

28. G. Unruh and R. Ettenson, "Growing Green," *Harvard Business Review,* June 2010, pp. 94–100; G. Zoppo, "Corporate Sustainability," *DiversityInc,* May 2010, pp. 76–80; and KPMG Global Sustainability Services, *Sustainability Insights,* October 2007.

29. *Symposium on Sustainability: Profiles in Leadership,* New York, October 2001.

30. C. Hausman, "Ethics, Economics, and Injuries Dominate Sports News," *Ethics Newsline Online,* February 7, 2011; S. Armour and T. Frank, "Ex-Worker: Law Firm Ran 'Foreclosure Mill,'" *USA Today,* October 19, 2010, p. 3B; and N. Clark, "Rogue Trader at Société Générale Gets Jail Term," *New York Times Online,* October 5, 2010.

31. S. A. DiPiazza, "Ethics in Action," *Executive Excellence,* January 2002, pp. 15–16.

32. This example is based on J. F. Viega, T. D. Golden, and K. Dechant, "Why Managers Bend Company Rules," *Academy of Management Executive* (May 2004), pp. 84–90.

33. G. F. Cavanaugh, D. J. Moberg, and M. Valasquez, "The Ethics of Organizational Politics," *Academy of Management Journal* (June 1981), pp. 363–374.

34. J. Liedtka, "Ethics and the New Economy," *Business and Society Review,* Spring 2002, p. 1.

35. R. M. Kidder, "Can Disobedience Save Wall Street?" *Ethics Newsline,* www.globalethics.org (May 3, 2010).

36. P. M. Lencioni, "Make Your Values Mean Something," *Harvard Business Review,* July 2002, p. 113.

37. D. H. Schepers, "Setting Global Standards: Guidelines for Creating Codes of Conduct in Multinational Corporations," *Business and Society,* December 2003, p. 496; and B. R. Gaummitz and J. C. Lere, "Contents of Codes of Ethics of Professional Business Organizations in the United States," *Journal of Business Ethics* (January 2002), pp. 35–49.

38. M. Weinstein, "Survey Says: Ethics Training Works," *Training* (November 2005), p. 15.

39. J. E. Fleming, "Codes of Ethics for Global Corporations," *Academy of Management News,* June 2005, p. 4.

40. T. F. Shea, "Employees' Report Card on Supervisors' Ethics: No Improvement," *HR Magazine,* April 2002, p. 29.

41. See also A. G. Peace, J. Weber, K. S. Hartzel, and J. Nightingale, "Ethical Issues in eBusiness: A Proposal for Creating the eBusiness Principles," *Business and Society Review,* Spring 2002, pp. 41–60.

42. D. Jones, "CEO's Moral Compass Steers Siemens," *USA Today,* February 15, 2010, p. 3B.

43. E. Finkel, "Yahoo Takes New 'Road' on Ethics Training," *Workforce Management Online,* July 2010.

44. T. A. Gavin, "Ethics Education," *Internal Auditor,* April 1989, pp. 54–57.

45. L. Myyry and K. Helkama, "The Role of Value Priorities and Professional Ethics Training in Moral Sensitivity," *Journal of Moral Education,* 31, no. 1 (2002), pp. 35–50; W. Penn and B. D. Collier, "Current Research in Moral Development as a Decision Support System," *Journal of Business Ethics* (January 1985), pp. 131–136.

46. J. A. Byrne, "After Enron: The Ideal Corporation," *BusinessWeek,* August 19, 2002, pp. 68–71; D. Rice and C. Dreilinger, "Rights and Wrongs of Ethics Training," *Training & Development Journal* (May 1990), pp. 103–109; and J. Weber, "Measuring the Impact of Teaching Ethics to Future Managers: A Review, Assessment, and

Recommendations," *Journal of Business Ethics* (April 1990), pp. 182–190.

47. S. Caminiti, "The Diversity Factor," *Fortune,* October 19, 2007, pp. 95–105; and B. Velez, "People and Places," *DiversityInc Online,* www.diversityinc.com (October 2006).

48. R. Anand and M. Frances Winters, "A Retrospective View of Corporate Diversity Training from 1964 to the Present," *Academy of Management Learning & Education,* September 2008, pp. 356–372.

49. N. Gibbs, "What Women Want Now," *Time,* October 26, 2009, pp. 24–33.

50. Right or Wrong box based on DiversityInc Staff, "Does McDonald's Web Site Stereotype Blacks?" *DiversityInc.com Online,* www.diversityinc.com (August 25, 2009).

51. M. Bello, USA Today, "Controversy Shrouds Scarves," *Springfield, Missouri News-Leader,* April 17, 2010, p. 8A.

52. "Facts & Figures: Number of Religious Discrimination Complaints Received," *DiversityInc,* November–December 2009, p. 52.

53. P. Wang and J. L. Schwartz, "Stock Price Reactions to GLBT Nondiscrimination Policies," *Human Resource Management,* March–April 2010, pp. 195–216.

54. L. Sullivan, "Sexual Orientation—The Last 'Acceptable' Bias," *Canadian HR Reporter,* December 20, 2004, pp. 9–11.

55. F. Colgan, T. Wright, C. Creegan, and A. McKearney, "Equality and Diversity in the Public Services: Moving

Forward on Lesbian, Gay and Bisexual Equality?" *Human Resource Management Journal,* 19, no. 3 (2009), pp. 280–301.

56. J. Hempel, "Coming Out in Corporate America," *BusinessWeek,* December 15, 2003, pp. 64–72.

57. See, for instance, P. Cappelli, J. Constantine, and C. Chadwick, "It Pays to Value Family: Work and Family Trade-Offs Reconsidered," *Industrial Relations,* April 2000, pp. 175–198; R. C. Barnett and D. T. Hall, "How to Use Reduced Hours to Win the War for Talent," *Organizational Dynamics,* March 2001, p. 42; and M. A. Verespej, "Balancing Act," *Industry Week,* May 15, 2000, pp. 81–85.

58. M. Conlin, "The New Debate over Working Moms," *BusinessWeek,* November 18, 2000, pp. 102–103.

59. M. Elias, "The Family-First Generation," *USA Today,* December 13, 2004, p. 5D.

60. J. Revell, C. Bigda, and D. Rosato, "The Rise of Freelance Nation," *CNNMoney,* cnnmoney.com (June 12, 2009).

61. Ibid.

62. Ibid.

63. S. Armour, "Generation Y: They've Arrived at Work with a New Attitude," *USA Today,* November 6, 2005, pp. 1B+; B. Moses, "The Challenges of Managing Gen Y," *Globe and Mail,* March 11 2005, p. C1; and C. A. Martin, *Managing Generation Y* (Amherst, MA: HRD Press, 2001).

YOUR TURN TO BE A MANAGER

Integrative Managerial Issues

Skill Development: Building High Ethical Standards

Ethics encompasses the rules and principles we use to define right and wrong conduct. Many organizations have formally written ethical codes to guide managers and employees in their decisions and actions. But individuals need to establish their own personal ethical standards. If managers are to successfully lead others, they need to be seen as trustworthy and ethical.

Personal Insights: How Do My Ethics Rate?

Indicate your level of agreement with these 15 statements using the following scale:

1 = Strongly disagree
2 = Disagree

3 = Neither agree or disagree
4 = Agree
5 = Strongly agree

1. The only moral of business is making money.	1 2 3 4 5
2. A person who is doing well in business does not have to worry about moral problems.	1 2 3 4 5
3. Act according to the law, and you can't go wrong morally.	1 2 3 4 5
4. Ethics in business is basically an adjustment between expectations and the ways people behave.	1 2 3 4 5
5. Business decisions involve a realistic economic attitude and not a moral philosophy.	1 2 3 4 5
6. "Business ethics" is a concept for public relations only.	1 2 3 4 5
7. Competitiveness and profitability are important values.	1 2 3 4 5
8. Conditions of a free economy will best serve the needs of society; limiting competition can only hurt society and actually violates basic natural laws.	1 2 3 4 5
9. As a consumer, when making an auto insurance claim, I try to get as much as possible regardless of the extent of the damage.	1 2 3 4 5
10. While shopping at the supermarket, it is appropriate to switch price tags on packages.	1 2 3 4 5
11. As an employee, I can take home office supplies; it doesn't hurt anyone.	1 2 3 4 5
12. I view sick days as vacation days that I deserve.	1 2 3 4 5
13. Employees' wages should be determined according to the laws of supply and demand.	1 2 3 4 5
14. The business world has its own rules.	1 2 3 4 5
15. A good businessperson is a successful businessperson.	1 2 3 4 5

Source: Adapted from A. Reichel and Y. Neumann, "Attitude Towards Business Ethics Questionnaire," *Journal of Instructional Psychology* (March 1988), pp. 25–53. With permission of the authors.

Analysis and Interpretation

No decision is completely value-free. It undoubtedly will have some ethical dimensions. This instrument presents philosophical positions and practical situations. Rather than specify "right" answers, this instrument works best when you compare your answers to those of others. With that in mind, here are mean responses from a group of 243 management students. How did your responses compare?

1. 3.09	6. 2.88	11. 1.58
2. 1.88	7. 3.62	12. 2.31
3. 2.54	8. 3.79	13. 3.36
4. 3.41	9. 3.44	14. 3.79
5. 3.88	10. 1.33	15. 3.38

Do you tend to be more or less ethical than the student norms presented above? On which items did you differ most? Your answers to these questions can provide insights into how well your ethical standards match other people with whom you will be working in the future. Large discrepancies might be a warning that others don't hold the same ethical values that you do.

Skill Basics

What You can do:

Know your values. What's important to you? Where do you draw the line?

Think before you act. Will your actions injure someone? What are your ulterior motives? Will your actions jeopardize your reputation?

Consider all consequences. If you make the wrong decision, what will happen? Every decision comes with consequences and you should be sure you've considered their implications.

Apply the "publicity test." What would your family and friends think if your actions were described in detail on the front page of your local newspaper or on the local TV news?

Seek opinions from others. Ask advice from others you respect. Use their experience and listen to their perspectives.

What Your Organization Can Do:

Create a formal ethics code. Organizations should set down their ethical standards and policies in a formal ethical code. The code should be widely distributed to all employees.

Set an ethical culture. Visibly reward employees who set a high ethical standard and visibly punish those who engage in unethical practices.

Ensure managers are role models. Employees look to their immediate superior and upper management for cues as to what is or is not acceptable behavior. Managers need to be positive ethical role models.

Offer ethics workshops. Employees should participate in regular ethics training to reinforce the importance of high ethical standards, to interpret the organization's ethical code, and to allow employees to clarify what they may see as "gray areas."

Appoint an ethics "advisor." A senior executive should be available for employees to meet and confer with to confidentially discuss ethical concerns.

Protect employees who report unethical practices. Mechanisms need to be put in place that protect employees from retributions or other negative consequences should they reveal unethical practices that are a threat to others.

Based on L. Nash, "Ethics Without the Sermon," *Harvard Business Review*, November–December 1981, pp. 78–92; W. D. Hall, *Making the Right Decision: Ethics for Managers* (New York: John Wiley, 1993); and L. K. Trevino and K. A. Nelson, *Managing Business Ethics: Straight Talk About How to Do It Right* (New York: John Wiley, 1995).

Skill Application

Form into teams of four or five people. Obtain a copy of your college's code of conduct. How many of the team members were aware of the code? How many had read it? Evaluate the code's provisions and policies. Are you uncomfortable with any of the code's provisions? Why? How effective do you think they have been in shaping student and faculty behavior? If they haven't been effective, what could be done to improve them?

Be prepared to present your team's findings to the class.

Skill Practice

1. On a scale of 1 to 10 (with 10 being high), how ethical would you describe yourself? What factors would you say have most shaped your views on ethics? Do you think your ethics have changed over time? If so, how and why? Do you think there is such a thing as "situational ethics"? If so, what situational factors would you consider relevant to your ethical behavior?

2. Research a recent highly publicized story of unethical behavior in business. What did this person or persons do? What do you think motivated the behavior? What could the organization have done better to have lessened the likelihood of such behavior? Had you been in the same situation, would you have acted similarly? Why or why not?

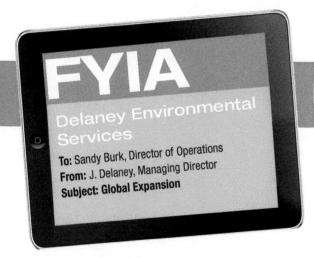

FYIA

Delaney Environmental Services

To: Sandy Burk, Director of Operations
From: J. Delaney, Managing Director
Subject: Global Expansion

For Your Immediate Action

Sandy, we need to start looking at expanding our global market opportunities. We've had a successful track record here in San Antonio providing environmental consulting and design services, and I believe that with our experience we have a lot to offer the Latin American market, particularly in Mexico.

Please research the potential problems we might face in moving into the Mexican market. Focus on: (1) cultural differences; (2) the current currency rate of exchange and how it's changed over the last three years; and (3) any legal or political situations we need to be aware of. Because this is just an initial analysis, please keep your report to one page or less.

This fictionalized company and message were created for educational purposes only, and not meant to reflect positively or negatively on management practices by any company that may share this name.

Case Application:
A Level Playing Field? Part 2

What is Deutsche Telekom doing to achieve its goal of bringing more women into management positions? One action the company is taking is to increase and improve recruiting of female university graduates. In fact, the company has committed to having at least 30 percent of the places in executive development programs held by women.

Other steps being taken by the company revolve around the work environment and work-family issues. The company plans to expand its parental-leave programs and introduce more flexible working hours for managers. Right now, fewer than 1 percent of the company's managers work part time. In addition, the company plans to double the number of available places in company child-care programs.

DISCUSSION QUESTIONS

1.   What do you think of this "quota" approach that Deutsche Telekom is pursuing? What benefits and drawbacks does such an approach have?

2.   What issues might Deutsche Telekom face in recruiting female university graduates? How could they address these issues?

3.   What issues might the company face in introducing changes in work-family programs? Again, how could they address these issues?

4.   Using the GLOBE highlights from the list within this chapter, find the dimensions where Germany is rated. How might those cultural realities affect actions that Deutsche Telekom wishes to pursue?

Foundations of Decision Making

Foundations of Decision Making

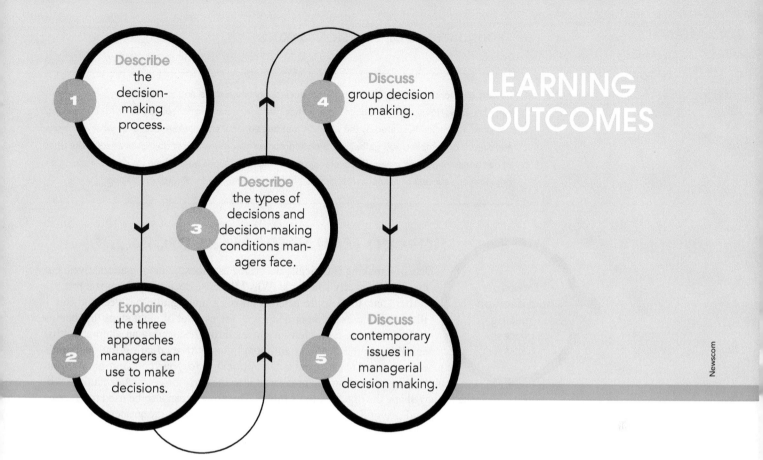

Describe the decision-making process.

1

Explain the three approaches managers can use to make decisions.

2

Describe the types of decisions and decision-making conditions managers face.

3

Discuss group decision making.

4

Discuss contemporary issues in managerial decision making.

5

Newscom

Lift Off

Over the years, NASA (National Aeronautics and Space Administration) has provided us with some spectacular moments—from Neil Armstrong's first steps on the moon to the Hubble Telescope's mesmerizing photos of distant stars and galaxies.[1] NASA's vision—to understand and protect our home planet, to explore the Universe and search for life, and to inspire the next generation of explorers—has guided its management team over the years as decisions were made about projects, missions, and programs. When the space shuttle program—NASA's main project mission—ended in 2011, the organization floundered. In fact, one agency program manager described NASA's future as "a period of sustained ambiguity." Possible new goals for NASA proposed by the president included getting to an asteroid by 2025 and putting astronauts on Mars by 2030. It's clear that NASA needs to chart a new course. As its managers contemplate that future, decision making will be crucial to plotting a course that takes the organization efficiently and effectively in a desirable direction.

Making decisions, especially during times of uncertainty when there are no precedents to guide you, can't be easy. However, that doesn't mean that managers can just forget about or ignore making decisions. Rather, as illustrated by the situation that decision makers at NASA face, even when decisions are difficult or complex, you gather the best information you can and just do it. Managers make a lot of decisions—minor and major. The overall quality of those decisions goes a long way in determining an organization's success or failure. In this chapter, we examine the basics of decision making.

HOW DO MANAGERS MAKE DECISIONS?

1 Describe the decision-making process.

Decision making is typically described as choosing among alternatives, but this view is overly simplistic. Why? Because decision making is a process rather than the simple act of choosing among alternatives. Exhibit 1 illustrates the **decision-making process** as a set of eight steps that begins with identifying a problem; it moves through selecting an alternative that can alleviate the problem and concludes with evaluating the decision's effectiveness. This process is as applicable to your decision about what you're going to do on spring break as it is to the decisions NASA executives will make as they shape the organization's future. The process can also be used to describe both individual and group decisions. Let's take a closer look at the process in order to understand what each step entails.

What Defines a Decision Problem?

The decision-making process begins with the identification of a **problem** (step 1) or, more specifically, a discrepancy between an existing and a desired state of affairs.[2] Let's develop an example illustrating this point to use throughout this section. For the sake of simplicity, we'll make it an example most of us can relate to: the decision to buy a car. Take the case of a new-product manager for the Netherlands-based food company Royal Ahold. The manager spent nearly $6,000 on auto repairs over the past few years, and now the car has a blown engine. Repair estimates indicate that it is not economical to repair the car. Furthermore, convenient public transportation is unavailable.

So now we have a problem that results from the disparity between the manager's need to have a car that works and the fact that her current one doesn't. Unfortunately, this example doesn't tell us much about how managers identify problems. In the real world, most problems don't come with neon signs identifying them as such. A blown engine is a clear signal to the manager that she needs a new car, but few problems are that obvious. Instead, problem identification is subjective. Furthermore, the manager who mistakenly solves the wrong problem perfectly is just as likely to perform poorly as the manager who fails to identify the right problem and does nothing. Problem identification is neither a simple nor

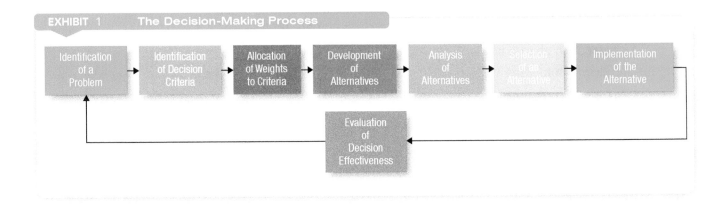

EXHIBIT 1   The Decision-Making Process

Identification of a Problem → Identification of Decision Criteria → Allocation of Weights to Criteria → Development of Alternatives → Analysis of Alternatives → Selection of an Alternative → Implementation of the Alternative → Evaluation of Decision Effectiveness

an unimportant part of the decision-making process.[3] How do managers become aware they have a discrepancy? They have to make a comparison between the current state of affairs and some standard, which can be past performance, previously set goals, or the performance of some other unit within the organization or in other organizations. In our car-buying example, the standard is previous performance—a car that runs.

What Is Relevant in the Decision-Making Process?

Once a manager has identified a problem that needs attention, the decision criteria that will be important in solving the problem must be identified (step 2).

In our vehicle-buying example, the product manager assesses the factors that are relevant in her decision, which might include criteria such as price, model (two-door or four-door), size (compact or intermediate), manufacturer (French, Japanese, South Korean, German, American), optional equipment (navigation system, side-impact protection, leather interior), and repair records. These criteria reflect what she thinks is relevant in her decision. Every decision maker has criteria—whether explicitly stated or not—that guide his or her decision making. Note that in this step in the decision-making process, what is not identified is as important as what is. If the product manager doesn't consider fuel economy to be a criterion, then it will not influence her choice of car. Thus, if a decision maker does not identify a particular factor in this second step, it's treated as irrelevant.

How Does the Decision Maker Weight the Criteria and Analyze Alternatives?

In many decision-making situations, the criteria are not all equally important.[4] It's necessary, therefore, to allocate weights to the items listed in step 2 in order to give them their relative priority in the decision (step 3). A simple approach is to give the most important criterion a weight of 10 and then assign weights to the rest against that standard. Thus, in contrast to a criterion that you gave a 5, the highest-rated factor would be twice as important. The idea is to use your personal preferences to assign priorities to the relevant criteria in your decision as well as to indicate their degree of importance by assigning a weight to each. Exhibit 2 lists the criteria and weights that our manager developed for her vehicle

The steps involved in buying a vehicle provide a good example of the decision-making process, which applies to both individual and group decisions. For this young woman, the process starts with a problem: She needs a car to drive to a new job. Then she identifies decision criteria (price, color, size, and performance); assigns priorities to the criteria; develops, analyzes, and selects alternatives; and implements the alternative. In the last step of the decision-making process she evaluates the effectiveness of her decision.

EXHIBIT 2	Important Criteria and Weights in a Car-Buying Decision

CRITERION	WEIGHT
Price	10
Interior comfort	8
Durability	5
Repair record	5
Performance	3
Handling	1

decision-making process
A set of eight steps that includes identifying a problem, selecting a solution, and evaluating the effectiveness of the solution

problem
A discrepancy between an existing and a desired state of affairs

decision criteria
Factors that are relevant in a decision

EXHIBIT 3   Assessment of Possible Car Alternatives

ALTERNATIVES	INITIAL PRICE	INTERIOR COMFORT	DURABILITY	REPAIR RECORD	PERFORMANCE	HANDLING	TOTAL
Jeep Compass	2	10	8	7	5	5	37
Ford Focus	9	6	5	6	8	6	40
Hyundai Elantra	8	5	6	6	4	6	35
Ford Fiesta SES	9	5	6	7	6	5	38
Volkswagen Golf	5	6	9	10	7	7	44
Toyota Prius	10	5	6	4	3	3	31
Mazda 3 MT	4	8	7	6	8	9	42
Kia Soul	7	6	8	6	5	6	38
BMW 335	9	7	6	4	4	7	37
Nissan Cube	5	8	5	4	10	10	42
Toyota Camry	6	5	10	10	6	6	43
Honda Fit Sport MT	8	6	6	5	7	8	40

replacement decision. Price is the most important criterion in her decision, with performance and handling having low weights.

Then the decision maker lists the alternatives that could succeed in resolving the problem (step 4). No attempt is made in this step to appraise these alternatives, only to list them.[5] Let's assume that our manager has identified 12 cars as viable choices: Jeep Compass, Ford Focus, Hyundai Elantra, Ford Fiesta SES, Volkswagen Golf, Toyota Prius, Mazda 3 MT, Kia Soul, BMW 335, Nissan Cube, Toyota Camry, and Honda Fit Sport MT.

Once the alternatives have been identified, the decision maker must critically analyze each one (step 5). Each alternative is evaluated by appraising it against the criteria. The strengths and weaknesses of each alternative become evident as they're compared with the criteria and weights established in steps 2 and 3. Exhibit 3 shows the assessed values that the manager put on each of her 12 alternatives after she had test-driven each car. Keep in mind that the ratings shown in Exhibit 3 are based on the assessment made by the new-product manager. Again, we're using a scale of 1 to 10. Some assessments can be achieved in a relatively objective fashion. For instance, the purchase price represents the best price the manager can get from local dealers, and consumer magazines report data from owners on frequency of repairs. However, the assessment of handling is clearly a personal judgment. Our point: most decisions contain judgments. They're reflected in the criteria chosen in step 2, the weights given to the criteria, and the evaluation of alternatives. The influence of personal judgment explains why two car buyers with the same amount of money may look at two totally distinct sets of alternatives or even look at the same alternatives and rate them differently.

Exhibit 3 shows only an assessment of the 12 alternatives against the decision criteria; it does not reflect the weighting done in step 3. If one choice had scored 10 on every criterion, you wouldn't need to consider the weights. Similarly, if the weights were all equal, you could evaluate each alternative merely by summing up the appropriate lines in Exhibit 3. For instance, the Ford Fiesta SES would have a score of 38, and the Toyota Camry a score of 43. If you multiply each alternative assessment against its weight, you get the figures in Exhibit 4. For instance, the Kia Soul scored a 40 on durability, which was determined by multiplying the weight given to durability [5] by the manager's appraisal of Kia on this criterion [8]. The sum of these scores represents an evaluation of each alternative against the previously established criteria and weights. Notice that the weighting of the criteria has changed the ranking of alternatives in our example. The Volkswagen Golf, for example, has gone from first to third. From our analysis, both initial price and interior comfort worked against the Volkswagen.

What Determines the Best Choice?

Step 6 is the critical act of choosing the best alternative from among those assessed. Since we determined all the pertinent factors in the decision, weighted them appropriately, and identified the viable alternatives, we merely have to choose the alternative that generated

EXHIBIT 4	Evaluation of Car Alternatives: Assessment Criteria × Criteria Weight											
ALTERNATIVES	INITIAL PRICE [10]		INTERIOR COMFORT [8]		DURABILITY [5]		REPAIR RECORD [5]		PERFORMANCE [3]		HANDLING [1]		TOTAL
Jeep Compass	2	20	10	80	8	40	7	35	5	15	5	5	195
Ford Focus	9	90	6	48	5	25	6	30	8	24	6	6	223
Hyundai Elantra	8	80	5	40	6	30	6	30	4	12	6	6	198
Ford Fiesta SES	9	90	5	40	6	30	7	35	6	18	5	5	218
Volkswagen Golf	5	50	6	48	9	45	10	50	7	21	7	7	221
Toyota Prius	10	100	5	40	6	30	4	20	3	9	3	3	202
Mazda 3 MT	4	40	8	64	7	35	6	30	8	24	9	9	202
Kia Soul	7	70	6	48	8	40	6	30	5	15	6	6	209
BMW 335	9	90	7	56	6	30	4	20	4	12	7	7	215
Nissan Cube	5	50	8	64	5	25	4	20	10	30	10	10	199
Toyota Camry	6	60	5	40	10	50	10	50	6	18	6	6	224
Honda Fit Sport MT	8	80	6	48	6	30	5	25	7	21	8	8	212

the highest score in step 5. In our vehicle example (Exhibit 4), the decision maker would choose the Toyota Camry. On the basis of the criteria identified, the weights given to the criteria, and the decision maker's assessment of each car on the criteria, the Toyota scored highest [224 points] and, thus, became the best alternative.

What Happens in Decision Implementation?

Although the choice process is completed in the previous step, the decision may still fail if it's not implemented properly (step 7). Therefore, this step is concerned with putting the decision into action. Decision implementation includes conveying the decision to those affected and getting their commitment to it.[6] The people who must carry out a decision are most likely to enthusiastically endorse the outcome if they participate in the decision-making process. Also, as we'll discuss later in this chapter, groups or committees can help a manager achieve commitment.

What Is the Last Step in the Decision Process?

In the last step in the decision-making process (step 8), managers appraise the result of the decision to see whether the problem was resolved. Did the alternative chosen in step 6 and implemented in step 7 accomplish the desired result? Evaluating the results of a decision is part of the managerial control process.

What Common Errors Are Committed in the Decision-Making Process?

When managers make decisions, they not only use their own particular style, but may use "rules of thumb" or heuristics, to simplify their decision making.[7] Rules of thumb can be useful because they help make sense of complex, uncertain, and ambiguous information. Even though managers may use rules of thumb, that doesn't mean those rules are reliable. Why? Because they may lead to errors and biases in processing and evaluating information. Exhibit 5 identifies 12 common decision errors and biases that managers make. Let's look briefly at each.[8]

When decision makers tend to think they know more than they do or hold unrealistically positive views of themselves and their performance, they're exhibiting the *over-confidence bias*. The *immediate gratification bias* describes decision makers who tend to want immediate rewards and to avoid immediate costs. For these individuals, decision

decision implementation
Putting a decision into action

heuristics
Judgmental shortcuts or "rules of thumb" used to simplify decision making

EXHIBIT 5   Common Decision-Making Errors and Biases

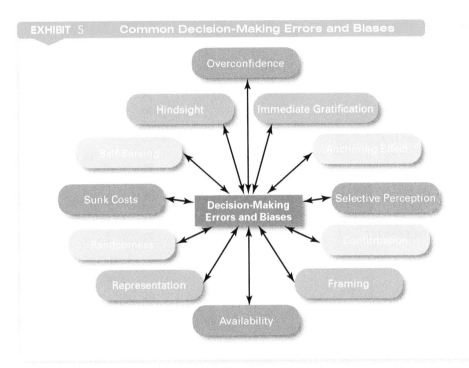

As sales manager of Prudential Realty in Brea, California, Tom Pelton makes decisions every day in performing the functions of planning, organizing, leading, and controlling. With home sales at his office dropping to an average of 54 sales per month, Pelton decided to develop a plan for attracting more first-time buyers and investors and then issued a challenge to his 75 agents to motivate them to sell 100 homes in a month. If they reached the goal, Pelton promised he would wear a dress to work. Pelton's decisions resulted in 102 home sales, setting a record for the office. The 6-foot-5, 260-pound Pelton made good on his promise by sashaying into the office with Aerosmith's "Dude Looks like a Lady" blaring over a loudspeaker, while his colleagues cheered, laughed, and took pictures to capture the fun-loving moment.

choices that provide quick payoffs are more appealing than those in the future. The *anchoring effect* describes when decision makers fixate on initial information as a starting point and then, once set, fail to adequately adjust for subsequent information. First impressions, ideas, prices, and estimates carry unwarranted weight relative to information received later. When decision makers selectively organize and interpret events based on their biased perceptions, they're using the *selective perception bias*. This influences the information they pay attention to, the problems they identify, and the alternatives they develop. Decision makers who seek out information that reaffirms their past choices and discount information that contradicts past judgments exhibit the *confirmation bias*. These people tend to accept at face value information that confirms their preconceived views and are critical and skeptical of information that challenges these views. The *framing bias* happens when decision makers select and highlight certain aspects of a situation while excluding others. By drawing attention to specific aspects of a situation and highlighting them, while at the same time downplaying or omitting other aspects, they distort what they see and create incorrect reference points. The *availability bias* occurs when decision makers tend to remember events that are the most recent and vivid in their memory. The result? It distorts their ability to recall events in an objective manner and results in distorted judgments and probability estimates. When decision makers assess the likelihood of an event based on how closely it resembles other events or sets of events, that's the *representation bias*. Managers exhibiting this bias draw analogies and see identical situations where they don't exist. The *randomness bias* describes when decision makers try to create meaning out of random events. They do this because most decision makers have difficulty dealing with chance even though random events happen to everyone and there's nothing that can be done to predict them. The *sunk costs error* takes place when decision makers forget that current choices can't correct the past. They incorrectly fixate

Joshua Sudock/Newscom

on past expenditures of time, money, or effort in assessing choices rather than on future consequences. Instead of ignoring sunk costs, they can't forget them. Decision makers who are quick to take credit for their successes and to blame failure on outside factors are exhibiting the *self-serving bias.* Finally, the *hindsight bias* is the tendency for decision makers to falsely believe that they would have accurately predicted the outcome of an event once that outcome is actually known.

Managers can avoid the negative effects of these decision errors and biases by being aware of them and then not using them! Beyond that, managers also should pay attention to "how" they make decisions and try to identify the heuristics they typically use and critically evaluate how appropriate those are. Finally, managers could ask colleagues to help identify weaknesses in their decision-making style and then work on improving those weaknesses.

WHAT ARE THREE APPROACHES MANAGERS CAN USE TO MAKE DECISIONS?

Explain the three approaches managers can use to make decisions.

2

Although everyone in an organization makes decisions, decision making is particularly important to managers. As Exhibit 6 shows, it's part of all four managerial functions. In fact, that's why we say that decision making is the essence of management.[9] And that's why managers—as they plan, organize, lead, and control—are called *decision makers*.

The fact that almost everything a manager does involves making decisions doesn't mean that decisions are always time-consuming, complex, or evident to an outside observer. Most decision making is routine. Every day of the year you make a decision about what to eat for dinner. It's no big deal. You've made the decision thousands of times before. It's a pretty simple decision and can usually be handled quickly. It's the type of

---

EXHIBIT 6   Decisions Managers May Make

PLANNING

- What are the organization's long-term objectives?
- What strategies will best achieve those objectives?
- What should the organization's short-term objectives be?
- How difficult should individual goals be?

ORGANIZING

- How many employees should I have report directly to me?
- How much centralization should there be in the organization?
- How should jobs be designed?
- When should the organization implement a different structure?

LEADING

- How do I handle employees who appear to be low in motivation?
- What is the most effective leadership style in a given situation?
- How will a specific change affect worker productivity?
- When is the right time to stimulate conflict?

CONTROLLING

- What activities in the organization need to be controlled?
- How should those activities be controlled?
- When is a performance deviation significant?
- What type of management information system should the organization have?

decision you almost forget *is* a decision. And managers also make dozens of these routine decisions every day, such as, for example, which employee will work what shift next week, what information should be included in a report, or how to resolve a customer's complaint. Keep in mind that even though a decision seems easy or has been faced by a manager a number of times before, it still is a decision. Let's look at three perspectives on how managers make decisions.

What Is the Rational Model of Decision Making?

When Hewlett-Packard (HP) acquired Compaq, the company did no research on how customers viewed Compaq products until "months after then-CEO Carly Fiorina publicly announced the deal and privately warned her top management team that she didn't want to hear any dissent pertaining to the acquisition."[10] By the time they discovered that customers perceived Compaq products as inferior—just the opposite of what customers felt about HP products—it was too late. HP's performance suffered and Fiorina lost her job.

We assume that managers' decision making will be **rational decision making**; that is, they'll make logical and consistent choices to maximize value.[11] After all, managers have all sorts of tools and techniques to help them be rational decision makers. (See the Technology and the Manager's Job box for additional information.) But as the HP example illustrates, managers aren't always rational. What does it mean to be a "rational" decision maker?

A rational decision maker would be fully objective and logical. The problem faced would be clear and unambiguous, and the decision maker would have a clear and specific goal and know all possible alternatives and consequences. Finally, making decisions rationally would consistently lead to selecting the alternative that maximizes the likelihood of achieving that goal. These assumptions apply to any decision—personal or managerial. However, for managerial decision making, we need to add one additional assumption—decisions are made in the best interests of the organization. These assumptions of rationality aren't very realistic, but the next concept can help explain how most decisions get made in organizations.

TECHNOLOGY AND THE MANAGER'S JOB — MAKING BETTER DECISIONS WITH TECHNOLOGY

Information technology is providing managers with a wealth of decision-making support, including expert systems, neural networks, groupware, and specific problem-solving software.[12] *Expert systems* use software programs to encode the relevant experience of an expert and allow a system to act like that expert in analyzing and solving ill-structured problems. The essence of expert systems is that (1) they use specialized knowledge about a particular problem area rather than general knowledge that would apply to all problems; (2) they use qualitative reasoning rather than numerical calculations; and (3) they perform at a level of competence that is higher than that of nonexpert humans. They guide users through problems by asking them a set of sequential questions about the situation and drawing conclusions based on the answers given. The conclusions are based on programmed rules that have been modeled on the actual reasoning processes of experts who have confronted similar problems before. Once in place, these systems allow employees and lower-level managers to make high-quality decisions that previously could have been made only by senior managers.

Neural networks are the next step beyond expert systems. They use computer software to imitate the structure of brain cells and connections among them. Sophisticated robotics use neural networks for their intelligence. Neural networks are able to distinguish patterns and trends too subtle or complex for human beings. For instance, people can't easily assimilate more than two or three variables at once, but neural networks can perceive correlations among hundreds of variables. As a result, they can perform many operations simultaneously, recognizing patterns, making associations, generalizing about problems they haven't been exposed to before, and learning through experience. For instance, most banks today use neural networks to flag potential credit card fraud. In the past they relied on expert systems to track millions of credit card transactions, but these earlier systems could look at only a few factors, such as the size of a transaction. Consequently, thousands of potential defrauding incidents were "flagged," most of which were false positives. Now with neural networks, significantly fewer numbers of cases are being identified as problematic—and it's more likely now that the majority of those identified will be actual cases of fraud. Furthermore, with the neural network system, fraudulent activities on a credit card can be uncovered in a matter of hours, rather than the two to three days it took prior to the implementation of neural networks. This is just one example of the power of IT to enhance an organization's—and its managers'—decision-making capabilities.

Think About:

· Can a manager have too much data when making decisions? Explain.

· Does information technology, such as expert systems and neural networks, make decisions, or is it simply a tool for managers? Discuss.

· How can technology help managers make better decisions?

· "Decision making is both science and art." Do you agree? Why or why not?

○ From the Past to the Present ○

Herbert A. Simon, who won a Nobel Prize in economics for his work on decision making, was primarily concerned with how people use logic and psychology to make choices.[13] He proposed that individuals were limited in their ability to "grasp the present and anticipate the future," and this bounded rationality made it difficult for them to "achieve the best possible decisions." Thus, people made "good enough" or "satisficing" choices. He went on to describe all administrative activity as group activity in which an organization took some decision-making autonomy from the individual and substituted it for an organizational decision-making process. Simon believed that such a process was necessary since it was impossible for any single individual to achieve any "high degree of objective rationality."

Simon's important contributions to management thinking came through his belief that to study and understand organizations meant studying the complex network of decisional processes that were inherent. His work in bounded rationality helps us make sense of how managers can behave rationally and still make satisfactory decisions, even given the limits of their capacity to process information.

Think About:

- Do you think satisficing is settling for second best? Discuss.
- In what decisions have you made "satisficing" choices? Were you happy with those choices?
- How does knowing about bounded rationality help make you a better decision maker?

What Is Bounded Rationality?

Despite the unrealistic assumptions, managers are expected to act rationally when making decisions.[14] They understand that "good" decision makers are supposed to do certain things and exhibit good decision-making behaviors as they identify problems, consider alternatives, gather information, and act decisively but prudently. When they do so, they show others that they're competent and that their decisions are the result of intelligent deliberation. However, a more realistic approach to describing how managers make decisions is the concept of bounded rationality, which says that managers make decisions rationally, but are limited (bounded) by their ability to process information.[15] Because they can't possibly analyze all information on all alternatives, managers satisfice, rather than maximize. That is, they accept solutions that are "good enough." They're being rational within the limits (bounds) of their ability to process information. Let's look at an example.

Suppose that you're a finance major and upon graduation you want a job, preferably as a personal financial planner, with a minimum salary of $45,000 and within a hundred miles of your hometown. You accept a job offer as a business credit analyst—not exactly a personal financial planner but still in the finance field—at a bank 50 miles from home at a starting salary of $39,000. If you had done a more comprehensive job search, you would have discovered a job in personal financial planning at a trust company only 25 miles from your hometown and starting at a salary of $43,000. You weren't a perfectly rational decision maker because you didn't maximize your decision by searching all possible alternatives and then choosing the best. But because the first job offer was satisfactory (or "good enough"), you behaved in a bounded rationality manner by accepting it.

Most decisions that managers make don't fit the assumptions of perfect rationality, so managers satisfice. However, keep in mind that their decision making is also likely influenced by the organization's culture, internal politics, power considerations, and by a phenomenon called escalation of commitment, which is an increased commitment to a previous decision despite evidence that it may have been wrong.[16]

---

rational decision making
Describes choices that are consistent and value-maximizing within specified constraints

bounded rationality
Making decisions that are rational within the limits of a manager's ability to process information

satisfice
Accepting solutions that are "good enough"

escalation of commitment
An increased commitment to a previous decision despite evidence that it may have been a poor decision

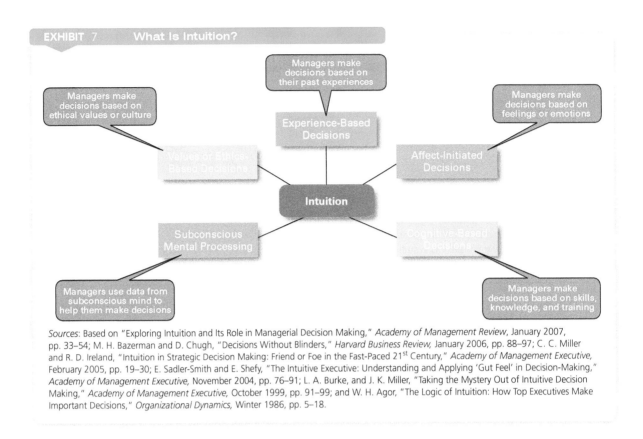

EXHIBIT 7   What Is Intuition?

Managers make decisions based on their past experiences

Managers make decisions based on ethical values or culture

Managers make decisions based on feelings or emotions

Experience-Based Decisions

Values or Ethics-Based Decisions

Affect-Initiated Decisions

Intuition

Subconscious Mental Processing

Cognitive-Based Decisions

Managers use data from subconscious mind to help them make decisions

Managers make decisions based on skills, knowledge, and training

Sources: Based on "Exploring Intuition and Its Role in Managerial Decision Making," *Academy of Management Review,* January 2007, pp. 33–54; M. H. Bazerman and D. Chugh, "Decisions Without Blinders," *Harvard Business Review,* January 2006, pp. 88–97; C. C. Miller and R. D. Ireland, "Intuition in Strategic Decision Making: Friend or Foe in the Fast-Paced 21st Century," *Academy of Management Executive,* February 2005, pp. 19–30; E. Sadler-Smith and E. Shefy, "The Intuitive Executive: Understanding and Applying 'Gut Feel' in Decision-Making," *Academy of Management Executive,* November 2004, pp. 76–91; L. A. Burke, and J. K. Miller, "Taking the Mystery Out of Intuitive Decision Making," *Academy of Management Executive,* October 1999, pp. 91–99; and W. H. Agor, "The Logic of Intuition: How Top Executives Make Important Decisions," *Organizational Dynamics,* Winter 1986, pp. 5–18.

Why would decision makers escalate commitment to a bad decision? Because they don't want to admit that their initial decision may have been flawed. Rather than search for new alternatives, they simply increase their commitment to the original solution.

What Role Does Intuition Play in Managerial Decision Making?

When Diego Della Valle, chairman of Italy-based Tod's luxury shoe empire, wants to know if a new style of shoes will work in the marketplace, he doesn't use focus groups or poll testing. Nope . . . he wears them. After a few days, if they're not to his liking, he renders his verdict: "These won't go into production." His intuitive decision approach has helped him turn Tod's into a successful multinational, multibillion-dollar company.[17] Like Della Valle, managers often use their intuition to help their decision making. What is intuitive decision making? It's making decisions on the basis of experience, feelings, and accumulated judgment. It's been described as "unconscious reasoning."[18] Researchers studying managers' use of intuitive decision making have identified five different aspects of intuition, which we describe in Exhibit 7.[19] How common is intuitive decision making? One survey found that almost half of the executives surveyed "used intuition more often than formal analysis to run their companies."[20]

Intuitive decision making can complement both rational and boundedly rational decision making.[21] First of all, a manager who has had experience with a similar type of problem or situation often can act quickly with what appears to be limited information because of that past experience. In addition, a recent study found that individuals who experienced intense feelings and emotions when making decisions actually achieved higher decision-making performance, especially when they understood their feelings as they were making decisions. The old belief that managers should ignore emotions when making decisions may not be the best advice.[22]

WHAT TYPES OF DECISIONS AND DECISION-MAKING CONDITIONS DO MANAGERS FACE?

Describe the types of decisions and decision-making conditions managers face.

3

Laura Ipsen is a senior vice president and general manager at Smart Grid, a business unit of Cisco Systems, which is working on helping utility companies find ways to build open, interconnected systems. She describes her job as "like having to put together a 1,000-piece puzzle, but with no box top with the picture of what it looks like and with some pieces missing."[23] Decision making in that type of environment is quite different from decision making done by a manager of a local Gap outlet store.

The types of problems managers face in decision-making situations often determine how a problem is treated. In this section, we present a categorization scheme for problems and for types of decisions. Then we show how the type of decision making a manager uses should reflect the characteristics of the problem.

How Do Problems Differ?

Some problems are straightforward. The goal of the decision maker is clear, the problem familiar, and information about the problem easily defined and complete. Examples might include a supplier who is late with an important delivery, a customer who wants to return an Internet purchase, a TV news team that has to respond to an unexpected and fast-breaking event, or a university that must help a student who is applying for financial aid. Such situations are called structured problems. They align closely with the assumptions underlying perfect rationality.

Many situations faced by managers, however, are unstructured problems. They are new or unusual. Information about such problems is ambiguous or incomplete. Examples of unstructured problems include the decision to enter a new market segment, to hire an architect to design a new office park, or to merge two organizations. So, too, is the decision to invest in a new, unproven technology. For instance, when Andrew Mason founded his online coupon start-up Groupon, he faced a situation best described as an unstructured problem.[24]

How Does a Manager Make Programmed Decisions?

Just as problems can be divided into two categories, so, too, can decisions. Programmed, or routine, decision making is the most efficient way to handle structured problems. However, when problems are unstructured, managers must rely on nonprogrammed decision making in order to develop unique solutions.

An auto mechanic damages a customer's rim while changing a tire. What does the manager do? Because the company probably has a standardized method for handling this type of problem, it is considered a programmed decision. For example, the manager may replace the rim at the company's expense. Decisions are programmed to the extent that they are repetitive and routine and to the extent that a specific approach has been worked out for handling them. Because the problem is well structured, the manager does not have to go to the trouble and expense of an involved decision process. Programmed decision making is relatively simple and tends to rely heavily on previous solutions. The develop-the-alternatives stage in the decision-making process is either nonexistent or given little attention. Why? Because once the structured problem is defined, its solution is usually

---

intuitive decision making
Making decisions on the basis of experience, feelings, and accumulated judgment

structured problem
A straightforward, familiar, and easily defined problem

unstructured problem
A problem that is new or unusual for which information is ambiguous or incomplete

programmed decision
A repetitive decision that can be handled using a routine approach

Policies for programmed decisions provide guidelines to channel a manager's thinking in a specific direction. Nestlé has corporate policies that guide decision making in the areas of nutrition, health, and wellness; consumer communication; and quality assurance and product safety. The company's quality policy covers all Nestlé products, including these Swiss chocolate cows made at a Nestlé plant in Switzerland. The quality policy is "to build trust by offering products and services that match consumer expectation and preference, and to comply with all internal and external food safety, regulatory, and quality requirements."

self-evident or at least reduced to only a few alternatives that are familiar and that have proved successful in the past. In many cases, programmed decision making becomes decision making by precedent. Managers simply do what they and others have done previously in the same situation. The damaged rim does not require the manager to identify and weight decision criteria or develop a long list of possible solutions. Rather, the manager falls back on a systematic procedure, rule, or policy.

PROCEDURES. A procedure is a series of interrelated sequential steps that a manager can use when responding to a well-structured problem. The only real difficulty is identifying the problem. Once the problem is clear, so is the procedure. For instance, a purchasing manager receives a request from computing services for licensing arrangements to install 250 copies of Norton Antivirus Software. The purchasing manager knows that a definite procedure is in place for handling this decision. Has the requisition been properly filled out and approved? If not, he can send the requisition back with a note explaining what is deficient. If the request is complete, the approximate costs are estimated. If the total exceeds $8,500, three bids must be obtained. If the total is $8,500 or less, only one vendor need be identified and the order placed. The decision-making process is merely the execution of a simple series of sequential steps.

RULES. A rule is an explicit statement that tells a manager what he or she ought—or ought not—to do. Rules are frequently used by managers who confront a structured problem because they're simple to follow and ensure consistency. In the preceding example, the $8,500 cutoff rule simplifies the purchasing manager's decision about when to use multiple bids.

POLICIES. A third guide for making programmed decisions is a policy. It provides guidelines to channel a manager's thinking in a specific direction. The statement that "we promote from within, whenever possible" is an example of a policy. In contrast to a rule, a policy establishes parameters for the decision maker rather than specifically stating what should or should not be done. It's at this point that one's ethical standards will come into play. As an analogy, think of the Ten Commandments as rules and the U.S. Constitution as policy. The latter requires judgment and interpretation; the former do not.

How Do Nonprogrammed Decisions Differ from Programmed Decisions?

Examples of nonprogrammed decisions include deciding whether to acquire another organization, deciding which global markets offer the most potential, or deciding whether to sell off an unprofitable division. Such decisions are unique and nonrecurring. When a manager confronts an unstructured problem, no cut-and-dried solution is available. A custom-made, nonprogrammed response is required.

The creation of a new organizational strategy is a nonprogrammed decision. This decision is different from previous organizational decisions because the issue is new; a different set of environmental factors exists, and other conditions have changed. For example, Amazon.com's Jeff Bezos's strategy to "get big fast" helped the company grow tremendously. But this strategy came at a cost—perennial financial losses. To turn a profit, Bezos made decisions regarding "sorting orders, anticipating demand, more efficient shipping, foreign partnerships, and opening a marketplace allowing other sellers to sell their books at Amazon." As a result, for the first time in company history, Amazon is profitable.[25]

How Are Problems, Types of Decisions, and Organizational Level Integrated?

Exhibit 8 describes the relationship among types of problems, types of decisions, and level in the organization. Structured problems are responded to with programmed decision making. Unstructured problems require nonprogrammed decision making. Lower-level managers essentially confront familiar and repetitive problems; therefore, they most typically rely on programmed decisions such as standard operating procedures. However, the problems confronting managers are likely to become less structured as they move up the organizational hierarchy. Why? Because lower-level managers handle the routine decisions themselves and pass upward only decisions that they find unique or difficult. Similarly, managers pass down routine decisions to their employees in order to spend their time on more problematic issues.

Few managerial decisions in the real world are either fully programmed or fully nonprogrammed. Most decisions fall somewhere in between. Few programmed decisions eliminate individual judgment completely. At the other extreme, even the most unusual situation requiring a nonprogrammed decision often can be helped by programmed routines. A final point we want to make is that organizational efficiency is facilitated by programmed decision making—a fact that may explain its wide popularity. Whenever possible, management decisions are likely to be programmed. Obviously, this approach isn't too realistic at the top of the organization, because most of the problems that top-level managers confront are of a nonrecurring nature. However, the necessity to control costs and other variables motivate them to create policies, standard operating procedures, and rules to guide other lower-level managers.

Programmed decisions minimize the need for managers to exercise discretion. This factor is important because discretion costs money. The more nonprogrammed decision making a manager is required to do, the greater the judgment needed. Because sound judgment is an uncommon quality, it costs more to acquire the services of managers who possess it.

What Decision-Making Conditions Do Managers Face?

When making decisions, managers may face three different conditions: certainty, risk, and uncertainty. Let's look at the characteristics of each.

The ideal situation for making decisions is one of certainty, which is a situation where a manager can make accurate decisions because the outcome of every alternative is known. For example, when South Dakota's state treasurer decides where to deposit excess state

EXHIBIT 8   Types of Problems, Types of Decisions, and Organizational Level

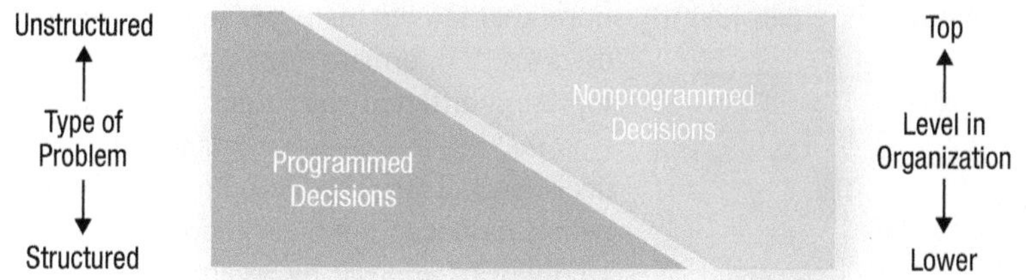

procedure
A series of interrelated, sequential steps used to respond to a structured problem

rule
An explicit statement that tells employees what can or cannot be done

policy
A guideline for making decisions

nonprogrammed decision
A unique and nonrecurring decision that requires a custom-made solution

certainty
A situation in which a decision maker can make accurate decisions because all outcomes are known

funds, he knows exactly the interest rate being offered by each bank and the amount that will be earned on the funds. He is certain about the outcomes of each alternative. As you might expect, most managerial decisions aren't like this.

A far more common situation is one of risk, conditions in which the decision maker is able to estimate the likelihood of certain outcomes. Under risk, managers have historical data from past personal experiences or secondary information that lets them assign probabilities to different alternatives.

What happens if you face a decision where you're not certain about the outcomes and can't even make reasonable probability estimates? We call this condition uncertainty. Managers do face decision-making situations of uncertainty. Under these conditions, the choice of alternative is influenced by the limited amount of available information and by the psychological orientation of the decision maker.

HOW DO GROUPS MAKE DECISIONS?

4 Discuss group decision making.

Do managers make a lot of decisions in groups? You bet they do! Many decisions in organizations, especially important decisions that have far-reaching effects on organizational activities and personnel, are typically made in groups. It's a rare organization that doesn't at some time use committees, task forces, review panels, work teams, or similar groups as vehicles for making decisions. Why? In many cases, these groups represent the people who will be most affected by the decisions being made. Because of their expertise, these people are often best qualified to make decisions that affect them.

Studies tell us that managers spend a significant portion of their time in meetings. Undoubtedly, a large portion of that time is involved with defining problems, arriving at solutions to those problems, and determining the means for implementing the solutions. It's possible, in fact, for groups to be assigned any of the eight steps in the decision-making process.

What Are the Advantages of Group Decision Making?

Individual and group decisions have their own set of strengths. Neither is ideal for all situations. Let's begin by reviewing the advantages that group decisions have over individual decisions.

Group decisions provide more complete information than do individual ones.[27] There is often truth to the saying that two heads are better than one. A group will bring a diversity of experiences and perspectives to the decision process that an individual acting alone cannot.[28] Groups also generate more alternatives. Because groups have a greater quantity and diversity of information, they can identify more alternatives than can an individual. Quantity and diversity of information are greatest when group members represent different specialties. Furthermore, group decision making increases acceptance of a solution.[29] Many decisions fail after the final choice has been made because people do not accept the solution. However, if the people who will be affected by a certain solution, and who will help implement it, participate in the decision they will be more likely to accept the decision and encourage others to accept it. And, finally, this process increases legitimacy. The group decision-making process is consistent with democratic ideals; therefore, decisions made by groups may be perceived as more legitimate than decisions made by a single person. The fact that the individual decision maker has complete power and has not consulted others can create a perception that a decision was made autocratically and arbitrarily.

An advantage of group decision making is that it brings a diversity of experiences and perspectives to the decision process. Group decision making is more effective than individual decision making at WLC Architects, where multiethnic design teams of professionals from various disciplines work on complex design and construction projects ranging from schools to civic centers. The group members representing many different specialties of architects and engineers generate more decision alternatives because they have a greater quantity and diversity of information. The decisions resulting from WLC's integrated team approach determine the success of its projects in terms of affordability, functionality, and creativity.

What Are the Disadvantages of Group Decision Making?

If groups are so good, how did the phrase "a camel is a racehorse put together by a committee" become so popular? The answer, of course, is that group decisions are not without their drawbacks. First, they're *time-consuming*. It takes time to assemble a group. In addition, the interaction that takes place once the group is in place is frequently inefficient. Groups almost always take more time to reach a solution than an individual would take to make the decision alone. They may also be subject to *minority domination*, where members of a group are never perfectly equal.[30] They may differ in rank in the organization, experience, knowledge about the problem, influence on other members, verbal skills, assertiveness, and the like. This imbalance creates the opportunity for one or more members to dominate others in the group. A minority that dominates a group frequently has an undue influence on the final decision.

Another problem focuses on the *pressures to conform* in groups. For instance, have you ever been in a situation in which several people were sitting around discussing a particular item and you had something to say that ran contrary to the consensus views of the group, but you remained silent? Were you surprised to learn later that others shared your views and also had remained silent? What you experienced is what Irving Janis called groupthink.[31] In this form of conformity, group members withhold deviant, minority, or unpopular views in order to give the appearance of agreement. As a result, groupthink undermines critical thinking in the group and eventually harms the quality of the final decision. And, finally, *ambiguous responsibility* can become a problem. Group members share responsibility, but who is actually responsible for the final outcome?[32] In an individual decision, it's clear who is responsible. In a group decision, the responsibility of any single member is watered down.

Groupthink affects a group's ability to appraise alternatives objectively and may jeopardize the arrival at a quality decision. Because of pressures for conformity, groups often deter individuals from critically appraising unusual, minority, or unpopular views. Consequently, an individual's mental efficiency, reality testing, and moral judgment deteriorate. How does groupthink occur? The following are examples of situations in which groupthink is evident:

- Group members rationalize any resistance to the assumptions they have made.
- Members apply direct pressures on those who momentarily express doubts about any of the group's shared views or who question the validity of arguments favored by the majority.
- Those members who have doubts or hold differing points of view seek to avoid deviating from what appears to be group consensus.
- An illusion of unanimity is pervasive. If someone does not speak, it is assumed that he or she is in full accord.

Does groupthink really hinder decision making? Yes. Several research studies have found that groupthink symptoms were associated with poorer quality decision outcomes. But groupthink can be minimized if the group is cohesive, fosters open discussion, and has an impartial leader who seeks input from all members.[33]

When Are Groups Most Effective?

Whether groups are more effective than individuals depends on the criteria you use for defining effectiveness, such as accuracy, speed, creativity, and acceptance. Group decisions tend to be more accurate. On average, groups tend to make better decisions than individuals, although groupthink may occur.[34] However, if decision effectiveness is defined in terms of speed, individuals are superior. If creativity is important, groups tend to

---

risk

A situation in which a decision maker is able to estimate the likelihood of certain outcomes

uncertainty

A situation in which a decision maker has neither certainty nor reasonable probability estimates available

groupthink

When a group exerts extensive pressure on an individual to withhold his or her different views in order to appear to be in agreement

RIGHT ? OR WRONG

MTV has long been known for pushing the envelope in television programming.[35] It pioneered reality television in 1992 with *The Real World*, in which seven young adult strangers live together in a house in some city and have their lives videotaped. When the show first aired, concerns were raised over what was being presented. Yet, the show is still going strong after 20 years. However, one of MTV's current shows, *Skins*, is generating much more significant controversy. The series, which deals with "explicitly teenage characters doing explicit things," is quite graphic in its portrayals of situations. The show has a TV-MA (meant for mature audiences) rating and MTV has suggested in press releases that the show is "specifically designed to be viewed by adults." However, critics contend that the show is "meant to offend adults and create did-you-see chatter among young people." Critics have also accused the show of violating child porn laws and several mainstream advertisers have backed out.

Think About:

- What do you think about this situation? What potential ethical issues do you see here? How do legal aspects figure into your assessment?

- Obviously, the more controversial a television program (or book or movie or Web site) becomes, the more that viewers might be attracted to it. Is that unethical? Discuss.

- What stakeholders do you think are most important in this situation and what concerns might those stakeholders have?

- Is there anything that MTV might do to "look better" (i.e., more responsible and ethical)?

- Using what you've learned about decision making, what would you suggest MTV executives do next?

Epilogue: In early summer 2011, MTV executives pulled the plug on the U.S. version of Skins. A network executive said in a written statement that, "Skins is a global television phenomenon that, unfortunately, didn't connect with a U.S. audience as much as we had hoped."

be more effective than individuals. And if effectiveness means the degree of acceptance the final solution achieves, the nod again goes to the group.

The effectiveness of group decision making is also influenced by the size of the group. The larger the group, the greater the opportunity for heterogeneous representation. On the other hand, a larger group requires more coordination and more time to allow all members to contribute. This factor means that groups probably should not be too large: A minimum of five to a maximum of about fifteen members is best. Groups of five to seven individuals appear to be the most effective. Because five and seven are odd numbers, decision deadlocks are avoided. Effectiveness should not be considered without also assessing efficiency. Groups almost always stack up as a poor second in efficiency to the individual decision maker. With few exceptions, group decision making consumes more work hours than does individual decision making. In deciding whether to use groups, then, primary consideration must be given to assessing whether increases in effectiveness are more than enough to offset the losses in efficiency.

How Can You Improve Group Decision Making?

Three ways of making group decisions more creative are brainstorming, the nominal group technique, and electronic meetings.

WHAT IS BRAINSTORMING? Brainstorming is a relatively simple idea-generating process that specifically encourages any and all alternatives while withholding any criticism of those alternatives.[36] In a typical brainstorming session, a half-dozen to a dozen people sit around a table. Of course, technology is changing where that "table" is. The group leader states the problem in a clear manner that is understood by all participants. Members then "freewheel" as many alternatives as they can in a given time. No criticism is allowed, and all the alternatives are recorded for later discussion and analysis.[37] Brainstorming, however, is merely a process for generating ideas. The next method, the nominal group technique, helps groups arrive at a preferred solution.[38]

HOW DOES THE NOMINAL GROUP TECHNIQUE WORK? The nominal group technique restricts discussion during the decision-making process, hence the term. Group members must be present, as in a traditional committee meeting, but they are required to operate independently. They secretly write a list of general problem areas or potential solutions to a problem. The chief advantage of this technique is that it permits the group to meet formally but does not restrict independent thinking, as so often happens in the traditional interacting group.[39]

HOW CAN ELECTRONIC MEETINGS ENHANCE GROUP DECISION MAKING? The most recent approach to group decision making blends the nominal group technique with computer technology and is called the electronic meeting.

Newscom

Once the technology for the meeting is in place, the concept is simple. Numerous people sit around a table that's empty except for a series of computer terminals. Issues are presented to the participants, who type their responses onto their computer screens. Individual comments, as well as aggregate votes, are displayed on a projection screen in the room.

The major advantages of electronic meetings are anonymity, honesty, and speed.[40] Participants can anonymously type any message they want, and it will flash on the screen for all to see with a keystroke. It allows people to be brutally honest with no penalty. And it is fast—chitchat is eliminated, discussions do not digress, and many participants can "talk" at once without interrupting the others.

Electronic meetings are significantly faster and much cheaper than traditional face-to-face meetings.[41] Nestlé, for instance, continues to use the approach for many of its meetings, especially globally focused meetings.[42] However, as with all other forms of group activities, electronic meetings do experience some drawbacks. Those who type quickly can outshine those who may be verbally eloquent but lousy typists; those with the best ideas don't get credit for them; and the process lacks the informational richness of face-to-face oral communication. However, group decision making is likely to include extensive usage of electronic meetings.[43]

A variation of the electronic meeting is the videoconference. By linking together media from different locations, people can have face-to-face meetings even when they are thousands of miles apart. This capability has enhanced feedback among the members, saved countless hours of business travel, and ultimately saved companies such as Nestlé and Logitech hundreds of thousands of dollars. As a result, they're more effective in their meetings and have increased the efficiency with which decisions are made.[44] Many companies utilized these approaches during the global recession.

WHAT CONTEMPORARY DECISION-MAKING ISSUES DO MANAGERS FACE?

Discuss contemporary issues in managerial decision making.

5

Today's business world revolves around making decisions, often risky ones, usually with incomplete or inadequate information, and under intense time pressure. Most managers make one decision after another; and as if that weren't challenging enough, more is at stake than ever before. Bad decisions can cost millions. We're going to look at two important issues—national culture and creativity—that managers face in today's fast-moving and global world.

How Does National Culture Affect Managers' Decision Making?

Research shows that, to some extent, decision-making practices differ from country to country.[45] The way decisions are made—whether by group, by team members, participatively, or autocratically by an individual manager—and the degree of risk a decision maker is willing to take are just two examples of decision variables that reflect a country's cultural environment. For example, in India, power distance and uncertainty avoidance are high. There, only very senior-level managers make decisions, and they are likely to make safe decisions. In contrast, in Sweden, power distance and uncertainty avoidance are low. Swedish managers are not afraid to make risky decisions. Senior managers in Sweden also push decisions down in the ranks. They encourage lower-level

---

brainstorming
An idea-generating process that encourages alternatives while withholding criticism

nominal group technique
A decision-making technique in which group members are physically present but operate independently

electronic meeting
A type of nominal group technique in which participants are linked by computer

Creativity based on expertise in developing video games made an important contribution to decision making at Rovio Mobile, the Finnish firm that created the Angry Birds game. One decision that led to Angry Birds' success was to invest time and money during the game's development to produce an innovative physics-based game that made it easy to learn, created depth for advanced players in later stages, and appealed to people of all ages. After studying the iPhone apps system, Rovio decided to launch the game on iPhone where it quickly became the most popular paid application in 61 countries. Rovio also decided to focus on player retention by issuing free regular game updates. Shown here is an Angry Bird on display at Rovio's offices.

managers and employees to take part in decisions that affect them. In countries such as Egypt, where time pressures are low, managers make decisions at a slower and more deliberate pace than managers do in the United States. And in Italy, where history and traditions are valued, managers tend to rely on tried and proven alternatives to resolve problems.

Decision making in Japan is much more group oriented than in the United States.[46] The Japanese value conformity and cooperation. Before making decisions, Japanese CEOs collect a large amount of information, which is then used in consensus-forming group decisions called ringisei. Because employees in Japanese organizations have high job security, managerial decisions take a long-term perspective rather than focusing on short-term profits, as is often the practice in the United States.

Senior managers in France and Germany also adapt their decision styles to their countries' cultures. In France, for instance, autocratic decision making is widely practiced, and managers avoid risks. Managerial styles in Germany reflect the German culture's concern for structure and order. Consequently, German organizations generally operate under extensive rules and regulations. Managers have well-defined responsibilities and accept that decisions must go through channels.

As managers deal with employees from diverse cultures, they need to recognize common and accepted behavior when asking them to make decisions. Some individuals may not be as comfortable as others with being closely involved in decision making, or they may not be willing to experiment with something radically different. Managers who accommodate the diversity in decision-making philosophies and practices can expect a high payoff if they capture the perspectives and strengths that a diverse workforce offers.

Why Is Creativity Important in Decision Making?

A decision maker needs creativity: the ability to produce novel and useful ideas. These ideas are different from what's been done before but are also appropriate to the problem or opportunity presented. Why is creativity important to decision making? It allows the decision maker to appraise and understand the problem more fully, including "seeing" problems others can't see. However, creativity's most obvious value is in helping the decision maker identify all viable alternatives.

Most people have creative potential that they can use when confronted with a decision-making problem. But to unleash that potential, they have to get out of the psychological ruts most of us get into and learn how to think about a problem in divergent ways.

We can start with the obvious. People differ in their inherent creativity. Einstein, Edison, Dali, and Mozart were individuals of exceptional creativity. Not surprisingly, exceptional creativity is scarce. A study of lifetime creativity of 461 men and women found that fewer than 1 percent were exceptionally creative. But 10 percent were highly creative, and about 60 percent were somewhat creative. These findings suggest that most of us have creative potential, if we can learn to unleash it.

Given that most people have the capacity to be at least moderately creative, what can individuals and organizations do to stimulate employee creativity? The best answer to this question lies in the three-component model of creativity based on an extensive body of research.[47] This model proposes that individual creativity essentially requires expertise, creative-thinking skills, and intrinsic task motivation. Studies confirm that the higher the level of each of these three components, the higher the creativity.

Expertise is the foundation of all creative work. Dali's understanding of art and Einstein's knowledge of physics were necessary conditions for them to be able to make creative contributions to their fields. And you wouldn't expect someone with a minimal knowledge of programming to be highly creative as a software engineer. The potential for creativity is enhanced when individuals have abilities, knowledge, proficiencies, and similar expertise in their fields of endeavor.

The second component is *creative-thinking skills*. It encompasses personality characteristics associated with creativity, the ability to use analogies, as well as the talent to see the familiar in a different light. For instance, the following individual traits have been found to be associated with the development of creative ideas: intelligence, independence, self-confidence, risk taking, internal locus of control, tolerance for ambiguity, and perseverance in the face of frustration. The effective use of analogies allows decision makers to apply an idea from one context to another. One of the most famous examples in which analogy resulted in a creative breakthrough was Alexander Graham Bell's observation that it might be possible to take concepts that operate in the ear and apply them to his "talking box." He noticed that the bones in the ear are operated by a delicate, thin membrane. He wondered why, then, a thicker and stronger piece of membrane shouldn't be able to move a piece of steel. Out of that analogy the telephone was conceived. Of course, some people have developed their skill at being able to see problems in a new way. They're able to make the strange familiar and the familiar strange. For instance, most of us think of hens laying eggs. But how many of us have considered that a hen is only an egg's way of making another egg?

The final component in our model is *intrinsic task motivation*—the desire to work on something because it's interesting, involving, exciting, satisfying, or personally challenging. This motivational component is what turns creative *potential* into *actual* creative ideas. It determines the extent to which individuals fully engage their expertise and creative skills. So creative people often love their work, to the point of seeming obsessed. Importantly, an individual's work environment and the organization's culture can have a significant effect on intrinsic motivation. Specifically, five organizational factors have been found that can impede your creativity: (1) expected evaluation—focusing on how your work is going to be evaluated; (2) surveillance—being watched while you're working; (3) external motivators—emphasizing external, tangible rewards; (4) competition—facing win–lose situations with your peers; and (5) constrained choices—being given limits on how you can do your work.

ringisei
Japanese consensus-forming group decisions

creativity
The ability to produce novel and useful ideas

Review

1 **Describe the decision-making process.** The decision-making process consists of eight steps: (1) identify a problem, (2) identify decision criteria, (3) weight the criteria, (4) develop alternatives, (5) analyze alternatives, (6) select alternative, (7) implement alternative, and (8) evaluate decision effectiveness. As managers make decisions, they may use heuristics to simplify the process, which can lead to errors and biases in their decision making. The 12 common decision-making errors and biases include overconfidence, immediate gratification, anchoring, selective perception, confirmation, framing, availability, representation, randomness, sunk costs, self-serving bias, and hindsight.

2 **Explain the three approaches managers can use to make decisions.** The first approach is the rational model. The assumptions of rationality are as follows: the problem is clear and unambiguous; a single, well-defined goal is to be achieved; all alternatives and consequences are known; and the final choice will maximize the payoff. The second approach, bounded rationality, says that managers make rational decisions but are bounded (limited) by their ability to process information. In this approach, managers satisfice, which is when decision makers accept solutions that are good enough. Finally, intuitive decision making is making decisions on the basis of experience, feelings, and accumulated judgment.

3 **Describe the types of decisions and decision-making conditions managers face.** Programmed decisions are repetitive decisions that can be handled by a routine approach and are used when the problem being resolved is straightforward, familiar, and easily defined (structured). Nonprogrammed decisions are unique decisions that require a custom-made solution and are used when the problems are new or unusual (unstructured) and for which information is ambiguous or incomplete. Certainty involves a situation in which a manager can make accurate decisions because all outcomes are known. With risk, a manager can estimate the likelihood of certain outcomes in a situation. Uncertainty is a situation in which a manager is not certain about the outcomes and can't even make reasonable probability estimates.

4 **Discuss group decision making.** Groups offer certain advantages when making decisions—more complete information, more alternatives, increased acceptance of a solution, and greater legitimacy. On the other hand, groups are time-consuming, can be dominated by a minority, create pressures to conform, and cloud responsibility. Three ways of improving group decision making are brainstorming (utilizing an idea-generating process that specifically encourages any and all alternatives while withholding any criticism of those alternatives), the nominal group technique (a technique that restricts discussion during the decision-making process), and electronic meetings (the most recent approach to group decision making, which blends the nominal group technique with sophisticated computer technology).

5 **Discuss contemporary issues in managerial decision making.** As managers deal with employees from diverse cultures, they need to recognize common and accepted behavior when asking them to make decisions. Some individuals may not be as comfortable as others with being closely involved in decision making, or they may not be willing to experiment with something radically different. Also, managers need to be creative in their decision making because creativity allows them to appraise and understand the problem more fully, including "seeing" problems that others can't see.

MyManagementLab   For more resources, please visit **www.mymanagementlab.com**

UNDERSTANDING THE CHAPTER

1. Why is decision making often described as the essence of a manager's job?

2. Describe the eight steps in the decision-making process.

3. All of us bring biases to the decisions we make. What would be the drawbacks of having biases? Could there be any advantages to having biases? Explain. What are the implications for managerial decision making?

4. "Because managers have software tools to use, they should be able to make more rational decisions." Do you agree or disagree with this statement? Why?

5. Is there a difference between wrong decisions and bad decisions? Why do good managers sometimes make wrong decisions? Bad decisions? How might managers improve their decision-making skills?

6. Describe a decision you've made that closely aligns with the assumptions of perfect rationality. Compare this decision with the process you used to select your college. Did you depart from the rational model in your college decisions? Explain.

7. Explain how a manager might deal with making decisions under conditions of uncertainty.

8. Why do you think organizations have increased the use of groups for making decisions? When would you recommend using groups to make decisions?

9. Find two examples each of procedures, rules, and policies. Bring your examples to class and be prepared to share them.

10. Do a Web search on the phrase "dumbest moments in business" and get the most current version of this list. Choose three of the examples and describe what happened. What's your reaction to each example? How could the managers in each have made better decisions?

Endnotes

1. J. Dean, "Boldness of '81 Test Flight Unlikely to Be Repeated," *USA Today,* April 11, 2011, p. 7A; G. Griffin, "As Shuttle Retires, A Vote for Commercial Space Flight," *USA Today,* April 6, 2011, p. 9A; A. K. Donahue, "More to Learn from NASA About Learning, Unlearning, and Forgetting," *Journal of Public Administration Research* (April 2011), pp. 391–395; C. Chaplain, "Additional Cost Transparency and Design Criteria Needed for National Aeronautics and Space Administration (NASA) Projects," *GAO Reports,* March 3, 2011, pp. 1–11; A. Pasztor, "U.S. News: NASA Budget Plan Restricts Spending on Private Rockets," *Wall Street Journal,* February 14, 2011, p. A2; "NASA's Space-Shuttle Program Ends," *Fast Company,* February 2011, p. 22; H. Hickam, "How About a Moon Base?" *Wall Street Journal,* December 14, 2010, p. A19; J. Penn, "NASA's Plan Is Not Sustainable," *Aviation Week & Space Technology,* December 6, 2010, p. 74; P. M. Barrett, "Lost in Space," *Bloomberg BusinessWeek,* November 1–7, 2010, pp. 66–73; A. Pasztor, "NASA Chief Bolden Seeks 'Plan B' for the Space Agency," *Wall Street Journal,* March 4, 2010, p. A6; A. Pasztor, "NASA Gets Flak on New Course," *Wall Street Journal,* March 1, 2010, p. A6; B. Mintz Testa, "New Workforce Orbit-Relaunch at NASA," *Workforce Management Online,* February 16, 2010; L. B. Jabs, "Communicative Rules and Organizational Decision Making," *Journal of Business Communication* (July 2005), pp. 265–288; T. M. Garrett, "Whither *Challenger*, Wither *Columbia*: Management Decision Making and the Knowledge Analytic," *American Review of*

Public Administration, December 2004, pp. 389–402; M. Maier "Teaching from Tragedy: An Interdisciplinary Module on the Space Shuttle *Challenger*," *THE Journal* (September 1993), pp. 91–94; and G. Moorhead, R. Ference, and C. P. Neck, "Group Decision Fiascoes Continue: Space Shuttle *Challenger* and a Revised Groupthink Framework," *Human Relations,* June 1991, pp. 539–550.

2. See, for example, A. Nagurney, J. Dong, and P. L. Mokhtarian, "Multicriteria Network Equilibrium Modeling with Variable Weights for Decision-Making in the Information Age with Applications to the Telecommuting and Teleshopping," *Journal of Economic Dynamics and Control* (August 2002), pp. 1629–1650.

3. J. Flinchbaugh, "Surfacing Problems Daily: Advice for Building a Problem-Solving Culture," *Industry Week,* April 2011, p. 12; "Business Analysis Training Helps Leaders Achieve an Enterprise-Wide Perspective," *Leader to Leader,* Fall 2010, pp. 63–65; D. Okes, "Common Problems with Basic Problem Solving," *Quality,* September 2010, pp. 36–40; J. Sawyer, "Problem-Solving Success Tips," *Business and Economic Review,* April–June 2002, pp. 23–24.

4. See J. Figueira and B. Ray, "Determining the Weights of Criteria in the Electre Type of Methods with a Revised Simons' Procedure," *European Journal of Operational Research,* June 1, 2002, pp. 317–326.

5. For instance, see M. Elliott, "Breakthrough Thinking," *IIE Solution,* October 2001, pp. 22–25; and B. Fazlollahi and

R. Vahidov, "A Method for Generation of Alternatives by Decision Support Systems," *Journal of Management Information Systems* (Fall 2001), pp. 229–250.

6. D. Miller, Q. Hope, R. Eisenstat, N. Foote, and J. Galbraith, "The Problem of Solutions: Balancing Clients and Capabilities," *Business Horizons,* March–April 2002, pp. 3–12.

7. E. Teach, "Avoiding Decision Traps," *CFO,* June 2004, pp. 97–99; and D. Kahneman and A. Tversky, "Judgment Under Uncertainty: Heuristics and Biases," *Science* 185 (1974), pp. 1124–1131.

8. Information for this section taken from S. P. Robbins, *Decide & Conquer* (Upper Saddle River, NJ: Financial Times/Prentice Hall, 2004).

9. T. A. Stewart, "Did You Ever Have to Make Up Your Mind?" *Harvard Business Review,* January 2006, p. 12; and E. Pooley, "Editor's Desk," *Fortune,* June 27, 2005, p. 16.

10. J. Pfeffer and R. I. Sutton, "Why Managing by Facts Works," *Strategy & Business,* Spring 2006, pp. 9–12.

11. See T. Shavit and A. M. Adam, "A Preliminary Exploration of the Effects of Rational Factors and Behavioral Biases on the Managerial Choice to Invest in Corporate Responsibility," *Managerial and Decision Economics,* April 2011, pp. 205–213; A. Langley, "In Search of Rationality: The Purposes Behind the Use of Formal Analysis in Organizations," *Administrative Science Quarterly*, December 1989, pp. 598–631; and H. A. Simon, "Rationality in Psychology and Economics," *Journal of Business* (October 1986), pp. 209–224.

12. Technology and the Manager's Job box based on M. Xu, V. Ong, Y. Duan, and B. Mathews, "Intelligent Agent Systems for Executive Information Scanning, Filtering, and Interpretation: Perceptions and Challenges," *Information Processing & Management,* March 2011, pp. 186–201; J. P. Kallunki, E. K. Laitinen, and H. Silvola, "Impact of Enterprise Resource Planning Systems on Management Control Systems and Firm Performance," *International Journal of Accounting Information Systems* (March 2011), pp. 20–39; H. W. K. Chia, C. L. Tan, and S. Y. Sung, "Enhancing Knowledge Discovery via Association-Based Evolution of Neural Logic Networks," *IEEE Transactions on Knowledge and Data Engineering* (July 2006), pp. 889–901; F. Harvey, "A Key Role in Detecting Fraud Patterns: Neural Networks," *Financial Times,* January 23, 2002, p. 3; D. Mitchell and R. Pavur, "Using Modular Neural Networks for Business Decisions," *Management Decision,* January–February 2002, pp. 58–64; B. L. Killingsworth, M. B. Hayden, and R. Schellenberger, "A Network Expert System Management System of Multiple Domains," *Journal of Information Science* (March–April 2001), p. 81; and S. Balakrishnan, N. Popplewell, and M. Thomlinson, "Intelligent Robotic Assembly," *Computers & Industrial Engineering,* December 2000, p. 467.

13. From the Past to the Present box based on M. Ibrahim, "Theory of Bounded Rationality," *Public Management,* June 2009, pp. 3–5; D. A. Wren, *The Evolution of Management Thought* Fourth Edition (New York: John Wiley & Sons, Inc., 1994), p. 291; and H. A. Simon, *Administrative Behavior* (New York: Macmillan Company, 1945).

14. J. G. March, "Decision-Making Perspective: Decisions in Organizations and Theories of Choice," in A. H. Van de Ven and W. F. Joyce (eds.), *Perspectives on Organization Design and Behavior* (New York: Wiley-Interscience, 1981), pp. 232–233.

15. See D. R. A. Skidd, "Revisiting Bounded Rationality," *Journal of Management Inquiry* (December 1992), pp. 343–347; B. E. Kaufman, "A New Theory of Satisficing," *Journal of Behavioral Economics* (Spring 1990), pp. 35–51; and N. McK. Agnew and J. L. Brown, "Bounded Rationality: Fallible Decisions in Unbounded Decision Space," *Behavioral Science*, July 1986, pp. 148–161.

16. See, for example, G. McNamara, H. Moon, and P. Bromiley, "Banking on Commitment: Intended and Unintended Consequences of an Organization's Attempt to Attenuate Escalation of Commitment," *Academy of Management Journal* (April 2002), pp. 443–452; V. S. Rao and A. Monk, "The Effects of Individual Differences and Anonymity on Commitment to Decisions," *Journal of Social Psychology* (August 1999), pp. 496–515; C. F. Camerer and R. A. Weber, "The Econometrics and Behavioral Economics of Escalation of Commitment: A Re-examination of Staw's Theory," *Journal of Economic Behavior and Organization* (May 1999), pp. 59–82; D. R. Bobocel and J. P. Meyer, "Escalating Commitment to a Failing Course of Action: Separating the Roles of Choice and Justification," *Journal of Applied Psychology* (June 1994), pp. 360–363; and B. M. Staw, "The Escalation of Commitment to a Course of Action," *Academy of Management Review*, October 1981, pp. 577–587.

17. L. Alderman, "A Shoemaker That Walks but Never Runs," *New York Times Online,* October 8, 2010.

18. C. Flora, "When to Go with Your Gut," *Women's Health,* June 2009, pp. 68–70.

19. See J. Evans, "Intuition and Reasoning: A Dual-Process Perspective," *Psychological Inquiry,* October–December 2010, pp. 313–326; T. Betsch and A. Blockner, "Intuition in Judgment and Decision Making: Extensive Thinking Without Effort," *Psychological Inquiry,* October–December 2010, pp. 279–294; R. Lange and J. Houran, "A Transliminal View of Intuitions in the Workplace," *North American Journal of Psychology,* 12, no. 3 (2010), pp. 501–516; E. Dane and M. G. Pratt, "Exploring Intuition and Its Role in Managerial Decision Making," *Academy of Management Review,* January 2007, pp. 33–54; M. H. Bazerman and D. Chugh, "Decisions Without Blinders," *Harvard Business Review,* January 2006, pp. 88–97; C. C. Miller and R. D. Ireland, "Intuition in Strategic Decision Making: Friend or Foe in the Fast-Paced 21st Century," *Academy of Management Executive,* February 2005, pp. 19–30; E. Sadler-Smith and E. Shefy, "The Intuitive Executive: Understanding and Applying 'Gut Feel' in Decision-Making," *Academy of Management Executive,* November 2004, pp. 76–91; and L. A. Burke and M. K. Miller, "Taking the Mystery Out of Intuitive Decision Making," *Academy of Management Executive*, October 1999, pp. 91–99.

20. C. C. Miller and R. D. Ireland, "Intuition in Strategic Decision Making: Friend or Foe," p. 20.

21. E. Sadler-Smith and E. Shefy, "Developing Intuitive Awareness in Management Education," *Academy of Management Learning & Education,* June 2007, pp. 186–205.

22. M. G. Seo and L. Feldman Barrett, "Being Emotional During Decision Making—Good or Bad? An Empirical Investigation," *Academy of Management Journal* (August 2007), pp. 923–940.

23. "Next: Big Idea," *Fast Company,* December 2010–January 2011, pp. 39–40.

24. B. Stone and D. Macmillan, "Groupon's $6 Billion Snub," *Bloomberg BusinessWeek,* December 13–19, 2010, pp. 6–7; E. M. Rusli and J. Wortham, "Google Gambit for Groupon Raises Concerns," *New York Times Online,* November 30, 2010;

D. Lyons, "Click and Save," *Newsweek,* November 29, 2010, p. 25; and J. Goltz, "Doing the Math on a Groupon Deal," *New York Times Online,* November 23, 2010.

25. R. D. Hof and H. Green, "How Amazon Cleared That Hurdle," *BusinessWeek,* February 4, 2002, p. 59.

26. And the Survey Says box based on P. Wang, "To Make Better Choices, Choose Less," *Money,* June 2010, pp. 111–114; B. Dumaine, "The Trouble with Teams," *Fortune,* September 5, 1994, pp. 86–92; A. S. Wellner, "A Perfect Brainstorm," *Inc.,* October 2003, pp. 31–35; "The Poll," *BusinessWeek,* August 21–28, 2006, p. 44; "Hurry Up and Decide," *BusinessWeek,* May 14, 2001, p. 16; J. MacIntyre, "Bosses and Bureaucracy," *Springfield, Missouri Business Journal,* August 1–7, 2005, p. 29; J. Crick, "Hand Jive," *Fortune,* June 13, 2005, pp. 40–41; and "On the Road to Invention," *Fast Company,* February 2005, p. 16.

27. See, for instance, S. Schulz-Hardt, A. Mojzisch, F. C. Brodbeck, R. Kerschreiter, and D. Frey, "Group Decision Making in Hidden Profile Situations: Dissent as a Facilitator for Decision Quality," *Journal of Personality and Social Psychology,* (December 2006), pp. 1080–1083; and C. K. W. DeDreu and M. A. West, "Minority Dissent and Team Innovation: The Importance of Participation in Decision Making." *Journal of Applied Psychology* (December 2001), pp. 1191–1201.

28. S. Mohammed, "Toward an Understanding of Cognitive Consensus in a Group Decision-Making Context," *Journal of Applied Behavioral Science* (December 2001), p. 408.

29. M. J. Fambrough and S. A. Comerford, "The Changing Epistemological Assumptions of Group Theory," *Journal of Applied Behavioral Science* (September 2006), pp. 330–349.

30. R. A. Meyers, D. E. Brashers, and J. Hanner, "Majority-Minority Influence: Identifying Argumentative Patterns and Predicting Argument-Outcome Links," *Journal of Communication* (Autumn 2000), pp. 3–30.

31. I. L. Janis, *Groupthink* (Boston: Houghton Mifflin, 1982). See also J. Chapman, "Anxiety and Defective Decision Making: An Elaboration of the Groupthink Mode," *Management Decision,* October 2006, pp. 1391–1404.

32. See, for instance, T. Horton, "Groupthink in the Boardroom," *Directors and Boards,* Winter 2002, p. 9.

33. See, for example, T. W. Costello and S. S. Zalkind, eds., *Psychology in Administration: A Research Orientation* (Upper Saddle River, NJ: Prentice Hall, 1963), pp. 429–430; R. A. Cooke and J. A. Kernaghan, "Estimating the Difference Between Group versus Individual Performance on Problem Solving Tasks," *Group and Organization Studies,* September 1987, pp. 319–342; and L. K. Michaelsen, W. E. Watson, and R. H. Black, "A Realistic Test of Individual Versus Group Consensus Decision Making," *Journal of Applied Psychology* (October 1989), pp. 834–839. See also J. Hollenbeck, D. R. Ilgen, J. A. Colquitt, and A. Ellis, "Gender Composition, Situational Strength, and Team Decision-Making Accuracy: A Criterion Decomposition Approach," *Organizational Behavior and Human Decision Processes,* May 2002, pp. 445–475.

34. See, for example, L. K. Michaelsen, W. E. Watson, and R. H. Black, "A Realistic Test of Individual versus Group Consensus Decision Making," *Journal of Applied Psychology* (October 1989), pp. 834–839; and P. W. Pease, M. Beiser, and M. E. Tubbs, "Framing Effects and Choice Shifts in Group Decision Making," *Organizational Behavior and Human Decision Processes,* October 1993, pp. 149–165.

35. Right or Wrong box based on C. A. MacKenzie, "MTV Cancels 'Skins'; Season 2 Not Happening," *From Inside the Box Blog* [http://blog.zap2it.com/frominsidethebox/2011/06/mtv-cancels-skins-season-2-not-happening.html (June 9, 2011); J. Hibbard, "MTV's *Skins* Rises for Finale, but Will TV's Most Controversial Drama Return?" www.insidetv.ew.com (March 22, 2011); J. Alston, "Why *The Real World* Still Matters," *The Daily Beast Blog,* March 9, 2011; D. Groner, "As MTV Premiers Its 25th Season, Critics Ask If *The Real World* Is Still Relevant?" www.mediaite.com/tv (March 9, 2011); D. Holloway, "Barely Legal," *Back Stage,* February 17, 2011, pp. 2–3; B. Grossman, "On Corporate Responsibility," *Broadcasting & Cable,* February 7, 2011, p. 26; A. Silver, "Brief History: Sex on TV," *Time,* February 7, 2011, p. 19; L. A. E. Schuker, "Skins Audience Flattens Out," *Wall Street Journal Online,* February 2, 2011; J. Lafayette, "MTV Upfront: More Than *Skins* Deep," *Broadcasting & Cable,* January 31, 2011, p. 16; L. A. E. Schuker, "Skins Audience Sinks 51%," *Wall Street Journal,* January 26, 2011, p. B8; S. Roberts, "Skins Is Not Being Canceled by MTV, Despite Ratings Drop from 3.3 to 1.6 Million: Network Rep," *New York Daily News Online,* January 26, 2011; C. Hausman, "Teen Drama Pushes Envelope on Depictions of Sex, Drug Use," *Ethics Newsline Online,* January 24, 2011; and D. Carr, "MTV's Naked Calculation Gone Bad," *New York Times Online,* January 23, 2011.

36. J. Wagstaff, "Brainstorming Requires Drinks," *Far Eastern Economic Review,* May 2, 2002, p. 34.

37. T. Kelley, "Six Ways to Kill a Brainstormer," *Across the Board,* March–April 2002, p. 12.

38. K. L. Dowling and R. D. St. Louis, "Asynchronous Implementation of the Nominal Group Technique: Is It Effective," *Decision Support Systems,* October 2000, pp. 229–248.

39. See also B. Andersen and T. Fagerhaug, "The Nominal Group Technique," *Quality Progress,* February 2000, p. 144.

40. J. Burdett, "Changing Channels: Using the Electronic Meeting System to Increase Equity in Decision Making," *Information Technology, Learning, and Performance Journal* (Fall 2000), pp. 3–12.

41. "Fear of Flying," *Business Europe,* October 3, 2001, p. 2.

42. "VC at Nestlé," *Business Europe,* October 3, 2001, p. 3.

43. M. Roberti, "Meet Me on the Web," *Fortune: Tech Supplement,* Winter 2002, p. 10.

44. See also, J. A. Hoxmeier and K. A. Kozar, "Electronic Meetings and Subsequent Meeting Behavior: Systems as Agents of Change," *Journal of Applied Management Studies* (December 2000), pp. 177–195.

45. See, for instance, P. Berthon, L. F. Pitt, and M. T. Ewing, "Corollaries of the Collective: The Influence of Organizational Culture and Memory Development on Perceived Decision-Making Context," *Academy of Marketing Science Journal* (Spring 2001), pp. 135–150.

46. J. de Haan, M. Yamamoto, and G. Lovink, "Production Planning in Japan: Rediscovering Lost Experiences or New Insights," *International Journal of Production Economics* (May 6, 2001), pp. 101–109.

47. T. M. Amabile, "Motivating Creativity in Organizations," *California Management Review* (Fall 1997), pp. 39–58.

Skill Development: Using Your Creativity in Decision Making

Many decisions that managers make are routine, so they can fall back on experience and "what's worked in the past." But other decisions—especially those made by upper-level managers—are unique and haven't been confronted before. These are decisions that require creativity—the ability to produce novel and useful ideas. If managers are to successfully progress upward in an organization, they will find an increasing need to develop creative decisions.

Personal Insights: How Creative Am I?

Review the 30 adjectives listed here. Being honest and forthright with your answers, identify only those items that accurately describe you.

1. affected	11. honest	21. reflective
2. capable	12. humorous	22. resourceful
3. cautious	13. individualistic	23. self-confident
4. clever	14. informal	24. sexy
5. commonplace	15. insightful	25. sincere
6. confident	16. intelligent	26. snobbish
7. conservative	17. inventive	27. submissive
8. conventional	18. mannerly	28. suspicious
9. dissatisfied	19. narrow interests	29. unconventional
10. egotistical	20. original	30. wide interests

Source: H. G. Gough, "A Creative Personality Scale for the Adjective Check List," *Journal of Personality and Social Psychology* (August 1979), pp. 1398–1405.

Analysis and Interpretation

Creativity is the ability to combine ideas in a unique way or to make unusual associations between ideas. A creative person develops novel approaches to doing work or unique solutions to problems.

This questionnaire was developed to identify creative talent and potential. It has been widely used and replicated. It is composed of 30 items—18 of which have been found to be positively associated with creativity, and 12 that are negatively correlated.

To calculate your score, give yourself +1 if you described yourself using items 2, 4, 6, 10, 12, 13, 14, 15, 16, 17, 20, 21, 22, 23, 24, 26, 29, and 30. Give yourself a −1 for any of the remaining items you said accurately described you.

Your score will range between −12 and +18. The higher your positive score, the more you display characteristics associated with a creative personality.

For managers, creativity is useful in decision making. It helps them to see problems and alternatives that others might not. All jobs, of course, don't require high creativity. And highly creative individuals, when faced with routine and structured jobs, often become frustrated and dissatisfied.

Skill Basics

The uniqueness and variety of problems that managers face demand that they be able to solve problems creatively.

Creativity is partly a frame of mind. You need to expand your mind's capabilities—that is, open yourself up to new ideas. Every individual has the ability to improve his or her creativity, but many people simply don't try to develop that ability.

You can be more effective at solving problems creatively if you use the following 10 suggestions.

1. *Think of yourself as creative.* Research shows that if you think you can't be creative, you won't be. Believing in your ability to be creative is the first step in becoming more creative.

2. *Pay attention to your intuition.* Every individual has a subconscious mind that works well. Sometimes answers will come to you when you least expect them. Listen to that "inner voice." In fact, most creative people will keep a notepad near their bed and write down ideas when the thoughts come to them.

3. *Move away from your comfort zone.* Every individual has a comfort zone in which certainty exists. But creativity and the known often do not mix. To be creative, you need to move away from the status quo and focus your mind on something new.

4. *Determine what you want to do.* This includes such things as taking time to understand a problem before beginning to try to resolve it, getting all the facts in mind, and trying to identify the most important facts.

5. *Think outside the box.* Use analogies whenever possible (for example, could you approach your problem like a fish out of water and look at what the fish does to cope? Or can you use the things you have to do to find your way when it's foggy to help you solve your problem?). Use different problem-solving strategies such as verbal, visual, mathematical, or theatrical. Look at your problem from a different perspective or ask yourself what someone else, like your grandmother, might do if faced with the same situation.

6. *Look for ways to do things better.* This may involve trying consciously to be original, not worrying about looking foolish, keeping an open mind, being alert to odd or puzzling facts, thinking of unconventional ways to use objects and the environment, discarding usual or habitual ways of doing things, and striving for objectivity by being as critical of your own ideas as you would those of someone else.

7. *Find several right answers.* Being creative means continuing to look for other solutions even when you think you have solved the problem. A better, more creative solution just might be found.

8. *Believe in finding a workable solution.* Like believing in yourself, you also need to believe in your ideas. If you don't think you can find a solution, you probably won't.

9. *Brainstorm with others.* Creativity is not an isolated activity. Bouncing ideas off of others creates a synergistic effect.

10. *Turn creative ideas into action.* Coming up with creative ideas is only part of the process. Once the ideas are generated, they must be implemented. Keeping great ideas in your mind, or on papers that no one will read, does little to expand your creative abilities.

Based on J. V. Anderson, "Mind Mapping: A Tool for Creative Thinking," *Business Horizons*, January –February 1993, pp. 42–46; and T. Proctor, *Creative Problem Solving for Managers* (New York: Routledge, 2005).

Skill Application

Every time the phone rings, your stomach clenches and your palms start to sweat. And it's no wonder! As sales manager for Brinkers, a machine tool parts manufacturer, you're besieged by calls from customers who are upset about late deliveries. Your boss, Carter Hererra, acts as both production manager and scheduler. Every time your sales representatives negotiate a sale, it's up to Carter to determine whether production can actually meet the delivery date the customer specifies. And Carter invariably says, "No problem." The good thing about this is that you make a lot of initial sales. The bad news is that production hardly ever meets the shipment dates that Carter authorizes. And he doesn't seem to be all that concerned about the aftermath of late deliveries. He says, "Our customers know they're getting outstanding quality at a great price. Just let them try to match that anywhere. It can't be done. So even if they have to wait a couple of extra days or weeks, they're still getting the best deal they can." Somehow the customers don't see it that way. And they let you know about their unhappiness. Then it's up to you to try to soothe the relationship. You know this problem has to be taken care of, but what possible solutions are there? After all, how are you going to keep from making your manager mad or making the customers mad?

Break into groups of three. Assume you're the sales manager. What creative solutions can your group come up with to deal with this problem?

Skill Practice

1. How many words can you make using the letters in the word *brainstorm*? There are at least 95.

2. Take 20 minutes to list as many medical or health-related jobs as you can that begin with the letter *r* (for instance, radiologist, registered nurse). If you run out of listings before time is up, it's OK to quit early, but try to be as creative as you can.

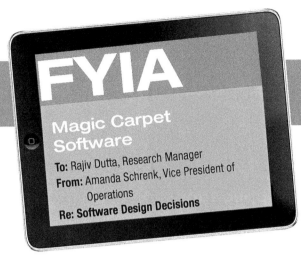

FYIA

Magic Carpet Software

To: Rajiv Dutta, Research Manager
From: Amanda Schrenk, Vice President of Operations
Re: Software Design Decisions

For Your Immediate Action

Rajiv, we have a problem in our software design unit. Our diverse pool of extremely talented and skilled designers is, undoubtedly, one of our company's most important assets. However, I'm concerned that our designers' emotional attachment to the software they've created overshadows other important factors that should be considered in the decision whether to proceed with the new product design. At this point, I'm not sure how to approach this issue. The last thing I want to do is stifle their creativity. But I'm afraid if we don't come up with an action plan soon, the problem may get worse.

I need you to research the role of emotions in decision making. What do the "experts" say? Is it even an issue that we need to be concerned about? What's the best way to deal with it? Please provide me with a one-page bulleted list of the important points you find from your research. And be sure to cite your sources in case I need to do some follow-up.

This fictionalized company and message were created for educational purposes only, and not meant to reflect positively or negatively on management practices by any company that may share this name.

Bringing the Real World to Life

Case Application:
Lift-Off: Part 2

NASA was established by the National Aeronautics and Space Act on July 29, 1958. Since that time, it has led U.S. efforts in space exploration including the Apollo lunar landing missions, the Skylab space station, the reusable manned spacecraft—which we know better as the Space Shuttle. As we stated in the chapter opener, NASA is facing uncertainty over its purpose and budget. "Implicitly acknowledging NASA's lack of direction, the White House has instructed the agency to take a deep breath, marshal resources, and chart a new course." Critics complain that the agency's space programs are too slow and too costly. A couple of possibilities being proposed are more international cooperation on space exploration and outsourcing certain tasks to private contractors. Although NASA's managers have important decisions to make about its future, we want to look at some past decisions where the outcomes were anything but what had been hoped for.

In an organization like NASA where equipment costs millions of dollars and where people's lives can be at stake, consistently making good decisions is not only expected, it's imperative. Over the years, NASA has had many successful endeavors. Getting men on the moon, not once, but six times, reflects outstanding technological prowess, far superior to any other country. Putting a rocket into space with a shuttle that then comes back to earth and lands on its own is a reflection of the incredible talent base that NASA has. Despite those successes, however, NASA has also had some spectacular disasters, which can be traced to errors in the decision-making process.

"Ever winter NASA revisits a week of tragedy during which the nation lost 17 astronauts and three space flight vehicles—*Apollo I* in 1967, space shuttle *Challenger* in 1986, and space shuttle *Columbia* in 2003. We are naturally drawn to ask why these accidents occurred—especially at such an accomplished organization working at the cutting edge of technology and exploration—and whether they could have been prevented."

The events leading up to the tragic end of the *Challenger* have been studied by many different people from many different perspectives—technological failures, poor decision-making practices, organizational culture, and so forth. That fateful launch day, January 28, 1986, was a sunny, but bitterly cold day in Florida. And the launch was perfect . . . until 73 seconds into flight when *Challenger* exploded. During the resulting presidential commission investigation, engineers for Morton Thiokol, the contractor for NASA's failed rocket boosters, revealed that they had issued repeated warnings about launching in the bitterly cold conditions. They strongly believed that the joint design of the solid rocket booster seals was unsafe in those types of conditions. Furthermore, with management approval, the Morton Thiokol engineers had officially recommended against launching. When NASA's team refused to accept the conservative "unsafe to fly" recommendation, Thiokol's managers overruled the concerns of the engineers and reversed the earlier decision, giving NASA the green light to launch. Why did NASA officials not pass the Thiokol concerns to those higher up in the launch decision chain of command? Virtually all of them said that they responded identically because "ultimately all parties were in agreement that no launch commit criteria were violated," and "proper procedures were followed." As one Thiokol engineer later related, "There was no miscommunication that night. We clearly told NASA it would be unsafe to launch, but they wouldn't listen to us."

For space shuttle *Columbia*, a problem during launch—damage sustained when a piece of foam insulation the size of a small briefcase broke off from the external tank and damaged the shuttle's thermal protection system on its left wing—led to its demise on return. NASA's original shuttle specifications said that any debris (including foam) were safety issues that "needed to be resolved before a launch was cleared. However, over the years, launches were often given the go-ahead as engineers came to see that foam shedding and debris strikes were inevitable and unresolvable. Most shuttle launches have had such foam or debris strikes on the thermal tiles. And NASA's senior managers saw fit to overlook that risk, as it did at *Columbia's* launch. However, on February 1, 2003, as *Columbia* was on its return from its space mission, heat build-up destroyed the shuttle's wing structure and it disintegrated over Texas and Louisiana resulting in the deaths of all seven crew members. The investigative report concluded that "the beleaguered space agency, battling a declining budget, learned little from the 1986 *Challenger* explosion, which also killed seven astronauts, and that a sense of infallibility permeated its decision making." One investigator also wrote, "NASA had conflicting goals of cost, schedule, and safety. Unfortunately, safety lost out."

DISCUSSION QUESTIONS

1. In doing what the agency is in business to do, do you think NASA managers deal more with structured or unstructured problems? Explain.

2. Would NASA's decision-making conditions be considered certainty, risk, or uncertainty? Explain.

3. What evidences of groupthink and escalation of commitment do you see in the preceding story? How could these decision-making problems have been prevented? What could other organizations learn from NASA's decision-making mistakes?

4. How could NASA managers best utilize the decision-making process as they shape its post-shuttle future?

5. How might international cooperative space efforts and outsourcing certain tasks to private contractors affect the decision making done at NASA?

Quantitative Module

QUANTITATIVE DECISION-MAKING AIDS

In this module we'll look at several decision-making aids and techniques, as well as some popular tools for managing projects.[1] Specifically, we'll introduce you to payoff matrices, decision trees, break-even analysis, ratio analysis, linear programming, queuing theory, and economic order quantity. The purpose of each method is to provide managers with a tool to assist in the decision-making process and to provide more complete information to make better-informed decisions.

Payoff Matrices

Although uncertainty plays a critical role by limiting the amount of information available to managers, another factor is their psychological orientation. For instance, the optimistic manager will typically follow a *maximax* choice (maximizing the maximum possible payoff); the pessimist will often pursue a *maximin* choice (maximizing the minimum possible payoff); and the manager who desires to minimize his "regret" will opt for a *minimax* choice. Let's briefly look at these different approaches using an example.

Consider the case of a marketing manager at Visa International in New York. He has determined four possible strategies (we'll label these S1, S2, S3, and S4) for promoting the Visa card throughout the northeastern United States. However, he is also aware that one of his major competitors, American Express, has three competitive strategies (CA1, CA2, and CA3) for promoting its own card in the same region. In this case, we'll assume that the Visa executive has no previous knowledge that would allow him to place probabilities on the success of any of his four strategies. With these facts, the Visa card manager formulates the matrix in Exhibit 1 to show the various Visa strategies and the resulting profit to Visa, depending on the competitive action chosen by American Express.

In this example, if our Visa manager is an optimist, he'll choose S4 because that could produce the largest possible gain ($28 million). Note that this choice maximizes the maximum possible gain (maximax choice). If our manager is a pessimist, he'll assume only the worst can occur. The worst outcome for each strategy is as follows: S1 = $11 million; S2 = $9 million; S3 = $15 million; and S4 = $14 million. Following the maximin choice, the pessimistic manager would maximize the minimum payoff—in other words, he'd select S3.

In the third approach, managers recognize that once a decision is made it will not necessarily result in the most profitable payoff. What could occur is a "regret" of profits forgone (given up)—regret referring to the amount of money that could have been made had a different strategy been used. Managers calculate regret by subtracting all possible payoffs in each category from the maximum possible payoff for each given—in this case, for each

EXHIBIT 1	Payoff Matrix for Visa		
VISA MARKETING STRATEGY	**AMERICAN EXPRESS'S RESPONSE (in $millions)**		
	CA1	**CA2**	**CA3**
S1	13	14	11
S2	9	15	18
S3	24	21	15
S4	18	14	28

EXHIBIT 2 — Regret Matrix for Visa

VISA MARKETING STRATEGY	AMERICAN EXPRESS'S RESPONSE (in $millions)		
	CA1	CA2	CA3
S1	11	7	17
S2	15	6	10
S3	0	0	13
S4	6	7	0

competitive action. For our Visa manager, the highest payoff, given that American Express engages in CA1, CA2, or CA3, is $24 million, $21 million, or $28 million, respectively (the highest number in each column). Subtracting the payoffs in Exhibit 1 from these figures produces the results in Exhibit 2.

The maximum regrets are S1 = $17 million; S2 = $15 million; S3 = $13 million; and S4 = $7 million. The minimax choice minimizes the maximum regret, so our Visa manager would choose S4. By making this choice, he'll never have a regret of profits forgone of more than $7 million. This result contrasts, for example, with a regret of $15 million had he chosen S2 and American Express had taken CA1.

Decision Trees

Decision trees are a useful way to analyze hiring, marketing, investment, equipment purchases, pricing, and similar decisions that involve a progression of decisions. They're called decision trees because, when diagrammed, they look a lot like a tree with branches. Typical decision trees encompass expected value analysis by assigning probabilities to each possible outcome and calculating payoffs for each decision path.

Exhibit 3 illustrates a decision facing Harrington, the midwestern region site selection supervisor for Walden bookstores. Becky supervises a small group of specialists

EXHIBIT 3

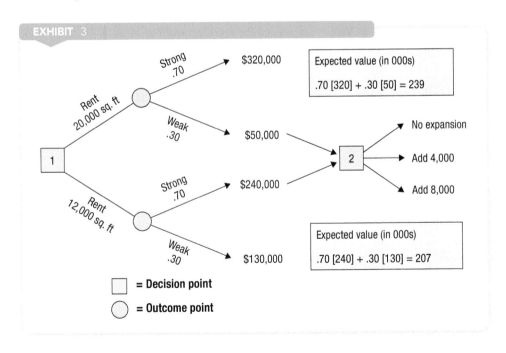

Strong .70 → $320,000

Expected value (in 000s)
.70 [320] + .30 [50] = 239

Weak .30 → $50,000

Rent 20,000 sq. ft

Strong .70 → $240,000

Rent 12,000 sq. ft

Weak .30 → $130,000

No expansion

Add 4,000

Add 8,000

Expected value (in 000s)
.70 [240] + .30 [130] = 207

☐ = Decision point

◯ = Outcome point

decision trees
A diagram used to analyze a progression of decisions. When diagrammed, a decision tree looks like a tree with branches.

who analyze potential locations and make store site recommendations to the midwestern region's director. The lease on the company's store in Winter Park, Florida, is expiring, and the property owner has decided not to renew it. Becky and her group have to make a relocation recommendation to the regional director. Becky's group has identified an excellent site in a nearby shopping mall in Orlando. The mall owner has offered her two comparable locations: one with 12,000 square feet (the same as she has now) and the other a larger, 20,000-square-foot space. Becky's initial decision concerns whether to recommend renting the larger or smaller location. If she chooses the larger space and the economy is strong, she estimates the store will make a $320,000 profit. However, if the economy is poor, the high operating costs of the larger store will mean that the profit will be only $50,000. With the smaller store, she estimates the profit at $240,000 with a good economy and $130,000 with a poor one.

As you can see from Exhibit 3, the expected value for the larger store is $239,000 [(.70 × 320) + (.30 × 50)]. The expected value for the smaller store is $207,000 [(.70 × 240) + (.30 × 130)]. Given these projections, Becky is planning to recommend the rental of the larger store space. What if Becky wants to consider the implications of initially renting the smaller space and then expanding if the economy picks up? She can extend the decision tree to include this second decision point. She has calculated three options: no expansion, adding 4,000 square feet, and adding 8,000 square feet. Following the approach used for Decision Point 1, she could calculate the profit potential by extending the branches on the tree and calculating expected values for the various options.

Break-Even Analysis

How many units of a product must an organization sell in order to break even—that is, to have neither profit nor loss? A manager might want to know the minimum number of units that must be sold to achieve his or her profit objective or whether a current product should continue to be sold or should be dropped from the organization's product line. **Break-even analysis** is a widely used technique for helping managers make profit projections.[2]

Break-even analysis is a simplistic formulation, yet it is valuable to managers because it points out the relationship among revenues, costs, and profits. To compute the break-even point (BE), the manager needs to know the unit price of the product being sold (P), the variable cost per unit (VC), and the total fixed costs (TFC).

An organization breaks even when its total revenue is just enough to equal its total costs. But total cost has two parts: a fixed component and a variable component. Fixed costs are expenses that do not change, regardless of volume, such as insurance premiums and property taxes. Fixed costs, of course, are fixed only in the short term because, in the long run, commitments terminate and are, thus, subject to variation. Variable costs change in proportion to output and include raw materials, labor costs, and energy costs.

The break-even point can be computed graphically or by using the following formula:

$$BE = [TFC/(P - VC)]$$

This formula tells us that (1) total revenue will equal total cost when we sell enough units at a price that covers all variable unit costs, and (2) the difference between price and variable costs, when multiplied by the number of units sold, equals the fixed costs.

When is break-even analysis useful? To demonstrate, assume that, at Jose's Bakersfield Espresso, Jose charges $1.75 for an average cup of coffee. If his fixed costs (salary, insurance, etc.) are $47,000 a year and the variable costs for each cup of espresso are $0.40, Jose can compute his break-even point as follows: $47,000/(1.75 − 0.40) = 34,815 (about 670 cups of espresso sold each week), or when annual revenues are approximately $60,926. This same relationship is shown graphically in Exhibit 4.

How can break-even analysis serve as a planning and decision-making tool? As a planning tool, break-even analysis could help Jose set his sales objective. For example, he could establish the profit he wants and then work backward to determine what sales level is needed

EXHIBIT 4

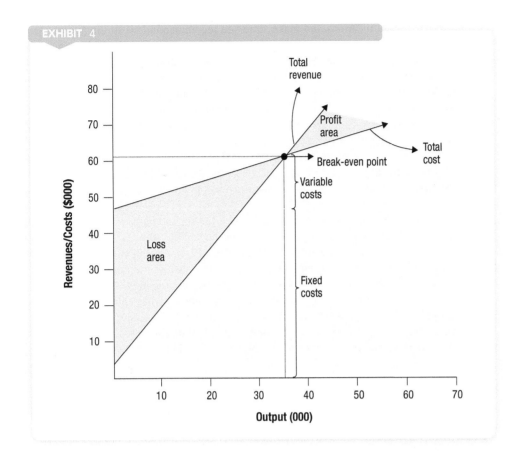

to reach that profit. As a decision-making tool, break-even analysis could also tell Jose how much volume has to increase in order to break even if he is currently operating at a loss, or how much volume he can afford to lose and still break even if he is currently operating profitably. In some cases, such as the management of professional sports franchises, break-even analysis has shown the projected volume of ticket sales required to cover all costs to be so unrealistically high that management's best choice is to sell or close the business.

Ratio Analysis

We know that investors and stock analysts make regular use of an organization's financial documents to assess its worth. These documents can be analyzed by managers as planning and decision-making aids.

Managers often want to examine their organization's balance sheet and income statements to analyze key ratios, that is, to compare two significant figures from the financial statements and express them as a percentage or ratio. This practice allows managers to compare current financial performance with that of previous periods and other organizations in the same industry. Some of the more useful ratios evaluate liquidity, leverage, operations, and profitability. These ratios are summarized in Exhibit 5.

What are liquidity ratios? *Liquidity* is a measure of the organization's ability to convert assets into cash in order to meet its debt obligations. The most popular liquidity ratios are the current ratio and the acid test ratio.

The *current ratio* is defined as the organization's current assets divided by its current liabilities. Although there is no magic number that is considered safe, the accountant's rule

break-even analysis
A technique for identifying the point at which total revenue is just sufficient to cover total costs.

EXHIBIT 5	Popular Financial Controls		
OBJECTIVE	RATIO	CALCULATION	MEANING
Liquidity test	Current ratio	$\dfrac{\text{Current assets}}{\text{Current liabilities}}$	Tests the organization's ability to meet short-term obligations
	Acid test	$\dfrac{\text{Current assets less inventories}}{\text{Current liabilities}}$	Tests liquidity more accurately when inventories turn over slowly or are difficult to sell
Leverage test	Debt to assets	$\dfrac{\text{Total debt}}{\text{Total assets}}$	The higher the ratio, the more leveraged the organization
	Times interest earned	$\dfrac{\text{Profits before interest and taxes}}{\text{Total interest charges}}$	Measures how far profits can decline before the organization is unable to meet its interest expenses
Operations test	Inventory turnover	$\dfrac{\text{Cost of sales}}{\text{Inventory}}$	The higher the ratio, the more efficiently inventory assets are being used
	Total assets turnover	$\dfrac{\text{Revenues}}{\text{Total assets}}$	The fewer assets used to achieve a given level of sales, the more efficiently management is using the organization's total assets
Profitability	Profit margin on revenues	$\dfrac{\text{Net profit after taxes}}{\text{Total revenues}}$	Identifies the profits that various products are generating
	Return on investment	$\dfrac{\text{Net profit after taxes}}{\text{Total assets}}$	Measures the efficiency of assets to generate profits

of thumb for the current ratio is 2:1. A significantly higher ratio usually suggests that management is not getting the best return on its assets. A ratio at or below 1:1 indicates potential difficulty in meeting short-term obligations (accounts payable, interest payments, salaries, taxes, etc.).

The *acid test ratio* is the same as the current ratio except that current assets are reduced by the dollar value of inventory held. When inventories turn slowly or are difficult to sell, the acid test ratio may more accurately represent the organization's true liquidity. That is, a high current ratio heavily based on an inventory that is difficult to sell overstates the organization's true liquidity. Accordingly, accountants typically consider an acid test ratio of 1:1 to be reasonable.

Leverage ratios refer to the use of borrowed funds to operate and expand an organization. The advantage of leverage occurs when funds can be used to earn a rate of return well above the cost of those funds. For instance, if management can borrow money at 8 percent and can earn 12 percent on it internally, it makes good sense to borrow, but there are risks to overleveraging. The interest on the debt can be a drain on the organization's cash resources and can, in extreme cases, drive an organization into bankruptcy. The objective, therefore, is to use debt wisely. Leverage ratios such as *debt to assets ratio* (computed by dividing total debt by total assets) or the *times interest earned ratio* (computed as profits before interest and taxes divided by total interest charges) can help managers control debt levels.

Operating ratios describe how efficiently management is using the organization's resources. The most popular operating ratios are inventory turnover and total assets turnover. The *inventory turnover ratio* is defined as revenue divided by inventory. The higher the ratio, the more efficiently inventory assets are being used. Revenue divided by total assets represents an organization's *total assets turnover ratio*. It measures the level of assets needed to generate the organization's revenue. The fewer the assets used to achieve a given level of revenue, the more efficiently management is using the organization's total assets.

Profit-making organizations want to measure their effectiveness and efficiency. Profitability ratios serve such a purpose. The better known of these ratios are profit margin on revenues and return on investment.

Managers of organizations that have a variety of products want to put their efforts into those products that are most profitable. The *profit margin on revenues ratio*, computed as net profit after taxes divided by total revenues, is a measure of profits per dollar revenues.

One of the most widely used measures of a business firm's profitability is the *return on investment ratio*. It's calculated by dividing net profits by total assets. This percentage recognizes that absolute profits must be placed in the context of assets required to generate those profits.

Linear Programming

Matt Free owns a software development company. One product line involves designing and producing software that detects and removes viruses. The software comes in two formats: Windows and Mac versions. He can sell all of these products that he can produce, which is his dilemma. The two formats go through the same production departments. How many of each type should he make to maximize his profits?

A close look at Free's operation tells us he can use a mathematical technique called **linear programming** to solve his resource allocation dilemma. As we will show, linear programming is applicable to his problem, but it cannot be applied to all resource allocation situations. Besides requiring limited resources and the objective of optimization, it requires that there be alternative ways of combining resources to produce a number of output mixes. A linear relationship between variables is also necessary, which means that a change in one variable will be accompanied by an exactly proportional change in the other. For Free's business, this condition would be met if it took exactly twice the time to produce two diskettes—irrespective of format—as it took to produce one.

Many different types of problems can be solved with linear programming. Selecting transportation routes that minimize shipping costs, allocating a limited advertising budget among various product brands, making the optimum assignment of personnel among projects, and determining how much of each product to make with a limited number of resources are just a few. To give you some idea of how linear programming is useful, let's return to Free's situation. Fortunately, his problem is relatively simple, so we can solve it rather quickly. For complex linear programming problems, computer software has been designed specifically to help develop solutions.

First, we need to establish some facts about the business. He has computed the profit margins to be $18 for the Windows format and $24 for the Mac. He can, therefore, express his objective function as maximum profit = $18R + $24S, where R is the number of Windows-based CDs produced and S is the number of Mac CDs. In addition, he knows how long it takes to produce each format and the monthly production capacity for virus software: 2,400 hours in design and 900 hours in production (see Exhibit 6). The

EXHIBIT 6	Production Data for Virus Software		
	NUMBER OF HOURS REQUIRED PER UNIT		
DEPARTMENT	WINDOWS VERSION	MAC VERSION	MONTHLY PRODUCT CAPACITY (HOURS)
Design	4	6	2,400
Manufacture	2.0	2.0	900
Profit per unit	$18	$24	

linear programming
A mathematical technique that solves resource allocation problems.

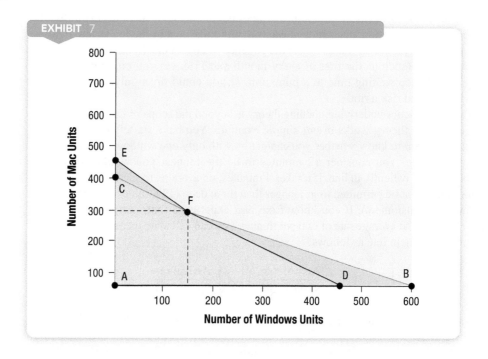

EXHIBIT 7

production capacity numbers act as constraints on his overall capacity. Now Free can establish his constraint equations:

$$4R + 6S < 2,400$$

$$2R + 2S < 900$$

Of course, because a software format cannot be produced in a volume less than zero, Matt can also state that R > 0 and S > 0. He has graphed his solution as shown in Exhibit 7. The beige shaded area represents the options that do not exceed the capacity of either department. What does the graph mean? We know that total design capacity is 2,400 hours. So if Matt decides to design only the Windows format, the maximum number he can produce is 600 (2,400 hours ÷ 4 hours of design for each Windows version). If he decides to produce all Mac versions, the maximum he can produce is 400 (2,400 hours ÷ 6 hours of design for Mac). This design constraint is shown in Exhibit 7 as line BC. The other constraint Matt faces is that of production. The maximum of either format he can produce is 450, because each takes two hours to copy, verify, and package. This production constraint is shown in the exhibit as line DE.

Free's optimal resource allocation will be defined at one of the corners of this feasibility region (area ACFD). Point F provides the maximum profits within the constraints stated. At point A, profits would be zero because neither virus software version is being produced. At points C and D, profits would be $9,600 (400 units @ $24) and $8,100 (450 units @ $18), respectively. At point F profits would be $9,900 (150 Windows units @ $18 + 300 Mac units @ $24).[3]

Queuing Theory

You are a supervisor for a branch of Bank of America outside of Cleveland, Ohio. One of the decisions you have to make is how many of the six teller stations to keep open at any given time. Queuing theory, or what is frequently referred to as waiting line theory, could help you decide.

A decision that involves balancing the cost of having a waiting line against the cost of service to maintain that line can be made more easily with queuing theory. These types of common situations include determining how many gas pumps are needed at gas stations, tellers at bank windows, toll takers at toll booths, or check-in lines at airline ticket counters. In each situation, management wants to minimize cost by having as few stations open as possible yet not so few as to test the patience of customers. In our teller example, on certain days (such as the first of every month and Fridays) you could open all six windows and keep waiting time to a minimum, or you could open only one, minimize staffing costs, and risk a riot.

The mathematics underlying queuing theory is beyond the scope of this book, but you can see how the theory works in our simple example. You have six tellers working for you, but you want to know whether you can get by with only one window open during an average morning. You consider 12 minutes to be the longest you would expect any customer to wait patiently in line. If it takes 4 minutes, on average, to serve each customer, the line should not be permitted to get longer than three deep (12 minutes ÷ 4 minutes per customer = 3 customers). If you know from past experience that, during the morning, people arrive at the average rate of two per minute, you can calculate the probability (P) of customers waiting in line as follows:

$$P_n = \left[1 - \left(\frac{\text{Arrival rate}}{\text{Service rate}} \right) \right] \times \left[\frac{\text{Arrival rate}}{\text{Service rate}} \right]^n$$

where $n = 3$ customers, arrival rate = 2 per minute, and service rate = 4 minutes per customer.

Putting these numbers into the foregoing formula generates the following:

$$P_n = [1 - 2/4] \times [2/4]^3 = (1/2) \times (8/64) = (8/128) = 0.0625$$

What does a P of 0.0625 mean? It tells you that the likelihood of having more than three customers in line during the average morning is 1 chance in 16. Are you willing to live with four or more customers in line 6 percent of the time? If so, keeping one teller window open will be enough. If not, you will have to assign more tellers to staff more windows.

Economic Order Quantity Model

When you order checks from a bank, have you noticed that the reorder form is placed about two-thirds of the way through your supply of checks? This practice is a simple example of a fixed-point reordering system. At some preestablished point in the process, the system is designed to "flag" the fact that the inventory needs to be replenished. The objective is to minimize inventory carrying costs while at the same time limiting the probability of *stocking out* of the inventory item. In recent years, retail stores have increasingly been using their computers to perform this reordering activity. Their cash registers are connected to their computers, and each sale automatically adjusts the store's inventory record. When the inventory of an item hits the critical point, the computer tells management to reorder.

One of the best-known techniques for mathematically deriving the optimum quantity for a purchase order is the economic order quantity (EOQ) model (see Exhibit 8). The EOQ model seeks to balance four costs involved in ordering and carrying inventory: the purchase costs (purchase price plus delivery charges less discounts); the ordering costs (paperwork, follow-up, inspection when the item arrives, and other processing costs); carrying costs (money tied up in inventory, storage, insurance, taxes, etc.); and stock-out costs (profits forgone from orders lost, the cost of reestablishing goodwill, and additional

queuing theory
Also known as waiting line theory, it a way of balancing the cost of having a waiting line versus the cost of maintaining the line. Management wants to have as few stations open to minimize costs without testing the patience of its customers.

fixed-point reordering system
A method for a system to "flag" the need to reorder inventory at some preestablished point in the process.

economic order quantity (EOQ)
A model that seeks to balance the costs involved in ordering and carrying inventory, thus minimizing total costs associated with carrying and ordering costs.

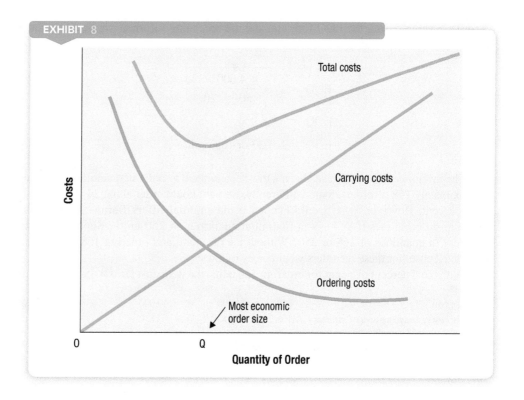

EXHIBIT 8

expenses incurred to expedite late shipments). When these four costs are known, the model identifies the optimal order size for each purchase.

The objective of the economic order quantity (EOQ) model is to minimize the total costs associated with the carrying and ordering costs. As the amount ordered gets larger, average inventory increases and so do carrying costs. For example, if annual demand for an inventory item is 26,000 units, and a firm orders 500 each time, the firm will place 52 [26,000/500] orders per year. This order frequency gives the organization an average inventory of 250 [500/2] units. If the order quantity is increased to 2,000 units, fewer orders (13) [26,000/2,000] will be placed. However, average inventory on hand will increase to 1,000 [2,000/2] units. Thus, as holding costs go up, ordering costs go down, and vice versa. The optimum economic order quantity is reached at the lowest point on the total cost curve. That's the point at which ordering costs equal carrying costs—or the economic order quantity (see point Q in Exhibit 8).

To compute this optimal order quantity, you need the following data: forecasted demand for the item during the period (D); the cost of placing each order (OC); the value or purchase price of the item (V); and the carrying cost (expressed as a percentage) of maintaining the total inventory (CC). Given these data, the formula for EOQ is as follows:

$$EOQ = \sqrt{\frac{2 \times D \times OC}{V \times CC}}$$

Let's work an example of determining the EOQ. Take, for example, Barnes Electronics, a retailer of high-quality sound and video equipment. The owner, Sam Barnes, wishes to determine the company's economic order quantities of high-quality sound and video equipment. The item in question is a Sony compact voice recorder. Barnes forecasts sales of 4,000 units a year. He believes that the cost for the sound system should be $50. Estimated costs of placing an order for these systems are $35 per order and annual insurance, taxes, and other carrying costs at 20 percent of the recorder's value. Using the EOQ formula, and the preceding information, he can calculate the EOQ as follows:

$$EOQ = \sqrt{\frac{2 \times 4{,}000 \times 35}{50 \times .20}}$$

$$EOQ = \sqrt{28{,}000}$$

$$EOQ = 167.33 \text{ or } 168 \text{ units}$$

The inventory model suggests that it's most economical to order in quantities or lots of approximately 168 recorders. Stated differently, Barnes should order about 24 [4,000/168] times a year. However, what would happen if the supplier offers Barnes a 5 percent discount on purchases if he buys in minimum quantities of 250 units? Should he now purchase in quantities of 168 or 250? Without the discount, and ordering 168 each time, the annual costs for these recorders would be as follows:

With the 5 percent discount for ordering 250 units, the item cost [$50 \times ($50 \times 0.05)]

Purchase cost:	$50	× $4,000	=	$200,000
Carrying cost (average number of inventory units times value of item times percentage):	168/2	× $50 × 0.2	=	840
Ordering costs (number of orders times cost to place order):	24	× $35	=	840
Total cost:			=	$201,680

would be $47.5. The annual inventory costs would be as follows:

Purchase cost:	$47.50	× $4,000	=	$190,000.00
Carrying cost:	250/2	× $47.50 × 0.2	=	1,187.50
Ordering cost:	16	× $35	=	560.00
Total cost:			=	$191,747.50

These calculations suggest to Barnes that he should take advantage of the 5 percent discount. Even though he now has to stock larger quantities, the annual savings amounts to nearly $10,000. A word of caution, however, needs to be added. The EOQ model assumes that demand and lead times are known and constant. If these conditions can't be met, the model shouldn't be used. For example, it generally shouldn't be used for manufactured component inventory because the components are taken out of stock all at once, in lumps, or odd lots, rather than at a constant rate. Does this caveat mean that the EOQ model is useless when demand is variable? No. The model can still be of some use in demonstrating trade-offs in costs and the need to control lot sizes. However, more sophisticated lot sizing models are available for handling demand and special situations. The mathematics for EOQ, like the mathematics for queuing theory, go far beyond the scope of this text.

Endnotes

1. Readers are encouraged to see B. Render, R. M. Stair, and M. E. Hanna, *Quantitative Analysis for Management*, 9th ed. (Upper Saddle River, NJ: Prentice Hall, 2005).

2. J. Schmid, "Getting to Breakeven," *Catalog Age*, November 2001, pp. 89–90.

3. We want to acknowledge and thank Professor Jeff Storm of Virginia Western Community College for his assistance in this example.

Foundations
of Planning

Foundations of Planning

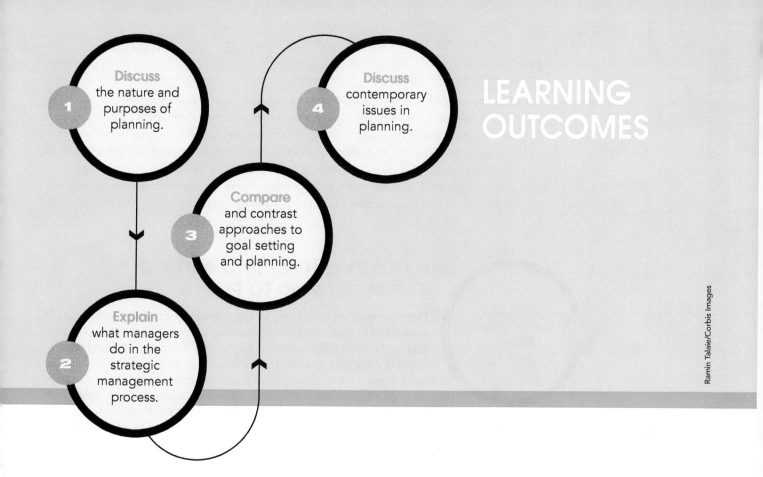

1 **Discuss** the nature and purposes of planning.

2 **Explain** what managers do in the strategic management process.

3 **Compare** and contrast approaches to goal setting and planning.

4 **Discuss** contemporary issues in planning.

Ramin Talaie/Corbis Images

Flip Flop

You've probably seen them at weddings or graduations, and maybe even at parties. No, they're not "crashers," they're the handheld Flip video camcorder. Flip was the brainchild of some San Francisco entrepreneurs whose idea was to create a pocket-size, inexpensive, and easy-to-use video camera. Considering that most video cameras were big, bulky, complicated, and expensive, that idea seemed right on target. And it was! When Flip went on sale in 2007, it quickly dominated the camcorder market as some 2 million were sold in the first two years. "Then, in 2009, the founders cashed out and sold to Cisco Systems, the computer networking giant, for $590 million." Not a bad payday, huh! For Cisco, the acquisition was a key to its strategy of expanding in the consumer market, especially as homes became more media-enabled. However, two years later, in April 2011, Cisco announced it was "killing" Flip and laying off 550 employees. Even in the frenetic, chaotic tech world, that was a fast flip flop. As one analyst said, "It's a testament to the pace of innovation in consumer electronics and smartphone technology. More and more functionality is being integrated into smartphones."[1]

Cisco Systems, like other organizations, has a purpose, people, and a structure to support and enable those people in carrying out that purpose. Also, like other organizations, its managers must develop plans and strategies for how best to achieve that purpose. However, sometimes after evaluating the outcomes of those plans and strategies, managers have to change direction as conditions change. This chapter presents the basics of planning. You'll learn what planning is, how managers use strategic management, and how they set goals and establish plans. Finally, we'll look at some of the contemporary planning issues managers have to deal with.

WHAT IS PLANNING AND WHY DO MANAGERS NEED TO PLAN?

1 Discuss the nature and purposes of planning.

Planning is often called the primary management function because it establishes the basis for all the other things managers do as they organize, lead, and control. What is meant by the term *planning?* Planning encompasses defining the organization's objectives or goals, establishing an overall strategy for achieving those goals, and developing a comprehensive hierarchy of plans to integrate and coordinate activities. It's concerned with ends (*what* is to be done) as well as with means (*how* it's to be done).

Planning can be further defined in terms of whether it's *formal* or *informal.* All5managers plan, even if it's only informally. In informal planning, very little, if anything, is written down. What is to be accomplished is in the heads of one or a few people. Furthermore, the organization's goals are rarely verbalized. Informal planning generally describes the planning that takes place in many smaller businesses. The owner-manager has an idea of where he or she wants to go and how he or she expects to get there. The planning is general and lacks continuity. Of course, you'll see informal planning in some large organizations, while some small businesses will have sophisticated formal plans.

When we use the term *planning,* we're referring to formal planning. In formal planning, specific goals covering a specific time period are defined. These goals are written down and made available to organization members. Using these goals, managers develop specific plans that clearly define the path the organization will take to get from where it is to where it wants to be.

Why Should Managers Formally Plan?

Managers should plan for at least four reasons. (See Exhibit 1.) First, planning establishes coordinated effort. It gives direction to managers and nonmanagerial employees. When all organizational members understand where the organization is going and what they must contribute to reach the goals, they can begin to coordinate their activities, thus fostering teamwork and cooperation. On the other hand, a lack of planning can cause organizational members or work units to work against one another and keep the organization from moving efficiently toward its goals.

Second, by forcing managers to look ahead, anticipate change, consider the impact of change, and develop appropriate responses, planning reduces uncertainty. It also clarifies the consequences of the actions managers might take in response to change. Planning, then, is precisely what managers need in a changing environment.

Third, planning reduces overlapping and wasteful activities. Coordination before the fact is likely to uncover waste and redundancy. Furthermore, when means and ends are clear, inefficiencies become obvious.

Finally, planning establishes the goals or standards that facilitate control. If organizational members are unsure of what they are attempting to achieve, how can they assess whether they've achieved it? When managers plan, they develop goals and plans. When they

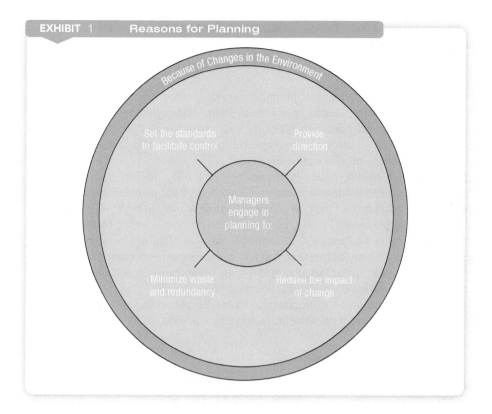

EXHIBIT 1   Reasons for Planning

Because of Changes in the Environment

Managers engage in planning to:

Set the standards to facilitate control

Provide direction

Minimize waste and redundancy

Reduce the impact of change

control, they see whether the plans have been carried out and the goals met. If significant deviations are identified, corrective action can be taken. Without planning, there would be no goals against which to measure or evaluate work efforts.

What Are Some Criticisms of Formal Planning?

Although it makes sense for an organization to establish goals and direction, critics have challenged some of the basic assumptions of planning.[2]

1. *Planning may create rigidity.* Formal planning efforts can lock an organization into specific goals to be achieved within specific timetables. Such goals may have been set under the assumption that the environment wouldn't change. Forcing a course of action when the environment is random and unpredictable can be a recipe for disaster. Instead, managers need to remain flexible and not be tied to a course of action simply because it's the plan.

2. *Formal plans can't replace intuition and creativity.* Successful organizations are typically the result of someone's vision, but these visions have a tendency to become formalized as they evolve. If formal planning efforts reduce the vision to a programmed routine, that too can lead to disaster. Planning should enhance and support intuition and creativity, not replace it.

3. *Planning focuses managers' attention on today's competition, not on tomorrow's survival.* Formal planning, especially strategic planning (which we'll discuss shortly), has a tendency to focus on how to best capitalize on existing business opportunities within the industry. Managers may not look at ways to re-create or reinvent the industry. Instead, when managers plan, they should be open to forging into uncharted waters if there are untapped opportunities.

4. *Formal planning reinforces success, which may lead to failure.* The American tradition has been that success breeds success. After all, if it's not broken, don't fix it. Right? Well maybe not! Success may, in fact, breed failure in an uncertain environment. It's hard to change or discard successful plans—to leave the comfort of what works for the uncertainty (and anxiety) of the unknown. Still, managers may need to face that unknown and be open to doing things in new ways to be even more successful.

Does Formal Planning Improve Organizational Performance?

Does it pay to plan? Or have the critics of planning won the debate? Let's look at the evidence.

Contrary to what the critics of planning say, the evidence generally supports the position that organizations should have formal plans. Although most studies that have looked at the relationship between planning and performance have shown generally positive relationships, we can't say that organizations that formally plan *always* outperform those that don't.[3] But what can we conclude?

First, formal planning generally means higher profits, higher return on assets, and other positive financial results. Second, the quality of the planning process and the appropriate implementation of the plan probably contribute more to high performance than does the extent of planning. Finally, in those organizations in which formal planning did not lead to higher performance, the environment was often to blame. For instance, governmental regulations, unforeseen economic challenges, and other environmental constraints reduce the impact of planning on an organization's performance. Why? Because managers will have fewer viable alternatives.

One important aspect of an organization's formal planning is strategic planning, which managers do as part of the strategic management process.

Explain
what managers
do in the
strategic
management
process.

2

WHAT DO MANAGERS NEED TO KNOW ABOUT STRATEGIC MANAGEMENT?

German engineering giant Siemens AG is rethinking its strategic goal of becoming a major player in the nuclear power industry. U.K. drug maker GlaxoSmithKline PLC has decided to sell off Alli, its over-the-counter diet drug. Best Buy Co. is shrinking its "big-box store" strategy to better position itself to compete online against Amazon.com. Burberry Group PLC is outfitting its stores in China with the latest digital technology including touch screens for customers and iPads for staff in an attempt to win over younger customers.[4] These are just a few of the business news stories from a single week, and each one is about a company's strategies. Strategic management is very much a part of what managers do.

What Is Strategic Management?

Strategic management is what managers do to develop an organization's strategies. What are an organization's **strategies**? They're the plans for how the organization will do what it's in business to do, how it will compete successfully, and how it will attract and satisfy its customers in order to achieve its goals.

Why Is Strategic Management Important?

Unlike many other mall-based clothing chains experiencing disastrous sales declines, retailer Buckle Inc. suffered from weak sales only during the last stages of the recent economic downturn. And it didn't take long for Buckle to regain its footing. What's the company's strategy? One important part has been its location strategy. Only a few of its 400-plus stores were located in states that suffered the worst from the recession. Another part of its strategy was to offer customer perks such as custom pants fittings and free hemming on its jeans. Such "customer-service investments can go a long way in differentiating Buckle in the congested teen market."[5] This company's managers obviously understand why strategic management is important!

Why *is* strategic management so important? One reason is that it can make a difference in how well an organization performs. Why do some businesses succeed and others fail, even when faced with the same environmental conditions? Research has found a generally positive relationship between strategic planning and performance.[6] Those companies that plan strategically appear to have better financial results than those organizations that don't.

Another reason it's important has to do with the fact that managers in organizations of all types and sizes face continually changing situations. They cope with this uncertainty by using the strategic management process to examine relevant factors in planning future actions.

Finally, strategic management is important because organizations are complex and diverse. Each part needs to work together to achieve the organization's goals; strategic management helps do this. For example, with more than 2.1 million employees worldwide working in various departments, functional areas, and stores, Walmart uses strategic management to help coordinate and focus employees' efforts on what's important.

Strategic management isn't just for business organizations. Even organizations such as government agencies, hospitals, educational institutions, and social agencies need strategic management. For example, the skyrocketing costs of a college education, competition from for-profit companies offering alternative educational environments, state budgets being slashed because of declining revenues, and cutbacks in federal aid for students and research have led many university administrators to assess their colleges' aspirations and identify a market niche in which they can survive and prosper.

Felipe T Garcia/Newscom

China is playing a significant role in the strategic plans of British fashion house Burberry Group PLC. Recognizing that young Chinese shoppers are driving the growth of the global luxury industry, Burberry's CEO Angela Ahrendts has selected China as the first market to launch the firm's digital retail model in a worldwide campaign that targets young consumers. Winning Chinese customers is critical to Burberry's growth strategy, with China expected to become the world's largest market for luxury goods by 2020. Shown here addressing the World Retail Congress, Ahrendts describes how Burberry is using in-store digital technology plus its own online shopping site, Chinese social networking sites, and Internet television to attract young buyers.

What Are the Steps in the Strategic Management Process?

The strategic management process (see Exhibit 2) is a six-step process that encompasses strategy planning, implementation, and evaluation. Although the first four steps describe the planning that must take place, implementation and evaluation are just as important! Even the best strategies can fail if management doesn't implement or evaluate them properly.

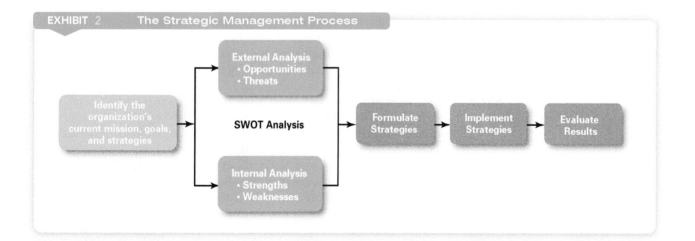

EXHIBIT 2   The Strategic Management Process

Identify the organization's current mission, goals, and strategies →

External Analysis
• Opportunities
• Threats

SWOT Analysis

Internal Analysis
• Strengths
• Weaknesses

→ Formulate Strategies → Implement Strategies → Evaluate Results

---

strategic management
What managers do to develop an organization's strategies

strategies
Plans for how the organization will do what it's in business to do, how it will compete successfully, and how it will attract its customers in order to achieve its goals

strategic management process
A six-step process that encompasses strategy planning, implementation, and evaluation

---

EXHIBIT 3   What a Mission Statement Includes

Customers: Who are the firm's customers?

Markets: Where does the firm compete geographically?

Concern for survival, growth, and profitability: Is the firm committed to growth and financial stability?

Philosophy: What are the firm's basic beliefs, values, and ethical priorities?

Concern for public image: How responsive is the firm to societal and environmental concerns?

Products or services: What are the firm's major products or services?

Technology: Is the firm technologically current?

Self-concept: What are the firm's major competitive advantage and core competencies?

Concern for employees: Are employees a valuable asset of the firm?

Source: Based on F. David, *Strategic Management,* 11th ed. (Upper Saddle River, NJ: Prentice Hall, 2007), p. 70.

STEP 1: Identifying the organization's current mission, goals, and strategies. Every organization needs a mission—a statement of its purpose. Defining the mission forces managers to identify what it's in business to do. For instance, the mission of Avon is "To be the company that best understands and satisfies the product, service, and self-fulfillment needs of women on a global level." The mission of Facebook is "a social utility that connects you with the people around you." The mission of the National Heart Foundation of Australia is to "reduce suffering and death from heart, stroke, and blood vessel disease in Australia." These statements provide clues to what these organizations see as their purpose. What should a mission statement include? Exhibit 3 describes some typical components.

It's also important for managers to identify the current goals and strategies. Why? So managers have a basis for assessing whether they need to be changed.

STEP 2: Doing an external analysis. Analyzing the external environment is a critical step in the strategic management process. Managers do an external analysis so they know, for instance, what the competition is doing, what pending legislation might affect the organization, or what the labor supply is like in locations where it operates. In an external analysis, managers should examine all components of the environment (economic, demographic, political/legal, sociocultural, technological, and global) to see the trends and changes.

Once they've analyzed the environment, managers need to pinpoint opportunities that the organization can exploit and threats that it must counteract or buffer against. Opportunities are positive trends in the external environment; threats are negative trends.

STEP 3: Doing an internal analysis. Now we move to the internal analysis, which provides important information about an organization's specific resources and capabilities. An organization's resources are its assets—financial, physical, human, and intangible—that it uses to develop, manufacture, and deliver products to its customers. They're "what" the organization has. On the other hand, its capabilities are its skills and abilities in doing the work activities needed in its business—"how" it does its work. The major value-creating capabilities of the organization are known as its core competencies.[7] Both resources and core competencies determine the organization's competitive weapons.

After completing an internal analysis, managers should be able to identify organizational strengths and weaknesses. Any activities the organization does well or any unique resources that it has are called strengths. Weaknesses are activities the organization doesn't do well or resources it needs but doesn't possess.

The combined external and internal analyses are called the SWOT analysis because it's an analysis of the organization's *s*trengths, *w*eaknesses, *o*pportunities, and *t*hreats. After completing the SWOT analysis, managers are ready to formulate appropriate strategies—that is, strategies that (1) exploit an organization's strengths and external opportunities, (2) buffer or protect the organization from external threats, or (3) correct critical weaknesses.

STEP 4: Formulating strategies. As managers formulate strategies, they should consider the realities of the external environment and their available resources and capabilities and design strategies that will help an organization achieve its goals. Managers typically formulate three main types of strategies: corporate, business, and functional. We'll describe each shortly.

STEP 5: Implementing strategies. Once strategies are formulated, they must be implemented. No matter how effectively an organization has planned its strategies, performance will suffer if the strategies aren't implemented properly.

STEP 6: Evaluating results. The final step in the strategic management process is evaluating results. How effective have the strategies been at helping the organization reach its goals? What adjustments are necessary? For instance, when Anne Mulcahy, Xerox's former CEO, was first named to that post, she assessed the results of previous strategies and determined that changes were needed. She made strategic adjustments—cutting jobs, selling assets, and reorganizing management—to regain market share and improve her company's bottom line.

Baofan/Photoshot Holdings

In examining the external environment to assess trends and changes, Baidu's chief executive Robin Li sees opportunities for his company to grow. Baidu is the largest Chinese language search engine. With more than two-thirds of China's population not yet Internet users, Li believes search advertising will continue as the company's main growth driver for the next decade. Li also sees China's fast-growing mobile Internet market as a huge opportunity for Baidu due to the rapid growth in the number of mobile phone subscribers. According to Li, the decision of competitor Google to move its China search engine service to Hong Kong benefited Baidu because it drew attention to the search business and helped educate the advertisers that search is one of the best ways for them to reach their targeted consumers.

What Strategies Do Managers Use?

Strategies need to be formulated for all levels in the organization: corporate, business, and functional (see Exhibit 4). Let's look closer at each of these types of strategies.

CORPORATE STRATEGY. A corporate strategy is an organizational strategy that specifies what businesses a company is in or wants to be in and what it wants to do with those businesses. It's based on the mission and goals of the organization and the roles that each business unit of the organization will play. We can see both of these aspects with PepsiCo, for instance. Its mission is: To be the world's premier consumer products company focused on convenient foods and beverages. It pursues that mission with a corporate strategy that has put it in different businesses including PepsiCo Americas Beverage, PepsiCo International, Frito-Lay North America, Quaker Foods North America, and Latin America Foods. The other part of corporate strategy is when top managers decide what to do with those businesses. The three main types of corporate strategies are growth, stability, and renewal.

mission
A statement of an organization's purpose

opportunities
Positive trends in the external environment

threats
Negative trends in the external environment

resources
An organization's assets that it uses to develop, manufacture, and deliver products to its customers

capabilities
An organization's skills and abilities in doing the work activities needed in its business

core competencies
The major value-creating capabilities of an organization

strengths
Any activities the organization does well or any unique resources that it has

weaknesses
Activities the organization doesn't do well or resources it needs but doesn't possess

SWOT analysis
The combined external and internal analyses

corporate strategy
An organizational strategy that specifies what businesses a company is in or wants to be in and what it wants to do with those businesses

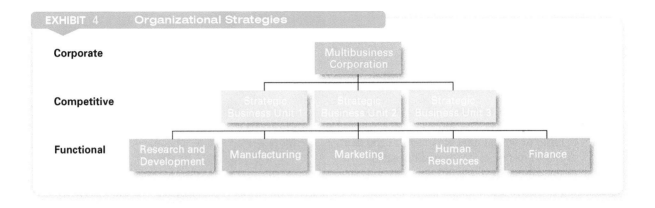

EXHIBIT 4 Organizational Strategies

Corporate — Multibusiness Corporation

Competitive — Strategic Business Unit 1 | Strategic Business Unit 2 | Strategic Business Unit 3

Functional — Research and Development | Manufacturing | Marketing | Human Resources | Finance

Growth Strategy.   Even though Walmart is the world's largest retailer, it continues to grow internationally and in the United States. A growth strategy is when an organization expands the number of markets served or products offered, either through its current business(es) or through new business(es). Because of its growth strategy, an organization may increase revenues, number of employees, or market share. Organizations grow by using concentration, vertical integration, horizontal integration, or diversification.

An organization that grows using *concentration* focuses on its primary line of business and increases the number of products offered or markets served in this primary business. For instance, Beckman Coulter, Inc., a Fullerton, California-based organization with annual revenues of almost $3.7 billion has used concentration to become one of the world's largest medical diagnostics and research equipment companies. The company has been so successful at this strategy that its largest rival acquired it for nearly $7 billion.

A company also might choose to grow by *vertical integration*, either backward, forward, or both. In backward vertical integration, the organization becomes its own supplier so it can control its inputs. For instance, eBay owns an online payment business that helps it provide more secure transactions and control one of its most critical processes. In forward vertical integration, the organization becomes its own distributor and is able to control its outputs. For example, Apple has some 380 retail stores around the globe to distribute its product.

In *horizontal integration*, a company grows by combining with competitors. For instance, French cosmetics giant L'Oréal acquired The Body Shop. Horizontal integration has been used in a number of industries in the last few years—financial services, consumer products, airlines, department stores, and software, among others. The U.S. Federal Trade Commission usually scrutinizes these combinations closely to see if consumers might be harmed by decreased competition. Other countries may have similar restrictions. For instance, managers at Oracle Corporation had to get approval from the European Commission, the "watchdog" for the European Union, before it could acquire rival business-software maker PeopleSoft.

Finally, an organization can grow through *diversification*, either related or unrelated. Related diversification is when a company combines with other companies in different, but related, industries. For example, American Standard Companies is in a variety of businesses including bathroom fixtures, air conditioning and heating units, plumbing parts, and pneumatic brakes for trucks. Although this mix of businesses seems odd, the company's "strategic fit" is the efficiency-oriented manufacturing techniques developed in its primary business of bathroom fixtures, which it has transferred to all its other businesses. Unrelated diversification is when a company combines with firms in different and unrelated industries. For instance, the Tata Group of India has businesses in chemicals, communications and IT, consumer products, energy, engineering, materials, and services. Again, an odd mix. But in this case, no strategic fit exists among the businesses. Each business is expected to compete and thrive on its own.

Stability Strategy.   During periods of economic uncertainty, many companies choose to maintain things as they are. In this stability strategy, an organization continues to do what it is currently doing. Examples of this strategy include continuing to serve the same clients by offering the same product or service, maintaining market share, and sustaining the organization's current business operations. The organization doesn't grow, but doesn't fall behind, either.

Renewal Strategy. In 2010, Federal National Mortgage Association (Fannie Mae) lost $14 billion after losing almost $72 billion in 2009. Its "brother" Freddie Mac (Federal Home Loan Mortgage Corporation) lost $14 billion in 2010 and $21.5 billion in 2009. Hitachi had a loss of $1.1 billion in 2010 and over $8 billion in 2009. When an organization is in trouble, something needs to be done. Managers need strategies that address declining performance. These strategies are called **renewal strategies**, of which there are two main types. A *retrenchment strategy* is a short-run renewal strategy used for minor performance problems. This strategy helps it stabilize operations, revitalize organizational resources and capabilities, and prepare to compete once again. When an organization's problems are more serious, more drastic action—the *turnaround strategy*—is needed. Managers do two things for both renewal strategies: cut costs and restructure organizational operations. However, in a turnaround strategy, these measures are more extensive than in a retrenchment strategy.

COMPETITIVE STRATEGY. A **competitive strategy** is a strategy for how an organization will compete in its business(es). For a small organization in only one line of business or a large organization that has not diversified into different products or markets, its competitive strategy describes how it will compete in its primary or main market. For organizations in multiple businesses, however, each business will have its own competitive strategy that defines its competitive advantage, the products or services it will offer, the customers it wants to reach, and the like. For example, the French company LVMH-Moët Hennessy Louis Vuitton SA has different competitive strategies for its businesses, which include Bliss cosmetics, Donna Karan fashions, Louis Vuitton leather goods, Guerlain perfume, TAG Heuer watches, Dom Perignon champagne, and other luxury products. Its selective retail division includes Sephora cosmetics stores, Le Bon Marché Paris department stores, and a majority holding of DFS Group duty-free shops. When an organization is in several different businesses, those single businesses that are independent and formulate their own competitive strategies are often called **strategic business units (SBUs)**.

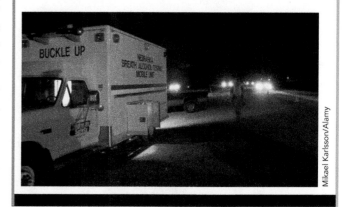

Mikael Karlsson/Alamy

---

growth strategy
A corporate strategy in which an organization expands the number of markets served or products offered either through its current business(es) or through new business(es)

stability strategy
A corporate strategy in which an organization continues to do what it is currently doing

renewal strategy
A corporate strategy that addresses declining organizational performance

competitive strategy
An organizational strategy for how an organization will compete in its business(es)

strategic business units (SBUs)
An organization's single businesses that are independent and formulate their own competitive strategies

The Role of Competitive Advantage. Michelin has mastered a complex technological process for making superior radial tires. Coca-Cola has created the world's best brand using specialized marketing and merchandising capabilities. The Ritz-Carlton hotels have a unique ability to deliver personalized customer service. Each of these companies has created a competitive advantage.

Developing an effective competitive strategy requires an understanding of competitive advantage, which is what sets an organization apart; that is, its distinctive edge. That distinctive edge comes from the organization's core competencies by doing something that others cannot do or doing it better than others can do it. For example, Southwest Airlines has a competitive advantage because of its skills at giving passengers what they want—convenient, reliable, and inexpensive service. Or competitive advantage can come from the company's resources—the organization has something that its competitors do not have. For instance, Walmart's state-of-the-art information system allows it to monitor and control inventories and supplier relations more efficiently than its competitors, which Walmart has turned into a cost advantage.

Choosing a Competitive Strategy. One of the leading researchers in strategy formulation is Michael Porter of Harvard's Graduate School of Business. His competitive strategies framework argues that managers can choose among three generic competitive strategies.[9] According to Porter, no firm can successfully achieve an above-average profitability by trying to be all things to all people. Rather, Porter proposed that managers must choose a competitive strategy that will give it a distinct advantage by capitalizing on the strengths of the organization and the industry it is in. His three competitive strategies are cost-leadership, differentiation, and focus.

When an organization competes on the basis of having the lowest costs in its industry, it's following a cost leadership strategy. A low-cost leader is highly efficient. Overhead is kept to a minimum, and the firm does everything it can to cut costs. You won't find expensive art or interior décor at offices of low-cost leaders. For example, at Walmart's headquarters in Bentonville, Arkansas, office furnishings are functional, not elaborate, maybe not what you'd expect for the world's largest retailer. Although a low-cost leader doesn't place a lot of emphasis on "frills," its product must be perceived as comparable in quality to that offered by rivals or at least be acceptable to buyers.

A company that competes by offering unique products that are widely valued by customers is following a differentiation strategy. Product differences might come from exceptionally high quality, extraordinary service, innovative design, technological capability, or an unusually positive brand image. Practically any successful consumer product or service can be identified as an example of the differentiation strategy; for instance, Nordstrom's (customer service); 3M Corporation (product quality and innovative design); Coach (design and brand image); and Apple (product design).

Although these two competitive strategies are aimed at the broad market, the final type of competitive strategy—the focus strategy—involves a cost advantage (cost focus) or a differentiation advantage (differentiation focus) in a narrow segment or niche. Segments can be based on product variety, customer type, distribution channel, or geographical location. For example, Denmark's Bang & Olufsen, whose revenues are more than $455 million, focuses on high-end audio equipment sales. Whether a focus strategy is feasible depends on the size of the segment and whether the organization can make money serving that segment.

By offering unique products that are widely valued by customers, Whole Foods Market uses a differentiation strategy for competing in the retail food industry. Since its inception, Whole Foods has focused on selling the highest-quality natural and organic products that benefit customers' health and following environment-friendly operating practices. This competitive strategy reflects the company's motto of "Whole Foods—Whole People—Whole Planet." The retailer is committed to buying fruits and vegetables from local farmers who are dedicated to sustainable agriculture. In this photo a mom and her kids shopping at a Whole Foods store pick up their fresh vegetables grown by a small local farmer.

What happens if an organization can't develop a cost or differentiation advantage? Porter called that being *stuck in the middle* and warned that it's not a good place to be.

Sustaining Competitive Advantage. Every organization has resources (assets) and capabilities (how work gets done). So what makes some organizations more successful than others? Why do some professional baseball teams consistently win championships or draw large crowds? Why do some organizations have consistent and continuous growth in revenues and profits? Why do some colleges, universities, or departments experience continually increasing enrollments? Why do some companies consistently appear at the top of lists ranking the "best," or the "most admired," or the "most profitable"? The answer is that not every organization is able to effectively exploit its resources and to develop the core competencies that can provide it with a competitive advantage. And it's not enough simply to create a competitive advantage. The organization must be able to sustain that advantage; that is, to keep its edge despite competitors' actions or evolutionary changes in the industry. But that's not easy to do! Market instabilities, new technology, and other changes can challenge managers' attempts at creating a long-term, sustainable competitive advantage. However, by using strategic management, managers can better position their organizations to get a sustainable competitive advantage.

FUNCTIONAL STRATEGY. The final type of strategy managers use is the functional strategy, which includes those strategies used by an organization's various functional departments to support the competitive strategy. For instance, when Starbucks found itself facing increased competition from the likes of McDonald's and Dunkin' Donuts, it put additional emphasis on its marketing, product research and development, and customer service strategies. We don't cover specific functional strategies here since you'll cover them in other business courses you take.

What Strategic Weapons Do Managers Have?

In today's intensely competitive and chaotic marketplace, organizations are looking for whatever "weapons" they can use to do what they're in business to do and to achieve their goals. Some of these weapons include customer service, employee skills and loyalty, innovation, and quality.

QUALITY AS A STRATEGIC WEAPON. When W. K. Kellogg started manufacturing his cornflake cereal in 1906, his goal was to provide his customers with a high-quality, nutritious product that was enjoyable to eat. That emphasis on quality is still important today. Every Kellogg employee has a responsibility to maintain the high quality of its products.

Many organizations are employing quality practices to build competitive advantage and attract and hold a loyal customer base. If implemented properly, quality can be a way for an organization to create a sustainable competitive advantage.[11] And if a business is

---

competitive advantage
What sets an organization apart; its distinctive edge

cost leadership strategy
When an organization competes on the basis of having the lowest costs in its industry

differentiation strategy
When an organization competes on the basis of having unique products that are widely valued by customers

focus strategy
When an organization competes in a narrow segment or niche with either a cost focus or a differentiation focus

functional strategy
Strategy used in an organization's various functional departments to support the competitive strategy

TECHNOLOGY AND THE MANAGER'S JOB

IT AND STRATEGY

How important is IT to a company's strategy?[10] Very important . . . as two examples will illustrate! Harrah's Entertainment, the world's largest gaming company, is fanatical about customer service, and for good reason. Company research showed that customers who were satisfied with the service they received at a Harrah's casino increased their gaming expenditures by 10 percent, and those who were extremely satisfied increased their gaming expenditures by 24 percent. It discovered this important customer service-expenditures connection because of its incredibly sophisticated information system. But an organization's IT may not always have such a positive payoff as the next example shows! At Prada's Manhattan flagship store, store designers were hoping for a "radically new shopping experience" that combined "cutting-edge architecture and twenty-first-century customer service." Or at least that was the strategy. Prada invested almost one-fourth of the new store's budget into IT, including wireless networks linked to an inventory database. As envisioned, sales staff would roam the store armed with PDAs so they could check whether items were in stock. Even the dressing rooms would have touch screens so customers could do the same. But the strategy didn't work as planned. The equipment malfunctioned and the staff was overwhelmed with trying to cope with crowds and equipment that didn't work. It's no wonder the multimillion-dollar investment might not have been the best strategy. When an organization's IT "works," it can be a very powerful strategic tool!

Think About:

· How should managers ensure that their IT efforts contribute to their strategies?

· Could the problems at Prada have been prevented? How might goals and plans have prevented these problems?

· How do IT applications help you be a better planner in your personal life? (Think smartphone organizers and calendars, text and voice messaging, etc.)

able to continuously improve the quality and reliability of its products, it may have a competitive advantage that can't be taken away.[12] Incremental improvement is something that becomes an integrated part of an organization's operations and can develop into a considerable advantage.

BENCHMARKING TO PROMOTE QUALITY.   Managers in such diverse industries as health care, education, and financial services are discovering what manufacturers have long recognized—the benefits of **benchmarking**, which is the search for the best practices among competitors or noncompetitors that lead to their superior performance. The basic idea of benchmarking is that managers can improve quality by analyzing and then copying the methods of the leaders in various fields.

In 1979, Xerox undertook what is widely regarded as the first benchmarking effort in the United States. Until then, the Japanese had been aggressively copying the successes of others by traveling around, watching what others were doing, and then using their new knowledge to improve their products and processes. Xerox's managers couldn't figure out how Japanese manufacturers could sell midsized copiers in the United States for considerably less than Xerox's production costs. So the company's head of manufacturing took a team to Japan to make a detailed study of its competition's costs and processes. The team got most of their information from Xerox's own joint venture partner, Fuji-Xerox, which knew its competition well. What the team found was shocking. Their Japanese rivals were light-years ahead of Xerox in efficiency. Benchmarking those efficiencies was the beginning of Xerox's recovery in the copier field. Today, many organizations use benchmarking practices. For instance, the American Medical Association developed more than 100 standard performance measures to improve medical care. Carlos Ghosn, CEO of Nissan, benchmarked Walmart's operations in purchasing, transportation, and logistics. And Southwest Airlines studied Indy 500 pit crews, who can change a race car's tire in under 15 seconds, to see how their gate crews could make their gate turnaround times even faster.[13]

Once managers have the organization's strategies in place, it's time to set goals and develop plans to pursue those strategies.

Teachers participating in the Weightless Flights of Discovery program are helping Northrop Grumman Foundation achieve its goal of inspiring more students to pursue careers in science, technology, engineering, and math. Concerned about our nation's shortage of future engineers and technologists, the aerospace and defense firm launched its program for middle school math and science teachers so they can bring unique learning opportunities to their classrooms. The program puts teachers in a zero-gravity aircraft flight where they learn about the physics of weightlessness, conduct experiments captured by a video camera, and then use their videotaped experience to show their students how math and science can be the basis for a fascinating career.

Rusty Costanza/Photoshot Holdings

HOW DO MANAGERS SET GOALS AND DEVELOP PLANS?

Planning involves two important aspects: goals and plans. **Goals (objectives)** are desired outcomes or targets. They guide managers' decisions and form the criteria against which work results are measured. **Plans** are documents that outline how goals are going to be met. They usually include resource allocations, budgets, schedules, and other necessary actions to accomplish the goals. As managers plan, they develop both goals and plans.

Compare and contrast approaches to goal setting and planning. **3**

What Types of Goals Do Organizations Have and How Do They Set Those Goals?

Although it might seem that organizations have a single goal—for businesses, to make a profit and for not-for-profit organizations, to meet the needs of some constituent group(s)—an organization's success can't be determined by a single goal. In reality, all organizations have multiple goals. For instance, businesses may want to increase market share, keep employees motivated, or work toward more environmentally sustainable practices. And a church provides a place for religious practices, but also assists economically disadvantaged individuals in its community and acts as a social gathering place for church members.

TYPES OF GOALS. Most company's goals can be classified as either strategic or financial. Financial goals are related to the financial performance of the organization while strategic goals are related to all other areas of an organization's performance. For instance, McDonald's financial targets include 3 to 5 percent average annual sales and revenue growth, 6 to 7 percent average annual operating income growth, and returns on invested capital in the high teens.[14] An example of a strategic goal would be the request by Nissan's CEO for the company's GT-R supercar: match or beat the performance of Porsche's 911 Turbo.[15] These goals are **stated goals**—official statements of what an organization says, and what it wants its stakeholders to believe, its goals are. However, stated goals—which can be found in an organization's charter, annual report, public relations announcements, or in public statements made by managers—are often conflicting and influenced by what various stakeholders think organizations should do. Such statements can be vague and probably better represent management's public relations skills instead of being meaningful guides to what the organization is actually trying to accomplish. It shouldn't be surprising then to find that an organization's stated goals are often irrelevant to what's actually done.[16]

If you want to know an organization's **real goals**—those goals an organization actually pursues—observe what organizational members are doing. Actions define priorities. Knowing that real and stated goals may differ is important for recognizing what you might otherwise think are inconsistencies.

SETTING GOALS. Goals provide the direction for all management decisions and actions and form the criterion against which actual accomplishments are measured. Everything organizational members do should be oriented toward achieving goals. These goals can be set either through a process of traditional goal setting or by using management by objectives.

benchmarking
The search for the best practices among competitors or noncompetitors that lead to their superior performance

goals (objectives)
Desired outcomes or targets

plans
Documents that outline how goals are going to be met

stated goals
Official statements of what an organization says, and wants its stakeholders to believe, its goals are

real goals
Those goals an organization actually pursues as shown by what the organization's members are doing

Traditional Goal Setting. In traditional goal setting, goals set by top managers flow down through the organization and become subgoals for each organizational area. (See Exhibit 5.) This traditional perspective assumes that top managers know what's best because they see the "big picture." And the goals passed down to each succeeding level guide individual employees as they work to achieve those assigned goals. Take a manufacturing business, for example. The president tells the vice president of production what he expects manufacturing costs to be for the coming year and tells the marketing vice president what level he expects sales to reach for the year. These goals are passed to the next organizational level and written to reflect the responsibilities of that level, passed to the next level, and so forth. Then, at some later time, performance is evaluated to determine whether the assigned goals have been achieved. Or that's the way it's supposed to happen. But in reality, it doesn't always do so. Turning broad strategic goals into departmental, team, and individual goals can be a difficult and frustrating process.

Another problem with traditional goal setting is that when top managers define the organization's goals in broad terms—such as achieving "sufficient" profits or increasing "market leadership"—these ambiguous goals have to be made more specific as they flow down through the organization. Managers at each level define the goals and apply their own interpretations and biases as they make them more specific. Clarity is often lost as the goals make their way down from the top of the organization to lower levels. But it doesn't have to be that way. For example, at Tijuana-based dj Orthopedics de Mexico, employee teams see the impact of their daily work output on company goals. The company's human resource manager says, "When people get a close connection with the result of their work, when they know every day what they are supposed to do and how they achieved the goals, that makes a strong connection with the company and their job."[17]

When the hierarchy of organizational goals *is* clearly defined, as it is at dj Orthopedics, it forms an integrated network of goals, or a means-ends chain. Higher-level goals (or ends) are linked to lower-level goals, which serve as the means for their accomplishment. In other words, the goals achieved at lower levels become the means to reach the goals (ends) at the next level. And the accomplishment of goals at that level becomes the means to achieve the goals (ends) at the next level and on up through the different organizational levels. That's how traditional goal setting is supposed to work.

Management by Objectives. Instead of using traditional goal setting, many organizations use management by objectives (MBO), a process of setting mutually agreed-upon goals and using those goals to evaluate employee performance. If a manager were to use this approach, he would sit down with each member of his team and set goals and periodically review whether progress was being made toward achieving those goals. MBO programs have four elements: goal specificity, participative decision making, an

Management by objectives (MBO) is not new. The concept can be traced back to Peter Drucker, who first popularized the term in his 1954 book *The Practice of Management*.[18] Its appeal lies in its emphasis on converting overall objectives into specific objectives for organizational units and individual members.

MBO makes goals operational by a process in which they cascade down through the organization. The organization's overall objectives are translated into specific objectives for each succeeding level—division, departmental, individual—in the organization. The result is a hierarchy that links objectives at one level to those at the next level. For the individual employee, MBO provides specific personal performance objectives. If all the individuals achieve their goals, then the unit's goals will be attained. Likewise, if all the units attain their goals, then the divisional goals will be met until ultimately the organization's overall goals will become a reality.

Does MBO work? Assessing the effectiveness of MBO is a complex task. But goal-setting research can give us some answers. For instance, research has shown that specific, difficult-to-achieve goals produce a higher level of output than do no goals or generalized goals such as "do your best." Also, feedback favorably affects performance because it lets a person know whether his or her level of effort is sufficient or needs to be increased. These findings are consistent with MBO's emphasis on specific goals and feedback. What about participation, though, since MBO strongly advocates that goals be set participatively? Research comparing participatively set goals with assigned goals has not shown any strong or consistent relationship to performance. One critical factor in the success of any MBO program, however, is top management commitment to the process. When top managers had a high commitment to MBO and were personally involved in its implementation, productivity gains were higher than if this commitment was lacking.

Think About:

- Why do you think management commitment is so important to the success of MBO programs?

- Do you set goals for yourself? Do you feel that setting goals helps you perform better? Discuss.

- Could MBO be useful in your personal life? How? What would you need to do to set up an MBO-like approach to your personal goals?

explicit time period, and performance feedback.[19] Instead of using goals to make sure employees are doing what they're supposed to be doing, MBO uses goals to motivate them as well. The appeal is that it focuses on employees working to accomplish goals they've had a hand in setting. (See the From the Past to the Present box for more information on MBO.)

Studies of actual MBO programs have shown that it can increase employee performance and organizational productivity. For example, one review of MBO programs found productivity gains in almost all of them.[20] But is MBO relevant for today's organizations? If it's viewed as a way of setting goals, then yes, research shows that goal setting can be an effective approach to motivating employees.[21]

Characteristics of Well-Written Goals. No matter which approach is used, goals have to be written, and some goals more clearly indicate what the desired outcomes are. Managers should develop well-written goals. Exhibit 6 lists the characteristics.[22] With these characteristics in mind, managers are now ready to actually set goals.

EXHIBIT 6   Well-Written Goals

- Written in terms of outcomes rather than actions
- Measurable and quantifiable
- Clear as to a time frame
- Challenging yet attainable
- Written down
- Communicated to all necessary organizational members

---

traditional goal setting
Goals set by top managers flow down through the organization and become subgoals for each organizational area

means-ends chain
An integrated network of goals in which higher-level goals are linked to lower-level goals, which serve as the means for their accomplishment

management by objectives (MBO)
A process of setting mutually agreed-upon goals and using those goals to evaluate employee performance

Steps in Goal Setting. Managers should follow six steps when setting goals.

1. *Review the organization's mission and employees' key job tasks.* An organization's mission statement will provide an overall guide to what organizational members think is important. Managers should review the mission before writing goals because goals should reflect that mission. In addition, it's important to define what you want employees to accomplish as they do their tasks.

2. *Evaluate available resources.* You don't want to set goals that are impossible to achieve given your available resources. Even though goals should be challenging, they should be realistic. After all, if the resources you have to work with won't allow you to achieve a goal no matter how hard you try or how much effort is exerted, you shouldn't set that goal. That would be like the person with a $50,000 annual income and no other financial resources setting a goal of building an investment portfolio worth $1 million in three years. No matter how hard he or she works at it, it's not going to happen.

3. *Determine the goals individually or with input from others.* The goals reflect desired outcomes and should be congruent with the organizational mission and goals in other organizational areas. These goals should be measurable, specific, and include a time frame for accomplishment.

4. *Make sure goals are well-written and then communicate them to all who need to know.* Writing down and communicating goals forces people to think them through. The written goals also become visible evidence of the importance of working toward something.

5. *Build in feedback mechanisms to assess goal progress.* If goals aren't being met, change them as needed.

6. *Link rewards to goal attainment.* It's natural for employees to ask "What's in it for me?" Linking rewards to goal achievement will help answer that question.

Once the goals have been established, written down, and communicated, managers are ready to develop plans for pursuing the goals.

What Types of Plans Do Managers Use and How Do They Develop Those Plans?

Managers need plans to help them clarify and specify how goals will be met. Let's look first at the types of plans managers use.

TYPES OF PLANS. The most popular ways to describe plans are in terms of their *breadth* (strategic versus tactical), *time frame* (long term versus short), *specificity* (directional versus specific), and *frequency of use* (single-use versus standing). As Exhibit 7 shows, these types of plans aren't independent. That is, strategic plans are usually long term, directional, and single-use. Let's look at each type of plan.

Breadth. Strategic plans are those that apply to an entire organization and encompass the organization's overall goals. Tactical plans (sometimes referred to as operational plans) specify the details of how the overall goals are to be achieved. When McDonald's invested in its Redbox kiosk business, it was the result of strategic planning. Deciding when, where, and how to actually operate the business was the result of tactical plans in marketing, logistics, finance, and so forth.

Time Frame. The number of years used to define short-term and long-term plans has declined considerably due to environmental uncertainty. *Long term* used to mean anything

EXHIBIT 7	Types of Plans		
BREADTH OF USE	TIME FRAME	SPECIFICITY	FREQUENCY OF USE
Strategic	Long term	Directional	Single-use
Tactical	Short term	Specific	Standing

over seven years. Try to imagine what you're likely to be doing in seven years. It seems pretty distant, doesn't it? Now, you can begin to understand how difficult it is for managers to plan that far in the future. Thus, long-term plans are now defined as plans with a time frame beyond three years. Short-term plans cover one year or less.

Specificity. Intuitively, it would seem that specific plans would be preferable to directional, or loosely guided, plans. Specific plans are plans that are clearly defined and leave no room for interpretation. For example, a manager who wants to increase his work unit's output by 8 percent over the next 12 months might establish specific procedures, budget allocations, and work schedules to reach that goal. However, when uncertainty is high and managers must be flexible in order to respond to unexpected changes, they'd likely use directional plans, flexible plans that set general guidelines. For example, Sylvia Rhone, president of Motown Records, had a simple goal—to "sign great artists."[23] She could create a specific plan to produce and market 10 albums from new artists this year. Or she might formulate a directional plan to use a network of people around the world to alert her to new and promising talent so she can increase the number of artists she has under contract. Sylvia, and any manager who engages in planning, must keep in mind that you have to weigh the flexibility of directional plans against the clarity you can get from specific plans.

Frequency of Use. Some plans that managers develop are ongoing, while others are used only once. A single-use plan is a one-time plan specifically designed to meet the needs of a unique situation. For instance, when Dell began developing a pocket-sized device for getting on the Internet, managers used a single-use plan to guide their decisions. In contrast, standing plans are ongoing plans that provide guidance for activities performed repeatedly. For example, when you register for classes for the upcoming semester, you're using a standardized registration plan at your college or university. The dates change, but the process works the same way semester after semester.

DEVELOPING PLANS. The process of developing plans is influenced by three contingency factors and by the planning approach followed.

Contingency Factors in Planning. Look back at our chapter-opening case. How will Cisco executives proceed now that the decision has been made to abandon its Flip business? Three contingency factors affect the choice of plans: organizational level, degree of environmental uncertainty, and length of future commitments.[24]

Exhibit 8 shows the relationship between a manager's level in the organization and the type of planning done. For the most part, lower-level managers do operational (or tactical) planning while upper-level managers do strategic planning.

The second contingency factor is environmental uncertainty. When uncertainty is high, plans should be specific, but flexible. Managers must be prepared to change or amend plans as they're implemented. For example, at Continental Airlines, the former CEO and his management team established a specific goal of focusing on what customers wanted most—on-time flights—to help the company become more competitive in the highly uncertain airline industry. Because of that uncertainty, the management team identified a "destination, but not a flight plan," and changed plans as necessary to achieve its goal of on-time service.

---

strategic plans
Plans that apply to the entire organization and encompass the organization's overall goals

tactical plans
Plans that specify the details of how the overall goals are to be achieved

long-term plans
Plans with a time frame beyond three years

short-term plans
Plans with a time frame of one year or less

specific plans
Plans that are clearly defined and leave no room for interpretation

directional plans
Plans that are flexible and set general guidelines

single-use plan
A one-time plan specifically designed to meet the needs of a unique situation

standing plans
Plans that are ongoing and provide guidance for activities performed repeatedly

EXHIBIT 8   Planning and Organizational Level

The last contingency factor also is related to the time frame of plans. The commitment concept says that plans should extend far enough to meet those commitments made when the plans were developed. Planning for too long or too short a time period is inefficient and ineffective. We can see the importance of the commitment concept, for example, with the plans that organizations make to increase their computing capabilities. At the data centers where companies' computers are housed, many have found their "power-hungry computers" generate so much heat that their electric bills have skyrocketed because of the increased need for air conditioning.[25] How does this illustrate the commitment concept? As organizations expand their computing technology, they're "committed" to whatever future expenses are generated by that plan. They have to live with the plan and its consequences.

Approaches to Planning.   Federal, state, and local government officials are working together on a plan to boost populations of wild salmon in the northwestern United States. Managers in the Global Fleet Graphics division of the 3M Company are developing detailed plans to satisfy increasingly demanding customers and to battle more aggressive competitors. Emilio Azcárraga Jean, chairman, president, and CEO of Grupo Televisa, gets input from many different people before setting company goals and then turns over the planning for achieving the goals to various executives. In each of these situations, planning is done a little differently. *How* an organization plans can best be understood by looking at *who* does the planning.

In the traditional approach, planning is done entirely by top level managers who often are assisted by a formal planning department, a group of planning specialists whose sole responsibility is to help write the various organizational plans. Under this approach, plans developed by top-level managers flow down through other organizational levels, much like the traditional approach to goal-setting. As they flow down through the organization, the plans are tailored to the particular needs of each level. Although this approach makes managerial planning thorough, systematic, and coordinated, all too often the focus is on developing "the plan," a thick binder (or binders) full of meaningless information, that's stuck away on a shelf and never used by anyone for guiding or coordinating work efforts. In fact, in a survey of managers about formal top-down organizational planning processes, over 75 percent said that their company's planning approach was unsatisfactory.[26] A common complaint was that "plans are documents that you prepare for the corporate planning staff and later forget." Although this traditional top-down approach to planning is used by many organizations, it can be effective only if managers understand the importance of creating documents that organizational members actually use, not documents that look impressive but are never used.

Another approach to planning is to involve more organizational members in the process. In this approach, plans aren't handed down from one level to the next, but instead are developed by organizational members at the various levels and in the various work units to meet their specific needs. For instance, at Dell, employees from production, supply management, and channel management meet weekly to make plans based on current product demand and supply. In addition, work teams set their own daily schedules and track their progress against those schedules. If a team falls behind, team members develop "recovery" plans to try to get back on schedule.[28] When organizational members are more actively involved in planning, they see that the plans are more than just something written down on paper. They can actually see that the plans are used in directing and coordinating work.

WHAT CONTEMPORARY PLANNING ISSUES DO MANAGERS FACE?

Discuss contemporary issues in planning.

4

We conclude this chapter by addressing two contemporary issues in planning. Specifically, we're going to look at planning effectively in dynamic environments and then at how managers can use environmental scanning, especially competitive intelligence.

How Can Managers Plan Effectively in Dynamic Environments?

The external environment is continually changing. For instance, Wi-Fi has revolutionized all kinds of industries from airlines to automobile manufacturing to supermarkets. Social networking sites are being used by companies for connecting with customers. Amounts spent on eating out instead of cooking at home are predicted to decline. And experts believe that China and India are transforming the twenty-first-century global economy.

How can managers effectively plan when the external environment is continually changing? We already discussed uncertain environments as one of the contingency factors that affect the types of plans managers develop. Because dynamic environments are more the norm than the exception, let's look at how they can effectively plan in such environments.

In an uncertain environment, managers should develop plans that are specific, but flexible. Although this may seem contradictory, it's not. To be useful, plans need some specificity, but the plans should not be set in stone. Managers need to recognize that planning is an ongoing process. The plans serve as a road map although the destination may change due to dynamic market conditions. They should be ready to change directions if environmental conditions warrant. This flexibility is particularly important as plans are implemented. Managers need to stay alert to environmental changes that may impact implementation and respond as needed. Keep in mind, also, that even when the environment is highly uncertain, it's important to continue formal planning in order to see any effect on organizational performance. It's the persistence in planning that contributes to significant performance improvement. Why? It seems that, as with most activities, managers "learn to plan" and the quality of their planning improves when they continue to do it.[29] Finally, make the organizational hierarchy flatter to effectively plan in dynamic environments. A flatter hierarchy means lower organizational levels can set goals and develop plans because organizations have little time for goals and plans to flow down from the top. Managers should teach their employees how to set goals and to plan and then trust them to do it. And you need look no further than Bangalore, India, to find a company that effectively understands this. Just a decade ago, Wipro Limited was "an anonymous conglomerate selling cooking oil and personal computers, mostly in India." Today, it's a $6 billion-a-year global company with most of its business (over 75 percent) coming from information-technology services.[30] Accenture, EDS, IBM, and the big U.S. accounting firms know all too well the competitive threat Wipro represents. Not only are Wipro's

---

commitment concept
The idea that plans should extend far enough to meet those commitments made when the plans were developed

formal planning department
A group of planning specialists whose sole responsibility is to help write the various organizational plans

Knowledgeable and skilled employees play an important role in planning at Wipro, a global information technology services company serving more than 800 clients including governments, educational institutions, and business enterprises. Operating in a dynamic environment, Wipro empowers its customer engagement managers to set goals and make plans in analyzing clients' ever-changing business needs and devising innovative solutions that help them function faster, simpler, and more efficiently. Giving these frontline employees responsibility for planning is part of Wipro's ownership-oriented approach of empowering them to function as mini-CEOS. Shown here are Wipro employees at company headquarters in Bangalore, India.

employees economical, they're knowledgeable and skilled. And they play an important role in the company's planning. Since the information services industry is continually changing, employees are taught to analyze situations and to define the scale and scope of a client's problems in order to offer the best solutions. These employees are the ones on the front line with the clients and it's their responsibility to establish what to do and how to do it. It's an approach that positions Wipro for success no matter how the industry changes.

How Can Managers Use Environmental Scanning?

A manager's analysis of the external environment may be improved by **environmental scanning**, which involves screening large amounts of information to detect emerging trends. One of the fastest-growing forms of environmental scanning is **competitive intelligence**, which is accurate information about competitors that allows managers to anticipate competitors' actions rather than merely react to them.[31] It seeks basic information about competitors: Who are they? What are they doing? How will what they're doing affect us?

Many who study competitive intelligence suggest that much of the competitor-related information managers need to make crucial strategic decisions is available and accessible to the public.[32] In other words, competitive intelligence isn't organizational espionage. Advertisements, promotional materials, press releases, reports filed with government agencies, annual reports, want ads, newspaper reports, information on the Internet, and industry studies are readily accessible sources of information. Specific information on an industry and associated organizations is increasingly available through electronic databases. Managers can literally tap into this wealth of competitive information by purchasing access to databases. Attending trade shows and debriefing your own sales staff also can be good sources of information on competitors. In addition, many organizations even regularly buy competitors' products and ask their own employees to evaluate them to learn about new technical innovations.[33]

In a changing global business environment, environmental scanning and obtaining competitive intelligence can be quite complex, especially when information must be gathered from around the world. However, managers could subscribe to news services that review newspapers and magazines from around the globe and provide summaries to client companies.

Managers do need to be careful about the way information, especially competitive intelligence, is gathered to prevent any concerns about whether it's legal or ethical. For instance, Starwood Hotels sued Hilton Hotels alleging that two former employees stole trade secrets and helped Hilton develop a new line of luxury, trendy hotels designed to appeal to a young demographic.[34] The court filing said, "This is the clearest imaginable case of corporate espionage, theft of trade secrets, unfair competition, and computer fraud." Competitive intelligence becomes illegal corporate spying when it involves the theft of proprietary materials or trade secrets by any means. The Economic Espionage Act makes it a crime in the United States to engage in economic espionage or to steal a trade secret.[35] Difficult decisions about competitive intelligence arise because often there's a fine line between what's considered *legal and ethical* and what's considered *legal but unethical.* Although the top manager at one competitive intelligence firm contends that 99.9 percent of intelligence gathering is legal, there's no question that some people or companies will go to any lengths—some unethical—to get information about competitors.[36]

---

environmental scanning
An analysis of the external environment, which involves screening large amounts of information to detect emerging trends

competitive intelligence
A type of environmental scanning that gives managers accurate information about competitors

Review

CHAPTER SUMMARY

1 Discuss the nature and purposes of planning. As the primary management function, planning establishes the basis for all the other things that managers do. The planning we're concerned with is formal planning; that is, specific goals covering a specific time period are defined and written down and specific plans are developed to make sure those goals are met. There are four reasons why managers should plan: (1) it establishes coordinated efforts; (2) it reduces uncertainty; (3) it reduces overlapping and wasteful activities; and (4) it establishes the goals or standards that are used in controlling work. Although criticisms have been directed at planning, the evidence generally supports the position that organizations benefit from formal planning.

2 Explain what managers do in the strategic management process. Managers develop the organization's strategies in the strategic management process, which is a six-step process encompassing strategy planning, implementation, and evaluation. The six steps are as follows: (1) Identify the organization's current mission, goals, and strategies; (2) do an external analysis; (3) do an internal analysis; steps 2 and 3 together are called SWOT analysis; (4) formulate strategies; (5) implement strategies; and (6) evaluate results. The end result of this process is a set of corporate, competitive, and functional strategies that allow the organization to do what it's in business to do and to achieve its goals.

3 Compare and contrast approaches to goal setting and planning. Most company's goals are classified as either strategic or financial. We can also look at goals as either stated or real. In traditional goal setting, goals set by top managers flow down through the organization and become subgoals for each organizational area. Organizations could also use management by objectives, which is a process of setting mutually agreed-upon goals and using those goals to evaluate employee performance. Plans can be described in terms of their breadth, time frame, specificity, and frequency of use. Plans can be developed by a formal planning department or by involving more organizational members in the process.

4 Discuss contemporary issues in planning. One contemporary planning issue is planning in dynamic environments, which usually means developing plans that are specific but flexible. Also, it's important to continue planning even when the environment is highly uncertain. Finally, because there's little time in a dynamic environment for goals and plans to flow down from the top, lower organizational levels should be allowed to set goals and develop plans. Another contemporary planning issue is using environmental scanning to help do a better analysis of the external environment. One form of environmental scanning, competitive intelligence, can be especially helpful in finding out what competitors are doing.

MyManagementLab For more resources, please visit www.mymanagementlab.com

---

UNDERSTANDING THE CHAPTER

1. Contrast formal with informal planning. Discuss why planning is beneficial.

2. Describe in detail the six-step strategic management process.

3. What is a SWOT analysis, and why is it important to managers?

4. "Organizations that fail to plan are planning to fail." Do you agree or disagree with this statement? Explain your position.

5. Under what circumstances do you believe MBO would be most useful? Discuss.

6. Find examples in current business periodicals of each of Porter's generic strategies. Name the company, describe the strategy being used, and explain why it's an example of that strategy. Be sure to cite your sources.

7. "The primary means of sustaining a competitive advantage is to adjust faster to the environment than

your competitors do." Do you agree or disagree with this statement? Explain your position.

8. What types of planning do you do in your personal life? Describe these plans in terms of being (a) strategic or operational, (b) short term or long term, (c) specific or directional, and (d) single-use or standing.

9. Do a personal SWOT analysis. Assess your personal strengths and weaknesses (skills, talents, abilities). What are you good at? What are you not so good at? What do you enjoy doing? Not enjoy doing? Then, identify career opportunities and threats by

researching job prospects in the industry you're interested in. Look at trends and projections. You might want to check out the information the Bureau of Labor Statistics provides on job prospects. Once you have all this information, write a specific career action plan. Outline five-year career goals and what you need to do to achieve those goals.

10. "The concept of competitive advantage is as important for not-for-profit organizations as it is for for-profit organizations." Do you agree or disagree with this statement? Explain, using examples to make your case.

Endnotes

1. R. Cheng and D. Clark, "Cisco Flips Consumer Strategy," *Wall Street Journal,* April 13, 2011, p. B3; J. Swartz, "Cisco to Close Flip Video-Camera Business," *USA Today,* April 13, 2011, p. 2B; S. Grobart and E. M. Rusli, "For Flip Video Camera, Four Years from Hot Start-Up to Obsolete," *New York Times Online,* April 12, 2011; D. Goldman, "Cisco Kills Flip, Cuts 550 Workers," *CNNMoney.com,* April 12, 2011; C. Tuna, "Head of Cisco's Consumer Business to Depart," *Wall Street Journal Online,* February 11, 2011; "Recognizing Excellence," *New Zealand Management,* December 2010, pp. 97–101; T. Dreier, "Cheap Flicks," *Money,* July 2010, p. 18; R. Karlgaard, "Three Joy-Giving Products," *Forbes,* June 22, 2009, p. 21; "Cisco Buying Flip Video Camera Maker," *Networkworld.com,* March 23, 2009, p. 10; S. H. Wildstrom, "Cisco Pushes Further into Consumer Technology," *BusinessWeek Online,* March 20, 2009; and K. Boehret, "The Mossberg Solution: An Easier Way to Make and Share Videos," *Wall Street Journal,* September 12, 2007, p. D3.
2. M. C. Mankins and R. Steele, "Stop Making Plans—Start Making Decisions," *Harvard Business Review,* January 2006, pp. 76–84; L. Bossidy and R. Charan, *Execution: The Discipline of Getting Things Done* (New York: Crown/Random House), 2002; P. Roberts, "The Art of Getting Things Done," *Fast Company,* June 2000, p. 162; H. Mintzberg, *The Rise and Fall of Strategic Planning* (New York: Free Press, 1994); G. Hamel and C. K. Prahalad, *Competing for the Future* (Boston: Harvard Business School Press, 1994); and D. Miller, "The Architecture of Simplicity," *Academy of Management Review,* January 1993, pp. 116–138.
3. See, for example, F. Delmar and S. Shane, "Does Business Planning Facilitate the Development of New Ventures?" *Strategic Management Journal* (December 2003), pp. 1165–1185; R. M. Grant, "Strategic Planning in a Turbulent Environment: Evidence from the Oil Majors," *Strategic Management Journal* (June 2003), pp. 491–517; P. J. Brews and M. R. Hunt, "Learning to Plan and Planning to Learn: Resolving the Planning School/Learning School Debate," *Strategic Management Journal* (December 1999), pp. 889–913; C. C. Miller and L. B. Cardinal, "Strategic Planning and Firm Performance: A Synthesis of More Than Two Decades of Research," *Academy of Management Journal* (March 1994), pp. 1649–1685; N. Capon, J. U. Farley, and J. M. Hulbert, "Strategic Planning and Financial Performance: More Evidence," *Journal of Management Studies* (January 1994), pp. 22–38; D.K. Sinha, "The Contribution of Formal Planning to Decisions," *Strategic Management Journal* (October 1990), pp. 479–492; J. A. Pearce II, E. B. Freeman, and R. B. Robinson Jr., "The Tenuous Link Between Formal Strategic Planning and Financial Performance," *Academy of Management Review,* October 1987, pp. 658–675; L. C. Rhyne, "Contrasting Planning Systems in High, Medium, and Low Performance Companies," *Journal of Management Studies* (July 1987), pp. 363–385; and J. A. Pearce II, K. K. Robbins, and R. B. Robinson, Jr., "The Impact of Grand Strategy and Planning Formality on Financial Performance," *Strategic Management Journal* (March–April 1987), pp. 125–134.
4. V. Fuhrmans, "Siemens Rethinks Nuclear Ambitions," *Wall Street Journal,* April 15, 2011, p. B1+; J. Whalen, "Glaxo to Shed Its OTC Diet Drug, Alli," *Wall Street Journal,* April 15, 2011, p. B1; M. Bustillo, "Best Buy to Shrink 'Big-Box' Store Strategy," *Wall Street Journal,* April 15, 2011, p. B7; and L. Burkitt, "Burberry Dresses Up China Stores with Digital Strategy," *Wall Street Journal,* April 14, 2011, p. B9.
5. A. J. Karr, "December Comp Crux," *Women's Wear Daily,* January 7, 2011, p. 4; A. Steigrad, "Specialty Retailers Show Weak Spots in Quarter," *Women's Wear Daily,* August 20, 2010, p. 14; K. Peterson, "Buckle Bends as Claiborne, Orbitz Climb, Ambow Sinks," *Wall Street Journal,* August 6, 2010, p. C6;

N. Casey, "Teen Idols: Aeropostale, Buckle Post Big Gains as Rivals Swoon," *Wall Street Journal,* May 22, 2009, p. B8; V. Dagher, "Hot Topic Goes Cold, Buckle Wears a Smile," *Wall Street Journal,* May 22, 2009, p. C6; and J. B. Stewart, "A Retailer Bucks a Trend with Sales Success in Its Jeans," *Wall Street Journal,* May 13, 2009, p. D1.

6. M. Gruber, F. Heinemann, M. Brettel, and S. Hungeling, "Configurations of Resources and Capabilities and Their Performance Implications: An Exploratory Study on Technology Ventures," *Strategic Management Journal* (December 2010), pp. 1337–1356; T. H. Poister, "The Future of Strategic Planning in the Public Sector: Linking Strategic Management and Performance," *Public Administration Review,* December 2010, pp. S246–S254; J. González-Benito and Isabel Suárez-González, "A Study of the Role Played by Manufacturing Strategic Objectives and Capabilities in Understanding the Relationship Between Porter's Generic Strategies and Business Performance," *British Journal of Management,* vol. 21, (2010), pp. 1027–1043; J. A. Parnell and E. B. Dent, "The Role of Luck in the Strategy-Performance Relationship," *Management Decision,* vol. 47, no. 6, (2009), pp. 1000–1021; H. J. Cho and V. Pucik, "Relationship Between Innovativeness, Quality, Growth, Profitability, and Market Value," *Strategic Management Journal* (June 2005), pp. 555–575; W. F. Joyce, "What Really Works," *Organizational Dynamics,* May 2005, pp. 118–129; M. A. Roberto, "Strategic Decision-Making Processes," *Group & Organization Management,* December 2004, pp. 625–658; A. Carmeli and A. Tischler, "The Relationships Between Intangible Organizational Elements and Organizational Performance," *Strategic Management Journal* (December 2004), pp. 1257–1278; D. J. Ketchen, C. C. Snow, and V. L. Street, "Improving Firm Performance by Matching Strategic Decision-Making Processes to Competitive Dynamics," *Academy of Management Executive,* November 2004, pp. 29–43; E. H. Bowman and C. E. Helfat, "Does Corporate Strategy Matter?" *Strategic Management Journal,* 22 (2001), pp. 1–23; P. J. Brews and M. R. Hunt, "Learning to Plan and Planning to Learn: Resolving the Planning School-Learning School Debate," *Strategic Management Journal,* 20 (1999), pp. 889–913; D. J. Ketchen Jr., J. B. Thomas, and R. R. McDaniel Jr., "Process, Content and Context; Synergistic Effects on Performance," *Journal of Management,* 22, no. 2 (1996), pp. 231–257; C. C. Miller and L. B. Cardinal, "Strategic Planning and Firm Performance: A Synthesis of More Than Two Decades of Research," *Academy of Management Journal* (December 1994), pp. 1649–1665; and N. Capon, J. U. Farley, and J. M. Hulbert, "Strategic Planning and Financial Performance: More Evidence," *Journal of Management Studies* (January 1994), pp. 105–110.

7. C. K. Prahalad and G. Hamel, "The Core Competence of the Corporation," *Harvard Business Review,* May–June 1990, pp. 79–91.

8. Right or Wrong box based on R. Stross, "Helping Drunken Drivers Avoid Tickets, But Not Wrecks," *New York Times Online,* April 16, 2011; "Senators Ask App Stores to End DUI Evasion Aids," *Telecommunications Reports,* April 1, 2011, p. 24; J. R. Quain, "DUI Checkpoint Apps Draw Ire and Fire," *Fox News.com,* March 29, 2011; M. Esteban and KOMO Staff, "App Designed to Sniff Out DUI Checkpoints Snuffed Out by Senators," *KOMO News.com,* March 25, 2011; and Associated Press, "Group Urges Sobriety Checkpoints," *Wall Street Journal,* January 13, 2005, p. A1.

9. C. H. Green, "Competitive Theory and Business Legitimacy," *BusinessWeek Online,* June 23, 2010; S. Parthasarathy, "Business Strategy" *Financial Management,* June 2010, pp. 32–33; M. E. Porter, *On Competition, Updated and Expanded Edition* (Boston: Harvard Business School), 2008; O. Ormanidhi and O. Stringa, "Porter's Model of Generic Competitive Strategies," *Business Economics,* July 2008, pp. 55–64; M. E. Porter, "The Five Competitive Forces That Shape Strategy," *Harvard Business Review,* January 2008, pp. 78–93; N. Argyres and A. M. McGahan, "Introduction: Michael Porter's Competitive Strategy," *Academy of Management Executive,* May 2002, pp. 41–42; and N. Argyres and A. M. McGahan, "An Interview with Michael Porter," *Academy of Management Executive,* May 2002, pp. 43–52.

10. Managers and Technology box based on D. McGinn, "From Harvard to Las Vegas," *Newsweek,* April 18, 2005, pp. E8–E14; G. Lindsay, "Prada's High-Tech Misstep," *Business 2.0,* March 2004, pp. 72–75; G. Loveman, "Diamonds in the Data Mine," *Harvard Business Review,* May 2003, pp. 109–113; and L. Gary, "Simplify and Execute: Words to Live By in Times of Turbulence," *Harvard Management Update,* January 2003, p. 12.

11. N. A. Shepherd, "Competitive Advantage: Mapping Change and the Role of the Quality Manager of the Future," *Annual Quality Congress,* May 1998, pp. 53–60; T. C. Powell, "Total Quality Management as Competitive Advantage: A Review and Empirical Study," *Strategic Management Journal* (January 1995), pp. 15–37; and R. D. Spitzer, "TQM: The Only Source of Sustainable Competitive Advantage," *Quality Progress,* June 1993, pp. 59–64.

12. See R. J. Schonenberger, "Is Strategy Strategic? Impact of Total Quality Management on Strategy," *Academy of Management Executive,* August 1992, pp. 80–87; C. A. Barclay, "Quality Strategy and TQM Policies: Empirical Evidence," *Management International Review,* Special Issue 1993, pp. 87–98; R. Jacob, "TQM: More Than a Dying Fad?" *Fortune,* October 18, 1993, pp. 66–72; R. Krishnan, A. B. Shani, R. M. Grant, and R. Baer, "In Search of Quality Improvement Problems of Design and Implementation," *Academy of Management Executive,* November 1993, pp. 7–20; B. Voss, "Quality's Second Coming," *Journal of Business Strategy,* March–April 1994, pp. 42–46; and special issue of *Academy of Management Review* devoted to TQM, July 1994, pp. 390–584.

13. R. Pear, "A.M.A. to Develop Measure of Quality of Medical Care," *New York Times Online,* February 21, 2006; and A. Taylor III, "Double Duty," *Fortune,* March 7, 2005, pp. 104–110.

14. McDonald's Annual Report 2007, www.mcdonalds.com (April 21, 2008).

15. S. Zesiger Callaway, "Mr. Ghosn Builds His Dream Car," *Fortune,* February 4, 2008, pp. 56–58.

16. See, for instance, J. Pfeffer, *Organizational Design* (Arlington Heights, IL: AHM Publishing, 1978), pp. 5–12; and C. K. Warriner, "The Problem of Organizational Purpose," *Sociological Quarterly* (Spring 1965), pp. 139–146.

17. D. Drickhamer, "Braced for the Future," *Industry Week,* October 2004, pp. 51–52.

18. From the Past to the Present box based on P. F. Drucker, *The Practice of Management* (New York: Harper & Row, 1954); J. F. Castellano and H. A. Roehm, "The Problem with

Managing by Objectives and Results," *Quality Progress,* March 2001, pp. 39–46; J. Loehr and T. Schwartz, "The Making of a Corporate Athlete," *Harvard Business Review,* January 2001, pp. 120–128; A. J. Vogl, "Drucker, of Course," *Across the Board,* November–December 2000, p. 1. For information on goals and goal setting, see, for example, E. A. Locke, "Toward a Theory of Task Motivation and Incentives," *Organizational Behavior and Human Performance*, May 1968, pp. 157–189; E. A. Locke, K. N. Shaw, L. M. Saari, and G. P. Latham, "Goal Setting and Task Performance: 1969–1980," *Psychological Bulletin,* July 1981, pp. 12–52; E. A. Locke and G. P. Latham, *A Theory of Goal Setting and Task Performance* (Upper Saddle River, NJ: Prentice Hall, 1990); P. Ward and M. Carnes, "Effects of Posting Self-Set Goals on Collegiate Football Players' Skill Execution During Practice and Games," *Journal of Applied Behavioral Analysis,* (Spring 2002), pp. 1–12; D. W. Ray, "Productivity and Profitability," *Executive Excellence,* October 2001, p. 14; D. Archer, "Evaluating Your Managed System," *CMA Management,* January 2000, pp. 12–14; and C. Antoni, "Management by Objectives: An Effective Tool for Teamwork," *International Journal of Human Resource Management* (February 2005), pp. 174–184. For information on participation in goal setting, see, for example, T. D. Ludwig and E. S. Geller, "Intervening to Improve the Safety of Delivery Drivers: A Systematic Behavioral Approach," *Journal of Organizational Behavior Management* (April 4, 2000), pp. 11–24; P. Latham and L. M. Saari, "The Effects of Holding Goal Difficulty Constant on Assigned and Participatively Set Goals," *Academy of Management Journal* (March 1979), pp. 163–168; M. Erez, P. C. Earley, and C. L. Hulin, "The Impact of Participation on Goal Acceptance and Performance: A Two Step Model," *Academy of Management Journal* (March 1985), pp. 50–66; and G. P. Latham, M. Erez, and E. A. Locke, "Resolving Scientific Disputes by the Joint Design of Crucial Experiments by the Antagonists: Application to the Erez Latham Dispute Regarding Participation in Goal Setting," *Journal of Applied Psychology* (November 1988), pp. 753–772. For information on effectiveness of MBO, see, for example, F. Dahlsten, A. Styhre, and M. Williander, "The Unintended Consequences of Management by Objectives: The Volume Growth Target at Volvo Cars," *Leadership & Organization Development Journal* (July 2005), pp. 529–541; J. R. Crow, "Crashing with the Nose Up: Building a Cooperative Work Environment," *Journal for Quality and Participation* (Spring 2002), pp. 45–50; and E. C. Hollensbe and J. P. Guthrie, "Group Pay-for-Performance Plans: The Role of Spontaneous Goal Setting," *Academy of Management Review,* October 2000, pp. 864–72.

19. P. N. Romani, "MBO by Any Other Name Is Still MBO," *Supervision,* December 1997, pp. 6–8; and A. W. Schrader and G. T. Seward, "MBO Makes Dollar Sense," *Personnel Journal* (July 1989), pp. 32–37.

20. R. Rodgers and J. E. Hunter, "Impact of Management by Objectives on Organizational Productivity," *Journal of Applied Psychology* (April 1991), pp. 322–336.

21. G. P. Latham, "The Motivational Benefits of Goal-Setting," *Academy of Management Executive,* November 2004, pp. 126–129.

22. For additional information on goals, see, for instance, P. Drucker, *The Executive in Action* (New York: HarperCollins Books, 1996), pp. 207–214; and E. A. Locke and G. P. Latham,

A Theory of Goal Setting and Task Performance (Upper Saddle River, NJ: Prentice Hall, 1990).

23. J. L. Roberts, "Signed, Sealed, Delivered?" *Newsweek,* June 20, 2005, pp. 44–46.

24. Several of these factors were suggested by R. K. Bresser and R. C. Bishop, "Dysfunctional Effects of Formal Planning: Two Theoretical Explanations," *Academy of Management Review,* October 1983, pp. 588–599; and J. S. Armstrong, "The Value of Formal Planning for Strategic Decisions: Review of Empirical Research," *Strategic Management Journal,* (July–September 1982), pp. 197–211.

25. K. Garber, "Powering the Information Age," *U.S. News & World Report,* April 2009, pp. 46–48; and S. Hamm, "It's Too Darn Hot," *BusinessWeek,* March 31, 2008, pp, 60–63.

26. A. Campbell, "Tailored, Not Benchmarked: A Fresh Look at Corporate Planning," *Harvard Business Review*, March–April 1999, pp. 41–50.

27. And the Survey Says box based on American Management Association, "Mercer Study Shows Workforce Priorities for 2010," www.amanet.org (October 21, 2009); M. Weinstein, "Coming Up Short? Join the Club," *Training* (April 2006), p. 14; J. Yang and M. E. Mullins, "Employee's Concerns in Mergers and Acquisitions," *USA Today,* June 6, 2007, p. 1B; J. Choi, D. Lovallo, and A. Tarasova, "Better Strategy for Business Units: A McKinsey Global Survey," *McKinsey Quarterly Online,* www.mckinseyquarterly.com (July 2007); G. Kranz, "Workers Unprepared," *Workforce Management Online,* March 13, 2008; and American Management Association, "2003 Survey on Leadership Challenges," www.amanet.org.

28. J. H. Sheridan, "Focused on Flow," *IW,* October 18, 1999, pp. 46–51.

29. Brews and Hunt, "Learning to Plan and Planning to Learn: Resolving the Planning School/Learning School Debate."

30. R. J. Newman, "Coming and Going," *U.S. News and World Report,* January 23, 2006, pp. 50–52; T. Atlas, "Bangalore's Big Dreams," *U.S. News and World Report,* May 2, 2005, pp. 50–52; and K. H. Hammonds, "Smart, Determined, Ambitious, Cheap: The New Face of Global Competition," *Fast Company,* February 2003, pp. 90–97.

31. See, for example, P. Tarraf and R. Molz, "Competitive Intelligence," *SAM Advanced Management Journal* (Autumn 2006), pp. 24–34; W. M. Fitzpatrick, "Uncovering Trade Secrets: The Legal and Ethical Conundrum of Creative Competitive Intelligence," *SAM Advanced Management Journal* (Summer 2003), pp. 4–12; L. Lavelle, "The Case of the Corporate Spy," *BusinessWeek,* November 26, 2001, pp. 56–58; C. Britton, "Deconstructing Advertising: What Your Competitor's Advertising Can Tell You About Their Strategy," *Competitive Intelligence,* January/February 2002, pp. 15–19; and L. Smith, "Business Intelligence Progress in Jeopardy," *InformationWeek,* March 4, 2002, p. 74.

32. S. Greenbard, "New Heights in Business Intelligence," *Business Finance,* March 2002, pp. 41–46; K. A. Zimmermann, "The Democratization of Business Intelligence," *KN World,* May 2002, pp. 20–21; and C. Britton, "Deconstructing Advertising: What Your Competitor's Advertising Can Tell You About Their Strategy," *Competitive Intelligence,* January–February 2002, pp. 15–19.

33. C. Hausman, "Business-Ethics News Featured in World-Press Reports," *Ethics Newsline,* March 14, 2011; and L. Weathersby, "Take This Job and ***** It," *Fortune,* January 7, 2002, p. 122.

34. P. Lattiman, "Hilton and Starwood Settle Dispute," *New York Times Online,* December 22, 2010; "Starwood vs. Hilton," *Hotels' Investment Outlook,* June 2009, p. 14; R. Kidder, "Hotel Industry Roiled by Corporate Espionage Claim," *Ethics Newsline,* www.globalethicslorg/newsline; Reuters, "Hilton Hotels Is Subpoenaed in Espionage Case," *New York Times Online,* April 22, 2009; T. Audi, "U.S. Probes Hilton Over Theft Claims,"

Wall Street Journal, April 22, 2009, p. B1; and T. Audi, "Hilton Is Sued Over Luxury Chain," *Wall Street Journal,* April 17, 2009, p. B1.

35. B. Rosner, "HR Should Get a Clue: Corporate Spying Is Real," *Workforce,* April 2001, pp. 72–75.

36. K. Western, "Ethical Spying," *Business Ethics,* September–October 1995, pp. 22–23.

YOUR TURN TO BE A MANAGER

Foundations of **Planning**

Skill Development: Goal Setting

It's been said that if you don't know where you're going, any road will get you there. It has also been said that the shortest distance between two points is a straight line. These two "adages" emphasize the importance of goals. Managers are typically judged on their ability to achieve goals. If individuals or units in the organization lack goals, there can be no direction or unity of effort. So successful managers are good at setting their own goals and helping others set goals.

Personal Insights: What's My Goal Orientation?

People have different views about how they approach work. Please read each of the following statements and select the response that reflects how much you agree or disagree with the statement.

1 = Strongly disagree

2 = Disagree

3 = Sort of disagree

4 = Neither

5 = Sort of agree

6 = Agree

7 = Strongly agree

1. I am willing to select a challenging work assignment that I can learn a lot from.

2. I often look for opportunities to develop new skills and knowledge.

3. I enjoy challenging and difficult tasks at work where I'll learn new skills.

4. For me, further development of my work ability is important enough to take risks.

5. I like to show that I can perform better than my coworkers.

6. I try to figure out what it takes to prove my ability to others at work.

7. I enjoy it when others at work are aware of how well I am doing.

8. I prefer to work on projects where I can prove my ability to others.

9. I would avoid taking on a new task if there was a chance that I would appear rather incompetent to others.

10. Avoiding a show of low ability is more important to me than learning a new skill.

11. I'm concerned about taking on a task at work if my performance would reveal that I had low ability.

12. I prefer to avoid situations at work where I might perform poorly.

Source: D. VandeWalle, "Development and Validation of a Work Domain Goal Orientation Instrument," *Educational and Psychological Measurement,* December 1997, pp. 995–1015. With permission. Adaptations suggested in correspondence with the author. Sample comparative data was obtained from D. VandeWalle, W. L. Cron, and J. W. Slocum, Jr., "The Role of Goal Orientation Following Performance Feedback," *Journal of Applied Psychology* (August 2001), pp. 629–640.

Analysis and Interpretation

This questionnaire assesses your views toward developing or demonstrating ability in achievement situations. It breaks down goal orientations into three categories: (1) *learning orientation*—a desire to develop yourself by acquiring new skills, mastering new situations, and improving your competence (items 1–4); (2) *prove performance orientation*—the desire to prove your competence and to gain favorable judgments about it (items 5–8); and (3) *avoiding orientation*—the desire to avoid the disproving of your competence and to avoid negative judgments about it (items 9–12).

Add up your scores separately for the three categories and divide by 4. Your scores will range from 1 to 7 in each. The higher your score in a category, the greater your goal preferences in achievement situations. For instance, the higher your learning goal orientation, the more adaptive you are in demonstrating persistence, escalated effort, and engaging in solution-oriented self-instruction. No specific guidelines are offered for interpreting your score, but a sample of 102 undergraduate business students had mean scores of 5.12, 4.41, and 4.31 in the three respective categories.

Skill Basics

In addition to your own focus on goals, employees should also have a clear understanding of what they're attempting to accomplish. Managers have the responsibility to help employees with this understanding as they set work goals.

You can be more effective at setting goals if you use the following eight suggestions.

1. *Identify an employee's key job tasks.* Goal setting begins by defining what it is that you want your employees to accomplish. The best source for this information is each employee's job description.

2. *Establish measurable, specific, and challenging goals for each key task.* Identify the level of performance expected of each employee. Specify the target toward which the employee is working.

3. *Specify the deadlines for each goal.* Putting deadlines on each goal reduces ambiguity. Deadlines, however, should not be set arbitrarily. Rather, they need to be realistic given the tasks to be completed.

4. *Allow the employee to participate actively.* When employees participate in goal setting, they're more likely to accept the goals. However, it must be sincere participation. That is, employees must perceive that you are truly seeking their input, not just going through the motions.

5. *Prioritize goals.* When you give someone more than one goal, it's important to rank the goals in order of importance. The purpose of prioritizing is to encourage the employee to take action and expend effort on each goal in proportion to its importance.

6. *Rate goals for difficulty and importance.* Goal setting should not encourage people to choose easy goals. Instead, goals should be rated for their difficulty and importance. When goals are rated, individuals can be given credit for trying difficult goals, even if they don't fully achieve them.

7. *Build in feedback mechanisms to assess goal progress.* Feedback lets employees know whether their level of

effort is sufficient to attain the goal. Feedback should be both self-generated and supervisor-generated. Feedback should also be frequent and recurring.

8. *Link rewards to goal attainment.* It's natural for employees to ask, "What's in it for me?" Linking rewards to the achievement of goals will help answer that question.

Based on E. A. Locke and G. P. Latham, *Goal-Setting: A Motivational Technique That Works!* (Upper Saddle River, NJ: Prentice Hall, 1984); and E. A. Locke and G. P. Latham, "Building a Practically Useful Theory of Goal Setting and Task Motivation," *American Psychologist,* September 2002, pp. 705–717.

Skill Application

You worked your way through college while holding down a part-time job bagging groceries at the Food Town supermarket chain. You liked working in the food industry, and when you graduated, you accepted a position with Food Town as a management trainee. Three years have passed and you've gained experience in the grocery store industry and in operating a large supermarket. Several months ago, you received a promotion to store manager at one of the chain's locations. One of the things you've liked about Food Town is that it gives store managers a great deal of autonomy in running their stores. The company provides very general guidelines to its managers. Top management is concerned with the bottom line;

for the most part, how you get there is up to you. Now that you're finally a store manager, you want to establish an MBO-type program in your store. You like the idea that everyone should have clear goals to work toward and then be evaluated against those goals.

Your store employs 70 people, although except for the managers, most work only 20 to 30 hours per week. You have six people reporting to you: an assistant manager; a weekend manager; and grocery, produce, meat, and bakery managers. The only highly skilled jobs belong to the butchers who have strict training and regulatory guidelines. Other less-skilled jobs include cashier, shelf stocker, maintenance worker, and grocery bagger.

Specifically describe how you would go about setting goals in your new position. Include examples of goals for the jobs of butcher, cashier, and bakery manager.

Skill Practice

1. Set personal and academic goals you want to achieve by the end of this college term. Prioritize and rate them for difficulty.

2. Where do you want to be in five years? Do you have specific five-year goals? Establish three goals you want to achieve in five years. Make sure these goals are specific, challenging, and measurable.

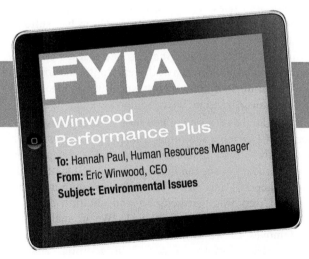

For Your Immediate Action

Winwood Performance Plus

To: Hannah Paul, Human Resources Manager
From: Eric Winwood, CEO
Subject: Environmental Issues

Hannah, as you know our entertainment consulting business has had a remarkable couple of years. The success we've achieved wouldn't be possible without the hard work our associates do, and I'm honored to be surrounded by such committed and talented individuals. I feel that our next push as

a company should be to become more environmentally responsible. All of us (me included) generate a lot of paper as we do our work, so I think our first step (and main focus right now) should be on controlling paper waste. I would like you to create a company-wide program for controlling paper waste. Before we get our associates involved, I'd like you to set some goals and develop some plans for this program. Get me your report (keep it to one page, please) outlining these goals and plans as soon as you can.

This fictionalized company and message were created for educational purposes only, and not meant to reflect positively or negatively on management practices by any company that may share this name.

Case Application:
Flip Flop: Part 2

Four years. That's all it took for the Flip video camera, the most popular video camera in the United States, to go from hot start-up to obsolete. But even in the life cycle of tech products where things happen fast, this seemed to be in the blink of an eye—unusually fast, as one analyst said, especially for a "hot" product. What happened?

The Flip camera broke new ground when it was introduced. Customers loved that it was pocketable, inexpensive, and easy to use. Flip's name came from the arm that flips out of the camera body and lets the user connect it directly to a computer. The camera also had video-editing software that opened when it was connected to the computer. Although the actual video camera seemed tiny, it recorded remarkably good footage for a camera of its size. In addition, unlike other video cameras, the Flip could be held comfortably in front of you so you didn't feel "removed" from the event being recorded. The product was exactly what the founders envisioned—a practical pocket-sized, inexpensive, and easy-to-use video camera.

When Cisco Systems decided to acquire Flip, one of the hottest consumer products to hit store shelves in a while, many industry analysts questioned that decision, believing it was an "odd fit" for the company that's best known for its business enterprise networking services. The Flip camera was the first true consumer product under the Cisco umbrella. In its announcement, Cisco said that the acquisition was a key to its strategy to expand momentum in the media-enabled home. There was no doubt that Cisco was serious about the company's desire to expand its market from technical components into true consumer electronics. And there was another variable at work here, as well. The acquisition of Pure Digital Technologies (the actual company behind the Flip camera) was another sign that Cisco was making a statement by aggressively pushing into new markets when many of its competitors were floundering during the economic downturn.

Pure Digital became a part of Cisco's Consumer Business Group, which also included Linksys home networking, audio, and media-storage products. When Cisco acquired Pure Digital it also named Jonathan Kaplan, Pure Digital's CEO, as Cisco's senior vice president and general manager in charge of consumer products. Kaplan was to help set Cisco's strategy in this area. And Cisco did what it thought was necessary to compete in the consumer market using Flip as a key focus. It spent heavily on consumer branding, hiring celebrities such as Ellen Page to star in its television commercials and

paying for product placement in shows such as *24*. Even Cisco's CEO, John Chambers (who owned eight Flips), shot videos on a Flip and constantly had it in view during television interviews. It even had Sean "Diddy" Combs design a custom Flip camera. Flip sales during fiscal 2010 were $317 million. However, it must not have been enough. Cisco had suffered several quarters of disappointing financial results and challenges in its core businesses. Analysts said that the company had been trying to do too many different things and losing its focus on what made it great. In retrospect, it was easy to see that major strategic changes were looming.

First, Cisco announced in February that Jonathan Kaplan was leaving Cisco to pursue "other career opportunities." Then, CEO Chambers said in an interview that "revenue from consumer products over the holiday season fell short of the company's hopes." Then came the announcement in mid-April 2011 that Cisco was restructuring and shutting down its Flip video-camera unit. Chambers said, "We are making key, targeted moves as we align operations in support of our network-centric platform strategy." In addition, analysts pointed to the rapid innovation of smartphones as one of the most disruptive trends ever seen. As phones with built-in cameras and editing apps hit the market, it was only a matter of time until Flip became obsolete.

DISCUSSION QUESTIONS

1. "I don't think there's an analyst on the planet who thought that Flip was a good acquisition for Cisco." Why do you think these analysts felt that way?

2. Evaluate Cisco's consumer marketing efforts. Why might it be difficult for a company accustomed to selling to businesses to sell products to consumers?

3. Could Cisco have done anything else to build up its consumer products including the Flip? What were Flip's strengths? What external threats were happening during this time period?

4. Why do you think Cisco decided to shut down the Flip business rather than try to sell it?

5. What type of strategies do you see described in this case? Be specific.

6. What role would goal setting and planning have played in: (a) Flip's founding, (b) Cisco's acquisition of Flip, (c) Cisco's managing of the Flip business unit, and (d) Cisco's strategic decision to shut down the Flip business unit?

Organizational Structure and Design

Organizational Structure and Design

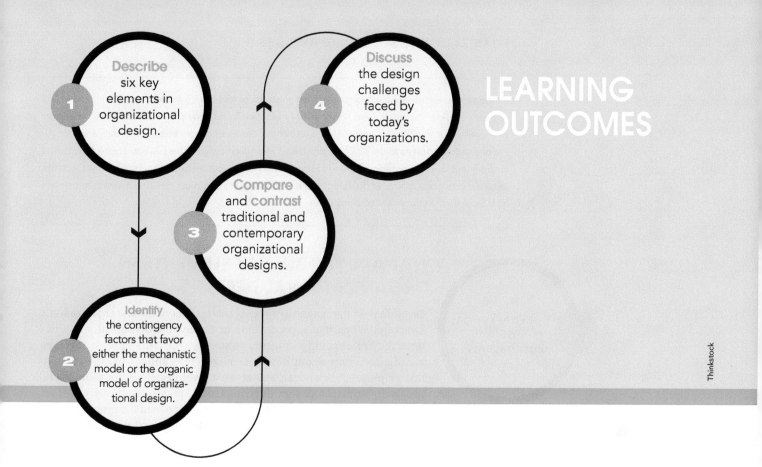

LEARNING OUTCOMES

1 **Describe** six key elements in organizational design.

2 **Identify** the contingency factors that favor either the mechanistic model or the organic model of organizational design.

3 **Compare** and **contrast** traditional and contemporary organizational designs.

4 **Discuss** the design challenges faced by today's organizations.

Thinkstock

Volunteers Work

They're individuals you might never have thought of as being part of an organization's structure, but for many organizations, volunteers provide a much-needed source of labor.[1] Maybe you've volunteered at a Habitat for Humanity build, a homeless shelter, or some nonprofit organization. However, what if the volunteer assignment was at a for-profit business and the job description read like this: "Spend a few hours a day, at your computer, supplying answers online to customer questions about technical matters like how to set up an Internet home network or how to program a new high-definition television," all for no pay. Many large corporations, start-up companies, and venture capitalists are betting that this "emerging corps of Web-savvy helpers will transform the field of customer service."

Welcome to the fascinating world of organization structure and design in the twenty-first century! Did you ever consider that businesses might actually have work tasks completed by someone other than employees...for free? In this chapter, we present the basics of organizational structure and design. We define the concepts and their key components and how managers use these to create a structured environment in which organizational members can do their work efficiently and effectively. Once the organization's goals, plans, and strategies are in place, managers must develop a structure that will best facilitate the attainment of those goals.

1 Describe six key elements in organizational design.

WHAT ARE THE SIX KEY ELEMENTS IN ORGANIZATIONAL DESIGN?

Organizing is the function of management that creates the organization's structure. When managers develop or change the organization's structure, they're engaging in **organization design**. This process involves making decisions about how specialized jobs should be, the rules to guide employees' behaviors, and at what level decisions are to be made. Although organization design decisions are typically made by top-level managers, it's important for everyone involved to understand the process. Why? Because each of us works in some type of organization structure, and we need to know how and why things get done. In addition, given the changing environment and the need for organizations to adapt, you should begin understanding what tomorrow's structures may look like—they will be the settings you'll be working in.

Few topics in management have undergone as much change in the past few years as that of organizing and organizational structure. Managers are reevaluating traditional approaches and exploring new structural designs that best support and facilitate employees doing the organization's work—designs that can achieve efficiency but are also flexible.

The basic concepts of organization design formulated by management writers such as Henri Fayol and Max Weber offered structural principles for managers to follow. Almost 80 years have passed since many of those principles were originally proposed. Given that length of time and all the changes that have taken place, you'd think that those principles would be mostly worthless today. Surprisingly, they're not. They still provide valuable insights into designing effective and efficient organizations. Of course, we've also gained a great deal of knowledge over the years as to their limitations. In the following sections, we discuss the six basic elements of organizational structure: work specialization, departmentalization, authority and responsibility, span of control, centralization versus decentralization, and formalization.

What Is Work Specialization?

At the Wilson Sporting Goods factory in Ada, Ohio, workers make every football used in the National Football League and most of those used in college and high school football games. To meet daily output goals, the workers specialize in job tasks such as molding, stitching and sewing, lacing, and so forth.[2] This is an example of **work specialization**, which is dividing work activities into separate job tasks. Individual employees "specialize" in doing part of an activity rather than the entire activity in order to increase work output. It's also known as division of labor.

Wilson Sporting Goods Company uses work specialization in making some 700,000 footballs a year for the Pee Wee leagues to the National Football Association. The activities involved in handcrafting a Wilson football are divided into 13 separate job tasks, beginning with cutting panels from leather and ending with putting the balls into a form and filling them with high pressure. Shown here is an employee specializing in the task of lacing the ball. Also known as division of labor, work specialization is an organizing mechanism that helps employees boost their productivity and makes efficient use of workers' diverse skills.

Jeff Haynes/Newscom

Work specialization allows organizations to efficiently use the diversity of skills that workers have. In most organizations, some tasks require highly developed skills; others can be performed by employees with lower skill levels. If all workers were engaged in all the steps of, say, a manufacturing process, all would need the skills necessary to perform both the most demanding and the least demanding jobs. Thus, except when performing the most highly skilled or highly sophisticated tasks, employees would be working below their skill levels. In addition, skilled workers are paid more than unskilled workers, and, because wages tend to reflect the highest level of skill, all workers would be paid at highly skilled rates to do easy tasks—an inefficient use of resources. This concept explains why you rarely find a cardiac surgeon closing up a patient after surgery. Instead, doctors doing their residencies in open-heart surgery and learning the skill usually stitch and staple the patient after the surgeon has finished the surgery.

Early proponents of work specialization believed that it could lead to great increases in productivity. At the beginning of the twentieth century, that generalization was reasonable. Because specialization was not widely practiced, its introduction almost always generated higher productivity. But a good thing can be carried too far. At some point, the human diseconomies—boredom, fatigue, stress, low productivity, poor quality, increased absenteeism, and high turnover—exceed the economic advantages (see Exhibit 1).[3]

WHAT IS TODAY'S VIEW OF SPECIALIZATION? Most managers today see work specialization as an important organizing mechanism because it helps employees be more efficient. For example, McDonald's uses high specialization to get its products made and delivered to customers efficiently. However, managers also have to recognize its limitations. That's why companies such as Avery-Dennison, Ford Australia, Hallmark, and American Express use minimal work specialization and instead give employees a broad range of tasks to do.

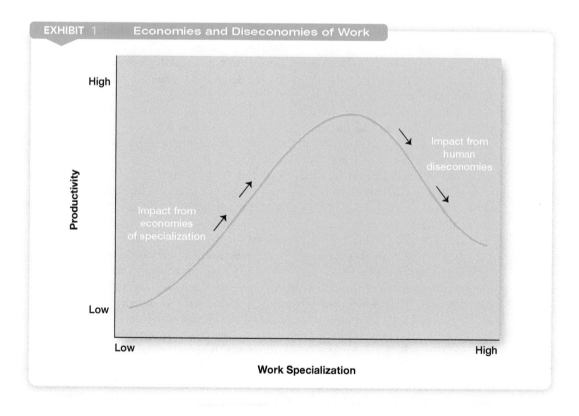

EXHIBIT 1   Economies and Diseconomies of Work

---

organizing
The function of management that creates the organization's structure

organization design
When managers develop or change the organization's structure

work specialization
Dividing work activities into separate job tasks; also called division of labor

EXHIBIT 2   Types of Departmentalization

• **Functional**	Groups employees based on work performed (e.g., engineering, accounting, information systems, human resources)
• **Product**	Groups employees based on major product areas in the corporation (e.g., women's footwear, men's footwear, and apparel and accessories)
• **Customer**	Groups employees based on customers' problems and needs (e.g., wholesale, retail, government)
• **Geographic**	Groups employees based on location served (e.g., North, South, Midwest, East)
• **Process**	Groups employees based on the basis of work or customer flow (e.g., testing, payment)

What Is Departmentalization?

Early management writers argued that after deciding what job tasks will be done by whom, common work activities needed to be grouped back together so work gets done in a coordinated and integrated way. How jobs are grouped together is called departmentalization. There are five common forms of departmentalization (see Exhibit 2) although an organization may use its own unique classification. No single method of departmentalization was advocated by the early writers. The method or methods used should reflect the grouping that would best contribute to the attainment of the goals of the organization and the individual units.

HOW ARE ACTIVITIES GROUPED?   One of the most popular ways to group activities is by functions performed, or functional departmentalization. A manager might organize the workplace by separating engineering, accounting, information systems, human resources, and purchasing specialists into departments. Functional departmentalization can be used in all types of organizations. Only the functions change to reflect the organization's objectives and activities. The major advantage to functional departmentalization is the achievement of economies of scale by placing people with common skills and specializations into common units.

Product departmentalization focuses attention on major product areas in the corporation. Each product is under the authority of a senior manager who is a specialist in, and is responsible for, everything having to do with his or her product line. One company that uses product departmentalization is Nike. Its structure is based on its varied product lines, which include athletic and dress/casual footwear, sports apparel and accessories, and performance equipment. If an organization's activities were service related rather than product related, each service would be autonomously grouped. The advantage of product grouping is that it increases accountability for product performance, because all activities related to a specific product are under the direction of a single manager.

The particular type of customer an organization seeks to reach can also dictate employee grouping. The sales activities in an office supply firm, for instance, can be divided into three departments that serve retail, wholesale, and government customers. A large law office can segment its staff on the basis of whether it serves corporate or individual clients. The assumption underlying customer departmentalization is that customers in each department have a common set of problems and needs that can best be met by specialists.

Another way to departmentalize is on the basis of geography or territory— geographic departmentalization. The sales function might have western, southern, midwestern, and eastern regions. If an organization's customers are scattered over a large geographic area, this form of departmentalization can be valuable. For instance, the organization structure of Coca-Cola reflects the company's operations in two broad geographic areas—the North American sector and the international sector (which includes the Pacific Rim, the European Community, Northeast Europe and Africa, and Latin America).

The final form of departmentalization is called process departmentalization, which groups activities on the basis of work or customer flow—like that found in many states' motor vehicle offices or in health care clinics. Units are organized around common skills needed to complete a certain process. If you've ever been to a state motor vehicle office to get a driver's license, you've probably experienced process departmentalization. With separate departments to handle applications, testing, information and photo processing, and payment collection, customers "flow" through the various departments in sequence to get their licenses.

WHAT IS TODAY'S VIEW OF DEPARTMENTALIZATION? Most large organizations continue to use most or all of the departmental groups suggested by the early management writers. Black & Decker, for instance, organizes its divisions along functional lines, its manufacturing units around processes, its sales around geographic regions, and its sales regions around customer groupings. However, many organizations use cross-functional teams, which are teams made up of individuals from various departments and that cross traditional departmental lines. These teams have been useful especially as tasks have become more complex and diverse skills are needed to accomplish those tasks.[4]

Finally, today's competitive environment has refocused the attention of management on its customers. To better monitor the needs of customers and to be able to respond to changes in those needs, many organizations are giving greater emphasis to customer departmentalization.

What Are Authority and Responsibility?

To understand authority and responsibility, you also have to be familiar with the chain of command, the line of authority extending from upper organizational levels to lower levels, which clarifies who reports to whom. Managers need to consider it when organizing work because it helps employees with questions such as "Who do I report to?" or "Who do I go to if I have a problem?" So, what *are* authority and responsibility?

Authority refers to the rights inherent in a managerial position to give orders and expect the orders to be obeyed. Authority was a major concept discussed by the early management writers as they viewed it as the glue that held an organization together.[5] It was delegated downward to lower-level managers, giving them certain rights while prescribing certain limits within which to operate. Each management position had specific inherent rights that incumbents acquired from the position's rank or title. Authority, therefore, is related to one's position within an organization and has nothing to do with the personal characteristics of an individual manager. When a position of authority is vacated, the person who has left the position no longer has any authority. The authority remains with the position and its new incumbent.

When managers delegate authority, they must allocate commensurate responsibility. That is, when employees are given rights, they also assume a corresponding obligation to perform. And they should be held accountable for their performance! Allocating authority without responsibility and accountability creates opportunities for abuse. Likewise, no one should be held responsible or accountable for something over which he or she has no authority.

At Dell, customer departmentalization allows the computer firm to better understand its customers and respond to their needs. Dell organizes its customers into eight segments: home and home office, small and medium business, large business, state and local government, federal government, K through 12 institutions, higher education institutions, and health care. To reach more home and home-office users, Dell has adopted a retail strategy that enables consumers to buy its personal computers in retail outlets worldwide. Through a partnership with Gome Group, China's largest electronics retailer, Dell plans to expand its laptop and desktop sales. Shown here are Dell products on display at a Gome store in Beijing.

Ng Han Guan/AP Images

departmentalization
How jobs are grouped together

functional departmentalization
Grouping activities by functions performed

product departmentalization
Grouping activities by major product areas

customer departmentalization
Grouping activities by customer

geographic departmentalization
Grouping activities on the basis of geography or territory

process departmentalization
Grouping activities on the basis of work or customer flow

cross-functional teams
Teams made up of individuals from various departments and that cross traditional departmental lines

chain of command
The line of authority extending from upper organizational levels to lower levels, which clarifies who reports to whom

authority
The rights inherent in a managerial position to give orders and expect the orders to be obeyed

responsibility
An obligation to perform assigned duties

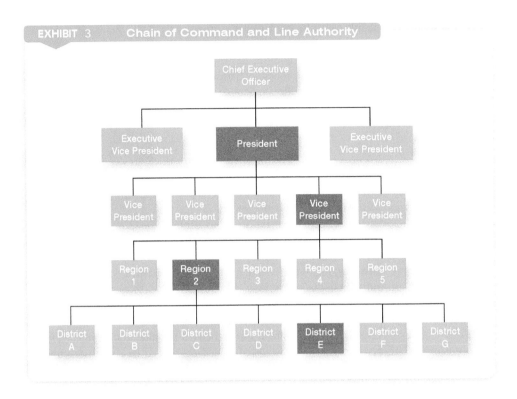

EXHIBIT 3 Chain of Command and Line Authority

WHAT ARE THE DIFFERENT TYPES OF AUTHORITY RELATIONSHIPS?   The early management writers distinguished between two forms of authority: line authority and staff authority. Line authority entitles a manager to direct the work of an employee. It is the employer–employee authority relationship that extends from the top of the organization to the lowest echelon, according to the chain of command, as shown in Exhibit 3. As a link in the chain of command, a manager with line authority has the right to direct the work of employees and to make certain decisions without consulting anyone. Of course, in the chain of command, every manager is also subject to the direction of his or her superior.

Keep in mind that sometimes the term *line* is used to differentiate line managers from staff managers. In this context, *line* refers to managers whose organizational function contributes directly to the achievement of organizational objectives. In a manufacturing firm, line managers are typically in the production and sales functions, whereas managers in human resources and payroll are considered staff managers with staff authority. Whether a manager's function is classified as line or staff depends on the organization's objectives. For example, at Staff Builders, a supplier of temporary employees, interviewers have a line function. Similarly, at the payroll firm of ADP, payroll is a line function.

As organizations get larger and more complex, line managers find that they do not have the time, expertise, or resources to get their jobs done effectively. In response, they create staff authority functions to support, assist, advise, and generally reduce some of their informational burdens. The hospital administrator cannot effectively handle the purchasing of all the supplies the hospital needs, so she creates a purchasing department, a staff department. Of course, the head of the purchasing department has line authority over the purchasing agents who work for him. The hospital administrator might also find that she is overburdened and needs an assistant. In creating the position of her assistant, she has created a staff position. Exhibit 4 illustrates line and staff authority.

WHAT IS UNITY OF COMMAND?   An employee who has to report to two or more bosses might have to cope with conflicting demands or priorities.[6] Accordingly, the early writers believed that each employee should report to only one manager, a term called unity of command. In those rare instances when the unity of command had to be violated, a clear separation of activities and a supervisor responsible for each was always explicitly designated.

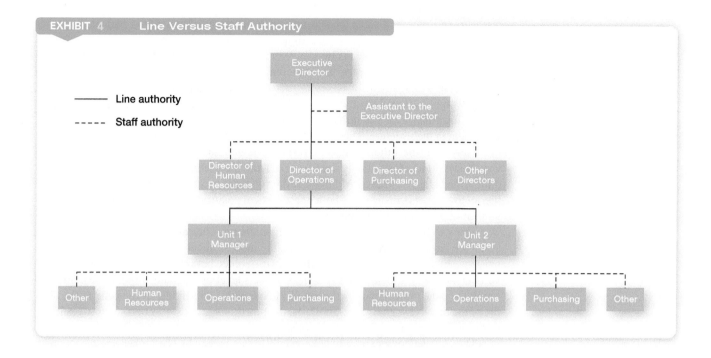

EXHIBIT 4   Line Versus Staff Authority

Unity of command was logical when organizations were relatively simple. Under some circumstances it is still sound advice and organizations continue to adhere to it. But advances in technology, for instance, allow access to organizational information that was once accessible only to top managers. Moreover, with computers, employees can communicate with anyone else in the organization without going through the formal communication channels of the chain of command. As such, in some instances, strict adherence to the unity of command creates a degree of inflexibility that hinders an organization's performance.

HOW DOES TODAY'S VIEW OF AUTHORITY AND RESPONSIBILITY DIFFER FROM THE HISTORICAL VIEW?   The early management writers were enamored of authority. They assumed that the rights inherent in one's formal position in an organization were the sole source of influence, and they believed that managers were all-powerful. This assumption might have been true 60 or even 30 years ago. Organizations were simpler. Staff was less important. Managers were only minimally dependent on technical specialists. Under such conditions, influence is the same as authority. And the higher a manager's position in the organization, the more influence he or she had. However, those conditions no longer exist. Researchers and practitioners of management now recognize that you don't have to be a manager to have power and that power is not perfectly correlated with one's level in the organization.

Authority is an important concept in organizations, but an exclusive focus on authority produces a narrow, unrealistic view of influence. Today, we recognize that authority is but one element in the larger concept of power.

HOW DO AUTHORITY AND POWER DIFFER?   Authority and power are often considered the same thing, but they're not. Authority is a right. Its legitimacy is based on an authority figure's position in the organization. Authority goes with the job. Power, on the other hand,

---

line authority
Authority that entitles a manager to direct the work of an employee

staff authority
Positions with some authority that have been created to support, assist, and advise those holding line authority

unity of command
Structure in which each employee reports to only one manager

power
An individual's capacity to influence decisions

refers to an individual's capacity to influence decisions. Authority is part of the larger concept of power. That is, the formal rights that come with an individual's position in the organization are just one means by which an individual can affect the decision process.

Exhibit 5 visually depicts the difference between authority and power. The two-dimensional arrangement of boxes in part A portrays authority. The area in which the authority applies is defined by the horizontal dimension. Each horizontal grouping represents a functional area. The influence one holds in the organization is defined by the vertical dimension in the structure. The higher one is in the organization, the greater one's authority.

Power, on the other hand, is a three-dimensional concept (the cone in part B of Exhibit 5). It includes not only the functional and hierarchical dimensions but also a third dimension called centrality. Although authority is defined by one's vertical position in the hierarchy, power is made up of both one's vertical position and one's distance from the organization's power core or center.

Think of the cone in Exhibit 5 as an organization. The center of the cone is the power core. The closer you are to the power core, the more influence you have on decisions. The existence of a power core is, in fact, the only difference between A and B in Exhibit 5. The vertical hierarchy dimension in A is merely one's level on the outer edge of the cone. The top of the cone corresponds to the top of the hierarchy, the middle of the cone to the middle of the hierarchy, and so on. Similarly, the functional groups in A become wedges in the cone. Each wedge represents a functional area.

The cone analogy explicitly acknowledges two facts: (1) The higher one moves in an organization (an increase in authority), the closer one moves to the power core; and (2) it is not necessary to have authority in order to wield power because one can move horizontally inward toward the power core without moving up. For instance, assistants often are

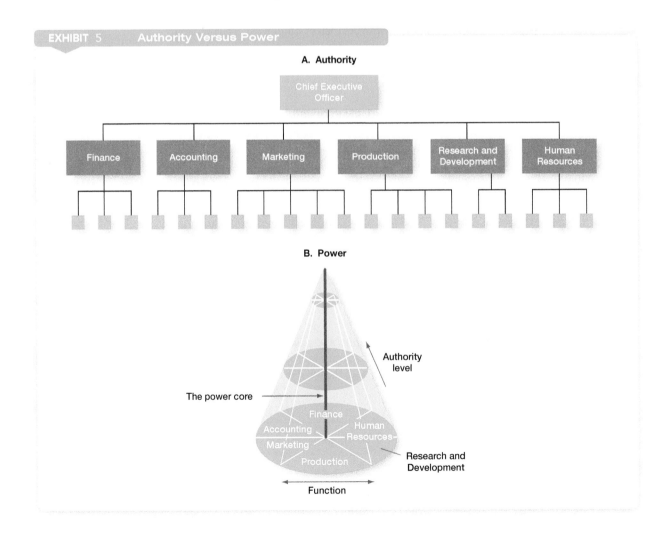

EXHIBIT 5   Authority Versus Power

A. Authority

B. Power

EXHIBIT 6	Types of Power
Coercive power	Power based on fear.
Reward power	Power based on the ability to distribute something that others value.
Legitimate power	Power based on one's position in the formal hierarchy.
Expert power	Power based on one's expertise, special skill, or knowledge.
Referent power	Power based on identification with a person who has desirable resources or personal traits.

powerful in a company even though they have little authority. As gatekeepers for their bosses, these assistants have considerable influence over whom their bosses see and when they see them. Furthermore, because they're regularly relied upon to pass information on to their bosses, they have some control over what their bosses hear. It's not unusual for a $105,000-a-year middle manager to tread carefully in order not to upset the boss's $45,000-a-year administrative assistant. Why? Because the assistant has power. This individual may be low in the authority hierarchy but close to the power core.

Likewise, low-ranking employees who have relatives, friends, or associates in high places might also be close to the power core. So, too, are employees with scarce and important skills. The lowly production engineer with 20 years of experience in a company might be the only one in the firm who knows the inner workings of all the old production machinery. When pieces of this old equipment break down, only this engineer understands how to fix them. Suddenly, the engineer's influence is much greater than it would appear from his or her level in the vertical hierarchy. What do these examples tell us about power? They indicate that power can come from different areas. French and Raven identified five sources, or bases, of power: coercive, reward, legitimate, expert, and referent.[7] We summarize them in Exhibit 6.

What Is Span of Control?

How many employees can a manager efficiently and effectively supervise? This question of span of control received a great deal of attention from early management writers. Although early writers came to no consensus on a specific number, most favored small spans—typically no more than six workers—in order to maintain close control.[8] However, several writers did acknowledge level in the organization as a contingency variable. They argued that as a manager rises in an organization, he or she has to deal with a greater number of unstructured problems, so top managers need a smaller span than do middle managers, and middle managers require a smaller span than do supervisors. Over the last decade, however, we've seen some change in theories about effective spans of control.[9]

Many organizations are increasing their spans of control. The span for managers at such companies as General Electric and Kaiser Aluminum has expanded significantly in the past decade. It has also expanded in the federal government, where efforts to increase the span of control are being implemented to save time in making decisions.[10] The span of control is increasingly being determined by looking at contingency variables. It's obvious that the more training and experience employees have, the less direct supervision they need. Managers who have well-trained and experienced employees can function with a wider span. Other contingency variables that determine the appropriate span include similarity of employee tasks, the complexity of those tasks, the physical

Decentralization is key to the success of the Nordstrom department store chain. Empowering employees, like the managers and salespeople at a new store opening shown here, is a primary reason why Nordstrom stands out as the model of customer service in the retail industry. Nordstrom has built a strong corporate culture that empowers buyers, store managers, department managers, and salespeople to make decisions in the best interest of their customers. Buyers are given the freedom to acquire merchandise that reflects local lifestyles and tastes, salespeople are empowered to accept returned merchandise, and department managers have the authority to make decisions about hiring, training, and evaluating their sales teams.

Jeff Gritchen/Newscom

span of control
The number of employees a manager can efficiently and effectively supervise

It's probably an understatement to say that people were excited about the introduction of Apple's iPad.[11] Then the news broke that a small group of computer experts calling themselves Goatse Security had hacked into AT&T's Web site and found numbers that identified iPads connected to AT&T's mobile network and those numbers allowed the group to uncover 114,000 e-mail addresses of thousands of first-adopter iPad customers including prominent officials in companies, politics, and the military. AT&T called it an act of malice, condemned the hackers, and apologized to its affected customers. The group that exposed the flaw said that it did a "public service." One analyst for CNET also said that the group did a good thing. "Ethical hacking" was a phrase used. "Security researchers often disclose holes to keep vendors honest. Many sources complain that they notify companies of security vulnerabilities and that the companies take months, or even years, to provide a fix to customers. In the meantime, malicious hackers could have discovered the same hole and used it to steal data, infect computers, or attack systems without the computer owner knowing there is even a risk."

Think About:

- What do you think? Is there such a thing as "ethical hacking"?

- What ethical issues do you see here?

- What are the implications for various stakeholders in this situation?

proximity of employees, the degree to which standardized procedures are in place, the sophistication of the organization's management information system, the strength of the organization's value system, and the preferred managing style of the manager.[12]

How Do Centralization and Decentralization Differ?

One of the questions that needs to be answered when organizing is "At what level are decisions made?" Centralization is the degree to which decision making takes place at upper levels of the organization. Decentralization is the degree to which lower-level managers provide input or actually make decisions. Centralization-decentralization is not an either-or concept. Rather, it's a matter of degree. What we mean is that no organization is completely centralized or completely decentralized. Few, if any, organizations could effectively function if all their decisions were made by a select few people (centralization) or if all decisions were pushed down to the level closest to the problems (decentralization). Let's look, then, at how the early management writers viewed centralization as well as at how it exists today.

Early management writers proposed that centralization in an organization depended on the situation.[13] Their goal was the optimum and efficient use of employees. Traditional organizations were structured in a pyramid, with power and authority concentrated near the top of the organization. Given this structure, historically centralized decisions were the most prominent, but organizations today have become more complex and responsive to dynamic changes in their environments. As such, many managers believe that decisions need to be made by those individuals closest to the problems, regardless of their organizational level. In fact, the trend over the past several decades—at least in U.S. and Canadian organizations—has been a movement toward more decentralization in organizations.[14]

WHAT IS TODAY'S VIEW OF CENTRALIZATION-DECENTRALIZATION? Today, managers often choose the amount of centralization or decentralization that will allow them to best implement their decisions and achieve organizational goals.[15] What works in one organization, however, won't necessarily work in another, so managers must determine the amount of decentralization for each organization and work units within it. When managers empower employees and delegate to them the authority to make decisions on those things that affect their work and to change the way that they think about work, that's decentralization. Notice, however, that it doesn't imply that top-level managers no longer make decisions.

What Is Formalization?

Formalization refers to how standardized an organization's jobs are and the extent to which employee behavior is guided by rules and procedures. In highly formalized organizations, there are explicit job descriptions, numerous organizational rules, and clearly defined procedures covering work processes. Employees have little discretion over what's done, when it's done, and how it's done. However, where formalization is low, employees have more discretion in how they do their work. Early management writers expected organizations to be fairly formalized, as formalization went hand-in-hand with bureaucratic-style organizations.

WHAT IS TODAY'S VIEW OF FORMALIZATION? Although some formalization is necessary for consistency and control, many organizations today rely less on strict rules and standardization to guide and regulate employee behavior. For instance, consider the following situation:

> A customer comes into a branch of a large national drug store chain and drops off a roll of film for same-day developing 37 minutes after the store's cut-off time. Although the sales clerk knows he's supposed to follow the rules, he also knows he could get the film developed with no problem and wants to accommodate the customer. So he accepts the film and hopes that his manager won't find out.[16]

Did this employee do something wrong? He did "break" the rule. But by "breaking" the rule, he actually brought in revenue and provided good customer service.

Considering there are numerous situations where rules may be too restrictive, many organizations have allowed employees some latitude, giving them sufficient autonomy to make those decisions that they feel are best under the circumstances. It doesn't mean throwing out all organizational rules because there always *will* be rules that are important for employees to follow—and these rules should be explained so employees understand why it's important to adhere to them. But for other rules, employees may be given some leeway.[17]

WHAT CONTINGENCY VARIABLES AFFECT STRUCTURAL CHOICE?

The most appropriate structure to use will depend on contingency factors. In this section, we address two generic organization structure models and then look at the more popular contingency variables—strategy, size, technology, and environment.

Identify the contingency factors that favor either the mechanistic model or the organic model of organizational design.

2

How Is a Mechanistic Organization Different from an Organic Organization?

Exhibit 7 describes two organizational forms.[18] The mechanistic organization (or bureaucracy) was the natural result of combining the six elements of structure. Adhering to the chain-of-command principle ensured the existence of a formal hierarchy of authority, with each person controlled and supervised by one superior. Keeping the span of control small at increasingly higher levels in the organization created tall, impersonal structures. As the distance between the top and the bottom of the organization expanded, top management would increasingly impose rules and regulations. Because top managers couldn't control lower-level activities through direct observation and ensure the use of standard practices, they substituted rules and regulations. The early management writers' belief in a high degree of work specialization created jobs that were simple, routine, and standardized. Further specialization through the use of

---

centralization
The degree to which decision making takes place at upper levels of the organization

decentralization
The degree to which lower-level managers provide input or actually make decisions

formalization
How standardized an organization's jobs are and the extent to which employee behavior is guided by rules and procedures

mechanistic organization
A bureaucratic organization; a structure that's high in specialization, formalization, and centralization

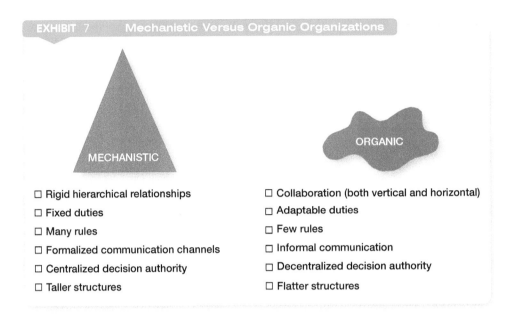

EXHIBIT 7   Mechanistic Versus Organic Organizations

MECHANISTIC

☐ Rigid hierarchical relationships

☐ Fixed duties

☐ Many rules

☐ Formalized communication channels

☐ Centralized decision authority

☐ Taller structures

ORGANIC

☐ Collaboration (both vertical and horizontal)

☐ Adaptable duties

☐ Few rules

☐ Informal communication

☐ Decentralized decision authority

☐ Flatter structures

departmentalization increased impersonality and the need for multiple layers of management to coordinate the specialized departments.

The organic organization is a highly adaptive form that is as loose and flexible as the mechanistic organization is rigid and stable. Rather than having standardized jobs and regulations, the organic organization's loose structure allows it to change rapidly as required.[19] It has division of labor, but the jobs people do are not standardized. Employees tend to be professionals who are technically proficient and trained to handle diverse problems. They need few formal rules and little direct supervision because their training has instilled in them standards of professional conduct. For instance, a petroleum engineer doesn't need to be given procedures on how to locate oil sources miles offshore. The engineer can solve most problems alone or after conferring with colleagues. Professional standards guide his or her behavior. The organic organization is low in centralization so that the professional can respond quickly to problems and because top-level managers cannot be expected to possess the expertise to make necessary decisions.

Top managers typically put a great deal of thought into designing an appropriate structure. What that appropriate structure is depends on four contingency variables: the organization's strategy, size, technology, and degree of environmental uncertainty. Let's look at these contingency variables.

How Does Strategy Affect Structure?

An organization's structure should facilitate goal achievement. Because goals are an important part of the organization's strategies, it's only logical that strategy and structure are closely linked. Alfred Chandler initially researched this relationship.[20] He studied several large U.S. companies and concluded that changes in corporate strategy led to changes in an organization's structure that supported the strategy. Specifically, he found that organizations usually begin with a single product or line. The simplicity of the strategy required only a simple or loose form of structure to execute it. As such, decisions could be centralized in the hands of a single senior manager, and complexity and formalization were low. However, as organizations grew, their strategies become more ambitious and elaborate.

Research has shown that certain structural designs work best with different organizational strategies.[21] For instance, the flexibility and free-flowing information of the organic structure works well when an organization is pursuing meaningful and unique innovations. The mechanistic organization with its efficiency, stability, and tight controls works best for companies wanting to tightly control costs.

How Does Size Affect Structure?

There's considerable evidence that an organization's size affects its structure.[22] Large organizations—typically considered to be those with more than 2,000 employees—tend to have more specialization, departmentalization, centralization, and rules and regulations than do small organizations. However, once an organization grows past a certain size, size has less influence on structure. Why? Essentially, once there are around 2,000 employees, it's already fairly mechanistic. Adding another 500 employees won't impact the structure much. On the other hand, adding 500 employees to an organization that has only 300 employees is likely to make it more mechanistic.

How Does Technology Affect Structure?

Every organization uses some form of technology to convert its inputs into outputs. For instance, workers at Whirlpool's Brazilian facility build microwave ovens and air conditioners on a standardized assembly line. Employees at FedEx Kinko's do custom design and print jobs for individual customers. And employees at Bayer's facility in Pakistan make pharmaceutical products using a continuous-flow production line. The initial research on technology's effect on structure can be traced to Joan Woodward.[23] For more information on her ground-breaking work, see the From the Past to the Present box.

From the Past to the Present

Joan Woodward, a British management scholar, studied small manufacturing firms in southern England to determine the extent to which structural design elements were related to organizational success.[24] She couldn't find any consistent pattern until she divided the firms into three distinct technologies that had increasing levels of complexity and sophistication. The first category, **unit production**, described the production of items in units or small batches. The second category, **mass production**, described large-batch manufacturing. Finally, the third and most technically complex group, **process production**, included continuous-process production. A summary of her findings regarding technology and appropriate organizational structure is shown in Exhibit 8.

Woodward's study of technology and organizational structure is one of the earliest studies of contingency theory. Her answer to the "it depends on" question would be that appropriate organizational design depends on what the organization's technology is. Other more recent studies also have shown that organizations adapt their structures to their technology depending on how routine their technology is for transforming inputs into outputs. In general, the more routine the technology, the more mechanistic the structure can be, and organizations with more nonroutine technology are more likely to have organic structures.

Think About:

- Give some examples of products produced by each of the three distinct technologies.

- Why would a mechanistic structure be more appropriate for an organization with a routine technology?

- Likewise, why would an organic structure be more appropriate for an organization with a nonroutine technology?

- Do you think Woodward's framework would still apply to today's organizations? Why or why not?

EXHIBIT 8	Woodward's Findings on Technology and Structure		
	UNIT PRODUCTION	MASS PRODUCTION	PROCESS PRODUCTION
Structural characteristics:	Low vertical differentiation	Moderate vertical differentiation	High vertical differentiation
	Low horizontal differentiation	High horizontal differentiation	Low horizontal differentiation
	Low formalization	High formalization	Low formalization
Most effective structure:	Organic	Mechanistic	Organic

---

organic organization
A structure that's low in specialization, formalization, and centralization

unit production
The production of items in units or small batches

mass production
Large-batch manufacturing

process production
Continuous flow or process production

How Does the Environment Affect Structure?

An organization's environment is a constraint on managerial discretion. It also has a major effect on an organization's structure. Essentially, mechanistic organizations are most effective in stable environments. Organic organizations are best matched with dynamic and uncertain environments.

The evidence on the environment–structure relationship helps to explain why so many managers have restructured their organizations to be lean, fast, and flexible.[25] Global competition, accelerated product innovation by competitors, knowledge management, and increased demands from customers for higher quality and faster deliveries are examples of dynamic environmental forces.[26] Mechanistic organizations tend to be ill equipped to respond to rapid environmental change. As a result, managers, such as those at Samsung Electronics, are redesigning their organizations in order to make them more organic.[27]

WHAT ARE SOME COMMON ORGANIZATIONAL DESIGNS?

3 Compare and contrast traditional and contemporary organizational designs.

In making structural decisions, managers have some common designs from which to choose: traditional ones and more contemporary ones. Let's look at some of the various types of organization designs.

What Traditional Organizational Designs Can Managers Use?

When designing a structure, managers may choose one of the traditional organizational designs. These structures—simple, functional, and divisional—tend to be more mechanistic in nature. (See Exhibit 9 for a summary of the strengths and weaknesses of each.)

WHAT IS THE SIMPLE STRUCTURE? Most companies start as entrepreneurial ventures using a simple structure, which is an organizational design with low departmentalization, wide spans of control, authority centralized in a single person, and little formalization.[28] The simple structure is most widely used in smaller businesses and its strengths should be obvious. It's fast, flexible, and inexpensive to maintain, and accountability is clear. However, it becomes increasingly inadequate as an organization grows, because its few policies or rules to guide operations and its high centralization result in information overload at the top. As size increases, decision making becomes slower and can eventually come to a standstill as the single executive tries to continue making all the decisions. If the

---

EXHIBIT 9   Traditional Organization Designs

Simple Structure

- **Strengths:** Fast; flexible; inexpensive to maintain; clear accountability.
- **Weaknesses:** Not appropriate as organization grows; reliance on one person is risky.

Functional Structure

- **Strengths:** Cost-saving advantages from specialization (economies of scale, minimal duplication of people and equipment); employees are grouped with others who have similar tasks.
- **Weaknesses:** Pursuit of functional goals can cause managers to lose sight of what's best for the overall organization; functional specialists become insulated and have little understanding of what other units are doing.

Divisional Structure

- **Strengths:** Focuses on results—division managers are responsible for what happens to their products and services.
- **Weaknesses:** Duplication of activities and resources increases costs and reduces efficiency.

structure is not changed and adapted to its size, the firm can lose momentum and is likely to eventually fail. The simple structure's other weakness is that it's risky: Everything depends on one person. If anything happens to the owner-manager, the organization's information and decision-making center is lost. As employees are added, however, most small businesses don't remain as simple structures. The structure tends to become more specialized and formalized. Rules and regulations are introduced, work becomes specialized, departments are created, levels of management are added, and the organization becomes increasingly bureaucratic. Two of the most popular bureaucratic design options grew out of functional and product departmentalizations and are called the functional and divisional structures.

WHAT IS THE FUNCTIONAL STRUCTURE?   A functional structure is an organizational design that groups similar or related occupational specialties together. You can think of this structure as functional departmentalization applied to the entire organization. For example, Revlon, Inc., is organized around the functions of operations, finance, human resources, and product research and development.

The strength of the functional structure lies in the advantages that accrue from work specialization. Putting like specialties together results in economies of scale, minimizes duplication of personnel and equipment, and makes employees comfortable and satisfied because it gives them the opportunity to talk the same language as their peers. The most obvious weakness of the functional structure, however, is that the organization frequently loses sight of its best interests in the pursuit of functional goals. No one function is totally responsible for results, so members within individual functions become insulated and have little understanding of what people in other functions are doing.

WHAT IS THE DIVISIONAL STRUCTURE?   The divisional structure is an organizational structure made up of separate business units or divisions.[29] In this structure, each division has limited autonomy, with a division manager who has authority over his or her unit and is responsible for performance. In divisional structures, however, the parent corporation typically acts as an external overseer to coordinate and control the various divisions, and often provides support services such as financial and legal. Health care giant Johnson & Johnson, for example, has three divisions: pharmaceuticals, medical devices and diagnostics, and consumer products. In addition, it has several subsidiaries that also manufacture and market diverse health care products.

The chief advantage of the divisional structure is that it focuses on results. Division managers have full responsibility for a product or service. The divisional structure also frees the headquarters staff from being concerned with day-to-day operating details so that they can pay attention to long-term and strategic planning. The major disadvantage of the divisional structure is duplication of activities and resources. Each division, for instance, may have a marketing research department. If there weren't any divisions, all of an organization's marketing research might be centralized and done for a fraction of the cost that divisionalization requires. Thus, the divisional form's duplication of functions increases the organization's costs and reduces efficiency.

What Contemporary Organizational Designs Can Managers Use?

Managers are finding that the traditional designs often aren't appropriate for today's increasingly dynamic and complex environment. Instead, organizations need to be lean, flexible, and innovative; that is, more organic. So managers are finding creative ways to

---

simple structure
An organizational design with low departmentalization, wide spans of control, authority centralized in a single person, and little formalization

functional structure
An organizational design that groups similar or related occupational specialties together

divisional structure
An organizational structure made up of separate business units or divisions

EXHIBIT 10 Contemporary Organization Designs

TEAM STRUCTURE

- **What it is:** A structure in which the entire organization is made up of work groups or teams.
- **Advantages:** Employees are more involved and empowered. Reduced barriers among functional areas.
- **Disadvantages:** No clear chain of command. Pressure on teams to perform.

MATRIX-PROJECT STRUCTURE

- **What it is:** Matrix is a structure that assigns specialists from different functional areas to work on projects but who return to their areas when the project is completed. Project is a structure in which employees continuously work on projects. As one project is completed, employees move on to the next project.
- **Advantages:** Fluid and flexible design that can respond to environmental changes. Faster decision making.
- **Disadvantages:** Complexity of assigning people to projects. Task and personality conflicts.

BOUNDARYLESS STRUCTURE

- **What it is:** A structure that is not defined by or limited to artificial horizontal, vertical, or external boundaries; includes *virtual* and *network* types of organizations.
- **Advantages:** Highly flexible and responsive. Utilizes talent wherever it is found.
- **Disadvantages:** Lack of control. Communication difficulties.

structure and organize work and are using designs such as team-based structures, matrix and project structures, and boundaryless structures.[30] (See Exhibit 10 for a summary of these designs.)

These Google employees gather for a team meeting in the offices of the Internet search engine's European headquarters in Dublin, Ireland. At offices around the globe, Googlers work in small focused teams to perform organizational tasks, create new ideas, and resolve problems. Google's team structure is critical to the firm's focus on innovation. The company's commitment to innovation depends on team members sharing ideas and opinions, testing them, and putting them into practice. Google gives empowered team members the authority to make decisions that will get innovations to market as quickly as possible.

WHAT ARE TEAM STRUCTURES? Larry Page and Sergey Brin, co-founders of Google, have created a corporate structure that "tackles most big projects in small, tightly focused teams."[31] A **team structure** is one in which the entire organization is made up of work teams that do the organization's work.[32] In this structure, employee empowerment is crucial because there is no line of managerial authority from top to bottom. Rather, employee teams design and do work in the way they think is best, but are also held responsible for all work performance results in their respective areas. In large organizations, the team structure complements what is typically a functional or divisional structure. This allows the organization to have the efficiency of a bureaucracy while providing the flexibility of teams. For instance, companies such as Amazon, Boeing, Hewlett-Packard, Louis Vuitton, Motorola, and Xerox extensively use employee teams to improve productivity.

Although team structures have been positive, simply arranging employees into teams is not enough. Employees must be trained to work on teams, receive cross-functional skills training, and be compensated accordingly. Without a properly implemented team-based pay plan, many of the benefits of a team structure may be lost.[33]

WHAT ARE MATRIX AND PROJECT STRUCTURES? In addition to team-based structures, other popular contemporary designs are the matrix and project structures. The **matrix structure** assigns specialists from different functional departments to work on projects led by a project manager. When employees finish work on an assigned project, they go back to their functional departments. One unique aspect of this design is that it creates a *dual chain of command* since employees in a matrix organization have two managers: their functional area manager and their product or project manager, who share authority.

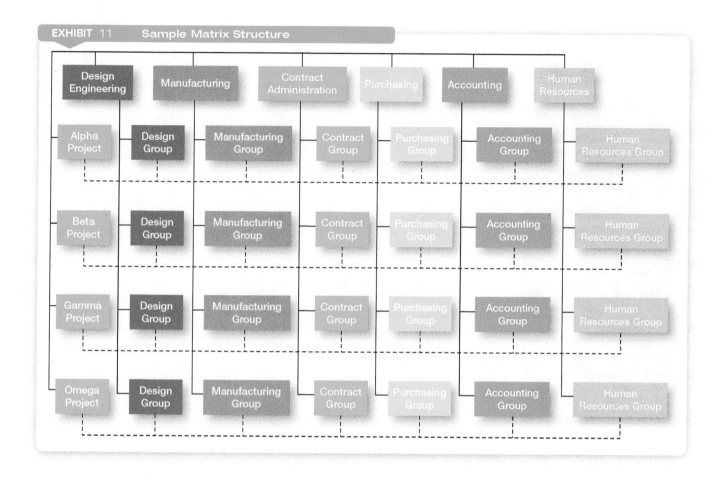

EXHIBIT 11 — Sample Matrix Structure

(See Exhibit 11.) The project manager has authority over the functional members who are part of his or her project team in areas related to the project's goals. However, any decisions about promotions, salary recommendations, and annual reviews typically remain the functional manager's responsibility. To work effectively, both managers have to communicate regularly, coordinate work demands on employees, and resolve conflicts together.

The primary strength of the matrix is that it can facilitate coordination of a multiple set of complex and interdependent projects while still retaining the economies that result from keeping functional specialists grouped together. The major disadvantages of the matrix are the confusion it creates and its propensity to foster power struggles. When you dispense with the chain of command and unity of command principles, you significantly increase ambiguity. Confusion can arise over who reports to whom. The confusion and ambiguity, in turn, are what trigger the power struggles.

Instead of a matrix structure, many organizations are using a **project structure**, in which employees continuously work on projects. Unlike the matrix structure, a project structure has no formal departments where employees return at the completion of a project. Instead, employees take their specific skills, abilities, and experiences to other projects. Also, all work in project structures is performed by teams of employees. For instance, at design firm IDEO, project teams form, disband, and form again as the work requires. Employees "join" project teams because they bring needed skills and abilities to that project. Once a project is completed, however, they move on to the next one.[34]

team structure
A structure in which the entire organization is made up of work teams

matrix structure
A structure in which specialists from different functional departments are assigned to work on projects led by a project manager

project structure
A structure in which employee continuously work on projects

Project structures tend to be more flexible organizational designs. The major advantage of that is that employees can be deployed rapidly to respond to environmental changes. Also, there's no departmentalization or rigid organizational hierarchy to slow down making decisions or taking action. In this structure, managers serve as facilitators, mentors, and coaches. They eliminate or minimize organizational obstacles and ensure that teams have the resources they need to effectively and efficiently complete their work. The two major disadvantages of the project structure are the complexity of assigning people to projects and the inevitable task and personality conflicts that arise.

WHAT IS A BOUNDARYLESS ORGANIZATION?   Another contemporary organizational design is the boundaryless organization, which is an organization whose design is not defined by, or limited to, the horizontal, vertical, or external boundaries imposed by a predefined structure.[36] Former GE chairman Jack Welch coined the term because he wanted to eliminate vertical and horizontal boundaries within GE and break down external barriers between the company and its customers and suppliers. Although the idea of eliminating boundaries may seem odd, many of today's most successful organizations are finding that they can operate most effectively by remaining flexible and *un*structured: that the ideal structure for them is *not* having a rigid, bounded, and predefined structure.[37]

What do we mean by "boundaries"? There are two types: (1) *internal*—the horizontal ones imposed by work specialization and departmentalization and the vertical ones that separate employees into organizational levels and hierarchies; and (2) *external*—the boundaries that separate the organization from its customers, suppliers, and other stakeholders. To minimize or eliminate these boundaries, managers might use virtual or network structural designs.

A virtual organization consists of a small core of full-time employees and outside specialists temporarily hired as needed to work on projects.[38] An example is StrawberryFrog, a global advertising agency with offices in New York, Amsterdam, Mumbai, and São Paulo. Work gets done with a minimal administrative staff and a global network of freelancers who are assigned client work. By relying on these freelancers, the company enjoys a network of talent without all the unnecessary overhead and structural complexity.[39] The inspiration for this structural approach comes from the film industry. There, people are essentially "free agents" who move from project to project applying their skills—directing, talent casting, costuming, makeup, set design, and so forth—as needed.

Another structural option for managers wanting to minimize or eliminate organizational boundaries is a network organization, which is one that uses its own employees to do some work activities and networks of outside suppliers to provide other needed product components or work processes.[40] This organizational form is sometimes called a modular organization by manufacturing firms.[41] This structural approach allows organizations to concentrate on what they do best by contracting out other activities to companies that do those activities best. Many companies are using such an approach for certain organizational work activities. For instance, the head of development for Boeing's 787 airplane manages thousands of employees and some 100 suppliers at more than 100 sites in different countries.[42] Sweden's Ericsson contracts its manufacturing and even some of its research and development to more cost-effective contractors in New Delhi, Singapore, California, and other global locations.[43] And at Penske Truck Leasing, dozens of business processes such as securing permits and titles, entering data from drivers' logs, and processing data for tax filings and accounting have been outsourced to Mexico and India.[44]

Newscom

STAR Collaborative is a virtual staffing network launched by cofounders Ed Lefkow (left in photo) and Dan Olson. STAR is a specialty consultant group comprised of 150-plus freelance project and change management professionals who help primarily *Fortune* 500 companies achieve business results by finding ways to increase communication, foster collaboration, and develop leadership. A virtual structure enables STAR to provide the high-quality resources of skilled and experienced consultants offered by large consulting firms without the unnecessary overhead and structural complexity. In this photo, Lefkow and Olson conduct business in a coffee shop, one of many virtual offices they work from so they can be close to their clients.

WHAT ARE TODAY'S ORGANIZATIONAL DESIGN CHALLENGES?

As managers look for organizational designs that will best support and facilitate employees doing their work efficiently and effectively, there are certain challenges with which they must contend. These include keeping employees connected, managing global structural issues, building a learning organization, and designing flexible work arrangements.

Discuss the design challenges faced by today's organizations.

4

How Do You Keep Employees Connected?

Many organizational design concepts were developed during the twentieth century when work tasks were fairly predictable and constant, most jobs were full-time and continued indefinitely, and work was done at an employer's place of business under a manager's supervision.[45] That's not what it's like in many organizations today, as you saw in our preceding discussion of virtual and network organizations. A major structural design challenge for managers is finding a way to keep widely dispersed and mobile employees connected to the organization. The Technology and the Manager's Job box describes ways that information technology can help.

How Do Global Differences Affect Organizational Structure?

Are there global differences in organizational structures? Are Australian organizations structured like those in the United States? Are German organizations structured like those in France or Mexico? Given the global nature of today's business environment, this is an issue

TECHNOLOGY AND THE MANAGER'S JOB — THE CHANGING WORLD OF WORK

It's fair to say that the world of work will never be like it was 10 years ago.[46] IT has opened up new possibilities for employees to do their work in locations as remote as Patagonia or in the middle of downtown Seattle. Although organizations have always had employees who traveled to distant corporate locations to take care of business, these employees no longer have to find the nearest pay phone or wait to get back to "the office" to see what problems have cropped up. Instead, mobile computing and communication have given organizations and employees ways to stay connected and to be more productive. Let's look at some of the technologies that are changing the way work is done.

· Handheld devices with e-mail, calendars, and contacts can be used anywhere there's a wireless network. And these devices can be used to log into corporate databases and company intranets.

· Employees can videoconference using broadband networks and Webcams.

· Many companies are giving employees key fobs with constantly changing encryption codes that allow them to log onto the corporate network to access e-mail and company data from any computer hooked up to the Internet.

· Cell phones switch seamlessly between cellular networks and corporate Wi-Fi connections.

The biggest issue in doing work anywhere, anytime is security. Companies must protect their important and sensitive information. However, software and other disabling devices have minimized security issues considerably. Even insurance providers are more comfortable giving their mobile employees access to information. For instance, Health Net Inc. gave BlackBerrys to many of its managers so they can tap into customer records from anywhere. As one tech company CEO said, "Companies now can start thinking about innovative apps [applications] they can create and deliver to their workers anywhere."

Think About:

· What benefits do you see with being able to do work anywhere, anytime? (Think in terms of benefits for an organization and for its human resources.)

· What other issues, besides security, do you see with being able to do work anywhere, anytime? (Again, think about this for an organization and for its employees.)

· How do you use IT to do your work as a student?

· What challenges do you find in doing so?

boundaryless organization
An organization whose design is not defined by, or limited to, boundaries imposed by a predefined structure

virtual organization
An organization that consists of a small core of full-time employees and outside specialists temporarily hired as needed to work on projects

network organization
An organization that uses its own employees to do some work activities and networks of outside suppliers to provide other needed product components or work processes

with which managers need to be familiar. Researchers have concluded that the structures and strategies of organizations worldwide are similar, "while the behavior within them is maintaining its cultural uniqueness."[47] What does this mean for designing effective and efficient structures? When designing or changing structure, managers may need to think about the cultural implications of certain design elements. For instance, one study showed that formalization—rules and bureaucratic mechanisms—may be more important in less economically developed countries and less important in more economically developed countries where employees may have higher levels of professional education and skills.[48] Other structural design elements may be affected by cultural differences as well.

How Do You Build a Learning Organization?

Doing business in an intensely competitive global environment, British retailer Tesco realized how important it was for its stores to run well behind the scenes. And it does so using a proven "tool" called Tesco in a Box, which promotes consistency in operations as well as being a way to share innovations. Tesco is an example of a learning organization, an organization that has developed the capacity to continuously learn, adapt, and change.[49] The concept of a learning organization doesn't involve a specific organizational design per se, but instead describes an organizational mind-set or philosophy that has significant design implications. In a learning organization, employees are practicing knowledge management by continually acquiring and sharing new knowledge and are willing to apply that knowledge in making decisions or performing their work. Some organizational design theorists even go so far as to say that an organization's ability to learn and to apply that learning as they perform the organization's work may be the only sustainable source of competitive advantage.

What would a learning organization look like? As you can see in Exhibit 12, the important characteristics of a learning organization revolve around organizational design, information sharing, leadership, and culture. Let's take a closer look at each.

What types of organizational design elements would be necessary for learning to take place? In a learning organization, it's critical for members to share information and collaborate on work activities throughout the entire organization—across different functional specialties and even at different organizational levels—through minimizing or eliminating the existing structural and physical boundaries. In this type of boundaryless environment, employees are free to work together and collaborate in doing the organization's work the

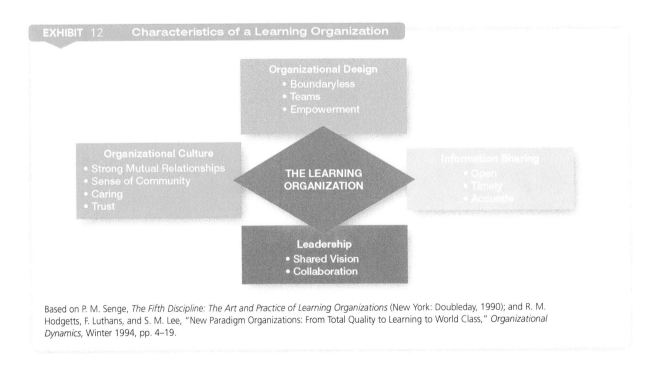

EXHIBIT 12   Characteristics of a Learning Organization

Organizational Design
• Boundaryless
• Teams
• Empowerment

Organizational Culture
• Strong Mutual Relationships
• Sense of Community
• Caring
• Trust

THE LEARNING ORGANIZATION

Information Sharing
• Open
• Timely
• Accurate

Leadership
• Shared Vision
• Collaboration

Based on P. M. Senge, *The Fifth Discipline: The Art and Practice of Learning Organizations* (New York: Doubleday, 1990); and R. M. Hodgetts, F. Luthans, and S. M. Lee, "New Paradigm Organizations: From Total Quality to Learning to World Class," *Organizational Dynamics*, Winter 1994, pp. 4–19.

best way they can, and to learn from each other. Because of this need to collaborate, teams also tend to be an important feature of a learning organization's structural design. Employees work in teams on whatever activities need to be done, and these employee teams are empowered to make decisions about doing their work or resolving issues. Empowered employees and teams have little need for "bosses" who direct and control. Instead, managers serve as facilitators, supporters, and advocates for employee teams.

Learning can't take place without information. For a learning organization to "learn," information must be shared among members; that is, organizational employees must engage in knowledge management by sharing information openly, in a timely manner, and as accurately as possible. Because few structural and physical barriers exist in a learning organization, the environment is conducive to open communication and extensive information sharing.

Leadership plays an important role as an organization moves toward becoming a learning organization. What should leaders do in a learning organization? One of their most important functions is facilitating the creation of a shared vision for the organization's future and then keeping organizational members working toward that vision. In addition, leaders should support and encourage the collaborative environment that's critical to learning. Without strong and committed leadership throughout the organization, it would be extremely difficult to be a learning organization.

Finally, the organizational culture is an important aspect of being a learning organization. In a learning organization's culture, everyone agrees on a shared vision and everyone recognizes the inherent interrelationships among the organization's processes, activities, functions, and external environment. It also fosters a strong sense of community, caring for each other, and trust. In a learning organization, employees feel free to communicate openly, share, experiment, and learn without fear of criticism or punishment.

How Can Managers Design Efficient and Effective Flexible Work Arrangements?

Accenture consultant Keyur Patel's job arrangement is becoming the norm, rather than the exception.[50] During a recent consulting assignment, he had three clocks on his desk: one set to Manila time (where his software programmers were), one to Bangalore (where another programming support team worked), and the third for San Francisco, where he was spending four days a week helping a major retailer implement IT systems to track and improve sales. And his cell phone kept track of the time in Atlanta, his home, where he headed on Thursday evenings.

For this new breed of professionals, life is a blend of home and office, work and leisure. Thanks to technology, work can now be done anywhere, anytime. As organizations adapt their structural designs to these new realities, we see more of them adopting flexible working arrangements. Such arrangements not only exploit the power of technology, but give organizations the flexibility to deploy employees when and where needed. In this section, we're going to take a look at some different types of flexible work arrangements including telecommuting; compressed workweeks, flextime, and job sharing; and contingent workforce. As with the other structural options we've looked at, managers must evaluate these in light of the implications for decision making, communication, authority relationships, work task accomplishment, and so forth.

WHAT'S INVOLVED IN TELECOMMUTING?   Information technology has made telecommuting possible and external environmental changes have made it necessary for many organizations. Telecommuting is a work arrangement in which employees work at home and are linked to the workplace by computer. Needless to say, not every job is a candidate for telecommuting. But many are.

---

learning organization
An organization that has developed the capacity to continuously learn, adapt, and change

telecommuting
A work arrangement in which employees work at home and are linked to the workplace by computer

When you call to book a flight with JetBlue Airlines, there's a good chance that you'll make a reservation with an agent working from home. That's because 80 percent of JetBlue's reservation agents are telecommuters. JetBlue reports that allowing its agents to work from home saves the company money and expensive office space and increases worker productivity. Telecommuting also gives JetBlue the flexibility to deploy more employees when call volume is high and fewer employees during slow call periods. The flexible work arrangement is a popular initiative with employees because it saves them traveling time and gas money and gives them more time to spend with their family.

Working from home used to be considered a "cushy perk" for a few lucky employees and such an arrangement wasn't allowed very often. Now, many businesses view telecommuting as a business necessity. For instance, at SCAN Health Plan, the company's chief financial officer said that getting more employees to telecommute provided the company a way to grow without having to incur any additional fixed costs such as office buildings, equipment, or parking lots.[51] In addition, some companies view the arrangement as a way to combat high gas prices and to attract talented employees who want more freedom and control over their work.

Despite its apparent appeal, many managers are reluctant to have their employees become "laptop hobos."[52] They argue that employees might waste time surfing the Internet or playing online games instead of working, ignore clients, and desperately miss the camaraderie and social exchanges of the workplace. In addition, managers worry about how they'll "manage" these employees? How do you interact with an employee and gain his or her trust when they're not physically present? And what if their work performance isn't up to par? How do you make suggestions for improvement? Another significant challenge is making sure that company information is kept safe and secure when employees are working from home.

Employees often express the same concerns about working remotely, especially when it comes to the isolation of not being "at work." At Accenture, where employees are scattered around the world, the chief human resources officer says that it isn't easy to maintain that esprit de corps.[53] However, the company put in place a number of programs and processes to create that sense of belonging for its workforce including webconferencing tools, assigning each employee to a career counselor, and holding quarterly community events at its offices. In addition, the telecommuter employee may find that the line between work and home becomes even more blurred, which can be stressful.[54] These are important organizing issues and ones that managers and organizations must address when moving toward having employees telecommute.

HOW CAN ORGANIZATIONS USE COMPRESSED WORKWEEKS, FLEXTIME, AND JOB SHARING?   During the most recent economic crisis in the United Kingdom, accounting firm KPMG needed to reduce costs and decided to use flexible work options as a way of doing so.[55] The company's program, called Flexible Futures, offered employees four options to choose from: a four-day workweek with a 20 percent salary reduction; a two-to twelve-week sabbatical at 30 percent of pay; both options; or continue with their regular schedule. Some 85 percent of the U.K. employees agreed to the reduced-work-week plan. "Since so many people agreed to the flexible work plans, KPMG was able to cap the salary cut at about 10 percent for the year in most cases." The best thing, though, was that as a result of the plan, KPMG didn't have to do large-scale employee layoffs.

As this example shows, organizations sometimes find they need to restructure work using other forms of flexible work arrangements. One approach is a compressed workweek in which employees work longer hours per day but fewer days per week. The most common arrangement is four 10-hour days (a 4-40 program). Another alternative is flextime (also known as flexible work hours), which is a scheduling system in which employees are required to work a specific number of hours a week but are free to vary those hours within certain limits. In a flextime schedule, most companies designate certain common core hours when all employees are required to be on the job, but starting, ending, and lunch-hour times are flexible. Another type of job scheduling is called job sharing—the practice of having two or more people split a full-time job. Organizations might offer job sharing to professionals who want to work but don't want the demands and hassles of a full-time position. For instance, at Ernst & Young, employees in many of the company's locations can choose from a variety of flexible work arrangements including job sharing. Many companies use job sharing during economic downturns to avoid employee layoffs.[56]

WHAT IS A CONTINGENT WORKFORCE?   "When Julia Lee first heard of Tongal, she thought it was a scam. Tongal pays people—anyone with a good idea, really—to create online videos for companies such as Mattel, Allstate, and Popchips."[57] Tongal divides projects into stages and pays cash for the top-five ideas. On Lee's first submission—which only took three hours of work—she got $1,000. On another, she earned $4,000. In a year's time, she's earned some $6,000 for about 100 hours of work. Tongal isn't the only business doing this. The idea of breaking up a job into small pieces and using the Internet to find workers to do those tasks was pioneered by LiveOps about a decade ago and followed by Amazon.com's Mechanical Turk in 2005.

"Companies want a workforce they can switch on and off as needed."[58] Although this quote may shock you, the truth is that the labor force already has begun shifting away from traditional full-time jobs toward contingent workers—temporary, freelance, or contract workers whose employment is *contingent* upon demand for their services. In today's economy, many organizations have responded by converting full-time permanent jobs into contingent jobs. It's predicted that by the end of the next decade the number of contingent employees will have grown to about 40 percent of the workforce. (It's at 30 percent today.)[59] In fact, one compensation and benefits expert says that "a growing a number of workers will need to structure their careers around this model."[60] That's likely to include you!

What are the implications for managers and organizations? Since contingent employees are not "employees" in the traditional sense of the word, managing them has its own set of challenges and expectations. Managers must recognize that because contingent workers lack the stability and security of permanent employees, they may not identify with the organization or be as committed or motivated. Managers may need to treat contingent workers differently in terms of practices and policies. However, with good communication and leadership, an organization's contingent employees can be just as valuable a resource to an organization as permanent employees are. Today's managers must recognize that it will be their responsibility to motivate their entire workforce, full-time and contingent, and to build their commitment to doing good work![61]

No matter what structural design managers choose for their organizations, the design should help employees do their work in the best, most efficient and effective way they can. The structure needs to help, not hinder, organizational members as they carry out the organization's work. After all, the structure is simply a means to an end.

---

compressed workweek
A workweek where employees work longer hours per day but fewer days per week

flextime (also known as flexible work hours)
A work scheduling system in which employees are required to work a specific number of hours per week but can vary when they work those hours within certain limits

job sharing
When two or more people split a full-time job

contingent workers
Temporary, freelance, or contract workers whose employment is *contingent* upon demand for their services

Review

1 Describe six key elements in organizational design.
The first element, *work specialization*, refers to dividing work activities into separate job tasks. The second, *departmentalization,* is how jobs are grouped together, which can be one of five types: functional, product, customer, geographic, or process. The third—*authority, responsibility, and power* all have to do with getting work done in an organization. Authority refers to the rights inherent in a managerial position to give orders and expect those orders to be obeyed. Responsibility refers to the obligation to perform when authority has been delegated. Power is the capacity of an individual to influence decisions and is not the same as authority. The fourth, *span of control*, refers to the number of employees a manager can efficiently and effectively manage. The fifth, *centralization and decentralization*, deals with where the majority of decisions are made—at upper organizational levels or pushed down to lower-level managers. The sixth, *formalization*, describes how standardized an organization's jobs are and the extent to which employees' behavior is guided by rules and procedures.

2 Identify the contingency factors that favor either the mechanistic model or the organic model of organizational design. A *mechanistic* organization design is quite bureaucratic whereas an *organic* organization design is more fluid and flexible. The *strategy*-determines-structure factor says that as organizational strategies move from single product to product diversification, the structure will move from organic to mechanistic. As an organization's *size* increases, so does the need for a more mechanistic structure. The more nonroutine the *technology*, the more organic a structure should be. Finally, stable *environments* are better matched with mechanistic structures, but dynamic ones fit better with organic structures.

3 Compare and contrast traditional and contemporary organizational designs. Traditional structural designs include simple, functional, and divisional. A *simple structure* is one with low departmentalization, wide spans of control, authority centralized in a single person, and little formalization. A *functional structure* is one that groups similar or related occupational specialties together. A *divisional structure* is one made up of separate business units or divisions. Contemporary structural designs include *team-based structures* (the entire organization is made up of work teams); *matrix and project structures* (where employees work on projects for short periods of time or continuously); and *boundaryless organizations* (where the structural design is free of imposed boundaries). A boundaryless organization can either be a virtual or a network organization.

4 Discuss the design challenges faced by today's organizations. One design challenge lies in keeping employees connected, which can be accomplished through using information technology. Another challenge is understanding the global differences that affect organizational structure. Although structures and strategies of organizations worldwide are similar, the behavior within them differs, which can influence certain design elements. Another challenge is designing a structure around the mind-set of being a learning organization. Finally, managers are looking for organizational designs with efficient and effective flexible work arrangements. They're using options such as telecommuting, compressed workweeks, flextime, job sharing, and contingent workers.

MyManagementLab   For more resources, please visit **www.mymanagementlab.com**

---

1. Describe what is meant by the term *organization design.*

2. Discuss the traditional and contemporary views of each of the six key elements of organizational design.

3. Can an organization's structure be changed quickly? Why or why not? Should it be changed quickly? Why or why not?

4. "An organization can have no structure." Do you agree or disagree with this statement? Explain.

5. Contrast mechanistic and organic organizations.

6. Explain the contingency factors that affect organizational design.

7. With the availability of information technology that allows employees to work anywhere, anytime, is organizing still an important managerial function? Why or why not?

8. Researchers are now saying that efforts to simplify work tasks actually have negative results for both companies and their employees. Do you agree? Why or why not?

9. "The boundaryless organization has the potential to create a major shift in the way we work." Do you agree or disagree with this statement? Explain.

10. Draw an organization chart of an organization with which you're familiar (where you work, a student organization to which you belong, your college or university, etc.). Be very careful in showing the departments (or groups) and especially be careful to get the chain of command correct. Be prepared to share your chart with the class.

Endnotes

1. A. Fox, "Pave the Way for Volunteers," *HR Magazine,* June 2010, pp. 70–74; G. Morse, "The Power of Unwitting Workers," *Harvard Business Review,* October 2009, pp. 27–27; S. Lohr, "Customer Service? Ask a Volunteer," *New York Times Online,* April 26, 2009; and B. Xu, D. R. Jones, and B. Shao, "Volunteers' Involvement in Online Community Based Software Development," *Information & Management,* April 2009, pp. 151–158.

2. M. Boyle, "Super Bucks," *Fortune,* February 4, 2008, pp. 8–9; and M. Hiestand, "Making a Stamp on Football," *USA Today,* January 25, 2005, pp. 1C+.

3. S. E. Humphrey, J. D. Nahrgang, and F. P. Morgeson, "Integrating Motivational, Social, and Contextual Work Design Features: A Meta-Analytic Summary and Theoretical Expansion of the Work Design Literature," *Journal of Applied Psychology* (September 2007), pp. 1332–1356.

4. E. Kelly, "Keys to Effective Virtual Global Teams," *Academy of Management Executive,* May 2001, pp. 132–133; and D. Ancona, H. Bresman, and K. Kaeufer, "The Comparative Advantage of X-Team," *MIT Sloan Management Review,* Spring 2002, pp. 33–39.

5. R. S. Benchley, "Following Orders," *Chief Executive,* March 2002, p. 6.

6. R. Preston, "Inside Out," *Management Today,* September 2001, p. 37; and R. D. Clarke, "Over Their Heads," *Black Enterprise,* December 2000, p. 79.

7. See J. R. P. French and B. Raven, "The Bases of Social Power," in D. Cartwright and A. F. Zander, eds., *Group Dynamics: Research and Theory* (New York: Harper & Row, 1960), pp. 607–623.

8. L. Urwick, *The Elements of Administration* (New York: Harper & Row, 1944), pp. 52–53. See also, J. H. Gittel, "Supervisory Span, Relational Coordination, and Flight Departure Performance: A Reassessment of Post-Bureaucracy Theory," *Organizational Science,* July–August 2001, pp. 468–483.

9. S. Harrison, "Is There a Right Span of Control? Simon Harrison Assesses the Relevance of the Concept of Span of Control to Modern Businesses," *Business Review,* February 2004, pp. 10–13.

10. P. C. Light, "From Pentagon to Pyramids: Whacking at Bloat," *Government Executive,* July 2001, p. 100.

11. Right or Wrong box based on C. Bray, "Hackers Are Arrested in iPad Breach," *Wall Street Journal,* January 19, 2011, p. B1; C. Hausman, "Was AT&T's iPad Security Breach 'Ethical' Hacking?" *Ethics Newsline,* www.globalethics.org (June 21, 2010); S. E. Ante and B. Worthen, "FBI to Probe iPad Breach— Group That Exposed AT&T Flaw to See Addresses Says It Did a Public Service," *Wall Street Journal,* June 11, 2010, p. B1; and S. E. Ante, "AT&T Discloses Breach of iPad Owner Data," *Wall Street Journal Online,* June 9, 2010.

12. See, for instance, D. Van Fleet, "Span of Management Research and Issues," *Academy of Management Journal* (September 1983), pp. 546–552; and S. H. Cady and P. M. Fandt, "Managing Impressions with Information: A Field Study of Organizational Realities," *Journal of Applied Behavioral Science* (June 2001), pp. 180–204.

13. Henri Fayol, *General and Industrial Management*, trans. C. Storrs (London: Pitman Publishing, 1949), pp. 19–42.

14. J. Zabojnik, "Centralized and Decentralized Decision Making in Organizations," *Journal of Labor Economics* (January 2002), pp. 1–22.

15. See P. Kenis and D. Knoke, "How Organizational Field Networks Shape InterOrganizational Tie-Formation Rates," *Academy of Management Review,* April 2002, pp. 275–293.

16. E. W. Morrison, "Doing the Job Well: An Investigation of Pro-Social Rule Breaking," *Journal of Management* (February 2006), pp. 5–28.

17. Ibid.

18. T. Burns and G. M. Stalker, *The Management of Innovation* (London: Tavistock, 1961).

19. D. Dougherty, "Re-imagining the Differentiation and Integration of Work for Sustained Product Innovation," *Organization Science,* September–October 2001, pp. 612–631.

20. A. D. Chandler, Jr., *Strategy and Structure: Chapters in the History of the Industrial Enterprise* (Cambridge, MA: MIT Press, 1962).

21. See, for instance, L. L. Bryan and C. I. Joyce, "Better Strategy Through Organizational Design," *McKinsey Quarterly,* no. 2 (2007), pp. 21–29; D. Jennings and S. Seaman, "High and Low Levels of Organizational Adaptation: An Empirical Analysis of Strategy, Structure, and Performance," *Strategic Management Journal* (July 1994), pp. 459–475; D. C. Galunic and K. M. Eisenhardt, "Renewing the Strategy-Structure-Performance Paradigm," in B. M. Staw and L. L. Cummings (eds.), *Research in Organizational Behavior,* vol. 16 (Greenwich, CT: JAI Press, 1994), pp. 215–255; R. Parthasarthy and S. P. Sethi, "Relating Strategy and Structure to Flexible Automation: A Test of Fit and Performance Implications," *Strategic Management Journal,* 14, no. 6 (1993), pp. 529–549; H. A. Simon, "Strategy and Organizational Evolution," *Strategic Management Journal* (January 1993), pp. 131–142; H. L. Boschken, "Strategy and Structure: Re-conceiving the Relationship," *Journal of Management* (March 1990), pp. 135–150; D. Miller, "The Structural and Environmental Correlates of Business Strategy," *Strategic Management Journal* (January–February 1987), pp. 55–76; and R. E. Miles and C. C. Snow, *Organizational Strategy, Structure, and Process* (New York: McGraw-Hill, 1978).

22. See, for instance, P. M. Blau and R. A. Schoenherr, *The Structure of Organizations* (New York: Basic Books, 1971); D. S. Pugh, "The Aston Program of Research: Retrospect and Prospect," in A. H. Van de Ven and W. F. Joyce (eds.), *Perspectives on Organization Design and Behavior* (New York: John Wiley, 1981), pp. 135–166; and R. Z. Gooding and J. A. Wagner III, "A Meta-Analytic Review of the Relationship Between Size and Performance: The Productivity and Efficiency of Organizations and Their Subunits," *Administrative Science Quarterly*, December 1985, pp. 462–481.

23. J. Woodward, *Industrial Organization: Theory and Practice* (London: Oxford University Press, 1965).

24. From the Past to the Present box based on J. Woodward, *Industrial Organization: Theory and Practice*. Also, see, for instance, C. Perrow, "A Framework for the Comparative Analysis of Organizations," *American Sociological Review*, April 1967, pp. 194–208; J. D. Thompson, *Organizations in Action* (New York: McGraw-Hill, 1967); J. Hage and M. Aiken, "Routine Technology, Social Structure, and Organizational Goals," *Administrative Science Quarterly*, September 1969, pp. 366–377; C. C. Miller, W. H. Glick, Y. D. Wang, and G. Huber, "Understanding Technology-Structure Relationships: Theory Development and Meta-Analytic Theory Testing," *Academy of Management Journal* (June 1991), pp. 370–399; D. M. Rousseau and R. A. Cooke, "Technology and Structure: The Concrete, Abstract, and Activity Systems of Organizations," *Journal of Management* (Fall–Winter 1984), pp. 345–361; and D. Gerwin, "Relationships between Structure and Technology," in P.C. Nystrom and W. H. Starbuck (eds.), *Handbook of Organizational Design*, vol. 2 (New York: Oxford University Press, 1981), pp. 3–38.

25. See, for example, H. M. O'Neill, "Restructuring, Reengineering and Rightsizing: Do the Metaphors Make Sense?" *Academy of Management Executive* 8, no. 4 (1994), pp. 9–30; R. K. Reger, J. V. Mullane, L. T. Gustafson, and S. M. Demarie, "Creating Earthquakes to Change Organizational Mindsets," *Academy of Management Executive* 8, no. 4 (1994), pp. 31–41; and J. Tan, "Impact of Ownership Type on Environment–Strategy Linkage and Performance: Evidence from a Transitional Company," *Journal of Management Studies* (May 2002), pp. 333–354.

26. J. C. Linder and S. Cantrell, "It's All in the Mind(set)," *Across the Board*, May–June 2002, pp. 38–42; and B. Holland, "Management's Sweet Spot," *New Zealand Management*, March 2002, pp. 60–61.

27. M. Song, "Samsung Electronics Net Rises 54%," *Wall Street Journal*, April 22, 2002, p. B4.

28. H. Mintzberg, *Structure in Fives: Designing Effective Organizations* (Upper Saddle River, NJ: Prentice Hall, 1983), p. 157.

29. D. A. Garvin and L. C. Levesque, "The Multiunit Enterprise," *Harvard Business Review*, June 2008, pp. 106–117; and R. J. Williams, J. J. Hoffman, and B. T. Lamont, "The Influence of Top Management Team Characteristics on M-Form Implementation Time," *Journal of Managerial Issues* (Winter 1995), pp. 466–480.

30. See, for example, R. Greenwood and D. Miller, "Tackling Design Anew: Getting Back to the Heart of Organization Theory," *Academy of Management Perspectives*, November 2010, pp. 78–88; G. J. Castrogiovanni, "Organization Task Environments: Have They Changed Fundamentally Over Time?" *Journal of Management*, vol. 28, no. 2 (2002), pp. 129–150; D. F. Twomey, "Leadership, Organizational Design, and Competitiveness for the 21st Century," *Global Competitiveness*, Annual 2002, pp. S31–S40; M. Hammer, "Processed Change: Michael Hammer Sees Process as 'the Clark Kent of Business Ideas'—A Concept That Has the Power to Change a Company's Organizational Design," *Journal of Business Strategy*,

(November–December 2001), pp. 11–15; T. Clancy, "Radical Surgery: A View from the Operating Theater," *Academy of Management Executive*, February 1994, pp. 73–78; I. I. Mitroff, R. O. Mason, and C. M. Pearson, "Radical Surgery: What Will Tomorrow's Organizations Look Like?" *Academy of Management Executive*, February 1994, pp. 11–21; and R. E. Hoskisson, C. W. L. Hill, and H. Kim, "The Multidivisional Structure: Organizational Fossil or Source of Value?" *Journal of Management* 19, no. 2 (1993), pp. 269–298.

31. Q. Hardy, "Google Thinks Small," *Forbes*, November 14, 2005, pp. 198–202.

32. See, for example, D. R. Denison, S. L. Hart, and J. A. Kahn, "From Chimneys to Cross-Functional Teams: Developing and Validating a Diagnostic Model," *Academy of Management Journal* (December 1996), pp. 1005–1023; D. Ray and H. Bronstein, *Teaming Up: Making the Transition to a Self-Directed Team-Based Organization* (New York: McGraw Hill, 1995); J. R. Katzenbach and D. K. Smith, *The Wisdom of Teams* (Boston: Harvard Business School Press, 1993); J. A. Byrne, "The Horizontal Corporation," *BusinessWeek*, December 20, 1993, pp. 76–81; B. Dumaine, "Payoff from the New Management," *Fortune*, December 13, 1993, pp. 103–110; and H. Rothman, "The Power of Empowerment," *Nation's Business*, June 1993, pp. 49–52.

33. C. Garvey, "Steer Teams with the Right Pay," *HR Magazine*, May 2002, pp. 70–78.

34. P. Kaihla, "Best-Kept Secrets of the World's Best Companies," *Business 2.0*, April 2006, p. 83; C. Taylor, "School of Bright Ideas," *Time Inside Business*, April 2005, pp. A8–A12; and B. Nussbaum, "The Power of Design," *Business Week*, May 17, 2004, pp. 86–94.

35. And the Survey Says box based on J. Schramm, "At Work in a Virtual World," *HR Magazine*, June 2010, p. 152; J. Yang and A. Gonzalez, "Top Peeves About Someone Working from Home," *USA Today*, May 27, 2010, p. 1B; J. Jusko, "A Team Effort," *Industry Week*, January 2007, pp. 42+; P. Coy, M. Conlin, and M. Herbst, "The Disposable Worker," *Bloomberg BusinessWeek*, January 18, 2010, p. 36; "Employee Loyalty Increases During Recession," *Workforce Management Online*, March 9, 2010; "Study: Flexibility Programs Gain Ground in Hard Times," *Workforce Management Online*, July 23, 2009; and J. Hyatt, "Taking It Personally," *CFO*, July–August 2009, p. 29.

36. See, for example, G. G. Dess, A. M. A. Rasheed, K. J. McLaughlin, and R. L. Priem, "The New Corporate Architecture," *Academy of Management Executive*, August 1995, pp. 7–20.

37. For additional readings on boundaryless organizations, see Rausch and Birkinshaw, June 2008; M. F. R. Kets de Vries, "Leadership Group Coaching in Action: The Zen of Creating High Performance Teams," *Academy of Management Executive*, February 2005, pp. 61–76; J. Child and R. G. McGrath, "Organizations Unfettered: Organizational Form in an Information-Intensive Economy," *Academy of Management Journal* (December 2001), pp. 1135–1148; M. Hammer and S. Stanton, "How Process Enterprises Really Work," *Harvard Business Review*, November–December 1999, pp. 108–118; T. Zenger and W. Hesterly, "The Disaggregation of Corporations: Selective Intervention, High-Powered Incentives,

and Modular Units," *Organization Science,* vol. 8 (1997), pp. 209–222; R. Ashkenas, D. Ulrich, T. Jick, and S. Kerr, *The Boundaryless Organization: Breaking the Chains of Organizational Structure* (San Francisco: Jossey-Bass, 1997); R. M. Hodgetts, "A Conversation with Steve Kerr," *Organizational Dynamics,* Spring 1996, pp. 68–79; and J. Gebhardt, "The Boundaryless Organization," *Sloan Management Review,* Winter 1996, pp. 117–119. For another view of boundaryless organizations, see B. Victor, "The Dark Side of the New Organizational Forms: An Editorial Essay," *Organization Science*, November 1994, pp. 479–482.

38. See, for instance, Y. Shin, "A Person-Environment Fit Model for Virtual Organizations," *Journal of Management* (December 2004), pp. 725–743; D. Lyons, "Smart and Smarter," *Forbes,* March 18, 2002, pp. 40–41; W. F. Cascio, "Managing a Virtual Workplace," *Academy of Management Executive,* August 2000, pp. 81–90; G. G. Dess, A. M. A. Rasheed, K. J. McLaughlin, and R. L. Priem, "The New Corporate Architecture"; H. Chesbrough and D. Teece, "When Is Virtual Virtuous: Organizing for Innovation," *Harvard Business Review,* January–February 1996, pp. 65–73; and W. H. Davidow and M. S. Malone, *The Virtual Corporation* (New York: Harper Collins, 1992).

39. "Could Your Brand Pass the Tee Shirt Test?" *Fortune,* May 28, 2007, p. 122; M. Maddever, "The New School: An Inconvenient Truth," www.strategymag.com (April 2007); K. Hugh, "Goodson Forecasts Future Shock," www.adweek.com (March 5, 2007); J. Ewing, "Amsterdam's Red-Hot Ad Shops," *BusinessWeek,* December 18, 2006, p. 52; and T. Howard, "Strawberry Frog Hops to a Different Drummer," *USA Today,* October 10, 2005 p. 4B.

40. R. E. Miles, C. C. Snow, J. A. Matthews, G. Miles, and H. J. Coleman, Jr., "Organizing in the Knowledge Age: Anticipating the Cellular Form," *Academy of Management Executive,* November 1997, pp. 7–24; C. Jones, W. Hesterly, and S. Borgatti, "A General Theory of Network Governance: Exchange Conditions and Social Mechanisms," *Academy of Management Review,* October 1997, pp. 911–945; R. E. Miles and C. C. Snow, "The New Network Firm: A Spherical Structure Built on Human Investment Philosophy," *Organizational Dynamics,* Spring 1995, pp. 5–18; and R. E. Miles and C. C. Snow, "Causes of Failures in Network Organizations," *California Management Review,* vol. 34, no. 4 (1992), pp. 53–72.

41. G. Hoetker, "Do Modular Products Lead to Modular Organizations?" *Strategic Management Journal* (June 2006), pp. 501–518; C. H. Fine, "Are You Modular or Integral?" *Strategy & Business,* Summer 2005, pp. 44–51; D. A. Ketchen, Jr. and G. T. M. Hult, "To Be Modular or Not to Be? Some Answers to the Question," *Academy of Management Executive,* May 2002, pp. 166–167; M. A. Schilling, "The Use of Modular Organizational Forms: An Industry-Level Analysis," *Academy of Management Journal* (December 2001), pp. 1149–1168; D. Lei, M. A. Hitt, and J. D. Goldhar, "Advanced Manufacturing Technology: Organizational Design and Strategic Flexibility," *Organization Studies,* vol. 17 (1996), pp. 501–523; R. Sanchez and J. Mahoney, "Modularity Flexibility and Knowledge Management in Product and Organization Design," *Strategic Management Journal,* vol. 17 (1996), pp. 63–76; and R. Sanchez, "Strategic Flexibility in Product Competition," *Strategic Management Journal,* vol. 16 (1995), pp. 135–159.

42. C. Hymowitz, "Have Advice, Will Travel," *Wall Street Journal,* June 5, 2006, pp B1+.

43. S. Reed, A. Reinhardt, and A. Sains, "Saving Ericsson," *BusinessWeek,* November 11, 2002, pp. 64–68.

44. P. Engardio, "The Future of Outsourcing," *BusinessWeek,* January 30, 2006, pp. 50–58.

45. C. E. Connelly and D. G. Gallagher, "Emerging Trends in Contingent Work Research," *Journal of Management* (November 2004), pp. 959–983.

46. Technology and the Manager's Job box based on R. Cheng, "So You Want to Use Your iPhone for Work? How the Smartest Companies Are Letting Employees Use Their Personal Gadgets to Do Their Jobs," *Wall Street Journal,* April 25, 2011, pp. R1+; B. Roberts, "Mobile Workforce Management," *HR Magazine,* March 2011, pp. 67–70; D. Darlin, "Software That Monitors Your Work, Wherever You Are," *New York Times Online* www.nytimesonline.com (April 12, 2009); D. Pauleen and B. Harmer, "Away from the Desk…Always," *Wall Street Journal,* December 15, 2008, p. R8; J. Marquez, "Connecting a Virtual Workforce," *Workforce Management Online* www.workforce.com (September 22, 2008); R. Yu, "Work Away from Work Gets Easier with Technology," *USA Today,* November 28, 2006, p. 8B; M. Weinstein, "GOing Mobile," *Training,* September 2006, pp. 24–29; C. Cobbs, "Technology Helps Boost Multitasking," *Springfield, Missouri News-Leader,* June 15, 2006, p. 5B; C. Edwards, "Wherever You Go, You're On the Job," *BusinessWeek,* June 20, 2005, pp. 87–90; and S. E. Ante, "The World Wide Work Space," *BusinessWeek,* June 6, 2005, pp. 106–108.

47. N. M. Adler, *International Dimensions of Organizational Behavior,* 5th ed. (Cincinnati, OH: South-Western), 2008, p. 62.

48. P. B. Smith and M. F. Peterson, "Demographic Effects on the Use of Vertical Sources of Guidance by Managers in Widely Differing Cultural Contexts," *International Journal of Cross Cultural Management* (April 2005), pp. 5–26.

49. P. Olson, "Tesco's Landing," *Forbes,* June 4, 2007, pp. 116–118; and P. M. Senge, *The Fifth Discipline: The Art and Practice of Learning Organizations* (New York: Doubleday, 1990).

50. J. Marquez, "Connecting a Virtual Workforce," *Workforce Management Online,* February 3, 2009.

51. M. Conlin, "Home Offices: The New Math," *BusinessWeek,* March 9, 2009, pp. 66–68.

52. Ibid.

53. J. Marquez, "Connecting a Virtual Workforce."

54. S. Jayson, "Working at Home: Family-Friendly," *USA Today,* April 15, 2010, pp. 1A+; T. D. Hecht and N. J. Allen, "A Longitudinal Examination of the Work-Nonwork Boundary Strength Construct," *Journal of Organizational Behavior* (October 2009), pp. 839–862; and G. E. Kreiner, E. C. Hollensbe, and M. L. Sheep, "Balancing Borders and Bridges: Negotiating the Work-Home Interface via Boundary Work Tactics," *Academy of Management Journal* (August 2009), pp. 704–730.

55. J. T. Marquez, "The Future of Flex," *Workforce Management Online,* January 2010.

56. S. Greenhouse, "Work-Sharing May Help Companies Avoid Layoffs," *New York Times Online,* June 16, 2009.

57. R. King, "Meet the Microworkers," *Bloomberg BusinessWeek Online,* February 1, 2011; and R. King, "Mechanical Serfdom Is Just That," *Bloomberg BusinessWeek Online,* February 1, 2011.

58. K. Bennhold, "Working (Part-Time) in the 21st Century," *New York Times Online,* December 29, 2010; and J. Revell, C. Bigda, and D. Rosato, "The Rise of Freelance Nation," *CNNMoney,* cnnmoney.com, June 12, 2009.

59. Revell, Bigda, and Rosato, "The Rise of Freelance Nation."

60. Ibid.

61. H. G. Jackson, "Flexible Workplaces: The Next Imperative," *HR Magazine,* March 2011, p. 8; E. Frauenheim, "Companies Focus Their Attention on Flexibility," *Workforce Management Online,* February 2011; P. Davidson, "Companies Do More with Fewer Workers," *USA Today,* February 23, 2011, pp. 1B+; M. Rich, "Weighing Costs, Companies Favor Temporary Help," *New York Times Online,* December 19, 2010; and P. Davidson, "Temporary Workers Reshape Companies, Jobs," *USA Today,* October 13, 2010, pp. 1B+.

YOUR TURN TO BE A MANAGER

Organization Structure and Design

Skill Development: Developing Your Power Base

Managerial jobs come with the power of authority. But sometimes that authority isn't enough to get things done. And other times you may not want to use your formal authority as a means of getting people to do what you want. You may, for instance, want to rely more on your persuasive skills than the power of your title. So effective managers increase their power by developing multiple sources of influence.

Personal Insights: How Power-Oriented Am I?

For each of statement, select the response that most closely resembles your attitude. Use the following ratings scale for your responses:

1 = Disagree a lot
2 = Disagree a little
3 = Neutral
4 = Agree a little
5 = Agree a lot

1. The best way to handle people is to tell them what they want to hear. 1 2 3 4 5

2. When you ask someone to do something for you, it is best to give the real reason for wanting it rather than giving reasons that might carry more weight. 1 2 3 4 5

3. Anyone who completely trusts anyone else is asking for trouble. 1 2 3 4 5

4. It is hard to get ahead without cutting corners here and there. 1 2 3 4 5

5. It is safest to assume that all people have a vicious streak, and it will come out when they are given a chance. 1 2 3 4 5

6. One should take action only when it is morally right. 1 2 3 4 5

7. Most people are basically good and kind. 1 2 3 4 5

8. There is no excuse for lying to someone else.   1 2 3 4 5

9. Most people more easily forget the death of their father than the loss of their property.   1 2 3 4 5

10. Generally speaking, people won't work hard unless they're forced to do so.   1 2 3 4 5

Source: R. Christie and F. L. Geis, *Studies in Machiavellianism.* ©Academic Press 1970. With permission.

Analysis and Interpretation

This instrument was designed to compute your Machiavellianism (Mach) score. Machiavelli wrote in the sixteenth century on how to gain and manipulate power. An individual with a high-Mach score is pragmatic, maintains emotional distance, and believes that ends can justify means.

To obtain your score, add your responses to questions 1, 3, 4, 5, 9, and 10. For the other four questions, reverse your scores (5 becomes 1, 4 becomes 2, and so on). The National Opinion Research Center, which used this instrument in a random sample of American adults, found that the national average was 25.

High-Machs are more likely to manipulate more, win more, are persuaded less, and persuade others more than do low-Machs. High-Machs are also more likely to shade the truth or act unethically in ambiguous situations where the outcome is important to them.

Skill Basics

You can increase the likelihood that you'll survive and thrive in your organization if you learn how to develop a power base. Remember, because you have power doesn't mean you have to use it. But it's nice to be able to call upon it when you do need it.

Four sources of power can be derived from your job. Another three sources are based on your personal unique characteristics.

All management jobs come with the power to coerce, reward, and impose authority. *Coercive power* is based on fear. If you can dismiss, suspend, demote, assign unpleasant work tasks, or write a negative performance review on someone, you hold coercive power over that person. Conversely, if you can give someone something of positive value or remove something of negative value—like control pay rates, raises, bonuses, promotions, or work assignments—you have *reward power*. And all managerial positions provide some degree—though within specific limitations—to exert authority over subordinates. If you can tell someone to do something and they see this request to be within your formal job description, you have *authority power* over them.

In addition to coercive, reward, and authoritative power, many managerial positions also possess *information power* that comes from access to and control over information. If you have data or knowledge that others need, and which only you have access to, it gives you power. Of course, you don't have to be a manager to have information power. Many employees are quite skilled at operating in secrecy, hiding technical short-cuts, or avoiding showing others exactly what they do—all with the intention of keeping important knowledge from getting into others' hands.

You don't have to be a manager or control information to have power in an organization. You can also exert influence based on your expertise, admiration that others might have for you, and through charismatic qualities. If you have a special skill or unique knowledge that others in the organization depend on, you hold *expert power*. In our current age of specialization, this source of power is increasingly potent. If others identify with you and look up to you to the extent that they want to please you, you have *referent power*. It develops out of admiration and the desire to be like someone else. The final source of influence is *charismatic power*, which is an extension of referent power. If others will follow you because they admire your heroic qualities, you have charismatic power over them.

Based on these sources of power, we can say that you can increase your power in organizations by taking on managerial responsibilities, gaining access to important information, developing an expertise that the organization needs, or displaying personal characteristics that others admire.

Based on J. R. P. French, Jr. and B. Raven, "The Bases of Social Power," in D. Cartwright (ed.), *Studies in Social Power* (Ann Arbor: University of Michigan Institute of Social Research, 1959), pp. 150–167; B. J. Raven, "The Bases of Power: Origin and Recent Developments," *Journal of Social Issues,* 49 (1993), pp. 227–251; E. A. Ward, "Social Power Bases of Managers: Emergence of a New Factor," *Journal of Social Psychology* (February 2001), pp. 144–147; and B. H. Raven, "The Bases of Power and the Power/Interaction Model of Interpersonal Influence," *Analyses of Social Issues and Public Policy,* December 2008, pp. 1–22.

Skill Application

Margaret is a supervisor in the online sales division of a large clothing retailer. She has let it be known that she is devoted to the firm and plans to build her career there. Margaret is hardworking and reliable, has volunteered for extra projects, has taken in-house development courses, and joined a committee dedicated to improving employee safety on the job. She undertook an assignment to research ergonomic office furniture for the head of the department and gave up several lunch hours to consult with the head of human resources about her report. Margaret filed the report late, but she explained the delay by saying that her assistant lost several pages that she had to redraft over the weekend. The report was well received, and several of Margaret's colleagues think she should be promoted when the next opening arises.

Evaluate Margaret's skill in building a power base. What actions has she taken that are helpful to her in reaching her goal? Is there anything she should have done differently?

Skill Practice

1. What can you do to improve your Mach score? Create a specific one-year plan to implement a program that will lead to an improved score.

2. Identify someone—a boss, coworker, friend, parent, sibling, significant other—with whom you would like to increase your power. Determine what tactic(s) might work, then cautiously practice your tactic(s).

FYIA

For Your Immediate Action

Ontario Electronics Ltd.

To: Claude Fortier, Special Assistant to the President

From: Ian Campbell, President

Subject: Learning Organizations

First of all, thanks for keeping everything "going" while I attended the annual meeting of the Canadian Electronics Manufacturers Industry Association last week. Our luncheon speaker on the final day talked about how important it is for organizations to be responsive to customer and marketplace needs. One approach she discussed for doing this was becoming a learning organization. I'm now convinced that our company's future may well depend on how well we're able to "learn."

I'd like you to find some current information on learning organizations. Although I'm sure you'll be able to find numerous articles about the topic, limit your report to five of what you consider to be the best sources of information on the topic. Write a one-paragraph summary for each of these five articles, being sure to note all the bibliographic information in case we need to find the article later. Since I'd like our executive team to move on this idea fairly quickly, please have your report back to me by the end of the week.

This fictionalized company and message were created for educational purposes only, and not meant to reflect positively or negatively on management practices by any company that may share this name.

Bringing the Real World to Life

Case Application: Volunteers Work: Part 2

Self check-outs. Self check-ins. Pumping your own gas (although most of you are probably too young to remember having an attendant that pumped your gas, checked your oil, and washed your windshield). Filling out online forms. Businesses have become very good at getting customers to do free work. Now, they're taking the concept even further, especially in customer service settings, by getting "volunteers" to perform specialized work tasks.

The role that these volunteer "enthusiasts" have played, especially in contributing innovations to research and development efforts, has been closely researched in recent years. For example, case studies highlight the product tweaks made by early skateboarders and mountain bikers to their gear. Researchers have

also studied the programmers behind open-source software like the Linux operating system. It seems that individuals who do this type of "volunteering" are motivated mainly by a payoff in enjoyment and respect among their peers and to some extent the skills they're able to develop. Now, as the concept of individuals volunteering for work tasks moves to the realm of customer service, can it work and what does it mean for managers?

For instance, at Verizon's high-speed fiber optic Internet, television, and telephone service, "volunteers" are answering customer questions about technical matters on a company-sponsored customer-service Web site for no pay. Mark Studness, director of Verizon's e-commerce unit was familiar with Web sites where users offered tips and answered questions. His challenge? Find a way to use that potential resource for customer service. His solution? "Super" or lead users—that is, users who provided the best answers and dialogue in Web forums.

The experiment at Verizon "suggests that company-sponsored online communities for customer service, if handled adeptly, hold considerable promise." Studness says that "you have to make an environment that attracts these super users of the world, because that's where the magic happens." A company that worked with Verizon to set up its structure said that "the mentality of super-users in online customer-service communities is similar to that of devout gamers." So they set up the structure with an elaborate rating system for contributors with ranks, badges, and "kudos counts." So far, Studness is happy with how it's gone. He says the company-sponsored customer-service site is "a very productive tool, partly because it absorbs many thousands of questions that would otherwise be expensive calls to a Verizon call center."

DISCUSSION QUESTIONS

1. What do you think about using "volunteers" to do work that other people get paid to do?

2. If you were in Mark Studness's position, what would you be most concerned about in this arrangement? How would you "manage" that concern?

3. How do these "volunteers" fit into an organization's structure? Take each of the six elements of organization design and discuss how each would affect this structural approach.

4. Do you think this approach could work for other types of work being done or in other types of organizations? Explain.

Managing Human Resources

Managing Human Resources

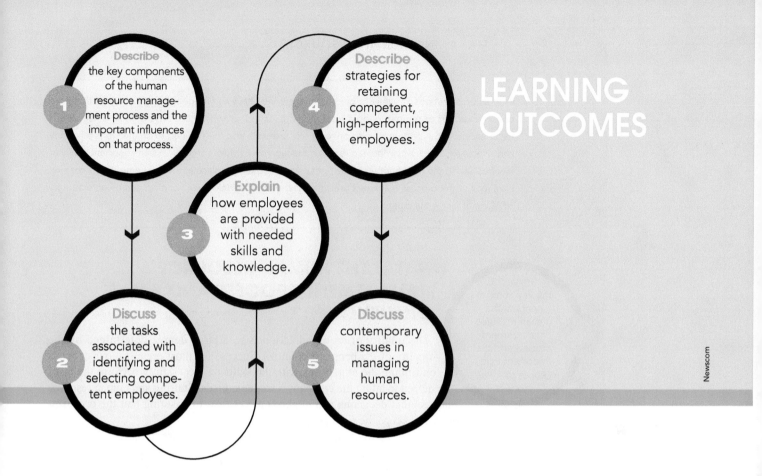

Describe the key components of the human resource management process and the important influences on that process.

1

Describe strategies for retaining competent, high-performing employees.

4

Explain how employees are provided with needed skills and knowledge.

3

Discuss the tasks associated with identifying and selecting competent employees.

2

Discuss contemporary issues in managing human resources.

5

Newscom

Thinking Outside the Box

It's the world's largest package delivery company with the instantly recognizable brown trucks.[1] Every day United Parcel Service (UPS) transports some 15 million packages and documents throughout the United States and to more than 215 countries and territories (and more than 430 million packages alone during the month before Christmas). And delivering those packages quickly and correctly is what it gets paid to do. In fact, UPS has been described as an "efficiency freak." That massive effort wouldn't be possible without its 99,000-plus drivers. However, UPS recognizes that it has an HR challenge: hiring and training some 25,000 drivers over the next five years to replace retiring Baby Boomers. But the company has a plan in place that combines its tested business model of uniformity and efficiency (for instance, drivers are trained to hold their keys on a pinky finger so they don't waste time fumbling in their pockets for the keys) with a new approach to driver training.

With an organization's structure in place, managers then have to find people to fill the jobs that have been created or to remove people from jobs if business circumstances require it. And like UPS is experiencing, those people have to be recruited, selected, and then trained to do their jobs efficiently and effectively. That's where human resource management (HRM) comes in. It's an important task that involves having the right number of the right people in the right place at the right time. In this chapter, we'll look at the process managers use to do just that. In addition, we'll look at some contemporary HRM issues facing managers.

Describe the key components of the human resource management process and the important influences on that process.

1

WHAT IS THE HUMAN RESOURCE MANAGEMENT PROCESS AND WHAT INFLUENCES IT?

The quality of an organization is to a large degree determined by the quality of the people it employs. Success for most organizations depends on finding the employees with the skills to successfully perform the tasks required to attain the company's strategic goals. Staffing and human resource management decisions and methods are critical to ensuring that the organization hires and keeps the right people.

Some of you may be thinking, "Sure, personnel decisions are important. But aren't most of them made by people who specifically handle human resource issues?" It's true that, in many organizations, a number of the activities grouped under the label **human resource management (HRM)** are done by specialists. In other cases, HRM activities may be outsourced to companies, domestic or global. Not all managers have HRM staff support, though. Many small business managers, for instance, frequently must do their own hiring without the assistance of HRM specialists. Even managers in larger organizations are often involved in recruiting candidates, reviewing application forms, interviewing applicants, orienting new employees, making decisions about employee training, providing career advice to employees, and evaluating employees' performance. So, even if an organization provides HRM support activities, every manager is involved with human resource decisions in his or her unit.[2]

Exhibit 1 introduces the key components of an organization's HRM process. It represents eight activities (the yellow boxes) that, if properly executed, will staff an organization with competent, high-performing employees who are capable of sustaining their performance level over the long term.

After an organization's strategy has been established and the organization structure designed, it's time to add the people. That's one of the most critical roles for HRM and one that has increased the importance of human resource managers to the organization. The first three activities in the HRM process represent employment planning: the addition of staff through recruitment, the reduction in staff through downsizing, and selection. When executed properly, these steps lead to the identification and selection of competent employees and assist organizations in achieving their strategic directions.

Once you select competent people, you need to help them adapt to the organization and ensure that their job skills and knowledge are kept current. These next two activities in the HRM process are accomplished through orientation and training. The last steps in the HRM process are designed to identify performance goals, correct performance problems if necessary, and help employees sustain a high level of performance over their entire work life. The activities involved include performance appraisal, and compensation and benefits. HRM also includes safety and health issues, but we're not covering those topics in this book.

Notice in Exhibit 1 that the entire process is influenced by the external environment.

EXHIBIT 1   The Human Resource Management Process

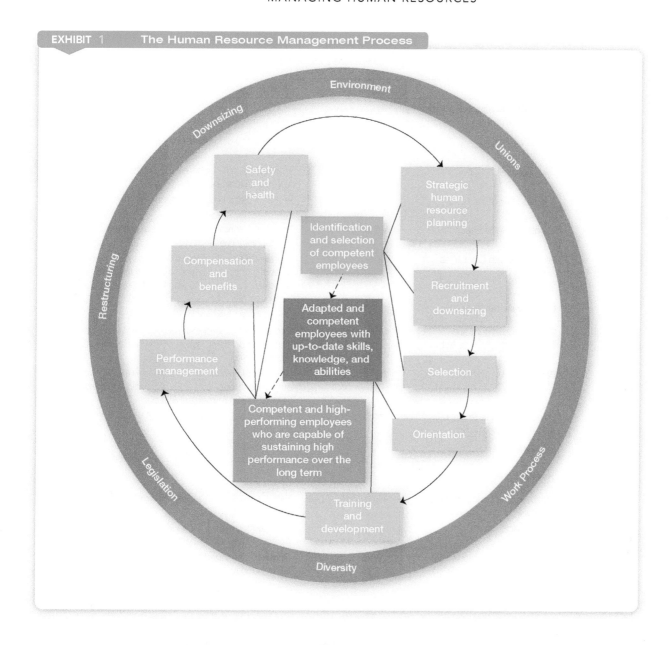

Before we review the HRM process, let's examine one primary environmental force that affects it—the legal environment, and employment and discrimination laws in particular.

What Is the Legal Environment of HRM?

HRM practices are governed by laws, which vary from country to country. Within countries, state or provincial and local regulations further influence specific practices. Consequently, it's impossible to provide you with all the information you need about the relevant regulatory environment. As a manager, it will be important for you to know what you can and cannot do, legally.

human resource management (HRM)
The management function concerned with getting, training, motivating, and keeping competent employees

EXHIBIT 2   Major HRM Laws

LAWS		
LAW OR RULING	YEAR	DESCRIPTION
Equal Employment Opportunity and Discrimination		
Equal Pay Act	1963	Prohibits pay differences for equal work based on gender
Civil Rights Act, Title VII	1964 (amended in 1972)	Prohibits discrimination based on race, color, religion, national origin, or gender
Age Discrimination in Employment Act	1967 (amended in 1978)	Prohibits discrimination against employees 40 years and older
Vocational Rehabilitation Act	1973	Prohibits discrimination on the basis of physical or mental disabilities
Americans with Disabilities Act	1990	Prohibits discrimination against individuals who have disabilities or chronic illnesses; also requires reasonable accommodations for these individuals
Compensation/Benefits		
Worker Adjustment and Retraining Notification Act	1990	Requires employers with more than 100 employees to provide 60 days' notice before a mass layoff or facility closing
Family and Medical Leave Act	1993	Gives employees in organizations with 50 or more employees up to 12 weeks of unpaid leave each year for family or medical reasons
Health Insurance Portability and Accountability Act	1996	Permits portability of employees' insurance from one employer to another
Lilly Ledbetter Fair Pay Act	2009	Changes the statute of limitations on pay discrimination to 180 days from each paycheck
Health/Safety		
Occupational Safety and Health Act (OSHA)	1970	Establishes mandatory and health standards in organizations
Privacy Act	1974	Gives employees the legal right to examine personnel files and letters of reference
Consolidated Omnibus Reconciliation Act (COBRA)	1985	Requires continued health coverage following termination (paid by employee)

WHAT ARE THE PRIMARY U.S. LAWS AFFECTING HRM?   Since the mid-1960s, the federal government in the United States has greatly expanded its influence over HRM by enacting a number of laws and regulations (see Exhibit 2 for examples). Although we've not seen many laws enacted recently at the federal level, many state laws have been passed that add to the provisions of the federal laws. For instance, in many states today, it's illegal to discriminate against an individual based on sexual orientation. As a result, today's employers must ensure that equal employment opportunities exist for job applicants and current employees. Decisions regarding who will be hired, for example, or which employees will be chosen for a management training program must be made without regard to race, sex, religion, age, color, national origin, or disability. Exceptions can occur only when special circumstances exist. For instance, a community fire department can deny employment to a firefighter applicant who is confined to a wheelchair, but if that same individual is applying for a desk job, such as a fire department dispatcher, the disability cannot be used as a reason to deny employment. The issues involved, however, are rarely that clear-cut. For example, employment laws protect most employees whose religious beliefs require a specific style of dress—robes, long shirts, long hair, and the like. However, if the specific style of dress may be hazardous or unsafe in the work setting (e.g., when operating machinery), a company could refuse to hire a person who would not adopt a safer dress code.

From the Past to the Present

Hugo Munsterberg was a pioneer in the field of industrial psychology and is "generally credited with creating the field."[3] As an admirer of Frederick W. Taylor and the scientific management movement, Munsterberg stated that "Taylor had introduced most valuable suggestions which the industrial world cannot ignore." Drawing on Taylor's works, Munsterberg stressed "the importance of efficiently using workers to achieve economic production." His research and work in showing organizations ways to improve the performance and well-being of workers was fundamental to the emerging field of management in the early 1900s.

Today, industrial-organizational psychology is defined as the scientific study of the workplace. Industrial-organizational (I/O) psychologists use scientific principles and research-based designs to generate knowledge about workplace issues. (Check out the Society for Industrial and Organizational Psychology at www.siop.org.) They study organizational topics such as job performance, job analysis, performance appraisal, compensation, work/life balance, work sample tests, employee training, employment law, personnel recruitment and selection, and so forth. Their research has contributed much to the field that we call human resource management. And all of this is due to the early work done by Hugo Munsterberg.

Think About:

- Why is it important to scientifically study the workplace?

- Do you think it's easier today to scientifically study the workplace than it was back in Munsterberg's days? Why or why not?

- How has I/O psychology contributed to HRM?

- Go to the SIOP Web site. Find the student section and the discussion of what I/O psychologists really do. In a bulleted list, summarize one of the individual profiles.

Trying to balance the "shoulds and should-nots" of these laws often falls within the realm of affirmative action programs. Many organizations operating in the United States have affirmative action programs to ensure that decisions and practices enhance the employment, upgrading, and retention of members from protected groups such as minorities and females. These organizations refrain from discrimination and actively seek to enhance the status of members from protected groups.

U.S. managers are not completely free to choose whom they hire, promote, or fire. Although these regulations have significantly helped to reduce employment discrimination and unfair employment practices, they have, at the same time, reduced management's discretion over HR decisions.

ARE HRM LAWS THE SAME GLOBALLY? HRM laws aren't the same globally. You need to know the laws and regulations that apply in your locale. Let's look at some of the federal legislation in countries such as Canada, Mexico, Australia, and Germany.

Canadian HRM laws closely parallel those in the United States. The Canadian Human Rights Act prohibits discrimination on the basis of race, religion, age, marital status, sex, physical or mental disability, or national origin. This law governs practices throughout the country. Canada's HRM environment, however, is somewhat different from that in the United States in that it involves more decentralization of lawmaking to the provincial level. For example, discrimination on the basis of language is not prohibited anywhere in Canada except in Quebec.

In Mexico, employees are more likely to be unionized than they are in the United States. Labor issues in Mexico are governed by the Mexican Federal Labor Law. One hiring law states that an employer has 28 days to evaluate a new employee's work performance. After that period, the employee is granted job security and termination is quite difficult and expensive. Those who violate the Mexican Federal Labor Law are subject to severe penalties, including criminal action that can result in steep fines and even jail sentences for employers who fail to pay, for example, the minimum wage.

Australia's discrimination laws were not enacted until the 1980s, and generally apply to discrimination and affirmative action for women. Yet, gender opportunities for women in Australia appear to lag behind those in the United States. In Australia,

affirmative action programs
Programs that ensure that decisions and practices enhance the employment, upgrading, and retention of members of protected groups

however, a significant proportion of the workforce is unionized. The higher percentage of unionized workers has placed increased importance on industrial relations specialists in Australia, and reduced the control of line managers over workplace labor issues. However, in 1997, Australia overhauled its labor and industrial relations laws with the objective of increasing productivity and reducing union power. The Workplace Relations Bill gives employers greater flexibility to negotiate directly with employees on pay, hours, and benefits. It also simplifies federal regulation of labor–management relations.

Our final example, Germany, is similar to most Western European countries when it comes to HRM practices. Legislation requires companies to practice representative participation, in which the goal is to redistribute power within the organization, putting labor on a more equal footing with the interests of management and stockholders. The two most common forms of representative participation are work councils and board representatives. Work councils link employees with management. They are groups of nominated or elected employees who must be consulted when management makes decisions involving personnel. Board representatives are employees who sit on a company's board of directors and represent the interest of the firm's employees.

Discuss the tasks associated with identifying and selecting competent employees.

2

HOW DO MANAGERS IDENTIFY AND SELECT COMPETENT EMPLOYEES?

Every organization needs people to do whatever work is necessary for doing what the organization is in business to do. How do organizations get those people? And more importantly what can they do to ensure they get competent, talented people? This first phase of the HRM process involves three tasks: employment planning, recruitment and downsizing, and selection.

What Is Employment Planning?

Internet start-ups across Silicon Valley are struggling to compete for talent as more-established companies such as Facebook, Twitter, and Zynga are looking to add employees as business continues to grow. During the last economic downturn, Boeing cut more than 3,000 jobs, mostly from its commercial airplanes unit. During the same time, it added 106 employees to its defense unit and was looking for several hundred more.[4] Like many companies, these start-ups and Boeing are juggling the supply of human resources to meet demand.

Employment planning is the process by which managers ensure that they have the right number and kinds of people in the right places at the right times, people who are capable of effectively and efficiently completing those tasks that will help the organization achieve its overall goals. Employment planning, then, translates the organization's mission and goals into an HR plan that will allow the organization to achieve those goals. The process can be condensed into two steps: (1) assessing current human resources and future human resource needs, and (2) developing a plan to meet those needs.

HOW DOES AN ORGANIZATION CONDUCT AN EMPLOYEE ASSESSMENT? Managers begin by reviewing the current human resource status. This review is typically done by generating a human resource inventory. It's not difficult to generate an inventory in most organizations since the information for it is derived from forms completed by employees. Such inventories might list the name, education, training, prior employment, languages spoken, capabilities, and specialized skills of each employee in the organization. This inventory allows managers to assess what talents and skills are currently available in the organization.

Another part of the current assessment is job analysis. Whereas the human resources inventory is concerned with telling management what individual employees can do, job analysis is more fundamental. It's typically a lengthy process, one in which workflows are analyzed and skills and behaviors that are necessary to perform jobs are identified. For instance, what does an international reporter who works for the *Wall Street Journal* do? What minimal knowledge, skills, and abilities are necessary for the adequate performance of this job? How do the job requirements for an international reporter compare with those for a domestic reporter or for a newspaper editor? Job analysis can answer these questions. Ultimately, the purpose of job analysis is to determine the kinds of skills, knowledge, and attitudes needed to successfully perform each job. This information is then used to develop or revise job descriptions and job specifications.

A **job description** is a written statement that describes the job—what a job holder does, how it's done, and why it's done. It typically portrays job content, environment, and conditions of employment. The **job specification** states the minimum qualifications that a person must possess to perform a given job successfully. It focuses on the person and identifies the knowledge, skills, and attitudes needed to do the job effectively. The job description and job specification are important documents when managers begin recruiting and selecting. For instance, the job description can be used to describe the job to potential candidates. The job specification keeps the manager's attention on the list of qualifications necessary for an incumbent to perform a job and assists in determining whether candidates are qualified. Furthermore, hiring individuals on the basis of the information contained in these two documents helps ensure that the hiring process does not discriminate.

3M Company needs a constant flow of creative scientists and engineers into its organization in order to achieve its goal of continually inventing new products through technological innovation. In a typical year, 3M hires several hundred scientists and technical experts. But faced with a future shortage of employees in these fields, 3M has developed a plan to replenish its supply of scientists. Part of the plan is an educational program that brings public high school students to 3M headquarters where they learn directly about science and technology from the company's researchers. In this photo, a 3M research specialist (left) works with a student in the company's adhesives laboratory.

HOW ARE FUTURE EMPLOYEE NEEDS DETERMINED? Future human resource needs are determined by the organization's strategic direction. Demand for human resources (employees) is a result of demand for the organization's products or services. On the basis of an estimate of total revenue, managers can attempt to establish the number and mix of people needed to reach that revenue. In some cases, however, the situation may be reversed. When particular skills are necessary and in scarce supply, the availability of needed human resources determines revenues. For example, managers of an upscale chain of assisted-living retirement facilities who find themselves with abundant business opportunities are limited in growing revenues by whether they can hire a qualified nursing staff to fully meet the needs of the residents. In most cases, however, the overall organizational goals and the resulting revenue forecast provide the major input in determining the organization's HR requirements.

After assessing both current capabilities and future needs, managers can estimate shortages—both in number and in kind—and highlight areas in which the organization is overstaffed. They can then develop a plan that matches these estimates with forecasts of future labor supply. Employment planning not only guides current staffing needs but also projects future employee needs and availability.

work councils
Groups of nominated or elected employees who must be consulted when management makes decisions involving personnel

board representatives
Employees who sit on a company's board of directors and represent the interest of employees

employment planning
The process by which managers ensure they have the right numbers and kinds of people in the right places at the right time

human resource inventory
A report listing important information about employees such as name, education, training, skills, languages spoken, and so forth

job analysis
An assessment that defines jobs and the behaviors necessary to perform them

job description
A written statement that describes a job

job specification
A written statement of the minimum qualifications that a person must possess to perform a given job successfully

How Do Organizations Recruit Employees?

Once managers know their current staffing levels—understaffed or overstaffed—they can begin to do something about it. If vacancies exist, they can use the information gathered through job analysis to guide them in recruitment—that is, the process of locating, identifying, and attracting capable applicants. On the other hand, if employment planning indicates a surplus, managers may want to reduce the labor supply within the organization and initiate downsizing or restructuring activities.

WHERE DOES A MANAGER RECRUIT APPLICANTS? Applicants can be found by using several sources, including the Internet. Exhibit 3 offers some guidance. The source that's used should reflect the local labor market, the type or level of position, and the size of the organization.

Which recruiting sources tend to produce superior applicants? Most studies have found that employee referrals generally produce the best applicants.[5] Why? First, applicants referred by current employees are prescreened by those employees. Because the recommenders know both the job and the person being recommended, they tend to refer well-qualified applicants.[6] Second, because current employees often feel that their reputation in the organization is at stake with a referral, they tend to make referrals only when they are reasonably confident that the referral won't make them look bad. However, managers shouldn't always opt for the employee-referred applicant; such referrals may not increase the diversity and mix of employees.

How Does a Manager Handle Layoffs?

Nokia reduces its global workforce by 7,000 (nearly 5% of its total workforce). Panasonic, the biggest Japanese maker of consumer electronic goods, cuts 17,000 jobs as it "adapts its business to a changing global environment." MySpace lays off 500 employees, cutting its staff count by 47 percent.[7]

In the past decade, and especially during the last couple of years, most global organizations, as well as many government agencies and small businesses, have been forced to shrink the size of their workforce or restructure their skill composition. Downsizing has become a relevant strategy for meeting the demands of a dynamic environment.

EXHIBIT 3	Recruiting Sources	
SOURCE	**ADVANTAGE**	**DISADVANTAGE**
Internal searches	Low cost; build employee morale; candidates are familiar with organization	Limited supply; may not increase proportion of protected group employees
Advertisements	Wide distribution can be targeted to specific groups	Generate many unqualified candidates
Employee referrals	Knowledge about the organization provided by current employees; can generate strong candidates because a good referral reflects on the recommender	May not increase the diversity and mix of employees
Public employment agencies	Free or nominal cost	Candidates tend to be lower skilled, although some skilled employees available
Private employment agencies	Wide contacts; careful screening; short-term guarantees often given	High cost
School placement	Large, centralized body of candidates	Limited to entry-level positions
Temporary help services	Fill temporary needs	Expensive
Employee leasing and independent contractors	Fill temporary needs but usually for more specific, longer-term projects	Little commitment to an organization other than current project

EXHIBIT 4   Downsizing Options

OPTION	DESCRIPTION
Firing	Permanent involuntary termination
Layoffs	Temporary involuntary termination; may last only a few days or extend to years
Attrition	Not filling openings created by voluntary resignations or normal retirements
Transfers	Moving employees either laterally or downward; usually does not reduce costs but can reduce intraorganizational supply–demand imbalances
Reduced workweeks	Having employees work fewer hours per week, share jobs, or through furloughs perform their jobs on a part-time basis
Early retirements	Providing incentives to older and more-senior employees for retiring before their normal retirement date
Job sharing	Having employees, typically two part-timers, share one full-time position

WHAT ARE DOWNSIZING OPTIONS?   Obviously, people can be fired, but other restructuring choices may be more beneficial to the organization. Exhibit 4 summarizes a manager's major downsizing options. Keep in mind that, regardless of the method chosen, employees may suffer. We discuss downsizing more fully—for both victims and survivors—later in this chapter.

How Do Managers Select Job Applicants?

Once the recruiting effort has developed a pool of applicants, the next step in the HRM process is to determine who is best qualified for the job. In essence, then, the selection process is a prediction exercise: It seeks to predict which applicants will be "successful" if hired; that is, who will perform well on the criteria the organization uses to evaluate its employees. In filling a network administrator position, for example, the selection process should be able to predict which applicants will be capable of properly installing, debugging, and managing the organization's computer network. For a position as a sales representative, it should predict which applicants will be successful at generating high sales volumes. Consider, for a moment, that any selection decision can result in four possible outcomes. As shown in Exhibit 5, two outcomes would indicate correct decisions, and two would indicate errors.

EXHIBIT 5   Selection Decision Outcomes

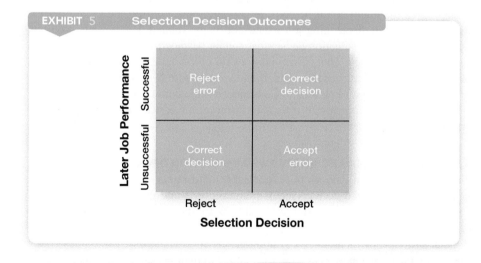

recruitment
Locating, identifying, and attracting capable applicants

selection process
Screening job applicants to ensure that the most appropriate candidates are hired

A decision is correct (1) when the applicant who was predicted to be successful (was accepted) and later proved to be successful on the job, or (2) when the applicant who was predicted to be unsuccessful (was rejected) and, if hired, would not have been able to do the job. In the former case, we have successfully accepted; in the latter case, we have successfully rejected. Problems occur, however, when we reject applicants who, if hired, would have performed successfully on the job (called *reject errors*) or accept those who subsequently perform poorly (*accept errors*). These problems are, unfortunately, far from insignificant. A generation ago, reject errors only meant increased selection costs because more applicants would have to be screened. Today, selection techniques that result in reject errors can open the organization to charges of employment discrimination, especially if applicants from protected groups are disproportionately rejected. Accept errors, on the other hand, have obvious costs to the organization, including the cost of training the employee, the costs generated or profits forgone because of the employee's incompetence, and the cost of severance and the subsequent costs of additional recruiting and selection screening. The major intent of any selection activity is, therefore, to reduce the probability of making reject errors or accept errors while increasing the probability of making correct decisions. We do this by using selection procedures that are both reliable and valid.

WHAT IS RELIABILITY? Reliability addresses whether a selection device measures the same characteristic consistently. For example, if a test is reliable, any individual's score should remain fairly stable over time, assuming that the characteristics it is measuring are also stable. The importance of reliability should be self-evident. No selection device can be effective if it's low in reliability. Using such a device would be the equivalent of weighing yourself every day on an erratic scale. If the scale is unreliable—randomly fluctuating, say, 10 to 15 pounds every time you step on it—the results will not mean much. To be effective predictors, selection devices must possess an acceptable level of consistency.

WHAT IS VALIDITY? Any selection device that a manager uses—such as application forms, tests, interviews, or physical examinations—must also demonstrate validity. Validity is based on a proven relationship between the selection device used and some relevant measure. For example, we mentioned earlier a firefighter applicant who was wheelchair bound. Because of the physical requirements of a firefighter's job, someone confined to a wheelchair would be unable to pass the physical endurance tests. In that case, denying employment could be considered valid, but requiring the same physical endurance tests for the dispatching job would not be job related. Federal law prohibits managers from using any selection device that cannot be shown to be directly related to successful job performance. That constraint goes for entrance tests, too; managers must be able to demonstrate that, once on the job, individuals with high scores on such a test outperform individuals with low scores. Consequently, the burden is on the organization to verify that any selection device it uses to differentiate applicants is related to job performance.

HOW EFFECTIVE ARE TESTS AND INTERVIEWS AS SELECTION DEVICES? Managers can use a number of selection devices to reduce accept and reject errors. The best-known devices include written and performance-simulation tests and interviews. Let's briefly review each device, giving particular attention to its validity in predicting job performance.

Typical *written tests* include tests of intelligence, aptitude, ability, and interest. Such tests have long been used as selection devices, although their popularity has run in cycles. Written tests were widely used after World War II, but beginning in the late 1960s, they fell out of favor. They were frequently characterized as discriminatory, and many organizations could not validate that their written tests were job related. Today, written tests have made a comeback although most of them are now Internet based.[8] Managers are increasingly aware that poor hiring decisions are costly and that properly designed tests can reduce the likelihood of making such decisions. In addition, the cost of developing and validating a set of written tests for a specific job has declined significantly.

A review of the evidence finds that tests of intellectual ability, spatial and mechanical ability, perceptual accuracy, and motor ability are moderately valid predictors for many semiskilled and unskilled operative jobs in an industrial organization.[9] However, an enduring criticism of written tests is that intelligence and other tested characteristics can be somewhat removed from the actual performance of the job itself.[10] For example, a high score on an intelligence test is not necessarily a good indicator that the applicant will perform well as a computer programmer. This criticism has led to an increased use of *performance-simulation tests*.

What better way to find out whether an applicant for a technical writing position at Apple can write technical manuals than to ask him or her to do it? That's why there's an increasing interest in performance-simulation tests. Undoubtedly, the enthusiasm for these tests lies in the fact that they're based on job analysis data and, therefore, should more easily meet the requirement of job relatedness than do written tests. Performance-simulation tests are made up of actual job behaviors rather than substitutes. The best-known performance-simulation tests are work sampling (a miniature replica of the job) and assessment centers (simulating real problems one may face on the job). The former is suited to persons applying for routine jobs, the latter to managerial personnel.

The advantage of performance simulation over traditional testing methods should be obvious. Because its content is essentially identical to job content, performance simulation should be a better predictor of short-term job performance and should minimize potential employment discrimination allegations. Additionally, because of the nature of their content and the methods used to determine content, well-constructed performance-simulation tests are valid predictors.

The *interview*, along with the application form, is an almost universal selection device. Few of us have ever gotten a job without undergoing one or more interviews. The irony of this is that the value of an interview as a selection device has been the subject of considerable debate.[11]

Interviews can be reliable and valid selection tools, but too often they're not. When interviews are structured and well organized, and when interviewers are held to relevant questioning, interviews are effective predictors.[12] But those conditions don't characterize many interviews. The typical interview in which applicants are asked a varying set of essentially random questions in an informal setting often provides little in the way of valuable information.

All kinds of potential biases can creep into interviews if they're not well structured and standardized. To illustrate, a review of the research leads us to the following conclusions:

◆ Prior knowledge about the applicant will bias the interviewer's evaluation.
◆ The interviewer tends to hold a stereotype of what represents a good applicant.
◆ The interviewer tends to favor applicants who share his or her own attitudes.
◆ The order in which applicants are interviewed will influence evaluations.
◆ The order in which information is elicited during the interview will influence evaluations.

Chris Seward/Newscom

The Container Store's business mission is to sell products that save customers space and time. The retailer hires salespeople who are energetic, display a positive and helpful attitude, love to sell, and can solve customers' one-of-a-kind storage and organization problems. To make interviews more valid and reliable, store managers use the behavioral or situational interview. In this photo, a Container Store recruiting manager leads a job candidate in a role-playing exercise as part of the interview. The recruiter presents the candidate with a realistic selling situation and then observes what she says and how she behaves. For The Container Store, the behavioral interview is an effective way to predict successful job performance.

---

reliability
The degree to which a selection device measures the same thing consistently

validity
The proven relationship between a selection device and some relevant criterion

performance-simulation tests
Selection devices based on actual job behaviors

◆ Negative information is given unduly high weight.

◆ The interviewer may make a decision concerning the applicant's suitability within the first four or five minutes of the interview.

◆ The interviewer may forget much of the interview's content within minutes after its conclusion.

◆ The interview is most valid in determining an applicant's intelligence, level of motivation, and interpersonal skills.

◆ Structured and well-organized interviews are more reliable than unstructured and unorganized ones.[13]

What can managers do to make interviews more valid and reliable? A number of suggestions that have been made over the years include reviewing the job description and job specification to help in assessing the applicant; preparing a structured set of questions to ask all applicants for the job; reviewing an applicant's résumé before meeting him or her; asking questions and listening carefully to the applicant's answer; and writing your evaluation of the applicant while the interview is still fresh in your mind.

One last popular modification to interviews has been the behavioral or situation interview.[14] In this type of interview, applicants are observed not only for what they say, but also how they behave. Applicants are presented with situations—often complex problems involving role playing—and are asked to "deal" with the situation. This type of interview provides an opportunity for interviewers to see how a potential employee will behave and how he or she will react under stress. Proponents of behavioral interviewing indicate such a process is much more indicative of an applicant's performance than simply having the individual tell the interviewer what he or she has done. In fact, research in this area indicates that behavioral interviews are nearly eight times more effective for predicting successful job performance.[15]

HOW CAN YOU "CLOSE THE DEAL"?   Interviewers who treat the recruiting and hiring of employees as if the applicants must be sold on the job and exposed only to an organization's positive characteristics are likely to have a workforce that is dissatisfied and prone to high turnover.[16]

During the hiring process, every job applicant acquires a set of expectations about the company and about the job for which he or she is interviewing. When the information an applicant receives is excessively inflated, a number of things happen that have potentially negative effects on the company. First, mismatched applicants are less likely to withdraw from the search process. Second, because inflated information builds unrealistic expectations, new employees are likely to become quickly dissatisfied and to resign prematurely. Third, new hires are prone to become disillusioned and less committed to the organization when they face the unexpected harsh realities of the job. In many cases, these individuals feel that they were misled during the hiring process and may become problem employees.

To increase job satisfaction among employees and reduce turnover, managers should consider a realistic job preview (RJP).[17] An RJP includes both positive and negative information about the job and the company. For example, in addition to the positive comments typically expressed in the interview, the applicant is told of the less attractive aspects of the job. For instance, he or she might be told that there are limited opportunities to talk to coworkers during work hours, that chances of being promoted are slim, or that work hours fluctuate so erratically that employees may be required to work during what are usually off hours (nights and weekends). Research indicates that applicants who have been given a realistic job preview hold lower and more realistic job expectations for the jobs they will be performing and are better able to cope with the frustrating elements of the job than are applicants who have been given only inflated information. The result is fewer unexpected resignations by new employees. For managers, realistic job previews offer a major insight into the HRM process. That is, it's just as important to *retain* good people as it is to *hire* them in the first place. Presenting only positive job aspects to an applicant may initially entice him or her to join the organization, but it may be a decision that both parties quickly regret.

HOW ARE EMPLOYEES PROVIDED WITH NEEDED SKILLS AND KNOWLEDGE?

If we've done our recruiting and selecting properly, we should have hired competent individuals who can perform successfully on the job. But successful performance requires more than possessing certain skills. New hires must be acclimated to the organization's culture and be trained and given the knowledge to do the job in a manner consistent with the organization's goals. To achieve this, HRM uses orientation and training.

Explain how employees are provided with needed skills and knowledge.

3

How Are New Hires Introduced to the Organization?

Once a job candidate has been selected, he or she needs to be introduced to the job and organization. This introduction is called orientation.[18] The major goals of orientation are to reduce the initial anxiety all new employees feel as they begin a new job; to familiarize new employees with the job, the work unit, and the organization as a whole; and to facilitate the outsider–insider transition. *Job orientation* expands on the information the employee obtained during the recruitment and selection stages. The new employee's specific duties and responsibilities are clarified as well as how his or her performance will be evaluated. Orientation is also the time to correct any unrealistic expectations new employees might hold about the job. *Work unit orientation* familiarizes an employee with the goals of the work unit, makes clear how his or her job contributes to the unit's goals, and provides an introduction to his or her coworkers. *Organization orientation* informs the new employee about the organization's goals, history, philosophy, procedures, and rules. This information includes relevant HR policies such as work hours, pay procedures, overtime requirements, and benefits. And a tour of the organization's physical facilities is often part of this orientation.

Managers have an obligation to make the integration of a new employee into the organization as smooth and anxiety-free as possible. Successful orientation, whether

TECHNOLOGY AND THE MANAGER'S JOB — DIGITAL HR

HR has gone digital.[19] Using software that automates many basic HR processes associated with recruiting, selecting, orienting, training, appraising performance, and storing and retrieving employee information, HR departments have cut costs and optimized service. One HR area where IT has contributed is in pre-employment assessments. For instance, at KeyBank, a Cleveland-based financial services organization, virtual "job tryout simulations" have been used in order to reduce 90-day turnover rates and create more consistency in staffing decisions. These simulations create an interactive multimedia experience and mimic key job tasks for competencies such as providing client service, adapting to change, supporting team members, following procedures, and working efficiently. Before using these virtual assessments, the bank was losing 13 percent of new tellers and call center associates in their first 90 days. After implementing the virtual assessments, that number dropped to 4 percent.

Another area where IT has had a significant impact is in training. In a survey by the American Society for Training and Development, 95 percent of the responding companies reported using some form of e-learning. Using technology to deliver needed knowledge, skills, and attitudes has had many benefits. As one researcher said, "The ultimate purpose of e-learning is not to reduce the cost of training, but to improve the way your organization does business." And in many instances, it seems to do that! For example, when Hewlett-Packard looked at how its customer service was affected by a blend of e-learning and other instructional methods, rather than just classroom training, it found that "sales representatives were able to answer questions more quickly and accurately, enhancing customer-service provider relations." And Unilever found that after e-learning training for sales employees, sales increased by several million dollars.

Think About:

· HR is supposed to be a "people-oriented" profession. Does the use of all this technology make it less so? Why or why not?

· Have you ever applied for a job on one of the many online job sites? What was your experience like? What benefits do these sites offer? What drawbacks do they have?

· You want a job after graduating from college. Knowing that you're likely to encounter online recruitment and selection procedures, how can you best prepare for making yourself stand out in the process?

---

realistic job preview (RJP)
A preview of a job that provides both positive and negative information about the job and the company

orientation
Introducing a new employee to the job and the organization

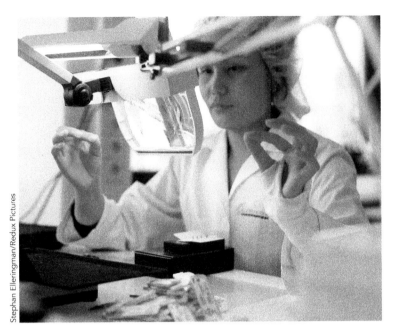

Ethicon, a subsidiary of Johnson & Johnson, is a global medical device firm that places a high priority on employee training. Working at an Ethicon plant in Germany, the employee shown here joins together under a microscope extremely fine threads and needles—finer than a human eyelash—that surgeons use during optical, neuron, and vascular surgery. Training for this type of work that requires great dexterity and accuracy takes about six months. Extensive and intensive employee training by Ethicon and other firms that make medical devices used by health care practitioners is important in promoting healing and speeding the recovery of millions of patients.

formal or informal, results in an outsider–insider transition that makes the new member feel comfortable and fairly well-adjusted, lowers the likelihood of poor work performance, and reduces the probability of a surprise resignation by the new employee only a week or two into the job.[20]

What Is Employee Training?

On the whole, planes don't cause airline accidents, people do. Most collisions, crashes, and other airline mishaps—nearly three-quarters of them—result from errors by the pilot or air traffic controller, or from inadequate maintenance. Weather and structural failures typically account for the remaining accidents.[21] We cite these statistics to illustrate the importance of training in the airline industry. Such maintenance and human errors could be prevented or significantly reduced by better employee training, as shown by the amazing "landing" of US Airways Flight 1549 in the Hudson River in January 2009 with no loss of life. Pilot Captain Chesley Sullenberger attributed the positive outcome to the extensive and intensive training that all pilots and flight crews undergo.[22]

Employee training is a learning experience that seeks a relatively permanent change in employees by improving their ability to perform on the job. Thus, training involves changing skills, knowledge, attitudes, or behavior.[23] This change may involve what employees know, how they work, or their attitudes toward their jobs, coworkers, managers, and the organization. It's been estimated, for instance, that U.S. business firms spend billions each a year on formal courses and training programs to develop workers' skills.[24] Managers, of course, are responsible for deciding when employees are in need of training and what form that training should take.

Determining training needs typically involves answering several questions. If some of these questions sound familiar, you've been paying close attention. It's precisely the type of analysis that takes place when managers develop an organizational structure to achieve their strategic goals—only now the focus is on the people.[25]

The questions in Exhibit 6 suggest the kinds of signals that can warn a manager when training may be necessary. The more obvious ones are related directly to productivity. Indications that job performance is declining include decreases in production numbers, lower quality, more accidents, and higher scrap or rejection rates. Any of these outcomes might suggest that worker skills need to be fine-tuned. Of course, we're assuming that an employee's performance decline is in no way related to lack of effort. Managers, too, must also recognize that training may be required because the workplace is constantly evolving. Changes imposed on employees as a result of job redesign or a technological breakthrough also require training.

HOW ARE EMPLOYEES TRAINED?   Most training takes place on the job. Why? It's simple and it usually costs less. However, on-the-job training can disrupt the workplace and result in an increase in errors while learning takes place. Also, some skill training is too complex to learn on the job and must take place outside the work setting.

Many different types of training methods are available. For the most part, we can classify them as on-the-job or off-the-job training. The more popular training methods are summarized in Exhibit 7.

HOW CAN MANAGERS ENSURE THAT TRAINING IS WORKING?   It's easy to generate a new training program, but if training efforts aren't evaluated, any can be rationalized. It would be nice if all companies could boast the returns on investments in training that Neil Huffman Auto Group executives do; they claim they receive $230 in increased

Stephan Elleringman/Redux Pictures

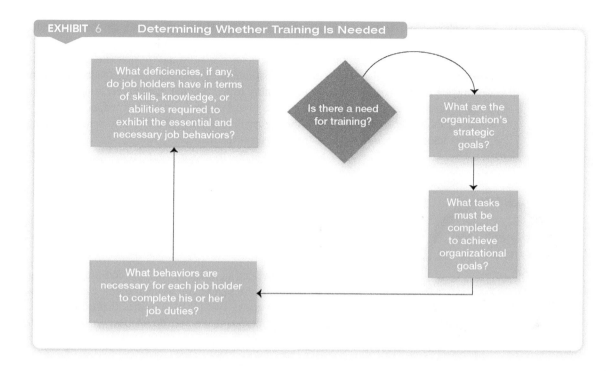

EXHIBIT 6   Determining Whether Training Is Needed

productivity for every dollar spent on training.[26] But such a claim cannot be made unless training is properly evaluated.

How are training programs typically evaluated? The following approach is probably generalizable across organizations: Several managers, representatives from HRM, and a group of workers who have recently completed a training program are asked for their opinions. If the comments are generally positive, the program may get a favorable evaluation and it's continued until someone decides, for whatever reason, that it should be eliminated or replaced.

EXHIBIT 7   Typical Training Methods

SAMPLE ON-THE-JOB TRAINING METHODS	
Job rotation	Lateral transfers allowing employees to work at different jobs. Provides good exposure to a variety of tasks.
Understudy assignments	Working with a seasoned veteran, coach, or mentor. Provides support and encouragement from an experienced worker. In the trades industry, this may also be an apprenticeship.

SAMPLE OFF-THE-JOB TRAINING METHODS	
Classroom lectures	Lectures designed to convey specific technical, interpersonal, or problem-solving skills.
Films and videos	Using media to explicitly demonstrate technical skills that are not easily presented by other training methods.
Simulation exercises	Learning a job by actually performing the work (or its simulation). May include case analyses, experiential exercises, role-playing, and group interaction.
Vestibule training	Learning tasks on the same equipment that one actually will use on the job but in a simulated work environment.

employee training
A learning experience that seeks a relatively permanent change in employees by improving their ability to perform on the job

Such reactions from participants or managers, while easy to acquire, are the least valid. Their opinions are heavily influenced by factors that may have little to do with the training's effectiveness—difficulty, entertainment value, or the personality characteristics of the instructor. However, trainees' reactions to the training may, in fact, provide feedback on how worthwhile the participants viewed the training to be. Beyond general reactions, however, training must also be evaluated in terms of how much the participants learned; how well they are using their new skills on the job (did their behavior change?); and whether the training program achieved its desired results (reduced turnover, increased customer service, etc.).[27]

Describe strategies for retaining competent, high-performing employees.

4

HOW DO ORGANIZATIONS RETAIN COMPETENT, HIGH-PERFORMING EMPLOYEES?

Once an organization has invested significant dollars in recruiting, selecting, orienting, and training employees, it wants to keep them, especially the competent, high-performing ones! Two HRM activities that play a role in this are managing employee performance and developing an appropriate compensation and benefits program.

What Is a Performance Management System?

It's important for managers to get their employees to achieve performance levels that the organization considers desirable. How do managers ensure that employees are performing as well as they're supposed to? In organizations, the formal means of assessing the work of employees is through a systematic performance appraisal process.

A **performance management system** is a process of establishing performance standards and evaluating performance in order to arrive at objective human resource decisions—such as pay increases and training needs—as well as to provide documentation to support any personnel actions. But how do you evaluate an employee's performance? We list specific appraisal techniques in Exhibit 8.

The *written essay* requires no complex forms or extensive training to complete. However, a "good" or "bad" appraisal may be determined as much by the evaluator's writing skill as by the employee's actual level of performance. The use of *critical incidents* focuses the evaluator's attention on critical or key behaviors. The appraiser writes down anecdotes describing whatever the employee did that was especially effective or ineffective. The key here is that specific behaviors are cited, not vaguely defined personality traits. One of the oldest and most popular methods of appraisal is by *adjective rating scales*. This method lists a set of performance factors such as quantity and quality of work, job knowledge,

EXHIBIT 8	Performance Appraisal Methods	
METHOD	**ADVANTAGE**	**DISADVANTAGE**
Written essay	Simple to use	More a measure of evaluator's writing ability than of employee's actual performance
Critical incidents	Rich examples; behaviorally based	Time-consuming; lack quantification
Graphic rating scales	Provide quantitative data; less time-consuming than others	Do not provide depth of job behavior assessed
BARS	Focus on specific and measurable job behaviors	Time-consuming; difficult to develop measures
Multiperson	Compares employees with one another	Unwieldy with large number of employees
MBO	Focuses on end goals; results oriented	Time-consuming
360° appraisal	More thorough	Time-consuming

cooperation, loyalty, attendance, honesty, and initiative. The evaluator then goes down the list and rates each factor on an incremental scale. An approach that has received renewed attention involves *behaviorally anchored rating scales (BARS)*.[28] These scales combine major elements from the critical incident and adjective rating scale approaches. The appraiser rates an employee according to items along a numerical scale, but the items are examples of actual behavior on a given job rather than general descriptions or traits.[29]

Finally, an appraisal device that seeks performance feedback from such sources as the person being rated, bosses, peers, team members, customers, and suppliers has become popular in organizations. It's called the 360-degree appraisal.[30] It's being used in approximately 90 percent of *Fortune* 1000 firms, including such companies as Otis Elevator, DuPont, Nabisco, Pfizer, ExxonMobil, Cook Children's Health Care System, General Electric, UPS, and Nokia.[31]

In today's dynamic organizations, traditional performance evaluation systems may be outdated.[32] Downsizing has given supervisors greater responsibility and more employees who report directly to them. Accordingly, it may be next to impossible for supervisors to have extensive job knowledge of each of their employees. Furthermore, the growth of project teams and employee involvement places the responsibility for evaluation where people are better able to make accurate assessments.[33]

The 360-degree feedback process also has some positive benefits for development concerns.[34] Many managers simply do not know how their employees view them and the work they have done. Research studies into the effectiveness of 360-degree performance appraisals report positive results including more accurate feedback, empowering employees, reducing the subjective factors in the evaluation process, and developing leadership in an organization.[35]

SHOULD PEOPLE BE COMPARED TO ONE ANOTHER OR AGAINST A SET OF STANDARDS?   The methods previously identified have one thing in common. They require us to evaluate employees on the basis of how well their performance matches established or absolute criteria. Multiperson comparisons, on the other hand, compare one person's performance with that of one or more individuals. These are relative, not absolute, measuring devices. The three most popular forms of this method are group-order ranking, individual ranking, and paired comparison.

The *group-order ranking* requires the evaluator to place employees into a particular classification such as "top fifth" or "second fifth." If a rater has 20 employees, only four can be in the top fifth, and, of course, four must be relegated to the bottom fifth. The *individual ranking* approach requires the evaluator to list the employees in order from highest to lowest. Only one can be "best." In an appraisal of 30 employees, the difference between the first and second employee is assumed to be the same as that between the twenty-first and twenty-second. Even though some employees may be closely grouped, no ties are allowed. In the *paired comparison*

Home Depot replaced a qualitative and subjective performance evaluation system that varied from region to region and store to store with a new companywide evaluation process based on mostly quantitative criteria. The new process includes the 360-degree appraisal for Home Depot's managers. Employees, customers, suppliers, and other sources now review managers by assigning points for specific behaviors such as "displays character" and "drives change." The new review has given Home Depot more accurate feedback and has reduced subjective factors in the process. Shown here talking with managers and employees who participate in the 360-degree appraisal is Ann-Marie Campbell, president of Home Depot's southern division.

Newscom

performance management system
A system that establishes performance standards that are used to evaluate employee performance

360-degree appraisal
An appraisal device that seeks feedback from a variety of sources for the person being rated

approach, each employee is compared with every other employee in the comparison group and rated as either the superior or weaker member of the pair. After all paired comparisons are made, each employee is assigned a summary ranking based on the number of superior scores he or she achieved. Although this approach ensures that each employee is compared against every other employee, it can become unwieldy when large numbers of employees are being assessed.

WHAT ABOUT MBO AS AN APPRAISAL APPROACH?   MBO is also a mechanism for appraising performance.

Employees are evaluated by how well they accomplish a specific set of objectives that are critical to the successful completion of their jobs. These objectives need to be tangible, verifiable, and measurable. MBO's popularity among managerial personnel is probably due to its focus on end goals. Managers tend to emphasize such results-oriented outcomes as profit, sales, and costs. This emphasis meshes with MBO's concern with quantitative measures of performance. Because MBO emphasizes ends rather than means, this appraisal method allows managers to choose the best path for achieving their goals.

What Happens If an Employee's Performance Is Not Up to Par?

So far this discussion has focused on the performance management system. But what if an employee is not performing in a satisfactory manner? What can you do?

If, for some reason, an employee is not meeting his or her performance goals, a manager needs to find out why. If it's because the employee is mismatched for the job (a hiring error) or because he or she does not have adequate training, the fix is relatively simple. The manager can either reassign the individual to a job that better matches his or her skills or train the employee to do the job more effectively. If the problem is associated with an employee's lack of desire to do the job, not with his or her abilities, it becomes a discipline problem. In that case, a manager can try counseling and, if necessary, take disciplinary action such as verbal and written warnings, suspensions, and even terminations.

Employee counseling is a process designed to help employees overcome performance-related problems. Rather than viewing the performance problem from a punitive standpoint (discipline), employee counseling attempts to uncover why employees have lost their desire or ability to work productively. More importantly, it's designed to find ways to fix the problem. In many cases, employees don't go from being productive one day to being unproductive the next. Rather, the change happens gradually and may be a function of what's occurring in their personal lives. Employee counseling attempts to assist employees in getting help to resolve whatever is bothering them. The premise behind employee counseling is fairly simple: It's beneficial to both the organization and the employee. Just as it's costly to have an employee quit shortly after being hired, it's costly to fire someone. The time spent recruiting and selecting, orienting, training, and developing employees translates into money. If, however, an organization can help employees overcome personal problems and get them back on the job quickly, it can avoid these costs. But make no mistake about it, employee counseling is not intended to lessen the effect of an employee's poor performance, nor is it intended to reduce his or her responsibility to change inappropriate work behavior. If the employee can't or won't accept help, then disciplinary actions must be taken.

How Are Employees Compensated?

Executives at Discovery Communications Inc. had an employee morale problem on their hands. Many of the company's top performers were making the same salaries as the poorer performers and the company's compensation program didn't allow for giving raises to people who stayed in the same position. The only way for managers to reward the top performers was to give them a bonus or promote them to another position. Executives were discovering that not only was that unfair, it was counterproductive. So they overhauled the program.[37]

AND THE SURVEY SAYS...[36]

36	percent of managers who contact references are most interested in a description of past job duties.
69	percent of employees say they've been asked to do things at work for which they have not received any training.
30	percent of students say that a company's market success was a preferred attribute.
60	percent of employers now offer wellness benefits.
31	percent of HR leaders say that the most important employee characteristic is fitting in with the organization's culture.
40	percent of employees say that their most appealing career model is working for two to three organizations throughout their career.
59	percent of HR recruiters said that the most neglected grooming for job interviews was fingernails.
75	percent of recruiters say that a chronological format is most preferred for a résumé.

Although there are exceptions, most of us work for money. What our jobs pay and what benefits we get fall under the heading of compensation and benefits. Determining levels of compensation isn't easy. However, most of us expect to receive appropriate compensation from our employer. Developing an effective and appropriate compensation system is an important part of the HRM process.[38] It can help attract and retain competent and talented individuals who help an organization accomplish its mission and goals. In addition, an organization's compensation system has been shown to have an impact on its strategic performance.[39] Managers must develop a compensation system that reflects the changing nature of work and the workplace in order to keep people motivated.

HOW ARE PAY LEVELS DETERMINED?   How does management decide who gets paid $15.85 an hour and who receives $325,000 a year? The answer lies in compensation administration. The goals of compensation administration are to design a cost-effective pay structure that will attract and retain competent employees and to provide an incentive for these individuals to exert high energy levels at work. Compensation administration also attempts to ensure that pay levels, once determined, will be perceived as fair by all employees. Fairness means that the established pay levels are adequate and consistent for the demands and requirements of the job. Therefore, the primary determination of pay is the kind of job an employee performs. Different jobs require different kinds and levels of skills, knowledge, and abilities, and these factors vary in their value to the organization. So, too, do the responsibility and authority of various positions. In short, the higher the skills, knowledge, and abilities—and the greater the authority and responsibility—the higher the pay.

So, how do managers determine who gets paid what? Several factors influence the compensation and benefit packages that different employees receive. Exhibit 9 summarizes

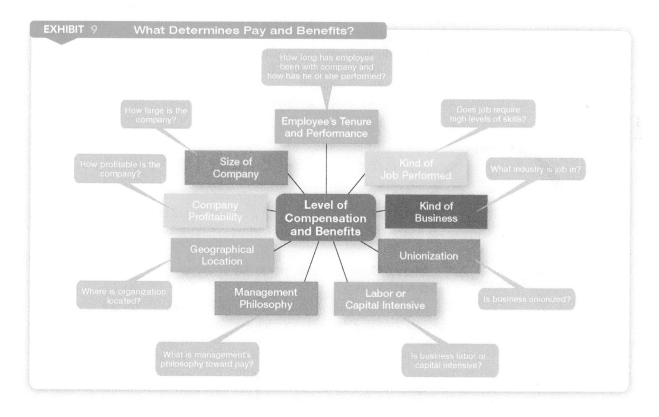

EXHIBIT 9   What Determines Pay and Benefits?

How long has employee been with company and how has he or she performed?

How large is the company?

Does job require high levels of skills?

How profitable is the company?

What industry is job in?

Employee's Tenure and Performance

Size of Company

Kind of Job Performed

Company Profitability

Level of Compensation and Benefits

Kind of Business

Geographical Location

Unionization

Where is organization located?

Management Philosophy

Labor or Capital Intensive

Is business unionized?

What is management's philosophy toward pay?

Is business labor or capital intensive?

---

discipline
Actions taken by a manager to enforce an organization's standards and regulations

employee counseling
A process designed to help employees overcome performance-related problems

compensation administration
The process of determining a cost-effective pay structure that will attract and retain employees, provide an incentive for them to work hard, and ensure that pay levels will be perceived as fair

these factors, which are job-based and business or industry-based. One factor that's critical is the organization's philosophy toward compensation. Some organizations, for instance, don't pay employees any more than they have to. In the absence of a union contract that stipulates wage levels, those organizations only have to pay minimum wage for most of their jobs. On the other hand, some organizations are committed to a compensation philosophy of paying their employees at or above area wage levels in order to emphasize that they want to attract and keep the best pool of talent.

Many organizations are using alternative approaches to determining compensation including skill-based pay and variable pay. Skill-based pay systems reward employees for the job skills and competencies they can demonstrate. Under this type of pay system, an employee's job title doesn't define his or her pay category, skills do.[40] Research shows that these types of pay systems tend to be more successful in manufacturing organizations than in service organizations and in organizations pursuing technical innovations.[41] On the other hand, many organizations use variable pay systems, in which an individual's compensation is contingent on performance—90 percent of U.S. organizations use variable pay plans, and 81 percent of Canadian and Taiwanese organizations do.[42]

WHY DO ORGANIZATIONS OFFER EMPLOYEE BENEFITS? When an organization designs its overall compensation package, it has to look further than just an hourly wage or annual salary. It has to take into account another element, employee benefits, which are nonfinancial rewards designed to enrich employees' lives. They have grown in importance and variety over the past several decades. Once viewed as "fringes," today's benefit packages reflect efforts to provide something that each employee values.

The benefits offered by an organization vary widely in scope. Most organizations are legally required to provide Social Security and workers' and unemployment compensation, but organizations may also provide an array of benefits such as paid time off from work, life and disability insurance, retirement programs, and health insurance.[43] The costs of some of these, such as retirement and health insurance benefits, may be paid by both the employer and the employee, although as you'll see in the next section, organizations are cutting back or putting stipulations on these two costly benefits.

Discuss contemporary issues in managing human resources.

5

WHAT CONTEMPORARY HRM ISSUES FACE MANAGERS?

HR issues that face today's managers include downsizing, workforce diversity, sexual harassment, workplace spirituality, and HR costs.

How Can Managers Manage Downsizing?

Downsizing is the planned elimination of jobs in an organization. Because downsizing typically involves shrinking the organization's workforce, it's an important issue in HRM. When an organization has too many employees—which may happen when it's faced with an economic crisis, declining market share, overly aggressive growth, or when it's been poorly managed—one option for improving profits is to eliminate excess workers. Over the last few years, many well-known companies have gone through several rounds of downsizing—Boeing, Volkswagen, Microsoft, Dell, General Motors, Unisys, Siemens, Merck, and Toyota, among others. How can managers best manage a downsized workforce?

After downsizing, disruptions in the workplace and in employees' personal lives are to be expected. Stress, frustration, anxiety, and anger are typical reactions of both individuals being laid off and the job survivors. And it may surprise you to learn that both victims and survivors experience those feelings.[44] Many organizations have

> **EXHIBIT 10   Tips for Managing Downsizing**
>
> - Communicate openly and honestly:
>   - Inform those being let go as soon as possible
>   - Tell surviving employees the new goals and expectations
>   - Explain impact of layoffs
> - Follow any laws regulating severance pay or benefits
> - Provide support/counseling for surviving employees
> - Reassign roles according to individuals' talents and backgrounds
> - Focus on boosting morale:
>   - Offer individualized reassurance
>   - Continue to communicate, especially one-on-one
>   - Remain involved and available

helped layoff victims by offering a variety of job-help services, psychological counseling, support groups, severance pay, extended health insurance benefits, and detailed communications. Although some individuals react negatively to being laid off (the worst cases involve individuals returning to their former organization and committing a violent act), offers of assistance reveal that an organization does care about its former employees. While those being laid off get to start over with a clean slate and a clear conscience, survivors don't. Unfortunately, the "survivors" who retain their jobs and have the task of keeping the organization going or even of revitalizing it seldom receive attention. One negative consequence appears to be what is being called **layoff-survivor sickness**, a set of attitudes, perceptions, and behaviors of employees who survive involuntary staff reductions.[45] Symptoms include job insecurity, perceptions of unfairness, guilt, depression, stress from increased workload, fear of change, loss of loyalty and commitment, reduced effort, and an unwillingness to do anything beyond the required minimum.

To show concern for job survivors, managers may want to provide opportunities for employees to talk to counselors about their guilt, anger, and anxiety.[46] Group discussions can be a way for the survivors to vent their feelings. Some organizations have used downsizing as the spark to implement increased employee participation programs such as empowerment and self-managed work teams. In short, to keep morale and productivity high, managers should make every attempt to ensure that those individuals still working in the organization know that they're valuable and much-needed resources. Exhibit 10 summarizes some ways that managers can reduce the trauma associated with downsizing.[47]

How Can Workforce Diversity Be Managed?

Workforce diversity affects such basic HRM activities as recruitment, selection, and orientation.[48]

Improving workforce diversity requires managers to widen their recruiting net. For example, the popular practice of relying on current employee referrals as a source of new job applicants tends to produce candidates who have similar characteristics to those of present employees. So managers have to look for applicants in places where they haven't typically looked before. To increase diversity, managers are increasingly

---

skill-based pay
A pay system that rewards employees for the job skills they demonstrate

variable pay
A pay system in which an individual's compensation is contingent on performance

employee benefits
Membership-based rewards designed to enrich employees' lives

downsizing
The planned elimination of jobs in an organization

layoff-survivor sickness
A set of attitudes, perceptions, and behaviors of employees who survive layoffs

RIGHT ⓘOR WRONG?

It's likely to be a challenging issue for HR managers.[49] "It" is the use of medical marijuana by employees. Fourteen states and the District of Columbia have laws or constitutional amendments that allow patients with certain medical conditions such as cancer, glaucoma, or chronic pain to use marijuana without fear of being prosecuted. Federal prosecutors have been directed by the current administration not to bring criminal charges against marijuana users who follow their states' laws. However, that puts employers in a difficult position as they try to accommodate state laws on medical marijuana use while having to enforce federal rules or company drug-use policies that are based on federal law. Although courts have generally ruled that companies do not have to accommodate medical marijuana users, legal guidance is still not all that clear. Legal experts have warned employers to "not run afoul of disability and privacy laws." In addition to the legal questions, employers are concerned about the challenge of maintaining a safe workplace.

Think About:

- What ethical issues do you see in this?

- How might this issue affect HR processes such as recruitment, selection, performance management, compensation and benefits, and safety and health?

- What other stakeholders might be impacted by this? In what ways might they be impacted?

ZUMA Press/Newscom

turning to nontraditional recruitment sources such as women's job networks, over-50 clubs, urban job banks, disabled people's training centers, ethnic newspapers, and gay rights organizations. This type of outreach should enable an organization to broaden its pool of applicants.

Once a diverse set of applicants exists, efforts must be made to ensure that the selection process does not discriminate. Moreover, applicants need to be made comfortable with the organization's culture and be made aware of management's desire to accommodate their needs. For instance, at TGI Friday's, company managers work diligently to accommodate differences and create workplace choices for a diverse workforce; so, too, do companies such as Sodexo, Johnson & Johnson, Ernst & Young, Marriott International, IBM, and Bank of America.[50]

Finally, orientation is often difficult for women and minorities. Many organizations, such as Lotus and Hewlett-Packard, provide special workshops to raise diversity consciousness among current employees as well as programs for new employees that focus on diversity issues. The thrust of these efforts is to increase individual understanding of the differences each of us brings to the workplace. A number of companies also have special mentoring programs to deal with the reality that lower-level female and minority managers have few role models with whom to identify.[51]

What Is Sexual Harassment?

Sexual harassment is a serious issue in both public and private sector organizations. Some 12,000 complaints are filed with the EEOC each year,[52] with more than 16 percent of the complaints filed by males.[53] Settlements in some of these cases incurred a substantial cost to the companies in terms of litigation. It's estimated that sexual harassment is the single largest financial risk facing companies today—and can result in decreases (sometimes greater than 30%) in a company's stock price.[54] At Mitsubishi, for example, the company paid out more than $34 million to 300 women for the rampant sexual harassment to which they were exposed.[55] But it's more than just jury awards. Sexual harassment results in millions lost in absenteeism, low productivity, and turnover.[56] Sexual harassment, furthermore, is not just a U.S. phenomenon. It's a global issue. For instance, nearly 10 percent of workers responding to a global survey reported that they had been harassed sexually or physically at work. The survey covered countries such as India, China, Saudi Arabia, Sweden, France, Belgium, Germany, Great Britain, and Poland, among others.[57] Even though discussions of sexual harassment cases often focus on the large awards granted by a court, employers face other concerns. Sexual harassment creates an unpleasant work environment for organization members and undermines their ability to perform their jobs. But just what is sexual harassment?

Any unwanted action or activity of a sexual nature that explicitly or implicitly affects an individual's employment, performance, or work environment can be regarded as **sexual harassment**. It can occur between members of the opposite or of the same sex—between employees of the organization or between employee and nonemployee.[58] Although such an activity has been generally prohibited under Title VII (sex discrimination) in the United States, in recent years this problem has gained more recognition. By most accounts, prior to the mid-1980s, occurrences were generally viewed as isolated incidents, with the individual committing the act being solely responsible (if at all) for his or her actions.[59] Today, charges of sexual harassment continue to appear in the headlines on an almost regular basis.

Much of the problem associated with sexual harassment is determining what constitutes this illegal behavior.[60] In 1993, the EEOC cited three situations in which sexual harassment can occur. In these instances, verbal or physical conduct toward an individual:

1. Creates an intimidating, offensive, or hostile environment.
2. Unreasonably interferes with an individual's work.
3. Adversely affects an employee's employment opportunities.

For many organizations, it's the offensive or hostile environment issue that's problematic.[61] What constitutes such an environment? Challenging hostile environment situations gained much support from the Supreme Court case of *Meritor Savings Bank v. Vinson*.[62] This case stemmed from a situation in which Ms. Vinson initially refused the sexual advances of her boss. However, out of fear of reprisal, she ultimately conceded. But according to court records, it didn't stop there. Vinson's boss continued to harass Vinson, subjecting her to severe hostility that affected her job.[63] In addition to supporting hostile environment claims, the *Meritor* case also identified employer liability; that is, in sexual harassment cases, an organization can be held liable for sexual harassment actions by its managers, employees, and even customers![64]

Although the *Meritor* case has implications for organizations, how do organizational members determine whether something is offensive? For instance, does sexually explicit language in the office create a hostile environment? How about off-color jokes? Pictures of women totally undressed? The answer is it could! It depends on the people in the organization and the environment in which they work. The point here is that we all must be attuned to what makes fellow employees uncomfortable—and if we don't know, then we should ask! Organizational success will, in part, reflect how sensitive each employee is toward another in the company. At DuPont, for example, the corporate culture and diversity programs are designed to eliminate sexual harassment through awareness and respect for all individuals.[65] It means understanding one another and, most importantly, respecting others' rights. Similar programs exist at FedEx, General Mills, and Levi-Strauss, among other companies.

If sexual harassment carries with it potential costs to the organization, what can a company do to protect itself?[66] The courts want to know two things—did the organization know about, or should it have known about, the alleged behavior? And what did managers do to stop it?[67] With the number and dollar amounts of the awards today, it's even more important for organizations and managers to educate all employees on sexual harassment matters and to have mechanisms available to monitor employees. Furthermore, "victims" no longer have to prove that their psychological well-being is seriously affected.

Kathleen Lange/AP Images

A peer-training program at the U.S. Naval Academy is designed to prevent sexual harassment, a high-profile problem not only at the military college but also in the U.S. Navy and U.S. Marine Corps. The Sexual Harassment and Assault Prevention Education (SHAPE) program is an open forum that gives midshipmen the opportunity to learn about and discuss many different aspects of sexual harassment, including gender discrimination and inappropriate language that can instigate harassment. Shown here are two student trainers guiding a class, one of 16 the midshipmen complete during their four years at the academy.

sexual harassment
Any unwanted action or activity of a sexual nature that explicitly or implicitly affects an individual's employment, performance, or work environment

The U.S. Supreme Court ruled in 1993, in the case of *Harris v. Forklift Systems, Inc.*, that victims do not have to suffer substantial mental distress to receive a jury award. Furthermore, in June 1998, the Supreme Court ruled that sexual harassment may have occurred even if the employee had not experienced any "negative" job repercussions. In this case, Kimberly Ellerth, a marketing assistant at Burlington Industries, filed harassment charges against her boss because he "touched her, suggested she wear shorter skirts, and told her during a business trip that he could make her job 'very hard or very easy.'" When Ellerth refused, the harasser never "punished" her; in fact, she even received a promotion during the time the harassment was ongoing. What the Supreme Court's decision in this case indicates is that "harassment is defined by the ugly behavior of the manager, not by what happened to the worker subsequently."[68]

Finally, in a sexual harassment matter, managers must remember that the harasser may have rights, too.[69] No action should be taken against someone until a thorough investigation has been conducted. Furthermore, the results of the investigation should be reviewed by an independent and objective individual before any action against the alleged harasser is taken. Even then, the harasser should be given an opportunity to respond to the allegation and have a disciplinary hearing if desired. Additionally, an avenue for appeal should also exist for the alleged harasser—an appeal heard by someone at a higher level of management who is not associated with the case.

What Is Workplace Spirituality?

What do organizations such as Southwest Airlines, Ford Motor Company, Tom's of Maine, Herman Miller, Tyson Foods, or Hewlett-Packard have in common? Among other characteristics, they're among a number of organizations that have embraced workplace spirituality.

Workplace spirituality is not about organized religious practices, theology, or one's spiritual leader.[70] Rather, workplace spirituality is about recognizing that employees have an inner life that nourishes and is nourished by meaningful work that takes place in the context of an organizational community. A recent study of the concept identified three factors: interconnection with a higher power, interconnection with human beings, and interconnection with nature and all living things.[71] Organizations that promote a spiritual culture recognize that employees have both a mind and a spirit, seek to find meaning and purpose in their work, and possess a desire to connect with other employees and be part of a community.

WHY THE EMPHASIS ON SPIRITUALITY IN TODAY'S ORGANIZATIONS? Historical management models had no room for spirituality.[72] These models typically focused on organizations that were efficiently run without feelings toward others. Similarly, concern about an employee's inner life had no role in managing organizations. But just as we've come to realize that the study of emotions improves our understanding of how and why people act the way they do in organizations, an awareness of spirituality can help one better understand employee work behavior in the twenty-first-century organization.

WHAT DOES A SPIRITUAL ORGANIZATION LOOK LIKE? The concept of spirituality draws on the ethics, values, motivation, work/life balance, and leadership elements of an organization. Spiritual organizations are concerned with helping employees develop and reach their full potential. They're also concerned with addressing problems created by work/life conflicts.

What differentiates spiritual organizations from their nonspiritual counterparts? Although research is fairly new in this arena, several characteristics tend to be associated with a spiritual organization.[73] We list them in Exhibit 11.

Although workplace spirituality has generated some interest in many organizations, it's not without its critics. Those who argue against spirituality in organizations

EXHIBIT 11   Characteristics of a Spiritual Organization

CHARACTERISTIC	DESCRIPTION
Strong sense of purpose	Organizational members know why the organization exists and what it values.
Focus on individual development	Employees are valuable and need to be nurtured to help them grow; this characteristic also includes a sense of job security.
Trust and openness	Organizational member relationships are characterized by mutual trust, honesty, and openness.
Employee empowerment	Employees are allowed to make work-related decisions that affect them, highlighting a strong sense of delegation of authority.
Tolerance of employee expression	The organizational culture encourages employees to be themselves and to express their moods and feelings without guilt or fear of reprimand.

typically focus on two issues. First is the question of legitimacy. Specifically, do organizations have the right to impose spiritual values on their employees? Second is the question of economics. Are spirituality and profits compatible? Let's briefly look at these issues.

The potential for an emphasis on spirituality to make some employees uneasy is clear. Critics argue that organizations have no business imposing spiritual values on employees. This criticism is undoubtedly valid when spirituality is defined as bringing religion and God into the workplace.[74] However, the criticism appears less stinging when the goal is limited to helping employees find meaning in their work lives.

The issue of whether spirituality and profits are compatible goals is certainly relevant for anyone in business. The evidence, although limited, indicates that the two may be compatible. Several studies show that organizations that have introduced spirituality into the workplace have witnessed improved productivity, reduced turnover, greater employee satisfaction, and increased organizational commitment.[75]

WHAT DOES HRM HAVE TO DO WITH SPIRITUALITY?   Ironically, introducing spirituality into the organization is nothing new for HR. In actuality, many of the areas that HRM addresses, and has done so for many years, are many of the same things that support spirituality.[76] For instance, matters such as work/life balances, proper selection of employees, setting performance goals and rewarding people for the work they do, are all components of making the organization more "spiritual." In fact, as you review the characteristics of a spiritual organization, in every case, HRM is either the leader in making such things happen, or is the vehicle by which the organization helps employees understand their responsibilities and offers the requisite training to make things happen. In the end, it's HRM that will make the workplace a supportive work environment, one where communication abounds and employees feel free to express themselves.

How and Why Are Organizations Controlling HR Costs?

HR costs are skyrocketing, especially those associated with employee health care and employee pensions. Organizations are looking for ways to control these costs.

workplace spirituality
A spiritual culture where organizational values promote a sense of purpose through meaningful work that takes place in the context of community

WHAT ABOUT EMPLOYEE HEALTH CARE COSTS? Employees at Paychex who undergo a confidential health screening and risk assessment, and for those who smoke who agree to enroll in a smoking cessation program, can get free annual physicals, colonoscopies, and 100 percent coverage of preventive care as well as lower deductibles and costs. At Black and Decker Corporation, employees and dependents who certify in an honor system that they have been tobacco-free for at least six months pay $75 less per month for their medical and dental coverage. At Amerigas Propane, employees were given an ultimatum: get their medical checkups or lose their health insurance. Some 67 percent of employers are concerned about the effects of obesity on medical claims expenses.[77]

All these examples illustrate how companies are trying to control skyrocketing employee health care costs. Since 2002, health care costs have risen an average of 15 percent a year and are expected to double by the year 2016 from the $2.2 trillion spent in 2007. The new federal health care mandates are expected to also add to those costs.[78] And smokers cost companies even more—about 25 percent more for health care than nonsmokers do.[79] However, the biggest health care cost for companies is obesity—an estimated $73 billion a year in medical expenditures and absenteeism.[80] A study of manufacturing organizations found that presenteeism, which is defined as employees not performing at full capacity, was 1.8 percent higher for workers with moderate to severe obesity than for all other employees. The reason for the lost productivity is likely the result of reduced mobility because of body size or pain problems such as arthritis. Another study found that injuries sustained by obese workers often require substantially more medical care and are more likely to lead to permanent disabilities than similar injuries suffered by employees who were not obese.[81]

Is it any wonder that organizations are looking for ways to control their health care costs? How? First, many organizations are providing opportunities for employees to lead healthy lifestyles. From financial incentives to company-sponsored health and wellness programs, the goal is to limit rising health care costs. About 41 percent of companies use some type of positive incentives aimed at encouraging healthy behavior, up from 34 percent in 1996.[82] Another study indicated that nearly 90 percent of companies surveyed planned to aggressively promote healthy lifestyles to their employees during the next three to five years.[83] Many are starting sooner: Google, Yamaha Corporation of America, Caterpillar, and others are putting health food in company break rooms, cafeterias, and vending machines; providing deliveries of fresh organic fruit; and putting "calorie taxes" on fatty foods. At Wegmans Food Markets, employees are challenged to eat five cups of fruits and vegetables and walk 10,000 steps a day. And the "competition" between departments and stores has proved to be very popular and effective.[84] In the case of smokers, however, some companies have taken a more aggressive stance by increasing the amount smokers pay for health insurance or by firing them if they refuse to stop smoking.

WHAT ABOUT EMPLOYEE PENSION PLAN COSTS? The other area where organizations are looking to control costs is employee pension plans. Corporate pensions have been around since the nineteenth century.[85] But the days when companies could afford to give employees a broad-based pension that provided them a guaranteed retirement income have changed. Pension commitments have become such an enormous burden that companies can no longer afford them. In fact, the corporate pension system has been described as "fundamentally broken."[86] It's not just struggling companies that have eliminated employee pension plans. Lots of reasonably sound companies—for instance, NCR, FedEx, Lockheed Martin, and Motorola—no longer provide pensions. Only 42 *Fortune* 100 companies now offer pension plans to their new hires. Even IBM, which closed its pension plan to new hires in December 2004, told employees that their pension benefits would be frozen.[87] Obviously, the pension issue is one that directly affects HR decisions. On the one hand, organizations want to attract talented, capable employees by offering them desirable benefits such as pensions. But on the other hand, organizations have to balance that with the costs of providing such benefits.

Review

① **Describe the key components of the human resource management process and the important influences on that process.** The HRM process consists of eight activities that will staff an organization with competent, high-performing employees who are capable of sustaining their performance level over the long term. The first three HR activities involve employment planning and include recruitment, downsizing, and selection. The next two steps involve helping employees adapt to the organization and ensuring that their skills and knowledge are kept current, and include the HR activities of orienting and training. The last steps involve identifying performance goals, correcting performance problems, and helping employees sustain high levels of performance. These are done using the HR activities of performance appraisal, compensation and benefits, and safety and health. The main influences on the HRM process are legal although other environmental conditions such as restructuring, downsizing, diversity, and so forth can impact it as well.

② **Discuss the tasks associated with identifying and selecting competent employees.** The first task is employment planning, which involves job analysis and the creation of job descriptions and job specifications. Then, if job needs are indicated, recruitment involves attempts to develop a pool of potential job candidates. Downsizing is used to reduce the labor supply. Selection involves determining who is best qualified for the job. Selection devices need to be both reliable and valid. Managers may want to give potential employees a realistic job preview.

③ **Explain how employees are provided with needed skills and knowledge.** New hires must be acclimated to the organization's culture and be trained and given

the knowledge to do the job in a manner consistent with the organization's goals. Orientation—job, work unit, and organizational—provides new employees with information to introduce them to the job. Training is used to help employees improve their ability to perform on the job.

④ **Describe strategies for retaining competent, high-performing employees.** Two HRM activities that play a role in this are managing employee performance and developing an appropriate compensation and benefits program. Managing employee performance involves establishing performance standards and then appraising performance to see if those standards have been met. There are various performance appraisal techniques managers can use. If an employee's performance is not up to par, managers need to assess why and take action. Compensation and benefits programs can help attract and retain competent and talented individuals. Managers have to determine who gets paid what and what benefits will be offered.

⑤ **Discuss contemporary issues in managing human resources.** Downsizing is the planned elimination of jobs and must be managed from the perspective of layoff victims and job survivors. Workforce diversity must be managed through HRM activities including recruitment, selection, and orientation. Sexual harassment is a significant concern of organizations and managers, which mean programs and mechanisms must be in place to educate all employees about it. Workplace spirituality involves attempts by organizations to make work more meaningful to employees. Finally, organizations are looking for ways to control HR costs, especially health care costs and pension costs.

MyManagementLab   For more resources, go to **www.mymanagementlab.com**

UNDERSTANDING THE CHAPTER

1. How does HRM affect all managers?
2. Should an employer have the right to choose employees without governmental interference? Support your position.
3. Some critics claim that corporate HR departments have outlived their usefulness and are not there to help

employees but to shield the organization from legal problems. What do you think? What benefits are there to having a formal HRM process? What are the drawbacks?

4. Do you think it's ethical for a prospective employer to delve into an applicant's life by means of interviews, tests, and background investigations? What if those

investigations involved looking at your Facebook page or personal blogs? Explain your position.

5. Discuss the advantages and drawbacks of the various recruiting sources.

6. Discuss the advantages and drawbacks of the various selection devices.

7. What are the benefits and drawbacks of realistic job previews? (Consider this question from both the perspective of the organization *and* the perspective of a potential employee.)

8. List the factors that influence employee compensation and benefits.

9. What, in your view, constitutes sexual harassment? Describe how companies can minimize sexual harassment in the workplace.

10. Research your chosen career by finding out what it's going to take to be successful in this career in terms of education, skills, experience, and so forth. Write a personal career guide that details this information.

Endnotes

1. A. Schwartz, "Leadership Development in a Global Environment: Lessons Learned from One of the World's Largest Employers," *Industrial and Commercial Training,* vol. 43, no. 1 (2011), pp. 13–16; "HR Trendbook 2011: Games at Work," *HR Magazine,* 2011, p. 70; "UPS to Deliver 430m Parcels in Month Before Christmas," *Commercial Motor,* December 2, 2010, p. 14; M. J. Credeur, "Squeezing More Green Out of Brown," *Bloomberg BusinessWeek,* September 20, 2010, p. 43; J. Casale, "Thorough Training Delivers Safer Drivers," *Business Insurance,* July 12, 2010, p. 1; J. Levitz, "UPS Thinks Outside the Box on Driver Training," *Wall Street Journal,* April 6, 2010, pp. B1+; and K. Kingsbury, "Road to Recovery," *Time,* March 8, 2010, pp. Global 14–16.

2. Material for this chapter is drawn from D. A. DeCenzo and S. P. Robbins, *Fundamentals of Human Resources Management,* 10th ed. (Hoboken, NJ: John Wiley & Sons, 2010).

3. From the Past to the Present box based on D. A. Wren and A. G. Bedeian, *The Evolution of Management Thought,* 6th ed. (Hoboken, NJ: John Wiley & Sons, 2009), pp. 198–200; "Building Better Organizations: Industrial-Organizational Psychology in the Workplace," *Society for Industrial and Organizational Psychology,* www.siop.org (July 13, 2009); and M. Munsterberg, *Hugo Munsterberg: His Life and Work* (New York: Appleton-Century-Crofts, 1922).

4. P. W. Tam and S. Woo, "Talent War Crunches Start-Ups," *Wall Street Journal,* February 28, 2011, pp. B1+; and C. Tuna, "Many Companies Hire as They Fire," *Wall Street Journal,* May 11, 2009, p. B6.

5. J. J. Salopek, "Employee Referrals Remain a Recruiter's Best Friend," *Workforce Management Online,* December 2010; L. G. Klaff, "New Internal Hiring Systems Reduce Cost and Boost Morale," *Workforce Management,* March 2004, pp. 76–79; M. N. Martinez, "The Headhunter Within," *HR Magazine,* August 2001, pp. 48–55; "Even Non-Recruiting Companies Must Maintain Hiring Networks," *HR Focus,* November 2001, p. 8; and L. Greenhalgh, A. T. Lawrence, and

R. I. Sutton, "Determinants of Work Force Reduction Strategies in Declining Organizations," *Academy of Management Review,* April 1988, pp. 241–254.

6. J. J. Salopek, "Employee Referrals Remain a Recruiter's Best Friend"; "Employee Referral Programs: Highly Qualified New Hires Who Stick Around," *Canadian HR Reporter,* June 4, 2001, p. 21; and C. Lachnit, "Employee Referral Saves Time, Saves Money, Delivers Quality," *Workforce,* June 2001, pp. 66–72.

7. C. Lawton, "Nokia to Cut 7,000 Globally," *Wall Street Journal,* April 28, 2011, p. B3; D. Jolly, "Panasonic to Cut 17,000 Jobs," *New York Times Online,* April 28, 2011; and L. Segall, "MySpace Slashes Its Staff in Half," *CNNMoney.com,* January 11, 2011.

8. J. Mooney, "Pre-Employment Testing on the Internet: Put Candidates a Click Away and Hire at Modem Speed," *Public Personnel Management,* Spring 2002, pp. 41–52.

9. See, for instance, R. D. Arvey and J. E. Campion, "The Employment Interview: A Summary and Review of Recent Research," *Personnel Psychology,* Summer 1982, pp. 281–322; and M. M. Harris, "Reconsidering the Employment Interview: A Review of Recent Literature and Suggestions for Future Research," *Personnel Psychology,* Winter 1989, pp. 691–726; J. H. Prager, "Nasty or Nice: 56-Question Quiz," *Wall Street Journal,* February 22, 2000, p. A4; and M. K. Zachary, "Labor Law for Supervisors," *Supervision,* March 2001, pp. 23–26.

10. See, for instance, G. Nicholsen, "Screen and Glean: Good Screening and Background Checks Help Make the Right Match for Every Open Position," *Workforce,* October 2000, p. 70.

11. R. A. Posthuma, F. P. Morgeson, and M. A. Campion, "Beyond Employment Interview Validity: A Comprehensive Narrative Review of Recent Research and Trends Over Time," *Personnel Psychology,* Spring 2002, pp. 1–81.

12. A. I. Huffcutt, J. M. Conway, P. L. Roth, and N. J. Stone, "Identification and Meta-Analysis Assessment of Psychological Constructs Measured in Employment Interviews," *Journal of Applied Psychology* (October 2001), pp. 897–913; and

A. I. Huffcutt, J. A. Weekley, W. H. Wiesner, T. G. Degroot, and C. Jones, "Comparison of Situational and Behavioral Description Interview Questions for Higher-Level Positions," *Personnel Psychology,* Autumn 2001, pp. 619–644.

13. See C. H. Middendorf and T. H. Macan, "Note-Taking in the Employment Interview: Effects on Recall and Judgments," *Journal of Applied Psychology* (April 2002), pp. 293–303; D. Butcher, "The Interview Rights and Wrongs," *Management Today,* April 2002, p. 4; P. L. Roth, C. H. Can Iddekinge, A. I. Huffcutt, C. E. Eidson, and P. Bobko, "Corrections for Range Restriction in Structured Interview Ethnic Group Differences: The Value May Be Larger than Researchers Thought," *Journal of Applied Psychology* (April 2002), pp. 369–376; and E. Hermelin and I. T. Robertson, "A Critique and Standardization of Meta-Analytic Coefficients in Personnel Selection," *Journal of Occupational and Organizational Psychology* (September 2001), pp. 253–277.

14. See J. Merritt, "Improv at the Interview," *BusinessWeek,* February 3, 2003, p. 63; P. J. Taylor and B. Small, "Asking Applicants What They Would Do Versus What They Did Do: A Meta-Analysis Comparison of Situation and Past Behavior Employment Interview Questions," *Journal of Occupational and Organizational Psychology* (September 2002), pp. 277–295; S. D. Mauer, "A Practitioner-Based Analysis of Interviewer Job Expertise and Scale Format as Contextual Factors in Situational Interviews," *Personnel Psychology,* Summer 2002, pp. 307–328; and J. M. Barclay, "Improving Selection Interviews with Structure: Organizations' Use of Behavioral Interviews," *Personnel Review* 30, no. 1 (2001), pp. 81–95.

15. J. Merrit, "Improv at the Interview," p. 63.

16. S. H. Applebaum and M. Donia, "The Realistic Downsizing Preview: A Management Intervention in the Prevention of Survivor Syndrome (Part II)," *Career Development International,* January 2001, pp. 5–19.

17. D. Zielinski, "Effective Assessments," *HRMagazine,* January 2011, pp. 61–64; W. L. Gardner, B. J. Reithel, R. T. Foley, C. C. Cogliser, and F. O. Walumbwa, "Attraction to Organizational Culture Profiles: Effects of Realistic Recruitment and Vertical and Horizontal Individualism-Collectivism," *Management Communication Quarterly,* February 2009, pp. 437–472; and S. L. Premack and J. P. Wanous, "A Meta-Analysis of Realistic Job Preview Experiments," *Journal of Applied Psychology* (November 1985), pp. 706–720.

18. C. Garvey, "The Whirlwind of a New Job," *HR Magazine,* June 2001, pp. 110–118.

19. Technology and the Manager's Job box based on D. Zielinski, "Effective Assessments;" R. E. DeRouin, B. A. Fritzsche, and E. Salas, "E-Learning in Organizations," *Journal of Management* (December 2005), pp. 920–940; K. O'Leonard, *HP Case Study: Flexible Solutions for Multi-Cultural Learners,* (Oakland: CA: Bersin & Associates), 2004; S. Greengard, "The Dawn of Digital HR," *Business Finance,* October 2003, pp. 55–59; and J. Hoekstra, "Three in One," *Online Learning,* vol. 5 (2001), pp. 28–32.

20. B. P. Sunoo, "Results-Oriented Customer Service Training," *Workforce* (May 2001), pp. 84–90.

21. See, for instance, E. G. Tripp, "Aging Aircraft and Coming Regulations: Political and Media Pressures Have Encouraged the FAA to Expand Its Pursuit of Real and Perceived Problems of Older Aircraft and Their Systems. Operators Will Pay," *Business and Commercial Aviation,* March 2001, pp. 68–75.

22. "A&S Interview: Sully's Tale," *Air & Space Magazine,* www.airspacemag.com (February 18, 2009); A. Altman, "Chesley B. Sullenberger III," *Time,* www.time.com (January 16, 2009); and K. Burke, P. Donohue, and C. Siemaszko, "US Airways Airplane Crashes in Hudson River—Hero Pilot Chesley Sullenberger III Saves All Aboard," *New York Daily News,* www.nydailynews.com (January 16, 2009).

23. C. S. Duncan, J. D. Selby-Lucas, and W. Swart, "Linking Organizational Goals and Objectives to Employee Performance: A Quantitative Perspective," *Journal of American Academy of Business* (March 2002), pp. 314–318.

24. "Training Expenditures," *Training* (November–December 2010), p. 19.

25. R. Langlois, "Fairmont Hotels: Business Strategy Starts with People," *Canadian HR Reporter,* November 5, 2001, p. 19.

26. M. Dalahoussaye, "Show Me the Results," *Training* (March 2002), p. 28.

27. See, for example, R. E. Catalano and D. L. Kirkpatrick, "Evaluating Training Programs: The State of the Art," *Training and Development Journal* (May 1968), pp. 2–9.

28. A. Tziner, C. Joanis, and K. R. Murphy, "A Comparison of Three Methods of Performance Appraisal with Regard to Goal Properties, Goal Perception, and Rate Satisfaction," *Group and Organization Management,* June 2000, pp. 175–190; and T. W. Kent and T. J. Davis, "Using Retranslation to Develop Operational Anchored Scales to Assess the Motivational Context of Jobs," *International Journal of Management* (March 2002), pp. 10–16.

29. See, also, C. A. Ramus and U. Steger, "The Roles of Supervisory Support Behaviors and Environmental Policy in Employee 'Ecoinitiatives' at Leading-Edge European Companies," *Academy of Management Journal* (August 2000), pp. 605–626.

30. See R. de Andrés, J. L. Garcia-Lapresta, and J. González-Pachón, "Performance Appraisal Based on Distance Function Methods," *European Journal of Operational Research* (December 2010), pp. 1599–1607; and L. Atwater and J. Brett, "Feedback Format: Does It Influence Manager's Reaction to Feedback," *Journal of Occupational and Organizational Psychology* (December 2006), pp. 517–532.

31. See "Performance Appraisals," *Business Europe,* April 3, 2002, p. 3.

32. M. A. Peiperl, "Getting 360 Feedback Right," *Harvard Business Review,* January 2001, pp. 142–147.

33. T. J. Maurer, D. R. D. Mitchell, and F. G. Barbeite, "Predictors of Attitudes Toward a 360-Degree Feedback System and Involvement in Post-Feedback Management Development Activity," *Journal of Occupational and Organizational Psychology* (March 2002), pp. 87–107.

34. A. Evans, "From Every Angle," *Training* (September 2001), p. 22.

35. R. de Andrés, J. L. Garcia-Lapresta, and J. González-Pachón, "Performance Appraisal Based on Distance Function Methods," *European Journal of Operational Research* (December 2010), pp. 1599–1607; J. Nelson, "How to Ace Your Yearly Review," *Canadian Business,* December 7, 2010, p. 94; G. P. Sillup and R. Klimberg, "Assessing the Ethics of Implementing Performance Appraisal Systems," *Journal of Management Development,* vol. 29, no. 1 (2010), pp. 38–55; T. Maylett, "360-Degree Feedback Revisited: The Transition from Development to Appraisal," *Compensation & Benefits Review,*

September–October 2009, pp. 52–59; P. Kamen, "The Way That You Use It: Full Circle Can Build Better Organizations with the Right Approach," *CMA Management,* April 2003, pp. 10–13; M. Kennett, "First Class Coach," *Management Today* (December 2001), p. 84; and T. A. Beehr, L. Ivanitsjaya, C. P. Hansen, D. Erofeev, and D. M. Gudanowski, "Evaluation of 360-Degree Feedback Ratings: Relationships with Each Other and with Performance and Selection Predictors," *Journal of Organizational Behavior* (November 2001), pp. 775–788.

36. By the Numbers box based on "Survey: 21 Percent of Job Seekers Dropped After Reference Checks," *Workforce Management Online,* June 23, 2010; J. Yang and A. Lewis, "Doing Jobs Without Training," *USA Today,* October 20, 2008, p. 1B; F. Di Meglio, "Dream Jobs: College Students Get Real," *Bloomberg BusinessWeek Online,* April 30, 2010; E. A. Grant, "Cookie Monster," *Fast Company,* June 2010, pp. 58–60; "Hiring for Fit," *Workforce Management Online,* May 28, 2010; J. Yang and A. Gonzalez, "Most Appealing Career Model for Me Is To . . ." *USA Today,* May 5, 2010, p. 1B; J. Yang and V. Salazar, "Most Neglected Grooming for Interviews," *USA Today,* December 31, 2009, p. 1B; and J. Yang and K. Simmons, "Preferred Résumé Format," *USA Today,* November 16, 2009, p. 1B.

37. J. D. Glater, "Seasoning Compensation Stew," *New York Times,* March 7, 2001, pp. C1+.

38. This section based on R. I. Henderson, *Compensation Management in a Knowledge-Based World,* 9th ed. (Upper Saddle River, NJ: Prentice Hall, 2003).

39. M. P. Brown, M. C. Sturman, and M. J. Simmering, "Compensation Policy and Organizational Performance: The Efficiency, Operational and Financial Implications of Pay Levels and Pay Structure," *Academy of Management Journal* (December 2003), pp. 752–762; J. D. Shaw, N. P. Gupta, and J. E. Delery, "Pay Dispersion and Workforce Performance: Moderating Effects of Incentives and Interdependence," *Strategic Management Journal* (June 2002), pp. 491–512; E. Montemayor, "Congruence between Pay Policy and Competitive Strategy in High-Performing Firms," *Journal of Management,* vol. 22, no. 6 (1996), pp. 889–908; and L. R. Gomez-Mejia, "Structure and Process of Diversification, Compensation Strategy, and Firm Performance," *Strategic Management Journal,* 13 (1992), pp. 381–397.

40. J. D. Shaw, N. Gupta, A. Mitra, and G. E. Ledford, Jr., "Success and Survival of Skill-Based Pay Plans," *Journal of Management* (February 2005), pp. 28–49; C. Lee, K. S. Law, and P. Bobko, "The Importance of Justice Perceptions on Pay Effectiveness: A Two-Year Study of a Skill-Based Pay Plan," *Journal of Management,* vol. 26, no. 6 (1999), pp. 851–873; G. E. Ledford, "Paying for the Skills, Knowledge and Competencies of Knowledge Workers," *Compensation and Benefits Review,* July–August 1995, pp. 55–62; and E. E. Lawler III, G. E. Ledford Jr., and L. Chang, "Who Uses Skill-Based Pay and Why," *Compensation and Benefits Review,* March–April 1993, p. 22.

41. J. D. Shaw, N. Gupta, A. Mitra, and G. E. Ledford Jr., "Success and Survival of Skill-Based Pay Plans."

42. Information from Hewitt Associates Studies: "As Fixed Costs Increase, Employers Turn to Variable Pay Programs as Preferred Way to Reward Employees," August 21, 2007; "Hewitt Study Shows Pay-for-Performance Plans Replacing Holiday Bonuses," December 6, 2005; "Salaries Continue to Rise in Asia Pacific, Hewitt Annual Study Reports," November 23, 2005; and "Hewitt Study Shows Base Pay Increases Flat for 2006 with Variable Pay Plans Picking Up the Slack," Hewitt Associates, LLC, www.hewittassociates.com (August 31, 2005).

43. "Mandated Benefits: 2002 Compliance Guide," *Employee Benefits Journal* (June 2002), p. 64; and J. J. Kim, "Smaller Firms Augment Benefits, Survey Shows," *Wall Street Journal,* June 6, 2002, p. D2.

44. P. P. Shah, "Network Destruction: The Structural Implications of Downsizing," *Academy of Management Journal* (February 2000), pp. 101–112.

45. See, for example, K. A. Mollica and B. Gray, "When Layoff Survivors Become Layoff Victims: Propensity to Litigate," *Human Resource Planning,* January 2001, pp. 22–32.

46. S. Koudsi, "You're Stuck," *Fortune,* December 10, 2001, pp. 271–274.

47. S. Berfield, "After the Layoff, The Redesign," *Business Week,* April 14, 2008, pp. 54–56; L. Uchitelle, "Retraining Laid-Off Workers, But for What?" *New York Times Online,* March 26, 2006; D. Tourish, N. Paulsen, E. Hobman, and P. Bordia, "The Downsides of Downsizing: Communication Processes and Information Needs in the Aftermath of a Workforce Reduction Strategy," *Management Communication Quarterly,* May 2004, pp. 485–516; J. Brockner, G. Spreitzer, A. Mishra, W. Hochwarter, L. Pepper, and J. Weinberg, "Perceived Control As an Antidote to the Negative Effects of Layoffs on Survivors' Organizational Commitment and Job Performance," *Administrative Science Quarterly,* 49 (2004), pp. 76–100; and E. Krell, "Defusing Downsizing," *Business Finance,* December 2002, pp. 55–57.

48. A. Joshi, "Managing the Organizational Melting Pot: Dilemmas of Workplace Diversity," *Administrative Science Quarterly,* December 2001, pp. 783–784.

49. Right or Wrong box based on R. Pyrillis, "Workers Using Medical Marijuana Hold Their Breath, but Employers Worry They'll Take a Hit," *Workforce Management Online,* April 2011; "Puffing Up Over Pot in Workplace," *Workforce Management,* March 2011, p. 41; D. Cadrain, "The Marijuana Exception," *HR Magazine,* November 2010, pp. 40–42; D. Cadrain, "Do Medical Marijuana Laws Protect Usage by Employees?" *HR Magazine,* November 2010, p. 12; A. K. Wiwi and N. P. Crifo, "The Unintended Impact of New Jersey's New Medical Marijuana Law on the Workplace," *Employee Relations Law Journal,* Summer 2010, pp. 33–37; S. Simon, "At Work, a Drug Dilemma," *Wall Street Journal,* August 3, 2010l, p. D1; and J. Greenwald, "Medical Marijuana Laws Create Dilemma for Firms," *Business Insurance,* February 15, 2010, pp. 1–20.

50. Top 50 Companies for Diversity, *DiversityInc,* June 2010, pp. 18–19.

51. See, for instance, K. Iverson, "Managing for Effective Workforce Diversity," *Cornell Hotel and Restaurant Administration Quarterly,* April 2000, pp. 31–38.

52. U.S. Equal Employment Opportunity Commission, "Sexual Harassment Charges EEOC and FEPAs Combined: FY 1997–FY 2010," http://www.eeoc.gov/eeoc/statistics/enforcement/sexual_harassment.

53. Ibid.

54. N. F. Foy, "Sexual Harassment Can Threaten Your Bottom Line," *Strategic Finance* (August 2000), pp. 56–57.

55. "Federal Monitors Find Illinois Mitsubishi Unit Eradicating Harassment," *Wall Street Journal* (September 7, 2000), p. A8.

56. L. J. Munson, C. Hulin, and F. Drasgow, "Longitudinal Analysis of Dispositional Influences and Sexual Harassment: Effects on Job and Psychological Outcomes," *Personnel Psychology* (Spring 2000), p. 21.

57. B. Leonard, "Survey: 10% of Employees Report Harassment at Work," *HR Magazine,* October 2010, p. 18.

58. *"Nichols v. Azteca Restaurant Enterprises,"* *Harvard Law Review,* May 2002, p. 2074; A. J. Morrell, "Non-Employee Harassment," *Legal Report* (January–February 2000), p. 1. See also S. Lim and L. M. Cortina, "Interpersonal Mistreatment in the Workplace: The Interface and Impact of General Incivility and Sexual Harassment," *Journal of Applied Psychology* (May 2005), pp. 483–496.

59. Although the male gender is referred to here, it is important to note that sexual harassment may involve people of either sex or the same sex. (See, for instance, *Oncale v. Sundowner Offshore Service, Inc.*, 118 S. Ct. 998.)

60. See also A. M. O'Leary-Kelly, L. Bowes-Sperry, C. A. Bates, and E. R. Lean, "Sexual Harassment at Work: A Decade (Plus) of Progress," *Journal of Management* (June 2009), pp. 503–536; M. Rotundo, D. H. Nguyen, and P. R. Sackett, "A Meta-Analytic Review of Gender Differences in Perceptions of Sexual Harassment," *Journal of Applied Psychology* (October 2001), pp. 914–922.

61. R. L. Wiener and L. E. Hurt, "How Do People Evaluate Social Sexual Conduct at Work? A Psychological Model," *Journal of Applied Psychology* (February 2000), p. 75.

62. *Meritor Savings Bank v. Vinson,* 477 U.S. 57 (1986).

63. R. D. Lee and P. S. Greenlaw, "Employer Liability for Employee Sexual Harassment: A Judicial Policy-Making Study," *Public Administration Review* (March–April 2000), p. 127.

64. Ibid.

65. "You and DuPont: Diversity," DuPont Company Documents (1999–2000), http://www.dupont.com/careers/you/diverse.html; and "DuPont Announces 2000 Dr. Martin Luther King, Days of Celebration," DuPont Company Documents, http://www.dupont.com/corp/whats-news/releases/00/001111.html (January 11, 2000).

66. It should be noted here that under the Title VII and the Civil Rights Act of 1991, the maximum award that can be given, under the Federal Act, is $300,000. However, many cases are tried under state laws that permit unlimited punitive damages.

67. J. W. Janove, "Sexual Harassment and the Big Three Surprises," *HR Magazine,* November 2001, pp. 123–130; and L. A. Baar, and J. Baar, "Harassment Case Proceeds Despite Failure to Report," *HR Magazine,* June 2005, p. 159.

68. W. L. Kosanovich, J. L. Rosenberg, and L. Swanson, "Preventing and Correcting Sexual Harassment: A Guide to the Ellerth/Faragher Affirmative Defense," *Employee Relations Law Journal* (Summer 2002), pp. 79–99; M. Zall, "Workplace Harassment and Employer Liability," *Fleet Equipment,* January 2000, p. B1. See also, "Ruling Allows Defense in Harassment Cases," *HR Magazine,* August 2004, p. 30.

69. See, for instance, P. W. Dorfman, A. T. Cobb, and R. Cox, "Investigations of Sexual Harassment Allegations: Legal Means Fair—Or Does It?" *Human Resources Management,* Spring 2000, pp. 33–39.

70. C. H. Liu and P. J. Robertson, "Spirituality in the Workplace," *Journal of Management Inquiry* (March 2011), pp. 35–50; and C. Cash and G. R. Gray, "A Framework for Accommodating Religion and Spirituality in the Workplace," *The Academy of Management Executive,* 14, no. 3 (August 2000), p. 124.

71. Liu and Robertson, "Spirituality in the Workplace;" and D. P. Ashmos and D. Duchon, "Spirituality at Work: A Conceptualization and Measure," *Journal of Management Inquiry* (June 2000), p. 139.

72. A. A. Mohamed, J. Wisnieski, M. Askar, and I. Syed, "Toward a Theory of Spirituality in the Workplace," *Competitiveness Review* 14, no. 1 (Winter–Fall 2004), pp. 102–107.

73. See F. Warner, "Professionals Tap a Higher Power in the Workplace," *Workforce Management Online,* April 2011; Liu and Robertson, "Spirituality in the Workplace;" E. J. Kutcher, J. D. Bragger, O. Rodriguez-Srednicki, and J. L. Masco, "The Role of Religiosity in Stress, Job Attitudes, and Organizational Citizenship Behavior," *Journal of Business Ethics* (August 2010), pp. 319–337; I. A. Mitroff and E. A. Denton, *A Spiritual Audit of Corporate America: A Hard Look at Spirituality, Religion, and Values in the Workplace* (San Francisco, CA: Jossey-Bass, 1999); J. Milliman, J. Ferguson, D. Trickett, and B. Condemi, "Spirit and Community at Southwest Airlines: An Investigation of a Spiritual Values-Based Model," *Journal of Organizational Change Management* 12, no. 3 (1999), pp. 221–233; E. H. Burack, "Spirituality in the Workplace," *Journal of Organizational Change Management* 12, no. 3 (1999), pp. 280–291; and F. Wagner-Marsh and J. Conley, "The Fourth Wave: The Spirituality-Based Firm," *Journal of Organizational Change Management* 12, no. 3 (1999), pp. 292–302.

74. M. Conlin, "Religion in the Workplace: The Growing Presence of Spirituality in Corporate America," *BusinessWeek,* November 1, 1999, pp. 151–158; and P. Paul, "A Holier Holiday Season," *American Demographics,* December 2001, pp. 41–45.

75. For a thorough review of the benefits of workplace spirituality, see J. Marques, S. Dhiman, and R. King, "Spirituality in the Workplace: Developing an Integral Model and a Comprehensive Definition," *Journal of American Academy of Business* (September 2005), pp. 81–92. See, also, M. Conlin, "Religion in the Workplace," p. 153; C. P. Neck and J. F. Milliman, "Thought Leadership: Finding Spiritual Fulfillment in Organizational Life," *Journal of Managerial Psychology* 9, no. 8 (1984), p. 9; D. W. McCormick, "Spirituality and Management," *Journal of Managerial Psychology* 9, no. 6 (1994), p. 5; E. Brandt, "Corporate Pioneers Explore Spirituality Peace," *HR Magazine,* April 1996, p. 82; P. Leigh, "The New Spirit at Work," *Training and Development* (February 1997), p. 193; and J. Milliman, A. Czaplewski, and J. Ferguson, "An Exploratory Empirical Assessment of the Relationship Between Spirituality and Employee Work Attitudes," paper presented at the national Academy of Management meeting, Washington, D.C. (August 2001).

76. See, for example, J. Marques, "HR's Crucial Role in the Establishment of Spirituality in the Workplace," *Journal of Academy of Business* (September 2005), pp. 27–31.

77. These examples taken from S. J. Wells, "Does Work Make You Fat?" *HR Magazine,* October 2010, pp. 26–32; R. King, "Slimming Down Employees to Cut Costs"; C. Tkaczyk, "Lowering Health-Care Costs," *Fortune,* November 23, 2009, p. 16; and A. W. Matthews, "When All Else Fails: Forcing Workers into Healthy Habits," *Wall Street Journal,* July 8, 2009, pp. D1+.

78. D. Mattioli, "Firms Feel Pain from Health Law," *Wall Street Journal,* December 13, 2010, pp. B1; L. Cornwell, "More Companies Penalize Workers with Health Risks," The Associated Press, *Springfield, Missouri News-Leader,* September 10, 2007, p. 10A; and A. Zimmerman, Matthews, and Hudson, "Can Employers Alter Hiring Policies to Cut Health Costs?"

79. B. Pyenson and K. Fitch, "Smoking May Be Hazardous to Your Bottom Line," *Workforce Online,* www.workforce.com (December 2007); and L. Cornwell, The Associated Press, "Companies Tack on Fees on Insurance for Smokers," *Springfield, Missouri News-Leader,* February 17, 2006, p. 5B.

80. J. Wojcik, "Research Shows Cost of Employee Obesity," *Business Insurance,* October 18, 2010, p. 24.

81. R. Ceniceros, "Obesity Can Exacerbate Workplace Injuries, Study Notes," *Workforce Management Online,* December 15, 2010; and "Obesity Weighs Down Production," *Industry Week,* March 2008, pp. 22–23.

82. J. Appleby, "Companies Step Up Wellness Efforts," *USA Today,* August 1, 2005, pp. 1A+.

83. G. Kranz, "Prognosis Positive: Companies Aim to Get Workers Healthy," *Workforce Management,* www.workforce.com (April 15, 2008).

84. S. J. Wells, "Does Work Make You Fat?"; and M. Conlin, "Hide the Doritos! Here Comes HR," *BusinessWeek,* April 28, 2008, pp. 94–96.

85. J. Fox, "Good Riddance to Pensions," *CNN Money,* January 12, 2006.

86. M. Adams, "Broken Pension System in Crying Need of a Fix," *USA Today,* November 15, 2005, p. 1B+.

87. "Prevalence of Retirement Plans by Type in the *Fortune* 100," *Pension Benefits,* September 2010, pp. 1–2; D. Kansas, "Has the 401(k) Failed?" *Fortune,* June 22, 2009, pp. 94–98; S. Block, "Company Pensions Are Out on a Limb," *USA Today,* May 22, 2009, pp. 1B+; A. Feldman, "Retiring the 401(k) Contribution," *BusinessWeek,* November 24, 2008, p. 32; J. Appleby, "Traditional Pensions Are Almost Gone. Is Employer-Provided Health Insurance Next?" *USA Today,* November 13, 2007, pp.1A+; S. Kelly, "FedEx, Goodyear Make Big Pension Plan Changes," *Workforce Management,* www.workforce.com, (March 1, 2007); G. Colvin, "The End of a Dream," *Fortune,* www.cnnmoney.com (June 22, 2006); E. Porter and M. Williams Nash, "Benefits Go the Way of Pensions," *NY Times Online,* February 9, 2006; and J. Fox, "Good Riddance to Pensions."

YOUR TURN TO BE A MANAGER

Managing Human Resources

Skill Development: Developing Interviewing Skills

Managers, by definition, get things done through and with other people. Part of their job is selecting competent people who can fill key roles on their teams. A major element in this selection process is interviewing prospective candidates. The better managers are at developing their interviewing skills, the greater the chance that they'll select new employees who are competent and fit well into the organization.

Personal Insights: What Do You Know About Effective Interviewing?

Indicate the degree to which you agree or disagree with these 10 statements.

1 = Strongly disagree
2 = Disagree
3 = Neither agree or disagree
4 = Agree
5 = Strongly agree

1. Prior knowledge about the applicant will improve the accuracy of my evaluation. 1 2 3 4 5

2. Most interviewers favor applicants who share the interviewer's attitudes. 1 2 3 4 5

3. The best interviews are those where the interviewer prepares a set of specific questions ahead of time. 1 2 3 4 5

4. Insights into an applicant's skills and abilities are improved when the applicant feels uncomfortable and uncertain. 1 2 3 4 5

5. Most interviewers give equal weight to positive and negative information. 1 2 3 4 5

6. The best interview questions can be answered with a direct "yes" or "no." 1 2 3 4 5

7. A good interviewer takes detailed notes during or immediately after the interview. 1 2 3 4 5

8. The best predictor of what an applicant will do in the future is what he or she has done in the past. 1 2 3 4 5

9. Interviews are more effective for selecting managers than blue-collar workers. 1 2 3 4 5

10. End interviews by telling the applicant how well he or she performed in the interview. 1 2 3 4 5

Source: Developed by Stephen P. Robbins.

Analysis and Interpretation

Add up your score for items 2, 3, 7, 8, and 9. For the other five items, reverse the score. A 1 should be scored as 5, a 2 as 4, and so on. Your total score will range between 10 and 50. Scores of 40 or better indicate a fairly accurate understanding of effective interviewing.

Source: Developed by Stephen P. Robbins

Skill Basics

Every manager needs to develop his or her interviewing skills. The following highlights the key behaviors associated with effective interviewing.

1. *Review the job description and job specification.* What does the job look like that the applicant will be filling? And what qualifications does the ideal candidate possess? Reviewing pertinent information about the job provides valuable information about how to assess the candidate. And relevant job requirements help to reduce interview bias.

2. *Prepare a structured set of questions to ask all applicants for the job.* By having a set of prepared questions, you ensure that the information you wish to elicit is attained. Furthermore, if you ask all applicants similar questions, you'll have a common base against which to compare their answers.

3. *Before meeting an applicant, review his or her application form and résumé.* Doing so helps you to create a complete picture of the applicant in terms of what is represented on the résumé or application and what the job requires. You will also begin to identify areas to explore in the interview. That is, areas that are not clearly defined on the résumé or application but that are essential for the job will become a focal point of your discussion with the applicant.

4. *Open the interview by putting the applicant at ease and providing a brief preview of the topics to be discussed.* Interviews are stressful for job applicants. By opening with small talk (e.g., the weather), you give the person time to adjust to the interview setting. By providing a preview of topics to come, you're giving the applicant an agenda that helps the individual begin framing what he or she will say in response to your questions.

5. *Ask your questions and listen carefully to the applicant's answers.* Ask questions that can't be merely answered with only a *yes* or *no.* Inquiries that begin with *how* or *why* tend to stimulate extended answers. Avoid leading questions that telegraph the desired response (such as "Would you say you have good interpersonal skills?") and bipolar questions that require the applicant to select an answer from only two choices (such as "Do you prefer working with people or working alone?"). Since the best predictor of future behavior is past behavior, the best questions tend to be those that focus on previous experiences that are relevant to the current job.

6. *Closing the interview.* Wrap up the interview by telling the applicant what's going to happen next. Be honest with the applicant regarding others who will be interviewed and the remaining steps in the hiring process. Tell the applicant how and when you will let him or her know about your decision.

7. *Concluding.* Once the interview is over, write your evaluation while it is fresh in your mind. Ideally, you kept notes or recorded the applicant's answers to your questions and made comments of your impressions. Now that the applicant is gone, take the time to assess the applicant's responses.

Based on W. C. Donaghy, *The Interview: Skills and Applications* (Glenview, Il: Scott, Foresman, 1984), pp. 245–280; E. D. Pulakos and N. Schmitt, "Experience-Based and Situational Interview Questions: Studies of Validity," *Personnel Psychology*, Summer 1995, pp. 289–308; W. W. Larson, *Ten Minute Guide to Conducting Job Interviews* (New York: Alpha, 2001); and C. Sun, "10 Tips on Conducting Effective Interviews," *TechRepublic*, October 28, 2008.

Skill Application

Each class member should bring in a copy of his or her résumé. If they don't have one, this is a good time to create one.

The class members should pair off. Using their partner's résumé, each will conduct a job interview. Here's a brief background about the job: Your college's admissions office is looking to fill a position of recruitment officer. The job requires no specific previous admissions experience but does assume some familiarity with the college, the college community, and the type of student it attracts. There are typically three people doing this job at the college—which includes meeting prospective students and parents; representing the college at regional college fairs; interviewing students; and evaluating prospective applicants—but one has tendered her resignation. So there is now a vacancy.

Each "interviewer" has up to 15 minutes to conduct his or her interview. After the first is complete, roles are reversed. Upon completion, each "interviewee" should critique his or her interviewer against the skills identified in the previous section.

Skill Practice

1. Select a job vacancy listed in your newspaper or online. Have a friend or relative play the role of job applicants and practice your skill at interviewing to fill the job vacancy.

2. Review your personal experiences in job interviews. How would you rate your interviewers' general effectiveness? What did they do right? What did they do wrong?

For Your Immediate Action

Western Montana Power & Light

To: Sandra Gillies, Director of Human Resources
From: William Mulroney, CEO
Re: Sexual Harassment

Sandra, I think we might have a problem. It appears that some of our employees aren't clear about the practices and actions that do or do not constitute sexual harassment. We can't have any ambiguity or uncertainty about this, as you know. We need to immediately develop a training program for all our employees and develop a workable procedure to handle any complaints that might arise.

I want this issue of sexual harassment to be the primary topic at next month's executive board meeting. To facilitate discussion, please give me a bulleted list describing the content of an initial two-hour employee workshop on sexual harassment.

This fictionalized company and message were created for educational purposes only, and not meant to reflect positively or negatively on management practices by any company that may share this name.

Bringing the Real World to Life

Case Application:
Thinking Outside the Box: Part 2

With more than 400,000 employees in 215 countries and territories, HRM is a significant and critical function for UPS. The company's top managers have recognized that if they want to position UPS to continue to grow in today's fast-changing global environment, they have to take a hard look at training policies and programs, especially in the way young workers are recruited, trained, and developed.

About five years ago, UPS began to notice a decline in the performance of young new drivers. "Previously, trainees needed 30 days to become proficient drivers. Younger drivers were now taking 90 to 180 days." These younger drivers were just as smart and had just as much potential, but the techniques that had been used for decades just were not clicking for these millennial trainees. In another sign that its traditional classroom driver training obviously wasn't working was that some 30 percent of its driver candidates didn't make it through the training period.

After much study (with the help of a $1.8 million grant from the Labor Department set up to look at the way millennials learn and with collaboration of higher education partners), the company was convinced that the twenty-somethings—the bulk of its driver recruits—responded best to high-tech instruction instead of books and lectures.

Thus, UPS invested in a "next-generation training facility called Integrad." Currently, UPS has two Integrad facilities—one outside of Baltimore and another outside of Chicago. There, trainees use video games, a "slip and fall simulator which combines a greased floor with slippery shoes," and an obstacle course around a mock village.

At the training center outside of Baltimore, applicants for a driver's job, which pays an average of $74,000 annually, spend one week practicing and training to be a driver. They move from one station to the next practicing the company's "340 Methods," which are techniques developed by industrial engineers "to save seconds and improve safety in every task from lifting and loading boxes to selecting a package from a shelf in the truck." Applicants play a video game where they're in the driver's seat and must identify obstacles. From computer simulations, they move to "Clarksville," a mock village with miniature houses and faux businesses. There, they drive a real truck and "must successfully execute five deliveries in 19 minutes." And, in the interest of safety and efficiency, trainees learn to carefully walk on ice with the slip and fall simulator.

How are the new training methods working? So far, so good. Of the 1,629 trainees who have completed it, "only 10 percent have failed the training program, which takes a total of six weeks overall including 30 days of driving a truck in the real world."

DISCUSSION QUESTIONS

1. What external factors were affecting UPS's HR practices? How did UPS respond to these trends?

2. Why is efficiency and safety so important to UPS? What role do the company's industrial engineers play in how employees do their work?

3. What changes did the company make to its driver training program? What do you think of these changes?

4. What advantages and drawbacks do you see to this training approach for (a) the trainee and (b) the company?

BUILDING YOUR CAREER

The term *career* has several meanings. In popular usage, it can mean advancement ("she is on a management career track"), a profession ("he has chosen a career in accounting"), or a lifelong sequence of jobs ("his career has included 12 jobs in six organizations"). For our purposes, we define a career as the sequence of work positions held by a person during his or her lifetime. Using this definition, it's apparent that we all have, or will have, a career. Moreover, the concept is as relevant to unskilled laborers as it is to software designers or physicians. But career development isn't what it used to be!

What Was Career Development Like, Historically?

Although career development has been an important topic in management courses for years, some dramatic changes have occurred in the concept. Career development programs used to be designed to help employees advance their work lives within a specific organization. The focus of such programs was to provide employees the information, assessment, and training needed to help them realize their career goals. Career development was also a way for organizations to attract and retain highly talented people. This approach has all but disappeared in today's workplace. Now, organizations that have such traditional career programs are few and far between. Downsizing, restructuring, and other organizational adjustments have brought us to one significant conclusion about career development: You—not the organization—will be responsible for designing, guiding, and developing your own career.

What Is Career Development Like, Now?

This idea of increased personal responsibility for one's career has been described as a boundaryless career. The challenge is that few hard-and-fast rules are available to guide you.

One of the first decisions you have to make is career choice. The optimum choice is one that offers the best match between what you want out of life and your interests, your abilities and personality, and market opportunities. Good career choices should result in a series of jobs that give you an opportunity to be a good performer, make you want to maintain your commitment to your career, lead to highly satisfying work, and give you the proper balance between work and personal life. A good career match, then, is one in which you are able to develop a positive self-concept, to do work that you think is important, and to lead the kind of life you desire. In a recent survey by Capital One Financial Corporation, 66 percent of college graduates said that a comprehensive benefits package (including, for example, health care, 401(k) program, child care, and domestic partner benefits) was the

---

career
The sequence of work positions held by a person during his or her lifetime

boundaryless career
When an individual takes personal responsibility for his or her own career

From Career Module of *Fundamentals of Management,* Eighth Edition. Stephen P. Robbins, David A. De Cenzo, Mary Coulter. Copyright © 2013 by Pearson Education, Inc. All rights reserved.

most important factor in their job search. Starting salary ranked second at 64 percent, with job location ranked third at 60 percent. Today's college grads are also looking to be rewarded or compensated (with comp time or matching donations, for instance) for their volunteer and philanthropic activities.

Once you've identified a career choice, it's time to initiate the job search. However, we aren't going to get into the specifics of job hunting, writing a résumé, or interviewing successfully, although those things are important. Let's fast-forward through all that and assume that your job search was successful. It's time to go to work! How do you survive and excel in your career?

How Can I Have a Successful Career?

What can you do to improve your chances for career success? You're already doing the *most* important thing: You're getting a college education! It's the surest way to increase your lifetime earnings. Currently, the average high school graduate earns $27,915 a year. His or her counterpart with a college degree earns $51,206. College graduates earn, on average, $800,000 more than high school graduates over their working career. Investing in your education and training is one of the best investments you'll make in your lifetime. What *else* can you do? The following suggestions are based on extensive research into career management.

Assess Your Personal Strengths and Weaknesses

Where do your natural talents lie? What can you do, relative to others, that gives you a competitive advantage? Are you particularly good with numbers? Have strong people skills? Good with your hands? Write better than most people? Everyone has some things that they do better than others and some areas where they're weak. Play to your strengths.

Identify Market Opportunities

Where are tomorrow's job opportunities? Regardless of your strengths, certain job categories are likely to decline in the coming decades—for instance, bank tellers, small farmers, movie projectionists, travel agents, and secretaries. In contrast, abundant opportunities are more likely to be created by an increasingly aging society, continued emphasis on technology, increased spending on education and training, and concern with personal security. These factors are likely to create excellent opportunities for jobs in gerontological counseling, network administration, training consultants, and security-alarm installers.

Take Responsibility for Managing Your Own Career

Historically, companies tended to assume responsibility for their employees' careers. Today, this is the exception rather than the rule. Employees are increasingly expected to take responsibility for their own careers.

Think of your career as your business and you're its CEO. To survive, you have to monitor market forces, head off competitors, and be ready to quickly take advantage of opportunities when they surface. You have to protect your career from harm and position yourself to benefit from changes in the environment.

Develop Your Interpersonal Skills

Interpersonal skills, especially the ability to communicate, top the list of almost every employer's "must have" skills. Whether it's getting a new job or a promotion, strong interpersonal skills are likely to give you a competitive edge.

Practice Makes Perfect

There's an increasing amount of evidence indicating that super-high achievers aren't fundamentally different from the rest of us. They just work harder and smarter. It's been found, based on studies of world-class performers in music, sports, chess, science, and business, that people like Tiger Woods, Mozart, and Bill Gates put in about 10,000 hours (or 10 years at 1,000 hours a year) of persistent, focused training and experience before they hit their peak performance level. If you want to excel in any field, you should expect to have to put in a lot of deliberate practice—consistently engaging in repeated activity specifically designed to improve performance beyond your current comfort and ability level.

Stay Up-to-Date

In today's dynamic world, skills can become obsolete quickly. To keep your career on track, you need to make learning a lifetime commitment. You should be continually "going to school"—if not taking formal courses, then reading books and journals to ensure that you don't get caught with obsolete skills.

Network

Networking refers to creating and maintaining beneficial relationships with others in order to accomplish your goals. It helps to have friends in high places. It also helps to have contacts who can keep you informed of changes that are going on in your organization and in your industry. Go to conferences. Maintain contact with former college friends and alumni. Get involved in community activities. Cultivate a broad set of relationships. And in today's increasingly interconnected world, join online business networking groups such as LinkedIn, Spoke, and Talkbiznow.

Stay Visible

Networking can increase your visibility. So, too, can writing articles in your professional journals, teaching classes or giving talks in your area of expertise, attending conferences and professional meetings, and making sure your accomplishments are properly promoted. You increase your mobility and value in the marketplace by keeping visible.

Seek a Mentor

Employees with mentors are likely to have enhanced mobility, increased knowledge of the organization's inside workings, greater access to senior executives, increased satisfaction, and increased visibility. For women and minorities, having mentors has been shown to be particularly helpful in promoting career advancement and success.

Leverage Your Competitive Advantage

Develop skills that will give you a competitive advantage in the marketplace. Especially focus on skills that are important to employers, skills that are scarce, and areas where you have limited competition. Try to avoid a worst-case scenario: You have a job that anyone can learn in 30 minutes. Remember that the harder it is for you to learn and develop a highly prized skill, the harder it'll also be for others to acquire it. Generally speaking, the more training necessary to do a job and the fewer people who have that training, the greater your security and influence.

Here's an insight from many years as a student and a professor: To succeed in school, you have to be a generalist and excel at everything. For instance, to earn a 4.0 GPA, you need to be a star in English, math, science, geography, languages, and so on. The "real world," on the other hand, rewards specialization. You don't have to be good at everything. You just need to be good at something that others aren't and that society values. You can be lousy in math or science and still be a very successful opera singer, artist, salesperson, or writer. You don't have to excel in English to be a computer programmer or electrician. The secret to life success is identifying your comparative advantage and then developing it. And as we've noted previously, you need to invest approximately 10,000 hours in honing your skills to achieve optimum proficiency.

Don't Shun Risks

Don't be afraid to take risks, especially when you're young and you don't have much to lose. Going back to school, moving to a new state or country, or quitting a job to start your own business can be the decision that will set your life in a completely new direction. Great accomplishments almost always require taking the path less traveled; and the road to nowhere is paved with fears of the unknown.

It's OK to Change Jobs

Past generations often believed "you don't leave a good job." That advice no longer applies. In today's fast-changing job market, staying put often only means that you're staying behind. Employers no longer expect long-term loyalty. And to keep your skills fresh, your income increasing, and your job tasks interesting, it will be increasingly likely that you'll need to change employers.

Opportunities, Preparation, and Luck = Success

Successful people are typically ambitious, intelligent, and hardworking. But they are also lucky. It's not by chance that many of the biggest technology success stories—Bill Gates and Paul Allen at Microsoft, Steve Jobs at Apple, Scott McNealy at Sun Microsystems, Eric Schmidt at Novell and Google—were born in a narrow three-year period between June 1953 and March 1956. They were smart. They were interested in computers and technology. But they were also lucky. They reached their teens and early 20s in 1975—at the dawn of the personal computer age. Those people with similar interests and talents but born in the mid-1940s were likely to have joined a firm like IBM out of college and been enamored with mainframe computers. Had they been born in the early 1960s, they would have missed getting in on the ground floor of the revolution.

Success is a matter of matching up opportunities, preparation, and luck. It's been suggested that few of us get more than a couple of special opportunities in our lifetime. If you're lucky, you will recognize those opportunities, have made the proper preparations, and then act on them.

You can't control when you were born, where you were born, your parents' finances, or the like. Those are the luck factors. But what you can control is your preparation and willingness to act when opportunity knocks.

Sources: Managing Your Career Module based on J. H. Greenhaus, V. M. Godstalk, and G. A. Callahan, *Career Management*, 3rd ed. (Cincinnati, OH: South–Western, 2000); K. A. Ericsson, "Deliberate Practice and the Modifiability of Body and Mind," *International Journal of Sports Psychology* (January–March 2007), pp. 4–34; J. P. Newport, "Mastery, Just 10,000 Hours Away," *Wall Street Journal*, March 14–15, 2009, p. W6; "Capital One Survey Highlights What Today's College Graduates Want from Employers," www.businesswire.com (June 10, 2008); M. Gladwell, *Outliers: The Story of Success* (New York: Little, Brown, 2008); R. N. Boles, *What Color Is Your Parachute? 2009: A Practical Manual for Job-Hunters and Career-Changers* (Berkeley, CA: Ten Speed Press, 2009); D. E. Super and D. T. Hall, "Career Development: Exploration and Planning," in M. R. Rosenzweig and L.W. Porter (eds.), *Annual Review of Psychology*, vol. 29 (Palo Alto, CA: Annual Reviews, 1978), p. 334; and M. B. Arthur and D. M. Rousseau, *The Boundaryless Career: A New Employment Principle for a New Organizational Era* (New York: Oxford University Press, 1996).

Managing Change
and **Innovation**

Managing Change and Innovation

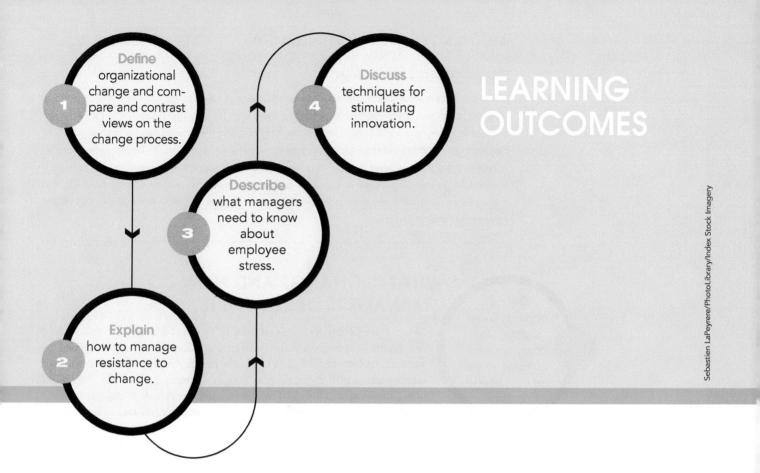

1. **Define** organizational change and compare and contrast views on the change process.

2. **Explain** how to manage resistance to change.

3. **Describe** what managers need to know about employee stress.

4. **Discuss** techniques for stimulating innovation.

Sebastien LaPeyrere/PhotoLibrary/Index Stock Imagery

Stress Kills

We know that too much stress can be bad for our health and well-being. That connection proved itself painfully and tragically at France Télécom.[1] Since early 2008, there have been more than 50 suicides of people who worked for the company. The situation captured the attention of the worldwide media, the public, and the French government because many of the suicides and more than a dozen failed suicide attempts were attributed to work-related problems. The masks worn by these protesting Telecom employees say "Lombard has killed me." Didier Lombard was the chairman of the board and chief executive officer of France Telecom when the suicides took place. Although France has a higher suicide rate than any other large Western country, this scenario was particularly troublesome. The spate of suicides highlighted a quirk at the heart of French society: "Even with robust labor protection, workers see themselves as profoundly insecure in the face of globalization, with many complaining about being pushed beyond their limits." France isn't the only country dealing with worker suicides. Workplace conditions at China's Foxconn, the world's largest maker of electronic components (including the iPhone, iPod, and iPad), were strongly criticized after 11 Foxconn employees committed suicide.

Stress can be an unfortunate consequence of change and anxiety, both at work and personally. However, change is a constant for organizations and thus for managers. Large companies, small businesses, entrepreneurial start-ups, universities, hospitals, and even the military are changing the way they do things. Although change has always been a part of a manager's job, it's become even more so in recent years. And because change can't be eliminated, managers must learn how to manage it successfully. In this chapter, we're going to look at organizational change efforts, the ways that managers can deal with the stress that exists in organizations, and how managers can stimulate innovation in their organizations.

WHAT IS CHANGE AND HOW DO MANAGERS DEAL WITH IT?

Define organizational change and compare and contrast views on the change process.

1

When John Lechleiter assumed the CEO's job at Eli Lilly, he sent each of his senior executives a gift—"a digital clock counting down, second by second, to October 23, 2011. That's the day Lilly's $5 billion-a-year schizophrenia pill, Zyprexa, was no longer under patent." By the end of 2016, Lilly stands to lose $10 billion in annual revenues as patents on three of its key drugs expire. Needless to say, the company has had to make some organizational changes as it picks up the pace of drug development.[2] Lilly's managers are doing what managers everywhere must do—implement change!

If it weren't for change, a manager's job would be relatively easy. Planning would be easier because tomorrow would be no different from today. The issue of organization design would be solved because the environment would be free from uncertainty and there would be no need to adapt. Similarly, decision making would be dramatically simplified because the outcome of each alternative could be predicted with near pinpoint accuracy. It would also simplify the manager's job if competitors never introduced new products or services, if customers didn't make new demands, if government regulations were never modified, if technology never advanced, or if employees' needs always remained the same. But that's not the way it is.

Change is an organizational reality. Most managers, at one point or another, will have to change some things in their workplace. We classify these changes as **organizational change**, which is any alteration of an organization's people, structure, or technology. (See Exhibit 1.) Let's look more closely at each of these three areas.

Changing *structure* includes any alteration in authority relationships, coordination mechanisms, degree of centralization, job design, or similar organization structure variables. For instance, in previous chapters, we've mentioned that work process engineering, restructuring, and empowering result in decentralization, wider spans of control, reduced work specialization, and work teams. These structural components give employees the authority and means to implement process improvements. For instance, the creation of work teams that cut across departmental lines allows those people who understand a problem best to solve that problem. In addition, cross-functional work teams encourage cooperative problem solving rather than "us versus them" situations. All of these situations may involve some type of structural change.

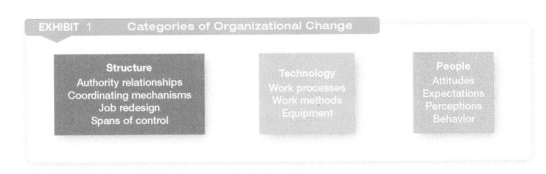

EXHIBIT 1 Categories of Organizational Change

Structure	Technology	People
Authority relationships	Work processes	Attitudes
Coordinating mechanisms	Work methods	Expectations
Job redesign	Equipment	Perceptions
Spans of control		Behavior

Changing *technology* encompasses modifications in the way work is done or the methods and equipment used. One organizational area, in particular, where managers deal with changing technology is continuous improvement initiatives, which are directed at developing flexible processes to support better-quality operations. Employees committed to continuous improvements are constantly looking for things to fix. Thus, work processes must be adaptable to continual change and fine-tuning. Such adaptability requires an extensive commitment to educating and training workers. Employees need skills training in problem solving, decision making, negotiation, statistical analysis, and team-building, and they must be able to analyze and act on data. For example, Campbell Soup Co. uses both technology and employee training to maintain its market-leading position in the soup industry.[3]

Changes in *people* refer to changes in employee attitudes, expectations, perceptions, or behaviors. The human dimension of change requires a workforce that's committed to quality and continuous improvement. Again, proper employee education and training are needed, as is a performance evaluation and reward system that supports and encourages those improvements. For example, successful programs put quality goals into bonus plans for executives and incentives for employees.

Why Do Organizations Need to Change?

Both external and internal forces constrain managers. These same forces also bring about the need for change. Let's briefly review these factors.

WHAT EXTERNAL FORCES CREATE A NEED TO CHANGE? The external forces that create the need for organizational change come from various sources. In recent years, the *marketplace* has affected firms such as AT&T and Lowe's because of new competition. AT&T, for example, faces competition from local cable companies and from free Internet services such as Skype. Lowe's, too, must now contend with a host of aggressive competitors such as Home Depot and Menard's. *Government laws and regulations* are also an impetus for change. For example, when the Americans with Disabilities Act was signed into law, thousands of businesses were required to widen doorways, reconfigure restrooms, and add ramps. Even today, organizations continue to deal with the requirements of improving accessibility for the disabled.

Technology also creates the need for organizational change. The Internet has changed the way we get information, how products are sold, and how we get our work done. Technological advancements have created significant economies of scale for many organizations. For instance, technology allows Scottrade to offer its clients the opportunity to make online trades without a broker. The assembly line in many industries has also undergone dramatic change as employers replace human labor with technologically advanced mechanical robots. Also, the fluctuation in *labor markets* forces managers to initiate changes. For example, the shortage of registered nurses in the United States has led many hospital administrators to redesign nursing jobs and to alter their rewards and benefits packages for nurses, as well as join forces with local universities to address the nursing shortage.

As the news headlines remind us, *economic* changes affect almost all organizations. For instance, prior to the mortgage market meltdown, low interest rates led to significant growth in the housing market. This growth meant more jobs, more employees hired, and significant increases in sales in other businesses that supported the building industry. However, as the economy soured, it had the opposite effect on the housing industry and other industries as credit markets dried up and businesses found it difficult to get the capital they needed to operate. And although it's been over a decade since 9/11, the airline industry is still dealing with the organizational changes forced on it by increased security measures and other environmental factors such as high fuel costs.

organizational change
Any alteration of an organization's people, structure, or technology

Newscom

Changes in the economic environment created a need for internal change at Intuit, Inc., a developer of tax-preparation and financial software. When the economic recession slowed the sales of Intuit's QuickBooks, Quicken, and TurboTax software, the firm's senior executives created an environment and established workplace practices that facilitated employee innovation. Developing an internal innovation program has transformed Intuit from a software maker to a provider of Web sites and new online and mobile software that are driving the company's long-term growth. Shown here at a business technology event is an Intuit vice president of innovation sharing how his firm boosted sales with new products and services.

WHAT INTERNAL FORCES CREATE A NEED TO CHANGE? Internal forces can also create the need for organizational change. These internal forces tend to originate primarily from the internal operations of the organization or from the impact of external changes. (It's also important to recognize that such changes are a normal part of the organizational life cycle.)[4]

When managers redefine or modify an organization's *strategy*, that action often introduces a host of changes. For example, Nokia bringing in new equipment is an internal force for change. Because of this action, employees may face job redesign, undergo training to operate the new equipment, or be required to establish new interaction patterns within their work groups. Another internal force for change is that the *composition of an organization's workforce* changes in terms of age, education, gender, nationality, and so forth. A stable organization in which managers have been in their positions for years might need to restructure jobs in order to retain more ambitious employees by affording them some upward mobility. The compensation and benefits systems might also need to be reworked to reflect the needs of a diverse workforce and market forces in which certain skills are in short supply. *Employee attitudes*, such as increased job dissatisfaction, may lead to increased absenteeism, resignations, and even strikes. Such events will, in turn, often lead to changes in organizational policies and practices.

Who Initiates Organizational Change?

Organizational changes need a catalyst. People who act as catalysts and assume the responsibility for managing the change process are called change agents.[5]

Any manager can be a change agent. When we talk about organizational change, we assume that it's initiated and carried out by a manager within the organization. However, the change agent could be a nonmanager—for example, an internal staff specialist or an outside consultant whose expertise is in change implementation. For major systemwide changes, an organization will often hire outside consultants for advice and assistance. Because these consultants come from the outside, they offer an objective perspective that insiders usually lack. However, the problem is that outside consultants may not understand the organization's history, culture, operating procedures, and personnel. They're also prone to initiating more drastic changes than insiders—which can be either a benefit or a disadvantage—because they don't have to live with the repercussions after the change is implemented. In contrast, internal managers who act as change agents may be more thoughtful (and possibly more cautious) because they must live with the consequences of their actions.

How Does Organizational Change Happen?

We often use two metaphors to clarify the change process.[6] The "calm waters" metaphor envisions the organization as a large ship crossing a calm sea. The ship's captain and crew know exactly where they're going because they've made the trip many times before. Change appears as the occasional storm, a brief distraction in an otherwise calm and predictable trip. In the "white-water rapids" metaphor, the organization is seen as a small raft navigating a raging river with uninterrupted white-water rapids. Aboard the raft are half a dozen people who have never worked together before, who are totally unfamiliar with the river, who are unsure of their eventual destination, and who, as if things weren't bad enough, are traveling at night. In the white-water rapids metaphor, change is the status quo and managing change is a continual process.

These two metaphors represent distinctly different approaches to understanding and responding to change. Let's look closer at each one.

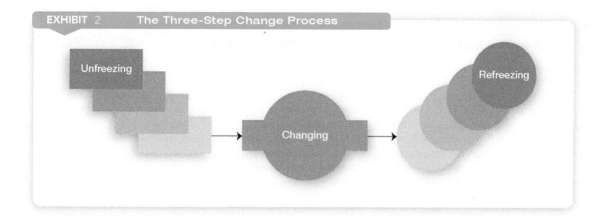

EXHIBIT 2   The Three-Step Change Process

Unfreezing

Changing

Refreezing

WHAT IS THE "CALM WATERS" METAPHOR?   Until recently, the "calm waters" metaphor dominated the thinking of practicing managers and academics. The prevailing model for handling change in such circumstances is best illustrated in Kurt Lewin's three-step description of the change process.[7] (See Exhibit 2.)

According to Lewin, successful change requires unfreezing the status quo, changing to a new state, and freezing the new change to make it permanent. The status quo can be considered an equilibrium state. Unfreezing is necessary to move from this equilibrium. It can be achieved in one of three ways:

- The driving forces, which direct behavior away from the status quo, can be increased.
- The restraining forces, which hinder movement from the existing equilibrium, can be decreased.
- The two approaches can be combined.

Once the situation has been unfrozen, the change itself can be implemented. However, the mere introduction of change doesn't ensure that it will take hold. The new situation, therefore, needs to be frozen so that it can be sustained over time. Unless this last step is done, it's likely that the change will be short-lived and employees will revert to the previous equilibrium state. The objective of freezing the entire equilibrium state, then, is to stabilize the new situation by balancing the driving and restraining forces.

Note how Lewin's three-step process treats change as a break in the organization's equilibrium state.[8] The status quo has been disturbed, and change is necessary to establish a new equilibrium state. Although this view might have been appropriate to the relatively calm environment faced by most organizations during the twentieth century, it's increasingly obsolete as a description of the kinds of "seas" that current managers have to navigate. (See the From the Past to the Present box for more information on Lewin and his organizational research.)

WHAT IS THE "WHITE-WATER RAPIDS" METAPHOR?   Susan Whiting is the chair of Nielsen Media Research, the company best known for its television ratings, which are frequently used to determine how much advertisers pay for TV commercials. The media research business isn't what it used to be, however, as the Internet, video on demand, cell phones, iPods, digital video recorders, and other changing technologies have made data collection much more challenging. Whiting says, "If you look at a typical week I have, it's a combination of trying to lead a company in change in an industry in change."[9] That's a

---

change agents
People who act as change catalysts and assume the responsibility for managing the change process

"calm waters" metaphor
A description of organizational change that likens that change to a large ship making a predictable trip across a calm sea and experiencing an occasional storm

"white-water rapids" metaphor
A description of organizational change that likens that change to a small raft navigating a raging river

"There is nothing so practical as a good theory."

"If you want truly to understand something, try to change it."

These two quotes by Kurt Lewin provide unique insights into who he was and how he approached studying management.[10] Lewin, who's often called the father of modern social psychology (a discipline that uses scientific methods to "understand and explain how the thought, feeling, and behavior of individuals are influenced by the actual, imagined, or implied presence of other human beings"), made his name in management circles through his studies of group dynamics. His approach was based on the belief that "group behavior is an intricate set of symbolic interactions and forces that not only affect group structure but also modify individual behavior."

One of his research studies that looked at modifying family food habits during World War II provided new and important insights into introducing change. He found that "changes were more easily induced through group decision making than through lectures and individual appeals." So what did this mean? His findings suggested that changes would be more readily accepted when people felt they had an opportunity to be involved in the change rather than when

they were simply asked or told to change. That's an important lesson for any manager, even today, to learn and apply.

Finally, another of Lewin's major contributions was the idea of force field analysis, a framework for looking at the factors (forces) that influenced a situation. Those forces could either be *driving* movement toward a goal or *blocking* movement toward a goal. When you view this idea in terms of managing change, you can see how this process also could contribute to understanding the dynamics of what makes change work and how managers can overcome resistance to change; that is, increase the driving forces, decrease the blocking forces, or both.

Think About:

- Using your own words, explain each of the two Lewin quotes above.

- Explain force field analysis and how it can be used in organizational change.

- What advice do you see in this information about Lewin's ideas that managers might use?

○

pretty accurate description of what change is like in our second change metaphor—white-water rapids. It's also consistent with a world that's increasingly dominated by information, ideas, and knowledge.[11]

To get a feeling of what managing change might be like in a white-water rapids environment, consider attending a college that had the following rules: Courses vary in length. When you sign up, you don't know how long a course will run. It might go for 2 weeks or 30 weeks. Furthermore, the instructor can end a course at any time with no prior warning. If that isn't challenging enough, the length of the class changes each time it meets: Sometimes the class lasts 20 minutes; other times it runs for 3 hours. And the time of the next class meeting is set by the instructor during this class. There's one more thing. All exams are unannounced, so you have to be ready for a test at any time. To succeed in this type of environment, you'd have to respond quickly to changing conditions. Students who were overly structured or uncomfortable with change wouldn't succeed.

DOES EVERY MANAGER FACE A WORLD OF CONSTANT AND CHAOTIC CHANGE?
No, not every manager faces such a world. However, the numbers who don't is dwindling. The stability and predictability of the calm waters metaphor don't exist. Disruptions in the status quo are not occasional and temporary, and they are not followed by a return to calm waters. Many managers never get out of the rapids. Like Susan Whiting, just described, they face constant forces in the environment (external *and* internal) that bring about the need for organizational change.

HOW DO ORGANIZATIONS IMPLEMENT PLANNED CHANGES? At the Wyndham Peachtree Conference Center in Georgia, businesses bring groups of employees to try their hand at the ancient Chinese water sport of dragon boat racing. Although the physical exercise is an added benefit, it's the team-building exercise in which participants learn about communication, collaboration, and commitment that's meant to be the longest-lasting benefit.[12]

We know that most changes employees experience in an organization don't happen by chance. Often managers make a concerted effort to alter some aspect of the organization. Whatever happens—in terms of structure or technology—ultimately affects organizational members. Efforts to assist organizational members with a planned change are referred to as **organization development (OD)**.

In facilitating long-term, organization-wide changes, OD focuses on constructively changing the attitudes and values of organization members so that they can more readily adapt to and be more effective in achieving the new directions of the organization.[13] When OD efforts are planned, organization leaders are, in essence, attempting to change the organization's culture.[14] However, a fundamental issue of OD is its reliance on employee participation to foster an environment in which open communication and trust exist.[15] Persons involved in OD efforts acknowledge that change can create stress for employees. Therefore, OD attempts to involve organizational members in changes that will affect their jobs and seeks their input about how the change is affecting them (just as Lewin suggested).

Any organizational activity that assists with implementing planned change can be viewed as an OD technique. However, the more popular OD efforts in organizations rely heavily on group interactions and cooperation and include survey feedback, process consultation, team-building, and intergroup development.

Survey feedback efforts are designed to assess employee attitudes about and perceptions of the change they are encountering. Employees are generally asked to respond to a set of specific questions regarding how they view such organizational aspects as decision making, leadership, communication effectiveness, and satisfaction with their jobs, coworkers, and management.[16] The data that a change agent obtains are used to clarify problems that employees may be facing. As a result of this information, the change agent takes some action to remedy the problems.

In **process consultation**, outside consultants help managers to perceive, understand, and act on organizational processes with which they must deal.[17] These elements might include, for example, workflow, informal relationships among unit members, and formal communications channels. Consultants give managers insight into what is going on. It's important to recognize that consultants are not there to solve these problems. Rather, they act as coaches to help managers diagnose the interpersonal processes that need improvement. If managers, with the consultants' help, cannot solve the problem, the consultants will often help managers find experts who can.

Organizations are made up of individuals working together to achieve some goals. Because organizational members must frequently interact with peers, a primary function of OD is to help them become a team. **Team-building** is generally an activity that helps work groups set goals, develop positive interpersonal relationships, and clarify the roles and responsibilities of each team member. It's not always necessary to address each area because the group may be in agreement and understand what's expected of it. The primary focus of team-building is to increase members' trust and openness toward one another.[18]

Whereas team-building focuses on helping a work group become more cohesive, **intergroup development** attempts to achieve the same results among different work groups. That is, intergroup development attempts to change attitudes, stereotypes, and perceptions that one group may have toward another group. In doing so, better coordination among the various groups can be achieved.

Xyratex, a data storage firm based in the United Kingdom, brings its managers and employees from around the world together to participate in philanthropic team-building events. This photo shows coworkers who gathered in Sacramento, California, for a team-building exercise to assemble bicycles and then give them to kids from local Boys & Girls Clubs. Team-building helps Xyratex employees increase their trust and openness toward one another and deepen their commitment to the firm's mission of "advancing digital innovation." By combining team building with philanthropy, Xyratex gives employees the opportunity to achieve a corporate goal of helping children who live near the firm's operations in Europe, Asia, and North America.

Randall Benton/Newscom

---

organization development (OD)
Efforts that assist organizational members with a planned change by focusing on their attitudes and values

survey feedback
A method of assessing employees' attitudes toward and perceptions of a change

process consultation
Using outside consultants to assess organizational processes such as workflow, informal intra-unit relationships, and formal communication channels

team-building
Using activities to help work groups set goals, develop positive interpersonal relationships, and clarify the roles and responsibilities of each team member

intergroup development
Activities that attempt to make several work groups more cohesive

HOW DO MANAGERS MANAGE RESISTANCE TO CHANGE?

2 Explain how to manage resistance to change.

We know that it's better for us to eat healthy and to be active, yet few of us follow that advice. We resist making changes in our lifestyle. Volkswagen Sweden and ad agency DDB Stockholm did an experiment to see if they could get people to change their behavior and take the healthier option of using the stairs instead of riding an escalator.[19] How? They put a working piano keyboard on a stairway in a Stockholm subway station (you can see a video of it on YouTube) to see if commuters would use it. The experiment was a resounding success as stair traffic rose 66 percent. The lesson—people can change if you make the change appealing.

Managers should be motivated to initiate change because they're concerned with improving their organization's effectiveness. But change isn't easy in any organization. It can be disruptive and scary. Organizations, and people within them, can build up inertia that causes them to resist any change, even if the change might be beneficial. In this section, we review why people in organizations resist change and what can be done to lessen that resistance.

Why Do People Resist Organizational Change?

It's often said that most people hate any change that doesn't jingle in their pockets. This resistance to change is well documented.[20] Why *do* people resist organizational change? The main reasons include uncertainty, habit, concern over personal loss, and the belief that the change is not in the organization's best interest.[21]

Change replaces the known with uncertainty. No matter how much you may dislike attending college (or certain classes), at least you know what's expected of you. When you leave college for the world of full-time employment, you'll trade the known for the unknown. Employees in organizations are faced with similar uncertainty. For example, when quality control methods based on statistical models are introduced into manufacturing plants, many quality control inspectors have to learn the new methods. Some may fear that they'll be unable to do so and may develop a negative attitude toward the change or behave poorly if required to use them.

Another cause of resistance is that we do things out of habit. Every day when you go to school or work you probably get there the same way, if you're like most people. We're creatures of habit. Life is complex enough—we don't want to have to consider the full range of options for the hundreds of decisions we make every day. To cope with this complexity, we rely on habits or programmed responses. But when confronted with change, our tendency to respond in our accustomed ways becomes a source of resistance.

The third cause of resistance is the fear of losing something already possessed. Change threatens the investment you've already made in the status quo. The more that people have invested in the current system, the more they resist change. Why? They fear losing status, money, authority, friendships, personal convenience, or other economic benefits that they value. This helps explain why older workers tend to resist change more than younger workers since they generally have more invested in the current system and more to lose by changing.

A final cause of resistance is a person's belief that the change is incompatible with the goals and interests of the organization. For instance, an employee who believes that a proposed new job procedure will reduce product quality can be expected to resist the change. This type of resistance can actually be beneficial to the organization if expressed in a positive way.

What Are Some Techniques for Reducing Resistance to Organizational Change?

At an annual 401(k) enrollment meeting, the CEO of North American Tool, frustrated at his employees' disinterest in maxing out their investments, brought in a big bag, unzipped it, and upended it over a table.[23] Cash poured out—$9,832 to be exact—the amount employees had failed to claim the prior year. He gestured at the money and said, "This is your money. It should be in your pocket. Next year, do you want it on the table or in your

EXHIBIT 3	Techniques for Reducing Resistance to Change		
TECHNIQUE	**WHEN USED**	**ADVANTAGE**	**DISADVANTAGE**
Education and communication	When resistance is due to misinformation	Clear up misunderstandings	May not work when mutual trust and credibility are lacking
Participation	When resisters have the expertise to make a contribution	Increase involvement and acceptance	Time-consuming; has potential for a poor solution
Facilitation and support	When resisters are fearful and anxiety-ridden	Can facilitate needed adjustments	Expensive; no guarantee of success
Negotiation	When resistance comes from a powerful group	Can "buy" commitment	Potentially high cost; opens doors for others to apply pressure too
Manipulation and co-optation	When a powerful group's endorsement is needed	Inexpensive, easy way to gain support	Can backfire, causing change agent to lose credibility
Coercion	When a powerful group's endorsement is needed	Inexpensive, easy way to gain support	May be illegal; may undermine change agent's credibility

pocket?" When the 401(k) enrollment forms were distributed, several individuals signed up. Sometimes to get people to change, you first have to get their attention.

When managers see resistance to change as dysfunctional, what can they do? Several strategies have been suggested in dealing with resistance to change. These approaches include education and communication, participation, facilitation and support, negotiation, manipulation and co-optation, and coercion. These tactics are summarized here and described in Exhibit 3. Managers should view these techniques as tools and use the most appropriate one depending on the type and source of the resistance.

Education and communication can help reduce resistance to change by helping employees see the logic of the change effort. This technique, of course, assumes that much of the resistance lies in misinformation or poor communication.

Participation involves bringing those individuals directly affected by the proposed change into the decision-making process. Their participation allows these individuals to express their feelings, increase the quality of the process, and increase employee commitment to the final decision.

Facilitation and support involve helping employees deal with the fear and anxiety associated with the change effort. This help may include employee counseling, therapy, new skills training, or a short paid leave of absence.

Negotiation involves exchanging something of value for an agreement to lessen the resistance to the change effort. This resistance technique may be quite useful when the resistance comes from a powerful source.

Manipulation and co-optation refer to covert attempts to influence others about the change. They may involve twisting or distorting facts to make the change appear more attractive.

Finally, *coercion* can be used to deal with resistance to change. Coercion involves the use of direct threats or force against the resisters.

WHAT REACTION DO EMPLOYEES HAVE TO ORGANIZATIONAL CHANGE?

Describe what managers need to know about employee stress.

3

For many employees, change creates stress. A dynamic and uncertain environment characterized by restructurings, downsizings, empowerment, and personal-life matters has caused large numbers of employees to feel overworked and "stressed out." As our opening case described, sometimes the stress gets to be so intense that individuals respond in a drastic (and tragic) way. In this section, we'll review specifically what is meant by the term *stress*, what the symptoms of stress are, what causes stress, and what managers can do to reduce anxiety.

What Is Stress?

Stress is the adverse reaction people have to excessive pressure placed on them from extraordinary demands, constraints, or opportunities.[24] Stress isn't always bad. Although it's often discussed in a negative context, stress can be positive, especially when it offers a potential gain. For instance, functional stress allows an athlete, stage performer, or employee to perform at his or her highest level at crucial times.

However, stress is more often associated with constraints and demands. A constraint prevents you from doing what you desire; demands refer to the loss of something desired. When you take a test at school or have your annual performance review at work, you feel stress because you confront opportunity, constraints, and demands. A good performance review may lead to a promotion, greater responsibilities, and a higher salary. But a poor review may keep you from getting a promotion. An extremely poor review might lead to your being fired.

One other thing to understand about stress is that just because the conditions are right for stress to surface doesn't always mean it will. Two conditions are necessary for *potential* stress to become *actual* stress.[25] First, there must be uncertainty over the outcome, and second, the outcome must be important.

What Are the Symptoms of Stress?

We see stress in a number of ways. For instance, an employee who is experiencing high stress may become depressed, accident prone, or argumentative; may have difficulty making routine decisions; may be easily distracted, and so on. As Exhibit 4 shows, stress symptoms can be grouped under three general categories: physical, psychological, and behavioral. All of these can significantly affect an employee's work.

Too much stress can also have tragic consequences. In Japan, there's a stress phenomenon called karoshi (pronounced kah-roe-she), which is translated literally as "death from overwork." During the late 1980s, "several high-ranking Japanese executives still in their prime years suddenly died without any previous sign of illness."[26] As public concern increased, even the Japanese Ministry of Labour got involved, and it now publishes statistics on the number of karoshi deaths. As Japanese multinational companies expand operations to China, Korea, and Taiwan, it's feared that the karoshi culture may follow.

What Causes Stress?

Stress can be caused by personal factors and by job-related factors called stressors. Clearly, change of any kind—personal or job-related—has the potential to cause stress because it involves demands, constraints, or opportunities. Organizations have no shortage of factors that can cause stress. Pressures to avoid errors or complete tasks in

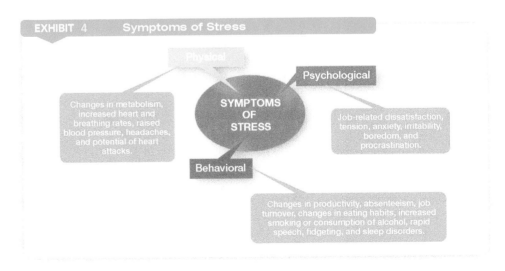

EXHIBIT 4   Symptoms of Stress

Physical
Changes in metabolism, increased heart and breathing rates, raised blood pressure, headaches, and potential of heart attacks.

Psychological
Job-related dissatisfaction, tension, anxiety, irritability, boredom, and procrastination.

SYMPTOMS OF STRESS

Behavioral
Changes in productivity, absenteeism, job turnover, changes in eating habits, increased smoking or consumption of alcohol, rapid speech, fidgeting, and sleep disorders.

a limited time period, changes in the way reports are filed, a demanding supervisor, and unpleasant coworkers are a few examples. Let's look at five categories of organizational stressors: task, role, and interpersonal demands; organization structure; and organizational leadership.

Task demands are factors related to an employee's job. They include the design of a person's job (autonomy, task variety, degree of automation), working conditions, and the physical work layout. Work quotas can put pressure on employees when their "outcomes" are perceived as excessive.[27] The more interdependence between an employee's tasks and the tasks of others, the more potential stress there is. *Autonomy*, on the other hand, tends to lessen stress. Jobs in which temperatures, noise, or other working conditions are dangerous or undesirable can increase anxiety. So, too, can working in an overcrowded room or in a visible location where interruptions are constant.

Role demands relate to pressures placed on an employee as a function of the particular role he or she plays in the organization. Role conflicts create expectations that may be hard to reconcile or satisfy. Role overload is experienced when the employee is expected to do more than time permits. Role ambiguity is created when role expectations are not clearly understood and the employee is not sure what he or she is to do.

Interpersonal demands are pressures created by other employees. Lack of social support from colleagues and poor interpersonal relationships can cause considerable stress, especially among employees with a high social need.

Organization structure can increase stress. Excessive rules and an employee's lack of opportunity to participate in decisions that affect him or her are examples of structural variables that might be potential sources of stress.

Organizational leadership represents the supervisory style of the organization's managers. Some managers create a culture characterized by tension, fear, and anxiety. They establish unrealistic pressures to perform in the short run, impose excessively tight controls, and routinely fire employees who don't measure up. This style of leadership filters down through the organization and affects all employees.

Personal factors that can create stress include family issues, personal economic problems, and inherent personality characteristics. Because employees bring their personal problems to work with them, a full understanding of employee stress requires a manager to be understanding of these personal factors.[28] Evidence also indicates that employees' personalities have an effect on how susceptible they are to stress. The most commonly used labels for these personality traits are Type A and Type B.

Chris Crisman/Redux Pictures

These top global executives of the JWT advertising agency have highly stressful jobs. As senior corporate executives leading an agency with more than 200 offices in 90 countries, they have a career that ranks high on the list of the most stressful jobs. Role and task demands make the jobs of senior executives stressful because as leaders they are expected to develop strategies and make decisions that keep their company profitable. This complex task requires an extensive knowledge of business and an understanding of industry trends, technological developments, and competitors' plans. On average, business leaders work 11 hours a day and face daily pressure to make decisions that affect employees, shareholders, and other stakeholders.

---

stress
The adverse reaction people have to excessive pressure placed on them from extraordinary demands, constraints, or opportunities

karoshi
A Japanese term that refers to a sudden death caused by overworking

stressors
Factors that cause stress

role conflicts
Work expectations that are hard to satisfy

role overload
Having more work to accomplish than time permits

role ambiguity
When role expectations are not clearly understood

RIGHT ? WRONG

One in five companies offers some form of stress management program.[29] Although such programs are available, many employees may choose not to participate. They may be reluctant to ask for help, especially if a major source of that stress is job insecurity. After all, there's still a stigma associated with stress. Employees don't want to be perceived as being unable to handle the demands of their job. Although they may need stress management now more than ever, few employees want to admit that they're stressed.

Think About:

- What can be done about this paradox?

- Do organizations even *have* an ethical responsibility to help employees deal with stress?

Madis Uudam/Shutterstock

The **Type A personality** is characterized by chronic feelings of a sense of time urgency, an excessive competitive drive, and difficulty accepting and enjoying leisure time. The opposite of Type A is the **Type B personality**. Type Bs never suffer from time urgency or impatience. Until quite recently, it was believed that Type As were more likely to experience stress on and off the job. A closer analysis of the evidence, however, has produced new conclusions. Studies show that only the hostility and anger associated with Type A behavior are actually associated with the negative effects of stress. And Type Bs are just as susceptible to the same anxiety-producing elements. For managers, what is important is to recognize that Type A employees are more likely to show symptoms of stress, even if organizational and personal stressors are low.

How Can Stress Be Reduced?

As mentioned earlier, not all stress is dysfunctional. Even though stress can never be totally eliminated from a person's life, managers want to reduce the stress that leads to dysfunctional work behavior. How? Through controlling certain organizational factors to reduce job-related stress, and to a more limited extent, offering help for personal stress.

Things that managers can do in terms of job-related factors begin with employee selection. Managers need to make sure that an employee's abilities match the job requirements. When employees are in over their heads, their stress levels typically will be high. A realistic job preview during the selection process can minimize stress by reducing ambiguity over job expectations. Improved organizational communications will keep ambiguity-induced stress to a minimum. Similarly, a performance planning program such as MBO will clarify job responsibilities, provide clear performance goals, and reduce ambiguity through feedback. Job redesign is also a way to reduce stress. If stress can be traced to boredom or to work overload, jobs should be redesigned to increase challenge or to reduce the workload. Redesigns that increase opportunities for employees to participate in decisions and to gain social support also have been found to lessen stress.[30] For instance, at U.K. pharmaceutical maker GlaxoSmithKline, a team-resilience program in which employees can shift assignments depending on people's workload and deadlines, has helped reduce work-related stress by 60 percent.[31]

No matter what you do to eliminate organizational stressors, some employees will still be "stressed out." And stress from an employee's personal life raises two problems. First, it's difficult for the manager to control directly. Second, there are ethical considerations. Specifically, does the manager have the right to intrude—even in the most subtle ways—in an employee's personal life? If a manager believes it's ethical and the employee is receptive, there are a few approaches the manager can consider.

To help deal with these issues, many companies offer employee assistance and wellness programs.[32] These employer-sponsored programs are designed to assist employees in areas where they might be having difficulties such as financial planning, legal matters, health, fitness, or stress.[33]

Contemporary **employee assistance programs (EAPs)** are extensions of programs that began in U.S. companies in the 1940s.[34] Companies such as DuPont, Standard Oil, and Kodak recognized that a number of their employees were experiencing problems with alcohol. Formal programs were implemented on the company's site to educate these workers about the dangers of alcohol and to help them overcome their addiction. The rationale for these programs, which still holds today, is getting a productive employee back on the job as quickly as possible. An organization also can benefit in terms of a return on investment. It's estimated that U.S. companies spend almost $1 billion each year on EAP programs. Studies suggest that most of these companies save up to $5 to $16 for every EAP dollar spent.[35] That's a significant return on investment!

In addition to EAP, many organizations are implementing wellness programs. A **wellness program** is designed to keep employees healthy.[36] These programs vary and may focus on such things as smoking cessation, weight control, stress management, physical fitness, nutrition education, high-blood-pressure control, violence protection, work team problem intervention, and so on.[37] Wellness programs are designed to help cut employer health costs and to lower absenteeism and turnover by preventing health-related problems.[38]

HOW CAN MANAGERS ENCOURAGE INNOVATION IN AN ORGANIZATION?

Discuss techniques for stimulating innovation.

4

"Innovation is the key to continued success." "We innovate today to secure the future."[39] These two quotes (the first by Ajay Banga, the CEO of MasterCard, and the second by Sophie Vandebroek, chief technology officer of Xerox Innovation Group) reflect how important innovation is to organizations. Success in business today demands innovation. In the dynamic, chaotic world of global competition, organizations must create new products and services and adopt state-of-the-art technology if they're going to compete successfully.[40]

What companies come to mind when you think of successful innovators? Maybe Apple with all its cool work and entertainment gadgets. Maybe Facebook for its 800 million-plus users. Maybe Nissan for creating the Leaf, the first mass-market all-electric car. Or even maybe Zynga (a company founded in 2007 and now worth over $500 million) for creating wildly popular games and dominating the social gaming market.[41] What's the secret to the success of these innovator champions? What can other managers do to make their organizations more innovative? In the following pages, we'll try to answer those questions as we discuss the factors behind innovation.

How Are Creativity and Innovation Related?

Creativity refers to the ability to combine ideas in a unique way or to make unusual associations between ideas.[42] A creative organization develops unique ways of working or novel solutions to problems. For instance, at Mattel, company officials introduced "Project Platypus," a special group that brings people from all disciplines—engineering, marketing, design, and sales—and tries to get them to "think outside the box" in order to "understand the sociology and psychology behind children's play patterns." To help make this kind of thinking happen, team members embarked on such activities as imagination exercises, group crying, and stuffed-bunny throwing. What does throwing stuffed bunnies have to do with creativity? It's part of a juggling lesson where team members tried to learn to juggle two balls and a stuffed bunny. Most people can easily learn to juggle two balls but can't let go of that third object. Creativity, like juggling, is learning to let go—that is, to "throw the bunny."[43] But creativity by itself isn't enough. The outcomes of the creative process need to be turned into useful products or work methods, which is defined as **innovation**. Thus,

---

Type A personality
People who have a chronic sense of urgency and an excessive competitive drive

Type B personality
People who are relaxed and easygoing and accept change easily

employee assistance programs (EAPs)
Programs offered by organizations to help employees overcome personal and health-related problems

wellness programs
Programs offered by organizations to help employees prevent health problems

creativity
The ability to produce novel and useful ideas

innovation
The process of taking a creative idea and turning it into a useful product, service, or method of operation

Groupon is an innovative organization that channeled creativity into a useful outcome. Company founder and CEO Andrew Mason describes his Groupon.com innovation as a "hybrid of local advertising and local commerce." An online group discount service targeted to local communities, Groupon has been called "the most exciting thing to happen to retail since eBay." The service offers daily deals from local merchants through group coupons, giving businesses a new way to advertise their products and services and giving consumers the chance to try new things at a huge discount. Shown here are employees of Groupon in Chicago, where the company was started in 2008 and has since expanded to cities throughout the world.

the innovative organization is characterized by its ability to channel creativity into useful outcomes. When managers talk about changing an organization to make it more creative, they usually mean they want to stimulate and nurture innovation.

What's Involved in Innovation?

Some people believe that creativity is inborn; others believe that with training, anyone can be creative. The latter group views creativity as a fourfold process consisting of perception, incubation, inspiration, and innovation.[44]

Perception involves the way you see things. Being creative means seeing things from a unique perspective. One person may see solutions to a problem that others cannot or will not see at all. The movement from perception to reality, however, doesn't occur instantaneously. Instead, ideas go though a process of *incubation*. Sometimes employees need to sit on their ideas, which doesn't mean sitting and doing nothing. Rather, during this incubation period, employees should collect massive amounts of data that are stored, retrieved, studied, reshaped, and finally molded into something new. During this period, it's common for years to pass. Think for a moment about a time you struggled for an answer on a test. Although you tried hard to jog your memory, nothing worked. Then suddenly, like a flash of light, the answer popped into your head. You found it! *Inspiration* in the creative process is similar. Inspiration is the moment when all your efforts successfully come together.

Although inspiration leads to euphoria, the creative work isn't complete. It requires an innovative effort. *Innovation* involves taking that inspiration and turning it into a useful product, service, or way of doing things. Thomas Edison is often credited with saying that "Creativity is 1 percent inspiration and 99 percent perspiration." That 99 percent, or the innovation, involves testing, evaluating, and retesting what the inspiration found. It's usually at this stage that an individual involves others more in what he or she has been working on. Such involvement is critical because even the greatest invention may be delayed, or lost, if an individual cannot effectively deal with others in communicating and achieving what the creative idea is supposed to do.

How Can a Manager Foster Innovation?

The systems model (inputs : transformation process : outputs) can help us understand how organizations become more innovative.[45] If an organization wants innovative products and work methods (*outputs*), it has to take its *inputs* and *transform* them into those outputs. Those *inputs* include creative people and groups within the organization. But as we said earlier, having creative people isn't enough. The *transformation process* requires having the right environment to turn those inputs into innovative products or work methods. This "right" environment—that is, an environment that stimulates innovation—includes three variables: the organization's structure, culture, and human resource practices. (See Exhibit 5.)

HOW DO STRUCTURAL VARIABLES AFFECT INNOVATION?
When Carol Bartz joined Yahoo! Inc. as CEO, one of the first things she noticed was how the organization's structure got in the way of innovation. Employees didn't know, when they wanted to try something different, whether they got to make the decision or somebody else did and what would happen if they went for it. Bartz's philosophy was that, "There's a freedom when you organize around the idea that you're clearly in charge and go for it." Today, Yahoo!'s structure has been changed so that there are clearer lines of responsibility and the freedom to make mistakes.[46]

Research into the effect of structural variables on innovation shows five things.[47] First, an organic-type structure positively influences innovation. Because this structure is

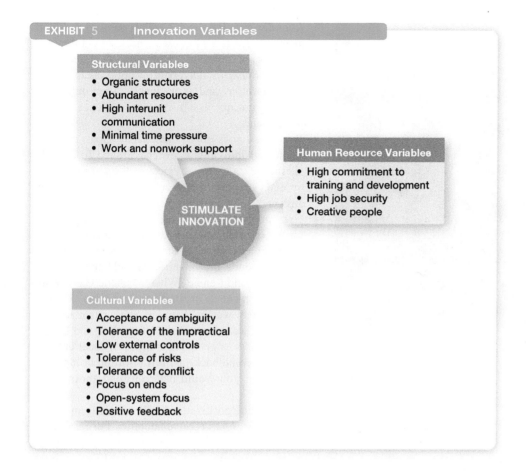

EXHIBIT 5 Innovation Variables

Structural Variables
- Organic structures
- Abundant resources
- High interunit communication
- Minimal time pressure
- Work and nonwork support

Human Resource Variables
- High commitment to training and development
- High job security
- Creative people

STIMULATE INNOVATION

Cultural Variables
- Acceptance of ambiguity
- Tolerance of the impractical
- Low external controls
- Tolerance of risks
- Tolerance of conflict
- Focus on ends
- Open-system focus
- Positive feedback

low in formalization, centralization, and work specialization, it facilitates the flexibility and sharing of ideas that are critical to innovation. Second, the availability of plentiful resources provides a key building block for innovation. With an abundance of resources, managers can afford to purchase innovations, can afford the cost of instituting innovations, and can absorb failures. Third, frequent communication between organizational units helps break down barriers to innovation.[48] Cross-functional teams, task forces, and other such organizational designs facilitate interaction across departmental lines and are widely used in innovative organizations. Fourth, innovative organizations try to minimize extreme time pressures on creative activities despite the demands of white-water-rapids-type environments. Although time pressures may spur people to work harder and may make them feel more creative, studies show that it actually causes them to be less creative.[49] Finally, studies have shown that when an organization's structure explicitly supports creativity, employees' creative performance can be enhanced. Beneficial kinds of support include encouragement, open communication, readiness to listen, and useful feedback.[50]

HOW DOES AN ORGANIZATION'S CULTURE AFFECT INNOVATION? Innovative organizations tend to have similar cultures.[51] They encourage experimentation; reward both successes and failures; and celebrate mistakes. An innovative organization is likely to have the following characteristics.

- *Accepts ambiguity.* Too much emphasis on objectivity and specificity constrains creativity.
- *Tolerates the impractical.* Individuals who offer impractical, even foolish, answers to what-if questions are not stifled. What at first seems impractical might lead to innovative solutions.
- *Keeps external controls minimal.* Rules, regulations, policies, and similar organizational controls are kept to a minimum.

Jim Wilson/Redux Pictures

Giving employees a sense of creative ownership is key to the innovation process at Zynga, a social network game developer. Shown here at company headquarters in San Francisco, Zynga's co-founder and chief executive Mark Pincus established "Be CEO: Own outcomes" as a core value to guide employees in how they do their jobs. Another core value—"Build games you and your friends love to play"—is supported by Zynga's organizational culture that gives employees the freedom to experiment, tolerates risk and conflict, and holds rules and regulations at a minimum. By also providing positive feedback and encouragement, Zynga supports employees' creative ideas that result in the development of popular games such as *CityVille*.

♦ *Tolerates risk.* Employees are encouraged to experiment without fear of consequences should they fail. Mistakes are treated as learning opportunities.

♦ *Tolerates conflict.* Diversity of opinions is encouraged. Harmony and agreement between individuals or units are *not* assumed to be evidence of high performance.

♦ *Focuses on ends rather than means.* Goals are made clear, and individuals are encouraged to consider alternative routes toward meeting the goals. Focusing on ends suggests that there might be several right answers to any given problem.

♦ *Uses an open-system focus.* Managers closely monitor the environment and respond to changes as they occur. For example, at Starbucks, product development depends on "inspiration field trips to view customers and trends." When Michelle Gass (who's now the president of Starbucks' division, Seattle's Best Coffee) was in charge of Starbucks marketing, she "took her team to Paris, Düsseldorf, and London to visit local Starbucks and other restaurants to get a better sense of local cultures, behaviors, and fashions." She says, "You come back just full of different ideas and different ways to think about things than you would had you read about it in a magazine or e-mail."[52]

♦ *Provides positive feedback.* Managers provide positive feedback, encouragement, and support so employees feel that their creative ideas receive attention. For instance, at Research In Motion, Mike Lazaridis, president and co-CEO says, "I think we have a culture of innovation here, and [engineers] have absolute access to me. I live a life that tries to promote innovation."[53]

WHAT HUMAN RESOURCE VARIABLES AFFECT INNOVATION? In this category, we find that innovative organizations actively promote the training and development of their members so their knowledge remains current; offer their employees high job security to reduce the fear of getting fired for making mistakes; and encourage individuals to become **idea champions**, actively and enthusiastically supporting new ideas, building support, overcoming resistance, and ensuring that innovations are implemented. Research finds that idea champions have common personality characteristics: extremely high self-confidence, persistence, energy, and a tendency toward risk taking. They also display characteristics associated with dynamic leadership. They inspire and energize others with their vision of the potential of an innovation and through their strong personal conviction in their mission. They're also good at gaining the commitment of others to support their mission. In addition, idea champions have jobs that provide considerable decision-making discretion. This autonomy helps them introduce and implement innovations in organizations.[54]

idea champions
Individuals who actively and enthusiastically support new ideas, build support for, overcome resistance to, and ensure that innovations are implemented

Review

CHAPTER SUMMARY

1 **Define organizational change and compare and contrast views on the change process.** Organizational change is any alteration of an organization's people, structure, or technology. The "calm waters" metaphor of change suggests that change is an occasional disruption in the normal flow of events and can be planned and managed as it happens, using Lewin's three-step change process (unfreezing, changing, and freezing). The "white-water rapids" view of change suggests that change is ongoing, and managing it is a continual process.

2 **Explain how to manage resistance to change.** People resist change because of uncertainty, habit, concern about personal loss, and the belief that a change is not in the organization's best interests. Techniques for managing resistance to change include education and communication (educating employees about and communicating to them the need for the change), participation (allowing employees to participate in the change process), facilitation and support (giving employees the support they need to implement the change), negotiation (exchanging something of value to reduce resistance), manipulation and co-optation (using negative actions to influence), selecting people who are open to and accept change, and coercion (using direct threats or force).

3 **Describe what managers need to know about employee stress.** Stress is the adverse reaction people have to excessive pressure placed on them from extraordinary demands, constraints, or opportunities.

The symptoms of stress can be physical, psychological, or behavioral. Stress can be caused by personal factors and by job-related factors. To help employees deal with stress, managers can address job-related factors by making sure an employee's abilities match the job requirements, improving organizational communications, using a performance planning program, or redesigning jobs. Addressing personal stress factors is trickier, but managers could offer employee counseling, time management programs, and wellness programs.

4 **Discuss techniques for stimulating innovation.** Creativity is the ability to combine ideas in a unique way or to make unusual associations between ideas. Innovation is turning the outcomes of the creative process into useful products or work methods. An innovative environment encompasses structural, cultural, and human resource variables.

Important structural variables include an organic-type structure, abundant resources, frequent communication between organizational units, minimal time pressure, and support. Important cultural variables include accepting ambiguity, tolerating the impractical, keeping external controls minimal, tolerating risk, tolerating conflict, focusing on ends not means, using an open-system focus, and providing positive feedback. Important human resource variables include high commitment to training and development, high job security, and encouraging individuals to be idea champions.

MyManagementLab   For more resources, please visit www.mymanagementlab.com

---

UNDERSTANDING THE CHAPTER

1. Why is managing change an integral part of every manager's job?

2. Contrast the calm waters and white-water rapids metaphors of change. Which of these would you use to describe your current life? Why is that one your choice?

3. Describe Lewin's three-step change process. How is it different from the change process needed in the white-water rapids metaphor of change?

4. How are opportunities, constraints, and demands related to stress? Give an example of each.

5. Organizations typically have limits to how much change they can absorb. As a manager, what signs would you look for that might suggest your organization has exceeded its capacity to change?

6. Why is organization development planned change? Explain how planned change is important for organizations in today's dynamic environment.

7. How do creativity and innovation differ? Give an example of each.

8. Research information on how to be a more creative person. Write down suggestions in a bulleted list format and be prepared to present your information in class.

9. How does an innovative culture make an organization more effective? Do you think an innovative culture could ever make an organization less effective? Why or why not?

10. When you find yourself experiencing dysfunctional stress, write down what's causing the stress, what stress symptoms you're exhibiting, and how you're dealing with the stress. Keep this information in a journal and evaluate how well your stress reducers are working and how you could handle stress better. Your goal is to get to a point where you recognize that you're stressed and can take positive actions to deal with the stress.

Endnotes

1. K. Dunn, "Employee Turnover and Suicide: It Turns Out the Response to Either Is the Same," *HR Capitalist Online,* May 9, 2011; S. Mahoney, "Stress Less, Accomplish More," *Good Housekeeping,* May 2010, p. 57; A. Chrisafis, "France Telecom Worker Kills Himself in Office Car Park," www.guardian.co.uk (April 27, 2011); Reuters, "France Telecom to Probe Employee Suicide by Fire," www.trust.org (April 27, 2011); A. R. Carey and P. Trap, "Aspect of the Job That Workers Find the Most Stressful," *USA Today,* April 20, 2011, p. 1A; "Survey," *Shape,* April 2011, p. 48; M. V. Rafter, "The Yawning of New Era," *Workforce Management Online,* December 2010; C. Hausman, "Millions of U.K. Workers Lie to Bosses About Stress-Induced Days," *Global Ethics Online,* November 8, 2010; E. Holbrook, "Beneath the Bell Jar: Companies Confront a Rise in Workplace Suicides," *Risk Management,* November 2010, pp. 6–8; "Survey: 30 Percent of Managers Under More Stress," *Workforce Management Online,* September 22, 2010; M. Colchester, "France Télécom Faces Inquiry Over Suicides," *New York Times Online,* April 12, 2010; M. Saltmarsh, "France Télécom Suicides Prompt an Investigation," *New York Times Online,* April 9, 2010; E. Frauenheim, "Suicides Spur Management Shake-Up at France Télécom," *Workforce Management,* March 2010, pp. 6–8; C. Stievenard, "France's Approach to Workplace 'Bullying,'" *Workforce Management Online,* www.workforce .com (March 2010); R. Bender and M. Colchester, "Morale Is Priority for France Télécom," *Wall Street Journal,* February 4, 2010, p. B2; The Associated Press, "Executive Quits After Suicides at France Télécom," *New York Times Online,* October 6, 2009; and D. Jolly and M. Saltmarsh, "Suicides in France Put Focus on Workplace," *New York Times Online,* September 30, 2009.

2. A. Weintraub and M. Tirrell, "Eli Lilly's Drug Assembly Line," *Bloomberg BusinessWeek,* March 8, 2010, pp. 56–57.

3. J. Katz, "Campbell Soup Cooking Up a New Recipe?" *Industry Week,* January 2011, p. 51.

4. K. Grzbowska, "The Social Aspect of Introducing Changes into the Organization," *International Journals of Human Resources Development and Management,* February 2, 2007, p. 67; and I. M. Jawahar and G. L. McLaughlin, "Toward a Descriptive Stakeholder Theory: An Organizational Life Cycle Approach," *Academy of Management Review,* July 2001, pp. 397–415.

5. E. Shannon, "Agent of Change," *Time,* March 4, 2002, p. 17; B. Kenney, "SLA Head Shaffer Resigns Abruptly: Did 'Change Agent' Move Too Fast in Aggressive Restructuring?" *Library Journal,* March 15, 2002, pp. 17–19; and T. Mudd, "Rescue Mission," *Industry Week,* May 1, 2000, pp. 30–37.

6. The idea for these metaphors came from P. Vaill, *Managing as a Performing Art: New Ideas for a World of Chaotic Change* (San Francisco: Jossey Bass, 1989).

7. K. Lewin, *Field Theory in Social Science* (New York: Harper & Row, 1951).

8. R. E. Levasseur, "People Skills: Change Management Tools— Lewin's Change Model," *Interfaces,* August 2001, pp. 71–74.

9. D. Lieberman, "Nielsen Media Has Cool Head at the Top," *USA Today,* March 27, 2006, p. 3B.

10. From the Past to the Present box based on D. A. Wren and A. G. Bedeian, *The Evolution of Management Thought,* 6th ed. (Hoboken, NJ: John Wiley & Sons, Inc., 2009); "Biography and Quotes of Kurt Lewin," *About.com,* psychology.about.com (July 15, 2009); and K. T. Lewin, "The Dynamics of Group Action," *Educational Leadership,* January 1944, pp. 195–200.

11. L. S. Lüscher and M. W. Lewis, "Organizational Change and Managerial Sensemaking: Working Through Paradox," *Academy of Management Journal* (April 2008), pp. 221–240; F. Buckley and K. Monks, "Responding to Managers' Learning Needs in an Edge-of-Chaos Environment: Insights from Ireland," *Journal of Management* (April 2008), pp. 146–163; and G. Hamel, "Take It Higher," *Fortune,* February 5, 2001, pp. 169–170.

12. L. Freifeld, "Paddle to Collaborate," *Training* (November– December 2010), p. 6.

13. S. Hicks, "What Is Organization Development?" *Training and Development* (August 2000), p. 65; and H. Hornstein, "Organizational Development and Change Management: Don't Throw the Baby Out with the Bath Water," *Journal of Applied Behavioral Science* (June 2001), pp. 223–227.

14. J. Wolfram and S. Minahan, "A New Metaphor for Organization Development," *Journal of Applied Behavioral Science* (June 2006), pp. 227–243.

15. See, for instance, H. B. Jones, "Magic, Meaning, and Leadership: Weber's Model and the Empirical Literature." *Human Relations,* June 2001, p. 753.

16. G. Akin and I. Palmer, "Putting Metaphors to Work for a Change in Organizations," *Organizational Dynamics,* Winter 2000, pp. 67–79.

17. J. Grieves, "Skills, Values or Impression Management: Organizational Change and the Social Processes of Leadership, Change Agent Practice, and Process Consultation," *Journal of Management Development* (May 2000), p. 407.

18. M. McMaster, "Team Building Tips," *Sales & Marketing Management,* January 2002, p. 140; and "How To: Executive Team Building," *Training and Development* (January 2002), p. 16.

19. S. Shinn, "Stairway to Reinvention," *BizEd,* January–February 2010, p. 6; M. Scott, "A Stairway to Marketing Heaven," *BusinessWeek,* November 2, 2009, p. 17; and The Fun Theory, http://thefuntheory.com (November 10, 2009).

20. See, for example, J. Robison and D. Jones, "Overcoming the Fear of Change," *Gallup Management Journal Online,* January 7, 2011; J. D. Ford, L. W. Ford, and A. D'Amelio, "Resistance to Change: The Rest of the Story," *Academy of Management Review,* April 2008, pp. 362–377; A. Deutschman, "Making Change: Why Is It So Hard to Change Our Ways?" *Fast Company,* May 2005, pp. 52–62; S. B. Silverman, C. E. Pogson, and A. B. Cober, "When Employees at Work Don't Get It: A Model for Enhancing Individual Employee Change in Response to Performance Feedback," *Academy of Management Executive,* May 2005, pp. 135–147; C. E. Cunningham, C. A. Woodward, H. S. Shannon, J. MacIntosh, B. Lendrum, D. Rosenbloom, and J. Brown, "Readiness for Organizational Change: A Longitudinal Study of Workplace, Psychological and Behavioral Correlates," *Journal of Occupational and Organizational Psychology* (December 2002), pp. 377–392; M. A. Korsgaard, H. J. Sapienza, and D. M. Schweiger, "Beaten Before Begun: The Role of Procedural Justice in Planning Change," *Journal of Management* 28, no. 4 (2002), pp. 497–516; R. Kegan and L. L. Lahey, "The Real Reason People Won't Change," *Harvard Business Review,* November

2001, pp. 85–92; S. K. Piderit, "Rethinking Resistance and Recognizing Ambivalence: A Multidimensional View of Attitudes Toward an Organizational Change," *Academy of Management Review,* October 2000, pp. 783–794; C. R. Wanberg and J. T. Banas, "Predictors and Outcomes of Openness to Changes in a Reorganizing Workplace," *Journal of Applied Psychology* (February 2000), pp. 132–142; A. A. Armenakis and A. G. Bedeian, "Organizational Change: A Review of Theory and Research in the 1990s," *Journal of Management* 25, no. 3 (1999), pp. 293–315; and B. M. Staw, "Counterforces to Change," in P.S. Goodman and Associates (eds.), *Change in Organizations* (San Francisco: Jossey-Bass, 1982), pp. 87–121.

21. A. Reichers, J. P. Wanous, and J. T. Austin, "Understanding and Managing Cynicism about Organizational Change," *Academy of Management Executive*, February 1997, pp. 48–57; P. Strebel, "Why Do Employees Resist Change?" *Harvard Business Review,* May–June 1996, pp. 86–92; and J. P. Kotter and L.A. Schlesinger, "Choosing Strategies for Change," *Harvard Business Review*, March–April 1979, pp. 107–109.

22. And the Survey Says box based on based on S. Schomer, "Under Pressure," *Fast Company,* April 2010, p. 112; "Organizational Change: Facebook Poll," *Harvard Business Review,* March 2010, p. 16; J. Yang and S. Ward, "I'd Rather Give Up," *USA Today,* March 4, 2010, p. 1B; M. Weinstein, "Missing Something," *Training* (January 2010), p. 6; J. MacIntyre, "Hard At Work," *Springfield Business Journal,* November 30–December 6, 2009, p. 16; J. MacIntyre, "Accidental Innovation," *Springfield Business Journal,* September 28–October 4, 2009, p. 22; and M. Healy and S. Ward, "Workplace Worries," *USA Today,* August 28, 2008, p. 1D.

23. D. Heath and C. Heath, "Passion Provokes Action," *Fast Company,* February 2011, pp. 28–30.

24. Adapted from the UK National Work-Stress Network, www.workstress.net.

25. R. S. Schuler, "Definition and Conceptualization of Stress in Organizations," *Organizational Behavior and Human Performance,* April 1980, p. 191.

26. A. Kanai, "Karoshi (Work to Death) in Japan," *Journal of Business Ethics* (January 2009) Supplement 2, pp. 209–216; The Associated Press, "Overwork Cited in Death of Japanese Worker," *New York Times Online,* July 10, 2008; "Jobs for Life," *Economist,* www.economist.com (December 19, 2007); and B. L. de Mente, "Karoshi: Death from Overwork," Asia Pacific Management Forum, www.apmforum.com (May 2002).

27. See, for example, "Stressed Out: Extreme Job Stress: Survivors' Tales," *Wall Street Journal* January 17, 2001, p. B1.

28. See, for instance, S. Bates, "Expert: Don't Overlook Employee Burnout," *HR Magazine,* August 2003, p. 14.

29. Right or Wrong? box based on D. Cole, "The Big Chill," *US News & World Report,* December 6, 2004, pp. EE2–EE5.

30. H. Benson, "Are You Working Too Hard?" *Harvard Business Review,* November 2005, pp. 53–58; B. Cryer, R. McCraty, and D. Childre, "Pull the Plug on Stress," *Harvard Business Review,* July 2003, pp. 102–107; C. Daniels, "The Last Taboo"; C. L. Cooper and S. Cartwright, "Healthy Mind, Healthy Organization—A Proactive Approach to Occupational Stress," *Human Relations,* April 1994, pp. 455–471; C. A. Heaney et al., "Industrial Relations, Worksite Stress Reduction and Employee Well-Being: A Participatory Action Research Investigation," *Journal of Organizational Behavior* (September 1993),

pp. 495–510; C. D. Fisher, "Boredom at Work: A Neglected Concept," *Human Relations,* March 1993, pp. 395–417; and S. E. Jackson, "Participation in Decision Making as a Strategy for Reducing Job-Related Strain," *Journal of Applied Psychology* (February 1983), pp. 3–19.

31. C. Mamberto, "Companies Aim to Combat Job-Related Stress," *Wall Street Journal,* August 13, 2007, p. B6.

32. T. Barton, "Brave Face," *Employee Benefits,* January 2011, p. 41; and "Employee Assistance Programs," *HR Magazine,* May 2003, p. 143.

33. S. Barrett, "Employee Assistance Programs," *Employee Benefits,* January 2011, pp. 49–52; "EAPs with the Most," *Managing Benefits Plans,* March 2003, p. 8; and K. Tyler, "Helping Employees Cope with Grief," *HR Magazine,* September 2003, pp. 55–58.

34. N. Faba, "The EAP Problem," *Benefits Canada,* March 2011, p. 7; D. A. Masi, "Redefining the EAP Field," *Journal of Workplace Behavioral Health* (January–March 2011), pp. 1–9; R. M. Weiss, "Brinksmanship Redux: Employee Assistance Programs' Precursors and Prospects," *Employee Responsibilities & Rights Journal* (December 2010), pp. 325–343; and F. Hansen, "Employee Assistance Programs (EAPs) Grow and Expand Their Reach," *Compensation and Benefits Review,* March–April 2000, p. 13.

35. F. Phillips, "Employee Assistance Programs: A New Way to Control Health Care Costs," *Employee Benefit Plan Review,* August 2003, pp. 22–24.

36. K. Lee, "EAP Diversity Detracts from Original Focus, Some Say," *Employee Benefits News,* July 1, 2003, p. 1.

37. See, for instance, P. Petesch, "Workplace Fitness or Workplace Fits?" *HR Magazine,* July 2001, pp. 137–140.

38. C. Petersen, "Value of Complementary Care Rises, But Poses Challenges," *Managed HealthCare,* November 2000, pp. 47–48.

39. A. Saha-Bubna and M. Jarzemsky, "MasterCard President Is Named CEO," *Wall Street Journal* April 13, 2010, p. C3; and S. Vandebook, "Quotable," *IndustryWeek,* April 2010, p. 18.

40. R. M. Kanter, "Think Outside the Building," *Harvard Business Review,* March 2010, p. 34; T. Brown, "Change By Design," *BusinessWeek,* October 5, 2009, pp. 54–56; J. E. Perry-Smith and C. E. Shalley, "The Social Side of Creativity: A Static and Dynamic Social Network Perspective," *Academy of Management Review,* January 2003, pp. 89–106; and P. K. Jagersma, "Innovate or Die: It's Not Easy, But It Is Possible to Enhance Your Organization's Ability to Innovate," *Journal of Business Strategy* (January–February 2003), pp. 25–28.

41. *Fast Company* staff, "The World's 50 Most Innovative Companies," *Fast Company,* March 2011, pp. 66+; and G. Colvin, "The World's Most Admired Companies," *Fortune,* March 21, 2011, pp. 109+.

42. These definitions are based on T. M. Amabile, *Creativity in Context* (Boulder, CO: Westview Press, 1996).

43. C. Salter, "Mattel Learns to 'Throw the Bunny,'" *Fast Company,* November 2002, p. 22; and L. Bannon, "Think Tank in Toyland," *Wall Street Journal,* June 6, 2002, pp. B1, B3.

44. C. Vogel and J. Cagan, *Creating Breakthrough Products: Innovation from Product Planning to Program Approval* (Upper Saddle River, NJ: Prentice Hall, 2002).

45. R. W. Woodman, J. E. Sawyer, and R. W. Griffin, "Toward a Theory of Organizational Creativity," *Academy of Management Review*, April 1993, pp. 293–321.

46. K. Swisher, "A Question of Management," *Wall Street Journal* June 2, 2009, p. R4.

47. T. M. Egan, "Factors Influencing Individual Creativity in the Workplace: An Examination of Quantitative Empirical Research," *Advances in Developing Human Resources,* May 2005, pp. 160–181; N. Madjar, G. R. Oldham, and M. G. Pratt, "There's No Place Like Home? The Contributions of Work and Nonwork Creativity Support to Employees' Creative Performance," *Academy of Management Journal* (August 2002), pp. 757–767; T. M. Amabile, C. N. Hadley, and S. J. Kramer, "Creativity Under the Gun," *Harvard Business Review,* August 2002, pp. 52–61; J. B. Sorensen and T. E. Stuart, "Aging, Obsolescence, and Organizational Innovation," *Administrative Science Quarterly,* March 2000, pp. 81–112; G.R. Oldham and A. Cummings, "Employee Creativity: Personal and Contextual Factors at Work," *Academy of Management Journal* (June 1996), pp. 607–634; and F. Damanpour, "Organizational Innovation: A Meta-Analysis of Effects of Determinants and Moderators," *Academy of Management Journal* (September 1991), pp. 555–590.

48. P. R. Monge, M. D. Cozzens, and N. S. Contractor, "Communication and Motivational Predictors of the Dynamics of Organizational Innovations," *Organization Science,* May 1992, pp. 250–274.

49. T. M. Amabile, C. N. Hadley, and S. J. Kramer, "Creativity Under the Gun."

50. N. Madjar, G. R. Oldham, and M. G. Pratt, "There's No Place Like Home? The Contributions of Work and Nonwork Creativity Support to Employees' Creative Performance."

51. See, for instance, J. E. Perry-Smith, "Social Yet Creative: The Role of Social Relationships in Facilitating Individual Creativity," *Academy of Management Journal* (February 2006), pp. 85–101; C. E. Shalley, J. Zhou, and G. R. Oldham, "The Effects of Personal and Contextual Characteristics on Creativity: Where Should We Go from Here?" *Journal of Management,* 30, no. 6 (2004), pp. 933–958; J. E. Perry-Smith and C. E. Shalley, "The Social Side of Creativity: A Static and Dynamic Social Network Perspective"; J. M. George and J. Zhou, "When Openness to Experience and Conscientiousness Are Related to Creative Behavior: An Interactional Approach," *Journal of Applied Psychology* (June 2001), pp. 513–524; J. Zhou, "Feedback Valence, Feedback Style, Task Autonomy, and Achievement Orientation: Interactive Effects on Creative Behavior," *Journal of Applied Psychology,* 83 (1998), pp. 261–276; T. M. Amabile, R. Conti, H. Coon, J. Lazenby, and M. Herron, "Assessing the Work Environment for Creativity," *Academy of Management Journal* (October 1996), pp. 1154–1184; S. G. Scott and R. A. Bruce, "Determinants of Innovative People: A Path Model of Individual Innovation in the Workplace," *Academy of Management Journal* (June 1994), pp. 580–607; R. Moss Kanter, "When a Thousand Flowers Bloom: Structural, Collective, and Social Conditions for Innovation in Organization," in B. M. Staw and L. L. Cummings (eds.), *Research in Organizational Behavior,* vol. 10 (Greenwich, CT: JAI Press, 1988), pp. 169–211; and Amabile, *Creativity in Context.*

52. J. McGregor, "The World's Most Innovative Companies," *BusinessWeek,* April 24, 2006, p. 70.

53. Ibid.

54. J. Ramos, "Producing Change That Lasts," *Across the Board,* March 1994, pp. 29–33; T. Stjernberg and A. Philips, "Organizational Innovations in a Long-Term Perspective: Legitimacy and Souls-of-Fire as Critical Factors of Change and Viability," *Human Relations,* October 1993, pp. 1193–2023; and J. M. Howell and C. A. Higgins, "Champions of Change," *Business Quarterly,* Spring 1990, pp. 31–32.

YOUR TURN TO BE **A MANAGER**

Managing Change and **Innovation**

Skill Development: Reducing Workplace Stress

It's no secret that employees, in general, are more stressed out today than previous generations. Heavier workloads, longer hours, continual reorganizations, technology that breaks down traditional barriers between work and personal life, and reduced job security are among factors that have increased employee stress. This stress can lead to lower productivity, increased absenteeism, reduced job satisfaction, and higher quit rates. When stress is excessive, managers need to know how to reduce it.

Personal Insights: How Stressful Is My Life?

Review the following list of life events. Identify those that you have experienced in the last 12 months.

Life Event	Mean Value
1. Death of spouse	100
2. Divorce	73
3. Marital separation from mate	65
4. Detention in jail or other institution	63
5. Death of a close family member	63
6. Major personal injury or illness	53
7. Marriage	50
8. Being fired from job	47
9. Marital reconciliation with mate	45
10. Retirement from work	45
11. Major change in health or behavior of a family member	44
12. Pregnancy	40
13. Sexual difficulties	39
14. Gaining a new family member	39
15. Major business readjustment (merger, reorganization, bankruptcy, etc.)	39
16. Major change in financial state (positive or negative)	38
17. Death of a close friend	37
18. Changing to a different line of work	36
19. Major change in the number of arguments with spouse	35
20. Taking out a mortgage or loan for a major purchase (home, business, etc.)	31
21. Foreclosure on a mortgage or loan	30
22. Major change in responsibilities at work (promotion, demotion, transfer)	29
23. Son or daughter leaving home	29
24. In-law troubles	29
25. Outstanding personal achievement	28
26. Spouse beginning or ceasing work	26
27. Beginning or ceasing formal schooling	26
28. Major change in living conditions (building new house, remodeling, deterioration of neighborhood)	25
29. Revision of personal habits	24
30. Troubles with the boss	23
31. Major change in working hours or conditions	20
32. Change in residence	20
33. Changing to a new school	20
34. Major change in usual type and/or amount of recreation	19
35. Major change in church activities	19
36. Major change in social activities	18

(*continued*)

Life Event	Mean Value
37. Taking out a loan for a lesser purchase (car, TV, etc.)	17
38. Major change in sleeping habits.	16
39. Major change in number of family get-togethers	15
40. Major change in eating habits	15
41. Vacation	13
42. Christmas	12
43. Minor violation of the law (traffic tickets, disturbing the peace, etc.)	11

Source: T. H. Holmes and R. H. Rahe, "The Social Readjustment Rating Scale," *Journal of Psychometric Research* (1967), pp. 213–218.

Analysis and Interpretation

Life change events build up and create stress. This instrument weighs the events you've experienced in the past year in terms of their potential to create stress-induced illnesses or injuries during the next two-year period. Notice that positive events (marriage, a promotion, an inheritance) as well as negative ones can create stress.

Add up the mean values for the events that you've experienced in the past year. A cumulative score of 150 or less indicates a low susceptibility to stress-induced illnesses or injuries. A score of 151 to 300 indicates a 35 to 50 percent probability of stress-related health changes in the next two-year period. And scores of over 300 indicates an 80 percent chance of stress-induced health changes.

This instrument dramatizes that changes accumulate and, if they accumulate too much, they can overtake your body's ability to adjust. Of course, different personality types handle stress differently. Hardy types seem to do better at dealing with change and stress. These are people who believe they can control the events they encounter, are extremely committed to the activities in their lives, and who treat change in their lives as a challenge. If you're a hardy type, a high score on this instrument may not lead to negative health changes.

Skill Basics

Eliminating all stress at work isn't going to happen and it shouldn't. Stress is an unavoidable consequence of life. It also has a positive side—when it focuses concentration and creativity. But when it brings about anger, frustration, fear, sleeplessness, and the like, it needs to be addressed.

Many organizations have introduced stress-reduction interventions for employees. These include improved employee selection and placement, helping employees set realistic goals, training in time management, redesign of jobs, increased involvement of employees in decisions that affect them, expanded social support networks, improved organizational communications, and organizationally supported wellness programs. But what can *you* do, on your own, to reduce stress if your employer doesn't provide such programs or if you need to take additional action? The following individual interventions have been suggested:

Implement time-management techniques. Every person can improve his or her use of time. Time is a unique resource in that, if it's wasted, it can *never* be replaced. While people talk about *saving time*, it can never actually be saved. And if it's lost, it can't be retrieved. The good news is that it's a resource we all have in equal amounts. Everyone gets the same 24 hours a day, 7 days a week to use. When tasks seem to exceed the hours you have available, stress often results. But effective management of time can reduce stress. Time-management training can, for example, teach you how to prioritize tasks by importance and urgency, schedule activities according to those priorities, avoid confusing actions with accomplishments, and understand your productivity cycle so you can handle the most demanding tasks during the high part of your cycle when you are most alert and productive.

Create personal goals. Goal setting is designed to help you better prioritize your activities and better manage how you direct your efforts. Goals become, in effect, a personal planning tool. For instance, setting long-term goals provide general direction; while short-term goals—such as weekly or daily "to do" lists—reduce the likelihood that important activities will be overlooked and help you to maximize the use of your time.

Use physical exercise. A large body of evidence indicates that noncompetitive physical exercise can help you to release tension that builds up in stressful situations. These activities include aerobics, walking, jogging, swimming, and riding a bicycle. Physical exercise increases heart capacity, lowers the at-rest heart rate, provides a mental diversion from work pressures, and offers a means to "let off steam."

Practice relaxation training. You can teach yourself to reduce tension through meditation, deep-breathing exercises, and guided imaging. They work by taking your mind off the sources of stress, achieving a state of deep relaxation, and releasing body tension.

Expand your social support network. Having friends, family, or work colleagues to talk to provides an outlet when stress levels become excessive. Expanding your social support network, therefore, can be a means for tension reduction. It provides you with someone to hear your problems and to offer a more objective perspective on the situation.

Based on J. E. Newman and T. A. Beehr, "Personal and Organizational Strategies for Handling Job Stress," *Personnel Psychology*, Spring 1979, pp. 1–38; M. T. Matteson and J. M. Ivancevich, "Individual Stress Management Interventions: Evaluation of Techniques," *Journal of Management Psychology* (January 1987), pp. 24–30; and K. M. Richardson and H. R. Rothstein, "Effects of Occupational Stress Management Intervention Programs: A Meta-Analysis," *Journal of Occupational Health Psychology* (January 2008), pp. 69–93.

Skill Application

Dana had become frustrated in her job at Taylor Books—a chain of 22 bookstores in Georgia and Florida. After nearly 13 years as director of marketing, she felt she needed new challenges. When she was offered the job as senior account supervisor for Dancer Advertising in Tampa, she jumped at the opportunity. Now, after 4 months on the job, she's not so certain she made the right move.

At Taylor, she worked a basic 8-to-5 day. She was easily able to balance her work responsibilities with her personal responsibilities as a wife and mother of two children—ages 4 and 7. But her new job is very different. Clients call anytime—day, night, and weekends—with demands. People in Dancer's creative department are constantly asking for her input on projects. And Dana's boss expects her not only to keep her current clients happy, he also expects Dana to help secure new clients by preparing and participating in presentations and working up budgets. Last month, alone, Dana calculated that she spent 67 hours in the office plus another 12 at home working on Dancer projects. Short on sleep, frazzled by the hectic pace, having no time for her family or chores, she's lost five pounds and broken out in hives. Her doctor told her the hives were stress-induced and she needed to sort out her life.

Dana really likes her job as an account executive but feels the demands and pulls of the job are overwhelming. Yesterday she called her old boss at Taylor Books and inquired about coming back. His reply, "Dana, we'd love to have you back here but we filled your slot. We could find something for you in marketing but you wouldn't be director and the pay would be at least a third less."

If you were Dana, what would you do? Be specific.

Skill Practice

1. Think of a particularly stressful situation you had either at home or at work. What was the cause of the stress? How did you handle it? Was your approach effective? What might you have done differently to have obtained a better and/or faster result?

2. The next time you find yourself "stressed out," analyze the situation and apply one or more of the skill behaviors suggested earlier.

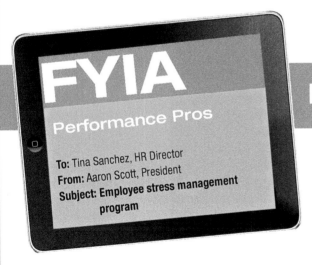

FYIA
Performance Pros

To: Tina Sanchez, HR Director
From: Aaron Scott, President
Subject: Employee stress management program

For Your Immediate Action

Well, Tina, we've made it through the initial phases of our restructuring efforts. The changes haven't been easy on any of us. But we've still got a long way to go, and that's where I need your assistance. To help minimize the pressures on our software developers and sales staff, I think we need to develop an employee stress management program that we could implement immediately. Due to finances, we don't have a lot of excess funds to spend on fitness equipment, so you're going to have to work within that constraint. Could you put together a brief (no more than one page) outline of what you think this program should include? Also, note the benefit(s) you think each suggestion would provide. I'd like some time to review your suggestions over the weekend, so please get me your report as soon as possible.

This fictionalized company and message were created for educational purposes only, and not meant to reflect positively or negatively on management practices by any company that may share this name.

Bringing the Real World to Life

Case Application: Stress Kills: Part 2

Here is what recent surveys are telling us about employee stress:

- 75 percent of Americans say their stress levels are high or moderate.
- 44 percent of Americans say their stress levels have gone up in the last five years.
- 81 percent of HR managers say that employee fatigue is a bigger problem than in past years.
- More than 50 percent of U.S. and Canadian workers say that they feel fatigued at the end of a workday. At least 40 percent of those workers say that their jobs made them depressed.
- 20 percent of U.K. workers say they have taken sick leave brought on by stress, but 90 percent have lied about the real reason for staying home.
- 30 percent of managers say they're more stressed at work today than a year ago.
- Reasons employees find work stressful: low pay, commuting, excessive workload, fear of being fired/laid off, annoying coworkers, and difficult bosses.

As you can see, stress and its effects on workers is (and should be) a serious concern for employers. When excessive pressure is placed on people from overwhelming demands or constraints they often feel they've got no choices or options. At France Télécom, the wave of employee suicides since 2008 was cause for concern. Trade union leaders "blame the allegedly brutal management culture of a company which has transformed itself over a decade from a ponderous state utility to a leading telecommunications company." However, for months, France Télécom management "dismissed the suicides as a contagious fad among its workforce." Unions then criticized the company for its poor choice of language.

The Paris prosecutor's office opened an investigation of the company over accusations of psychological harassment. The judicial inquiry stemmed from a complaint by the union Solidares Unitaires Démocratiques against France Télécom's former chief executive and two members of his top management team. The complaint accused management of conducting a "pathogenic restructuring." Excerpts of the inspector's report, although not made public, were published in the French media. It described a situation in which the company used various forms of psychological pressure in an effort to eliminate 22,000 jobs from 2006 to 2008. Company doctors alerted management about the possible psychological dangers of the stress that could accompany such drastic change. Despite these findings, a company lawyer denied that France Télécom had systematically pressured employees to leave.

Company executives realized that they needed to take drastic measures to address the issue. One of the first changes was a new CEO, Stéphane Richard, who said his priority "would be to rebuild the morale of staff who have been through trauma, suffering and much worse." The company also halted some workplace practices identified as being particularly disruptive, like involuntary transfers. It is also encouraging more supportive practices, including working from home. A company spokesperson says the company has completed two of six agreements with unions that cover a wide range of workplace issues like mobility and work/life balance and stress. Despite these measures, another France Télécom worker committed suicide in April 2011. A union official suggested that "the man had struggled with being made to frequently change jobs." The worker had written to management on several occasions about the situation and was believed to have had no reply. France Télécom's CEO, Stéphane Richard, promised a thorough investigation into the suicide. "We need to analyze in great depth and detail what happened. It is my intention that this investigation will be particularly painstaking and transparent."

DISCUSSION QUESTIONS

1. What is your reaction to the situation described in this case? What factors, both inside the company and externally, appear to have contributed to this situation?

2. What appeared to be happening in France Télécom's workplace? What stress symptoms might managers have looked for to be alerted to a problem?

3. Should managers be free to make decisions that are in the best interests of the company without worrying about employee reactions? Discuss. What are the implications for managing change?

4. What are France Télécom's executives doing to address the situation? Do you think it's enough? Are there other actions they might take? If so, describe those. If not, why not?

5. What could other companies and managers learn from this situation?

Foundations
of Individual Behavior

Foundations of Individual Behavior

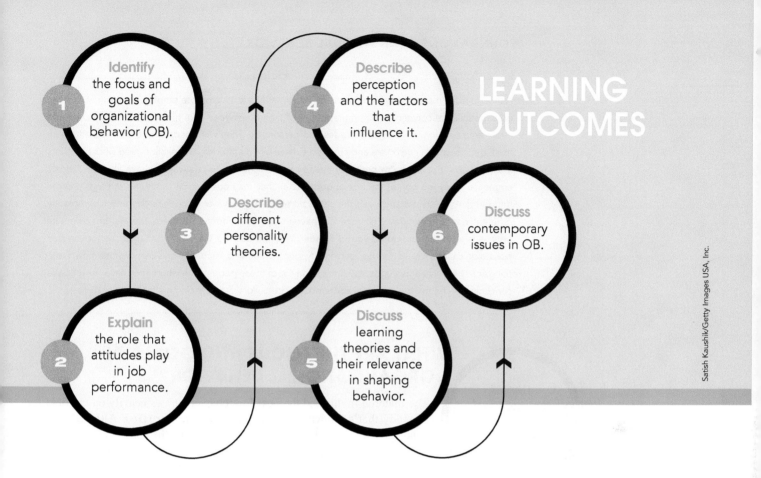

Learning Outcomes:

1. **Identify** the focus and goals of organizational behavior (OB).

2. **Explain** the role that attitudes play in job performance.

3. **Describe** different personality theories.

4. **Describe** perception and the factors that influence it.

5. **Discuss** learning theories and their relevance in shaping behavior.

6. **Discuss** contemporary issues in OB.

Employees First

"Employees first." That's the most important and crucial cultural value that HCL Technologies CEO Vineet Nayar believes will take his company into the future.[1] Although most managers think that customers should come first, Nayar's philosophy is that employee satisfaction needs to be the top priority.

As one of the largest companies in India, HCL sells various information technology product services, such as laptop, custom software development, and technology consulting. Luring and keeping top talent is one of the challenges HCL faces. And at its size, it doesn't have the atmosphere of a fun and quirky start-up.

Part of that "employee first" philosophy is a no-layoff policy, which was difficult to uphold during the pressures of the economic downturn. Like its competitors, HCL had excess employees and had suspended raises. But HCL kept its promise and didn't lay off any HCLite (Nayar's name for HCL employees). As business has picked up, however, employees begin looking at competitors' job offers. During the first quarter alone of 2010, HCL lost 22 percent of its workforce. Maybe it's time to monitor and track employee satisfaction.

Although most managers will not go as far as Vineet Nayar to promote employee satisfaction, many organizations are concerned with the attitudes of their employees. Like him, they want to attract and retain employees with the right attitudes and personality. They want people who show up and work hard, get along with coworkers and customers, have good attitudes, and exhibit good work behaviors in other ways. But as you're probably already aware, people don't always behave like that "ideal" employee. They job hop at the first opportunity or they may post critical comments in blogs. People differ in their behaviors and even the same person can behave one way one day and a completely different way another day. For instance, haven't you seen family members, friends, or coworkers behave in ways that prompted you to wonder: Why did they do that? In this chapter, we look at four psychological aspects—attitudes, personality, perception, and learning—and demonstrate how these things can help managers understand the behavior of those people with whom they have to work. We conclude the chapter by looking at contemporary behavioral issues facing managers.

WHAT ARE THE FOCUS AND GOALS OF ORGANIZATIONAL BEHAVIOR?

1 Identify the focus and goals of organizational behavior (OB).

The material in this and the next four chapters draws heavily on the field of study that's known as *organizational behavior (OB)*. Although it's concerned with the subject of behavior—that is, the actions of people—organizational behavior is the study of the actions of people at work.

One of the challenges in understanding organizational behavior is that it addresses issues that aren't obvious. Like an iceberg, OB has a small visible dimension and a much larger hidden portion. (See Exhibit 1.) What we see when we look at an organization is its visible aspects: strategies, objectives, policies and procedures, structure, technology, formal authority relationships, and chain of command. But under the surface are other elements that managers need to understand—elements that also influence how employees behave at work. As we'll show, OB provides managers with considerable insights into these important, but hidden, aspects of the organization.

What Is the Focus of OB?

Organizational behavior focuses on three major areas. First, OB looks at *individual behavior.* Based predominantly on contributions from psychologists, this area includes such topics as

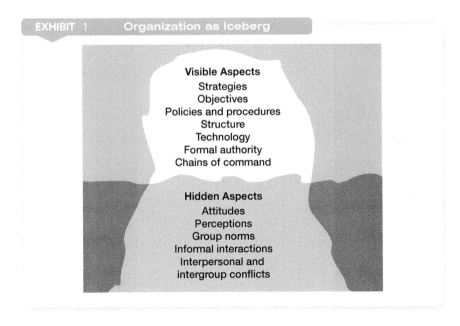

EXHIBIT 1   Organization as Iceberg

Visible Aspects
Strategies
Objectives
Policies and procedures
Structure
Technology
Formal authority
Chains of command

Hidden Aspects
Attitudes
Perceptions
Group norms
Informal interactions
Interpersonal and
intergroup conflicts

attitudes, personality, perception, learning, and motivation. Second, OB is concerned with *group behavior*, which includes norms, roles, team building, leadership, and conflict. Our knowledge about groups comes basically from the work of sociologists and social psychologists. Finally, OB also looks at *organizational* aspects including structure, culture, and human resource policies and practices. We've addressed organizational aspects in previous chapters. In this chapter, we'll look at individual behavior and in the following chapter, at group behavior.

What Are the Goals of Organizational Behavior?

The goals of OB are to *explain, predict,* and *influence* behavior. Managers need to be able to *explain* why employees engage in some behaviors rather than others, *predict* how employees will respond to various actions and decisions, and *influence* how employees behave.

What employee behaviors are we specifically concerned with explaining, predicting, and influencing? Six important ones have been identified: employee productivity, absenteeism, turnover, organizational citizenship behavior (OCB), job satisfaction, and workplace misbehavior. Employee productivity is a performance measure of both work efficiency and effectiveness. Managers want to know what factors will influence the efficiency and effectiveness of employees. Absenteeism is the failure to show up for work. It's difficult for work to get done if employees don't show up. Studies have shown that the total costs of all major types of absences cost organizations an average 35 percent of payroll with unscheduled absences costing companies around $660 per employee per year.[2] Although absenteeism can't be totally eliminated, excessive levels have a direct and immediate impact on the organization's functioning. Turnover is the voluntary and involuntary permanent withdrawal from an organization. It can be a problem because of increased recruiting, selection, and training costs and work disruptions. Just like absenteeism, managers can never eliminate turnover, but it is something they want to minimize, especially among high-performing employees. Organizational citizenship behavior is discretionary behavior that's not part of an employee's formal job requirements, but which promotes the effective functioning of the organization.[3] Examples of good OCB include helping others on one's work team, volunteering for extended job activities, avoiding unnecessary conflicts, and making constructive statements about one's work group and the organization. Organizations need individuals who will do more than their usual job duties and the evidence indicates that organizations that have such employees outperform those that don't.[4] However, drawbacks to OCB arise if employees experience work overload, stress, and work-family conflicts.[5] *Job satisfaction* refers to an employee's general attitude toward his or her job. Although job satisfaction is an attitude rather than a behavior, it's an outcome that concerns many managers because satisfied employees are more likely to show up for work, have higher levels of performance, and stay with an organization. Workplace misbehavior is any intentional employee behavior that is potentially

Organizational behavior focuses on job satisfaction and how it influences employee productivity, absenteeism, and turnover. Job satisfaction is high at the Lexus of Westminster auto dealership where Trung Pham, shown here, works as a mechanic. Pham and the dealership's 125 other employees have a positive feeling about their jobs and the company they work for. They say their employer, a family-owned and operated business, values the contributions they make, treats them with respect and integrity, and entrusts them with great responsibility in providing customers with a world-class Lexus ownership experience. Satisfied employees help the dealership maintain low absenteeism and turnover rates and high worker productivity.

Newscom

---

behavior
The actions of people

organizational behavior
The study of the actions of people at work

employee productivity
A performance measure of both work efficiency and effectiveness

absenteeism
The failure to show up for work

turnover
Voluntary and involuntary permanent withdrawal from an organization

organizational citizenship behavior
Discretionary behavior that's not part of an employee's formal job requirements, but that promotes the effective functioning of the organization

workplace misbehavior
Any intentional employee behavior that is potentially harmful to the organization or individuals within the organization

harmful to the organization or individuals within the organization. Workplace misbehavior shows up in organizations in four ways: deviance, aggression, antisocial behavior, and violence.[6] Such behaviors can range from playing loud music just to irritate coworkers to verbal aggression to sabotaging work, all of which can create havoc in any organization. In the following pages, we'll address how an understanding of four psychological factors—employee attitudes, personality, perception, and learning—can help us predict and explain these employee behaviors.

WHAT ROLE DO ATTITUDES PLAY IN JOB PERFORMANCE?

Explain the role that attitudes play in job performance.

2

Attitudes are evaluative statements, either favorable or unfavorable, concerning objects, people, or events. They reflect how an individual feels about something. When a person says, "I like my job," he or she is expressing an attitude about work.

What Are the Three Components of an Attitude?

To better understand attitude, we need to look at its three components: cognition, affect, and behavior.[7] The **cognitive component** of an attitude is made up of the beliefs, opinions, knowledge, and information held by a person. For example, shortly after the September 11, 2001, attacks on the World Trade Center and the Pentagon, Congress debated for weeks as to whether airport baggage screeners should be federal employees. Some claimed the current private airport screeners were adequately doing their jobs, even though evidence presented during the debate showed that knives, pepper spray, and a loaded gun were missed by airport screeners.[8] The belief held by some congressional leaders that private screeners were effective is an example of cognition. The **affective component** is the emotional or feeling part of an attitude. This component would be reflected in the statement, "I don't like Erica because she smokes." Cognition and affect can lead to behavioral outcomes. The **behavioral component** of an attitude refers to an intention to behave in a certain way toward someone or something. So, to continue our example, I might choose to avoid Erica because of my feelings about her. Looking at attitudes as being made up of three components—cognition, affect, and behavior—helps to illustrate the complexity of attitudes. For the sake of clarity, keep in mind that the term usually refers only to the affective component.

What Attitudes Might Employees Hold?

Naturally, managers are not interested in every attitude an employee might hold. Rather, they're specifically interested in job-related attitudes, and the three most important and most studied are job satisfaction, job involvement, and organizational commitment.[9] **Job satisfaction** is an employee's general attitude toward his or her job. When people speak of employee attitudes, more often than not they mean job satisfaction. **Job involvement** is the degree to which an employee identifies with his or her job, actively participates in it, and considers his or her job performance important for self-worth. Finally, **organizational commitment** represents an employee's orientation toward the organization in terms of his or her loyalty to, identification with, and involvement in the organization.

A new concept associated with job attitudes that's generating widespread interest is **employee engagement**, which happens when employees are connected to, satisfied with, and enthusiastic about their jobs.[10] Highly engaged employees are passionate about and deeply connected to their work. Disengaged employees have essentially "checked out" and don't care. They show up for work, but have no energy or passion for it. A global study of more than 12,000 employees found that respect ranked as the number one factor contributing to employee engagement. In addition to respect, the top five engagement factors included type of work, work/life balance, providing good service to customers, and base pay.[11]

Having highly engaged employees produces both benefits and costs. Highly engaged employees are two-and-a-half times more likely to be top performers than their less-engaged coworkers. In addition, companies with highly engaged employees have higher retention rates, which help keep recruiting and training costs low. And both of these outcomes—higher performance and lower costs—contribute to superior financial performance.[12]

Do Individuals' Attitudes and Behaviors Need to Be Consistent?

Did you ever notice how people change what they say so that it doesn't contradict what they do? Perhaps a friend of yours had consistently argued that American-manufactured cars were poorly built and that he'd never own anything but a foreign import. Then his parents gave him a late model American-made car, and suddenly they weren't so bad. Or when going through sorority rush, a new freshman believes that sororities are good and that pledging a sorority is important. If she's not accepted by a sorority, however, she may say, "Sorority life isn't all it's cracked up to be anyway."

Research generally concludes that people seek consistency among their attitudes and between their attitudes and their behavior.[13] Individuals try to reconcile differing attitudes and align their attitudes and behavior so that they appear rational and consistent. They do so by altering either the attitudes or the behavior or by developing a rationalization for the discrepancy.

What Is Cognitive Dissonance Theory?

Can we assume from this consistency principle that an individual's behavior can always be predicted if we know his or her attitude on a subject? The answer isn't a simple "yes" or "no." Why? Cognitive dissonance theory.

Cognitive dissonance theory, proposed by Leon Festinger in the 1950s, sought to explain the relationship between attitudes and behavior.[14] **Cognitive dissonance** is any incompatibility or inconsistency between attitudes or between behavior and attitudes. The theory argued that inconsistency is uncomfortable and that individuals will try to reduce the discomfort and thus, the dissonance.

Of course, no one can avoid dissonance. You know you should floss your teeth every day, but don't do it. There's an inconsistency between attitude and behavior. How do people cope with cognitive dissonance? The theory proposed that how hard we try to reduce dissonance is determined by three things: (1) the *importance* of the factors creating the dissonance, (2) the degree of *influence* the individual believes he or she has over those factors, and (3) the *rewards* that may be involved in dissonance.

Cognitive dissonance refers to any incompatibility or inconsistency between attitudes and behaviors. For example, most people may believe that they are safe drivers, yet many may create potentially unsafe road conditions by driving and texting at the same time. To reduce the dissonance, these drivers may either stop their habit of driving and texting, or they may rationalize that driving and texting doesn't really pose any threat to others' safety, that they are in control of the situation, or that everyone else is doing the same thing.

Robert Crum/Shutterstock

---

attitudes
Evaluative statements, either favorable or unfavorable, concerning objects, people, or events

cognitive component
The part of an attitude made up of the beliefs, opinions, knowledge, and information held by a person

affective component
The part of an attitude that's the emotional or feeling part

behavioral component
The part of an attitude that refers to an intention to behave in a certain way toward someone or something

job satisfaction
An employee's general attitude toward his or her job

job involvement
The degree to which an employee identifies with his or her job, actively participates in it, and considers his or her job performance important for self-worth

organizational commitment
An employee's orientation toward the organization in terms of his or her loyalty to, identification with, and involvement in the organization

employee engagement
When employees are connected to, satisfied with, and enthusiastic about their jobs

cognitive dissonance
Any incompatibility or inconsistency between attitudes or between behavior and attitudes

If the factors creating the dissonance are relatively unimportant, the pressure to correct the inconsistency will be low. However, if those factors are important, individuals may change their behavior, conclude that the dissonant behavior isn't so important, change their attitude, or identify compatible factors that outweigh the dissonant ones.

How much influence individuals believe they have over the factors also affects their reaction to the dissonance. If they perceive the dissonance is something about which they have no choice, they won't be receptive to attitude change or feel a need to do so. If, for example, the dissonance-producing behavior was required as a result of a manager's order, the pressure to reduce dissonance would be less than if the behavior had been performed voluntarily. Although dissonance exists, it can be rationalized and justified by the need to follow the manager's orders—that is, the person had no choice or control.

Finally, rewards also influence the degree to which individuals are motivated to reduce dissonance. Coupling high dissonance with high rewards tends to reduce the discomfort by motivating the individual to believe that there is consistency.

Let's look at an example. Tracey Ford, a corporate manager, believes strongly that no company should lay off employees. Unfortunately, Tracey has to make decisions that trade off her company's strategic direction against her convictions on layoffs. She knows that organizational restructuring means some jobs may no longer be needed. She also knows layoffs are in the best economic interest of her firm. What will she do? Undoubtedly, Tracey is experiencing a high degree of cognitive dissonance. Because of the *importance* of the issues in this example, she can't ignore the inconsistency. To deal with her dilemma, she can follow several steps. She can change her behavior (lay off employees). Or she can reduce dissonance by concluding that the dissonant behavior is not so important after all ("I've got to make a living, and in my role as a decision maker, I often have to place the good of my company above that of individual organizational members"). She might also change her attitude ("There is nothing wrong in laying off employees"). Finally, another choice would be to seek out more consonant elements to outweigh the dissonant ones ("The long-term benefits to the surviving employees from our restructuring more than offset the associated costs"). Let's explain her behavior.

The *degree of influence* that Tracey believes she has also impacts how she reacts to the dissonance. If she perceives the dissonance to be uncontrollable—something about which she has no choice—she's less likely to feel she needs to change her attitude. If, for example, her boss told her that she had to lay off employees, the pressure to reduce dissonance would be less than if Tracey was performing the behavior voluntarily. Dissonance would exist but it could be rationalized and justified. This tendency illustrates why it's critical in today's organizations for leaders to establish an ethical culture. Without the leaders' influence and support, employees won't feel as much dissonance when faced with decisions of whether to act ethically or unethically.[15]

Finally, *rewards* also influence how likely Tracy is to reduce dissonance. High dissonance, when accompanied by high rewards, tends to reduce the tension inherent in the dissonance. The reward reduces dissonance by adding to the consistency side of the individual's balance sheet. Tracey might feel because she is well compensated in her job that she sometimes has to make hard decisions, such as laying off employees.

So what can we say about dissonance and employee behavior? These moderating factors suggest that although individuals experience dissonance, they won't necessarily move toward consistency, that is, toward reducing the dissonance. If the issues underlying the dissonance are of minimal importance, if an individual perceives that the dissonance is externally imposed and is substantially uncontrollable, or if rewards are significant enough to offset the dissonance, the individual will not be under great tension to reduce the dissonance.[16]

How Can an Understanding of Attitudes Help Managers Be More Effective?

Managers should be interested in their employees' attitudes because they influence behavior. Satisfied and committed employees, for instance, have lower rates of turnover and absenteeism. If managers want to keep resignations and absences down—especially among their more productive employees—they'll want to do things that generate positive job attitudes.

Whether satisfied workers are productive workers is a debate that's been going on for almost 80 years. After the Hawthorne Studies, managers believed that happy workers were productive workers. Because it's not easy to determine whether job satisfaction "caused" job productivity or vice versa, some management researchers felt that the belief was generally wrong. However, we can say with some certainty that the correlation between satisfaction and productivity is fairly strong.[18] Satisfied employees do perform better on the job. So managers should focus on those factors that have been shown to be conducive to high levels of employee job satisfaction: making work challenging and interesting, providing equitable rewards, and creating supportive working conditions and supportive colleagues.[19] These factors are likely to help employees be more productive.

Managers should also survey employees about their attitudes. As one study put it, "A sound measurement of overall job attitude is one of the most useful pieces of information an organization can have about its employees."[20] However, research has also shown that attitude surveys can be more effective at pinpointing employee dissatisfaction if done multiple times rather than just at one point in time.[21]

Finally, managers should know that employees will try to reduce dissonance. If employees are required to do things that appear inconsistent to them or that are at odds with their attitudes, managers should remember that pressure to reduce the dissonance is not as strong when the employee perceives that the dissonance is externally imposed and uncontrollable. It's also decreased if rewards are significant enough to offset the dissonance. So the manager might point to external forces such as competitors, customers, or other factors when explaining the need to perform some work that the individual may have some dissonance about. Or the manager can provide rewards that an individual desires.

WHAT DO MANAGERS NEED TO KNOW ABOUT PERSONALITY?

Describe different personality theories.

3

"Incoming Bowling Green State University freshmen Erica Steele and Katelyn Devore had never met. But after they scored a 95 percent match on an online compatibility test, they signed up to room together."[22] If you've ever shared a living space with someone else (family or nonfamily), you know how important it can be for roommates to be compatible and to get along with each other. This compatibility is affected and influenced by our own and by other people's personalities.

Personality. We all have one. Some of us are quiet and passive; others are loud and aggressive. When we describe people using terms such as *quiet, passive, loud, aggressive, ambitious, extroverted, loyal, tense,* or *sociable,* we're describing their personalities. An individual's personality is a unique combination of emotional, thought, and behavioral patterns that affect how a person reacts to situations and interacts with others. Personality is most often described in terms of measurable traits that a person exhibits. We're interested in looking at personality because just like attitudes, it affects how and why people behave the way they do.

Can Personality Predict Behavior?

Literally dozens of behaviors are attributed to an individual's traits. So too are personality types influential in how people interact with one another and how they solve problems. Through the years, researchers attempted to focus specifically on which personality types

personality
A unique combination of emotional, thought, and behavioral patterns that affect how a person reacts to situations and interacts with others

and personality traits would identify information about the individual. Two of these efforts have been widely recognized: the Myers-Briggs Type Indicator® and the Big Five model of personality.

WHAT IS THE MYERS-BRIGGS TYPE INDICATOR?   One of the more widely used methods of identifying personalities is the Myers-Briggs Type Indicator (MBTI). The MBTI® assessment uses four dimensions of personality to identify 16 different personality types based on the responses to an approximately 100-item questionnaire. More than 2 million individuals take the MBTI assessment each year in the United States alone. It's used in such companies as Apple, Hallmark, AT&T, Exxon, 3M, as well as many hospitals, educational institutions, and the U.S. Armed Forces.

The 16 personality types are based on four dimensions: Extraversion versus Introversion (EI), Sensing versus Intuition (SN), Thinking versus Feeling (TF), and Judging versus Perceiving (JP). The EI dimension describes an individual's orientation toward the external world of the environment (E) or the inner world of ideas and experiences (I). The Sensing-Intuition dimension indicates an individual's preference for gathering data while focusing on a standard routine based on factual data (S) to focusing on the big picture and making connections among the facts (N). Thinking-Feeling reflects one's preference for making decisions in a logical and analytical manner (T) or on the basis of values and beliefs and the effects the decision will have on others (F). The Judging-Perceiving index reflects an attitude toward how one deals with the external world—either in a planned and orderly way (J) or preferring to remain flexible and spontaneous (P).[23]

Let's give you some examples. An ISTJ (Introversion - Sensing - Thinking - Judging) is quiet, serious, dependable, practical, and matter-of-fact. On the other hand, an ESFP (Extraversion - Sensing - Feeling - Perceiving) is outgoing, friendly, spontaneous, enjoys working with others, and learns best by trying a new skill with other people. An INFP (Introversion - Intuition - Feeling - Perceiving) is idealistic, loyal to personal values, and seeks to understand people and help them fulfill their potential. Finally, an ENTJ (Extraversion - Intuition - Thinking - Judging) is frank, decisive, and will assume leadership roles. This type also enjoys long-term planning and goal setting and is forceful in presenting ideas.[24]

How could the MBTI assessment help managers? Proponents of the instrument believe that it's important to know these personality types because they influence the way people interact and solve problems.[25] For example, if your boss prefers Intuition and you're a Sensing type, you'll deal with information in different ways. An Intuition preference indicates your boss is one who prefers gut reactions, whereas you, as a Sensing type, prefer to deal with the facts. To work well with your boss, you have to present more than just facts about a situation—you'll also have to discuss your gut feeling about the situation. The MBTI assessment has also been found to be useful in focusing on growth orientations for entrepreneurial types as well as profiles supporting emotional intelligence (something we'll look at shortly).[26]

WHAT IS THE BIG FIVE MODEL OF PERSONALITY?   Another way of viewing personality is through a five-factor model of personality—more typically called the Big Five model.[27] The Big Five factors are:

1 Extraversion	A personality dimension that describes the degree to which someone is sociable, talkative, and assertive.
2 Agreeableness	A personality dimension that describes the degree to which someone is good-natured, cooperative, and trusting.
3 Conscientiousness	A personality dimension that describes the degree to which someone is responsible, dependable, persistent, and achievement oriented.
4 Emotional stability	A personality dimension that describes the degree to which someone is calm, enthusiastic, and secure (positive) or tense, nervous, depressed, and insecure (negative).
5 Openness to experience	A personality dimension that describes the degree to which someone is imaginative, artistically sensitive, and intellectual.

The Big Five model provides more than just a personality framework. Research has shown that important relationships exist between these personality dimensions and job performance.[28] For example, one study reviewed five categories of occupations: professionals (e.g., engineers, architects, attorneys), police, managers, sales, and semiskilled and skilled employees. Job performance was defined in terms of employee performance ratings, training competency, and personnel data such as salary level. The results of the study showed that conscientiousness predicted job performance for all five occupational groups.[29] Predictions for the other personality dimensions depended on the situation and the occupational group. For example, extraversion predicted performance in managerial and sales positions, in which high social interaction is necessary.[30] Openness to experience was found to be important in predicting training competency. Ironically, emotional security was not positively related to job performance. Although it would seem logical that calm and secure workers would be better performers, that wasn't the case. Perhaps it's a function of the likelihood that emotionally stable workers often keep their jobs and emotionally unstable people may not. Given that all those participating in the study were employed, the variance on that dimension was probably small.

WHAT IS EMOTIONAL INTELLIGENCE?   People who understand their own emotions and are good at reading others' emotions may be more effective in their jobs. That, in essence, is the theme of the underlying research on emotional intelligence.[31]

Emotional intelligence (EI) refers to an assortment of noncognitive skills, capabilities, and competencies that influences a person's ability to cope with environmental demands and pressures.[32] It's composed of five dimensions:

- *Self-awareness*. Being aware of what you're feeling.
- *Self-management*. Managing your own emotions and impulses.
- *Self-motivation*. Persisting in the face of setbacks and failures.
- *Empathy*. Sensing how others are feeling.
- *Social skills*. Adapting to and handling the emotions of others.

Several studies suggest that EI may play an important role in job performance.[33] For instance, one study looked at the characteristics of Bell Lab engineers who were rated as stars by their peers. The scientists concluded that these stars were better at relating to others. That is, it was EI, not academic IQ, that characterized high performers. A second study of Air Force recruiters generated similar findings: Top-performing recruiters exhibited high levels of EI. Using these findings, the Air Force revamped its selection criteria. A follow-up investigation found that future hires who had high EI scores were 2.6 times more successful than those with low scores. Organizations such as American Express have found that implementing emotional intelligence programs has helped increase its effectiveness; other organizations also found similar results that emotional intelligence contributes to team effectiveness.[34] For instance, at Cooperative Printing in Minneapolis, a study of its 45 employees concluded that EI skills were twice as important in "contributing to excellence as intellect and expertise alone."[35] A poll of human resources managers asked this question: How important is it for your workers to demonstrate EI to move up the corporate ladder? Forty percent of the managers replied "very important." Another 16 percent said moderately important. Other studies also indicated that emotional intelligence can be beneficial to quality improvements in contemporary organizations.[36]

The implication is that employers should consider emotional intelligence as a criterion in their selection process—especially for those jobs that demand a high degree of social interaction.[37]

Myers-Briggs Type Indicator (MBTI)
A personality assessment that uses four dimensions of personality to identify different personality types

big five model
A personality trait model that examines five traits: extraversion, agreeableness, conscientiousness, emotional stability, and openness to experience

emotional intelligence (EI)
The ability to notice and to manage emotional cues and information

RIGHT ? WRONG

It's been called the "desperation hustle."[38] Employees who are "anxious about layoffs want to look irreplaceable." So they clean up their act. Those who might not have paid much attention to their manner of dress now do. Those who were mouthy and argumentative are now quiet and compliant. Those who used to "watch the clock" are now the last to leave. The fear is there and it's noticeable. "Managing that fear can be challenging."

Think About:

- What ethical issues might arise for both employees and for managers?

- How could managers approach these circumstances ethically?

- What information in this chapter might help managers help employees?

Superstock

Can Personality Traits Predict Practical Work-Related Behaviors?

Five specific personality traits have proven most powerful in explaining individual behavior in organizations. These are locus of control, Machiavellianism, self-esteem, self-monitoring, and risk propensity.

Who has control over an individual's behavior? Some people believe that they control their own fate. Others see themselves as pawns of fate, believing that what happens to them in their lives is due to luck or chance. The **locus of control** in the first case is internal. In the second case, it is external; these people believe that their lives are controlled by outside forces.[39] A manager might also expect to find that externals blame a poor performance evaluation on their boss's prejudice, their coworkers, or other events outside their control, whereas "internals" explain the same evaluation in terms of their own actions.

The second characteristic is called **Machiavellianism ("Mach")** after Niccolo Machiavelli, who provided instruction in the sixteenth century on how to gain and manipulate power. An individual who is high in Machiavellianism is pragmatic, maintains emotional distance, believes that ends can justify the means,[40] and may have beliefs that are less ethical.[41] The philosophy "if it works, use it" is consistent with a high Mach perspective. Do high Machs make good employees? That answer depends on the type of job and whether you consider ethical implications in evaluating performance. In jobs that require bargaining skills (a labor negotiator) or that have substantial rewards for winning (a commissioned salesperson), high Machs are productive. In jobs in which ends do not justify the means or that lack absolute standards of performance, it's difficult to predict the performance of high Machs.

People differ in the degree to which they like or dislike themselves. This trait is called **self-esteem (SE).**[42] The research on SE offers some interesting insights into organizational behavior. For example, SE is directly related to expectations for success. High SEs believe that they possess the ability to succeed at work. Individuals with high SE will take more risks in job selection and are more likely to choose unconventional jobs than are people with low SE.[43] The most common finding on self-esteem is that low SEs are more susceptible to external influence than are high SEs. Low SEs are dependent on positive evaluations from others. As a result, they're more likely to seek approval from others and more prone to conform to the beliefs and behaviors of those they respect than are high SEs. In managerial positions, low SEs will tend to be concerned with pleasing others and, therefore, will be less likely to take unpopular stands than will high SEs. Not surprisingly, self-esteem has also been found to be related to job satisfaction. A number of studies confirm that high SEs are more satisfied with their jobs than are low SEs.

Another personality trait researchers have identified is called **self-monitoring.**[44] Individuals high in self-monitoring can show considerable adaptability in adjusting their behavior to external, situational factors.[45] They're highly sensitive to external cues and can behave differently in different situations. High self-monitors are capable of presenting striking contradictions between their public persona and their private selves. Low self-monitors can't alter their behavior. They tend to display their true dispositions and attitudes in every situation; hence, they exhibit high behavioral consistency between who they are and what they do. Evidence suggests that high self-monitors tend to pay closer attention to the behavior of others and are more capable of conforming than are low self-monitors.[46] We might also hypothesize that high self-monitors will be more successful in managerial positions that require individuals to play multiple, and even contradicting, roles.

The final personality trait influencing worker behavior reflects the willingness to take chances—the propensity for *risk taking.* A preference to assume or avoid risk has been shown to have an impact on how long it takes individuals to make a decision and how much information they require before making their choice. For instance, in one classic study, 79 managers worked on a simulated human resources management exercise that required them to make hiring decisions.[47] High risk-taking managers made more rapid decisions and used less information in making their choices than did the low risk-taking managers. Interestingly, the decision accuracy was the same for both groups.

Although it's generally correct to conclude that managers in organizations are risk averse, especially in large companies and government bureaus,[48] individual differences are still found on this dimension.[49] As a result, it makes sense to recognize these differences and even to consider aligning risk-taking propensity with specific job demands. For instance, a high risk-taking propensity may lead to effective performance for a stock trader in a brokerage firm since this type of job demands rapid decision making. The same holds true for the entrepreneur.[50] On the other hand, this personality characteristic might prove a major obstacle to accountants performing auditing activities, which might be better done by someone with a low risk-taking propensity.

How Do We Match Personalities and Jobs?

"What if you're not happy in your job? Is it possible that you're in the wrong career entirely?"[51] As you do your job day-by-day, you may realize that your tasks don't mesh well with your personality or talents. Wouldn't it seem to make more sense to strive for a match between your personality and your chosen job or career path?

Obviously, individual personalities differ. So, too, do jobs. How do we match the two? The best-documented personality-job fit theory was developed by psychologist John Holland.[52] His theory states that an employee's satisfaction with his or her job, as well as his or her likelihood of leaving that job, depends on the degree to which the individual's personality matches the job environment. Holland identified six basic personality types as shown in Exhibit 2.

Holland's theory proposes that satisfaction is highest and turnover lowest when personality and occupation are compatible.[53] Social individuals should be in "people" type jobs, and so forth. The key points of this theory include the following: (1) there do appear to be intrinsic differences in personality among individuals; (2) there are different types of jobs; and (3) people in job environments compatible with their personality types should be more satisfied and less likely to resign voluntarily than people in incongruent jobs.

Do Personality Attributes Differ Across Cultures?

Do personality frameworks, like the Big Five model, transfer across cultures? Are dimensions like locus of control relevant in all cultures? Let's try to answer these questions.

---

locus of control
The degree to which people believe they control their own fate

machiavellianism ("Mach")
A measure of the degree to which people are pragmatic, maintain emotional distance, and believe that ends justify means

self-esteem (SE)
An individual's degree of like or dislike for himself or herself

self-monitoring
A personality trait that measures the ability to adjust behavior to external situational factors

EXHIBIT 2	Holland's Personality-Job Fit	
PERSONALITY TYPE	**CHARACTERISTICS**	**SAMPLE OCCUPATIONS**
Realistic Prefers physical activities that require skill, strength, and coordination	Shy, genuine, persistent, stable, conforming, practical	Mechanic, drill-press operator, assembly-line worker, farmer
Investigative Prefers activities involving thinking, organizing, and understanding	Analytical, original, curious, independent	Biologist, economist, mathematician, reporter
Social Prefers activities that involve helping and developing others	Sociable, friendly, cooperative, understanding	Social worker, teacher, counselor, clinical psychologist
Conventional Prefers rule-regulated, orderly, and unambiguous activities	Conforming, efficient, practical, unimaginative, inflexible	Accountant, corporate manager, bank teller, file clerk
Enterprising Prefers verbal activities that include opportunities to influence others and attain power	Self-confident, ambitious, energetic, domineering	Lawyer, real estate agent, public relations specialist, small business manager
Artistic Prefers ambiguous and unsystematic activities that allow creative expression	Imaginative, disorderly, idealistic, emotional, impractical	Painter, musician, writer, interior decorator

Source: Reproduced by special permission of the publisher, Psychological Assessment Resources, Inc., *Making Vocational Choices*, 3rd ed., copyright 1973, 1985, 1992, 1997 by Psychological Assessment Resources, Inc. All rights reserved.

Even though personality attributes appear in most cross-cultural studies, differences exist in the emphasis countries place on personality dimensions. Chinese culture, for example, places a high premium on conscientiousness and self-monitoring. Chinese employees are hard-working, efficient, responsible, dependable, and achievement oriented. As high self-monitors, they show considerable adaptability in adjusting their behavior to external factors. In China, employee conscientiousness and ability to adapt are key factors that drive the country's competitiveness. These personality traits influence the behavior of Landsha Group employees, shown here, who work for China's leading producer of socks and stockings.

Zhang Jiancheng/Newscom

The five personality factors studied in the Big Five model appear in almost all cross-cultural studies.[54] A wide variety of diverse cultures, such as China, Israel, Germany, Japan, Spain, Nigeria, Norway, Pakistan, and the United States, have been the setting for these studies. Differences are found in the emphasis on dimensions. Chinese, for example, use the category of conscientiousness more often and use the category of agreeableness less often than do Americans. But a surprisingly high amount of agreement is found, especially among individuals from developed countries. As a case in point, a comprehensive review of studies covering people from the European Community found that conscientiousness was a valid predictor of performance across jobs and occupational groups.[55] U.S. studies found the same results.

We know that there are certainly no common personality types for a given country. You can, for instance, find high risk takers and low risk takers in almost any culture. Yet a country's culture influences the *dominant* personality characteristics of its people. We can see this effect of national culture by looking at one of the personality traits we just discussed: locus of control.

National cultures differ in terms of the degree to which people believe they control their environment. For instance, North Americans believe that they can dominate their environment; other societies, such as those in Middle Eastern countries, believe that life is essentially predetermined. Notice how closely this distinction parallels the concept of internal and external locus of control. On the basis of this particular cultural characteristic, we should expect a larger proportion of internals in the U.S. and Canadian workforces than in the workforces of Saudi Arabia or Iran.

As we have seen throughout this section, personality traits influence employees' behavior. For global managers, understanding how personality traits differ takes on added significance when looking at it from the perspective of national culture.

How Can an Understanding of Personality Help Managers Be More Effective?

Some 62 percent of companies are using personality tests when recruiting and hiring.[56] And that's where the major value in understanding personality differences probably lies. Managers are likely to have higher-performing and more-satisfied employees if consideration is given to matching personalities with jobs. In addition, compatibility leads to other benefits. By recognizing that people approach problem solving, decision making, and job interactions differently, a manager can better understand why, for instance, an employee is uncomfortable with making quick decisions or why an employee insists on gathering as much information as possible before addressing a problem. For instance, managers can expect that individuals with an external locus of control may be less satisfied with their jobs than those with an internal locus and also that they may be less willing to accept responsibility for their actions.

WHAT IS PERCEPTION AND WHAT INFLUENCES IT?

"L ke y ur b ain, the n w L nd Rov r autom tic lly adj sts to anyth ng."[57] This advertisement for a Land Rover SUV illustrates the perceptual process at work. You were likely able to read the sentence even with the missing letters because you recognized the word patterns and organized and interpreted them in a way that made sense.

Describe perception and the factors that influence it.

4

Perception is a process by which we give meaning to our environment by organizing and interpreting sensory impressions. Research on perception consistently demonstrates that individuals may look at the same thing yet perceive it differently. One manager, for instance, can interpret the fact that her assistant regularly takes several days to make important decisions as evidence that the assistant is slow, disorganized, and afraid to make decisions. Another manager with the same assistant might interpret the same tendency as evidence that the assistant is thoughtful, thorough, and deliberate. The first manager would probably evaluate her assistant negatively; the second manager would probably evaluate the person positively. The point is that none of us see reality. We interpret what we see and call it reality. And, of course, as the example shows, we behave according to our perceptions.

What Influences Perception?

How do we explain the fact that Cathy, a marketing supervisor for a large commercial petroleum products organization, age 52, noticed Bill's nose ring during his employment interview, and Sean, a human resources recruiter, age 23, didn't? A number of factors operate to shape and sometimes distort perception. These factors can reside in the perceiver, in the object or target being perceived, or in the context of the situation in which the perception is made.

When an individual looks at a target and attempts to interpret what he or she sees, that individual's personal characteristics will heavily influence the interpretation. These personal characteristics include attitudes, personality, motives, interests, past experiences, and expectations. The characteristics of the target being observed can also affect what is perceived. Loud people are more likely than quiet people to be noticed in a group. So, too, are extremely attractive or unattractive individuals. Because targets

perception
A process by which we give meaning to our environment by organizing and interpreting sensory impressions

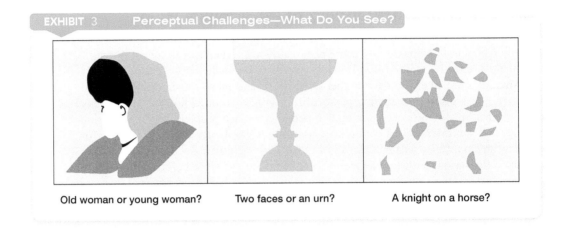

EXHIBIT 3   Perceptual Challenges—What Do You See?

Old woman or young woman?   Two faces or an urn?   A knight on a horse?

are not looked at in isolation, the relationship of a target to its background also influences perception (see Exhibit 3 for an example), as does our tendency to group close things and similar things together.

The context in which we see objects or events is also important. The time at which an object or event is seen can influence attention, as can location, lighting, temperature, and any number of other situational factors.

How Do Managers Judge Employees?

Much of the research on perception is directed at inanimate objects. Managers, though, are more concerned with human beings. Our perceptions of people differ from our perceptions of such inanimate objects as computers, robots, or buildings because we make inferences about the actions of people that we don't, of course, make about inanimate objects. When we observe people, we attempt to develop explanations of why they behave in certain ways. Our perception and judgment of a person's actions, therefore, will be significantly influenced by the assumptions we make about the person's internal state. Many of these assumptions have led researchers to develop attribution theory.

WHAT IS ATTRIBUTION THEORY?   Attribution theory has been proposed to explain how we judge people differently depending on what meaning we attribute to a given behavior.[58] Basically, the theory suggests that when we observe an individual's behavior, we attempt to determine whether it was internally or externally caused. Internally caused behavior is believed to be under the control of the individual. Externally caused behavior results from outside causes; that is, the person is seen as having been forced into the behavior by the situation. That determination, however, depends on three factors: distinctiveness, consensus, and consistency.

Distinctiveness refers to whether an individual displays a behavior in many situations or whether it is particular to one situation. Is the employee who arrived late to work today also the person coworkers see as a goof-off? What we want to know is whether this behavior is unusual. If it is, the observer is likely to give the behavior an external attribution. If this action is not unique, it will probably be judged as internal.

If everyone who is faced with a similar situation responds in the same way, we can say the behavior shows *consensus*. Our tardy employee's behavior would meet this criterion if all employees who took the same route to work today were also late. If consensus is high, you would be expected to give an external attribution to the employee's tardiness, whereas if other employees who took the same route made it to work on time, you would conclude the reason to be internal.

Finally, a manager looks for *consistency* in an employee's actions. Does the individual engage in the behaviors regularly and consistently? Does the employee respond the same way over time? Coming in 10 minutes late for work is not perceived in the same way if, for one employee, it represents an unusual case (she hasn't been late

 FOUNDATIONS OF INDIVIDUAL BEHAVIOR

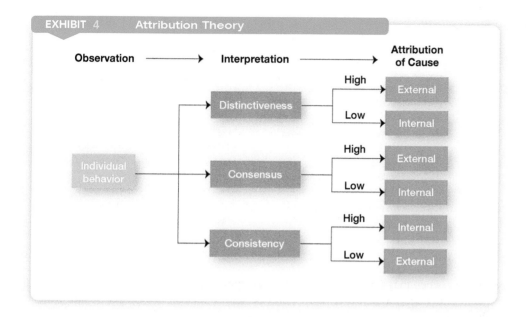

EXHIBIT 4 Attribution Theory

for several months), but for another it is part of a routine pattern (he is late two or three times a week). The more consistent the behavior, the more the observer is inclined to attribute it to internal causes.

Exhibit 4 summarizes the key elements in attribution theory. It would tell us, for instance, that if an employee, Mr. Flynn, generally performs at about the same level on other related tasks as he does on his current task (low distinctiveness), if other employees frequently perform differently—better or worse—than Mr. Flynn does on that current task (low consensus), and if Mr. Flynn's performance on this current task is consistent over time (high consistency), his manager or anyone else who is judging Mr. Flynn's work is likely to hold him primarily responsible for his task performance (internal attribution).

CAN ATTRIBUTIONS BE DISTORTED? One of the more interesting findings drawn from attribution theory is that errors or biases distort attributions. For instance, substantial evidence supports the hypothesis that when we make judgments about the behavior of other people, we have a tendency to underestimate the influence of external factors and overestimate the influence of internal or personal factors.[59] This **fundamental attribution error** can explain why a sales manager may be prone to attribute the poor performance of her sales agents to laziness rather than to the innovative product line introduced by a competitor. Individuals also tend to attribute their own successes to internal factors such as ability or effort while putting the blame for failure on external factors such as luck. This **self-serving bias** suggests that feedback provided to employees in performance reviews will be predictably distorted by them, whether it is positive or negative.

WHAT PERCEPTUAL SHORTCUTS DO WE USE? All of us, managers included, use a number of shortcuts to judge others. Perceiving and interpreting people's behavior is a lot of work, so we use shortcuts to make the task more manageable.[60] Such shortcuts can be

---

attribution theory
A theory used to explain how we judge people differently, based on what meaning we attribute to a given behavior

fundamental attribution error
The tendency to underestimate the influence of external factors and overestimate the influence of internal factors when making judgments about the behavior of others

self-serving bias
The tendency for individuals to attribute their successes to internal factors while putting the blame for failures on external factors

EXHIBIT 5	Perceptual Shortcuts	
SHORTCUT	**WHAT IT IS**	**DISTORTION**
Selectivity	People assimilate certain bits and pieces of what they observe depending on their interests, background, experience, and attitudes	"Speed reading" others may result in an inaccurate picture of them
Assumed similarity	People assume that others are like them	May fail to take into account individual differences, resulting in incorrect similarities
Stereotyping	People judge others on the basis of their perception of a group to which the others belong	May result in distorted judgments because many stereotypes have no factual foundation
Halo effect	People form an impression of others on the basis of a single trait	Fails to take into account the total picture of what an individual has done

valuable when they let us make accurate perceptions quickly and provide valid data for making predictions. However, they aren't perfect. They can and do get us into trouble. What are these perceptual shortcuts? (See Exhibit 5 for a summary.)

Individuals can't assimilate all they observe, so they're selective in their perception. They absorb bits and pieces. These bits and pieces are not chosen randomly; rather, they're selectively chosen depending on the interests, background, experience, and attitudes of the observer. Selective perception allows us to "speed read" others but not without the risk of drawing an inaccurate picture.

It's easy to judge others if we assume that they're similar to us. In assumed similarity, or the "like me" effect, the observer's perception of others is influenced more by the observer's own characteristics than by those of the person observed. For example, if you want challenges and responsibility in your job, you'll assume that others want the same. People who assume that others are like them can, of course, be right, but not always.

When we judge someone on the basis of our perception of a group he or she is part of, we're using the shortcut called stereotyping. For instance, "Married people are more stable employees than single persons" or "Older employees are absent more often from work" are examples of stereotyping. To the degree that a stereotype is based on fact, it may produce accurate judgments. However, many stereotypes aren't factual and distort our judgment.

When we form a general impression about a person on the basis of a single characteristic, such as intelligence, sociability, or appearance, we're being influenced by the halo effect. This effect frequently occurs when students evaluate their classroom instructor. Students may isolate a single trait such as enthusiasm and allow their entire evaluation to be slanted by the perception of this one trait. If an instructor who is quiet, assured, knowledgeable, and highly qualified has a classroom teaching style that lacks enthusiasm, that instructor might be rated lower on a number of other characteristics.

How Can an Understanding of Perception Help Managers Be More Effective?

Managers need to recognize that their employees react to perceptions, not to reality. So whether a manager's appraisal of an employee's performance is actually objective and unbiased or whether the organization's wage levels are among the highest in the community is less relevant than what employees perceive them to be. If individuals perceive appraisals to be biased or wage levels as low, they'll behave as if those conditions actually exist. Employees organize and interpret what they see, so there is always the potential for perceptual distortion. The message is clear: Pay close attention to how employees perceive both their jobs and management actions. Remember, the valuable employee who quits because of an inaccurate perception is just as great a loss to an organization as the valuable employee who quits for a valid reason.

HOW DO LEARNING THEORIES EXPLAIN BEHAVIOR?

Discuss learning theories and their relevance in shaping behavior.

5

When 20-year-old Elvis Andrus was signed by the Texas Rangers in 2009, he was excited to find out that the Rangers had signed another shortstop—11-time Gold Glove winner and fellow Venezuelan Omar Vizquel. Vizquel's role was clear: to be a mentor to the talented young player. Managers of major league baseball teams "regularly mix savvy veterans with talented young players, hoping tricks of the trade and advice on everything from how to turn a double play to how to avoid trouble in night spots on the road will rub off."[61]

Mentoring is a good example of the last individual behavior concept we're going to look at—learning. Learning is included in our discussion of individual behavior for the obvious reason that almost all behavior is learned. If we want to explain, predict, and influence behavior, we need to understand how people learn.

The psychologists' definition of learning is considerably broader than the average person's view that "it's what we do in school." Learning occurs all the time as we continuously learn from our experiences. A workable definition of learning is any relatively permanent change in behavior that occurs as a result of experience. Two learning theories help us understand how and why individual behavior occurs.

What Is Operant Conditioning?

Operant conditioning argues that behavior is a function of its consequences. People learn to behave to get something they want or to avoid something they don't want. Operant behavior is voluntary or learned behavior, not reflexive or unlearned behavior. The tendency to repeat learned behavior is influenced by reinforcement or lack of reinforcement that happens as a result of the behavior. Reinforcement strengthens a behavior and increases the likelihood that it will be repeated. Lack of reinforcement weakens a behavior and lessens the likelihood that it will be repeated.

B. F. Skinner's research widely expanded our knowledge of operant conditioning.[62] Behavior is assumed to be determined from without—that is, *learned*—rather than from within—reflexive or unlearned. Skinner argued that people will most likely engage in desired behaviors if they are positively reinforced for doing so, and rewards are most effective if they immediately follow the desired response. In addition, behavior that isn't rewarded or is punished, is less likely to be repeated. (For more information about Skinner's contributions, see the From the Past to the Present box.)

You see examples of operant conditioning everywhere. Any situation in which it's either explicitly stated or implicitly suggested that reinforcement (rewards) are contingent on some action on your part is an example of operant conditioning. Your instructor says that if you want a high grade in this course, you must perform well on tests by giving correct answers.

Small business owner Morgan Smith (left) applies social learning theory in teaching employees the skills they need to meet the firm's high standards of quality and efficiency. As owner and managing partner of Boneheads Restaurant, Smith serves as a trainer and role model in showing employees how to prepare food, use equipment, and serve customers. Under Smith's tutelage, employees learn through observation and direct experience and then practice what they learn. Smith is an important and influential model for employees. His goal for them is to reach their full potential, and he willingly invests time to achieve that goal. In this photo, Smith shows a chef at Boneheads how to adjust some equipment in the kitchen.

Newscom

---

selective perception
The tendency for people to only absorb parts of what they observe, which allows us to "speed read" others

assumed similarity
An observer's perception of others influenced more by the observer's own characteristics than by those of the person observed

stereotyping
When we judge someone on the basis of our perception of a group to which that person belongs

halo effect
When we form a general impression of a person on the basis of a single characteristic

learning
A relatively permanent change in behavior that occurs as a result of experience

operant conditioning
A theory of learning that says behavior is a function of its consequences

---

From the Past to the Present

Why does hearing Christmas carols evoke pleasant memories of childhood?[63] *Classical conditioning theory* would say it's because the songs are associated with a festive holiday spirit and make us remember all the fun and excitement. Classical conditioning can also explain why a scheduled visit by the "top brass" brings flurried activities of cleaning, straightening, and rearranging at a local outlet of a major retail company. However, classical conditioning is a passive theory. Something happens, and we react in a specific way. As such, it can explain simple reflexive behavior. But most behavior by people at work is voluntary rather than reflexive; that is, employees *choose* to arrive at work on time, ask their boss for help with some problem, or "goof off" when no one is watching. A better explanation for behavior is operant conditioning.

Operant conditioning says that people behave the way they do so they can get something they want or avoid something they don't want. It's voluntary or learned behavior, not reflexive or unlearned behavior. Harvard psychologist B. F. Skinner first identified the process of operant conditioning. He argued that creating pleasing consequences to follow specific forms of behavior would increase the frequency of that behavior. Skinner demonstrated that people will most likely engage in desired behaviors if they're positively reinforced for doing so; that rewards are most effective if they immediately follow the desired response (behavior); and that behavior that is not rewarded or is punished is less likely to be repeated. For example, a professor places a mark by a student's name each time the student makes a contribution to class discussions. Operant conditioning would argue that this practice is motivating because it conditions a student to expect a reward (earning class credit) each time she demonstrates a specific behavior (speaking up in class). Operant conditioning can be seen in work settings as well. And smart managers quickly recognize that they can use operant conditioning to shape employees' behaviors to get work done in the most effective and efficient manner possible.

Think About:

- How do classical conditioning and operant conditioning differ?
- How could managers use operant conditioning?
- What's the connection between operant conditioning and shaping behavior?
- What ethical concerns might arise in "shaping" someone's behavior?

A salesperson working on commission knows that earning a sizeable income is contingent upon generating high sales in his or her territory. Of course, the linkage between behavior and reinforcement can also work to teach the individual to behave in ways that work against the best interests of the organization. Assume that your boss tells you that if you'll work overtime during the next three-week busy season, you'll be compensated for it at the next performance appraisal. Then, when performance appraisal time comes, you are given no positive reinforcements (such as being praised for pitching in and helping out when needed). What will you do the next time your boss asks you to work overtime? You'll probably refuse. Your behavior can be explained by operant conditioning: If a behavior isn't positively reinforced, the probability that the behavior will be repeated declines.

What Is Social Learning Theory?

Some 60 percent of the Radio City Rockettes have danced in prior seasons. The veterans help newcomers with "Rockette style"—where to place their hands, how to hold their hands, how to keep up stamina, and so forth.[64]

As the Rockettes are well aware, individuals can also learn by observing what happens to other people and just by being told about something as well as by direct experiences. Much of what we have learned comes from watching others (models)—parents, teachers, peers, television and movie actors, managers, and so forth. This view that we can learn both through observation and direct experience is called social learning theory.[65]

The influence of others is central to the social learning viewpoint. The amount of influence that these models have on an individual is determined by four processes:

1. *Attentional processes.* People learn from a model when they recognize and pay attention to its critical features. We're most influenced by models who are attractive, repeatedly available, thought to be important, or seen as similar to us.
2. *Retention processes.* A model's influence will depend on how well the individual remembers the model's action, even after the model is no longer readily available.

3. *Motor reproduction processes.* After a person has seen a new behavior by observing the model, the watching must become doing. This process then demonstrates that the individual can actually do the modeled activities.

4. *Reinforcement processes.* Individuals will be motivated to exhibit the modeled behavior if positive incentives or rewards are provided. Behaviors that are reinforced will be given more attention, learned better, and performed more often.

How Can Managers Shape Behavior?

Managers should be concerned with how they can teach employees to behave in ways that most benefit the organization.[66] Thus, managers will often attempt to mold individuals by guiding their learning in graduated steps. This process is called shaping behavior.

Consider the situation in which an employee's behavior is significantly different from that desired by management. If management reinforced the individual only when he or she showed desirable responses, little reinforcement might happen at all.

We shape behavior by systematically reinforcing each successive step that moves the individual closer to the desired response. If an employee who has continually been 30 minutes late for work arrives only 20 minutes late, we can reinforce this improvement. Reinforcement would increase as responses more closely approximate the desired behavior.

Four ways can be used to shape behavior: positive reinforcement, negative reinforcement, punishment, or extinction. When a response is followed with something pleasant, such as when a manager praises an employee for a job well done, it is called *positive reinforcement.* Rewarding a response with the termination or withdrawal of something pleasant is called *negative reinforcement.* Managers who habitually criticize their employees for taking extended coffee breaks are using negative reinforcement. The only way these employees can stop the criticism is to shorten their breaks. *Punishment* penalizes undesirable behavior. Suspending an employee for two days without pay for showing up drunk is an example of punishment. Eliminating any reinforcement that is maintaining a behavior is called *extinction.* When a behavior isn't reinforced, it gradually disappears. Managers who wish to discourage employees from continually asking distracting or irrelevant questions in meetings can eliminate that behavior by ignoring those employees when they raise their hands to speak. Soon, the behavior will be diminished.

Both positive and negative reinforcement result in learning. They strengthen a desired response and increase the probability of repetition. Both punishment and extinction also result in learning; however, they weaken behavior and tend to decrease its subsequent frequency.

How Can an Understanding of Learning Help Managers Be More Effective?

Employees are going to learn on the job. The only issue is whether managers are going to manage their learning through the rewards they allocate and the examples they set, or allow it to occur haphazardly. If marginal employees are rewarded with pay raises and promotions, they will have little reason to change their behavior. In fact, productive employees, who see marginal performance rewarded, might change their behavior. If managers want behavior A, but reward behavior B, they shouldn't be surprised to find employees' learning to engage in behavior B. Similarly, managers should expect that employees will look to them as models. Managers who are consistently late to work, or take two hours for lunch, or help themselves to company office supplies for personal use should expect employees to read the message they are sending and model their behavior accordingly.

social learning theory
A theory of learning that says people can learn through observation and direct experience

shaping behavior
The process of guiding learning in graduated steps, using reinforcement or lack of reinforcement

6 Discuss contemporary issues in OB.

WHAT CONTEMPORARY OB ISSUES FACE MANAGERS?

By this point, you're probably well aware of why managers need to understand how and why employees behave the way they do. We conclude this chapter by looking at two OB issues having a major influence on managers' jobs today.

How Do Generational Differences Affect the Workplace?

They're young, smart, brash. They wear flip-flops to the office or listen to iPods at their desk. They want to work, but don't want work to be their life. This is Generation Y, some 70 million of them, embarking on their careers, taking their place in an increasingly multigenerational workplace.[67]

JUST WHO IS GEN Y? There's no consensus about the exact time span that Gen Y comprises, but most definitions include those individuals born from about 1982 to 1997. One thing is for sure—they're bringing new attitudes with them to the workplace. Gen Ys have grown up with an amazing array of experiences and opportunities. And they want their work life to provide that as well, as shown in Exhibit 6. For instance, Stella Kenyi, who is passionately interested in international development, was sent by her employer, the National Rural Electric Cooperative Association, to Yai, Sudan, to survey energy use.[68] At Best Buy's corporate offices, Beth Trippie, a senior scheduling specialist, feels that as long as the results are there, why should it matter how it gets done. She says, "I'm constantly playing video games, on a call, doing work, and the thing is, all of it gets done, and it gets done well."[69] And Katie Patterson, an assistant account executive in Atlanta says, "We are willing and not afraid to challenge the status quo. An environment where creativity and independent thinking are looked upon as a positive is appealing to people my age. We're very independent and tech savvy."[70]

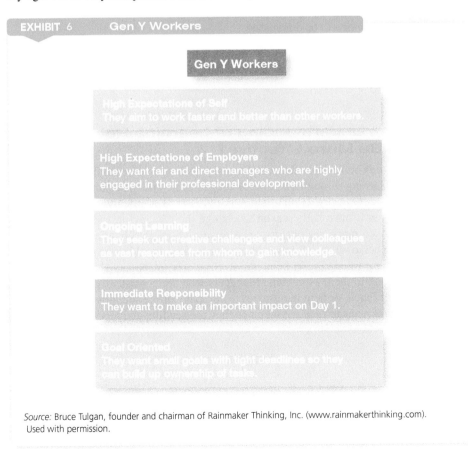

EXHIBIT 6   Gen Y Workers

Gen Y Workers

High Expectations of Self
They aim to work faster and better than other workers.

High Expectations of Employers
They want fair and direct managers who are highly engaged in their professional development.

Ongoing Learning
They seek out creative challenges and view colleagues as vast resources from whom to gain knowledge.

Immediate Responsibility
They want to make an important impact on Day 1.

Goal Oriented
They want small goals with tight deadlines so they can build up ownership of tasks.

Source: Bruce Tulgan, founder and chairman of Rainmaker Thinking, Inc. (www.rainmakerthinking.com). Used with permission.

DEALING WITH THE MANAGERIAL CHALLENGES. Managing Gen Y workers presents some unique challenges. Conflicts and resentment can arise over issues such as appearance, technology, and management style.

How flexible must an organization be in terms of "appropriate" office attire? It may depend on the type of work being done and the size of the organization. There are many organizations where jeans, T-shirts, and flip-flops are acceptable. However, in other settings, employees are expected to dress more conventionally. But even in those more conservative organizations, one possible solution to accommodate the more casual attire preferred by Gen Y is to be more flexible in what's acceptable. For instance, the guideline might be that when the person is not interacting with someone outside the organization, more casual wear (with some restrictions) can be worn.

What about technology? This generation has lived much of their lives with ATMs, DVDs, cell phones, e-mail, texting, laptops, and the Internet. When they don't have information they need, they just simply enter a few keystrokes to get it. Having grown up with technology, Gen Ys tend to be totally comfortable with it. They're quite content to meet virtually to solve problems, while bewildered baby boomers expect important problems to be solved with an in-person meeting. Baby boomers complain about Gen Y's inability to focus on one task, while Gen Ys see nothing wrong with multitasking. Again, flexibility from both is the key.

Finally, what about managing Gen Ys? Like the old car advertisement that used to say, "This isn't your father's Oldsmobile," we can say that "this isn't your father's or mother's way of managing." Gen Y employees want bosses who are open minded; experts in their field, even if they aren't tech-savvy; organized; teachers, trainers, and mentors; not authoritarian or paternalistic; respectful of their generation; understanding of their need for work/life balance; providing constant feedback; communicating in vivid and compelling ways; and providing stimulating and novel learning experiences.[71]

Gen Y employees have a lot to offer organizations in terms of their knowledge, passion, and abilities. Managers, however, have to recognize and understand the behaviors of this group in order to create an environment in which work can be accomplished efficiently, effectively, and without disruptive conflict.

How Do Managers Deal with Negative Behavior in the Workplace?

Jerry notices the oil is low in his forklift but continues to drive it until it overheats and can't be used. After enduring 11 months of repeated insults and mistreatment from her supervisor, Maria quits her job. An office clerk slams her keyboard and then shouts profanity whenever her computer freezes up. Rudeness, hostility, aggression, and other forms of workplace negativity have become all too common in today's organizations. In a survey of U.S. employees, 10 percent said they witnessed rudeness daily within their workplaces and 20 percent said that they personally were direct targets of incivility at work at least once a week. In a survey of Canadian workers, 25 percent reported seeing incivility daily and 50 percent said they were the direct targets at least once per week.[72] And it's been estimated that negativity costs the U.S. economy some $300 billion a year.[73] What can managers do to manage negative behavior in the workplace?

The main thing is to recognize that it's there. Pretending that negative behavior doesn't exist or ignoring such misbehaviors will only confuse employees about what is expected and acceptable behavior. Although researchers continue to debate about the preventive or responsive actions to negative behaviors, in reality, both are needed.[74] Preventing negative behaviors by carefully screening potential employees for certain personality traits and responding immediately and decisively to unacceptable negative behaviors can go a long way toward managing negative workplace behaviors. But it's also important to pay attention to employee attitudes, since negativity will show up there as well. As we said earlier, when employees are dissatisfied with their jobs, they *will* respond somehow.

Newscom

Blizzard Entertainment understands the new attitudes of millennials and has created a casual and fun environment that appeals to employees like the Web software engineer shown here taking a lunch break with her dog. A developer of gaming software, Blizzard promises employees challenging work that stimulates personal and professional growth. Employees are encouraged to pursue what they are passionate about and to freely give ideas for developing new products. They can rely on supportive managers and peers to help them gain the knowledge and training they need. Blizzard values its tech-savvy employees and encourages them to "embrace your inner geek" in creating great games that contribute to the company's success.

Review

1 Identify the focus and goals of organizational behavior (OB). OB focuses on three areas: individual behavior, group behavior, and organizational aspects. The goals of OB are to explain, predict, and influence employee behavior. Six important employee behaviors are as follows: Employee productivity is a performance measure of both efficiency and effectiveness. Absenteeism is the failure to report to work. Turnover is the voluntary and involuntary permanent withdrawal from an organization. Organizational citizenship behavior (OCB) is discretionary behavior that's not part of an employee's formal job requirements, but it promotes the effective functioning of an organization. Job satisfaction is an individual's general attitude toward his or her job. Workplace misbehavior is any intentional employee behavior that's potentially harmful to the organization or individuals within the organization.

2 Explain the role that attitudes play in job performance. Attitudes are evaluative statements concerning people, objects, or events. The cognitive component of an attitude refers to the beliefs, opinions, knowledge, or information held by a person. The affective component is the emotional or feeling part of an attitude. The behavioral component refers to an intention to behave in a certain way toward someone or something.

Four job-related attitudes include job satisfaction, job involvement, organizational commitment, and employee engagement. Job satisfaction refers to a person's general attitude toward his or her job. Job involvement is the degree to which an employee identifies with his or her job, actively participates in it, and considers his or her job performance to be important to his or her self-worth. Organizational commitment is the degree to which an employee identifies with a particular organization and its goals, and wishes to maintain membership in that organization. Employee engagement is when employees are connected to, satisfied with, and enthusiastic about their jobs.

According to cognitive dissonance theory, individuals try to reconcile attitude and behavior inconsistencies by altering their attitudes, altering their behavior, or rationalizing the inconsistency.

3 Describe different personality theories. The MBTI measures four dimensions: social interaction, preference for gathering data, preference for decision making, and style of making decisions. The Big Five Model consists of five personality traits: extraversion, agreeableness, conscientiousness, emotional stability, and openness to experience. Another way to view personality is through the five personality traits that help explain individual behavior in organizations: locus of control, Machiavellianism, self-esteem, self-monitoring, and risk taking.

Finally, how a person responds emotionally and how they deal with their emotions is a function of personality. A person who is emotionally intelligent has the ability to notice and to manage emotional cues and information.

4 Describe perception and the factors that influence it. Perception is how we give meaning to our environment by organizing and interpreting sensory impressions.

Attribution theory helps explain how we judge people differently. It depends on three factors. Distinctiveness is whether an individual displays different behaviors in different situations (that is, is the behavior unusual). Consensus is whether others facing a similar situation respond in the same way. Consistency is when a person engages in behaviors regularly and consistently. Whether these three factors are high or low helps managers determine whether employee behavior is attributed to external or internal causes.

The fundamental attribution error is the tendency to underestimate the influence of external factors and overestimate the influence of internal factors. The self-serving bias is the tendency to attribute our own successes to internal factors and to put the blame for personal failure on external factors. Shortcuts used in judging others are selective perception, assumed similarity, stereotyping, and the halo effect.

5 Discuss learning theories and their relevance in shaping behavior. Operant conditioning argues that behavior is a function of its consequences. Social learning theory says that individuals learn by observing what happens to other people and by directly experiencing something.

Managers can shape behavior by using positive reinforcement (reinforcing a desired behavior by giving something pleasant), negative reinforcement (reinforcing a desired response by withdrawing something unpleasant), punishment (eliminating undesirable behavior by applying penalties), or extinction (not reinforcing a behavior to eliminate it).

6 Discuss contemporary issues in OB. The challenge of managing Gen Y workers is that they bring new attitudes to the workplace. The main challenges are over issues such as appearance, technology, and management style.

Workplace misbehavior can be dealt with by recognizing that it's there; carefully screening potential employees for possible negative tendencies; and most importantly, by paying attention to employee attitudes through surveys about job satisfaction and dissatisfaction.

MyManagementLab   For more resources, please visit www.mymanagementlab.com

UNDERSTANDING THE CHAPTER

1. How is an organization like an iceberg? Use the iceberg metaphor to describe the field of organizational behavior.

2. Does the importance of knowledge of OB differ based on a manager's level in the organization? If so, how? If not, why not? Be specific.

3. Clarify how individuals reconcile inconsistencies between attitudes and behaviors.

4. Describe what is meant by the term *emotional intelligence.* Provide an example of how it's used in contemporary organizations.

5. "Instead of worrying about job satisfaction, companies should be trying to create environments where performance is enabled." What do you think this statement means? Explain. What's your reaction to this statement? Do you agree? Disagree? Why?

6. How might a manager use personality traits to improve employee selection in his or her department? Emotional intelligence? Discuss.

7. Describe the implications of social learning theory for managing people at work.

8. A Gallup Organization survey shows that most workers rate having a caring boss even higher than they value money or fringe benefits. How should managers interpret this information? What are the implications?

9. Write down three attitudes you have. Identify the cognitive, affective, and behavioral components of those attitudes.

10. Explain the challenges facing managers in managing generational differences and negative behavior in the workplace.

Endnotes

1. R. Mobbs, "The Employee Is Always Right," *In the Black,* April 2011, pp. 12–15; V. Nayar, "Employee Happiness: Zappos vs. HCL," *Bloomberg BusinessWeek.com,* January 5, 2011; G. Hamel, "Extreme Makeover," *Leadership Excellence,* January 2011, pp. 3–4; V. Nayar, "The World in 2036: Vineet Nayar Envisages Bottom-Up Leadership," *Economist,* November 27, 2010, p. 114; V. Nayar, "Employees First, Customers Second," *Chief Learning Officer,* October 2010, pp. 20–23; V. Nayar, "Back to Front," *People Management,* August 12, 2010, pp. 26–29; V. Nayar, "A Maverick CEO Explains How He Persuaded His Team to Leap into the Future," *Harvard Business Review,* June 2010, pp. 110–113; B. Einhorn and K. Gokhale, "Bangalore's Paying Again to Keep the Talent," *Bloomberg BusinessWeek,* May 24, 2010, pp. 14–16; M. Srivastava and S. Hamm, "Using the Slump to Get Bigger in Bangalore," *BusinessWeek,* September 3, 2009, pp. 50–51; and S. Lauchlan, "HCL Embraces Slumdog Effect," *Computer Weekly,* June 23, 2009, p. 8.

2. "Survey on the Total Financial Impact of Employee Absences," *Medical Benefits,* November 30, 2010, p. 9; and K. M. Kroll, "Absence-Minded," *CFO Human Capital,* 2006, pp. 12–14.

3. D. W. Organ, *Organizational Citizenship Behavior: The Good Soldier Syndrome* (Lexington, MA: Lexington Books, 1988), p. 4. See also J. L. Lavell, D. E. Rupp, and J. Brockner, "Taking a Multifoci Approach to the Study of Justice, Social Exchange, and Citizenship Behavior: The Target Similarity Model," *Journal of Management* (December 2007), pp. 841–866; and J. A. LePine, A. Erez, and D. E. Johnson, "The Nature and Dimensionality of Organizational Citizenship Behavior: A Critical Review and Meta-Analysis," *Journal of Applied Psychology* (February 2002), pp. 52–65.

4. J. R. Spence, D. L. Ferris, D. J. Brown, and D. Heller, "Understanding Daily Citizenship Behaviors: A Social Comparison Approach," *Journal of Organizational Behavior* (May 2011), pp. 547–571; L. M. Little, D. L. Nelson, J. C. Wallace, and P. D. Johnson, "Integrating Attachment Style,

Vigor at Work, and Extra-Role Performance," *Journal of Organizational Behavior* (April 2011), pp. 464–484; N. P. Podsakoff, P. M. Podsakoff, S. W. Whiting, and P. Mishra, "Effects of Organizational Citizenship Behavior on Selection Decisions in Employment Interviews," *Journal of Applied Psychology* (March 2011), pp. 310–326; T. M. Glomb, D. P. Bhave, A. G. Miner, and M. Wall, "Doing Good, Feeling Good: Examining the Role of Organizational Citizenship Behaviors in Changing Mood," *Personnel Psychology,* Spring 2011, pp. 191–223; T. P. Munyon, W. A. Hochwarter, P. L. Perrewé, and G. R. Ferris, "Optimism and the Nonlinear Citizenship Behavior—Job Satisfaction Relationship in Three Studies," *Journal of Management* (November 2010), pp. 1505–1528; R. Ilies, B. A. Scott, and T. A. Judge, "The Interactive Effects of Personal Traits and Experienced States on Intraindividual Patterns of Citizenship Behavior," *Academy of Management Journal* (June 2006), pp. 561–575; P. Cardona, B. S. Lawrence, and P. M. Bentler, "The Influence of Social and Work Exchange Relationships on Organizational Citizenship Behavior," *Group & Organization Management,* April 2004, pp. 219–247; M. C. Bolino and W. H. Turnley, "Going the Extra Mile: Cultivating and Managing Employee Citizenship Behavior," *Academy of Management Executive,* August 2003, pp. 60–73; M. C. Bolino, W. H. Turnley, and J. J. Bloodgood, "Citizenship Behavior and the Creation of Social Capital in Organizations," *Academy of Management Review,* October 2002, pp. 505–522; and P. M. Podsakoff, S. B. MacKenzie, J. B. Paine, and D. G. Bachrach, "Organizational Citizenship Behaviors: A Critical Review of the Theoretical and Empirical Literature and Suggestions for Future Research," *Journal of Management,* 26, no. 3 (2000), pp. 543–548.

5. M. C. Bolino and W. H. Turnley, "The Personal Costs of Citizenship Behavior: The Relationship Between Individual Initiative and Role Overload, Job Stress, and Work-Family Conflict," *Journal of Applied Psychology* (July 2005), pp. 740–748.

6. This definition adapted from R. W. Griffin and Y. P. Lopez, "Bad Behavior in Organizations: A Review and Typology for Future Research," *Journal of Management* (December 2005), pp. 988–1005.

7. S. J. Becker, "Empirical Validation of Affect, Behavior, and Cognition as Distinct Components of Behavior," *Journal of Personality and Social Psychology* (May 1984), pp. 1191–1205.

8. "A Case of Cognitive Dissonance," *US News and World Report,* November 26, 2001, p. 10.

9. S. P. Robbins and T. A. Judge, *Essentials of Organizational Behavior,* 11th ed. (Upper Saddle River, NJ: Prentice Hall, 2010).

10. M. S. Christian, A. S. Garza, and J. E. Slaughter, "Work Engagement: A Quantitative Review and Test of Its Relations with Task and Contextual Performance," *Personnel Psychology,* Spring 2011, pp. 89–136; V. T. Ho, S-S Wong, and C. H. Lee, "A Tale of Passion: Linking Job Passion and Cognitive Engagement to Employee Work Performance," *Journal of Management Studies* (January 2011), pp. 26–47; D. R. May, R. L. Gilson, and L. M. Harter, "The Psychological Conditions of Meaningfulness, Safety and Availability and the Engagement of the Human Spirit at Work," *Journal of Occupational and Organizational Psychology* (March 2004), pp. 11–37; R. T. Keller, "Job Involvement and Organizational Commitment as Longitudinal Predictors of Job Performance: A Study of Scientists and Engineers," *Journal of Applied Psychology* (August 1997), pp. 539–545; W. Kahn, "Psychological Conditions

of Personal Engagement and Disengagement at Work," *Academy of Management Journal* (December 1990), pp. 692–794; and P. P. Brooke, Jr., D. W. Russell and J. L. Price, "Discriminant Validation of Measures of Job Satisfaction, Job Involvement, and Organizational Commitment," *Journal of Applied Psychology* (May 1988), pp. 139–145. Also, see, for example, J. Smythe, "Engaging Employees to Drive Performance," *Communication World,* May–June 2008, pp. 20–22; A. B. Bakker and W. B. Schaufeli, "Positive Organizational Behavior: Engaged Employees in Flourishing Organizations," *Journal of Organizational Behavior* (February 2008), pp. 147–154; U. Aggarwal, S. Datta, and S. Bhargava, "The Relationship Between Human Resource Practices, Psychological Contract, and Employee Engagement—Implications for Managing Talent," *IIMB Management Review,* September 2007, pp. 313–325; M. C. Christian and J. E. Slaughter, "Work Engagement: A Meta-Analytic Review and Directions for Research in an Emerging Area," *AOM Proceedings,* August 2007, pp. 1–6; C. H. Thomas, "A New Measurement Scale for Employee Engagement: Scale Development, Pilot Test, and Replication," *AOM Proceedings,* August 2007, pp. 1–6; A. M. Saks, "Antecedents and Consequences of Employee Engagement," *Journal of Managerial Psychology,* 21, no. 7 (2006), pp. 600–619; and A. Parsley, "Road Map for Employee Engagement," *Management Services,* Spring 2006, pp. 10–11.

11. Mercer, *IndustryWeek,* April 2008, p. 24.

12. J. M. George, "The Wider Context, Costs, and Benefits of Work Engagement," *European Journal of Work & Organizational Psychology* (February 2011), pp. 53–59; and "Employee Engagement Report 2011," *BlessingWhite Research,* http://www.blessingwhite.com/eee__report.asp (January 2011), pp. 7–8.

13. A. J. Elliott and P. G. Devine, "On the Motivational Nature of Cognitive Dissonance: Dissonance as Psychological Discomfort," *Journal of Personality and Social Psychology* (September 1994), pp. 382–394.

14. L. Festinger, *A Theory of Cognitive Dissonance* (Stanford, CA: Stanford University Press, 1957); C. Crossen, "Cognitive Dissonance Became a Milestone in 1950s Psychology," *Wall Street Journal,* December 4, 2006, p. B1; and Y. "Sally" Kim, "Application of the Cognitive Dissonance Theory to the Service Industry," *Services Marketing Quarterly,* April–June 2011, pp. 96–112.

15. H. C. Koh and E. H. Y. Boo, "The Link Between Organizational Ethics and Job Satisfaction: A Study of Managers in Singapore," *Journal of Business Ethics,* February 15, 2001, p. 309.

16. See, for example, W. D. Crano and R. Prislin, "Attitudes and Persuasion," *Annual Review of Psychology,* 2006, pp. 345–374; and J. Jermias, "Cognitive Dissonance and Resistance to Change: The Influence of Commitment Confirmation and Feedback on Judgment Usefulness of Accounting Systems." *Accounting, Organizations, and Society,* March 2001, p. 141.

17. And the Survey Says box based on "Employee Engagement Correlates to Career Advancement and Training," *T&D,* February 2011, p. 21; J. Yang and S. Ward, "My Feeling Toward My Job Is ..." *USA Today,* February 7, 2011, p. 1B; E. Spitznagel, "The Tragic Decline of Business Casual," *Bloomberg BusinessWeek,* October 11–17, 2010, pp. 94–95; B. M. Testa, "Multiskilled Employees Sought as Versatility Becomes a Workplace Virtue," *Workforce Management Online,* September 24, 2010; J. Yang and P. Trap, "Top Workplace Break Room Annoyances," *USA Today,* August 30, 2010, p. 1B; E. Frauenheim, "Recession Unleashes Boss Bullying," *Workforce*

Management Online, April 2010; S. Jayson, "A Detailed Look at Millennials," *USA Today,* February 24, 2010, p. 10B; and T. Janisch, "Digital Marketplace: Welcoming Gen Y to the Workforce," http://wisetechnology.com/articles (May 19, 2009).

18. T. A. Judge, C. J. Thoresen, J. E. Bono, and G. K. Patton, "The Job Satisfaction–Job Performance Relationship: A Qualitative and Quantitative Review," *Psychological Bulletin,* May 2001, pp. 376–407.

19. L. Saari and T. A. Judge, "Employee Attitudes and Job Satisfaction," *Human Resource Management,* Winter 2004, pp. 395–407; and T. A. Judge and A. H. Church, "Job Satisfaction: Research and Practice," in C. L. Cooper and E. A. Locke (eds.), *Industrial and Organizational Psychology: Linking Theory with Practice* (Oxford, UK: Blackwell, 2000).

20. D. A. Harrison, D. A. Newman, and P. L. Roth, "How Important Are Job Attitudes?: Meta-Analytic Comparisons of Integrative Behavioral Outcomes and Time Sequences," *Academy of Management Journal* (April 2006), pp. 305–325.

21. G. Chen, R. E. Ployhart, H. C. Thomas, N. Anderson, and P. D. Bliese, "The Power of Momentum: A New Model of Dynamic Relationships Between Job Satisfaction Change and Turnover Intentions," *Academy of Management Journal* (February 2011), pp. 159–181.

22. I. Arnsdorf, "No More New Kid on Campus," *Wall Street Journal,* August 5, 2010, pp. D1+.

23. CPP, Inc., Myers-Briggs Type Indicator® (MBTI®), http://www.cpp.com/products/mbti/index.asp (2011); and J. Llorens, "Taking Inventory of Myers-Briggs," *T&D,* April 2010, pp. 18–19.

24. Ibid.

25. See, for instance, J. Overbo, "Using Myers-Briggs Personality Type to Create a Culture Adapted to the New Century," *T&D,* February 2010, pp. 70–72; K. Garrety, R. Badham, V. Morrigan, W. Rifkin, and M. Zanko, "The Use of Personality Typing in Organizational Change: Discourse, Emotions, and the Reflective Subject," *Human Relations,* February 2003, pp. 211–235.

26. P. Moran, "Personality Characteristics and Growth-Orientation of the Small Business Owner Manager," *Journal of Managerial Psychology* (July 2000), p. 651; and M. Higgs, "Is There a Relationship Between the Myers-Briggs Type Indicator and Emotional Intelligence?" *Journal of Managerial Psychology* (September–October 2001), pp. 488–513.

27. J. M. Digman, "Personality Structure: Emergence of the Five Factor Model," in M. R. Rosenweig and L. W. Porter, eds., *Annual Review of Psychology,* vol. 41 (Palo Alto, CA: Annual Reviews, 1990), pp. 417–440; O. P. John, "The Big Five Factor Taxonomy: Dimensions of Personality in the Natural Language and in Questionnaires," in L. A. Pervin, ed., *Handbook of Personality Theory and Research* (New York: Guilford Press, 1990), pp. 66–100; and M. K. Mount, M. R. Barrick, and J. P. Strauss, "Validity of Observer Ratings of the Big Five Personality Factors," *Journal of Applied Psychology* (April 1996), pp. 272–280.

28. See, for example, T. W. Yiu and H. K. Lee, "How Do Personality Traits Affect Construction Dispute Negotiation: Study of Big Five Personality Model," *Journal of Construction Engineering & Management* (March 2011), pp. 169–178; H. J. Kell, A. D. Rittmayer, A. E. Crook, and S. J. Motowidlo, "Situational Content Moderates the Association Between the Big Five Personality Traits and Behavioral Effectiveness," *Human Performance,* February 2010, pp. 213–228; R. D. Meyer, R. S. Dalal, and S. Bonaccio, "A Meta-Analytic Investigation into the Moderating Effects of Situational Strength on the Conscientiousness–Performance Relationship," *Journal of Organizational Behavior* (November 2009), pp. 1077–1102; G. Vittorio, C. Barbaranelli, and G. Guido, "Brand Personality: How to Make the Metaphor Fit," *Journal of Economic Psychology* (June 2001), p. 377; G. M. Hurtz and J. J. Donovan, "Personality and Job Performance: The Big Five Revisited," *Journal of Applied Psychology* (December 2000), p. 869; W. A. Hochwarter, L. A. Witt, and K. M. Kacmar, "Perceptions of Organizational Politics as a Moderator of the Relationship Between Conscientiousness and Job Performance," *Journal of Applied Psychology* (June 2000), p. 472; and M. R. Barrick and M. K. Mount, "The Big Five Personality Dimensions and Job Performance: A Meta-Analytic Study," *Personnel Psychology* 44 (1991), pp. 1–26.

29. Barrick and Mount, "Autonomy as a Moderator of the Relationship Between the Big Five Personality Dimensions and Job Performance."

30. See also M. R. Furtner and J. F. Rauthmann, "Relations Between Self-Leadership and Scores on the Big Five," *Psychological Reports,* October 2010, pp. 339–353; R. Barrick, M. Piotrowski, and G. L. Stewart, "Personality and Job Performance: Test of the Mediating Effects of Motivation Among Sales Representatives," *Journal of Applied Psychology* (February 2002), pp. 43–52; and I. T. Robertson, H. Baron, P. Gibbons, R. MacIver, and G. Nyfield, "Conscientiousness and Managerial Performance," *Journal of Occupational and Organizational Psychology* (June 2000), pp. 171–78.

31. See, for example, J. L. Kisamore, I. M. Jawahar, E. W. Liguori, T. L. Mharapara, and T. H. Stone, "Conflict and Abusive Workplace Behaviors: The Moderating Effects of Social Competencies," *Career Development International,* October 2010, pp. 583–600; P. S. Mishra and A. K. Das Mohapatra, "Relevance of Emotional Intelligence for Effective Job Performance: An Empirical Study," *Vikalpa: The Journal for Decision Makers* (January–March 2010), pp. 53–61; T-Y. Kim, D. M. Cable, S-P. Kim, and J. Wang, "Emotional Competence and Work Performance: The Mediating Effect of Proactivity and the Moderating Effect of Job Autonomy," *Journal of Organizational Behavior* (October 2009), pp. 983–1000; J. M. Diefendorff and G. J. Greguras, "Contextualizing Emotional Display Rules: Examining the Roles of Targets and Discrete Emotions in Shaping Display Rule Perceptions," *Journal of Management* (August 2009), pp. 880–898; J. Gooty, M. Gavin, and N. M. Ashkanasy, "Emotions Research in OB: The Challenges That Lie Ahead," *Journal of Organizational Behavior* (August 2009), pp. 833–838; N. M. Ashkanasy and C. S. Daus, "Emotion in the Workplace: The New Challenge for Managers," *Academy of Management Executive,* February 2002, pp. 76–86; N. M. Ashkanasy, C. E. J. Hartel, and C. S. Daus, "Diversity and Emotions: The New Frontiers in Organizational Behavior Research," *Journal of Management,* 28, no. 3 (2002), pp. 307–338; S. Fox, "Promoting Emotional Intelligence in Organizations: Make Training in Emotional Intelligence Effective," *Personnel Psychology,* Spring 2002, pp. 236–240; B. E. Ashforth, "The Handbook of Emotional Intelligence: Theory, Development, Assessment, and Application at Home, School, and in the Work Place: A Review," *Personnel Psychology,* Autumn 2001, pp. 721–724; and R. Bar-On and J. D. A. Parker, *The Handbook of Emotional Intelligence: Theory, Development, Assessment, and Application at Home, School, and in the Work Place* (San Francisco, CA: Jossey-Bass, 2000).

32. See, for instance, C. S. P. Fernandez, "Emotional Intelligence in the Workplace," *Journal of Public Health Management and Practice* (February 2007), pp. 80–82.

33. R. Pearman, "The Leading Edge: Using Emotional Intelligence to Enhance Performance," *T&D,* March 2011, pp. 68–71; C. Prentice and B. King, "The Influence of Emotional Intelligence on the Service Performance of Casino Frontline Employees," *Tourism & Hospitality Research,* January 2011, pp. 49–66; E. H. O'Boyle, Jr., R. H. Humphrey, J. M. Pollack, T. H. Hawver, and P. A. Story, "The Relation Between Emotional Intelligence and Job Performance: A Meta-Analysis," *Journal of Organizational Behavior Online,* www.interscience.wiley.com, June 2010; and P. J. Jordan, N. M. Ashkanasy, and C. E. J. Hartel, "Emotional Intelligence as a Moderator of Emotional and Behavioral Reactions to Job Insecurity," *Academy of Management Review,* July 2002, pp. 361–372.

34. C. Cherniss and R. D. Caplan, "A Case Study of Implementing Emotional Intelligence Programs in Organizations," *Journal of Organizational Excellence* (Winter 2001), pp. 763–786; and S. B. Vanessa-Urch and W. Deuskat, "Building the Emotional Intelligence of Groups," *Harvard Business Review,* March 2001, pp. 81–91.

35. "Can't We All Just Get Along," *BusinessWeek,* October 9, 2000, p. 18.

36. C. Moller and S. Powell, "Emotional Intelligence and the Challenges of Quality Management," *Leadership and Organizational Development Journal* (July–August 2001), pp. 341–345.

37. See L.A. Downey, V. Papageorgiou, and C. Stough, "Examining the Relationship Between Leadership, Emotional Intelligence, and Intuition in Female Managers," *Leadership & Organization Development Journal* (April 2006), pp. 250–264.

38. Right or Wrong? box based on C. Mindrum, "The Twitching Organization," *Chief Learning Officer,* March 2011, pp. 20–25; M. Conlin, "Are People in Your Office Acting Oddly?" *BusinessWeek*, April 13, 2009, p. 54; and J. Hoffman, "Working Hard to Look Busy," *New York Times Online,* January 25, 2009.

39. See, for instance, J. Silvester, F. M. Anderson-Gough, N. R. Anderson, and A. R. Mohamed, "Locus of Control, Attributions and Impression Management in the Selection Interview," *Journal of Occupational and Organizational Psychology* (March 2002), pp. 59–77; D. W. Organ and C. N. Greene, "Role Ambiguity, Locus of Control, and Work Satisfaction," *Journal of Applied Psychology* (February 1974), pp. 101–102; and T. R. Mitchell, C. M. Smyser and S. E. Weed, "Locus of Control: Supervision and Work Satisfaction," *Academy of Management Journal* (September 1975), pp. 623–631.

40. I. Zettler, N. Friedrich, and B. E. Hilbig, "Dissecting Work Commitment: The Role of Machiavellianism," *Career Development International,* February 2011, pp. 20–35; S. R. Kessler, A. C. Bandelli, P. E. Spector, W. C. Borman, C. E. Nelson, and L. M. Penney, "Re-Examining Machiavelli: A Three-Dimensional Model of Machiavellianism in the Workplace," *Journal of Applied Social Psychology* (August 2010), pp. 1868–1896; W. Amelia, "Anatomy of a Classic: Machiavelli's Daring Gift," *Wall Street Journal,* August 30–31, 2008, p. W10; S. A. Snook, "Love and Fear and the Modern Boss, *Harvard Business Review,* January 2008, pp. 16–17; and R. G. Vleeming, "Machiavellianism: A Preliminary Review," *Psychology Reports,* February 1979, pp. 295–310.

41. P. Harris, "Machiavelli and the Global Compass: Ends and Means in Ethics and Leadership," *Journal of Business Ethics* (June 2010), pp. 131–138; and P. Van Kenhove, I. Vermeir, and S. Verniers, "An Empirical Investigation of the Relationship Between Ethical Beliefs, Ethical Ideology, Political Preference and Need for Closure," *Journal of Business Ethics,* August 15, 2001, p. 347.

42. Based on J. Brockner, *Self-Esteem at Work: Research, Theory, and Practice* (Lexington, MA: Lexington Books, 1988), chs. 1–4.

43. See, for instance, R. Vermunt, D. van Knippenberg, B. van Knippenberg, and E. Blaauw, "Self-Esteem and Outcome Fairness: Differential Importance of Procedural and Outcome Considerations," *Journal of Applied Psychology* (August 2001), p. 621; T. A. Judge and J. E. Bono, "Relationship of Core Self-Evaluation Traits—Self-Esteem, Generalized Self Efficacy, Locus of Control, and Emotional Stability—With Job Satisfaction and Job Performance," *Journal of Applied Psychology* (February 2001), p. 80; and D. B. Fedor, J. M. Maslyn, W. D. Davis, and K. Mathieson, "Performance Improvement Efforts in Response to Negative Feedback: The Roles of Source Power and Recipient Self-Esteem," *Journal of Management* (January–February 2001), pp. 79–97.

44. M. Snyder, *Public Appearances, Private Realities: The Psychology of Self-Monitoring* (New York: W. H. Freeman, 1987).

45. See, for example, D. U. Bryant, M. Mitcham, A. R. Araiza, and W. M. Leung, "The Interaction of Self-Monitoring and Organizational Position on Perceived Effort," *Journal of Managerial Psychology,* 26, no. 2 (2011), pp. 138–154; B. B. Vilela and J. A. V. González, "Salespersons' Self-Monitoring: Direct, Indirect, and Moderating Effects on Salespersons' Organizational Citizenship Behavior," *Psychology & Marketing,* January 2010, pp. 71–89; and P. M. Fandt, "Managing Impressions with Information: A Field Study of Organizational Realities," *Journal of Applied Behavioral Science* (June 2001), pp. 180–205.

46. Ibid.

47. R. N. Taylor and M. D. Dunnette, "Influence of Dogmatism, Risk Taking Propensity, and Intelligence on Decision Making Strategies for a Sample of Industrial Managers," *Journal of Applied Psychology* (August 1974), pp. 420–423.

48. I. L. Janis and L. Mann, *Decision Making: A Psychological Analysis of Conflict, Choice, and Commitment* (New York: Free Press, 1977).

49. See, for instance, C. P. Cross, L. T. Copping, and A. Campbell, "Sex Differences in Impulsivity: A Meta-Analysis," *Psychological Bulletin,* January 2011, pp. 97–130; A. A. Schooler, K. Fujita, X. Zou, and S. J. Stroessner, "When Risk Seeking Becomes a Motivational Necessity," *Journal of Personality and Social Psychology* (August 2010), pp. 215–231; A. Chatterjee and D. C. Hambrick, "Executive Personality, Capability Cues, and Risk-Taking: How Narcissistic CEOs React to Their Successes and Stumbles," *Academy of Management Proceedings,* www.aomonline.org (2010); E. Soane, C. Dewberry, and S. Narendran, "The Role of Perceived Costs and Perceived Benefits in the Relationship Between Personality and Risk-Related Choices," *Journal of Risk Research* (April 2010), pp. 303–318; and N. Kogan and M. A. Wallach, "Group Risk Taking as a Function of Members' Anxiety and Defensiveness," *Journal of Personality* (March 1967), pp. 50–63.

50. H. Zhao, S. E. Seibert, and G. T. Lumpkin, "The Relationship of Personality to Entrepreneurial Intentions and Performance: A Meta-Analytic Review," *Journal of Management*

(March 2010), pp. 381–404; and K. Hyrshy, "Entrepreneurial Metaphors and Concepts: An Exploratory Study," *Journal of Managerial Psychology* (July 2000), p. 653; and B. McCarthy, "The Cult of Risk Taking and Social Learning: A Study of Irish Entrepreneurs," *Management Decision,* August 2000, pp. 563–575.

51. M. Goldman, "A Journey into Personality Self-Discovery, Vol. 2," *Bloomberg BusinessWeek Online,* March 22, 2011; M. Goldman, "A Journey into Personality Self-Discovery, Vol. 1," *Bloomberg BusinessWeek Online,* February 15, 2011; and P. Korkki, "The True Calling That Wasn't," *New York Times Online,* July 16, 2010.

52. J. L. Holland, *Making Vocational Choices: A Theory of Vocational Personalities and Work Environments* (Odessa, FL: Psychological Assessment Resources, 1997).

53. S. Bates, "Personality Counts: Psychological Tests Can Help Peg the Job Applicants Best Suited for Certain Jobs," *HR Magazine,* February 2002, pp. 28–38; and K. J. Jansen and A. K. Brown, "Toward a Multi-Level Theory of Person Environment Fit," *Academy of Management Proceedings from the Fifty-Eighth Annual Meeting of the Academy of Management,* San Diego, CA (August 7–12, 1998), pp. HR: FR1–FR8.

54. See, for instance, G. W. M. Ip and M. H. Bond, "Culture, Values, and the Spontaneous Self-Concept," *Asian Journal of Psychology,* vol. 1 (1995), pp. 30–36; J. E. Williams, J. L. Saiz, D. L. FormyDuval, M. L. Munick, E. E. Fogle, A. Adom, A. Haque, F. Neto, and J. Yu, "Cross-Cultural Variation in the Importance of Psychological Characteristics: A Seven-Year Country Study," *International Journal of Psychology* (October 1995), pp. 529–550; V. Benet and N. G. Walker, "The Big Seven Factor Model of Personality Description: Evidence for Its Cross-Cultural Generalizability in a Spanish Sample," *Journal of Personality and Social Psychology* (October 1995), pp. 701–718; R. R. McCrae and P. To. Costa Jr., "Personality Trait Structure as a Human Universal," *American Psychologist,* 1997, pp. 509–516; and M. J. Schmit, J. A. Kihm, and C. Robie, "Development of a Global Measure of Personality," *Personnel Psychology,* Spring 2000, pp. 153–193.

55. J. F. Salgado, "The Five Factor Model of Personality and Job Performance in the European Community," *Journal of Applied Psychology* (February 1997), pp. 30–43. Note: This study covered the 15-nation European community and did not include the 10 countries that joined in 2004.

56. G. Kranz, "Organizations Look to Get Personal in '07," *Workforce Management,* www.workforce.com (June 19, 2007).

57. H. H. Kelley, "Attribution in Social Interaction," in E. Jones et al. (eds.), *Behavior* (Morristown, NJ: General Learning Press, 1972).

58. Advertisement for Land Rover Discovery Series II.

59. G. Miller and T. Lawson, "The Effect of an Informational Option on the Fundamental Attribution Error," *Personality and Social Psychology Bulletin,* June 1989, pp. 194–204. See also G. Charness and E. Haruvy, "Self-Serving Bias: Evidence from a Simulated Labour Relationship," *Journal of Managerial Psychology* (July 2000), p. 655; and T. J. Elkins, J. S. Phillips, and R. Konopaske, "Gender-Related Biases in Evaluations of Sex Discrimination Allegations: Is Perceived Threat a Key?" *Journal of Applied Psychology* (April 2002), pp. 280–293.

60. S. T. Fiske, "Social Cognition and Social Perception," *Annual Review of Psychology,* 1993, pp. 155–194; G. N. Powell and Y. Kido, "Managerial Stereotypes in a Global Economy: A Comparative Study of Japanese and American Business Students' Perspectives," *Psychological Reports,* February 1994, pp. 219–26; and J. L. Hilton and W. von Hippel, "Stereotypes," in J. T. Spence, J. M. Darley, and D. J. Foss (eds.), *Annual Review of Psychology,* vol. 47 (Palo Alto, CA: Annual Reviews Inc., 1996), pp. 237–271.

61. P. White, "Baseball Elders Teach Lessons of the Game," *USA Today,* April 14, 2009, p. 1C+.

62. B. F. Skinner, *Contingencies of Reinforcement* (East Norwalk, CT: Appleton-Century-Crofts, 1971).

63. From the Past to the Present box based on B. F. Skinner, *Contingencies of Reinforcement;* and S. P. Robbins and T. A. Judge, *Organizational Behavior,* 14th ed. (Upper Saddle River, NJ: Pearson Prentice Hall, 2011).

64. A. Applebaum, "Linear Thinking," *Fast Company,* December 2004, p. 35.

65. A. Bandura, *Social Learning Theory* (Upper Saddle River, NJ: Prentice Hall, 1977).

66. For an interesting article on the subject, see D. Nitsch, M. Baetz, and J. C. Hughes, "Why Code of Conduct Violations Go Unreported: A Conceptual Framework to Guide Intervention and Future Research," *Journal of Business Ethics* (April 2005), pp. 327–341.

67. R. J. Alsop, "The Last Word: Youth and Consequences," *Workforce Management Online,* February 2011; M. Fertik, "Managing Employees in Their Twenties," *Bloomberg BusinessWeek Online,* January 19, 2011; M. Richtel, "Growing Up Digital: Wired for Distraction," *New York Times Online,* November 21, 2010; N. Lublin, "In Defense of Millennials," *Fast Company,* October 2010, pp. 72–74; A. D. Wright and T. D. Tapscott, "Millennials: Bathed in Bits," *HR Magazine,* July 2010, pp. 40–41; S. Jayson, "A Detailed Look at Millennials;" T. Janisch, "Digital Marketplace: Welcoming Gen Y to the Workforce"; and S. Armour, "Generation Y: They've Arrived at Work with a New Attitude," *USA Today,* November 6, 2005, pp. 1B+.

68. N. Ramachandran, "New Paths at Work," *US News & World Report,* March 20, 2006, p. 47.

69. D. Sacks, "Scenes from the Culture Clash," *Fast Company,* January–February 2006, p. 75.

70. S. Armour, "Generation Y: They've Arrived at Work with a New Attitude," p. 2B.

71. S. Armour, "Generation Y: They've Arrived at Work with a New Attitude"; B. Moses, "The Challenges of Managing Gen Y," *The Globe and Mail,* March 11, 2005, p. C1; and C. A. Martin, *Managing Generation Y* (Amherst, MA: HRD Press, 2001).

72. C. M. Pearson and C. L. Porath, "On the Nature, Consequences, and Remedies of Workplace Incivility: No Time for Nice? Think Again," *Academy of Management Executive,* February 2005, pp. 7–18.

73. J. Robison, "Be Nice: It's Good for Business," *Gallup Brain,* http://brain.gallup.com (August 12, 2004).

74. M. Sandy Hershcovis and J. Barling, "Towards a Multi-Foci Approach to Workplace Aggression: A Meta-Analytic Review of Outcomes from Different Perpetrators," *Journal of Organizational Behavior* (January 2010), pp. 24–44; R. E. Kidwell and S. R. Valentine, "Positive Group Context, Work Attitudes, and Organizational Behavior: The Case of Withholding Job Effort," *Journal of Business Ethics* (April 2009), pp. 15–28; P. Bordia and S. L. D . Resubog, "When Employees Strike Back: Investigating Mediating Mechanisms Between Psychological Contract Breach and Workplace Deviance," *Journal of Applied Psychology* (September 2008), pp. 1104–1117; and Y. Vardi and E. Weitz, *Misbehavior in Organizations* (Mahwah, NJ: Lawrence Erlbaum Associates, 2004), pp. 246–247.

YOUR TURN TO BE A MANAGER

Foundations of Individual Behavior

Skill Development: Reading Emotions

Employees bring their emotions with them to work every day. Although managers would like to think that employees are always rational, they aren't. And any manager who deals with people by ignoring how emotions—such as fear, anger, love, hate, joy, and grief—shape employees' day-to-day behavior, isn't likely to be a very effective manager.

Personal Insights: What's My EI Score?

Indicate your level of agreement with these 10 statements using the following scale:

1 = Strongly disagree
2 = Disagree
3 = Neither agree or disagree
4 = Agree
5 = Strongly agree

1. I am usually aware—from moment to moment—of my feelings as they change.	1 2 3 4 5
2. I act before I think.	1 2 3 4 5
3. When I want something, I want it NOW!	1 2 3 4 5
4. I bounce back quickly from life's setbacks.	1 2 3 4 5
5. I can pick up subtle social cues that indicate others' needs or wants.	1 2 3 4 5
6. I'm very good at handling myself in social situations.	1 2 3 4 5
7. I'm persistent in going after the things I want.	1 2 3 4 5
8. When people share their problems with me, I'm good at putting myself in their shoes.	1 2 3 4 5
9. When I'm in a bad mood, I make a strong effort to get out of it.	1 2 3 4 5
10. I can find common ground and build rapport with people from all walks of life.	1 2 3 4 5

Source: Based on D. Goleman, *Emotional Intelligence: Why It Can Matter More Than IQ* (New York: Bantam Book, 1995).

Analysis and Interpretation

Emotional intelligence (EI) is an assortment of skills and competencies that have been shown to influence a person's ability to succeed in coping with environmental demands and pressures. People with high EI have the ability to accurately perceive, evaluate, express, and regulate emotions and feelings.

This questionnaire taps the five basic dimensions in EI: self-awareness (items 1 and 9), self-management (2, 4), self-motivation (3,7), empathy (5,8), and social skills (6,10). To calculate your EI score, add up your responses to the 10 items; however, reverse your scores for items 2 and 3.

Your score will fall between 10 and 50. Although no definite cutoff scores are available, scores of 40 or higher indicate a high EI. Scores of 20 or less suggest a relatively low EI.

EI may be most predictive of performance in jobs such as sales or management where success is as dependent on interpersonal skills as technical ability. EI should also be relevant in selecting members to teams. People with low EI are likely to have difficulty managing others, making effective sales presentations, and working on teams.

Skill Basics

Understanding another person's felt emotions is a difficult task. But we can learn to read others' display emotions. We do this by focusing on actual behavior as well as verbal, nonverbal, and paralinguistic cues.

1. *Assess others' emotional intelligence (EI).* Some people are more in touch with their emotions than others. Those who understand and can manage their emotions are said to be high in EI. When people exhibit the following behaviors, you should find that they have less variance in their emotions and are easier to read. People high in EI understand the way they feel (self-aware), are sensitive to the feelings of others (empathetic), voluntarily help others (socially responsible), see things the way they are rather than they way they wish them to be (reality-oriented), reach out to others and show concern for others' interests (sociable), and manage their frustrations and anger (impulse control).

2. *Ask about emotions.* The easiest way to find out what someone is feeling is to ask them. Saying something as simple as "Are you OK? What's the problem?" can frequently provide you with the information to assess an individual's emotional state. But relying on a verbal response has two drawbacks. First, almost all of us conceal our emotions to some extent for privacy and to reflect social expectations. So we might be unwilling to share our true feelings. Second, even if we want to convey our feelings verbally, we may be unable to do so. Some people have difficulty understanding their own emotions and, hence, are unable to express them verbally. So, at best, verbal responses provide only partial information.

3. *Look for nonverbal cues.* You're talking with a coworker. Does the fact that his back is rigid, his teeth clenched, and his facial muscles tight tell you something about his emotional state? It probably should. Facial expressions, gestures, body movements, and physical distance are nonverbal cues that can provide additional insights into what a person is feeling. Facial expressions, for instance, are a window into a person's feelings. Notice differences in facial features: the height of the cheeks, the raising or lowering of the brow, the turn of the mouth, the positioning of the lips, and the configuration of muscles around the eyes. Even something as subtle as the distance at which someone chooses to position him- or herself from you can convey their feelings, or lack, of intimacy, aggressiveness, repugnance, or withdrawal.

4. *Look for how things are said.* As Janet and I talked, I noticed a sharp change in the tone of her voice and the speed at which she spoke. I was tapping into the third source of information on a person's emotions—*paralanguage.* This is communication that goes beyond the specific spoken words. It includes pitch, amplitude, rate, and voice quality of speech. Paralanguage reminds us that people convey their feelings not only in *what* they say, but also in *how* they say it.

Based on V. P. Richmond, J. C. McCroskey, and S. K. Payne, *Nonverbal Behavior in Interpersonal Relations*, 2nd ed. (Englewood Cliffs, NJ: Prentice Hall, 1991), pp. 117–138; R. Bar-On, *The Emotional Intelligence Inventory (EQ-I): Technical Manual* (Toronto: Multi-Health Systems, 1997); L. A. King, "Ambivalence over Emotional Expression and Reading Emotions in Situations and Faces," *Journal of Personality and Social Psychology* (March 1998), pp. 753–762; and M. Lewis, J. M. Haviland-Jones, and L. F. Barrett (eds.), *Handbook of Emotions*, 3rd ed. (New York: Guilford Press, 2011).

Skill Application

Part A. Form groups of two. Each person is to spend a couple of minutes thinking (without sharing with the other person) of a time in the past when he or she was emotional about something. Examples might include being upset with a parent, sibling, or friend; being excited or disappointed about an academic or athletic achievement; being angry with someone over an insult or slight; being disgusted by something someone has said or done; or being happy because of something good that happened.

Part B. Now you'll conduct two role plays. Each will be an interview. In the first, one person will play the interviewer and the other will play the job applicant. The job is for a summer management internship with a large retail chain. Each role play will last no longer than 10 minutes. The interviewer is to conduct a normal job interview except you are to continually rethink the emotional episode you envisioned in Part A. Try hard to convey this emotion while, at the same time, being professional in interviewing the job applicant.

Part C. Now reverse positions for the second role play. The interviewer becomes the job applicant, and vice versa. The new interviewer will conduct a normal job interview except that he or she will continually rethink the emotional episode chosen in Part A.

Part D. Spend 10 minutes deconstructing the interview, with specific attention focused on what emotion(s) you think the other was conveying? What cues did you pick up? How accurate were you in reading those cues?

Skill Practice

1. Rent a video of an emotionally laden film such as *Death of a Salesman* or *Twelve Angry Men.* Carefully watch the actors for clues to the emotions they are exhibiting. Try to determine the various emotions projected and explain how you arrived at your conclusion.

2. If you're currently working, spend a day specifically looking for emotional cues in interactions with colleagues. How accurate do you think your assessments of those emotions were? What, if anything, did you see that you would normally miss?

Skill Development: Reading Personality

People are all different. And one way we differentiate people is by their personality traits. The more insight managers have to the personality of the people they need to work with—bosses, colleagues, subordinates, customers—the better job they can do. Why? Because they can adjust their behavior to reflect the characteristics of the person or persons with whom they have to work.

Personal Insights: What's My Basic Personality?

Listed here are 15 adjective pairs. For each, select the number along the scale (you must choose a whole number) that most closely describes you or your preferences.

		1	2	3	4	5	
1.	Quiet	1	2	3	4	5	Talkative
2.	Tolerant	1	2	3	4	5	Critical
3.	Disorganized	1	2	3	4	5	Organized
4.	Tense	1	2	3	4	5	Calm
5.	Imaginative	1	2	3	4	5	Conventional
6.	Reserved	1	2	3	4	5	Outgoing
7.	Uncooperative	1	2	3	4	5	Cooperative
8.	Unreliable	1	2	3	4	5	Dependable
9.	Insecure	1	2	3	4	5	Secure
10.	New	1	2	3	4	5	Familiar
11.	Sociable	1	2	3	4	5	Loner
12.	Suspicious	1	2	3	4	5	Trusting
13.	Undirected	1	2	3	4	5	Goal-oriented
14.	Enthusiastic	1	2	3	4	5	Depressed
15.	Change	1	2	3	4	5	Status quo

Source: Based on O. P. John, "The 'Big Five' Factor Taxonomy: Dimensions of Personality in the Natural Language and in Questionnaires," in L. A. Pervin (ed.), *Handbook of Personality Theory and Research* (New York: Guilford Press, 1990), pp. 66–100; and D. L. Formy-Duval, J. E. Williams, D. J. Patterson, and E. E. Fogle, "A 'Big Five' Scoring System for the Item Pool of the Adjective Check List," *Journal of Personality Assessment*, 65 (1995), pp. 59–76.

Analysis and Interpretation

The five-factor model of personality—often referred to as the Big Five—has an impressive body of research supporting that five basic personality dimensions underlie human behavior. These five dimensions are defined as follows:

Extraversion—Someone who is sociable, talkative, and assertive. High scores indicate you're an extravert; low scores indicate you're an introvert.

Agreeableness—Someone who is good-natured, cooperative, and trusting. It is a measure of your propensity to defer to others. High scores indicate you value harmony; low scores indicate you prefer having your say or way on issues.

Conscientiousness—Someone who is responsible, dependable, persistent, and achievement oriented. High scores indicate that you pursue fewer goals in a purposeful way; while low scores indicate that you're more easily distracted, pursue many goals, and are more hedonistic.

Emotional stability—Someone who is calm, enthusiastic, and secure. High scores indicate positive emotional stability, with low scores indicating negative emotional stability.

Openness to experience—Someone who is imaginative, artistically sensitive, and intellectual. High scores indicate you have a wide range of interests and a fascination with novelty and innovation; low scores indicate you're more conventional and find comfort in the familiar.

To calculate your personality score, add up your points as follows (reverse scoring those items marked with an asterisk):

Items 1, 6, and 11*. This is your extraversion score.
Items 2*, 7, and 12. This is your agreeableness score.
Items 3, 8, and 13. This is your conscientiousness score.
Items 4, 9, and 14*. This is your emotional stability score.
Items 5*, 10*, and 15*. This is your openness-to-experience score.

What defines a high or low score? No definite cutoffs are available. However, reasonable cutoffs for each dimension would be 12–15 points = high; 7–11 = moderate; and 3–6 = low.

The most impressive evidence relates to the conscientiousness dimension. Studies show that conscientiousness predicts job performance for all occupational groups. The preponderance of evidence indicates that individuals who are dependable, reliable, thorough, organized, able to plan, and persistent (that is, high on conscientiousness) tend to have higher job performance in most if not all occupations. In addition, individuals who score high in conscientiousness develop higher levels of job knowledge, probably because highly conscientious people exert greater levels of effort on their job. The higher levels of job knowledge then contribute to higher levels of job performance.

Other insights from your scores: High scores on extraversion indicate you may be suited to a managerial or sales position.

These occupations require high social interaction. And high scores on openness-to-experience is a good predictor of your ability to achieve significant benefits from training efforts.

Skill Basics

Ideally, it would be nice to know the personality characteristics of individuals we have to deal with in our jobs. It would allow us to better communicate and help us predict responses to our actions. Unfortunately, people don't come with ID tags identifying their personality traits. And we don't typically have the luxury of testing them to have a reliable measure of those traits. So we're usually forced to try to make sense of others' personality characteristics through observations. With the caveat that these observations are likely to be poor substitutes for a more objective, questionnaire-based assessment, the following should help you to gain insights into others' personality:

- Is the person more extroverted and enthusiastic or reserved and quiet? This question taps the dimension of extroversion.
- Is the person more critical and quarrelsome or sympathetic and warm? This question taps the dimension of agreeableness.
- Is the person dependable and self-disciplined or disorganized and careless? This question taps the dimension of conscientiousness.
- Is the person more anxious and easily upset or calm and emotionally stable? This question taps the dimension of emotional stability.
- Is the person more open to new experiences and complex or conventional and uncreative? This question taps the dimension of openness to experience.

Based on S. D. Gosling, P. J. Rentfrow, and W. B. Swann Jr., "A Very Brief Measure of the Big-Five Personality Domains," *Journal of Research in Personality* (December 2003), pp. 504–528; and P. Y. Herzberg and E. Brahler, "Assessing the Big-Five Personality Domains via Short Forms: A Cautionary Note and a Proposal," *European Journal of Psychological Assessment*, 23, no. 3 (2006), pp. 139–148.

Skill Application

Form into teams of three. Each team is to identify four well-known people (film stars, television personalities, business executives, local celebrities) with whom all members of the team feel familiar. The team will then analyze each of these people in terms of how they would describe his or her personality. Team members should be able to provide specific behavioral examples to support their personality assessment.

How much agreement was there among team members in assessing each personality? Where was there disagreement? To what degree did this exercise support the view that it's possible to read personality traits?

Skill Practice

1. Identify a person you know well and with whom you feel comfortable sharing intimate information. Assess that person's personality using the preceding questions. Now share that assessment with the individual. To what degree did the person agree or disagree with your assessment? "It's easier to accurately rate the traits of celebrities than your normal work colleagues, friends, or relatives because they tend toward extremes." Do you agree or disagree with this statement and why?

2. How would you rate yourself on the five personality traits? Ask four or five of your friends to also rate you. How closely did the ratings match? Based on your personality profile, what jobs do you think you're well suited for? What jobs do you think would be a poor fit with your personality traits?

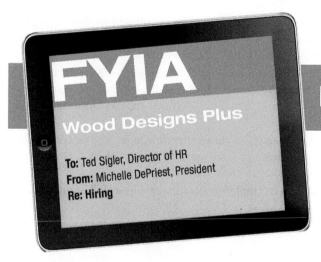

FYIA
Wood Designs Plus

To: Ted Sigler, Director of HR
From: Michelle DePriest, President
Re: Hiring

For Your Immediate Action

Ted, as we discussed last Friday, our manufacturing operations have grown to the point where we need to add a couple of people to our executive team; specifically, a corporate controller and a national sales director. The controller will be responsible for establishing operational and financial standards (in other words, a lot of number-crunching using financial and manufacturing statistics) for our various work units. The national sales director will be responsible for working closely with our sales staff to further develop long-lasting and mutually beneficial relationships with our customers.

I recall something from a management class I took in college that certain personality types fit best with certain types of jobs. Could you do some research on this topic for me? Write up a short report (no more than a page) describing the personality type that might be an appropriate match for each of these new positions. Get this to me by the end of the week.

This fictionalized company and message were created for educational purposes only, and not meant to reflect positively or negatively on management practices by any company that may share this name.

Bringing the Real World to Life

Case Application:
Employees First: Part 2

HCL Technologies is headquartered in the world's largest democracy, so it's quite fitting that the New Delhi—based company is attempting a radical experiment in workplace democracy. CEO Vineet Nayar is committed to creating a company where the job of company leaders is to enable people to find their own destiny by gravitating to their strengths. As we discussed in the chapter opener, one thing that Nayar has done is to pioneer a culture in which employees are first. What has he done to put employees first? Part of the cultural initiative dealt with the organization's structure. HCL inverted its organizational structure and placed more power in the hands of frontline employees, especially those in direct contact with customers and clients. It increased its investment in employee development and improved communication through greater transparency. Employees were encouraged to communicate directly with Nayar. Through a forum called U&I (You and I), Nayar fielded more than a hundred questions from employees every week. "I threw open the door and invited criticism," he said. However, the signature piece of the company's cultural mission is probably what HCL called "trust pay." In contrast to the industry standard in which the average employee's pay is 30 percent variable, HCL decided to pay higher fixed salaries and reduce the variable component.

Does the unique "employees first" culture at HCL Technologies attract unique employees? Rajeev Sawhney, HCL's European president would say it does. He uses *Slumdog Millionaire,* the movie that won the Academy Award for Best Picture in 2009, as a parallel. "It (the movie) is a reflection of the Indian race. It shows the adversity that creates the desire in people to reach out and create. . . . With each adversity they face, there is a greater desire to reach out and do something more." Sawhney says that entrepreneurialism is a key value of the HCL culture. "You can still tell an HCL person from a mile off. I think there is a particular DNA for an HCL person.

It includes a very high need for achievement and very persuasive skills. HCL people are very energetic; they want to do lots of things and to take risks on behalf of the company."

DISCUSSION QUESTIONS

1. What is your impression of an "employees first" culture? Would this work in other organizations? Why or why not? What would it take to make it work?

2. How might an understanding of organizational behavior help CEO Vineet Nayar lead his company? Be specific. How about first-line company supervisors? Again, be specific.

3. What aspects of personality do you see in this story about HCL? How have the personality traits of HCL employees contributed to make HCL what it is?

4. Design an employee attitude survey for HCL's employees.

Understanding Groups and Managing Work Teams

Understanding Groups and Managing Work Teams

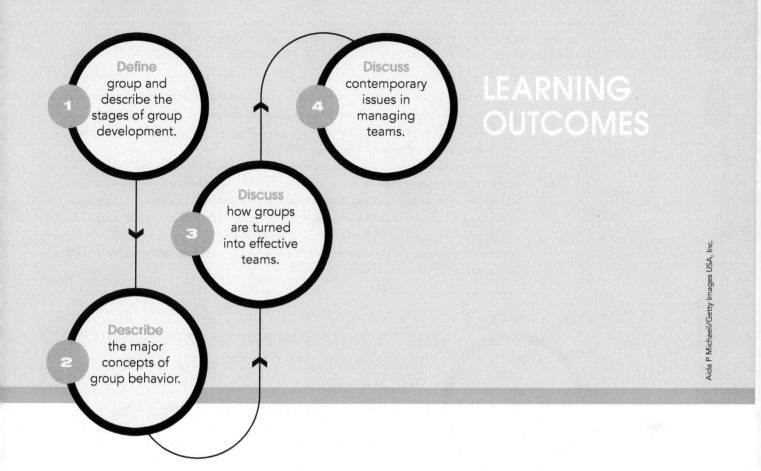

Aida P Michaeli/Getty Images USA, Inc.

LEARNING OUTCOMES

1 Define group and describe the stages of group development.

2 Describe the major concepts of group behavior.

3 Discuss how groups are turned into effective teams.

4 Discuss contemporary issues in managing teams.

Intel Inside...and Far Away

Located in Haifa on the Mediterranean coast, Intel's Israel Development Center was established in 1974 as the company's first development center outside the United States.[1] As the world's largest semiconductor manufacturer, Intel's components are used in more than 80 percent of the world's desktop and notebook computers and computer servers. Its technological capabilities are known the world over. For instance, a Russian bus manufacturer shortened vehicle development cycles and boosted product quality using Intel-based servers. Telecommunications provider Telefónica used Intel processors to launch its cloud services. And footwear company Adidas turned to Intel to help it create a virtual footwear wall. The Israeli team of engineers has been instrumental in developing many of the company's most successful innovations. The group has been described as having a "strong culture of debate and confrontation. Sometimes too much." However, a major challenge for this design group has been the geographical distance between it and other Intel design groups. Yet, Intel's managers have found ways to keep the teams connected and the innovations flowing.

Like company executives at Intel, managers today believe that the use of teams allows their organizations to increase sales or produce better products faster and at lower costs. Although the effort to create teams isn't always successful, well-planned teams can reinvigorate productivity and better position an organization to deal with a rapidly changing environment.

You've probably had a lot of experience working in groups—class project teams, maybe an athletic team, a fundraising committee, or even a sales team at work. Work teams are one of the realities—and challenges—of managing in today's dynamic global environment. Many organizations have made the move to restructure work around teams rather than individuals. Why? What do these teams look like? And how can managers build effective teams? These are some of the questions we'll be answering in this chapter. Before we can understand teams, however, we first need to understand some basics about groups and group behavior.

1 Define group and describe the stages of group development.

WHAT IS A GROUP AND WHAT STAGES OF DEVELOPMENT DO GROUPS GO THROUGH?

Each person in the group had his or her assigned role: The Spotter, the Back Spotter, the Gorilla, and the Big Player. For over 10 years, this group—former MIT students who were members of a secret Black Jack Club—used their extraordinary mathematical abilities, expert training, teamwork, and interpersonal skills to take millions of dollars from some of the major casinos in the United States.[2] Although most groups aren't formed for such dishonest purposes, the success of this group at its task was impressive. Managers would like their work groups to be successful at their tasks also. The first step is understanding what a group is and how groups develop.

What Is a Group?

A group is defined as two or more interacting and interdependent individuals who come together to achieve specific goals. *Formal groups* are work groups that are defined by the organization's structure and have designated work assignments and specific tasks directed at accomplishing organizational goals. Exhibit 1 provides some examples. *Informal groups* are social groups. These groups occur naturally in the workplace and tend to form around friendships and common interests. For example, five employees from different departments who regularly eat lunch together are an informal group.

EXHIBIT 1   Examples of Formal Work Groups

- **Command groups**—Groups that are determined by the organization chart and composed of individuals who report directly to a given manager.

- **Task groups**—Groups composed of individuals brought together to complete a specific job task; their existence is often temporary because when the task is completed, the group disbands.

- **Cross-functional teams**—Groups that bring together the knowledge and skills of individuals from various work areas or groups whose members have been trained to do each other's jobs.

- **Self-managed teams**—Groups that are essentially independent and that, in addition to their own tasks, take on traditional managerial responsibilities, such as hiring, planning and scheduling, and evaluating performance.

EXHIBIT 2   Stages of Group Development

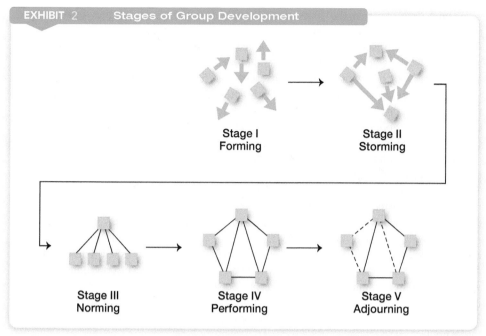

Stage I
Forming

Stage II
Storming

Stage III
Norming

Stage IV
Performing

Stage V
Adjourning

What Are the Stages of Group Development?

Research shows that groups develop through five stages.[3] As shown in Exhibit 2, these five stages are: *forming, storming, norming, performing,* and *adjourning.*

The forming stage has two phases. The first occurs as people join the group. In a formal group, people join because of some work assignment. Once they've joined, the second phase begins: defining the group's purpose, structure, and leadership. This phase involves a great deal of uncertainty as members "test the waters" to determine what types of behavior are acceptable. This stage is complete when members begin to think of themselves as part of a group.

The storming stage is appropriately named because of the intragroup conflict. There's conflict over who will control the group and what the group needs to be doing. When this stage is complete, a relatively clear hierarchy of leadership and agreement on the group's direction will be evident.

The norming stage is one in which close relationships develop and the group becomes cohesive. The group now demonstrates a strong sense of group identity and camaraderie. This stage is complete when the group structure solidifies and the group has assimilated a common set of expectations (or norms) regarding member behavior.

These assembly-line workers at the Samsung Electronics Company's factory in Gumi, South Korea, proudly display the company's new Galaxy S2 mobile phones they produce. The figure of 1 million marks the number of units sold just one month after the phone's release. This group of young women is an example of the performing stage of group development. As they work together they have a strong sense of group identity and camaraderie and focus their energies on their task of assembling the smartphones to meet the demands of the marketplace. For permanent work groups such as these assembly-line employees, performing is the last stage in the group development process

Newscom

---

group
Two or more interacting and interdependent individuals who come together to achieve specific goals

forming stage
The first stage of group development in which people join the group and then define the group's purpose, structure, and leadership

storming stage
The second stage of group development, which is characterized by intragroup conflict

norming stage
The third stage of group development, which is characterized by close relationships and cohesiveness

The fourth stage is the **performing stage**. The group structure is in place and accepted by group members. Their energies have moved from getting to know and understand each other to working on the group's task. This is the last stage of development for permanent work groups. However, for temporary groups—project teams, task forces, or similar groups that have a limited task to do—the final stage is the **adjourning stage**. In this stage, the group prepares to disband. Attention is focused on wrapping up activities instead of task performance. Group members react in different ways. Some are upbeat, thrilled about the group's accomplishments. Others may be sad over the loss of camaraderie and friendships.

Many of you have probably experienced these stages as you've worked on a group project for a class. Group members are selected or assigned and then meet for the first time. There's a "feeling out" period to assess what the group is going to do and how it's going to be done. This is usually followed by a battle for control: Who's going to be in charge? Once this issue is resolved and a "hierarchy" agreed on, the group identifies specific work that needs to be done, who's going to do each part of the project, and dates by which the assigned work needs to be completed. General expectations are established. These decisions form the foundation for what you hope will be a coordinated group effort culminating in a project that's been done well. Once the project is complete and turned in, the group breaks up. Of course, some groups don't get much beyond the forming or storming stages. These groups may have serious interpersonal conflicts, turn in disappointing work, and get lower grades.

Does a group become more effective as it progresses through the first four stages? Some researchers say yes, but it's not that simple.[5] That assumption may be generally true, but what makes a group effective is a complex issue. Under some conditions, high levels of conflict are conducive to high levels of group performance. There might be situations in which groups in the storming stage outperform those in the norming or performing stages. Also, groups don't always proceed sequentially from one stage to the next. Sometimes, groups are storming and performing at the same time. Groups even occasionally regress to previous stages. Therefore, don't assume that all groups precisely follow this process or that performing is always the most preferable stage. Think of this model as a general framework that underscores the fact that groups are dynamic entities and managers need to know the stage a group is in so they can understand the problems and issues that are most likely to surface.

2 Describe the major concepts of group behavior.

WHAT ARE THE MAJOR CONCEPTS OF GROUP BEHAVIOR?

The basic foundation for understanding group behavior includes roles, norms and conformity, status systems, group size, and group cohesiveness. Let's take a closer look at each of those aspects.

What Are Roles?

Managers aren't the only individuals in an organization who have roles. The concept of roles applies to all employees in organizations and to their lives outside the organization as well.

A **role** refers to behavior patterns expected of someone who occupies a given position in a social unit. Individuals play multiple roles, adjusting their roles to the group to which they belong at the time. In an organization, employees attempt to determine what behaviors are expected of them. They read their job descriptions, get suggestions from their bosses, and watch what their coworkers do. An individual who's confronted by divergent role expectations experiences role conflict. Employees in organizations often face such role conflicts. The credit manager expects her credit analysts to process a minimum of 30 applications a week, but the work group pressures members to restrict output to

20 applications a week so that everyone has work to do and no one gets laid off. A newly hired college instructor's colleagues want him to give out only a few high grades in order to maintain the department's reputation for high standards, whereas students want him to give out lots of high grades to enhance their grade point averages. To the degree that the instructor sincerely seeks to satisfy the expectations of both his colleagues and his students, he faces role conflict.

How Do Norms and Conformity Affect Group Behavior?

All groups have established norms, acceptable standards that are shared by the group's members. Norms dictate output levels, absenteeism rates, promptness or tardiness, the amount of socializing allowed on the job, and so on. Norms, for example, dictate the dress code of customer service representatives at a credit card processing company. Most workers who have little direct customer contact come to work dressed casually. However, on occasion, a newly hired employee will come to work dressed in a suit. Those who do are teased and pressured until their dress conforms to the group's standard.

Although each group has its own unique set of norms, common classes of norms appear in most organizations. These norms focus on effort and performance, dress, and loyalty. Probably the most widespread norms are related to levels of *effort and performance*. Work groups typically provide their members with explicit cues on how hard to work, what level of output to have, when to look busy, when it's acceptable to goof off, and the like. These norms are extremely powerful in affecting an individual employee's performance. They're so powerful that performance predictions based solely on an employee's ability and level of personal motivation often prove wrong.

Some organizations have formal *dress codes*—even describing what's considered acceptable for corporate casual dress. However, even in the absence of codes, norms frequently develop to dictate the kind of clothing that should be worn to work. College seniors, when interviewing for their first postgraduate job, pick up this norm quickly. Every spring, on college campuses around the country, students interviewing for jobs can be spotted; they're the ones walking around in the dark gray or blue pinstriped suits. They're enacting the dress norms they've learned are expected in professional positions. Of course, acceptable dress in one organization will be different from another's norms.

Few managers appreciate employees who ridicule the organization. Similarly, professional employees and those in the executive ranks recognize that most employers view persons who actively look for another job unfavorably. People who are unhappy know that they should keep their job searches secret. These examples demonstrate that *loyalty norms* are widespread in organizations. This concern for demonstrating loyalty, by the way, often explains why ambitious aspirants to top management positions

RIGHT ? WRONG
OR

When coworkers work closely on a team project, is there such a thing as TMI (too much information)?[6] At one company, a team that had just finished a major project went out to lunch to celebrate. During lunch, one colleague mentioned that he was training for a 20-mile bike race. In addition to a discussion of his new helmet and Lycra shorts, the person also described shaving his whole body to reduce aerodynamic drag. Afterwards, another team member said, "Why, why, why do we need to go there? This is information about a coworker, not someone I really consider a friend, and now it's forever burned in my brain."

Think About:

- What do you think? Why are work colleagues sharing increasingly personal information?

- What benefits/drawbacks arise from sharing information like this?

- How have social media and technology contributed to this type of information disclosure?

- What are the ethical implications of sharing such personal information in the workplace?

Thinkstock

---

performing stage
The fourth stage of group development, when the group is fully functional and works on the group task

adjourning stage
The final stage of group development for temporary groups, during which groups prepare to disband

role
Behavior patterns expected of someone who occupies a given position in a social unit

norms
Standards or expectations that are accepted and shared by a group's members

From the Past to the Present

Does the desire to be accepted as a part of a group leave one susceptible to conforming to the group's norms? Will the group exert pressure that's strong enough to change a member's attitude and behavior? According to the research by Solomon Asch, the answer appears to be yes.[7]

Asch's study involved groups of seven or eight people who sat in a classroom and were asked to compare two cards held by an investigator. One card had one line; the other had three lines of varying length. As shown in Exhibit 3, one of the lines on the three-line card was identical to the line on the one-line card. The difference in line length was quite obvious; under ordinary conditions, subjects made errors of less than 1 percent. The object was to announce aloud which of the three lines matched the single line. But what happens if all the members of the group begin to give incorrect answers? Will the pressure to conform cause the unsuspecting subject (USS) to alter his or her answers to align with those of the others? That's what Asch wanted to know. He arranged the group so that the USS was unaware that the experiment was fixed. The seating was prearranged so that the USS was the last to announce his or her decision.

The experiment began with two sets of matching exercises. All the subjects gave the right answers. On the third set, however, the first subject gave an obviously wrong answer—for example, saying C in Exhibit 3. The next subject gave the same wrong answer, and so did the others, until it was the unsuspecting subject's turn. He knew that "B" was the same as "X" but everyone else said "C."

The decision confronting the USS was this: Do you publicly state a perception that differs from the pre-announced position of the others? Or do you give an answer that you strongly believe to be incorrect in order to have your response agree with the other group members? Asch's subjects conformed in about 35 percent of many experiments and many trials. That is, the subjects gave answers that they knew were wrong but were consistent with the replies of other group members.

For managers, the Asch study provides considerable insight into group behaviors. The tendency, as Asch showed, is for individual members to go along with the pack. To diminish the negative aspects of conformity, managers should create a climate of openness in which employees are free to discuss problems without fear of retaliation.

Think About:

- DOES the desire to be accepted as a part of a group leave one susceptible to conforming to the group's norms? WILL a group exert pressure that's strong enough to change a member's attitude and behavior? What do YOU think?

- Think of groups that you've been part of (work or school). Were there times when you felt pressured to conform or when you pressured others to conform? What possible consequences (think in terms of people *and* outcomes) resulted or could have resulted?

- What can you use from this discussion to help you be a better manager?

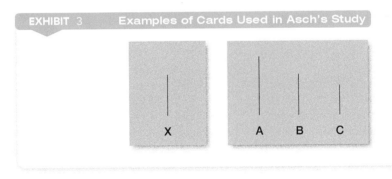

EXHIBIT 3   Examples of Cards Used in Asch's Study

willingly take work home at night, come in on weekends, and accept transfers to cities in which they would otherwise prefer not to live. Because individuals desire acceptance by the groups to which they belong, they're susceptible to conformity pressures. The impact of group pressures for conformity on an individual member's judgment and attitudes was demonstrated in the classic studies by Solomon Asch.[8] Asch's results suggest that group norms press us toward conformity. We desire to be one of the group and to avoid being visibly different. We can generalize this finding to say that when an individual's opinion of objective data differs significantly from that of others in the group, he or she feels extensive pressure to align his or her opinion to conform with those of the others. The From the Past to the Present, box has additional background information on Asch's contributions to group theory.

What Is Status and Why Is It Important?

Status is a prestige grading, position, or rank within a group. As far back as scientists have been able to trace human groupings, they've found status hierarchies: tribal chiefs and their followers, nobles and peasants, the haves and the have-nots. Status systems are important factors in understanding behavior. Status is a significant motivator that has behavioral consequences when individuals see a disparity between what they perceive their status to be and what others perceive it to be.

Status may be informally conferred by characteristics such as education, age, skill, or experience. However, anything can have status value if others in the group admire it. Of course, just because status is informal doesn't mean that it's unimportant or that there's disagreement on who has it or who doesn't. Members of groups have no problem placing people into status categories, and they usually agree about who's high, low, and in the middle.

It's important for employees to believe that the organization's formal status system is congruent. That is, there should be equity between the perceived ranking of an individual and the status symbols he or she is given by the organization. For instance, incongruence may occur when a supervisor earns less than his or her employees or when a desirable office is occupied by a lower-ranking individual. Employees may view such cases as a disruption to the general pattern of order and consistency in the organization.

Does Group Size Affect Group Behavior?

The size of a group affects that group's behavior. However, that effect depends on what criteria you're looking at.[9]

The evidence indicates, for instance, that small groups complete tasks faster than larger ones. However, if a group is engaged in problem solving, large groups consistently get better marks than their smaller counterparts. Translating these results into specific numbers is a bit trickier, but we can offer some parameters. Large groups—with a dozen or more members—are good for gaining diverse input. Thus, if the goal of the group is to find facts, larger groups should be more effective. On the other hand, smaller groups are better at doing something productive with those facts. Groups of approximately five to seven members tend to act more effectively.

One of the more disturbing findings is that, as groups get incrementally larger, the contribution of individual members often tends to lessen. That is, although the total productivity of a group of four is generally greater than that of a group of three, the individual productivity of each group member declines as the group expands. Thus, a group of four will tend to produce at a level of less than four times the average individual performance. The best explanation for this reduction of effort is that dispersion of responsibility encourages individuals to slack off; a behavior referred to as social loafing[10] When the results of the group can't be attributed to any single person, the relationship between an individual's input and the group's output is clouded. In such situations, individuals may be tempted to become "free riders" and coast on the group's efforts. In other words, efficiency is reduced when individuals think that their contributions cannot be measured. The obvious conclusion from this finding is that managers who use work groups should also provide a means by which individual efforts can be identified.

Are Cohesive Groups More Effective?

Intuitively, it makes sense that groups that experience a lot of internal disagreement and lack of cooperation are less effective than are groups in which individuals generally agree, cooperate, and like each other. Research has looked at group cohesiveness, the degree to which members are attracted to one another and share the

Group cohesiveness is high for the musical director and musicians of the Chicago Symphony Orchestra (CSO). Maestro Riccardo Muti (center) and the musicians of the orchestra share the group's goals of bringing unparalleled musical experiences to its audiences, preserving the legacy of symphonic music, and providing opportunities for everyone to have access to the art form. They also share the belief that the power of the music they perform can transform lives and communities, enact social change, and transcend cultural divides. As a highly cohesive group, the CSO is associated with excellent performances for audiences in Chicago and in musical venues around the world.

Todd Rosenberg/AP Images

---

status
A prestige grading, position, or rank within a group

social loafing
The tendency for individuals to expend less effort when working collectively than when working individually

group cohesiveness
The degree to which group members are attracted to one another and share the group's goals

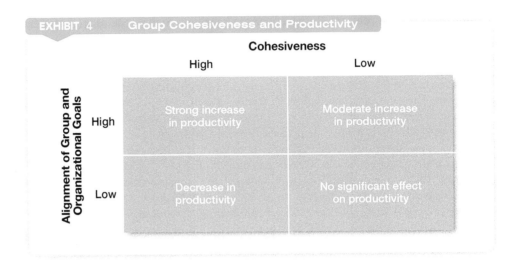

group's goals. The more that members are attracted to one another and the more that a group's goals align with each individual's goals, the greater the group's cohesiveness.

Previous research has generally shown that highly cohesive groups are more effective than are those with less cohesiveness, but the relationship between cohesiveness and effectiveness is more complex.[11] A key moderating variable is the degree to which the group's attitude aligns with its formal goals or those of the larger organization.[12] The more cohesive a group is, the more its members will follow its goals. If these goals are favorable (for instance, high output, quality work, cooperation with individuals outside the group), a cohesive group is more productive than a less cohesive group. But if cohesiveness is high and attitudes are unfavorable, productivity decreases. If cohesiveness is low and goals are supported, productivity increases, but not as much as when both cohesiveness and support are high. When cohesiveness is low and goals are not supported, cohesiveness has no significant effect on productivity. These conclusions are summarized in Exhibit 4.

HOW ARE GROUPS TURNED INTO EFFECTIVE TEAMS?

3 Discuss how groups are turned into effective teams.

When companies like W. L. Gore, Volvo, and Kraft Foods introduced teams into their production processes, it made news because no one else was doing it. Today, it's just the opposite—the organization that *doesn't* use teams would be newsworthy. It's estimated that some 80 percent of *Fortune* 500 companies have at least half of their employees on teams. In fact, more than 70 percent of U.S. manufacturers use work teams.[13] Teams are likely to continue to be popular. Why? Research suggests that teams typically outperform individuals when the tasks being done require multiple skills, judgment, and experience.[14] Organizations are using team-based structures because they've found that teams are more flexible and responsive to changing events than are traditional departments or other permanent work groups. Teams have the ability to quickly assemble, deploy, refocus, and disband. In this section, we'll discuss what a work team is, the different types of teams that organizations might use, and how to develop and manage work teams.

Are Work Groups and Work Teams the Same?

At this point, you may be asking yourself: Are teams and groups the same thing? No. In this section, we clarify the difference between a work group and a work team.[15]

Most of you are probably familiar with teams especially if you've watched or participated in organized sports events. Work *teams* do differ from work *groups* and have their own unique traits (see Exhibit 5). Work groups interact primarily to share information and to

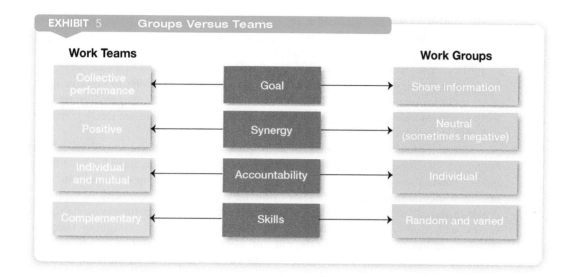

EXHIBIT 5   Groups Versus Teams

Work Teams		Work Groups
Collective performance	Goal	Share information
Positive	Synergy	Neutral (sometimes negative)
Individual and mutual	Accountability	Individual
Complementary	Skills	Random and varied

make decisions to help each member do his or her job more efficiently and effectively. There's no need or opportunity for work groups to engage in collective work that requires joint effort. On the other hand, work teams are groups whose members work intensely on a specific, common goal using their positive synergy, individual and mutual accountability, and complementary skills.

These descriptions should help clarify why so many organizations have restructured work processes around teams. Managers are looking for that positive synergy that will help the organization improve its performance.[16] The extensive use of teams creates the potential for an organization to generate greater outputs with no increase in (or even fewer) inputs. For example, until the economic downturn hit, investment teams at Wachovia's Asset Management Division (which is now a part of Wells Fargo & Company) were able to significantly improve investment performance. As a result, these teams helped the bank improve its Morningstar financial rating.[17]

Recognize, however, that such increases are simply "potential." Nothing inherently magical in the creation of work teams guarantees that this positive synergy and its accompanying productivity will occur. Accordingly, merely calling a group a team doesn't automatically increase its performance.[18] As we show later in this chapter, successful or high-performing work teams have certain common characteristics. If managers hope to gain increases in organizational performance, it will need to ensure that its teams possess those characteristics.

What Are the Different Types of Work Teams?

Teams can do a variety of things. They can design products, provide services, negotiate deals, coordinate projects, offer advice, and make decisions.[19] For instance, at Rockwell Automation's facility in North Carolina, teams are used in work process optimization projects. At Arkansas-based Acxiom Corporation, a team of human resource professionals planned and implemented a cultural

Team-based work is a key ingredient to the success of Facebook. Throughout the company, small work teams that require multiple skills, judgment, and experience work on a specific, common goal in creating new products and finding solutions for problems. For Facebook, work teams are more flexible and responsive to the company's dynamic business environment than are individuals, traditional departments, or other permanent work groups. Facebook's security team shown in this photo includes Max Kelly (standing in front), head of Internet security, and other team members whose task is to filter inappropriate content on the site. The team stands in front of the "Wall of Shame," a wall that highlights unusual correspondence and postings on the site.

David Butow/Redux Pictures

work teams
Groups whose members work intensely on specific, common goals using their positive synergy, individual and mutual accountability, and complementary skills

change. And every summer weekend at any NASCAR race, you can see work teams in action during drivers' pit stops.[20] The four most common types of work teams are problem-solving teams, self-managed work teams, cross-functional teams, and virtual teams.

When work teams first became popular, most were problem-solving teams, which are teams from the same department or functional area involved in efforts to improve work activities or to solve specific problems. Members share ideas or offer suggestions on how work processes and methods can be improved. However, these teams are rarely given the authority to implement any of their suggested actions.

Although problem-solving teams were helpful, they didn't go far enough in getting employees involved in work-related decisions and processes. This need led to another type of team, a self-managed work team, which is a formal group of employees who operate without a manager and are responsible for a complete work process or segment. A self-managed team is responsible for getting the work done *and* for managing themselves, and usually includes planning and scheduling of work, assigning tasks to members, collective control over the pace of work, making operating decisions, and taking action on problems. For instance, teams at Corning have no shift supervisors and work closely with other manufacturing divisions to solve production-line problems and coordinate deadlines and deliveries. The teams have the authority to make and implement decisions, finish projects, and address problems.[21] Other organizations such as Xerox, Boeing, PepsiCo, and Hewlett-Packard also use self-managed teams. It's estimated that about 30 percent of U.S. employers now use this form of team; and among large firms, the number is probably closer to 50 percent.[22] Most organizations that use self-managed teams find them to be effective.[23]

The third type of team is the cross-functional team, and is defined as a work team composed of individuals from various specialties. Many organizations use cross-functional teams. For example, ArcelorMittal, the world's largest steel company, uses cross-functional teams of scientists, plant managers, and salespeople to review and monitor product innovations.[24] The concept of cross-functional teams is even being applied in health care. For instance, at Suburban Hospital in Bethesda, Maryland, intensive care unit (ICU) teams composed of a doctor trained in intensive care medicine, a pharmacist, a social worker, a nutritionist, the chief ICU nurse, a respiratory therapist, and a chaplain meet daily with every patient's bedside nurse to discuss and debate the best course of treatment. The hospital credits this team care approach with reducing errors, shortening the amount of time patients spent in ICU, and improving communication between families and the medical staff.[25]

The final type of team is the virtual team, which is a team that uses technology to link physically dispersed members in order to achieve a common goal. For instance, a virtual team at Boeing-Rocketdyne played a pivotal role in developing a radically new product.[26] Another company, Decision Lens, uses a virtual team environment to generate and evaluate creative ideas.[27] In a virtual team, members collaborate online with tools such as wide-area

TECHNOLOGY AND THE MANAGER'S JOB

IT AND TEAMS

Work teams need information to do their work. With work teams often being not just steps away, but continents away from each other, it's important to have a way for team members to communicate and collaborate. That's where IT comes in. Technology has enabled greater online communication and collaboration within teams of all types.[28]

The idea of technologically aided collaboration actually originated with online search engines. The Internet itself was initially intended as a way for groups of scientists and researchers to share information. Then,

as more and more information was put "on the Web," users relied on a variety of search engines to help them find that information. Now, we see many examples of collaborative technologies such as wiki pages, blogs, and even multiplayer virtual reality games.

Today, online collaborative tools have given work teams more efficient and effective ways to get work done. For instance, engineers at Toyota use collaborative communication tools to share process improvements and innovations. They have developed a "widely disseminated, collectively owned pool of common

knowledge, which drives innovation at a speed few other corporate systems can match." And despite some recent "bumps," there's no disputing the successes Toyota has achieved. Managers everywhere should look to the power of IT to help work teams improve the way work gets done.

Think About:

· What challenges do managers face in managing teams that must rely on IT to communicate?

· Using, Exhibit 6, discuss how the four major components of team effectiveness would affect and be affected by a team's use of IT.

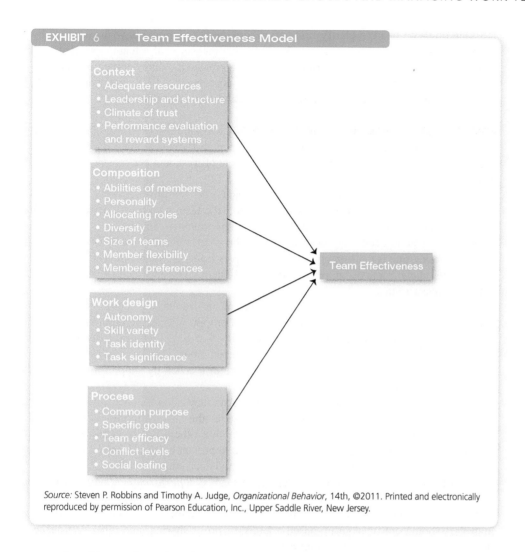

EXHIBIT 6   Team Effectiveness Model

Context
- Adequate resources
- Leadership and structure
- Climate of trust
- Performance evaluation and reward systems

Composition
- Abilities of members
- Personality
- Allocating roles
- Diversity
- Size of teams
- Member flexibility
- Member preferences

Work design
- Autonomy
- Skill variety
- Task identity
- Task significance

Process
- Common purpose
- Specific goals
- Team efficacy
- Conflict levels
- Social loafing

Team Effectiveness

Source: Steven P. Robbins and Timothy A. Judge, *Organizational Behavior*, 14th, ©2011. Printed and electronically reproduced by permission of Pearson Education, Inc., Upper Saddle River, New Jersey.

networks, videoconferencing, fax, e-mail, or Web sites where the team can hold online conferences.[29] Virtual teams can do all the things that other teams can—share information, make decisions, and complete tasks; however, they lack the normal give-and-take of face-to-face discussions. That's why virtual teams tend to be more task-oriented, especially if the team members have never personally met.

What Makes a Team Effective?

Much research has been done on what it is that makes a team effective.[30] Out of these efforts, we now have a fairly focused model identifying those characteristics.[31] Exhibit 6 summarizes what we currently know about what makes a team effective. As we look at this model, keep in mind two things. First, teams differ in form and structure. This model attempts to generalize across all teams, so you should only use it as a guide.[32] Secondly, the model assumes that managers have already determined that teamwork is preferable to individual work. Creating "effective" teams in situations in which individuals can do the job better would be wasted effort.

problem-solving teams
A team from the same department or functional area that's involved in efforts to improve work activities or to solve specific problems

self-managed work team
A type of work team that operates without a manager and is responsible for a complete work process or segment

cross-functional team
A work team composed of individuals from various specialties

virtual team
A type of work team that uses technology to link physically dispersed members in order to achieve a common goal

One thing we need to clarify first before looking at the model is what we mean by team effectiveness. Typically, it includes objective measures of a team's productivity, managers' ratings of the team's performance, and aggregate measures of member satisfaction. As you can see from the model, the four key components of effective teams include the context, the team's composition, work design, and process variables.

WHAT FACTORS IN THE CONTEXT APPEAR TO MAKE A TEAM EFFECTIVE?   Four contextual factors appear to be most significantly related to team performance. These factors include adequate resources, leadership and structure, a climate of trust, and performance evaluation and reward systems.

As part of the larger organization system, a team relies on resources outside the group to sustain it. If it doesn't have *adequate resources*, the team's ability to perform its job effectively is reduced. This factor appears to be so important to team performance that one research study concluded that "perhaps one of the most important characteristics of an effective work group is the support the group receives from the organization."[33] Resources can include timely information, proper equipment, encouragement, adequate staffing, and administrative assistance.

If a team can't agree on who is to do what or ensure that all members contribute equally in sharing the work load, it won't function properly. Agreeing on the specifics of work and how all the team members' individual skills fit together requires *team leadership and structure*. This aspect can come from the organization or from the team itself. Even in self-managed teams, a manager's job is to be more of a coach by supporting the team's efforts and managing outside (rather than inside) the team.

Members of effective teams *trust* each other. And they also trust their leaders.[34] Why is trust important? It facilitates cooperation, reduces the need to monitor each other's behavior, and bonds members around the belief that others on the team won't take advantage of them. Trusting the team leader is also important because it means the team is willing to accept and commit to the leader's goals and decisions.

The final contextual factor of an effective team is a *performance evaluation and reward system*. Team members have to be accountable both individually and jointly. So, in addition to evaluating and rewarding employees for their individual contributions, managers should consider group-based appraisals, profit-sharing, and other approaches that reinforce team effort and commitment.

WHAT TEAM COMPOSITION FACTORS LEAD TO EFFECTIVENESS?   Several team composition factors are important to a team's effectiveness. They include team member abilities, personality, role allocation, diversity, size of teams, member flexibility, and member preferences.

Part of a team's performance depends on its members' *knowledge, skills, and abilities*.[35] Research has shown that to perform effectively, a team needs three different types of skills. First, it needs people with technical expertise. Next, it needs members with problem-solving and decision-making skills. Finally, a team needs people with interpersonal skills. A team can't achieve its performance potential if it doesn't have or can't develop all these skills. And the right mix of these skills is also critical. Too much of one at the expense of another will lead to lower team performance. However, a team doesn't necessarily need all these skills immediately. It's not uncommon for team members to take responsibility for learning the skills in which the group is deficient. That way a team can achieve its full potential.

As we saw in the last chapter, *personality* significantly influences individual behavior. It's also true for team behavior. Research has shown that three of the Big Five dimensions are relevant to team effectiveness.[36] For instance, high levels of both conscientiousness and openness-to-experience tend to lead to higher team performance. Agreeableness also appears to matter. And teams that had one or more highly disagreeable members performed poorly. Maybe you've had that not-so-good experience in group projects that you've been part of!

Nine potential team *roles* have been identified. (See Exhibit 7.) High-performing work teams have people to fill all these roles who were selected to fulfill these roles based on their skills and preferences.[37] On many teams, individuals may play multiple roles.

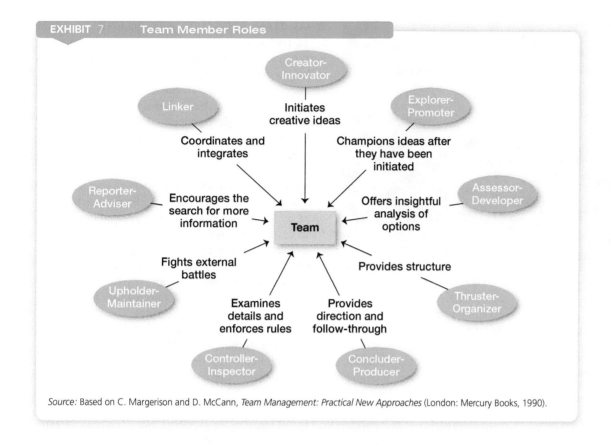

EXHIBIT 7   Team Member Roles

Source: Based on C. Margerison and D. McCann, *Team Management: Practical New Approaches* (London: Mercury Books, 1990).

It's important for managers to understand the individual strengths a person will bring to a team and select team members with those strengths in mind to ensure that these roles are filled.

Team *diversity* is another factor that can influence team effectiveness. Although many of us hold the optimistic view that diversity is desirable, research seems to show the opposite. One review found that "Studies on diversity in teams from the last 50 years have shown that surface-level social-category differences such as race/ethnicity, gender, and age tend to . . . have negative effects" on the performance of teams.[38] However, some evidence does show that the disruptive effects of diversity decline over time, but does not confirm that diverse teams perform better eventually.

What *size* should a work team be in order to be effective? At Amazon, work teams have considerable autonomy to innovate and to investigate ideas. Jeff Bezos, founder and CEO, uses a "two-pizza" philosophy; that is, a team should be small enough that it can be fed with two pizzas. This "two-pizza" philosophy usually limits groups to five to seven people, depending, of course, on team member appetites![39] Generally speaking, the most effective teams have five to nine members. And experts suggest using the smallest number of people who can do the task.

Team *member preferences* need to be considered. Why? Some people just prefer not to work on teams. Given the option, many employees will opt not to be part of a team. When people who would prefer to work alone are forced on a team, it creates a direct threat to the team's morale and to individual member satisfaction.[40]

HOW DOES WORK DESIGN AFFECT TEAM EFFECTIVENESS?   Effective teams need to work together and take collective responsibility for completing tasks. An effective team must be more than a "team in name only."[41] Important work design elements include *autonomy*, using a *variety of skills*, being able to complete a *whole and identifiable* task or product, and working on a task or project that has a *significant impact* on others. Research indicates that these characteristics enhance team member motivation and increase team effectiveness.[42]

Jim Dedmon/Newscom

Effective teams have a specific goal that facilitates communication and a common plan and purpose that provide direction, momentum, and commitment from team members. In this photo, the members of the pit crew team of NASCAR racer Kyle Busch work toward the goal of winning the race. While each crew member has a different job—such as jack man, tire carrier, fueler, and fire extinguisher—the team's plan is to function at top speed with no errors in checking the car, fixing parts, changing tires, and pumping gas. An effective pit crew can prevent problems and mean the difference between a victory and defeat. Here Busch's team is at work during a winning pit stop that qualified the racer for an all-star race.

WHAT TEAM PROCESSES ARE RELATED TO TEAM EFFECTIVENESS? Five team process variables have been shown to be related to team effectiveness. These include a common purpose, specific team goals, team efficacy, managed conflict, and minimal social loafing.

An effective team has a *common plan and purpose.* This common purpose provides direction, momentum, and commitment for team members.[43] Members of successful teams put a lot of time and effort into discussing, shaping, and agreeing on a purpose that belongs to them both individually and as a team.

Teams also need *specific goals.* Such goals facilitate clear communication and help teams maintain their focus on getting results.

Team efficacy emerges when teams believe in themselves and believe they can succeed.[44] Effective teams have confidence in themselves and in their members.

Effective teams need some *conflict.* Conflict on a team isn't necessarily bad and can actually improve team effectiveness.[45] But it has to be the right kind of conflict. Relationship conflicts—those based on interpersonal incompatibilities, tension, and autonomy toward others—are almost always dysfunctional. However, task conflicts—those based on disagreements about task content—can be beneficial because they may stimulate discussion, promote critical assessment of problems and options, and can lead to better team decisions.

Finally, effective teams work to minimize the tendency for *social loafing*, which we discussed earlier in this chapter. Successful teams make members individually and jointly accountable for the team's purpose, goals, and approach.[46]

How Can a Manager Shape Team Behavior?

A manager can do several things to shape a team's behavior including proper selection, employee training, and rewarding the appropriate team behaviors. Let's look at each.

WHAT ROLE DOES SELECTION PLAY? Some individuals already possess the interpersonal skills to be effective team players. When hiring team members, managers should check whether applicants have the technical skills required to successfully perform the job *and* whether they can fulfill team roles.

Some applicants may have been socialized around individual contributions and, consequently, lack team skills, which could also be true for some current employees being moved into teams due to organizational restructuring. When faced with this situation, a manager can do several things. First, and most obvious, if team skills are woefully lacking, don't hire the person. If successful performance is going to require interaction, not hiring the individual is appropriate. On the other hand, an applicant who has some basic skills can be hired on a probationary basis and required to undergo training to shape him or her into a team player. If the skills aren't learned or practiced, then the individual may have to be let go.

CAN INDIVIDUALS BE TRAINED TO BE TEAM PLAYERS? Performing well in a team involves a set of behaviors.[47] As we discussed in the preceding chapter, new behaviors *can* be learned. Even people who feel strongly about the importance of individual accomplishment can be trained to become team players. Training specialists can conduct exercises so employees can experience what teamwork is all about. The workshops can cover such topics as team problem solving, communications, negotiations, conflict resolution, and coaching skills. It's not unusual, too, for these individuals to be exposed to the five stages of team development that we discussed earlier.[48] At Verizon Communications, for example, trainers focus on how a team goes through various stages before it gels. And employees are reminded of the importance of patience, because teams take longer to do some things—such as make decisions—than do employees acting alone.[49]

WHAT ROLE DO REWARDS PLAY IN SHAPING TEAM PLAYERS? An organization's reward system needs to encourage cooperative efforts rather than competitive ones. For instance, Lockheed Martin's aeronautics division organized its some 20,000 employees into teams. Rewards are structured to return a percentage increase in the bottom line to the team members on the basis of achievements of the team's performance goals.

Promotions, pay raises, and other forms of recognition should be given to employees who are effective collaborative team members. Taking this approach doesn't mean that individual contribution is ignored, but rather that it's balanced with selfless contributions to the team. Examples of behaviors that should be rewarded include training new colleagues, sharing information with teammates, helping resolve team conflicts, and mastering new skills in which the team is deficient.[50] Finally, managers can't forget the inherent rewards that employees can receive from teamwork. Work teams provide camaraderie. It's exciting and satisfying to be an integral part of a successful team. The opportunity to engage in personal development and to help teammates grow can be a satisfying and rewarding experience for employees.[51]

WHAT CURRENT ISSUES DO MANAGERS FACE IN MANAGING TEAMS?

Few trends have influenced how work gets done in organizations as much as the use of work teams. The shift from working alone to working on teams requires employees to cooperate with others, share information, confront differences, and sublimate personal interests for the greater good of the team. Managers can build effective teams by understanding what influences performance and satisfaction. However, managers also face some current challenges in managing teams, including those associated with managing global teams and with understanding when teams aren't the answer.

> **Discuss contemporary issues in managing teams.**
>
> **4**

What's Involved with Managing Global Teams?

Two characteristics of today's organizations are obvious: they're global and work is increasingly done by teams. Because of those reasons, any manager is likely to have to manage a global team. What do we know about managing global teams? We know there are both drawbacks and benefits in using global teams (see Exhibit 8). What are some of the challenges associated with managing global teams?

HOW DO TEAM COMPOSITION FACTORS AFFECT MANAGING A GLOBAL TEAM? In global organizations, understanding the relationship between team effectiveness and team composition is more challenging because of the unique cultural characteristics represented

---

EXHIBIT 8   Global Teams

DRAWBACKS	BENEFITS
• Disliking team members	• Greater diversity of ideas
• Mistrusting team members	• Limited groupthink
• Stereotyping	• Increased attention on understanding others' ideas, perspectives, etc.
• Communication problems	
• Stress and tension	

Source: Based on N. Adler, *International Dimensions of Organizational Behavior*, 4th ed. (Cincinnati, OH: Southwestern Cengage Publishing, 2002), pp 141–147.

by members of a global team. In addition to recognizing team members' abilities, skills, knowledge, and personality, managers need to be familiar with and clearly understand the cultural characteristics of the groups and the group members they manage.[52] For instance, is the global team from a culture in which uncertainty avoidance is high? If so, members will not be comfortable dealing with unpredictable and ambiguous tasks. Also, as managers work with global teams, they need to be aware of the potential for stereotyping, which can lead to problems.

HOW DOES TEAM STRUCTURE AFFECT MANAGING A GLOBAL TEAM? Some of the structural areas where we see differences in managing global teams include conformity, status, social loafing, and cohesiveness.

Are conformity findings generalizable across cultures? Research suggests that Asch's findings are culture-bound.[53] For instance, as might be expected, conformity to social norms tends to be higher in collectivistic cultures than in individualistic cultures. However, groupthink tends to be less of a problem in global teams because members are less likely to feel pressured to conform to the ideas, conclusions, and decisions of the group.[54]

Also, the importance of status varies between cultures. The French, for example, are extremely status conscious. Also, countries differ on the criteria that confer status. For instance, in Latin America and Asia, status tends to come from family position and formal roles held in organizations. In contrast, while status is important in countries like the United States and Australia, it tends to be less "in your face." And it tends to be given based on accomplishments rather than on titles and family history. Managers must understand who and what holds status when interacting with people from a culture different from their own. An American manager who doesn't understand that office size isn't a measure of a Japanese executive's position or who fails to grasp the importance the British place on family genealogy and social class is likely to unintentionally offend others and lessen his or her interpersonal effectiveness.

Social loafing has a Western bias. It's consistent with individualistic cultures, like the United States and Canada, which are dominated by self-interest. It's not consistent with collectivistic societies, in which individuals are motivated by group goals. For instance, in studies comparing employees from the United States with employees from the People's Republic of China and Israel (both collectivistic societies), the Chinese and Israelis showed no propensity to engage in social loafing. In fact, they actually performed better in a group than when working alone.[55]

Cohesiveness is another group structural element that may create special challenges for managers. In a cohesive group, members are unified and "act as one." There's a great deal of camaraderie and group identity is high. In global teams, however, cohesiveness is often more difficult to achieve because of higher levels of "mistrust, miscommunication, and stress."[56]

The International Atomic Energy Agency and the government of Japan created an 18-member global team to study the Fukushima nuclear power station accident triggered by the 2011 earthquake in Japan. Comprised of experts with experience across a range of nuclear specialties, the team members came from 12 countries: Argentina, China, France, Hungary, India, Indonesia, Russia, South Korea, Spain, Turkey, the United Kingdom, and the United States. Using a global team brought a greater diversity of ideas to the team's mission of identifying lessons learned from the accident that can help improve nuclear safety around the world. In this photo the team begins its investigation by touring the crippled nuclear power plant.

HOW DO TEAM PROCESSES AFFECT MANAGING A GLOBAL TEAM? The processes that global teams use to do their work can be particularly challenging for managers. For one thing, communication issues often arise because not all team members may be fluent in the team's working language, which can lead to inaccuracies, misunderstandings, and inefficiencies.[57] However, research has also shown that a multicultural global team is better able to capitalize on the diversity of ideas represented if a wide range of information is used.[58]

Managing conflict in global teams isn't easy, especially when those teams are virtual teams. Conflict can interfere with how information is used by the team. However, research shows that in collectivistic cultures, a collaborative conflict management style can be most effective.[59]

TEPCO/Newscom

When Are Teams Not the Answer?

Teamwork takes more time and often more resources than does individual work.[60] Teams require managers to communicate more, manage conflicts, and run meetings. So, the benefits of using teams need to exceed the costs. And that's not always the case![61] In the rush to use teams, some managers have introduced them into situations in which it would have been better to have individuals do the work. So before implementing teams just because everyone's talking about their popularity, you should carefully evaluate whether the work requires or will benefit from a collective effort.

How do you know whether work is better done individually or by a group? Three "tests" have been suggested.[62] First, can the work be done better by more than one person? Task complexity would be a good indicator of a need for different perspectives. Simple tasks that don't require diverse input are probably better done by individuals. Second, does the work create a common purpose or set of goals for the people in the group that's more than the sum of individual goals? For instance, many car dealerships use teams to link customer-service personnel, mechanics, parts specialists, and sales representatives. Such teams can better meet the goal of outstanding customer satisfaction. The final test to assess whether teams or individuals are better suited for doing work is to look at the interdependence of the individuals. Using teams makes sense when there's interdependence between tasks; that is, when the success of everyone depends on the success of each person *and* the success of each person depends on the others. For example, soccer is an obvious team sport. Success requires a lot of coordination between interdependent players. On the other hand, swim teams aren't really teams, except on relays. They're groups of individuals, performing individually, whose total performance is merely the sum of their individual performances.

Review

CHAPTER SUMMARY

1 **Define group and describe the stages of group development.** A group is two or more interacting and interdependent individuals who come together to achieve specific goals. Formal groups are work groups that are defined by the organization's structure and have designated work assignments and specific tasks directed at accomplishing organizational goals. Informal groups are social groups.

The forming stage consists of two phases: joining the group and defining the group's purpose, structure, and leadership. The storming stage is one of intra-group conflict over who will control the group and what the group will be doing. The norming stage is when close relationships and cohesiveness develop as norms are determined. The performing stage is when group members work on the group's task. The adjourning stage happens when the group prepares to disband.

2 **Describe the major concepts of group behavior.** A role refers to a set of behavior patterns expected of someone occupying a given position in a social unit. At any given time, employees adjust their role behaviors to the group of which they are a part. Norms are standards shared by group members. They informally convey to employees which behaviors are acceptable and which are unacceptable. Status is another factor to know because it can be a significant motivator and it needs to be congruent. Also, group size affects group behavior in a number of ways. Smaller groups are generally faster at completing tasks than are larger ones. However, larger groups are frequently better at fact finding because of their diversified input. As a result, larger groups are generally better at problem solving. Finally, group cohesiveness is important because of its impact on a group's effectiveness at achieving its goals.

3 **Discuss how groups are turned into effective teams.** Effective teams have common characteristics. They have adequate resources, effective leadership, a climate of trust, and a performance evaluation and reward system that reflects team contributions. These teams have individuals with technical expertise as well as problem-solving, decision-making, and interpersonal skills and the right traits, especially conscientiousness and openness to new experiences. Effective teams also tend to be small, preferably of diverse backgrounds. They have members who fill role demands and who prefer to be part of a team. And the work that members do provides freedom and autonomy, the opportunity to use different skills and talents, the ability to complete a whole and identifiable task or product, and work that has a substantial impact on others. Finally, effective teams have members who believe in the team's capabilities and are committed to a common plan and purpose, specific team goals, a manageable level of conflict, and a minimal degree of social loafing.

4 **Discuss contemporary issues in managing teams.** The challenges of managing global teams can be seen in team composition factors, especially the diverse cultural characteristics; in team structure, especially conformity, status, social loafing, and cohesiveness; and in team processes, especially with communication and managing conflict; and the manager's role in making it all work.

Managers also need to know when teams are not the answer. They can do this by assessing whether the work can be done better by more than one person; by whether the work creates a common purpose or set of goals for the members of the team; and by the amount of interdependence among team members.

MyManagementLab   For more resources, please visit **www.mymanagementlab.com**

UNDERSTANDING THE CHAPTER

1. Think of a group to which you belong (or have belonged). Trace its development through the stages of group development as shown in Exhibit 2. How closely did its development parallel the group development model? How might the group development model be used to improve this group's effectiveness?

2. Contrast (a) self-managed and cross-functional teams, and (b) virtual and face-to-face teams.

3. How do you explain the popularity of work teams in countries such as the United States and Canada, whose national cultures place a high value on individualism?

4. "All work teams are work groups, but not all work groups are work teams." Do you agree or disagree with this statement? Discuss.

5. Would you prefer to work alone or as part of a team? Why?

6. "To have a successful team, first find a great leader." What do you think of this statement? Do you agree? Why or why not?

7. What traits do you think good team players have? Do some research to answer this question and write a short report detailing your findings using a bulleted list format.

8. Contrast the pros and cons of diverse teams.

9. How do you think scientific management theorists would react to the increased use of teams in organizations? How would behavioral science theorists react?

10. What challenges do managers face in managing global teams? How should those challenges be handled?

Endnotes

1. J. Terzakis, "Virtual Retrospectives for Geographically Dispersed Software Teams," *IEEE Computer Society,* May–June 2011, pp. 12–15; "Virtual Teams Must Function Correctly," *Strategic Direction,* April 2011, pp. 22–24; C. Scovotti and L. D. Spiller, "Cross-Border Student Collaborations: Opportunities for Videoconferencing," *Marketing Education Review,* Spring 2011, pp. 57–61; E. Markowitz, "Are the Best Leaders Revolutionaries?" *Inc. Online,* March 28, 2011; L. J. Gressgård, "Virtual Team Collaboration and Innovation in Organizations," *Team Performance Management,* March 2011, pp. 102–119; L. Tischler, "Intel's Virtual Footwear Wall for Adidas Turns Boutiques into Shoe-Topias," *Fast Company Online,* January 11, 2011; A. Gupta, S. Seshasai, R. Aron, and S. Pareek, "The 24-Hour Knowledge Factory: Work and Organizational Redesign and Associated Challenges," *Information Resources Management Journal* (October–December 2010), pp. 40–56; M. R. Haas, "The Double-Edged Swords of Autonomy and External Knowledge: Analyzing Team Effectiveness in a Multinational Organization," *Academy of Management Journal* (October 2010), pp. 989–1008; O. Coren, "Israel Offers Intel $110 Million for Commitment to Stay in the Country," *Haaretz.com,* August 26, 2010; M. B. O'Leary, "Go (Con)figure: Subgroups, Imbalance, and Isolates in Geographically Dispersed Teams," *Organization Science,* January–February 2010, pp. 115–131; and R. R. Nelson, "Project Retrospectives: Evaluating Project Success, Failure, and Everything In Between," *MIS Quarterly Executive,* September 2005, pp. 361–372.

2. B. Mezrich, *Bringing Down the House: The Inside Story of Six MIT Students Who Took Vegas for Millions* (New York: Free Press, 2002). The 2008 film *21* was a fictional work based loosely on the story.

3. B. W. Tuckman and M. C. Jensen, "Stages of Small-Group Development Revisited," *Group and Organizational Studies,* December 1977, pp. 419–427; and M. F. Maples, "Group Development: Extending Tuckman's Theory," *Journal for Specialists in Group Work* (Fall 1988), pp. 17–23.

4. And the Survey Says box based on J. Yang and P. Trap, "As a Manager, It's Most Challenging to . . . ," *USA Today,* April 19, 2011, p. 1B; J. Yang and K. Gelles, "Workplace Friendships," *USA Today,* April 13, 2010, p. 1B; K. Merriman, "Low-Trust Teams Prefer Individualized Pay," *Harvard Business Review,* November 2008, p. 32; B. J. West, J. L. Patera, and M. K. Carsten, "Team Level Positivity: Investigating Positive Psychological Capacities and Team Level Outcomes," *Journal of Organizational Behavior* (February 2009), p. 249; J. Yang and K. Simmons, "Traits of Good Team Players," *USA Today,* November 21, 2007, p. 1B; J. Yang and M. E. Mullins, "Workers More Productive in Small Groups," *USA Today,* January 10, 2007, p. 1B; and M. Weinstein, "Coming Up Short? Join the Club," *Training* (April 2006), p. 14.

5. L. N. Jewell and H. J. Reitz, *Group Effectiveness in Organizations* (Glenview, IL: Scott, Foresman, 1981); and M. Kaeter, "Repotting Mature Work Teams," *Training* (April 1994), pp. 54–56.

6. Right or Wrong box based on K. McCullum, "Hush, Hush," *OfficePro*, March–April 2011, pp. 18–22; and E. Bernstein, "You Did *What?* Spare the Office the Details," *Wall Street Journal*, April 6, 2010, pp. D1+.

7. From the Past to the Present box based on S. S. Wang, "Under the Influence: How the Group Changes What We Think," *Wall Street Journal*, May 3, 2011, pp. D1+; M. E. Shaw, *Group Dynamics: The Psychology of Small Group Behavior* (New York: McGraw-Hill, 1975); and E. J. Thomas and C. F. Fink, "Effects of Group Size," *Psychological Bulletin* (July 1963), pp. 371–384.

8. S. E. Asch, "Effects of Group Pressure upon the Modification and Distortion of Judgments," in H. Guetzkow (ed.), *Groups, Leadership, and Men* (Pittsburgh, PA: Carnegie Press, 1951), pp. 177–190.

9. Asch, "Effects of Group Pressure upon the Modification and Distortion of Judgments."

10. O. A. Alnuaimi, L. P. Robert Jr., and L. M. Maruping, "Team Size, Dispersion, and Social Loafing in Technology-Supported Teams: A Perspective on the Theory of Moral Disengagement," *Journal of Management Information Systems* (Summer 2010), pp. 203–230; C. Cheshire and J. Antin, "None of Us Is As Lazy As All of Us," *Information, Communication & Society*, June 2010, pp. 537–555; R. van Dick, J. Stellmacher, U. Wagner, G. Lemmer, and P. A. Tissington, "Group Membership Salience and Task Performance," *Journal of Managerial Psychology* 24, no. 7 (2009), pp. 609–626; A. Jassawalla, H. Sashittal, and A. Malshe, "Students' Perceptions of Social Loafing: Its Antecedents and Consequences in Undergraduate Business Classroom Teams," *Academy of Management Learning & Education*, March 2009, pp. 42–54; and R. Albanese and D. D. Van Fleet, "Rational Behavior in Groups: The Free Riding Tendency," *Academy of Management Review*, April 1985, pp. 244–255.

11. L. Berkowitz, "Group Standards, Cohesiveness, and Productivity," *Human Relations* November 1954, pp. 509–519.

12. See, for example, R. A. Henry, J. Kmet, and A. Landa, "Examining the Impact of Interpersonal Cohesiveness on Group Accuracy Interventions: the Importance of Matching Versus Buffering," *Organizational Behavior and Human Decision Processes* (January 2002), pp. 25–43.

13. Cited in T. Purdum, "Teaming, Take 2," *Industry Week*, May 2005, p. 43; and C. Joinson, "Teams at Work," *HR Magazine*, May 1999, p. 30.

14. See, for example, S. A. Mohrman, S. G. Cohen, and A. M. Mohrman, Jr., *Designing Team-Based Organizations* (San Francisco: Jossey-Bass, 1995); P. MacMillan, *The Performance Factor: Unlocking the Secrets of Teamwork* (Nashville, TN: Broadman & Holman, 2001); and E. Salas, C. A. Bowers, and E. Eden (eds.), *Improving Teamwork in Organizations: Applications of Resource Management Training* (Mahwah, NJ: Lawrence Erlbaum, 2002).

15. Information for this section is based on J. R. Katzenbach and D. K. Smith, *The Wisdom of Teams* (Boston: Harvard Business School Press, 1993), pp. 21, 45, 85; and D. C. Kinlaw, *Developing Superior Work Teams* (Lexington, MA: Lexington Books, 1991), pp. 3–21.

16. S. Adams and L. Kydoniefs, "Making Teams Work: Bureau of Labor Statistics Learns What Works and What Doesn't," *Quality Progress* (January 2000), pp. 43–49.

17. D. Hoffman, "At Wachovia, Fund Teams Work: Bank's Buddy System Improves Performance," *Investment News* (February 2001), p. 8.

18. T. Capozzoli, "How to Succeed with Self-Directed Work Teams," *Supervision* (February 2002), pp. 25–27.

19. See, for instance, E. Sunstrom, DeMeuse, and D. Futrell, "Work Teams: Applications and Effectiveness," *American Psychologist,* February 1990, pp. 120–133.

20. J. S. McClenahen, "Bearing Necessities," *Industry Week,* October 2004, pp. 63–65; P. J. Kiger, "Acxiom Rebuilds from Scratch," *Workforce,* December 2002, pp. 52–55; and T. Boles, "Viewpoint—Leadership Lessons from NASCAR," *Industry Week,* www.industryweek.com (May 21, 2002).

21. M. Cianni and D. Wanuck, "Individual Growth and Team Enhancement: Moving Toward a New Model of Career Development," *Academy of Management Executive,* February 1997, pp. 105–115.

22. C. Joinson, "Teams at Work," p. 30; and "Teams," *Training* (October 1996), p. 69.

23. J. P. Millikin, P. W. Hom, and C. C. Manz, "Self-Management Competencies in Self-Managing Teams: Their Impact on Multi-Team System Productivity," *Leadership Quarterly,* October 2010, pp. 687–702; O. Turel and Y. Zhang, "Does Virtual Team Composition Matter? Trait and Problem-Solving Configuration Effects on Team Performance," *Behavior & Information Technology,* July–August 2010, pp. 363–375; J. S. Bunderson and P. Boumgarden, "Structure and Learning in Self-Managed Teams: Why 'Bureaucratic' Teams Can Be Better Learners," *Organization Science,* May–June 2010, pp. 609–624; and G. M. Spreitzer, S. G. Cohen, and G. E. Ledford, Jr., "Developing Effective Self-Managing Work Teams in Service Organizations," *Group & Organization Management*, September 1999, pp. 340–366.

24. "Meet the New Steel," *Fortune*, October 1, 2007, pp. 68–71.

25. J. Appleby and R. Davis, "Teamwork Used to Save Money; Now It Saves Lives," *USA Today*, www.usatoday.com (March 1, 2001).

26. A. Malhotra, A. Majchrzak, R. Carman, and V. Lott, "Radical Innovation without Collocation: A Case Study at Boeing-Rocketdyne," *MIS Quarterly*, June 2001, pp. 229–249.

27. A. Stuart, "Virtual Agreement," *CFO*, November 2007, p. 24.

28. Technology and the Manager's Job box based on "Virtual Team Collaboration and Innovation in Organizations," *Team Performance Management*, March 2011, pp. 109–119; M. Flammia, Y. Cleary, and D. M. Slattery, "Leadership Roles, Socioemotional Strategies, and Technology Use of Irish and US Students in Virtual Teams," *IEEE Transactions on Professional Communication*, June 2010, pp. 89–101; P. Evans, "The Wiki Factor," *BizEd*, January–February 2006, pp. 28–32; and M. McCafferty, "A Human Inventory," *CFO*, April 2005, pp. 83–85.

29. "Virtual Team Collaboration and Innovation in Organizations"; M. Flammia, Y. Cleary, and D. M. Slattery, "Leadership Roles, Socioemotional Strategies, and Technology Use of Irish and U.S. Students in Virtual Teams"; A. Malhotra, A. Majchrzak, and B. Rosen, "Leading Virtual Teams," *Academy of Management Perspectives,* February 2007, pp. 60–70; B. L. Kirkman and J. E. Mathieu, "The Dimensions and Antecedents of Team Virtuality," *Journal of Management* (October 2005), pp. 700–718; J. Gordon, "Do Your Virtual Teams Deliver Only Virtual Performance?" *Training* (June 2005), pp. 20–25; L. L. Martins, L. L. Gilson, and M. T. Maynard, "Virtual Teams: What Do We Know and Where Do We Go from Here?" *Journal of Management* (December 2004), pp. 805–835; S. A. Furst, M. Reeves, B. Rosen, and R. S. Blackburn,

"Managing he Life Cycle of Virtual Teams," *Academy of Management Executive,* May 2004, pp. 6–20; B. L. Kirkman, B. Rosen, P. E. Tesluk, and C. B. Gibson, "The Impact of Team Empowerment on Virtual Team Performance: The Moderating Role of Face-to-Face Interaction," *Academy of Management Journal* (April 2004), pp. 175–192; F. Keenan and S. E. Ante, "The New Teamwork," *Business Week e.biz,* February 18, 2002, pp. EB12–EB16; and G. Imperato, "Real Tools for Virtual Teams," *Fast Company*, July 2000, pp. 378–387.

30. See, for instance, D. C. Jones and T. Kato, "The Impact of Teams on Output, Quality, and Downtime: An Empirical Analysis Using Individual Panel Data," *Industrial and Labor Relations Review,* January 2011, pp. 215–240; A. Gilley, J. W. Gilley, C. W. McConnell, and A. Veliquette, "The Competencies Used by Effective Managers to Build Teams: An Empirical Study," *Advances in Developing Human Resources,* February 2010, pp. 29–45; M. A. Campion, G. J. Medsker, and C. A. Higgs, "Relations Between Work Group Characteristics and Effectiveness: Implications for Designing Effective Work Groups," *Personnel Psychology,* Winter 1993, pp. 823–850; and J. R. Hackman, "The Design of Work Teams," in J. W. Lorsch (ed.), *Handbook of Organizational Behavior* (Upper Saddle River, NJ: Prentice Hall, 1987), pp. 315–342.

31. This model is based on M. A. Campion, E. M. Papper, and G. J. Medsker, "Relations Between Work Team Characteristics and Effectiveness: A Replication and Extension," *Personnel Psychology,* Summer 1996, pp. 429–452; D. E. Hyatt and T. M. Ruddy, "An Examination of the Relationship Between Work Group Characteristics and Performance: Once More into the Breech," *Personnel Psychology,* Autumn 1997, pp. 553–585; S. G. Cohen and D. E. Bailey, "What Makes Teams Work: Group Effectiveness Research from the Shop Floor to the Executive Suite," *Journal of Management* (September 1997), pp. 239–290; L. Thompson, *Making the Team* (Upper Saddle River, NJ: Prentice Hall, 2000), pp. 18–33; and J. R. Hackman, *Leading Teams: Setting the Stage for Great Performance* (Boston: Harvard Business School Press, 2002).

32. See M. Mattson, T. V. Mumford, and G. S. Sintay, "Taking Teams to Task: A Normative Model for Designing or Recalibrating Work Teams," paper presented at the National Academy of Management Conference, Chicago, August 1999; and G. L. Stewart and M. R. Barrick, "Team Structure and Performance: Assessing the Mediating Role of Intrateam Process and the Moderating Role of Task Type," *Academy of Management Journal* (April 2000), pp. 135–148.

33. R. I. Sutton, "The Boss as Human Shield," *Harvard Business Review,* September 2010, pp. 106–109; and Hyatt and Ruddy, "An Examination of the Relationship Between Work Group Characteristics and Performance," p. 577.

34. M. E. Palanski, S. S. Kahai, and F. J. Yammarino, "Team Virtues and Performance: An Examination of Transparency, Behavioral Integrity, and Trust," *Journal of Business Ethics* (March 2011), pp. 201–216; H. H. Chang, S. S. Chuang, and S. H. Chao, "Determinants of Cultural Adaptation, Communication Quality, and Trust in Virtual Teams' Performance," *Total Quality Management and Business Excellence,* March 2011, pp. 305–329; A. C. Costa and N. Anderson, "Measuring Trust in Teams: Development and Validation of a Multifaceted Measure of Formative and Reflective Indicators of Team Trust," *European Journal of Work & Organizational Psychology* (February 2011), pp. 119–154; M. Mach, S. Dolan, and S. Tzafrir,

"The Differential Effect of Team Members' Trust on Team Performance: The Mediation Role of Team Cohesion," *Journal of Occupational and Organizational Psychology* (September 2010), pp. 771–794; B. A. DeJong and T. Elfring, "How Does Trust Affect the Performance of Ongoing Teams? The Mediating Role of Reflexivity, Monitoring, and Effort," *Academy of Management Journal* (June 2010), pp. 535–549; M. Williams, "In Whom We Trust: Group Membership as an Affective Context for Trust Development," *Academy of Management Review,* July 2001, pp. 377–396; and K. T. Dirks, "Trust in Leadership and Team Performance: Evidence from NCAA Basketball," *Journal of Applied Psychology* (December 2000), pp. 1004–1012.

35. R. R. Hirschfeld, M. J. Jordan, H. S. Field, W. F. Giles, and A. A. Armenakis, "Becoming Team Players: Team Members' Mastery of Team Knowledge as a Predictor of Team Task Proficiency and Observed Teamwork Effectiveness," *Journal of Applied Psychology* 91, no. 2 (2006), pp. 467–474.

36. S. T. Bell, "Deep-Level Composition Variables as Predictors of Team Performance: A Meta-Analysis," *Journal of Applied Psychology* 92, no. 3 (2007), pp. 595–615; and M. R. Barrick, G. L. Stewart, M. J. Neubert, and M. K. Mount, "Relating Member Ability and Personality to Work-Team Processes and Team Effectiveness," *Journal of Applied Psychology* (June 1998), pp. 377–391.

37. M. Costello, "Team Weaver," *People Management*, January 2011, pp. 26–27; and C. Margerison and D. McCann, *Team Management: Practical New Approaches* (London: Mercury Books, 1990).

38. K. H. T. Yu and D. M. Cable, "Unpacking Cooperation in Diverse Teams," *Team Performance Management*, March 2011, pp. 63–82; A. Nederveen Pieterse, D. van Knippenberg, and W. P. van Ginkel, "Diversity in Goal Orientation, Team Reflexivity, and Team Performance," *Organizational Behavior and Human Performance,* March 2011, pp. 153–164; M.-E. Roberge and R. van Dick, "Recognizing the Benefits of Diversity: When and How Does Diversity Increase Group Performance," *Human Resource Management Review,* December 2010, pp. 295–208; and E. Mannix and M. A. Neale, "What Differences Make a Difference: The Promise and Reality of Diverse Teams in Organizations," *Psychological Science in the Public Interest,* October 2005, pp. 31–55.

39. A. Deutschman, "Inside the Mind of Jeff Bezos," *Fast Company,* August 2004, pp. 50–58.

40. Hyatt and Ruddy, "An Examination of the Relationship Between Work Group Characteristics and Performance"; J. D. Shaw, M. K. Duffy, and E. M. Stark, "Interdependence and Preference for Group Work: Main and Congruence Effects on the Satisfaction and Performance of Group Members," *Journal of Management* (June 2000), pp. 259–279; and S. A. Kiffin-Peterson and J. L. Cordery, "Trust, Individualism, and Job Characteristics of Employee Preference for Teamwork," *International Journal of Human Resource Management* (February 2003), pp. 93–116.

41. J. S. Bunderson and P. Boumgarden, "Structure and Learning in Self-Managed Teams: Why 'Bureaucratic' Teams Can Be Better Learners"; and R. Wageman, "Critical Success Factors for Creating Superb Self-Managing Teams," *Organizational Dynamics,* Summer 1997, p. 55.

42. Campion, Papper, and Medsker, "Relations Between Work Team Characteristics and Effectiveness," p. 430; B. L. Kirkman and B. Rosen, "Powering Up Teams," *Organizational Dynamics,* Winter 2000, pp. 48–66; and D. C. Man and S. S. K. Lam, "The

Effects of Job Complexity and Autonomy on Cohesiveness in Collectivist and Individualist Work Groups: A Cross-Cultural Analysis," *Journal of Organizational Behavior* (December 2003), pp. 979–1001.

43. A. Mehta, H. Feild, A. Armenakis, and N. Mehta, "Team Goal Orientation and Team Performance: The Mediating Role of Team Planning," *Journal of Management* (August 2009), pp. 1026–1046; K. Blanchard, D. Carew, and E. Parisi-Carew, "How to Get Your Group to Perform Like a Team," *Training and Development* (September 1996), pp. 34–37; K. D. Scott and A. Townsend, "Teams: Why Some Succeed and Others Fail," *HR Magazine,* August 1994, pp. 62–67; and K. Hess, *Creating the High-Performance Team* (New York: Wiley, 1987); Katzenbach and Smith, *The Wisdom of Teams,* pp. 43–64.

44. H. van Emmerik, I. M. Jawahar, B. Schreurs, and N. de Cuyper, "Social Capital, Team Efficacy and Team Potency: The Mediating Role of Team Learning Behaviors," *Career Development International* (February 2011), pp. 82–99; T. Lewis, "Assessing Social Identity and Collective Efficacy as Theories of Group Motivation at Work," *International Journal of Human Resource Management* (February 2011), pp. 963–980; K. Tasa, G. J. Sears, and A. C. H. Schat, "Personality and Teamwork Behavior in Context: The Cross-Level Moderating Role of Collective Efficacy," *Journal of Organizational Behavior* (January 2011), pp. 65–85; J. A. Goncalo, E. Polman, and C. Maslach, "Can Confidence Come Too Soon? Collective Efficacy, Conflict and Group Performance Over Time," *Organizational Behavior & Human Decision Processes,* September 2010, pp. 13–24; K. Tasa, S. Taggar, and G. H. Seijts, "The Development of Collective Efficacy in Teams: A Multilevel and Longitudinal Perspective," *Journal of Applied Psychology* (January 2007), pp. 17–27; C. B. Gibson, "The Efficacy Advantage: Factors Related to the Formation of Group Efficacy," *Journal of Applied Social Psychology* (October 2003), pp. 2153–2186; and D. I. Jung and J. J. Sosik, "Group Potency and Collective Efficacy: Examining Their Predictive Validity, Level of Analysis, and Effects of Performance Feedback on Future Group Performance," *Group & Organization Management,* September 2003, pp. 366–391.

45. K. C. Kostopoulos and N. Bozionelos, "Team Exploratory and Exploitative Learning: Psychological Safety, Task Conflict, and Team Performance," *Group & Organization Management,* June 2011, pp. 385–415; K. J. Behfar, E. A. Mannix, R. S. Peterson, and W. M. Trochim, "Conflict in Small Groups: The Meaning and Consequences of Process Conflict," *Small Group Research,* April 2011, pp. 127–176; R. S. Peterson and K. J. Behfar, "The Dynamic Relationship Between Performance Feedback, Trust, and Conflict in Groups: A Longitudinal Study," *Organizational Behavior and Human Decision Processes,"* September–November 2003, pp. 102–112; and K. A. Jehn, "A Qualitative Analysis of Conflict Types and Dimensions in Organizational Groups," *Administrative Science Quarterly,* September 1997, pp. 530–557.

46. O. A. Alnuaimi, L. P. Robert Jr., and L. M. Maruping, "Team Size, Dispersion, and Social Loafing in Technology-Supported Teams: A Perspective on the Theory of Moral Disengagement"; C. Cheshire and J. Antin, "None of Us Is As Lazy As All of Us"; R. van Dick, J. Stellmacher, U. Wagner, G. Lemmer, and P. A. Tissington, "Group Membership Salience and Task Performance"; A. Jassawalla, H. Sashittal, and A. Malshe, "Students' Perceptions of Social Loafing: Its Antecedents and Consequences in Undergraduate Business Classroom Teams";

K. H. Price, D. A. Harrison, and J. H. Gavin, "Withholding Inputs in Team Contexts: Member Composition, Interaction Processes, Evaluation Structure, and Social Loafing," *Journal of Applied Psychology* (December 2006), pp. 1375–1384; and R. Albanese and D. D. Van Fleet, "Rational Behavior in Groups: The Free Riding Tendency," *Academy of Management Review,* April 1985, pp. 244–255.

47. "Helping Hands," *HR Magazine,* May 2011, p. 18; M. O'Neil, "Leading the Team," *Supervision,* April 2011, pp. 8–10; J. Beeson, "Build a Strong Team," *Leadership Excellence,* February 2011, p. 15; S. Brutus and M. B. L. Donia, "Improving the Effectiveness of Students in Groups With a Centralized Peer Evaluation System," *Academy of Management Learning & Education,* December 2010, pp. 652–662; and N. H. Woodward, "Make the Most of Team Building," *HR Magazine,* September 2006, pp. 73–76.

48. R. M. Yandrick, "A Team Effort," *HR Magazine,* June 2001, pp. 136–141.

49. Ibid.

50. "How Should We Recognize Team Goals Over Individual?" *Workforce Management Online,* February 2011; S. J. Goerg, S. Kube, and R. Zultan, "Treating Equals Unequally: Incentives in Teams, Workers' Motivation, and Production Technology," *Journal of Labor Economics* (October 2010), pp. 747–772; T. Taylor, "The Challenge of Project Team Incentives," *Compensation & Benefits Review,* September–October 2010, pp. 411–419; M. J. Pearsall, M. S. Christian, and A. P. J. Ellis, "Motivating Interdependent Teams: Individual Rewards, Shared Rewards, or Something in Between?" *Journal of Applied Psychology* (January 2010), pp. 183–191; M. A. Marks, C. S. Burke, M. J. Sabella, and S. J. Zaccaro, "The Impact of Cross-Training on Team Effectiveness," *Journal of Applied Psychology* (February 2000), pp. 3–14; and M. A. Marks, S. J. Zaccaro, and J. E. Mathieu, "Performance Implications of Leader Briefings and Team Interaction for Team Adaptation to Novel Environments," *Journal of Applied Psychology* (December 2000), p. 971.

51. C. Garvey, "Steer Teams with the Right Pay: Team-Based Pay Is a Success When It Fits Corporate Goals and Culture, and Rewards the Right Behavior," *HR Magazine,* May 2002, pp. 71–77.

52. F. Niederman and F. B. Tan, "Emerging Markets Managing Global IT Teams: Considering Cultural Dynamics," *Communications of the ACM,* April 2011, pp. 24–27; R. M. B. Boyle and S. Nicholas, "Cross-Cultural Group Performance," *The Learning Organization,* March 2011, pp. 94–101; G. K. Stahl, M. L. Maznevski, A. Voigt, and K. Jonsen, "Unraveling the Effects of Cultural Diversity in Teams: A Meta-Analysis of Research on Multicultural Work Groups," *Journal of International Business Studies* (May 2010), pp. 690–709; and M. R. Haas, "The Double-Edged Sword of Autonomy and External Knowledge: Analyzing Team Effectiveness in a Multinational Organization."

53. R. Bond and P. B. Smith, "Culture and Conformity: A Meta-Analysis of Studies Using Asch's [1952, 1956] Line Judgment Task," *Psychological Bulletin,* January 1996, pp. 111–137.

54. I. L. Janis, *Groupthink,* 2nd ed. (New York: Houghton Mifflin Company, 1982), p. 175.

55. See P. C. Earley, "Social Loafing and Collectivism: A Comparison of the United States and the People's Republic of China," *Administrative Science Quarterly,* December 1989, pp. 565–581; and P. C. Earley, "East Meets West Meets

Mideast: Further Explorations of Collectivistic and Individualistic Work Groups," *Academy of Management Journal* (April 1993), pp. 319–348.

56. N. J. Adler, *International Dimensions of Organizational Behavior,* 4th ed. (Cincinnati, OH: Southwestern, 2002), p. 142.

57. K. B. Dahlin, L. R. Weingart, and P. J. Hinds, "Team Diversity and Information Use," *Academy of Management Journal* (December 2005), pp. 1107–1123.

58. Adler, *International Dimensions of Organizational Behavior,* p. 142.

59. S. Paul, I. M. Samarah, P. Seetharaman, and P. P. Mykytyn, "An Empirical Investigation of Collaborative Conflict Management Style in Group Support System-Based Global Virtual Teams," *Journal of Management Information Systems* (Winter 2005), pp. 185–222.

60. This section is based on S. P. Robbins and T. A. Judge, *Organizational Behavior*, 14th ed. (Upper Saddle River, NJ: Pearson Prentice Hall, 2011).

61. C. E. Naquin and R. O. Tynan, "The Team Halo Effect: Why Teams Are Not Blamed for Their Failures," *Journal of Applied Psychology* (April 2003), pp. 332–340.

62. A. B. Drexler and R. Forrester, "Teamwork—Not Necessarily the Answer," *HRMagazine,* January 1998, pp. 55–58. See also R. Saavedra, P. C. Earley, and L. Van Dyne, "Complex Interdependence in Task-Performing Groups," *Journal of Applied Psychology* (February 1993), pp. 61–72; and K. A. Jehn, G. B. Northcraft, and M. A. Neale, "Why Differences Make a Difference: A Field Study of Diversity, Conflict, and Performance in Work Groups," *Administrative Science Quarterly,* December 1999, pp. 741–763.

YOUR TURN TO BE A MANAGER

Understanding Groups and Managing Work Teams

Skill Development: Working with Teams

Organizations have become increasingly designed around teams. Twenty years ago, the individual was the basic building block of an organization; today it's teams. And the manager who can't effectively be part of a team or lead a team is likely to have a short tenure in his or her management position.

Personal Insights: How Good Am I at Building and Leading a Team?

Use the following rating scale to respond to the 18 questions on building and leading an effective team:

1 = Strongly disagree
2 = Disagree
3 = Slightly disagree
4 = Slightly agree
5 = Agree
6 = Strongly agree

1. I am knowledgeable about the different stages of development that teams can go through in their life cycles. 1 2 3 4 5 6

2. When a team forms, I make certain that all team members are introduced to one another at the outset. 1 2 3 4 5 6

3. When the team first comes together, I provide directions, answer team members' questions, and clarify goals, expectations, and procedures. 1 2 3 4 5 6

4. I help team members establish a foundation of trust among one another and between themselves and me. 1 2 3 4 5 6

5. I ensure that standards of excellence—not mediocrity or mere acceptability—characterize the team's work. 1 2 3 4 5 6

6. I provide a great deal of feedback to team members regarding their performance. 1 2 3 4 5 6

7. I encourage team members to balance individual autonomy with interdependence among other team members. 1 2 3 4 5 6

8. I help team members become at least as committed to the success of the team as to their own personal success. 1 2 3 4 5 6

9. I help members learn to play roles that assist the team in accomplishing its tasks as well as building strong interpersonal relationships. 1 2 3 4 5 6

10. I articulate a clear, exciting, passionate vision of what the team can achieve. 1 2 3 4 5 6

11. I help team members become committed to the team vision. 1 2 3 4 5 6

12. I encourage a win/win philosophy in the team; that is, when one member wins, every member wins. 1 2 3 4 5 6

13. I help the team avoid "groupthink" or making the group's survival more important than accomplishing its goal. 1 2 3 4 5 6

322

14. I use formal process management procedures to help the group become faster, more efficient, and more productive, and to prevent errors.   1 2 3 4 5 6

15. I encourage team members to represent the team's vision, goals, and accomplishments to outsiders.   1 2 3 4 5 6

16. I diagnose and capitalize on the team's core competence.   1 2 3 4 5 6

17. I encourage the team to achieve dramatic breakthrough innovations as well as small continuous improvements.   1 2 3 4 5 6

18. I help the team work toward preventing mistakes, not just correcting them after-the-fact.   1 2 3 4 5 6

Source: Adapted from D. A. Whetten and K. S. Cameron, *Developing Management Skills*, 3rd ed. (New York: HarperCollins, 1995), pp. 534–535.

Analysis and Interpretation

The authors of this instrument propose that it assesses team development behaviors in five areas: diagnosing team development (items 1, 16); managing the forming stage (2–4); managing the conforming stage (6–9, 13); managing the storming stage (10–12, 14, 15), and managing the performing stage (5, 17, 18).

To calculate your total score, add up your scores on the 18 individual items. Your score will range between 18 and 108.

Based on a norm group of 500 business students, the following can help estimate where you are relative to others:

Total score of 95 or above = You're in the top quartile

72–94 = You're in the second quartile

60–71 = You're in the third quartile

Below 60 = You're in the bottom quartile

Skill Basics

Managers and team leaders need to be able to create effective teams. You can increase the effectiveness of your teams if you use the following nine behaviors.

1. *Establish a common purpose.* An effective team needs a common purpose to which all members aspire. This purpose is a vision. It's broader than any specific goals. This common purpose provides direction, momentum, and commitment for team members.

2. *Assess team strengths and weaknesses.* Team members will have different strengths and weaknesses. Knowing these strengths and weaknesses can help the team leader build on the strengths and compensate for the weaknesses.

3. *Develop specific individual goals.* Specific individual goals help lead team members to achieve higher performance. In addition, specific goals facilitate clear communication and help maintain the focus on getting results.

4. *Get agreement on a common approach for achieving goals.* Goals are the ends a team strives to attain. Defining and agreeing on a common approach ensures that the team is unified on the *means* for achieving those ends.

5. *Encourage acceptance of responsibility for both individual and team performance.* Successful teams make members individually and jointly accountable for the team's purpose, goals, and approach. Members understand what they are individually responsible for and what they are jointly responsible for.

6. *Build mutual trust among members.* When there is *trust,* team members believe in the integrity, character, and ability of each other. When trust is lacking, members are unable to depend on each other. Teams that lack trust tend to be short-lived.

7. *Maintain an appropriate mix of team member skills and personalities.* Team members come to the team with different skills and personalities. To perform effectively, teams need three types of skills. They need people with technical expertise, people with problem-solving and decision-making skills, and people with good interpersonal skills.

8. *Provide needed training and resources.* Team leaders need to make sure that their teams have both the training and the resources they need to accomplish their goals.

9. *Create opportunities for small achievements.* Building an effective team takes time. Team members have to learn to think and work as a team. New teams can't be expected to hit home runs every time they come to bat, especially at the beginning. Instead, team members should be encouraged to try for small achievements initially.

Based on J. R. Katzenback and D. K. Smith, *The Wisdom of Teams* (Boston: Harvard Business Press, 1993); M. Hanlan, *High Performance Teams: How to Make Them Work* (New York: Praeger, 2005); and L. Thompson, *Making the Team,* 3rd ed. (Upper Saddle River, NJ: Prentice Hall, 2008).

Skill Application

You're the leader of a five-member project team that's been assigned the task of moving your engineering firm into the growing area of high-speed intercity rail construction. You and your team members have been researching the field, identifying specific business opportunities, negotiating alliances with equipment vendors, and evaluating high-speed rail experts and consultants from around the world. Throughout the process, Tonya, a highly qualified and respected engineer, has challenged a number of things you've said during team meetings and in the workplace. For example, at a meeting two weeks ago, you presented the team with a list of 10 possible high-speed rail projects and started evaluating your organization's ability to compete for them. Tonya contradicted virtually all your comments, questioned your statistics, and was quite pessimistic about the possibility of getting contracts on these projects. After this latest display of displeasure, two other group members, Bryan and Maggie, came to you and complained that Tonya's actions were damaging the team's effectiveness. You originally put Tonya on the team for her unique expertise and insight. You'd like to find a way to reach her and get the team on the right track to its fullest potential.

Form three-member teams in class. Each team should analyze the leader's problem and suggest solutions. Each team should be prepared to present its conclusions to the class.

Skill Practice

1. Interview three managers at different organizations. Ask them about their experiences in managing teams. Have each describe teams that they thought were effective and why they succeeded. Have each also describe teams that they thought were ineffective and the reasons that might have caused this.

2. Think about teams of which you've been a member: Contrast a team in which members trusted each other with another team in which members lacked trust with each other. How did these conditions develop? What were the consequences in terms of interaction patterns and performance?

Skill Development: Resolving Conflicts

Studies have found that managing conflicts is one of the top activities consuming a manager's time. Therefore, how effective a manager is in handling conflicts will go a long way in determining how successful he or she will be on the job.

Personal Insights: What's My Preferred Conflict-Handling Style?

When you differ with someone, how do you respond? Use the following rating scale to record your answers:

1 = Practically never
2 = Once in a great while
3 = Sometimes
4 = Fairly often
5 = Very often

1. I work to come out victorious, no matter what.	1 2 3 4 5
2. I try to put the needs of others above my own.	1 2 3 4 5
3. I look for a mutually satisfactory solution.	1 2 3 4 5
4. I try not to get involved in conflicts.	1 2 3 4 5
5. I strive to investigate issues thoroughly and jointly.	1 2 3 4 5
6. I never back away from a good argument.	1 2 3 4 5
7. I strive to foster harmony.	1 2 3 4 5
8. I negotiate to get a portion of what I propose.	1 2 3 4 5
9. I avoid open discussions of controversial subjects.	1 2 3 4 5
10. I openly share information with others in resolving disagreements.	1 2 3 4 5
11. I would rather win than end up compromising.	1 2 3 4 5
12. I go along with suggestions of others.	1 2 3 4 5
13. I look for a middle ground to resolve disagreements.	1 2 3 4 5
14. I keep my true opinions to myself to avoid hard feelings.	1 2 3 4 5
15. I encourage the open sharing of concerns and issues.	1 2 3 4 5
16. I am reluctant to admit I am wrong.	1 2 3 4 5
17. I try to help others avoid losing face in a disagreement.	1 2 3 4 5
18. I stress the advantages of give-and-take.	1 2 3 4 5
19. I agree early on, rather than argue about a point.	1 2 3 4 5
20. I state my position as only one point of view.	1 2 3 4 5

Source: Based on conflict dimensions defined in K. W. Thomas, "Conflict and Conflict Management," in M. Dunnette (ed.), *Handbook of Industrial and Organizational Psychology* (Chicago: Rand McNally, 1976), pp. 889–935.

Analysis and Interpretation

Research has identified five conflict-handling styles. They are defined as follows:

> Competing = A desire to satisfy one's interests, regardless of the impact on the other party to the conflict. Items 1, 6, 11, and 16 in this instrument tap this style.
>
> Collaborating = Where the parties to a conflict each desire to satisfy fully the concerns of all parties. Items 5, 10, 15, and 20 in this instrument.
>
> Avoiding = The desire to withdraw from or suppress the conflict. Items 4, 9, 14, and 19 in this instrument.
>
> Accommodating = Willingness of one party in a conflict to place the opponent's interests above his or her own. Items 2, 7, 12, and 17 in this instrument.
>
> Compromising = Where each party to a conflict is willing to give up something. Items 3, 8, 13, and 18 in this instrument.

To calculate your conflict-handling score, add up your totals for each of the five categories. Your score within each category will range from 4 to 20. The category you score highest in is your preferred conflict-handling style. Your next-highest total is your secondary style.

Ideally, we should adjust our conflict-handling style to the situation. For instance, avoidance works well when a conflict is trivial, when emotions are running high and time is needed to cool them down, or when the potential disruption from a more assertive action outweighs the benefits of a resolution. In contrast, competing works well when you need a quick resolution on important issues where unpopular actions must be taken, or when commitment by others to your solution is not critical. But the evidence indicates that we all have a preferred style for handling conflicts. When "push comes to shove," this is the style we tend to rely on.

Skill Basics

To manage conflict effectively, you need to know yourself, as well as the conflicting parties; to understand the situation that has created the conflict; and to be aware of your options.

What's your underlying conflict-handling style? Most of us have the ability to vary our conflict response according to the situation, but each of us has a preferred style for handling conflicts. These styles include *collaborating* (accommodating various points of view to seek a win-win solution); *compromising* (we both give up something so there is no clear winner or loser); *accommodating* (self-sacrificing by putting others' interests above your own); *forcing* (satisfying your own interest regardless of the impact on others); and *avoiding* (withdrawing from or suppressing differences).

Selectively choose the conflicts you want to handle. Not every conflict justifies your attention. Avoidance may appear to be a cop-out, but it can sometimes be the most appropriate response. Avoid trivial conflicts and save your efforts for the ones that count.

Evaluate the conflict parties. Who is involved in the conflict? What interests do you or they represent? What are each party's values, personality, feelings, and resources?

Assess the source of the conflict. The most common sources of interpersonal conflicts in organizations are communication differences, structural differences (i.e., rules, territorial battles, budget conflicts, questions of authority), and personality and value differences. Communication conflicts are typically the easiest to resolve, while personality and value differences the most difficult. Knowing the source of a conflict will narrow your choices of resolution techniques.

Select the best option. In addition to the five preferred-styles of handling conflict noted above, additional resolution techniques include expanding the scarce resource (such as a budget or promotion opportunities) that is causing the conflict; creating a shared goal that requires all parties to the conflict to cooperate on; behavioral-change intervention and counseling; and reorganizing jobs or departments.

Based on S. P. Robbins, *Managing Organizational Conflict* (Englewood Cliffs, NJ: Prentice Hall, 1974); K. W. Thomas, "Conflict and Conflict Management," in Marvin Dunnette (ed.), *Handbook of Industrial and Organizational Psychology* (Chicago: Rand McNally, 1976), pp. 889–935; and K. Cloke and J. Goldsmith, *Resolving Conflicts at Work: Eight Strategies for Everyone on the Job*, rev. ed. (San Francisco: Jossey-Bass, 2006).

Skill Application

Form teams of three. Analyze each of the following scenarios and formulate a conflict-handling strategy:

> *Situation 1.* You are a staff specialist and have been assigned two projects: one by your immediate supervisor and one by the supervisor of another department. There is adequate time to complete both projects by the deadline date, however, neither project would be completed with the degree of excellence required by your organization. What would you do?
>
> *Situation 2.* You are the moderator of a group session with five other people. The purpose of the session is to formulate a plan that requires consent from all participants. One of the participants is so involved with the important details of the plan that he is delaying the group from reaching agreement. As moderator, what would you do in this situation?
>
> *Situation 3.* Your boss has called you into his office and you find that he wants your opinion about the performance of one of your coworkers. The coworker is your best friend and neighbor, but you are inclined to believe that his performance is substandard. What would you tell the boss?

Skill Practice

1. Interview several managers to learn (a) what they think their basic conflict-handling style is; (b) how flexible they perceive themselves to be in adjusting their style to changing situations; (c) and how effective they have been in mastering the skills of conflict management.

2. Think of three conflict situations you've faced in recent months. How did you handle the conflict? How effective was your approach? What could you have done differently to improve the outcome?

FYIA

Colorado State High School Sports Association

To: Eric Gershman, Manager, Program Infractions Investigations
From: Audrey Costa, Director of Association Services
Subject: Conflicts on Investigation Teams

For Your Immediate Action

Eric, we've got a problem. I've been receiving complaints that the members of the five-person investigation teams we're sending out to high schools to investigate allegations of rules infractions are having conflicts. Because team members have to work closely together in interviewing people, interpreting the rules, and writing up reports, I'm worried that this conflict may be hurting the quality of the teams' investigation process. We've got to address this problem immediately in order to protect our reputation for being fair and reasonable in our rules enforcement. Please send me a bulleted list (no longer than a page) describing how you're going to address this problem and get it to me as soon as possible. Once I've had a chance to look it over, we'll get together to discuss it.

This fictionalized company and message were created for educational purposes only, and not meant to reflect positively or negatively on management practices by any company that may share this name.

Bringing the Real World to Life

Case Application:
Intel Inside . . . and Far Away:
Part 2

As one of Intel's premier research and development labs, the Israel Development Center (IDC) has employed engineers for almost 40 years. The technology behind the highly successful Centrino chips for laptops came out of this lab, as have processors for servers, PCs, and laptops. The group atmosphere at IDC, although quite confrontational, actually helped Centrino get off the ground and become a marketplace and financial success for Intel. Getting there, however, wasn't easy.

During the initial design stages of Centrino, the focus, as always, was on processor chip speed. But the reality is that fast

chips consume more power and shorten battery life. And when designing a product for use in wireless computers, that's not a good thing. An engineer at IDC came to the team leader and suggested that by giving up half the chip speed that power consumption could also be cut by half as well. Such a suggestion probably wouldn't have survived long at the home office because it involved challenging everything that the company stood for. However, here in a location where the group wasn't bound by such cultural constraints, it led to the development of a winning product.

Another benefit of having design groups thousands of miles away from headquarters in Santa Clara, California (some 28 percent of the company's R&D employees are located in more than 20 countries outside the United States), is that these off-site locations don't suffer from bureaucratic inertia associated with constant meetings and committees.

However, the challenge for Intel's geographically dispersed teams is that when team members live and work in different countries, time zones, diverse cultures, and dissimilar languages "add complexities to the difficult tasks associated with successful teamwork." One thing that has worked for Intel is the virtual retrospective.

A retrospective is "a formal method for evaluating project performance, extracting lessons learned, and making recommendations for the future." Because Intel's design teams are geographically dispersed, they collaborate virtually over an audio or video connection. Such retrospectives allow Intel's teams to connect and collaborate. The major problems, though, are simple things like finding a common time to meet. For instance, setting up a virtual retrospective between IDC and an Intel team in Hillsboro, Oregon, involved a 10-hour time difference. However, they resolved it as the Israeli team members agreed to shift their work day and start the retrospective at 5 P.M. Haifa time, which was 7 A.M. Hillsboro time. Another challenge is that these virtual meetings usually last longer than normal simply because the teams usually have numerous issues to discuss. Also, team leaders need to take into account cultural differences (speaking styles, family commitments), safety (establishing an environment where all participants feel free to express observations and opinions), and fairness (locations with a large number of participants can dominate the discussion and limit input from sites with fewer participants).

Despite the challenges, Intel's project managers have found that having a way for their geographically dispersed teams to collaborate and connect is vital and valuable.

DISCUSSION QUESTIONS

1. What challenges have Intel's managers faced in connecting their geographically dispersed teams?

2. How have they dealt with these challenges?

3. Would a "confrontational" atmosphere be appropriate in all team situations? Explain.

4. Discuss how roles, norms, status, group size, and cohesiveness might affect these geographically dispersed teams.

5. Compare the team characteristics described here against the characteristics of effective teams as shown in Exhibit 10–6 (see p. 259). Which ones does the IDC team appear to have?

Motivating and Rewarding Employees

From Chapter 11 of *Fundamentals of Management,* Eighth Edition. Stephen P. Robbins, David A. De Cenzo, Mary Coulter. Copyright © 2013 by Pearson Education, Inc. All rights reserved.

Motivating and Rewarding Employees

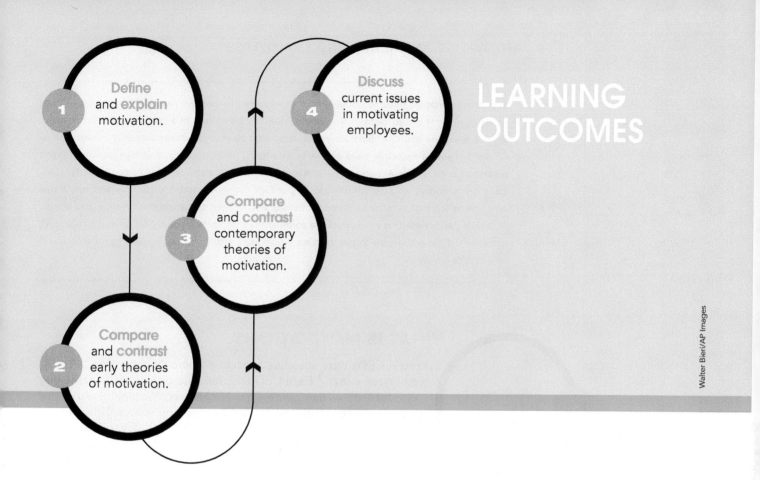

LEARNING OUTCOMES

1 Define and **explain** motivation.

2 Compare and **contrast** early theories of motivation.

3 Compare and **contrast** contemporary theories of motivation.

4 Discuss current issues in motivating employees.

Searching For?

Google gets more than 3,000 job applications a day.[1] And it's no wonder! With a massage every other week, onsite laundry, swimming pool and spa, free delicious all-you-can-eat gourmet meals, and fun diversions like a huge slide in the workplace, what more could an employee want? Sounds like an ideal job, doesn't it? However, many people are demonstrating by their decisions to leave the company that all those perks (and these are just a few) aren't enough to keep them there.

Google is number one on the list of "ideal" employers and has been in the top five of *Fortune*'s list of "best companies to work for" for five years running and was number one on the list for two of those years. But make no mistake, Google's executives offer these fabulous perks for several reasons: to attract the best knowledge workers it can in an intensely competitive, cutthroat market; to help employees work long hours and not have to deal with time-consuming personal chores; to show employees they're valued; and to have employees remain Googlers (the name used for employees) for many years. Yet, employees continue to jump ship. As one analyst said, "Yes, Google's making gobs of money. Yes, it's full of smart people. Yes, it's a wonderful place to work. So why are so many people leaving?"

Successful managers need to understand that what motivates them personally may have little or no effect on others. Just because you're motivated by being part of a cohesive work team, don't assume everyone is. Or just because you're motivated by your job doesn't mean that everyone is. Or just because employees have access to free food, free massages, and free laundry doesn't mean those extras are enough to keep them from looking elsewhere for career opportunities. Effective managers who get employees to put forth maximum effort know how and why those employees are motivated and tailor motivational practices to satisfy their needs and wants. Motivating and rewarding employees are some of the manager's most important and challenging activities. To get employees to put forth maximum work effort, managers need to know how and why they're motivated.

WHAT IS MOTIVATION?

① Define and explain motivation.

Several CEOs were attending a meeting where the topic was "What do employees want?"[2] Each CEO took turns describing the benefits they provided and how they gave out free M&Ms every Wednesday and offered their employees stock options and free parking spaces. However, the meeting's main speaker made the point that "employees don't want M&Ms; they want to love what they do." Half expecting his audience to laugh, the speaker was pleasantly surprised as the CEOs stood up one-by-one to agree. They all recognized that "the value in their companies comes from the employees who are motivated to be there."

These CEOs understand how important employee motivation is. Like them, all managers need to be able to motivate their employees, which requires understanding what motivation is. Let's begin by pointing out what motivation is not. Why? Because many people incorrectly view motivation as a personal trait; that is, they think some people are motivated and others aren't. Our knowledge of motivation tells us that we can't label people that way because individuals differ in motivational drive and their overall motivation varies from situation to situation. For instance, you're probably more motivated to work hard and do well in some classes than in others.

Motivation refers to the process by which a person's efforts are energized, directed, and sustained toward attaining a goal.[3] This definition has three key elements: energy, direction, and persistence.[4]

The *energy* element is a measure of intensity or drive. A motivated person puts forth effort and works hard. However, the quality of the effort must be considered as well as its intensity. High levels of effort don't necessarily lead to favorable job performance unless the effort is channeled in a *direction* that benefits the organization. Effort that's directed toward, and consistent with, organizational goals is the kind of effort we want from employees. Finally, motivation includes a *persistence* dimension. We want employees to persist in putting forth effort to achieve those goals.

Motivating high levels of employee performance is an important organizational concern and managers keep looking for answers. For instance, a Gallup poll found that a large majority of U.S. employees—some 73 percent—are not excited about their work. As the researchers stated, "These employees are essentially 'checked out.' They're sleep-walking through their workday, putting time, but not energy or passion, into their work."[6] It's no wonder then that both managers and academics want to understand and explain employee motivation.

WHAT DO THE EARLY THEORIES OF MOTIVATION SAY?

Compare and contrast early theories of motivation. 2

The 1950s and 1960s were a fruitful time for the development of motivation concepts. Four specific theories formulated during this period are probably still the best-known explanations of employee motivation although they've been criticized and questioned. They include the hierarchy of needs theory, Theories X and Y, the two-factor theory, and three-needs theory. Although more valid explanations of motivation have been developed, you should know these early theories for at least two reasons. First, they represent the foundation from which contemporary theories grew. Second, practicing managers regularly use these theories and their terminology in explaining employee motivation. Let's take a look at them.

What Is Maslow's Hierarchy of Needs Theory?

Having a car to get to work is a necessity for many workers. When two crucial employees of Taleo/Vurv Technology in Jacksonville, Florida, had trouble getting to work, the owner decided to buy two inexpensive used cars for the employees. He said, "I felt that they were good employees and a valuable asset to the company." One of the employees who got one of the cars said, "It wasn't the nicest car. It wasn't the prettiest car. But boy did my overwhelming feeling of dread go from that to enlightenment. The 80-hour weeks we worked after that never meant anything. It was give and take. I was giving and the company was definitely giving back."[7] This manager understood employee needs (reliable transportation being an essential need for employees to be able to get to work) and their impact on motivation. The first motivation theory we're going to look at addresses employee needs.

The best-known motivation theory is probably Abraham Maslow's hierarchy of needs theory.[8] Maslow was a psychologist who proposed that within every person is a hierarchy of five needs:

1. **Physiological needs:** Food, drink, shelter, sex, and other physical requirements
2. **Safety needs:** Security and protection from physical and emotional harm, as well as assurance that physical needs will continue to be met
3. **Social needs:** Affection, belongingness, acceptance, and friendship
4. **Esteem needs:** Internal esteem factors such as self-respect, autonomy, and achievement and external esteem factors such as status, recognition, and attention
5. **Self-actualization needs:** Growth, achieving one's potential, and self-fulfillment; the drive to become what one is capable of becoming

Maslow argued that each level in the needs hierarchy must be substantially satisfied before the next need becomes dominant. An individual moves up the needs hierarchy from one level to the next. (See Exhibit 1.) In addition, Maslow separated the five needs into higher and lower levels. Physiological and safety needs were considered *lower-order needs*; social, esteem, and self-actualization needs were considered *higher-order needs*. Lower-order needs are predominantly satisfied externally while higher-order needs are satisfied internally.

How does Maslow's theory explain motivation? Managers using Maslow's hierarchy to motivate employees do things to satisfy employees' needs. But the theory also says that once a need is substantially satisfied, an individual isn't motivated to satisfy that need. Therefore, to motivate someone, you need to understand what need level that person is on in the hierarchy and focus on satisfying needs at or above that level.

motivation
The process by which a person's efforts are energized, directed, and sustained toward attaining a goal

hierarchy of needs theory
Maslow's theory that there is a hierarchy of five human needs: physiological, safety, social, esteem, and self-actualization

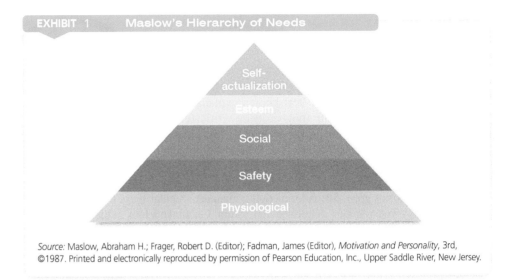

EXHIBIT 1 Maslow's Hierarchy of Needs

Self-actualization

Esteem

Social

Safety

Physiological

Source: Maslow, Abraham H.; Frager, Robert D. (Editor); Fadman, James (Editor), *Motivation and Personality*, 3rd, ©1987. Printed and electronically reproduced by permission of Pearson Education, Inc., Upper Saddle River, New Jersey.

Maslow's need theory is widely recognized, especially among practicing managers. Its popularity probably can be attributed to the theory's intuitive logic and ease of understanding.[9] But Maslow provided no empirical support for his theory, and several studies that sought to validate it could not.[10]

What Are McGregor's Theory X and Theory Y?

General Motors' new CEO has been described as brash, blunt, and demanding. Critics say that his approach may not go over well in a company that is "rebuilding itself from the brink of extinction." A manufacturing plant manager in another industry described his managerial style as: "If you're not a fan of in-your-face management, don't work here."[11] Both these managers are examples of what Douglas McGregor called a Theory X manager.

Douglas McGregor is best known for proposing two assumptions about human nature: Theory X and Theory Y.[12] Very simply, **Theory X** is a negative view of people that assumes workers have little ambition, dislike work, want to avoid responsibility, and need to be closely controlled to work effectively. **Theory Y** is a positive view that assumes employees enjoy work, seek out and accept responsibility, and exercise self-direction. McGregor believed that Theory Y assumptions should guide management practice and proposed that participation in decision making, responsible and challenging jobs, and good group relations would maximize employee motivation.

Unfortunately, no evidence confirms that either set of assumptions is valid or that being a Theory Y manager is the only way to motivate employees. For instance, Jen-Hsun Huang, founder of Nvidia Corporation, an innovative and successful microchip manufacturer, has been known to use both reassuring hugs and tough love in motivating employees. But he has little tolerance for screw-ups. "In one legendary meeting, he's said to have ripped into a project team for its tendency to repeat mistakes. 'Do you suck?' he asked the stunned employees. 'Because if you suck, just get up and say you suck.'"[13] His message, delivered in classic Theory X style, was that if you need help, ask for it. It's a harsh approach, but it has worked.

What Is Herzberg's Two-Factor Theory?

Frederick Herzberg's **two-factor theory** (also called motivation-hygiene theory) proposes that intrinsic factors are related to job satisfaction, while extrinsic factors are associated with job dissatisfaction.[14]

Berkshire Hathaway Chairman and CEO Warren Buffet is a Theory Y manager. He has a positive view of human nature and assumes that people enjoy work and accept responsibility. Buffet motivates employees by being approachable, trusting, and forgiving, by delegating decision-making authority, by giving them challenging work, and by making them feel valued. He constantly communicates that Berkshire Hathaway companies are well-managed, and he credits his managers for his success. Buffet is shown here playing the ukulele and singing with the Quebe Sisters band before participating in the company's annual shareholders' meeting.

Nati Harnick/AP Images

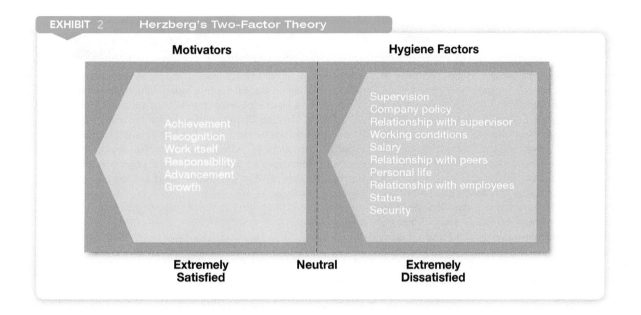

EXHIBIT 2 Herzberg's Two-Factor Theory

Motivators

Achievement
Recognition
Work itself
Responsibility
Advancement
Growth

Hygiene Factors

Supervision
Company policy
Relationship with supervisor
Working conditions
Salary
Relationship with peers
Personal life
Relationship with employees
Status
Security

Extremely Satisfied — **Neutral** — **Extremely Dissatisfied**

Herzberg wanted to know when people felt exceptionally good (satisfied) or bad (dissatisfied) about their jobs. (These findings are shown in Exhibit 2.) He concluded that the replies people gave when they felt good about their jobs were significantly different from the replies they gave when they felt badly. Certain characteristics were consistently related to job satisfaction (factors on the left side of the exhibit), and others to job dissatisfaction (factors on the right side). When people felt good about their work, they tended to cite intrinsic factors arising from the job itself such as achievement, recognition, and responsibility. On the other hand, when they were dissatisfied, they tended to cite extrinsic factors arising from the job context such as company policy and administration, supervision, interpersonal relationships, and working conditions.

In addition, Herzberg believed the data suggested that the opposite of satisfaction was not dissatisfaction, as traditionally had been believed. Removing dissatisfying characteristics from a job would not necessarily make that job more satisfying (or motivating). As shown in Exhibit 3, Herzberg proposed that a dual continuum existed: The opposite of "satisfaction" is "no satisfaction," and the opposite of "dissatisfaction" is "no dissatisfaction."

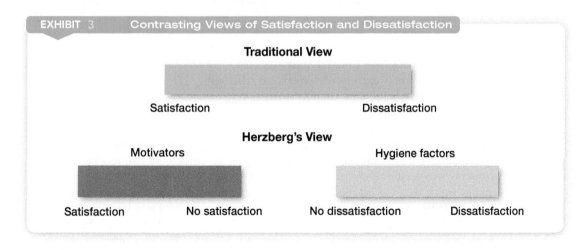

EXHIBIT 3 Contrasting Views of Satisfaction and Dissatisfaction

Traditional View

Satisfaction — Dissatisfaction

Herzberg's View

Motivators — Hygiene factors

Satisfaction — No satisfaction — No dissatisfaction — Dissatisfaction

theory X
The assumption that employees dislike work, are lazy, avoid responsibility, and must be coerced to work

theory Y
The assumption that employees are creative, enjoy work, seek responsibility, and can exercise self-direction

two-factor theory
Herzberg's motivation theory, which proposes that intrinsic factors are related to job satisfaction and motivation, whereas extrinsic factors are associated with job dissatisfaction

Deciding how work tasks should be performed has long been of interest to managers.[15] From scientific management's attempts to find the "one best way" to do work to the Hawthorne Studies that attempted to unravel patterns of human behavior at work, researchers have been curious about the ideal approach to work design. In the 1950s, Frederick Herzberg and his associates began research to "discover the importance of attitudes toward work and the experiences both good and bad, that workers reported." He wanted to know the kinds of things that made people at their work happy and satisfied or unhappy and dissatisfied. What he discovered changed the way we view job design. The fact that job dissatisfaction and job satisfaction were the results of different aspects of the work environment was an important finding. Herzberg's two-factor theory gave practicing managers insights into both job context and job content. And if you wanted to motivate

employees, you'd better focus more on the job content aspects (the motivators) than on the job context aspects (the hygiene factors).

In addition, Herzberg's research stimulated additional interest in work design. The Job Characteristics model, for one, built upon Herzberg's findings in identifying the five core job dimensions, especially autonomy. As managers and organizations continue to search for work designs that will energize and engage employees, Herzberg's study of when people felt good and felt bad at work continues as a classic.

Think About:

- Why do you think jobs need to be "designed"?

- How can job design contribute to employee motivation?

- What would your "ideal" job look like?

Again, Herzberg believed that the factors that led to job satisfaction were separate and distinct from those that led to job dissatisfaction. Therefore, managers who sought to eliminate factors that created job dissatisfaction could keep people from being dissatisfied but not necessarily motivate them. The extrinsic factors that create job dissatisfaction were called hygiene factors. When these factors are adequate, people won't be dissatisfied, but they won't be satisfied (or motivated) either. To motivate people, Herzberg suggested emphasizing motivators, the intrinsic factors having to do with the job itself.

Herzberg's theory enjoyed wide popularity from the mid-1960s to the early 1980s, despite criticisms of his procedures and methodology. Although some critics said his theory was too simplistic, it has influenced how we currently design jobs. (See the From the Past to the Present box for additional information.)

What Is McClelland's Three-Needs Theory?

David McClelland and his associates proposed the three-needs theory, which says three acquired (not innate) needs are major motives in work.[16] These three needs include the need for achievement (nAch), which is the drive to succeed and excel in relation to a set of standards; the need for power (nPow), which is the need to make others behave in a way that they would not have behaved otherwise; and the need for affiliation (nAff), which is the desire for friendly and close interpersonal relationships. Of these three needs, the need for achievement has been researched the most.

People with a high need for achievement are striving for personal achievement rather than for the trappings and rewards of success. They have a desire to do something better or more efficiently than it's been done before.[17] They prefer jobs that offer personal responsibility for finding solutions to problems, in which they can receive rapid and unambiguous feedback on their performance in order to tell whether they're improving, and in which they can set moderately challenging goals. High achievers avoid what they perceive to be very easy or very difficult tasks. Also, a high need to achieve doesn't necessarily lead to being a good manager, especially in large organizations. That's because high achievers focus on their *own* accomplishments while good managers emphasize helping *others* accomplish their goals.[18] McClelland showed that employees can be trained to stimulate their achievement need by being in situations where they have personal responsibility, feedback, and moderate risks.[19]

The other two needs in this theory haven't been researched as extensively as the need for achievement. However, we do know that the best managers tend to be high in the need for power and low in the need for affiliation.[20]

HOW DO THE CONTEMPORARY THEORIES EXPLAIN MOTIVATION?

At Electronic Arts (EA), one of the world's largest video game designers, employees put in grueling hours developing games. However, EA takes care of its game developers by providing them with workday intramural sports leagues, pinball arcades, group fitness classes, and an open invite to pets at work.[21] With some 8,000 workers in more than 20 countries, EA's managers need to understand employee motivation.

Compare and contrast contemporary theories of motivation. ③

The theories we look at in this section represent current explanations of employee motivation. Although these theories may not be as well known as those we just discussed, they are supported by research.[22] These contemporary motivation approaches include goal-setting theory, job design theory, equity theory, and expectancy theory.

What Is Goal-Setting Theory?

Before a big assignment or major class project presentation, has a teacher ever encouraged you to "Just do your best"? What does that vague statement, "do your best" mean? Would your performance on a class project have been higher had that teacher said you needed to score a 93 percent to keep your A in the class? Research on goal-setting theory addresses these issues, and the findings, as you'll see, are impressive in terms of the effect that goal specificity, challenge, and feedback have on performance.[23]

Substantial research support has been established for **goal-setting theory**, which says that specific goals increase performance and that difficult goals, when accepted, result in higher performance than do easy goals. What does goal-setting theory tell us?

First, working toward a goal is a major source of job motivation. Studies on goal setting have demonstrated that specific and challenging goals are superior motivating forces.[24] Such goals produce a higher output than does the generalized goal of "do your best." The specificity of the goal itself acts as an internal stimulus. For instance, when a sales rep commits to making eight sales calls daily, this intention gives him a specific goal to try to attain.

Next, will employees try harder if they have the opportunity to participate in the setting of goals? Not always. In some cases, participatively set goals elicit superior performance; in other cases, individuals performed best when their manager assigned goals. However, participation is probably preferable to assigning goals when employees might resist accepting difficult challenges.[25]

Finally, we know that people will do better if they get feedback on how well they're progressing toward their goals because feedback helps identify discrepancies between what they've done and what they want to do.

Working toward a goal is a major source of motivation for Mary Kay Cosmetics independent beauty consultants who receive generous recognition and rewards for their accomplishments. Consultants set their own specific sales goals for achieving different categories of rewards that range from jewelry to luxury trips to electronic equipment. Shown here is Mary Kay consultant Patricia Schneider, who has been setting and meeting her ambitious sales goals for 19 years and earning rewards that include jewelry and a pink bike. As the company's top sales producer in Orange County, California, Schneider has earned the use of her fourth pink Cadillac career car.

Newscom

---

hygiene factors
Factors that eliminate job dissatisfaction but don't motivate

motivators
Factors that increase job satisfaction and motivation

three-needs theory
McClelland's theory, which says that three acquired (not innate) needs—achievement, power, and affiliation—are major motives at work

need for achievement (nAch)
The drive to succeed and excel in relation to a set of standards

need for power (nPow)
The need to make others behave in a way that they would not have behaved otherwise

need for affiliation (nAff)
The desire for friendly and close interpersonal relationships

goal-setting theory
The proposition that specific goals increase performance and that difficult goals, when accepted, result in higher performance than do easy goals

But all feedback isn't equally effective. Self-generated feedback—where an employee monitors his or her own progress—has been shown to be a more powerful motivator than feedback coming from someone else.[26]

Three other contingencies besides feedback influence the goal-performance relationship: goal commitment, adequate self-efficacy, and national culture.

First, goal-setting theory assumes that an individual is committed to the goal. Commitment is most likely when goals are made public, when the individual has an internal locus of control, and when the goals are self-set rather than assigned.[27]

Next, **self-efficacy** refers to an individual's belief that he or she is capable of performing a task.[28] The higher your self-efficacy, the more confidence you have in your ability to succeed in a task. So, in difficult situations, we find that people with low self-efficacy are likely to reduce their effort or give up altogether, whereas those with high self-efficacy will try harder to master the challenge.[29] In addition, individuals with high self-efficacy seem to respond to negative feedback with increased effort and motivation, whereas those with low self-efficacy are likely to reduce their effort when given negative feedback.[30]

Finally, the value of goal-setting theory depends on the national culture. It's well adapted to North American countries because its main ideas align reasonably well with those cultures. It assumes that subordinates will be reasonably independent (not a high score on power distance), that people will seek challenging goals (low in uncertainty avoidance), and that performance is considered important by both managers and subordinates (high in assertiveness). Don't expect goal setting to lead to higher employee performance in countries where the cultural characteristics aren't like this.

Exhibit 4 summarizes the relationships among goals, motivation, and performance. Our overall conclusion is that the intention to work toward hard and specific goals is a powerful motivating force. Under the proper conditions, it can lead to higher performance. However, we have no evidence that such goals are associated with increased job satisfaction.[31]

How Does Job Design Influence Motivation?

Because managers want to motivate individuals on the job, we need to look at ways to design motivating jobs. If you look closely at what an organization is and how it works, you'll find that it's composed of thousands of tasks. These tasks are, in turn, aggregated into jobs. We use the term **job design** to refer to the way tasks are combined to form complete jobs. The jobs that people perform in an organization should not evolve by chance. Managers should design jobs deliberately and thoughtfully to reflect the demands of the changing environment, the organization's technology, and employees' skills,

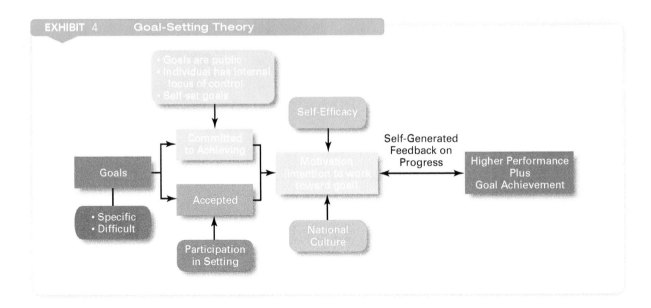

EXHIBIT 4   Goal-Setting Theory

abilities, and preferences.[32] When jobs are designed like that, employees are motivated to work hard. What are the ways that managers can design motivating jobs? We can answer that with the **job characteristics model (JCM)** developed by J. Richard Hackman and Greg R. Oldham.[33]

According to Hackman and Oldham, any job can be described in terms of the following five core job dimensions:

1. **Skill variety.** The degree to which the job requires a variety of activities so the worker can use a number of different skills and talents
2. **Task identity.** The degree to which the job requires completion of a whole and identifiable piece of work
3. **Task significance.** The degree to which the job affects the lives or work of other people
4. **Autonomy.** The degree to which the job provides freedom, independence, and discretion to the individual in scheduling the work and in determining the procedures to be used in carrying it out
5. **Feedback.** The degree to which carrying out the work activities required by the job results in the individual's obtaining direct and clear information about the effectiveness of his or her performance

Exhibit 5 presents the model. Notice how the first three dimensions—skill variety, task identity, and task significance—combine to create meaningful work. What we mean is that if these three characteristics exist in a job, we can predict that the person will view his or her job as being important, valuable, and worthwhile. Notice, too, that jobs that

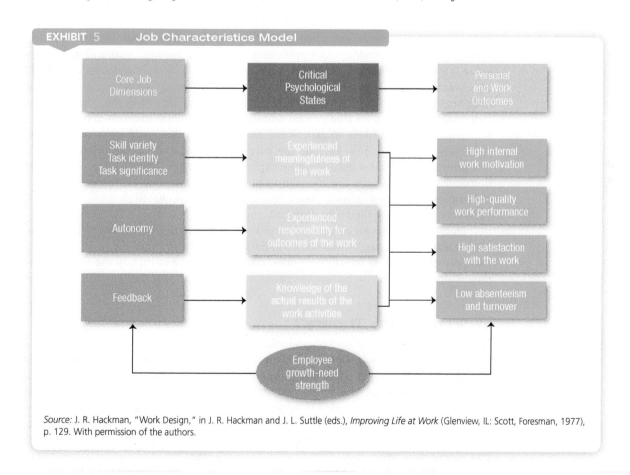

EXHIBIT 5   Job Characteristics Model

Source: J. R. Hackman, "Work Design," in J. R. Hackman and J. L. Suttle (eds.), *Improving Life at Work* (Glenview, IL: Scott, Foresman, 1977), p. 129. With permission of the authors.

---

self-efficacy
An individual's belief that he or she is capable of performing a task

job design
The way tasks are combined to form complete jobs

job characteristics model (JCM)
A framework for analyzing and designing jobs that identifies five primary core job dimensions, their interrelationships, and their impact on outcomes

339

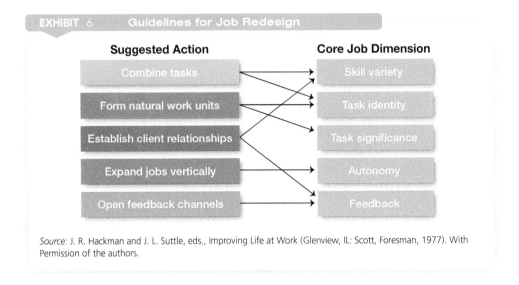

Source: J. R. Hackman and J. L. Suttle, eds., Improving Life at Work (Glenview, IL: Scott, Foresman, 1977). With Permission of the authors.

possess autonomy give the job incumbent a feeling of personal responsibility for the results and that, if a job provides feedback, the employee will know how effectively he or she is performing.

From a motivational point of view, the JCM suggests that internal rewards are obtained when an employee *learns* (knowledge of results through feedback) that he or she *personally* (experienced responsibility through autonomy of work) has performed well on a task that he or she *cares* about (experienced meaningfulness through skill variety, task identity, and/or task significance). The more these three conditions characterize a job, the greater the employee's motivation, performance, and satisfaction and the lower his or her absenteeism and the likelihood of resigning. As the model shows, the links between the job dimensions and the outcomes are moderated by the strength of the individual's growth need (the person's desire for self-esteem and self-actualization). Individuals are more likely to experience the critical psychological states and respond positively when their jobs include the core dimensions than are individuals with a low growth need. This distinction may explain the mixed results with job enrichment (vertical expansion of a job by adding planning and evaluation responsibilities): Individuals with low growth need don't tend to achieve high performance or satisfaction by having their jobs enriched.

The JCM provides significant guidance to managers for job design for both individuals and teams.[34] The suggestions shown in Exhibit 6, which are based on the JCM, specify the types of changes in jobs that are most likely to improve in each of the five core job dimensions.

What Is Equity Theory?

Do you ever wonder what kind of grade the person sitting next to you in class makes on a test or on a major class assignment? Most of us do! Being human, we tend to compare ourselves with others. If someone offered you $55,000 a year on your first job after graduating from college, you'd probably jump at the offer and report to work enthusiastic, ready to tackle whatever needed to be done, and certainly satisfied with your pay. How would you react, though, if you found out a month into the job that a coworker—another recent graduate, your age, with comparable grades from a comparable school, and with comparable work experience—was getting $60,000 a year? You'd probably be upset! Even though in absolute terms, $55,000 is a lot of money for a new graduate to make (and you know it!), that suddenly isn't the issue. Now you see the issue as what you believe is *fair*— what is *equitable*. The term *equity* is related to the concept of fairness and equitable treatment compared with others who behave in similar ways. There's considerable evidence that employees compare themselves to others and that inequities influence how much effort employees exert.[35]

Equity theory, developed by J. Stacey Adams, proposes that employees compare what they get from a job (outcomes) in relation to what they put into it (inputs) and then compare their inputs-outcomes ratio with the inputs-outcomes ratios of relevant others (Exhibit 7). If an employee perceives her ratio to be equitable in comparison to those of relevant others, there's no problem. However, if the ratio is inequitable, she views herself as underrewarded or overrewarded. When inequities occur, employees attempt to do something about it.[36] The result might be lower or higher productivity, improved or reduced quality of output, increased absenteeism, or voluntary resignation.

The referent—the other persons, systems, or selves individuals compare themselves against in order to assess equity—is an important variable in equity theory.[37] Each of the three referent categories is important. The "persons" category includes other individuals with similar jobs in the same organization but also includes friends, neighbors, or professional associates. Based on what they hear at work or read about in newspapers or trade journals, employees compare their pay with that of others. The "system" category includes organizational pay policies, procedures, and allocation. The "self" category refers to inputs-outcomes ratios that are unique to the individual. It reflects past personal experiences and contacts and is influenced by criteria such as past jobs or family commitments.

Originally, equity theory focused on distributive justice, which is the perceived fairness of the amount and allocation of rewards among individuals. More recent research has focused on looking at issues of procedural justice, which is the perceived fairness of the process used to determine the distribution of rewards. This research shows that distributive justice has a greater influence on employee satisfaction than procedural justice, while procedural justice tends to affect an employee's organizational commitment, trust in his or her boss, and intention to quit.[38] What are the implications for managers? They should consider openly sharing information on how allocation decisions are made, follow consistent and unbiased procedures, and engage in similar practices to increase the perception of procedural justice. By increasing the perception of procedural justice, employees are likely to view their bosses and the organization as positive even if they're dissatisfied with pay, promotions, and other personal outcomes.

RIGHT OR WRONG?

Book retailer Borders Group Inc. is in a mature and very competitive industry.[42] As a book seller, it's faced with the challenges of a product format that's evolved from physical to digital. Couple that with an economy in which consumers curtailed their spending and voila . . . you have a formula for financial failure, which is what happened. Borders filed for Chapter 11 bankruptcy protection in early 2011 and began immediately looking at ways to get lean, which included closing hundreds of stores, putting scores of employees out of work. Critics cried foul, however, when Borders continued with their plan to pay executives and other high-level employees $8.3 million in bonuses. A judge cleared an amended bonus pay plan that "ties the payments closer to the financial performance of Borders." Borders maintains that these bonuses were needed to "maintain its experienced work force" so that it could restructure and refocus for its eventual emergence from bankruptcy.

Think About:

- What do you think? Do you agree with Borders that this plan was needed, especially during this challenging period?

- What ethical issues do you see in this situation?

- What stakeholders might be impacted by this bonus plan? How might they be impacted?

- Could Borders have handled this differently? Discuss.

Mandel Ngan/Newscom

How Does Expectancy Theory Explain Motivation?

The most comprehensive explanation of how employees are motivated is Victor Vroom's expectancy theory.[39] Although the theory has its critics,[40] most research evidence supports it.[41]

---

job enrichment
The vertical expansion of a job by adding planning and evaluation responsibilities

equity theory
The theory that an employee compares his or her job's input-to-outcome ratio with that of relevant others and then corrects any inequity

referent
The persons, systems, or selves against which individuals compare themselves to assess equity

distributive justice
Perceived fairness of the amount and allocation of rewards among individuals

procedural justice
Perceived fairness of the process used to determine the distribution of rewards

expectancy theory
The theory that an individuals tends to act in a certain way, based on the expectation that the act will be followed by a given outcome and on the attractiveness of that outcome to the individual

EXHIBIT 7   Equity Theory Relationships

PERCEIVED RATIO COMPARISON*		EMPLOYEE'S ASSESSMENT
$\dfrac{\text{Outcomes A}}{\text{Inputs A}} < \dfrac{\text{Outcomes B}}{\text{Inputs B}}$		Inequity (underrewarded)
$\dfrac{\text{Outcomes A}}{\text{Inputs A}} = \dfrac{\text{Outcomes B}}{\text{Inputs B}}$		Equity
$\dfrac{\text{Outcomes A}}{\text{Inputs A}} > \dfrac{\text{Outcomes B}}{\text{Inputs B}}$		Inequity (overrewarded)

*Person A is the employee, and Person B is a relevant other or referent.

Expectancy theory states that an individual tends to act in a certain way based on the expectation that the act will be followed by a given outcome and on the attractiveness of that outcome to the individual. It includes three variables or relationships (see Exhibit 8):

1. *Expectancy* or *effort-performance linkage* is the probability perceived by the individual that exerting a given amount of effort will lead to a certain level of performance.
2. *Instrumentality* or *performance-reward linkage* is the degree to which the individual believes that performing at a particular level is instrumental in attaining the desired outcome.
3. *Valence* or *attractiveness of reward* is the importance that the individual places on the potential outcome or reward that can be achieved on the job. Valence considers both the goals and needs of the individual.

This explanation of motivation might sound complicated, but it really isn't. It can be summed up in the questions: How hard do I have to work to achieve a certain level of performance, and can I actually achieve that level? What reward will performing at that level get me? How attractive is the reward to me, and does it help me achieve my own personal goals? Whether you are motivated to put forth effort (that is, to work hard) at any given time depends on your goals and your perception of whether a certain level of performance is necessary to attain those goals. Let's look at an example. Many years ago, when a woman went to work for IBM as a sales rep, her favorite work "reward" became having an IBM corporate jet fly to pick up her best customers and her and take them for a weekend of golfing at some fun location. But to get that particular "reward," she had to achieve at a certain level of performance, which involved exceeding her sales goals by a specified percentage. How hard she was willing to work (that is, how motivated she was to put forth effort) was dependent on the level of performance that had to be met and the likelihood that if she achieved at that level of performance she would receive that reward. Because she "valued" that reward, she always worked hard to exceed her sales goals. And the performance-reward linkage was clear because her hard work and performance achievements were always acknowledged by the company with the reward she valued (access to a corporate jet).

The key to expectancy theory is understanding an individual's goal and the linkage between effort and performance, between performance and rewards, and finally, between rewards and individual goal satisfaction. It emphasizes payoffs, or rewards. As a result, we

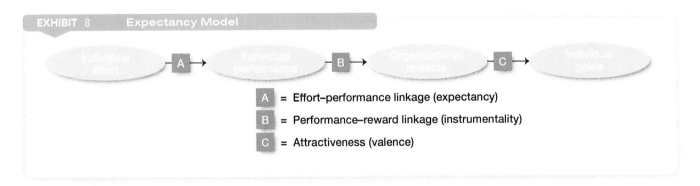

EXHIBIT 8   Expectancy Model

Individual effort →A→ Individual performance →B→ Organizational rewards →C→ Individual goals

A = Effort–performance linkage (expectancy)
B = Performance–reward linkage (instrumentality)
C = Attractiveness (valence)

have to believe that the rewards an organization offers align with what the individual wants. Expectancy theory recognizes that no universal principle explains what motivates individuals and thus stresses that managers understand why employees view certain outcomes as attractive or unattractive. After all, we want to reward individuals with those things they value positively. Also, expectancy theory emphasizes expected behaviors. Do employees know what is expected of them and how they'll be evaluated? Finally, the theory is concerned with perceptions. Reality is irrelevant. An individual's own perceptions of performance, reward, and goal outcomes, not the outcomes themselves, will determine his or her motivation (level of effort).

How Can We Integrate Contemporary Motivation Theories?

Many of the ideas underlying the contemporary motivation theories are complementary, and you'll understand better how to motivate people if you see how the theories fit together.[43] Exhibit 9 presents a model that integrates much of what we know about motivation. Its basic foundation is the expectancy model. Let's work through the model, starting on the left.

The individual effort box has an arrow leading into it. This arrow flows from the individual's goals. Consistent with goal-setting theory, this goals-effort link is meant to illustrate that goals direct behavior. Expectancy theory predicts that an employee will exert a high level of effort if he or she perceives a strong relationship between effort and performance, performance and rewards, and rewards and satisfaction of personal goals. Each

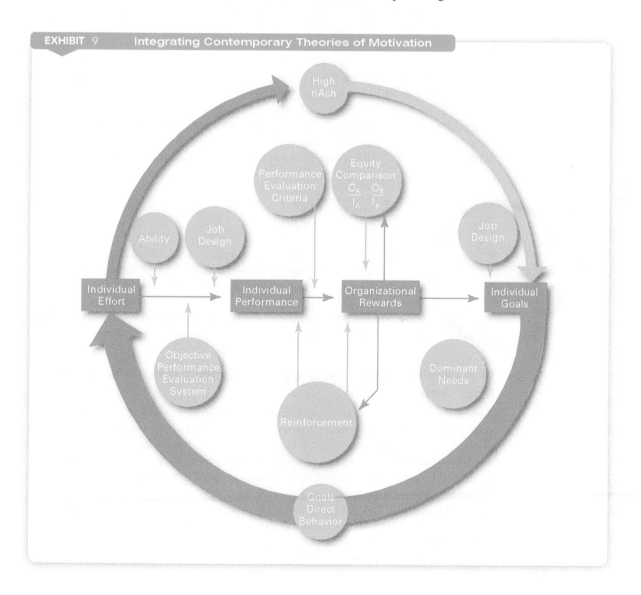

EXHIBIT 9   Integrating Contemporary Theories of Motivation

of these relationships is, in turn, influenced by certain factors. You can see from the model that the level of individual performance is determined not only by the level of individual effort but also by the individual's ability to perform and by whether the organization has a fair and objective performance evaluation system. The performance-reward relationship will be strong if the individual perceives that it is performance (rather than seniority, personal favorites, or some other criterion) that is rewarded. The final link in expectancy theory is the rewards-goal relationship. The traditional need theories come into play at this point. Motivation would be high to the degree that the rewards an individual received for his or her high performance satisfied the dominant needs consistent with his or her individual goals.

A closer look at the model also shows that it considers the achievement-need, reinforcement, equity, and JCM theories. The high achiever isn't motivated by the organization's assessment of his or her performance or organizational rewards, hence the jump from effort to individual goals for those with a high nAch. Remember that high achievers are internally driven as long as the jobs they're doing provide them with personal responsibility, feedback, and moderate risks. They're not concerned with the effort-performance, performance-reward, or rewards-goals linkages.

Reinforcement theory is seen in the model by recognizing that the organization's rewards reinforce the individual's performance. If managers have designed a reward system that is seen by employees as "paying off" for good performance, the rewards will reinforce and encourage continued good performance. Rewards also play a key part in equity theory. Individuals will compare the rewards (outcomes) they have received from the inputs or efforts they made with the inputs-outcomes ratio of relevant others. If inequities exist, the effort expended may be influenced.

Finally, the JCM is seen in this integrative model. Task characteristics (job design) influence job motivation at two places. First, jobs that are designed around the five job dimensions are likely to lead to higher actual job performance because the individual's motivation will be stimulated by the job itself—that is, they will increase the linkage between effort and performance. Second, jobs that are designed around the five job dimensions also increase an employee's control over key elements in his or her work. Therefore, jobs that offer autonomy, feedback, and similar task characteristics help to satisfy the individual goals of employees who desire greater control over their work.

Discuss current issues in motivating employees.

WHAT CURRENT MOTIVATION ISSUES DO MANAGERS FACE?

Understanding and predicting employee motivation is one of the most popular areas in management research. We've introduced you to several motivation theories. However, even current studies of employee motivation are influenced by some significant workplace issues—motivating in tough economic circumstances, managing cross-cultural challenges, motivating unique groups of workers, and designing appropriate rewards programs.

How Can Managers Motivate Employees When the Economy Stinks?

Zappos, the quirky Las Vegas–based online shoe retailer (now a part of Amazon.com), has always had a reputation for being a fun place to work.[44] However, during the economic recession, it, like many companies, had to cut staff—124 employees in total. CEO Tony Hsieh wanted to get out the news fast to lessen the stress for his employees. So he announced the layoff in an e-mail, on his blog, and on his Twitter account. Although some might think these are terrible ways to communicate that kind of news, most employees thanked him for being so open and so honest. The company also took good care of those being laid off. Laid-off employees with less than two years of service were paid through the end of the year. Longer-tenured employees got four weeks for every year of service. All got six months of continued paid health coverage and, at the request of the employees, got to keep their 40 percent merchandise discount through the Christmas season. Zappos had always been a model of how to nurture employees in good times, now it showed how to treat employees in bad times.

The economic recession of the last few years was difficult for many organizations, especially when it came to their employees. Layoffs, tight budgets, minimal or no pay raises, benefit cuts, no bonuses, long hours doing the work of those who had been laid off—this was the reality that many employees faced. As conditions deteriorated, employee confidence, optimism, and job engagement plummeted as well. As you can imagine, it wasn't an easy thing for managers to keep employees motivated under such challenging circumstances.

Managers came to realize that in an uncertain economy, they had to be creative in keeping their employees' efforts energized, directed, and sustained toward achieving goals. They were forced to look at ways to motivate employees that didn't involve money or that were relatively inexpensive.[45] So they relied on actions such as holding meetings with employees to keep the lines of communication open and to get their input on issues; establishing a common goal, such as maintaining excellent customer service, to keep everyone focused; creating a community feel so employees could see that managers cared about them and their work; and giving employees opportunities to continue to learn and grow. And, of course, an encouraging word always went a long way, as well.

How Does Country Culture Affect Motivation Efforts?

In today's global business environment, managers can't automatically assume that motivational programs that work in one geographic location are going to work in others. Most current motivation theories were developed in the United States by Americans and about Americans.[46] Maybe the most blatant pro-American characteristic in these theories is the strong emphasis on individualism and achievement. For instance, both goal-setting and expectancy theories emphasize goal accomplishment as well as rational and individual thought. Let's look at the cross-cultural transferability of the motivation theories.

Maslow's need hierarchy argues that people start at the physiological level and then move progressively up the hierarchy in order. This hierarchy, if it has any application at all, aligns with American culture. In countries such as Japan, Greece, and Mexico, where uncertainty avoidance characteristics are strong, security needs would be on top of the need hierarchy. Countries that score high on nurturing characteristics—Denmark, Sweden, Norway, the Netherlands, and Finland—would have social needs on top.[47] We would predict, for instance, that group work will be more motivating when the country's culture scores high on the nurturing criterion.

Another motivation concept that clearly has an American bias is the achievement need. The view that a high achievement need acts as an internal motivator presupposes two cultural characteristics—a willingness to accept a moderate degree of risk (which excludes countries with strong uncertainty avoidance characteristics) and a concern with performance (which applies almost singularly to countries with strong achievement characteristics). This combination is found in the Anglo-American countries of the United States, Canada, and Great Britain.[48] On the other hand, these characteristics are relatively absent in countries such as Chile and Portugal.

Equity theory has a relatively strong following in the United States, which is not surprising given that U.S.–style reward systems are based on the assumption that workers are highly sensitive to equity in reward allocations. In the United States, equity is meant to closely link pay to performance. However, recent evidence suggests that in collectivist cultures, especially in the former socialist countries of Central and Eastern Europe, employees expect rewards to reflect their individual needs as well as their performance.[49] Moreover, consistent with a legacy of communism and centrally planned economies, employees exhibited a greater "entitlement" attitude—that is, they expected outcomes to be greater than their inputs.[50] These findings suggest that U.S.–style pay practices may need to be modified in some countries in order to be perceived as fair by employees.

Despite these cross-cultural differences in motivation, a number of cross-cultural consistencies can be found. For instance, the desire for interesting work seems important to almost all workers, regardless of their national culture. In a study of seven countries, employees in Belgium, Britain, Israel, and the United States ranked "interesting work" number one among 11 work goals. It was ranked either second or third in Japan, the Netherlands, and Germany.[51] Similarly, in a study comparing job-preference outcomes among graduate students in the United States, Canada, Australia, and Singapore, growth, achievement, and responsibility were rated the top three and had identical rankings.[52] Both studies suggest some universality to the importance of intrinsic factors identified by Herzberg in his two-factor theory. Another recent study examining workplace motivation trends in Japan also seems to indicate that Herzberg's model is applicable to Japanese employees.[53]

How Can Managers Motivate Unique Groups of Workers?

Motivating employees has never been easy! Employees come into organizations with different needs, personalities, skills, abilities, interests, and aptitudes. They have different expectations of their employers and different views of what they think their employer has a right to expect of them. And they vary widely in what they want from their jobs. For instance, some employees get more satisfaction out of their personal interests and pursuits and only want a weekly paycheck—nothing more. They're not interested in making their work more challenging or interesting or in "winning" performance contests. Others derive a great deal of satisfaction in their jobs and are motivated to exert high levels of effort. Given these differences, how can managers do an effective job of motivating the unique groups of employees found in today's workforce? One thing is to understand the motivational requirements of these groups including diverse employees, professionals, and contingent workers.

MOTIVATING A DIVERSE WORKFORCE. To maximize motivation among today's workforce, managers need to think in terms of *flexibility*. For instance, studies tell us that men place more importance on having autonomy in their jobs than do women. In contrast, the opportunity to learn, convenient and flexible work hours, and good interpersonal relations are more important to women.[54] Having the opportunity to be independent and to be exposed to different experiences is important to Gen Y employees whereas older workers may be more interested in highly structured work opportunities.[55] Managers need to recognize that what motivates a single mother with two dependent children who's working full time to support her family may be very different from the needs of a single part-time employee or an older employee who is working only to supplement his or her retirement income. A diverse array of rewards is needed to motivate employees with such diverse needs. Many of the work/life balance programs that organizations have implemented are a response to the varied needs of a diverse workforce. In addition, many organizations have developed flexible work arrangements that recognize different needs. These types of programs (including telecommuting, compressed workweeks, flextime, and job sharing) may become even more popular as employers look for ways to help employees cope with high fuel prices.

Do flexible work arrangements motivate employees? Although such arrangements might seem highly motivational, both positive and negative relationships have been found. For instance, one study of the impact of telecommuting on job satisfaction found that job satisfaction initially increased as the extent of telecommuting increased, but as the number of hours spent telecommuting increased, job satisfaction started to level off, decreased slightly, and then stabilized.[56]

MOTIVATING PROFESSIONALS. In contrast to a generation ago, the typical employee today is more likely to be a professional with a college degree than a blue-collar factory worker. What special concerns should managers be aware of when trying to motivate a team of engineers at Intel's India Development

Motivating professional employees who have a strong and long-term commitment to their field of expertise is different from motivating other employees. Challenging work tends to be ranked high for financial services professionals such as Brenda Hung, the branch manager of TD Canada Trust, shown here cutting a ribbon to celebrate the opening of a renovated bank location. Hung and the other TD Canada Trust professionals enjoy tackling problems and finding solutions as they provide their customers with personal and commercial banking, wealth management, insurance, securities, and other financial products and services.

Jeff Vinnick/Newscom

Center, software designers at SAS Institute in North Carolina, or a group of consultants at Accenture in Singapore?

Professionals are different from nonprofessionals.[57] They have a strong and long-term commitment to their field of expertise. To keep current in their field, they need to regularly update their knowledge, and because of their commitment to their profession they rarely define their workweek as 8 A.M. to 5 P.M. five days a week.

What motivates professionals? Money and promotions typically are low on their priority list. Why? They tend to be well paid and enjoy what they do. In contrast, job challenge tends to be ranked high. They like to tackle problems and find solutions. Their chief reward is the work itself. Professionals also value support. They want others to think that what they're working on is important. That may be true for all employees, but professionals tend to be focused on their work as their central life interest, whereas nonprofessionals typically have other interests outside of work that can compensate for needs not met on the job.

MOTIVATING CONTINGENT WORKERS. As full-time jobs have been eliminated through downsizing and other organizational restructurings, the number of openings for part-time, contract, and other forms of temporary work have increased. Contingent workers don't have the security or stability that permanent employees have, and they don't identify with the organization or display the commitment that other employees do. Temporary workers also typically get little or no benefits such as health care or pensions.[58]

There's no simple solution for motivating contingent employees. For that small set of individuals who prefer the freedom of their temporary status, the lack of stability may not be an issue. In addition, temporariness might be preferred by highly compensated physicians, engineers, accountants, or financial planners who don't want the demands of a full-time job. But these are the exceptions. For the most part, temporary employees are not temporary by choice.

What will motivate involuntarily temporary employees? An obvious answer is the opportunity to become a permanent employee. In cases in which permanent employees are selected from a pool of temps, the temps will often work hard in hopes of becoming permanent. A less obvious answer is the opportunity for training. The ability of a temporary employee to find a new job is largely dependent on his or her skills. If an employee sees that the job he or she is doing can help develop marketable skills, then motivation is increased. From an equity standpoint, when temps work alongside permanent employees who earn more and get benefits too for doing the same job, the performance of temps is likely to suffer. Separating such employees or perhaps minimizing interdependence between them might help managers counteract potential problems.[59]

How Can Managers Design Appropriate Rewards Programs?

Blue Cross of California, one of the nation's largest health insurers, pays bonuses to doctors serving its health maintenance organization members based on patient satisfaction and other quality standards. FedEx's drivers are motivated by a pay system that rewards them for timeliness and how much they deliver.[60] There's no doubt that employee rewards programs play a powerful role in motivating appropriate employee behavior. Some of the more popular rewards programs include open-book management, employee recognition, and pay-for-performance.

HOW CAN OPEN-BOOK MANAGEMENT PROGRAMS MOTIVATE EMPLOYEES? Within 24 hours after managers of the Heavy Duty Division of Springfield Remanufacturing Company (SRC) gather to discuss a multipage financial document, every plant employee will have seen the same information. If the employees can meet shipment goals, they'll all share in a large year-end bonus.[61] Many organizations of various sizes involve their employees in workplace decisions by opening up the financial statements (the "books"). They share that information so that employees will be motivated to make better decisions about their work and better able to understand the implications of what they do, how they do it, and the ultimate impact on the bottom line. This approach is called

Each year Marriott International shines the spotlight on a select few employees by presenting them with the J. Willard Marriott Award of Excellence during a gala employee recognition celebration. Presented by J. W. Marriott (on the right), the hotelier's CEO and chairman, the award is Marriott's highest form of associate recognition. It honors employees who demonstrate achievement, character, dedication, effort, and perseverance in leading by example and exceeding expectations. Through many other awards and recognition programs, Marriott celebrates associates who exemplify the company's motto "Spirit to Serve" as they enhance the lives of customers, coworkers, and people in their communities.

open-book management and many organizations are using it.[62] At Best Buy, the "Donuts with Darren" sessions (held when Darren Jackson was the company's chief financial officer) were so popular that more than 600 employees regularly took part. His presentations covered the financials and the basics of finance.[63]

The goal of open-book management is to get employees to think like an owner by seeing the impact their decisions have on financial results. Because many employees don't have the knowledge or background to understand the financials, they have to be taught how to read and understand the organization's financial statements. Once employees have this knowledge, however, managers need to regularly share the numbers with them. By sharing this information, employees begin to see the link between their efforts, level of performance, and operational results.

HOW CAN MANAGERS USE EMPLOYEE RECOGNITION PROGRAMS? **Employee recognition programs** consist of personal attention and expressions of interest, approval, and appreciation for a job well done.[64] They can take numerous forms. For instance, Kelly Services, introduced a new version of its points-based incentive system to better promote productivity and retention among its employees. The program, called Kelly Kudos, gives employees more choices of awards and allows them to accumulate points over a longer time period. It's working. Participants generate three times more revenue and hours than employees not receiving points.[65] Most managers, however, use a far more informal approach. For example, when Julia Stewart—currently chairman and CEO of DineEquity, Inc.—was president of Applebee's Restaurants, she would frequently leave sealed notes on the chairs of employees after everyone had gone home.[66] These notes explained how important Stewart thought the person's work was or how much she appreciated the completion of a project. Stewart also relied heavily on voice mail messages left after office hours to tell employees how appreciative she was for a job well done. And recognition doesn't have to come only from managers. Some 35 percent of companies encourage coworkers to recognize peers for outstanding work efforts.[67] For instance, managers at Yum Brands Inc. (the Kentucky-based parent of food chains Taco Bell, KFC, and Pizza Hut) were looking for ways to reduce employee turnover. They found a successful customer-service program involving peer recognition at KFC restaurants in Australia. Workers there spontaneously rewarded fellow workers with "Champs cards, an acronym for attributes such as cleanliness, hospitality, and accuracy." Yum implemented the program in other restaurants around the world, and credits the peer recognition with reducing hourly employee turnover from 181 percent to 109 percent.[68]

A survey of organizations found that 84 percent had some type of program to recognize worker achievements.[69] And do employees think these programs are important? You bet! A survey of a wide range of employees asked them what they considered the most powerful workplace motivator. Their response? Recognition, recognition, and more recognition![70]

Consistent with reinforcement theory, rewarding a behavior with recognition immediately following that behavior is likely to encourage its repetition. And recognition can take many forms. You can personally congratulate an employee in private for a good job. You can send a handwritten note or e-mail message acknowledging something positive that the employee has done. For employees with a strong need for social acceptance, you can publicly recognize accomplishments. To enhance group cohesiveness and motivation, you can celebrate team successes. For instance, you can do something as simple as throw a pizza party to celebrate a team's accomplishments. Some of these things may seem simple, but they can go a long way in showing employees they're valued.

HOW CAN MANAGERS USE PAY-FOR-PERFORMANCE TO MOTIVATE EMPLOYEES? Here's a survey statistic that may surprise you: 40 percent of employees see no clear link between performance and pay.[71] You have to think: What are the companies where these employees work paying for? They're obviously not clearly communicating performance expectations.[72] **Pay-for-performance programs** are variable compensation plans that pay employees on the basis of some performance measure.[73] Piece-rate pay plans, wage incentive plans, profit-sharing, and lump-sum bonuses are examples. What differentiates these forms of pay from more traditional compensation plans is that instead of paying a person for time on the job, pay is adjusted to reflect some performance measure. These performance measures might include such things as individual productivity, team or work group productivity, departmental productivity, or the overall organization's profit performance.

Pay-for-performance is probably most compatible with expectancy theory. Individuals should perceive a strong relationship between their performance and the rewards they receive for motivation to be maximized. If rewards are allocated only on nonperformance factors—such as seniority, job title, or across-the-board pay raises—then employees are likely to reduce their efforts. From a motivation perspective, making some or all an employee's pay conditional on some performance measure focuses his or her attention and effort toward that measure, then reinforces the continuation of the effort with a reward. If the employee, team, or organization's performance declines, so does the reward. Thus, there's an incentive to keep efforts and motivation strong.

Pay-for-performance programs are popular. Some 80 percent of large U.S. companies have some form of variable pay plan.[74] These types of pay plans have also been tried in other countries such as Canada and Japan. About 30 percent of Canadian companies and 22 percent of Japanese companies have company-wide pay-for-performance plans.[75]

Do pay-for-performance programs work? For the most part, studies seem to indicate that they do. For instance, one study found that companies that used pay-for-performance programs performed better financially than those that did not.[76] Another study showed that pay-for-performance programs with outcome-based incentives had a positive impact on sales, customer satisfaction, and profits.[77] If an organization uses work teams, managers should consider group-based performance incentives that will reinforce team effort and commitment. But whether these programs are individual based or team based, managers need to ensure that they're specific about the relationship between an individual's pay and his or her expected level of appropriate performance. Employees must clearly understand exactly how performance—theirs and the organization's—translates into dollars on their paychecks.[78]

Gerald Herbert/AP Images

Trenise Duvernay teaches a fourth grade math class at a charter school in New Orleans. As a teacher, Duvernay wants to be rewarded for helping students succeed and supports the variable-pay initiative offered at her school. She is eligible for a merit bonus of $2,000 or more each year based on how well her students perform in classroom observations and on achievement tests. The pay plan motivates teachers by basing a portion of their pay on their performance in raising student achievement rather than on seniority or degrees. The move toward pay-for-performance plans to reward teachers for their individual efforts follows the widespread adoption of variable-pay plans in many businesses and government agencies.

A FINAL NOTE ON EMPLOYEE REWARDS PROGRAMS. During times of economic and financial uncertainty, managers' abilities to recognize and reward employees are often severely constrained. It's hard to keep employees productive during challenging times, even though it's especially critical. It's not surprising, then, that employees feel less connected to their work. In fact, a recent study by the Corporate Executive Board found that declining employee engagement has decreased overall productivity by 3 to 5 percent.[79] But there are actions managers can take to maintain and maybe even increase employees' motivation levels. One is to clarify each person's role in the organization. Show them how their efforts are contributing to improving the company's overall situation. It's also important to keep communication lines open and use two-way exchanges between top-level managers and employees to soothe fears and concerns. The key with taking any actions is continuing to show workers that the company cares about them. As we said at the beginning of the chapter, the value in companies comes from employees who are motivated to be there. Managers have to give employees a reason to want to be there.

---

open-book management
A motivational approach in which an organization's financial statements (the "books") are shared with all employees

employee recognition programs
Programs that consist of personal attention and expressions of interest, approval, and appreciation for a job well done

pay-for-performance programs
Variable compensation plans that pay employees on the basis of some performance measure

Review

1 Define and explain motivation. Motivation is the process by which a person's efforts are energized, directed, and sustained toward attaining a goal.

The *energy* element is a measure of intensity or drive. The high level of effort needs to be *directed* in ways that help the organization achieve its goals. Employees must *persist* in putting forth effort to achieve those goals.

2 Compare and contrast early theories of motivation. Individuals move up the hierarchy of five needs (physiological, safety, social, esteem, and self-actualization) as needs are substantially satisfied. A need that's substantially satisfied no longer motivates.

A Theory X manager believes that people don't like to work, or won't seek out responsibility, so they have to be threatened and coerced to work. A Theory Y manager assumes that people like to work and seek out responsibility, so they will exercise self-motivation and self-direction.

Herzberg's theory proposed that intrinsic factors associated with job satisfaction were what motivated people. Extrinsic factors associated with job dissatisfaction simply kept people from being dissatisfied.

Three-needs theory proposed three acquired needs that are major motives in work: need for achievement, need for affiliation, and need for power.

3 Compare and contrast contemporary theories of motivation. Goal-setting theory says that specific goals increase performance, and difficult goals, when accepted, result in higher performance than do easy goals. Important points in goal-setting theory include intention to work toward a goal as a major source of job motivation; specific hard goals to produce higher levels of output than generalized goals; participation in setting goals as preferable to assigning goals, but not always; feedback to guide and motivate behavior, especially self-generated feedback; and contingencies that affect goal setting, such as goal commitment, self-efficacy, and national culture.

The job characteristics model is based on five core job dimensions (skill variety, task identity, task significance, autonomy, and feedback) that are used to design motivating jobs.

Equity theory focuses on how employees compare their inputs-outcomes ratios to relevant others' ratios. A perception of inequity will cause an employee to do something about it. Procedural justice has a greater influence on employee satisfaction than does distributive justice.

Expectancy theory says that an individual tends to act in a certain way based on the expectation that the act will be followed by a desired outcome. Expectancy is the effort-performance linkage (how much effort do I need to exert to achieve a certain level of performance); instrumentality is the performance-reward linkage (achieving at a certain level of performance will get me what reward); and valence is the attractiveness of the reward (is the reward what I want).

4 Discuss current issues in motivating employees. During rough economic conditions, managers must look for creative ways to keep employees' efforts energized, directed, and sustained toward achieving goals.

Most motivational theories were developed in the United States and have a North American bias. Some theories (Maslow's need hierarchy, achievement need, and equity theory) don't work well for other cultures. However, the desire for interesting work seems important to all workers and Herzberg's motivator (intrinsic) factors may be universal.

Managers face challenges in motivating unique groups of workers. A diverse workforce is looking for flexibility. Professionals want job challenge and support, and are motivated by the work itself. Contingent workers want the opportunity to become permanent or to receive skills training.

Open-book management is when financial statements (the books) are shared with employees who have been taught what that information means. Employee recognition programs consist of personal attention, approval, and appreciation for a job well done. Pay-for-performance programs are variable compensation plans that pay employees on the basis of some performance measure.

UNDERSTANDING THE CHAPTER

1. Most of us have to work for a living, and a job is a central part of our lives. So why do managers have to worry so much about employee motivation issues?

2. What is motivation? Explain the three key elements of motivation.

3. Contrast lower-order and higher-order needs in Maslow's needs hierarchy.

4. What role would money play in (a) the hierarchy of needs theory, (b) two-factor theory, (c) equity theory, (d) expectancy theory, and (e) motivating employees with a high nAch?

5. What are some of the possible consequences of employees perceiving an inequity between their inputs and outcomes and those of others?

6. What are some advantages of using pay-for-performance programs to motivate employee performance? Are there drawbacks? Explain.

7. Many job design experts who have studied the changing nature of work say that people do their best work when they're motivated by a sense of purpose rather than by the pursuit of money. Do you agree? Explain your position. What are the implications for managers?

8. Could managers use any of the motivation theories or approaches to encourage and support workforce diversity efforts? Explain.

9. Can an individual be too motivated? Discuss.

10. What challenges do managers face in motivating today's workforce?

Endnotes

1. S. Levy, "The Problem with Success," *Wall Street Journal,* April 7, 2011, p. A15; S. Levy, *In the Plex: How Google Thinks, Works, and Shapes Our Lives* (New York: Simon & Schuster), 2011; C. C. Miller and J. Wortham, "Silicon Valley Hiring Perks: Meals, iPads, and a Cubicle for Spot," *New York Times Online,* March 26, 2011; J. Light, "Google Is No. 1 on List of Desired Employers," *Wall Street Journal,* March 21, 2011, p. B8; M Moskowitz, R. Levering, and C. Tkaczyk, "100 Best Companies to Work For," *Fortune,* February 7, 2011, pp. 91+; C. C. Miller and M. Helft, "Google Shake-Up Is Effort to Revive Start-Up Spark," *New York Times Online,* January 20, 2011; C. C. Miller, "Google Grows and Works to Retain Nimble Minds," *New York Times Online,* November 28, 2010; A. Efrati and P-W. Tam, "Google Battles to Keep Talent," *Wall Street Journal,* November 11, 2010, pp. B1+; L. Petrecca, "With 3,000 Applications a Day, Google Can Be Picky," *USA Today,* May 19, 2010, p. 2B; S. E. Ante and K. Weisul, "And Google Begat . . . ," *Bloomberg BusinessWeek,* March 8, 2010, pp. 39–42; A. Lashinsky, "Where Does Google Go Next?" *CNNMoney.com,* May 12, 2008; and "Perk Place: The Benefits Offered by Google and Others May Be Grand, But They're All Business," *Knowledge @ Wharton,* http://knowledge.wharton.upenn.edu/article (March 21, 2007).

2. P. Bronson, "What Should I Do with My Life Now?" *Fast Company,* April 2009, pp. 35–37.

3. R. M. Steers, R. T. Mowday, and D. L. Shapiro, "The Future of Work Motivation Theory," *Academy of Management Review,* July 2004, pp. 379–387.

4. N. Ellemers, D. De Gilder, and S. A. Haslam, "Motivating Individuals and Groups at Work: A Social Identity Perspective

on Leadership and Group Performance," *Academy of Management Review,* July 2004, pp. 459–478.

5. And the Survey Says box based on J. Yang and P. Trap, "Does Your Manager Acknowledge and Appreciate You at Work?" *USA Today,* March 24, 2011, p. 1B; A. R. Carey and K. Gelles, "Which of These Is Most Important About Your Job?" *USA Today,* January 31, 2011, p. 1A; J. Yang and S. Ward, "Who Appreciates You the Most at Work?" *USA Today,* June 2, 2010, p. 1B; E. Frauenheim, "Bosses Don't Drive Workers Away, Poll Concludes," *Workforce Management Online,* April 2010; J. Yang and K. Simmons, "What Primary Motivation Does Your Employer Provide?" *USA Today,* February 22, 2010, p. 1B; and A. R. Carey and S. Ward, "What Small Perks Workers Want," *USA Today,* March 31, 2010, p. 1A.

6. J. Krueger and E. Killham, "At Work, Feeling Good Matters," *Gallup Management Journal,* http://gmj.gallup.com (December 8, 2005).

7. M. Meece, "Using the Human Touch to Solve Workplace Problems," *New York Times Online,* April 3, 2008.

8. "Maslow Motion," *New Statesman,* March 15, 2010, p. 37; "Dialogue," *Academy of Management Review,* October 2000, pp. 696–701; M. L. Ambrose and C. T. Kulik, "Old Friends, New Faces: Motivation Research in the 1990s," *Journal of Management,* 25, no. 3 (1999), pp. 231–292; A. Maslow, D. C. Stephens, and G. Heil, *Maslow on Management* (New York: John Wiley & Sons, 1998); and A. Maslow, *Motivation and Personality* (New York: McGraw-Hill, 1954).

9. R. Coutts, "A Pilot Study for the Analysis of Dream Reports Using Maslow's Need Categories: An Extension to the Emotional Selection Hypothesis," *Psychological Reports,*

October 2010, pp. 659–673; E. A. Fisher, "Motivation and Leadership in Social Work Management: A Review of Theories and Related Studies," *Administration in Social Work,* October–December 2009, pp. 347–367; and N. K. Austin, "The Power of the Pyramid: The Foundation of Human Psychology and, Thereby, of Motivation, Maslow's Hierarchy Is One Powerful Pyramid," *Incentive* (July 2002), p. 10.

10. See, for example, M. L. Ambrose and C. T. Kulik, "Old Friends, New Faces: Motivation Research in the 1990s"; J. Rowan, "Ascent and Descent in Maslow's Theory," *Journal of Humanistic Psychology* (Summer 1999), pp. 125–133; J. Rowan, "Maslow Amended," *Journal of Humanistic Psychology,* (Winter 1998), pp. 81–92; R. M. Creech, "Employee Motivation," *Management Quarterly,* Summer 1995, pp. 33–39; E. E. Lawler III and J. L. Suttle, "A Causal Correlational Test of the Need Hierarchy Concept," *Organizational Behavior and Human Performance,* April 1972, pp. 265–287; and D. T. Hall and K. E. Nongaim, "An Examination of Maslow's Need Hierarchy in an Organizational Setting," *Organizational Behavior and Human Performance,* February 1968, pp. 12–35.

11. S. Terlep and J. S. Lublin, "New GM CEO: Brash, Blunt, Demanding," *Wall Street Journal,* August 16, 2010, pp. B1+; and S. Fitch, "Zero Tolerance," *Forbes,* January 28, 2008, p. 52.

12. R. E. Kopelman, D. J. Prottas, and A. L. Davis, "Douglas McGregor's Theory X and Y: Toward a Construct-Valid Measure," *Journal of Managerial Issues* (Summer 2008), pp. 255–271; and D. McGregor, *The Human Side of Enterprise* (New York: McGraw-Hill, 1960). For an updated description of Theories X and Y, see an annotated edition with commentary of *The Human Side of Enterprise* (McGraw-Hill, 2006); and G. Heil, W. Bennis, and D. C. Stephens, *Douglas McGregor, Revisited: Managing the Human Side of Enterprise* (New York: Wiley, 2000).

13. R. Parloff, "Has Intel Finally Met Its Match?" *Fortune,* August 16, 2010, pp. 21–22; and J. M. O'Brien, "The Next Intel," *Wired,* July 2002, pp. 100–107.

14. F. Herzberg, B. Mausner, and B. Snyderman, *The Motivation to Work* (New York: John Wiley, 1959); F. Herzberg, *The Managerial Choice: To Be Effective or to Be Human,* rev. ed. (Salt Lake City: Olympus, 1982); R. M. Creech, "Employee Motivation"; and M. L. Ambrose and C. T. Kulik, "Old Friends, New Faces: Motivation Research in the 1990s."

15. From the Past to the Present box based on C. M. Christensen, "How Will You Measure Your Life?" *Harvard Business Review,* July–August 2010, pp. 46–51; D. A. Wren and A. G. Bedeian, *The Evolution of Management Thought* (New York: John Wiley & Sons, Inc., 2009); F. Herzberg, *One More Time: How Do You Motivate Employees?* (Boston, MA: Harvard Business School Press, 2008); and F. Herzberg, B. Mausner, and B. B. Snyderman, *The Motivation to Work.*

16. D. C. McClelland, *The Achieving Society* (New York: Van Nostrand Reinhold, 1961); J. W. Atkinson and J. O. Raynor, *Motivation and Achievement* (Washington, DC: Winston, 1974); D. C. McClelland, *Power: The Inner Experience* (New York: Irvington, 1975); and M. J. Stahl, *Managerial and Technical Motivation: Assessing Needs for Achievement, Power, and Affiliation* (New York: Praeger, 1986).

17. McClelland, *The Achieving Society.*

18. McClelland, *Power: The Inner Experience*; D. C. McClelland and D. H. Burnham, "Power Is the Great Motivator," *Harvard Business Review,* March–April 1976, pp. 100–110.

19. D. Miron and D. C. McClelland, "The Impact of Achievement Motivation Training on Small Businesses," *California Management Review,* Summer 1979, pp. 13–28.

20. "McClelland: An Advocate of Power," *International Management,* July 1975, pp. 27–29.

21. J. Flint, "How to Be a Player," *Bloomberg BusinessWeek,* January 24–January 30, 2011, pp. 108–109.

22. R. M. Steers, R. T. Mowday, and D. L. Shapiro, "The Future of Work Motivation Theory"; E. A. Locke and G. P. Latham, "What Should We Do About Motivation Theory? Six Recommendations for the Twenty-First Century," *Academy of Management Review,* July 2004, pp. 388–403; and M. L. Ambrose and C. T. Kulik, "Old Friends, New Faces: Motivation Research in the 1990s."

23. M. L. Ambrose and C. T. Kulik, "Old Friends, New Faces: Motivation Research in the 1990s."

24. J. C. Naylor and D. R. Ilgen, "Goal Setting: A Theoretical Analysis of a Motivational Technique," in B. M. Staw and L. L. Cummings (eds.), *Research in Organizational Behavior,* vol. 6 (Greenwich, CT: JAI Press, 1984), pp. 95–140; A. R. Pell, "Energize Your People," *Managers Magazine,* December 1992, pp. 28–29; E. A. Locke, "Facts and Fallacies About Goal Theory: Reply to Deci," *Psychological Science,* January 1993, pp. 63–64; M. E. Tubbs, "Commitment as a Moderator of the Goal-Performance Relation: A Case for Clearer Construct Definition," *Journal of Applied Psychology* (February 1993), pp. 86–97; M. P. Collingwood, "Why Don't You Use the Research?" *Management Decision,* May 1993, pp. 48–54; M. E. Tubbs, D. M. Boehne, and J. S. Dahl, "Expectancy, Valence, and Motivational Force Functions in Goal-Setting Research: An Empirical Test," *Journal of Applied Psychology* (June 1993), pp. 361–373; E. A. Locke, "Motivation Through Conscious Goal Setting," *Applied and Preventive Psychology,* vol. 5 (1996), pp. 117–124; M. L. Ambrose and C. T. Kulik, "Old Friends, New Faces: Motivation Research in the 1990s; E. A. Locke and G. P. Latham, "Building a Practically Useful Theory of Goal Setting and Task Motivation: A 35-Year Odyssey," *American Psychologist,* September 2002, pp. 705–717; Y. Fried and L. H. Slowik, "Enriching Goal-Setting Theory with Time: An Integrated Approach," *Academy of Management Review,* July 2004, pp. 404–422; G. P. Latham, "The Motivational Benefits of Goal-Setting," *Academy of Management Executive,* November 2004, pp. 126–129; and G. Yeo, S. Loft, T. Xiao, and C. Kiewitz, "Goal Orientation and Performance: Differential Relationships Across Levels of Analysis and as a Function of Task Demands," *Journal of Applied Psychology* (May 2009), pp. 710–726.

25. J. A. Wagner III, "Participation's Effects on Performance and Satisfaction: A Reconsideration of Research and Evidence," *Academy of Management Review,* April 1994, pp. 312–330; J. George-Falvey, "Effects of Task Complexity and Learning Stage on the Relationship Between Participation in Goal Setting and Task Performance," *Academy of Management Proceedings on Disk,* 1996; T. D. Ludwig and E. S. Geller, "Assigned Versus Participative Goal Setting and Response Generalization: Managing Injury Control Among Professional Pizza Deliverers," *Journal of Applied Psychology* (April 1997), pp. 253–261; and S. G. Harkins and M. D. Lowe, "The Effects of Self-Set Goals on Task Performance," *Journal of Applied Social Psychology* (January 2000), pp. 1–40.

26. J. M. Ivancevich and J. T. McMahon, "The Effects of Goal Setting, External Feedback, and Self-Generated Feedback on Outcome Variables: A Field Experiment," *Academy of*

Management Journal (June 1982), pp. 359–372; and E. A. Locke, "Motivation Through Conscious Goal Setting."

27. J. R. Hollenbeck, C. R. Williams, and H. J. Klein, "An Empirical Examination of the Antecedents of Commitment to Difficult Goals," *Journal of Applied Psychology* (February 1989), pp. 18–23; see, also, J. C. Wofford, V. L. Goodwin, and S. Premack, "Meta-Analysis of the Antecedents of Personal Goal Level and of the Antecedents and Consequences of Goal Commitment," *Journal of Management* (September 1992), pp. 595–615; Tubbs, "Commitment as a Moderator of the Goal-Performance Relation"; J. W. Smither, M. London, and R. R. Reilly, "Does Performance Improve Following Multisource Feedback? A Theoretical Model, Meta-Analysis, and Review of Empirical Findings," *Personnel Psychology,* Spring 2005, pp. 171–203.

28. M. E. Gist, "Self-Efficacy: Implications for Organizational Behavior and Human Resource Management," *Academy of Management Review*, July 1987, pp. 472–485; and A. Bandura, *Self-Efficacy: The Exercise of Control* (New York: Freeman, 1997).

29. E. A. Locke, E. Frederick, C. Lee, and P. Bobko, "Effect of Self-Efficacy, Goals, and Task Strategies on Task Performance," *Journal of Applied Psychology* (May 1984), pp. 241–251; M. E. Gist and T. R. Mitchell, "Self-Efficacy: A Theoretical Analysis of Its Determinants and Malleability," *Academy of Management Review*, April 1992, pp. 183–211; A. D. Stajkovic and F. Luthans, "Self-Efficacy and Work-Related Performance: A Meta-Analysis," *Psychological Bulletin,* September 1998, pp. 240–261; A. Bandura, "Cultivate Self-Efficacy for Personal and Organizational Effectiveness," in E. Locke (ed.), *Handbook of Principles of Organizational Behavior* (Malden, MA: Blackwell, 2004), pp. 120–136; and F. Q. Fu, K. A. Richards, and E. Jones, "The Motivation Hub: Effects of Goal Setting and Self-Efficacy on Effort and New Product Sales," *Journal of Personal Selling & Sales Management* (Summer 2009), pp. 277–292.

30. A. Bandura and D. Cervone, "Differential Engagement in Self-Reactive Influences in Cognitively Based Motivation," *Organizational Behavior and Human Decision Processes*, August 1986, pp. 92–113; and R. Ilies and T. A. Judge, "Goal Regulation Across Time: The Effects of Feedback and Affect," *Journal of Applied Psychology* (May 2005), pp. 453–467.

31. See J. C. Anderson and C. A. O'Reilly, "Effects of an Organizational Control System on Managerial Satisfaction and Performance," *Human Relations*, June 1981, pp. 491–501; and J. P. Meyer, B. Schacht-Cole, and I. R. Gellatly, "An Examination of the Cognitive Mechanisms by Which Assigned Goals Affect Task Performance and Reactions to Performance," *Journal of Applied Social Psychology* 18, no. 5 (1988), pp. 390–408.

32. See, for example, R. W. Griffin, "Toward an Integrated Theory of Task Design," in L. L. Cummings and B. M. Staw (eds.), *Research in Organizational Behavior*, vol. 9 (Greenwich, CT: JAI Press, 1987), pp. 79–120; and M. Campion, "Interdisciplinary Approaches to Job Design: A Constructive Replication with Extensions," *Journal of Applied Psychology* (August 1988), pp. 467–481.

33. See J. R. Hackman and G. R. Oldham, "Motivation Through the Design of Work: Test of a Theory," *Organizational Behavior and Human Performance,* August 1976, pp. 250–279; Y. Fried and G. R. Ferris, "The Validity of the Job Characteristics Model: A Review and Meta Analysis," *Personnel Psychology,* Summer 1987, pp. 287–322; S. J. Zaccaro and E. F. Stone, "Incremental Validity of an Empirically Based Measure of Job Characteristics," *Journal of Applied Psychology* (May 1988), pp. 245–252; and R. W. Renn and R. J. Vandenberg, "The Critical Psychological States: An Underrepresented Component in Job Characteristics Model Research," *Journal of Management* (February 1995), pp. 279–303.

34. G. Van Der Vegt, B. Emans, and E. Van Der Vliert, "Motivating Effects of Task and Outcome Interdependence in Work Teams," *Journal of Managerial Psychology* (July 2000), p. 829; and B. Bemmels, "Local Union Leaders' Satisfaction with Grievance Procedures," *Journal of Labor Research* (Summer 2001), pp. 653–669.

35. J. S. Adams, "Inequity in Social Exchanges," in L. Berkowitz (ed.), *Advances in Experimental Social Psychology*, vol. 2 (New York: Academic Press, 1965), pp. 267–300; and M. L. Ambrose and C. T. Kulik, "Old Friends, New Faces: Motivation Research in the 1990s."

36. See, for example, R. L. Bell, "Addressing Employees' Feelings of Inequity," *Supervision,* May 2011, pp. 3–6; P. S. Goodman and A. Friedman, "An Examination of Adams' Theory of Inequity," *Administrative Science Quarterly*, September 1971, pp. 271–288; M. R. Carrell, "A Longitudinal Field Assessment of Employee Perceptions of Equitable Treatment," *Organizational Behavior and Human Performance*, February 1978, pp. 108–118; E. Walster, G. W. Walster, and W. G. Scott, *Equity: Theory and Research* (Boston: Allyn & Bacon, 1978); R. G. Lord and J. A. Hohenfeld, "Longitudinal Field Assessment of Equity Effects on the Performance of Major League Baseball Players," *Journal of Applied Psychology* (February 1979), pp. 19–26; J. E. Dittrich and M. R. Carrell, "Organizational Equity Perceptions, Employee Job Satisfaction, and Departmental Absence and Turnover Rates," *Organizational Behavior and Human Performance*, August 1979, pp. 29–40; and J. Greenberg, "Cognitive Reevaluation of Outcomes in Response to Underpayment Inequity," *Academy of Management Journal* (March 1989), pp. 174–184.

37. P. S. Goodman, "An Examination of Referents Used in the Evaluation of Pay," *Organizational Behavior and Human Performance*, October 1974, pp. 170–195; S. Ronen, "Equity Perception in Multiple Comparisons: A Field Study," *Human Relations*, April 1986, pp. 333–346; R. W. Scholl, E. A. Cooper, and J. F. McKenna, "Referent Selection in Determining Equity Perception: Differential Effects on Behavioral and Attitudinal Outcomes," *Personnel Psychology*, Spring 1987, pp. 113–127; and C. T. Kulik and M. L. Ambrose, "Personal and Situational Determinants of Referent Choice," *Academy of Management Review*, April 1992, pp. 212–237.

38. See, for example, R. C. Dailey and D. J. Kirk, "Distributive and Procedural Justice as Antecedents of Job Dissatisfaction and Intent to Turnover," *Human Relations,* March 1992, pp. 305–316; D. B. McFarlin and P. D. Sweeney, "Distributive and Procedural Justice as Predictors of Satisfaction with Personal and Organizational Outcomes," *Academy of Management Journal* (August 1992), pp. 626–637; M. A. Konovsky, "Understanding Procedural Justice and Its Impact on Business Organizations," *Journal of Management,* 26, no. 3 (2000), pp. 489–511; J. A. Colquitt, "Does the Justice of One Interact with the Justice of Many? Reactions to Procedural Justice in Teams," *Journal of Applied Psychology* (August 2004), pp. 633–646; J. Brockner, "Why It's So Hard to Be Fair," *Harvard Business Review,* March 2006, pp. 122–129; and B. M. Wiesenfeld, W. B. Swann, Jr., J. Brockner, and

C. A. Bartel, "Is More Fairness Always Preferred: Self-Esteem Moderates Reactions to Procedural Justice," *Academy of Management Journal* (October 2007), pp. 1235–1253.

39. V. H. Vroom, *Work and Motivation* (New York: John Wiley, 1964).

40. See, for example, H. G. Heneman III and D. P. Schwab, "Evaluation of Research on Expectancy Theory Prediction of Employee Performance," *Psychological Bulletin*, July 1972, pp. 1–9; L. Reinharth and M. Wahba, "Expectancy Theory as a Predictor of Work Motivation, Effort Expenditure, and Job Performance," *Academy of Management Journal* (September 1975), pp. 502–537; and K. T. Lambright, "An Update of a Classic: Applying Expectancy Theory to Understand Contracted Provider Motivation," *Administration & Society*, July 2010, pp. 375–403.

41. See, for example, V. H. Vroom, "Organizational Choice: A Study of Pre- and Postdecision Processes," *Organizational Behavior and Human Performance*, April 1966, pp. 212–225; L. W. Porter and E. E. Lawler III, *Managerial Attitudes and Performance* (Homewood, IL: Richard D. Irwin, 1968); W. Van Eerde and H. Thierry, "Vroom's Expectancy Models and Work-Related Criteria: A Meta-Analysis," *Journal of Applied Psychology* (October 1996), pp. 575–586; and M. L. Ambrose and C. T. Kulik, "Old Friends, New Faces: Motivation Research in the 1990s."

42. Right or Wrong box based on Borders Group, Inc., 2010 Form 10-K, www.borders.com (June 6, 2011); J. Checkler, "Judge Clears Bonuses at Borders," *Wall Street Journal*, April 23–24, 2011, p. B3; "News Briefs," *Publishers Weekly*, April 11, 2011, pp. 4+; P. Brickley, "Borders Seeks to Hand Out $8.3 Million in Bonuses," *Wall Street Journal*, March 26, 2011, p. B2; and J. A. Trachtenberg and M. Spector, "For Borders, A Scramble to Be Lean," *Wall Street Journal*, March 14, 2011, p. B1.

43. See, for instance, M. Siegall, "The Simplistic Five: An Integrative Framework for Teaching Motivation," *The Organizational Behavior Teaching Review* 12, no. 4 (1987–1988), pp. 141–143.

44. "100 Best Companies to Work For," *Fortune*, February 7, 2011, pp. 91+; V. Nayar, "Employee Happiness: Zappos vs. HCL," *Businessweek.com*, January 5, 2011; D. Richards, "At Zappos, Culture Pays," *Strategy+Business Online*, Autumn 2010; T. Hseih, "Zappos's CEO on Going to Extremes for Customers," *Harvard Business Review*, July–August 2010, pp. 41–45; A. Perschel, "Work-Life Flow: How Individuals, Zappos, and Other Innovative Companies Achieve High Engagement," *Global Business & Organizational Excellence*, July 2010, pp. 17–30; and J. M. O'Brien, "Zappos Know How to Kick It," *Fortune*, February 2, 2009, pp. 54–60.

45. T. Barber, "Inspire Your Employees Now," *Bloombeg BusinessWeek Online*, May 18, 2010; D. Mattioli, "CEOs Welcome Recovery to Look After Staff," *Wall Street Journal*, April 5, 2010, p. B5; J. Sullivan, "How Do We Keep People Motivated Following Layoffs?" *Workforce Management Online*, March 2010; S. Crabtree, "How to Bolster Employees' Confidence," *The Gallup Management Journal Online*, February 25, 2010; S. E. Needleman, "Business Owners Try to Motivate Employees," *Wall Street Journal*, January 14, 2010, p. B5; H. Mintzberg, "Rebuilding Companies as Communities," *Harvard Business Review*, July–August, 2009, pp. 140–143; and R. Luss, "Engaging Employees Through Periods of Layoffs," *Towers Watson*, www.towerswatson.com (March 3, 2009).

46. N. J. Adler with A. Gundersen, *International Dimensions of Organizational Behavior*, 5th ed. (Cincinnati, OH, 2008).

47. G. Hofstede, "Motivation, Leadership and Organization: Do American Theories Apply Abroad?" *Organizational Dynamics*, Summer 1980, p. 55.

48. Ibid.

49. J. K. Giacobbe-Miller, D. J. Miller, and V. I. Victorov, "A Comparison of Russian and U.S. Pay Allocation Decisions, Distributive Justice Judgments and Productivity Under Different Payment Conditions," *Personnel Psychology*, Spring 1998, pp. 137–163.

50. S. L. Mueller and L. D. Clarke, "Political-Economic Context and Sensitivity to Equity: Differences Between the United States and the Transition Economies of Central and Eastern Europe," *Academy of Management Journal* (June 1998), pp. 319–329.

51. I. Harpaz, "The Importance of Work Goals: An International Perspective," *Journal of International Business Studies* (First Quarter 1990), pp. 75–93.

52. G. E. Popp, H. J. Davis, and T. T. Herbert, "An International Study of Intrinsic Motivation Composition," *Management International Review*, January 1986, pp. 28–35.

53. R. W. Brislin, B. MacNab, R. Worthley, F. Kabigting Jr., and B. Zukis, "Evolving Perceptions of Japanese Workplace Motivation: An Employee-Manager Comparison," *International Journal of Cross-Cultural Management* (April 2005), pp. 87–104.

54. J. R. Billings and D. L. Sharpe, "Factors Influencing Flextime Usage Among Employed Married Women," *Consumer Interests Annual*, 1999, pp. 89–94; and I. Harpaz, "The Importance of Work Goals: An International Perspective," *Journal of International Business Studies* (First Quarter 1990), pp. 75–93.

55. N. Ramachandran, "New Paths At Work," *U.S. News & World Report*, March 20, 2006, p. 47; S. Armour, "Generation Y: They've Arrived at Work With a New Attitude," *USA Today*, November 6, 2005, pp. B1+; and R. Kanfer and P. L. Ackerman, "Aging, Adult Development, and Work Motivation," *Academy of Management Review*, July 2004, pp. 440–458.

56. T. D. Golden and J. F. Veiga, "The Impact of Extent of Telecommuting on Job Satisfaction: Resolving Inconsistent Findings," *Journal of Management* (April 2005), pp. 301–318.

57. See, for instance, M. Alpert, "The Care and Feeding of Engineers," *Fortune*, September 21, 1992, pp. 86–95; G. Poole, "How to Manage Your Nerds," *Forbes ASAP*, December 1994, pp. 132–136; T. J. Allen and R. Katz, "Managing Technical Professionals and Organizations: Improving and Sustaining the Performance of Organizations, Project Teams, and Individual Contributors," *Sloan Management Review*, Summer 2002, pp. S4–S5; and S. R. Barley and G. Kunda, "Contracting: A New Form of Professional Practice," *Academy of Management Perspectives*, February 2006, pp. 45–66.

58. K. Bennhold, "Working (Part-Time) in the 21st Century," *New York Times Online*, December 29, 2010; and J. Revell, C. Bigda, and D. Rosato, "The Rise of Freelance Nation," *CNNMoney*, cnnmoney.com (June 12, 2009); and R. J. Bohner, Jr. and E. R. Salasko, "Beware the Legal Risks of Hiring Temps," *Workforce*, October 2002, pp. 50–57.

59. H. G. Jackson, "Flexible Workplaces: The Next Imperative," *HR Magazine*, March 2011, p. 8; E. Frauenheim, "Companies Focus Their Attention on Flexibility," *Workforce Management Online*, February 2011; P. Davidson, "Companies Do More with Fewer Workers," *USA Today*, February 23, 2011, pp. 1B+; M. Rich, "Weighing Costs, Companies Favor Temporary Help," *New York Times Online*, December 19, 2010; P. Davidson, "Temporary Workers Reshape Companies, Jobs," *USA Today*, October 13, 2010, pp. 1B+; J. P. Broschak and A. Davis-Blake,

"Mixing Standard Work and Nonstandard Deals: The Consequences of Heterogeneity in Employment Arrangements," *Academy of Management Journal* (April 2006), pp. 371–393; M. L. Kraimer, S. J. Wayne, R. C. Liden, and R. T. Sparrowe, "The Role of Job Security in Understanding the Relationship Between Employees' Perceptions of Temporary Workers and Employees' Performance," *Journal of Applied Psychology* (March 2005), pp. 389–398; and C. E. Connelly and D. G. Gallagher, "Emerging Trends in Contingent Work Research," *Journal of Management* (November 2004), pp. 959–983.

60. C. Haddad, "FedEx: Gaining on the Ground," *BusinessWeek,* December 16, 2002, pp. 126–128; and L. Landro, "To Get Doctors to Do Better, Health Plans Try Cash Bonuses," *Wall Street Journal,* September 17, 2004, pp. A1+.

61. K. E. Culp, "Playing Field Widens for Stack's Great Game," *Springfield, Missouri, News-Leader,* January 9, 2005, pp. 1A+.

62. P. M. Buehler, "Opening Up Management Communication: Learning from Open Book Management," *Supervision,* August 2010, pp. 15–17; D. Drickhamer, "Open Books to Elevate Performance," *Industry Week,* November 2002, p. 16; J. Case, "Opening the Books," *Harvard Business Review*, March–April 1997, pp. 118–27; J. P. Schuster, J. Carpenter, and M. P. Kane, *The Power of Open-Book Management* (New York: John Wiley, 1996); and J. Case, "The Open-Book Revolution," *Inc.,* June 1995, pp. 26–50.

63. L. DeMars, "Glazed Over in a Good Way," *CFO,* July 2007, p. 80.

64. J. Singer, "Healing Your Workplace," *Supervision,* March 2011, pp. 11–13; P. Hart, "Benefits of Employee Recognition in the Workplace: Reduced Risk and Raised Revenues," *EHS Today,* February 2011, pp. 49–52; and F. Luthans and A. D. Stajkovic, "Provide Recognition for Performance Improvement," in E. A. Locke (ed.), *Principles of Organizational Behavior* (Oxford, England: Blackwell, 2000), pp. 166–180.

65. C. Huff, "Recognition That Resonates," *Workforce Management Online,* April 1, 2008.

66. J. Stewart, "I'm Standing Up for the Industry. Are You?" *Restaurant Business,* February 2011, pp. 36–37; and M. Littman, "Best Bosses Tell All," *Working Woman,* October 2000, p. 54.

67. E. White, "Praise from Peers Goes a Long Way," *Wall Street Journal,* December 19, 2005, p. B3.

68. Ibid.

69. K. J. Dunham, "Amid Sinking Workplace Morale, Employers Turn to Recognition," *Wall Street Journal,* November 19, 2002, p. B8.

70. See B. Nelson, "Try Praise," *Inc.,* September 1996, p. 115; and J. Wiscombe, "Rewards Get Results," *Workforce,* April 2002, pp. 42–48. Cited in S. Caudron, "The Top 20 Ways to Motivate Employees," *Industry Week,* April 3, 1995, pp. 15–16.

71. V. M. Barret, "Fight the Jerks," *Forbes,* July 2, 2007, pp. 52–54.

72. E. Krell, "All for Incentives, Incentives for All," *HR Magazine,* January 2011, pp. 35–38; and E. White, "The Best vs. the Rest," *Wall Street Journal,* January 30, 2006, pp. B1+.

73. R. K. Abbott, "Performance-Based Flex: A Tool for Managing Total Compensation Costs," *Compensation and Benefits Review*, March–April 1993, pp. 18–21; J. R. Schuster and P. K. Zingheim, "The New Variable Pay: Key Design Issues," *Compensation and Benefits Review*, March–April 1993, pp. 27–34; C. R. Williams and L. P. Livingstone, "Another Look at the Relationship Between Performance and Voluntary Turnover," *Academy of Management Journal* (April 1994), pp. 269–298; A. M. Dickinson and K. L. Gillette, "A Comparison of the Effects of Two Individual Monetary Incentive Systems on Productivity: Piece Rate Pay Versus Base Pay Plus Incentives," *Journal of Organizational Behavior Management* (Spring 1994), pp. 3–82; and C. B. Cadsby, F. Song, and F. Tapon, "Sorting and Incentive Effects of Pay for Performance: An Experimental Investigation," *Academy of Management Journal* (April 2007), pp. 387–405.

74. E. White, "Employers Increasingly Favor Bonuses to Raises," *Wall Street Journal,* August 28, 2006, p. B3.

75. "More Than 20 Percent of Japanese Firms Use Pay Systems Based on Performance," *Manpower Argus,* May 1998, p. 7; and E. Beauchesne, "Pay Bonuses Improve Productivity, Study Shows," *Vancouver Sun,* September 13, 2002, p. D5.

76. H. Rheem, "Performance Management Programs," *Harvard Business Review*, September–October 1996, pp. 8–9; G. Sprinkle, "The Effect of Incentive Contracts on Learning and Performance," *Accounting Review,* July 2000, pp. 299–326; and "Do Incentive Awards Work?" *HRFocus,* October 2000, pp. 1–3.

77. R.D. Banker, S.Y. Lee, G. Potter, and D. Srinivasan, "Contextual Analysis of Performance Impacts on Outcome-Based Incentive Compensation," *Academy of Management Journal* (August 1996), pp. 920–948.

78. S. A. Jeffrey and G. K. Adomza, "Incentive Salience and Improved Performance," *Human Performance,* 24, no. 1 (2011), pp. 47–59; T. Reason, "Why Bonus Plans Fail," *CFO,* January 2003, p. 53; and "Has Pay for Performance Had Its Day?" *McKinsey Quarterly,* no. 4 (2002), accessed at www.forbes.com.

79. E. Frauenheim, "Downturn Puts New Emphasis on Engagement," *Workforce Management Online,* July 21, 2009; S. D. Friedman, "Dial Down the Stress Level," *Harvard Business Review,* December 2008, pp. 28–29; and S. E. Needleman, "Allaying Workers' Fears During Uncertain Times," *Wall Street Journal,* October 6, 2008.

YOUR TURN TO BE A MANAGER

Motivating and Rewarding Employees

Skill Development: Applying Motivation Concepts

Great managers are great motivators. They're able to find the magic "potion" that stimulates employees to reach their full potential. The fact that there are hundreds of business books on motivation and dozens of experts who make a living by putting on motivation seminars only confirms the importance of this topic to managerial effectiveness.

Personal Insights: Do I Want an Enriched Job?

Listed here are 12 pairs of jobs. For each pair, indicate which job you would prefer—Job A or Job B. Assume that everything else about the jobs is the same. Use the following rating scale for your responses, and try to minimize your use of the "neutral" selection:

> **1** = Strongly prefer A
> **2** = Prefer A
> **3** = Slightly prefer A
> **4** = Neutral
> **5** = Slightly prefer B
> **6** = Prefer B
> **7** = Strongly prefer B

1. Job A   A job that offers little or no challenge.   1 2 3 4 5 6 7
   Job B   A job that requires you to be completely isolated from coworkers.

2. Job A   A job that pays very well.   1 2 3 4 5 6 7
   Job B   A job that allows considerable opportunity to be creative and innovative.

3. Job A   A job that often requires you to make important decisions.   1 2 3 4 5 6 7
   Job B   A job in which there are many pleasant people to work with.

4. Job A   A job with little security in a somewhat unstable organization.   1 2 3 4 5 6 7
   Job B   A job in which you have little or no opportunity to participate in decisions which affect your work.

5. Job A   A job in which greater responsibility is given to those who do the best work.   1 2 3 4 5 6 7
   Job B   A job in which great responsibility is given to loyal employees who have the most seniority.

6. Job A   A job with a supervisor who sometimes is highly critical.   1 2 3 4 5 6 7
   Job B   A job that does not require you to use much of your talent.

7. Job A   A very routine job.   1 2 3 4 5 6 7
   Job B   A job where your co-workers are not very friendly.

8. Job A   A job with a supervisor who respects you and treats you fairly.   1 2 3 4 5 6 7
   Job B   A job that provides constant opportunities for you to learn new and interesting things.

9. Job A   A job that gives you a real chance to develop yourself personally.   1 2 3 4 5 6 7
   Job B   A job with excellent vacations and fringe benefits.

10. Job A   A job where there is a real chance you could be laid off.   1 2 3 4 5 6 7
    Job B   A job with very little chance to do challenging work.

11. Job A   A job with little freedom and independence to do your work in the way you think best.   1 2 3 4 5 6 7
    Job B   A job with poor working conditions.

12. Job A   A job with very satisfying teamwork.   1 2 3 4 5 6 7
    Job B   A job that allows you to use your skills and abilities to the fullest extent.

Source: Adapted from J. R. Hackman and G. R. Oldham, *The Job Diagnostic Survey: An instrument for the Diagnosis of Jobs and the Evaluation of Job Redesign Projects.* Technical Report No. 4 (New Haven, CT: Yale University, Department of Administrative Sciences, 1974). With permission.

Analysis and Interpretation

This instrument is designed to assess the degree to which you desire complex, challenging work. A high need for growth suggests that you are more likely to experience the desired psychological states in the Job Characteristics Model when you have an enriched job.

This 12-item instrument taps the degree to which you have a strong versus weak desire to obtain growth satisfaction from your work. To calculate your growth need strength score, average the 12 items as follows:

1, 2, 7, 8, 11, and 12 (direct scoring)
3, 4, 5, 6, 9, and 10 (reverse scoring)

Average scores for typical respondents are close to the midpoint of 4.0. Research indicates that if you score high on this measure, you will respond positively to an enriched job.

Conversely, if you score low, you will tend *not* to find enriched jobs satisfying or motivating.

You should take away two insights from this exercise. First, it gives you an idea of your personal preference. Second, and more important in your role as a manager, it should remind you that everyone isn't like you. Some people have a greater need for growth and thus prefer characteristics like variety and autonomy in their jobs. But others prefer jobs that offer routine and standardized tasks. Don't automatically impose your needs onto others.

Skill Basics

Attempting to motivate others is a complex task. Unfortunately, no universal motivators are available that are guaranteed to work on anyone, anywhere. That said, we do know a lot about what works and doesn't work in terms of motivating others. The following suggestions summarize the essence of what we know is likely to be effective.

1. *Recognize individual differences.* People have different needs. Don't treat them all alike. Moreover, spend the time necessary to understand what's important to each person. This will allow you to individualize goals, level of involvement, and rewards to align with individual needs.

2. *Use goals and feedback.* People prefer to have goals. If you're in a position to assign or participate in setting goals for others, help them to set hard and specific goals. These are most likely to motivate. In addition, individuals are most likely to be motivated when they get feedback on how well they are faring in the pursuit of their goals.

3. *Allow people to participate in decisions that affect them.* If you are in a position to influence the level of participation, actively seek input from the person you seek to motivate. Employees are especially likely to respond positively when allowed to participate in setting work goals, choosing their benefit packages, solving productivity and quality problems, and the like.

4. *Link rewards to unsatisfied needs.* Recommendations #2 and #3 apply most directly to managers or team leaders trying to motivate their employees or team members. Effectively linking rewards to unsatisfied needs is a more generalizable action: It applies to motivating colleagues, friends, spouses, customers—as well as employees and team members. It builds on recommendation #1 and individual differences.

   Depending on your position in an organization and your resources, the rewards you control will vary. For example, senior-level executives typically can control pay increases, bonuses, promotion decisions, job assignments, and training decisions. They also can usually control job design such as allowing employees more freedom and control over their work, improving working conditions, increasing social interactions in the workplace, or modifying the workload. But everyone can offer others rewards such as recognition or providing sympathetic and sensitive help with problems. The key is identifying what needs are dominant and unsatisfied, then choosing rewards that will help satisfy those needs.

5. *Link rewards to performance.* The rewards you choose should be allocated so as to be contingent on performance. Importantly, the person you're trying to motivate must perceive a clear linkage. Regardless of how closely rewards are actually correlated to performance criteria, it's perception that counts. If individuals perceive this relationship to be low, motivation and performance will suffer.

6. *Maintain equity.* Rewards should be perceived by people in the organization as equating with the inputs they bring to their job. At a simplistic level, it means that experience, skills, abilities, effort, and other obvious inputs should explain differences in performance and, hence, pay, job assignments, and other obvious rewards.

Based on V. H. Vroom, *Work and Motivation* (New York: John Wiley, 1964); J. S. Adams, "Inequity in Social Exchanges," in L. Berkowitz (ed.), *Advances in Experimental Social Psychology* (New York: Academic Press, 1965),. pp. 267–300; and E. A. Locke and G. P. Latham, *A Theory of Goal Setting and Task Performance* (Upper Saddle River, NJ: Prentice Hall, 1990).

Skill Application

Sean's first job out of college is as a supervisor for Lyle's Catering Services. One of Lyle's main businesses is managing the food service operations at colleges and hospitals.

Sean has been given responsibility for the cafeteria at St. Paul College. He has a staff of approximately 12 full-time and 15 part-time workers. The cafeteria is open 7 days a week, from 6:30 A.M. until 8 P.M.

Sean has been in the job eight months and has become frustrated by the high employee turnover. Just since he's been on the job, 3 full-time and 6 part-time people have quit. Sean went back and looked at the personnel records for the past 5 years and this pattern has been a constant. He's frustrated by the cost and time involved in continually hiring and training new people. He's decided he needs to do something.

Sean has begun informally talking to employees. None seem particularly enthusiastic about their jobs. Even some of the "old timers"—who've worked in the cafeteria for six years or more—have little enthusiasm for their work. In fact, the part-timers seem more motivated than the full-timers even though the average part-timer makes only $11.50 an hour versus the full-timers' $15.00.

The class should form into small groups. Assume you are Sean. How can you improve the staff's motivation and reduce the turnover rate?

Skill Practice

1. Think of the worst job you've had. Was there anything management could have done to make the job better for you?

2. Interview a friend or family member who seems very satisfied in his or her job. What does this person like about his or job? What doesn't he or she like? What does he or she attribute this high job satisfaction to? How much of this person's high satisfaction do you think is attributable to the job and how much do you think is just inherent in the individual's personal outlook on life?

FYIA

La Mexican Kitchen

To: Linda Bustamante, Operations Manager
From: Matt Perkins, Shift Supervisor

For Your Immediate Action

Linda, HELP! We're having a difficult time keeping our food servers with us. It seems like I just get them trained and they leave. And we both know that our servers are key to our company's commitment to excellent customer service. We can have the best food in town (and do!) but if our servers aren't motivated to provide excellent service, we won't have any customers.

Although these positions pay minimum wage, you and I both know a motivated server can make additional money from tips. But it seems that this isn't enough to motivate them to stay. So what would you recommend? Could you jot down some ideas about how to better motivate our food servers and send those to me? Thanks!

This fictionalized company and message were created for educational purposes only, and not meant to reflect positively or negatively on management practices by any company that may share this name.

Bringing the Real World to Life

Case Application: Searching For?: Part 2

"For many people who work in the tech industry—fresh college grads and accomplished professionals alike—Google ranks near the top of lists of the most desirable employers." Yet, Google is now fighting off Facebook and other fast-growing Internet start-ups who want to poach its talented staff. It also has found itself losing employees who give up the fantastic benefits to go out on their own.

For instance, Sean Knapp and two colleagues, brothers Bismarck and Belsasar Lepe, came up with an idea on how to handle Web video. They left Google, or as one person put it, "expelled themselves from paradise to start their own company." When the threesome left the company, Google really wanted them and their project to stay. Google offered them a "blank check." But the trio realized they would do all the hard work and Google would own the product. So off they went, for the excitement of a start-up.

If this were an isolated occurrence, it would be easy to write off. But it's not. Other talented Google employees have done the same thing. In fact, there are so many of them who have left that they've formed an informal alumni club of ex-Googlers turned entrepreneurs.

Google is taking aggressive steps to retain its talent, especially those with start-up ambitions. One thing the company has done is give several engineers who said they wanted to leave to pursue their own ideas the opportunity to pursue those ideas within Google. These employees work independently and can recruit other engineers. In addition, Google's resources, such as its code base and computer servers, are available to them. In addition, from the very beginning, Google's founders (Larry Page and Sergey Brin) believed in giving everyone time—called 20 percent time—to work on their own projects.

Other Googlers have left because they felt Google had gotten too big and turned into a slow-moving bureaucratic company. Again, the company battled to keep the talent. For instance, when a Google product manager told his bosses that he was leaving to take a job at Facebook, they offered him a huge raise. But he told them it wasn't about the money. So they offered him a promotion, the opportunity to work in a different area, or even to start his own company inside Google. Yet, the former employee says that "At Facebook, I can see how quickly I could get things done compared to Google." However, there's one other thing that Facebook and other start-ups can offer experienced employees: They're still "private companies that

haven't gone public and can lure workers with pre-IPO (initial public offering) stock."

DISCUSSION QUESTIONS

1. What's it like to work at Google? (Hint: Go to Google's Web site and find the section on Jobs at Google and go from there.) What's your assessment of the company's work environment?

2. Google is doing a lot for its employees, but obviously not enough to retain several of its talented employees. Using what you've learned from studying the various motivation theories, what does this situation tell you about employee motivation?

3. What do you think is Google's biggest challenge in keeping employees motivated?

4. If you were managing a team of Google employees, how would you keep them motivated?

5. Reread the chapter section on motivating professionals. Using this information, what would you tell managers at Google?

Leadership and Trust

Leadership
and
Trust

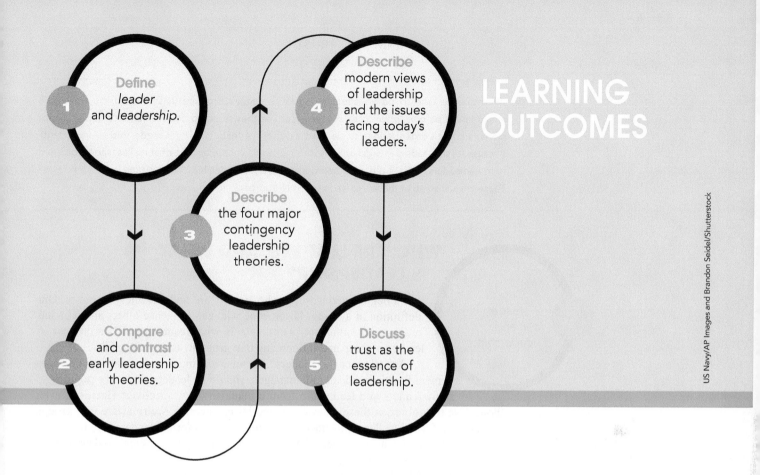

1 Define *leader* and *leadership.*

2 Compare and **contrast** early leadership theories.

3 Describe the four major contingency leadership theories.

4 Describe modern views of leadership and the issues facing today's leaders.

5 Discuss trust as the essence of leadership.

Master and Commander

With a father who was a Navy captain, Holly Graf, the first woman to command a Navy cruiser, had dreamed of doing just that since her high school days in Connecticut.[1] Upon graduation from the U.S. Naval Academy in 1985, colleagues sensed that she was on a fast track to leadership. Her assignments were well-rounded—from tours aboard a destroyer tender, a frigate, and a destroyer, to shore assignments at the Pentagon and as a Navy instructor at Villanova University. However, Graf's "darker side began to emerge when she was assigned to the destroyer U.S.S. *Curtis Wilbur* as the executive officer (XO) or second in command." One individual (now retired) says his tour on the *Curtis Wilbur* was "the worst time in my life." Graf's constant berating of the crew led him to complain to officials, but nothing was done. A few years later, Graf made U.S. Naval history by becoming the first female commander of a destroyer, the U.S.S. *Winston Churchill*. A Navy chaplain called his time aboard the *Churchill* as "the strangest of more than 200 such visits to ships in his career. Morale was the lowest he had ever encountered on any vessel." He tried to talk to Graf about what he was hearing from the crew and junior officers, but she cut him off and said she didn't want to talk to him about it. How effective do you think Graf could be with this kind of leader style?

What does it take to be an effective leader in today's organizations? Should the workplace environment be one in which employees feel like they're heard and trusted? It's important for managers in all organizations to be seen as effective leaders. Why is leadership so important? Because it's the leaders in organizations who make things happen. But what makes leaders different from nonleaders? What's the most appropriate style of leadership? What makes leaders effective? These are just some of the topics we're going to address in this chapter.

WHO ARE LEADERS, AND WHAT IS LEADERSHIP?

1 Define *leader* and *leadership*.

Let's begin by clarifying who leaders are and what leadership is. Our definition of a leader is someone who can influence others and who has managerial authority. Leadership is what leaders do. It's a process of leading a group and influencing that group to achieve its goals.

Are all managers leaders? Because leading is one of the four management functions, ideally all managers *should* be leaders. Thus, we're going to study leaders and leadership from a managerial perspective.[2] However, even though we're looking at these from a managerial perspective, we're aware that groups often have informal leaders who emerge. Although these informal leaders may be able to influence others, they have not been the focus of most leadership research and are not the types of leaders we're studying in this chapter.

Leaders and leadership, like motivation, are organizational behavior topics that have been researched a lot. Most of that research has been aimed at answering the question: "What is an effective leader?" We'll begin our study of leadership by looking at some early leadership theories that attempted to answer that question.

WHAT DO EARLY LEADERSHIP THEORIES TELL US ABOUT LEADERSHIP?

2 Compare and contrast early leadership theories.

People have been interested in leadership since they started coming together in groups to accomplish goals. However, it wasn't until the early part of the twentieth century that researchers actually began to study it. These early leadership theories focused on the *leader* (trait theories) and how the *leader interacted* with his or her group members (behavioral theories).

What Traits Do Leaders Have?

Ask the average person on the street what comes to mind when he or she thinks of leadership. You're likely to get a list of qualities such as intelligence, charisma, decisiveness, enthusiasm, strength, bravery, integrity, and self-confidence. These responses represent, in essence, trait theories of leadership. The search for traits or characteristics that differentiate leaders from nonleaders dominated early leadership research efforts. If the concept of traits were valid, all leaders would have to possess specific characteristics.

However, despite the best efforts of researchers, it proved impossible to identify a set of traits that would *always* differentiate a leader (the person) from a nonleader. Maybe it was a bit optimistic to think that there could be consistent and unique traits that would apply universally to all effective leaders, no matter whether they were in charge of Hyundai Motor Company, the Moscow Ballet, the country of Brazil, a local collegiate chapter of Alpha Chi Omega, or Ted's Malibu Surf Shop. However, later attempts to identify traits consistently associated with *leadership* (the process, not the person) were more successful. The seven traits shown to be associated with effective leadership are described briefly in Exhibit 1.[3]

EXHIBIT 1   Traits Associated with Leadership

1. *Drive*. Leaders exhibit a high effort level. They have a relatively high desire for achievement, they are ambitious, they have a lot of energy, they are tirelessly persistent in their activities, and they show initiative.

2. *Desire to lead*. Leaders have a strong desire to influence and lead others. They demonstrate the willingness to take responsibility.

3. *Honesty and integrity*. Leaders build trusting relationships with followers by being truthful, or nondeceitful, and by showing high consistency between word and deed.

4. *Self-confidence*. Followers look to leaders for an absence of self-doubt. Leaders, therefore, need to show self-confidence in order to convince followers of the rightness of their goals and decisions.

5. *Intelligence*. Leaders need to be intelligent enough to gather, synthesize, and interpret large amounts of information, and they need to be able to create visions, solve problems, and make correct decisions.

6. *Job-relevant knowledge*. Effective leaders have a high degree of knowledge about the company, industry, and technical matters. In-depth knowledge allows leaders to make well-informed decisions and to understand the implications of those decisions.

7. *Extraversion*. Leaders are energetic, lively people. They are sociable, assertive, and rarely silent or withdrawn.

Sources: Based on S. A. Kirkpatrick and E. A. Locke, "Leadership: Do Traits Really Matter?" *Academy of Management Executive,* May 1991, pp. 48–60; and T. A. Judge, J. E. Bono, R. Ilies, and M. W. Gerhardt, "Personality and Leadership: A Qualitative and Quantitative Review," *Journal of Applied Psychology* (August 2002), pp. 765–80.

Researchers eventually recognized that traits alone were not sufficient for identifying effective leaders because explanations based solely on traits ignored the interactions of leaders and their group members as well as situational factors. Possessing the appropriate traits only made it more likely that an individual would be an effective leader. Therefore, leadership research from the late 1940s to the mid-1960s concentrated on the preferred behavioral styles that leaders demonstrated. Researchers wondered whether there was something unique in what effective leaders *did*—in other words, in their *behavior*.

What Behaviors Do Leaders Exhibit?

It was hoped that the behavioral theories of leadership approach would provide more definitive answers about the nature of leadership and, if successful, also have practical implications quite different from those of the trait approach. If trait research had been successful, it would have provided a basis for selecting the right people to assume formal leadership positions in organizations. In contrast, if behavioral studies were to turn up critical behavioral determinants of leadership, people could be trained to be leaders, which is precisely the premise behind management development programs.

A number of studies looked at behavioral styles. We'll briefly review three of the most popular: Kurt Lewin's studies at the University of Iowa, the Ohio State studies, and the University of Michigan studies. Then we'll see how the concepts developed in those studies were used in a grid created for appraising leadership styles.

WHAT DID THE UNIVERSITY OF IOWA STUDIES TELL US ABOUT LEADERSHIP BEHAVIOR?

One of the first studies of leadership behavior was done by Kurt Lewin and his associates at the University of Iowa.[4] In their studies, the researchers explored three leadership

---

leader
Someone who can influence others and who has managerial authority

leadership
The process of leading a group and influencing that group to achieve its goals

trait theories of leadership
Theories that isolate characteristics (traits) that differentiate leaders from nonleaders

behavioral theories of leadership
Theories that isolate behaviors that differentiate effective leaders from ineffective leaders

Autocratic style describes the leadership of Martha Stewart, founder of Martha Stewart Living Omnimedia. In presiding over her many business ventures in publishing, broadcasting, and merchandising, Stewart's leadership behavior includes centralizing authority, dictating work methods, making unilateral decisions, and limiting employee participation. She is described as meticulous and highly demanding of her staff. Stewart is shown here shaking hands with the president of the Culinary Institute of America, where she delivered the commencement address and told graduates that she attributes her successful business career to passion, hard work, and generosity.

behaviors or styles: autocratic, democratic, and laissez-faire. An autocratic style is that of a leader who typically tends to centralize authority, dictate work methods, make unilateral decisions, and limit employee participation. A leader with a democratic style tends to involve employees in decision making, delegates authority, encourages participation in deciding work methods and goals, and uses feedback as an opportunity to coach employees. The democratic style can be further classified in two ways: consultative and participative. A *democratic-consultative leader* seeks input and hears the concerns and issues of employees but makes the final decision him- or herself. In this capacity, the democratic-consultative leader is using the input as an information-seeking exercise. A *democratic-participative leader* often allows employees to have a say in what's decided. Here, decisions are made by the group, with the leader providing one input to that group. Finally, the laissez-faire leader generally gives his or her employees complete freedom to make decisions and to complete their work in whatever way they see fit. A laissez-faire leader might simply provide necessary materials and answer questions.

Lewin and his associates wondered which one of the three leadership styles was most effective. On the basis of their studies of leaders from boys' clubs, they concluded that the laissez-faire style was ineffective on every performance criterion when compared with both democratic and autocratic styles. Quantity of work done was equal in groups with democratic and autocratic leaders, but work quality and group satisfaction were higher in democratic groups. The results suggest that a democratic leadership style could contribute to both good quantity and high quality of work.

Later studies of autocratic and democratic styles of leadership showed mixed results. For example, democratic leadership styles sometimes produced higher performance levels than autocratic styles, but at other times they produced group performance that was lower than or equal to that of autocratic styles. Nonetheless, more consistent results were generated when a measure of employee satisfaction was used.

Group members' satisfaction levels were generally higher under a democratic leader than under an autocratic one.[5] Did this finding mean that managers should always exhibit a democratic style of leadership? Two researchers, Robert Tannenbaum and Warren Schmidt, attempted to provide that answer.[6]

Tannenbaum and Schmidt developed a continuum of leader behaviors. The continuum illustrated that a range of leadership behaviors, from boss centered (autocratic) to employee centered (laissez-faire), is possible. In deciding which leader behavior from the continuum to use, Tannenbaum and Schmidt proposed that managers look at forces within themselves (such as comfort level with the chosen leadership style), forces within the employees (such as readiness to assume responsibility), and forces within the situation (such as time pressures). They suggested that managers should move toward more employee-centered styles in the long run because such behavior would increase employees' motivation, decision quality, teamwork, morale, and development.

This dual nature of leader behaviors—that is, focusing on the work to be done and focusing on the employees—is also a key characteristic of the Ohio State and University of Michigan studies.

WHAT DID THE OHIO STATE STUDIES SHOW?   The most comprehensive and replicated of the behavioral theories resulted from research that began at Ohio State University in the late 1940s.[7] These studies sought to identify independent dimensions of leader behavior. Beginning with more than 1,000 dimensions, the researchers eventually narrowed the list down to two categories that accounted for most of the leadership behavior described by employees. They called these two dimensions initiating structure and consideration.

○ From the Past to the Present ○

Both the Ohio State and Michigan studies added a lot to our understanding of effective leadership.[9] Prior to the completion of these studies, it was widely thought by researchers and practicing managers that one style of leadership was good and another bad. However, as the research showed, both leader behavior dimensions—job-centered and employee-centered in the Michigan studies, and initiating structure and consideration in the Ohio State studies—are necessary for effective leadership. That dual focus of "what" a leader does still holds today. Leaders are expected to focus on both the task and on the people he or she is leading. Even the later contingency leadership theories used the people/task distinction to define a leader's style. Finally, these early behavioral studies were important for the "systematic methodology they introduced and the increased awareness they generated concerning the importance of leader behavior." Although the behavioral theories may not have been the final chapter in the book on leadership, they "served as a springboard for the leadership research that followed."

Think About:

- Is saying that the leader's "job" is to focus on the task and focus on the people too simplistic? Explain.

- How did the behavioral theories serve as a springboard for the leadership research that followed?

Initiating structure refers to the extent to which a leader is likely to define and structure his or her role and those of employees in the search for goal attainment. It includes behavior that attempts to organize work, work relationships, and goals. For example, the leader who is characterized as high in initiating structure assigns group members to particular tasks, expects workers to maintain definite standards of performance, and emphasizes meeting deadlines.

Consideration is defined as the extent to which a leader has job relationships characterized by mutual trust and respect for employees' ideas and feelings. A leader who is high in consideration helps employees with personal problems, is friendly and approachable, and treats all employees as equals. He or she shows concern for his or her followers' comfort, well-being, status, and satisfaction.

Extensive research based on these definitions found that a leader who is high in initiating structure and consideration (a high-high leader) achieved high employee performance and satisfaction more frequently than one who rated low on either consideration, initiating structure, or both. However, the high-high style did not always yield positive results. For example, leader behavior characterized as high on initiating structure led to greater rates of grievances, absenteeism, and turnover, and lower levels of job satisfaction for workers performing routine tasks. Other studies found that high consideration was negatively related to performance ratings of the leader by his or her manager. In conclusion, the Ohio State studies suggested that the high-high style generally produced positive outcomes, but enough exceptions were found to indicate that situational factors needed to be integrated into the theory.

HOW DID THE UNIVERSITY OF MICHIGAN STUDIES DIFFER? Leadership studies undertaken at the University of Michigan's Survey Research Center, at about the same time as those being done at Ohio State, had similar research objectives: to locate the behavioral characteristics of leaders that were related to performance effectiveness. The Michigan group also came up with two dimensions of leadership behavior, which they labeled employee oriented and production oriented.[8] Leaders who were **employee oriented** emphasized

---

autocratic style
A leader who centralizes authority, dictates work methods, makes unilateral decisions, and limits employee participation

democratic style
A leader who involves employees in decision making, delegates authority, encourages participation in deciding work methods, and uses feedback to coach employees

laissez-faire
A leader who generally gives employees complete freedom to make decisions and to complete their work however they see fit

initiating structure
The extent to which a leader defines and structures his or her role and the roles of employees to attain goals

consideration
The extent to which a leader has job relationships characterized by mutual trust, respect for employees' ideas, and regard for their feelings

employee oriented
A leader who emphasizes the people aspects

British entrepreneur Richard Branson, chairman and CEO of Virgin Group, is an employee-oriented leader who emphasizes interpersonal relations, takes a personal interest in the needs of employees, and accepts individual differences among workers. Described as fun-loving and sensitive to the needs of others, Branson has built one of the most recognized and respected brands in the world for products and services in the areas of travel, entertainment, and lifestyle. In this photo, Branson poses in front of the Eiffel Tower with some of Virgin's employees in Paris who joined him in a promotional tour to launch the French translation of his autobiography.

interpersonal relations; they took a personal interest in the needs of their employees and accepted individual differences among members. Leaders who were **production oriented**, in contrast, tended to emphasize the technical or task aspects of the job, were concerned mainly with accomplishing their group's tasks, and regarded group members as a means to that end.

The conclusions of the Michigan researchers strongly favored leaders who were employee oriented. Employee-oriented leaders were associated with higher group productivity and higher job satisfaction. Production-oriented leaders were associated with lower group productivity and lower worker satisfaction.

What Is the Managerial Grid?

The behavioral dimensions from these early leadership studies provided the basis for the development of a two-dimensional grid for appraising leadership styles. This **managerial grid** used the behavioral dimensions "concern for people" and "concern for production" and evaluated a leader's use of these behaviors, ranking them on a scale from 1 (low) to 9 (high).[10] Although the grid had 81 potential categories into which a leader's behavioral style might fall, only five styles were named: impoverished management (1,1), task management (9,1), middle-of-the-road management (5,5), country club management (1,9), and team management (9,9). Of these five styles, the researchers concluded that managers performed best when using a 9,9 style. Unfortunately, the grid offered no answers to the question of what made a manager an effective leader; it only provided a framework for conceptualizing leadership style. In fact, little substantive evidence supports the conclusion that a 9,9 style is most effective in all situations.[11]

Leadership researchers were discovering that predicting leadership success involved something more complex than isolating a few leader traits or preferable behaviors. They began looking at situational influences. Specifically, which leadership styles might be suitable in different situations and what were these different situations?

3 Describe the four major contingency leadership theories.

WHAT DO THE CONTINGENCY THEORIES OF LEADERSHIP TELL US?

"The corporate world is filled with stories of leaders who failed to achieve greatness because they failed to understand the context they were working in."[12] In this section we examine four contingency theories—Fiedler, Hersey-Blanchard, leader-participation, and path-goal. Each looks at defining leadership style and the situation, and attempts to answer the *if-then* contingencies (that is, *if* this is the context or situation, *then* this is the best leadership style to use).

What Was the First Comprehensive Contingency Model?

The first comprehensive contingency model for leadership was developed by Fred Fiedler.[13] The **Fiedler contingency model** proposed that effective group performance depended upon properly matching the leader's style and the amount of control and influence in the situation. The model was based on the premise that a certain leadership style would be most effective in different types of situations. The keys were (1) to define those leadership styles and the different types of situations, and then (2) identify the appropriate combinations of style and situation.

Fiedler proposed that a key factor in leadership success was an individual's basic leadership style, either task oriented or relationship oriented. To measure a leader's style, Fiedler developed the **least-preferred co-worker (LPC) questionnaire**. This questionnaire contained 18 pairs of contrasting adjectives—for example, pleasant–unpleasant, cold–warm, boring–interesting, or friendly–unfriendly. Respondents were asked to think of all the co-workers they had ever had and to describe that one person they *least enjoyed* working with by rating him or her on a scale of 1 to 8 for each of the sets of adjectives (the 8 always described the positive adjective out of the pair and the 1 always described the negative adjective out of the pair).

If the leader described the least preferred co-worker in relatively positive terms (in other words, a "high" LPC score—a score of 64 or above), then the respondent was primarily interested in good personal relations with co-workers and the style would be described as *relationship oriented*. In contrast, if you saw the least preferred co-worker in relatively unfavorable terms (a low LPC score—a score of 57 or below), you were primarily interested in productivity and getting the job done; thus, your style would be labeled as *task oriented*. Fiedler did acknowledge that a small number of people might fall in between these two extremes and not have a cut-and-dried leadership style. One other important point is that Fiedler assumed a person's leadership style was fixed regardless of the situation. In other words, if you were a relationship-oriented leader, you'd always be one, and the same for task-oriented.

After an individual's leadership style had been assessed through the LPC, it was time to evaluate the situation in order to be able to match the leader with the situation. Fiedler's research uncovered three contingency dimensions that defined the key situational factors in leader effectiveness. These were:

- *Leader-member relations:* the degree of confidence, trust, and respect employees had for their leader; rated as either good or poor.
- *Task structure:* the degree to which job assignments were formalized and structured; rated as either high or low.
- *Position power:* the degree of influence a leader had over activities such as hiring, firing, discipline, promotions, and salary increases; rated as either strong or weak.

Each leadership situation was evaluated in terms of these three contingency variables, which when combined produced eight possible situations that were either favorable or unfavorable for the leader. (See the bottom of the chart in Exhibit 2). Situations I, II, and III were classified as highly favorable for the leader. Situations IV, V, and VI were moderately favorable for the leader. And situations VII and VIII were described as highly unfavorable for the leader.

Once Fiedler had described the leader variables and the situational variables, he had everything he needed to define the specific contingencies for leadership effectiveness. To do so, he studied 1,200 groups where he compared relationship-oriented versus task-oriented leadership styles in each of the eight situational categories. He concluded that task-oriented leaders performed better in very favorable situations and in very unfavorable situations. (See the top of Exhibit 2 where performance is shown on the vertical axis and situation favorableness is shown on the horizontal axis.)

production oriented
A leader who emphasizes the technical or task aspects

managerial grid
A two-dimensional grid for appraising leadership styles

fiedler contingency model
Leadership theory proposing that effective group performance depends on the proper match between a leader's style and the degree to which the situation allowed the leader to control and influence

least-preferred coworker (LPC) questionnaire
A questionnaire that measures whether a leader was task or relationship oriented

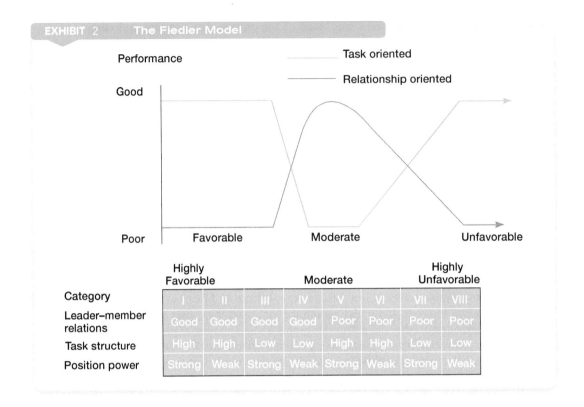

EXHIBIT 2   The Fiedler Model

Category	I	II	III	IV	V	VI	VII	VIII
Leader–member relations	Good	Good	Good	Good	Poor	Poor	Poor	Poor
Task structure	High	High	Low	Low	High	High	Low	Low
Position power	Strong	Weak	Strong	Weak	Strong	Weak	Strong	Weak

On the other hand, relationship-oriented leaders performed better in moderately favorable situations.

Because Fiedler treated an individual's leadership style as fixed, there were only two ways to improve leader effectiveness. First, you could bring in a new leader whose style better fit the situation. For instance, if the group situation was highly unfavorable but was led by a relationship-oriented leader, the group's performance could be improved by replacing that person with a task-oriented leader. The second alternative was to change the situation to fit the leader. This could be done by restructuring tasks; by increasing or decreasing the power that the leader had over factors such as salary increases, promotions, and disciplinary actions; or by improving the leader-member relations. Research testing the overall validity of Fiedler's model has shown considerable evidence to support the model.[14] However, his theory wasn't without criticisms. The major one is that it's probably unrealistic to assume that a person can't change his or her leadership style to fit the situation. Effective leaders can, and do, change their styles. Another is that the LPC wasn't very practical. Finally, the situation variables were difficult to assess.[15] Despite its shortcomings, the Fiedler model showed that effective leadership style needed to reflect situational factors.

How Do Followers' Willingness and Ability Influence Leaders?

Paul Hersey and Ken Blanchard developed a leadership theory that has had a strong following among management development specialists.[16] This model, called **situational leadership theory (SLT)**, is a contingency theory that focuses on followers' readiness. Before we proceed, there are two points we need to clarify: Why a leadership theory focuses on the followers, and what is meant by the term *readiness*.

The emphasis on the followers in leadership effectiveness reflects the reality that it *is* the followers who accept or reject the leader. Regardless of what the leader does, the group's effectiveness depends on the actions of the followers. This is an important dimension that has been overlooked or underemphasized in most leadership theories.

And readiness, as defined by Hersey and Blanchard refers to the extent to which people have the ability and willingness to accomplish a specific task.

SLT uses the same two leadership dimensions that Fiedler identified: task and relationship behaviors. However, Hersey and Blanchard go a step further by considering each as either high or low and then combining them into four specific leadership styles described as follows:

- *Telling* (high task–low relationship): The leader defines roles and tells people what, how, when, and where to do various tasks.
- *Selling* (high task–high relationship): The leader provides both directive and supportive behavior.
- *Participating* (low task–high relationship): The leader and followers share in decision making; the main role of the leader is facilitating and communicating.
- *Delegating* (low task–low relationship): The leader provides little direction or support.

The final component in the model is the four stages of follower readiness:

- *R1:* People are both *unable and unwilling* to take responsibility for doing something. Followers aren't competent or confident.
- *R2:* People are *unable but willing* to do the necessary job tasks. Followers are motivated but lack the appropriate skills.
- *R3:* People are *able but unwilling* to do what the leader wants. Followers are competent, but don't want to do something.
- *R4:* People are both *able and willing* to do what is asked of them.

SLT essentially views the leader-follower relationship as like that of a parent and a child. Just as a parent needs to relinquish control when a child becomes more mature and responsible, so, too, should leaders. As followers reach higher levels of readiness, the leader responds not only by decreasing control over their activities but also decreasing relationship behaviors. The SLT says if followers are at R1 (*unable* and *unwilling* to do a task), the leader needs to use the telling style and give clear and specific directions; if followers are at R2 (*unable* and *willing*), the leader needs to use the selling style and display high task orientation to compensate for the followers' lack of ability and high relationship orientation to get followers to "buy into" the leader's desires; if followers are at R3 (*able* and *unwilling*), the leader needs to use the participating style to gain their support; and if employees are at R4 (both *able* and *willing*), the leader doesn't need to do much and should use the delegating style.

SLT has intuitive appeal. It acknowledges the importance of followers and builds on the logic that leaders can compensate for ability and motivational limitations in their followers. However, research efforts to test and support the theory generally have been disappointing.[17] Possible explanations include internal inconsistencies in the model as well as problems with research methodology. Despite its appeal and wide popularity, we have to be cautious about any enthusiastic endorsement of SLT.

LiPo Ching/Newscom

Software engineers and Web developers at YouTube work together in small teams to design, develop, and roll out key features and products in short time frames. Employees work in a fast-paced, creative, and intellectually challenging environment where they apply their problem-solving skills and technical knowledge in displaying a wide variety of video content for the second most visited site in the world. They have a high level of follower readiness. As well educated and responsible employees, they are willing and able to complete their tasks under leadership that gives them the freedom to make and implement decisions. This leader-follower relationship is consistent with Hersey and Blanchard's situational leadership theory.

---

situational leadership theory (SLT)
A leadership contingency theory that focuses on followers' readiness

readiness
The extent to which people have the ability and willingness to accomplish a specific task

How Participative Should a Leader Be?

Back in 1973, Victor Vroom and Phillip Yetton developed a leader-participation model that related leadership behavior and participation to decision making.[19] Recognizing that task structures have varying demands for routine and nonroutine activities, these researchers argued that leader behavior must adjust to reflect the task structure. Vroom and Yetton's model was normative. That is, it provided a sequential set of rules to be followed in determining the form and amount of participation in decision making in different types of situations. The model was a decision tree incorporating seven contingencies (whose relevance could be identified by making yes or no choices) and five alternative leadership styles.

More recent work by Vroom and Arthur Jago has revised that model.[20] The new model retains the same five alternative leadership styles but expands the contingency variables to twelve—from the leader's making the decision completely by himself or herself to sharing the problem with the group and developing a consensus decision. These variables are listed in Exhibit 3.

Research on the original leader-participation model was encouraging.[21] But unfortunately, the model is far too complex for the typical manager to use regularly. In fact, Vroom and Jago have developed a computer program to guide managers through all the decision branches in the revised model. Although we obviously can't do justice to this model's sophistication in this discussion, it has provided us with some solid, empirically supported insights into key contingency variables related to leadership effectiveness. Moreover, the leader-participation model confirms that leadership research should be directed at the situation rather than at the person. That is, it probably makes more sense to talk about autocratic and participative situations than autocratic and participative leaders. As House did in his path-goal theory, Vroom, Yetton, and Jago argue against the notion that leader behavior is inflexible. The leader-participation model assumes that the leader can adapt his or her style to different situations.[22]

How Do Leaders Help Followers?

Another approach to understanding leadership is path-goal theory, which states that the leader's job is to assist followers in attaining their goals and to provide direction or support needed to ensure that their goals are compatible with the goals of the group or organization. Developed by Robert House, path-goal theory takes key elements from the expectancy theory of motivation.[23] The term *path-goal* is derived from the belief that effective leaders clarify the path to help their followers get from where they are to the achievement of their work goals and make the journey along the path easier by reducing roadblocks and pitfalls.

EXHIBIT 3   Contingency Variables in the Revised Leader-Participation Model

1. Importance of the decision
2. Importance of obtaining follower commitment to the decision
3. Whether the leader has sufficient information to make a good decision
4. How well structured the problem is
5. Whether an autocratic decision would receive follower commitment
6. Whether followers "buy into" the organization's goals
7. Whether there is likely to be conflict among followers over solution alternatives
8. Whether followers have the necessary information to make a good decision
9. Time constraints on the leader that may limit follower involvement
10. Whether costs to bring geographically dispersed members together are justified
11. Importance to the leader of minimizing the time it takes to make the decision
12. Importance of using participation as a tool for developing follower decision skills

Source: Stephen P. Robbins and Timothy A. Judge, *Organizational Behavior*, 13th, ©2009. Printed and electronically reproduced by permission of Pearson Education, Inc., Upper Saddle River, New Jersey.

House identified four leadership behaviors:

◆ *Directive leader:* Lets subordinates know what's expected of them, schedules work to be done, and gives specific guidance on how to accomplish tasks.

◆ *Supportive leader:* Shows concern for the needs of followers and is friendly.

◆ *Participative leader:* Consults with group members and uses their suggestions before making a decision.

◆ *Achievement-oriented leader:* Sets challenging goals and expects followers to perform at their highest level.

In contrast to Fiedler's view that a leader couldn't change his or her behavior, House assumed that leaders are flexible and can display any or all of these leadership styles depending on the situation.

As Exhibit 4 illustrates, path-goal theory proposes two situational or contingency variables that moderate the leadership behavior-outcome relationship: those in the *environment* that are outside the control of the follower (factors including task structure, formal authority system, and the work group) and those that are part of the personal characteristics of the *follower* (including locus of control, experience, and perceived ability). Environmental factors determine the type of leader behavior required if subordinate outcomes are to be maximized; personal characteristics of the follower determine how the environment and leader behavior are interpreted. The theory proposes that a leader's behavior won't be

Chung Mong-Koo, chairman and CEO of South Korea's Hyundai-Kia Motor Group, is an achievement-oriented leader. Since assuming leadership of Hyundai Motor Company in 1999, Chung Mong-Koo has set difficult goals and has motivated his employees to achieve them. His achievements include elevating product quality from poor to world class, increasing sales volume, and improving brand image and customer satisfaction. Confident and aggressive, Chung Mong-Koo has transformed Hyundai into a top global competitor and the world's fastest-growing major car maker. Chung Mong-Koo (left) is shown here preparing to deliver his annual New Year's address to employees.

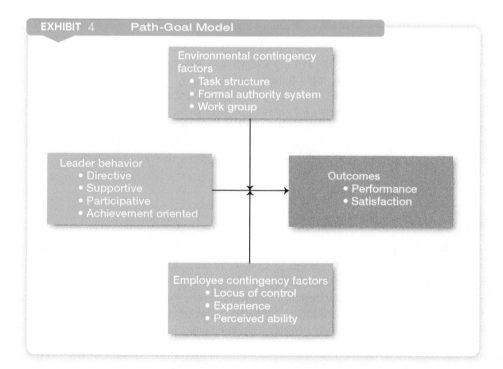

EXHIBIT 4   Path-Goal Model

Environmental contingency factors
- Task structure
- Formal authority system
- Work group

Leader behavior
- Directive
- Supportive
- Participative
- Achievement oriented

Outcomes
- Performance
- Satisfaction

Employee contingency factors
- Locus of control
- Experience
- Perceived ability

leader-participation model
A leadership contingency theory that's based on a sequential set of rules for determining how much participation a leader uses in decision making according to different types of situations

path-goal theory
A leadership theory that says the leader's job is to assist followers in attaining their goals and to provide direction or support needed to ensure that their goals are compatible with the organization's or group's goals

effective if it's redundant with what the environmental structure is providing or is incongruent with follower characteristics. For example, some predictions from path-goal theory are:

- Directive leadership leads to greater satisfaction when tasks are ambiguous or stressful than when they are highly structured and well laid out. The followers aren't sure what to do, so the leader needs to give them some direction.
- Supportive leadership results in high employee performance and satisfaction when subordinates are performing structured tasks. In this situation, the leader only needs to support followers, not tell them what to do.
- Directive leadership is likely to be perceived as redundant among subordinates with high perceived ability or with considerable experience. These followers are quite capable so they don't need a leader to tell them what to do.
- The clearer and more bureaucratic the formal authority relationships, the more leaders should exhibit supportive behavior and deemphasize directive behavior. The organizational situation has provided the structure as far as what is expected of followers, so the leader's role is simply to support.
- Directive leadership will lead to higher employee satisfaction when there is substantive conflict within a work group. In this situation, the followers need a leader who will take charge.
- Subordinates with an internal locus of control will be more satisfied with a participative style. Because these followers believe that they control what happens to them, they prefer to participate in decisions.
- Subordinates with an external locus of control will be more satisfied with a directive style. These followers believe that what happens to them is a result of the external environment so they would prefer a leader who tells them what to do.
- Achievement-oriented leadership will increase subordinates' expectancies that effort will lead to high performance when tasks are ambiguously structured. By setting challenging goals, followers know what the expectations are.

Research findings on the path-goal model have been mixed because the theory has so many variables to examine. Although not every study has found support, we can still say that evidence supports the logic underlying the theory.[24] That is, an employee's performance and satisfaction are likely to be positively influenced when the leader chooses a leadership style that compensates for shortcomings in either the employee or the work setting. However, if the leader spends time explaining tasks that are already clear or when the employee has the ability and experience to handle them without interference, the employee is likely to see such directive behavior as redundant or even insulting.

WHAT IS LEADERSHIP LIKE TODAY?

Describe modern views of leadership and the issues facing today's leaders.

What are the latest views of leadership, and what issues do today's leaders have to deal with? In this section, we're going to look at four contemporary views of leadership: leader-member exchange (LMX), transformational-transactional leadership, charismatic-visionary leadership, and team leadership. In addition, we'll discuss some issues that leaders have to face in leading effectively in today's environment.

What Do the Four Contemporary Views of Leadership Tell Us?

Remember our discussion at the beginning of this chapter where we said that leadership studies have long had the goal of describing what it takes to be an effective leader. That goal hasn't changed! Even the contemporary views of leadership are interested in answering that question. These views of leadership have a common theme: leaders who interact with, inspire, and support followers.

HOW DO LEADERS INTERACT WITH FOLLOWERS?   Have you ever been in a group in which the leader had "favorites" who made up his or her in-group? If so, that's the premise behind leader-member exchange (LMX) theory.[25] Leader-member exchange (LMX) theory says that leaders create in-groups and out-groups and those in the in-group will have higher performance ratings, less turnover, and greater job satisfaction.

LMX theory suggests that early on in the relationship between a leader and a given follower, a leader will implicitly categorize a follower as an "in" or as an "out." That relationship tends to remain fairly stable over time. Leaders also encourage LMX by rewarding those employees with whom they want a closer linkage and punishing those with whom they do not.[26] For the LMX relationship to remain intact, however, both the leader and the follower must "invest" in the relationship.

It's not exactly clear how a leader chooses who falls into each category, but evidence indicates that in-group members have demographic, attitude, personality, and even gender similarities with the leader or they have a higher level of competence than out-group members.[27] The leader does the choosing, but the follower's characteristics drive the decision.

Research on LMX has been generally supportive. It appears that leaders do differentiate among followers; that these disparities are not random; and followers with in-group status will have higher performance ratings, engage in more helping or "citizenship" behaviors at work, and report greater satisfaction with their boss.[28] These findings probably shouldn't be surprising when leaders are most likely to invest their time and other resources in those whom they expect to perform best.

HOW DO TRANSACTIONAL LEADERS DIFFER FROM TRANSFORMATIONAL LEADERS?
Many early leadership theories viewed leaders as transactional leaders; that is, leaders who lead primarily by using social exchanges (or transactions). Transactional leaders guide or motivate followers to work toward established goals by exchanging rewards for their productivity.[29] But another type of leader—a transformational leader—stimulates and inspires (transforms) followers to achieve extraordinary outcomes. Examples include Jim Goodnight of SAS Institute and Andrea Jung of Avon. They pay attention to the concerns and developmental needs of individual followers; they change followers' awareness of issues by helping those followers look at old problems in new ways; and they are able to excite, arouse, and inspire followers to exert extra effort to achieve group goals.

Transactional and transformational leadership shouldn't be viewed as opposing approaches to getting things done.[30] Transformational leadership develops from transactional leadership. Transformational leadership produces levels of employee effort and performance that go beyond what would occur with a transactional approach alone. Moreover, transformational leadership is more than charisma since the transformational leader attempts to instill in followers the ability to question not only established views but those views held by the leader.[31]

The evidence supporting the superiority of transformational leadership over transactional leadership is overwhelmingly impressive. For instance, studies that looked at managers in different settings, including the military and business, found that transformational leaders were evaluated as more effective, higher performers, more promotable than their transactional counterparts, and more interpersonally sensitive.[32] In addition, evidence indicates that transformational leadership is strongly correlated with lower turnover rates and higher levels of productivity, work engagement, employee satisfaction, creativity, goal attainment, and follower well-being.[33]

HOW DO CHARISMATIC LEADERSHIP AND VISIONARY LEADERSHIP DIFFER?   Jeff Bezos, founder and CEO of Amazon.com, is a person who exudes energy, enthusiasm, and drive.[34] He's fun-loving (his legendary laugh has been described as a flock

---

leader-member exchange (LMX) theory
A leadership theory that says leaders create in-groups and out-groups and those in the in-group will have higher performance ratings, less turnover, and greater job satisfaction

transactional leaders
Leaders who lead primarily by using social exchanges (or transactions)

transformational leaders
Leaders who stimulate and inspire (transform) followers to achieve extraordinary outcomes

Mark Richards/PhotoEdit

Amazon.com founder and chief executive Jeff Bezos is a charismatic leader. Described as energetic, enthusiastic, optimistic, and self-confident, Bezos has the drive to set and pursue goals for risky new ventures and to inspire his employees to work hard to achieve them. He started the company in 1994 with the vision of providing consumers with the service of an online bookstore, and he built it into the largest retailer on the Web. Bezos reinvented Amazon by introducing a product innovation, the Kindle electronic reader, that began with his long-term vision of "every book, ever printed, in any language, all available in less than 60 seconds." In this photo, Bezos uses his charisma to inspire employees working at an Amazon distribution center.

of Canadian geese on nitrous oxide), but has pursued his vision for Amazon with serious intensity and has demonstrated an ability to inspire his employees through the ups and downs of a rapidly growing company. Bezos is what we call a **charismatic leader**—that is, an enthusiastic, self-confident leader whose personality and actions influence people to behave in certain ways.

Several authors have attempted to identify personal characteristics of the charismatic leader.[35] The most comprehensive analysis identified five such characteristics: they have a vision, the ability to articulate that vision, willingness to take risks to achieve that vision, sensitivity to both environmental constraints and follower needs, and behaviors that are out of the ordinary.[36]

An increasing body of evidence shows impressive correlations between charismatic leadership and high performance and satisfaction among followers.[37] Although one study found that charismatic CEOs had no impact on subsequent organizational performance, charisma is still believed to be a desirable leadership quality.[38]

If charisma is desirable, can people learn to be charismatic leaders? Or are charismatic leaders born with their qualities? Although a small number of experts still think that charisma can't be learned, most believe that individuals can be trained to exhibit charismatic behaviors.[39] For example, researchers have succeeded in teaching undergraduate students to "be" charismatic. How? They were taught to articulate a far-reaching goal, communicate high performance expectations, exhibit confidence in the ability of subordinates to meet those expectations, and empathize with the needs of their subordinates; they learned to project a powerful, confident, and dynamic presence; and they practiced using a captivating and engaging voice tone. The researchers also trained the student leaders to use charismatic nonverbal behaviors including leaning toward the follower when communicating, maintaining direct eye contact, and having a relaxed posture and animated facial expressions. In groups with these "trained" charismatic leaders, members had higher task performance, higher task adjustment, and better adjustment to the leader and to the group than did group members who worked in groups led by noncharismatic leaders.

One last thing we should say about charismatic leadership is that it may not always be necessary to achieve high levels of employee performance. It may be most appropriate when the follower's task has an ideological purpose or when the environment involves a high degree of stress and uncertainty.[40] This aspect may explain why, when charismatic leaders surface, it's more likely to be in politics, religion, or wartime; or when a business firm is starting up or facing a survival crisis. For example, Martin Luther King Jr. used his charisma to bring about social equality through nonviolent means; and Steve Jobs achieved unwavering loyalty and commitment from Apple's technical staff in the early 1980s by articulating a vision of personal computers that would dramatically change the way people lived.

Although the term *vision* is often linked with charismatic leadership, **visionary leadership** is different: it's the ability to create and articulate a realistic, credible, and attractive vision of the future that improves upon the present situation.[41] This vision, if properly selected and implemented, is so energizing that it "in effect jump-starts the future by calling forth the skills, talents, and resources to make it happen."[42]

An organization's vision should offer clear and compelling imagery that taps into people's emotions and inspires enthusiasm to pursue the organization's goals. It should be able to generate possibilities that are inspirational and unique and offer new ways of doing things that are clearly better for the organization and its members. Visions that are clearly articulated and have powerful imagery are easily grasped and accepted. For instance, Michael Dell created a vision of a business that sells and delivers customized PCs directly to customers in less than a week. The late Mary Kay Ash's vision of women as entrepreneurs selling products that improved their self-image gave impetus to her cosmetics company, Mary Kay Cosmetics.

WHAT ABOUT LEADERS AND TEAMS? Because leadership is increasingly taking place within a team context and more organizations are using work teams, the role of the leader in guiding team members has become increasingly important. The role of team leader *is* different from the traditional leadership role, as J. D. Bryant, a supervisor at Texas Instruments' Forest Lane plant in Dallas, discovered.[43] One day he was contentedly overseeing a staff of 15 circuit board assemblers. The next day he was told that the company was going to use employee teams and he was to become a "facilitator." He said, "I'm supposed to teach the teams everything I know and then let them make their own decisions." Confused about his new role, he admitted, "There was no clear plan on what I was supposed to do." What *is* involved in being a team leader?

Many leaders are not equipped to handle the change to employee teams. As one consultant noted, "Even the most capable managers have trouble making the transition because all the command-and-control type things they were encouraged to do before are no longer appropriate. There's no reason to have any skill or sense of this."[44] This same consultant estimated that "probably 15 percent of managers are natural team leaders; another 15 percent could never lead a team because it runs counter to their personality—that is, they're unable to sublimate their dominating style for the good of the team. Then there's that huge group in the middle: Team leadership doesn't come naturally to them, but they can learn it."[45]

The definition of "friend" on social networking sites such as Facebook and MySpace is so broad that even strangers may tag you. But it doesn't feel weird because nothing really changes when a stranger does this. However, what if your boss, who isn't much older than you are, asks you to be a friend on these sites? What then?

Think About:

- What are the implications if you refuse the offer?
- What are the implications if you accept?
- What ethical issues might arise because of this situation?
- What would you do?

pressureUA/Shutterstock

The challenge for many managers is learning how to become an effective team leader. They have to learn skills such as patiently sharing information, being able to trust others and to give up authority, and understanding when to intervene. And effective team leaders have mastered the difficult balancing act of knowing when to leave their teams alone and when to get involved. New team leaders may try to retain too much control at a time when team members need more autonomy, or they may abandon their teams at times when the teams need support and help.[46]

One study looking at organizations that had reorganized themselves around employee teams found certain common responsibilities of all leaders. These responsibilities included coaching, facilitating, handling disciplinary problems, reviewing team and individual performance, training, and communication.[47] However, a more meaningful way to describe the team leader's job is to focus on two priorities: (1) managing the team's external boundary, and (2) facilitating the team process.[48] These priorities entail four specific leadership roles as shown in Exhibit 5.

charismatic leaders
Enthusiastic, self-confident leaders whose personalities and actions influence people to behave in certain ways

visionary leadership
The ability to create and articulate a realistic, credible, and attractive vision of the future that improves on the present situation

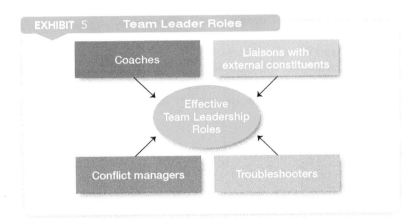

EXHIBIT 5   Team Leader Roles

What Issues Do Today's Leaders Face?

It's not easy being a chief information officer (CIO) today. A person responsible for managing a company's information technology activities faces a lot of external and internal pressures. Technology changes rapidly—almost daily, it sometimes seems. Business costs continue to rise. Competitors develop new strategies. Economic conditions continue to confound even the experts. Rob Carter, CIO of FedEx is on the hot seat facing such challenges.[49] He's responsible for all the computer and communication systems that provide around-the-clock and around-the-globe support for FedEx's products and services. If anything goes wrong, you know who takes the heat. However, Carter has been an effective leader in this seemingly chaotic environment.

Leading effectively in today's environment is likely to involve such challenges for many leaders. Twenty-first-century leaders face some important leadership issues. In this section, we look at these issues including empowering employees, cross-cultural leadership, and emotional intelligence and leadership.

WHY DO LEADERS NEED TO EMPOWER EMPLOYEES?   As we've described in different places throughout the text, managers are increasingly leading by not leading; that is, by empowering their employees. Empowerment involves increasing the decision-making discretion of workers. Millions of individual employees and employee teams are making the key operating decisions that directly affect their work. They're developing budgets, scheduling workloads, controlling inventories, solving quality problems, and engaging in similar activities that until very recently were viewed exclusively as part of the manager's job.[50] For instance, at The Container Store, any employee who gets a customer request has permission to take care of it. The company's chairman emeritus Garret Boone says, "Everybody we hire, we hire as a leader. Anybody in our store can take an action that you might think of typically being a manager's action."[51]

One reason more companies are empowering employees is the need for quick decisions by those people who are most knowledgeable about the issues—often those at lower organizational levels. If organizations want to successfully compete in a dynamic global economy, employees have to be able to make decisions and implement changes quickly. Another reason is that organizational downsizings left many managers with larger spans of control. In order to cope with the increased work demands, managers had to empower their people. Although empowerment is not a universal answer, it can be beneficial when employees have the knowledge, skills, and experience to do their jobs competently.

Technology also has contributed to the increases in employee empowerment. Managers face unique challenges in leading empowered employees who aren't physically present in the workplace as the Technology and the Manager's Job box discusses.

DOES NATIONAL CULTURE AFFECT LEADERSHIP?   One general conclusion that surfaces from leadership research is that effective leaders do not use a single style. They adjust their style to the situation. Although not mentioned explicitly, national culture is certainly

TECHNOLOGY AND THE MANAGER'S JOB

VIRTUAL LEADERSHIP

How do you lead people who are physically separated from you and with whom your interactions are primarily written digital communications?[52] That's the challenge of being a virtual leader. And unfortunately, leadership research has been directed mostly at face-to-face and verbal situations. But we can't ignore the reality that today's managers and their employees are increasingly being linked by technology rather than by geographic proximity. So what guidance would be helpful to leaders who must inspire and motivate dispersed employees?

It's easy to soften harsh words in face-to-face communication with nonverbal action. A smile or a comforting gesture can go a long way in lessening the blow behind strong words like *disappointed*, *unsatisfactory*,

inadequate, or *below expectations*. That nonverbal component doesn't exist in online interactions. The *structure* of words in a digital communication also has the power to motivate or demotivate the receiver. A manager who inadvertently sends a message in short phrases or in ALL CAPS may get a very different response than if the message had been sent in full sentences using appropriate punctuation.

To be an effective virtual leader, managers must recognize that they have choices in the words and structure of their digital communications. They also need to develop the skill of "reading between the lines" in the messages they receive. It's important to try and decipher the emotional content of a message as well as the written content. Also, virtual leaders need to think carefully about

what actions they want their digital messages to initiate. Be clear about what's expected and follow up on messages.

For an increasing number of managers, good interpersonal skills may include the abilities to communicate support and leadership through digital communication and to read emotions in others' messages. In this "new world" of communication, writing skills are likely to become an extension of interpersonal skills.

Think About:

· What challenges does a "virtual" leader face?

· Which is more important to a virtual leader: focusing on the task or focusing on the people? Explain your choice.

· How can virtual leaders use technology to help them be more effective leaders?

---

an important situational variable in determining which leadership style will be most effective. What works in China isn't likely to be effective in France or Canada. For instance, one study of Asian leadership styles revealed that Asian managers preferred leaders who were competent decision makers, effective communicators, and supportive of employees.[53] Another study of leadership in Sub-Saharan Africa found that charismatic leaders can help overcome cultural problems of corruption, poverty, tribalism, and violence.[54]

National culture affects leadership style because it influences how followers will respond. Leaders can't (and shouldn't) just choose their styles randomly. They're constrained by the cultural conditions their followers have come to expect. Exhibit 6 provides some

---

EXHIBIT 6 — Cross-Cultural Leadership

- Korean leaders are expected to be paternalistic toward employees.
- Arab leaders who show kindness or generosity without being asked to do so are seen by other Arabs as weak.
- Japanese leaders are expected to be humble and speak frequently.
- Scandinavian and Dutch leaders who single out individuals with public praise are likely to embarrass, not energize, those individuals.
- Effective leaders in Malaysia are expected to show compassion while using more of an autocratic than a participative style.
- Effective German leaders are characterized by high performance orientation, low compassion, low self-protection, low team orientation, high autonomy, and high participation.

Sources: Based on J.-H. Shin, R. L. Heath, and J. Lee, "A Contingency Explanation of Public Relations Practitioner Leadership Styles: Situation and Culture," *Journal of Public Relations Research* (April 2011), pp. 167–190; J. C. Kennedy, "Leadership in Malaysia: Traditional Values, International Outlook," *Academy of Management Executive*, August 2002, pp. 15–17; F. C. Brodbeck, M. Frese, and M. Javidan, "Leadership Made in Germany: Low on Compassion, High on Performance," *Academy of Management Executive*, February 2002, pp. 16–29; M. F. Peterson and J. G. Hunt, "International Perspectives on International Leadership," *Leadership Quarterly*, Fall 1997, pp. 203–231; R. J. House and R. N. Aditya, "The Social Scientific Study of Leadership: Quo Vadis?" *Journal of Management* 23, no. 3 (1997), p. 463; and R. J. House, "Leadership in the Twenty-First Century," in A. Howard (ed.), *The Changing Nature of Work* (San Francisco: Jossey-Bass, 1995), p. 442.

---

empowerment
The act of increasing the decision-making discretion of workers

findings from selected examples of cross-cultural leadership studies. Because most leadership theories were developed in the United States, they have an American bias. They emphasize follower responsibilities rather than rights; assume self-gratification rather than commitment to duty or altruistic motivation; assume centrality of work and democratic value orientation; and stress rationality rather than spirituality, religion, or superstition.[55] However, the GLOBE research program is the most extensive and comprehensive cross-cultural study of leadership ever undertaken. The GLOBE study has found that there are some universal aspects to leadership. Specifically, a number of elements of transformational leadership appear to be associated with effective leadership regardless of what country the leader is in.[56] These elements include vision, foresight, providing encouragement, trustworthiness, dynamism, positiveness, and proactiveness. The results led two members of the GLOBE team to conclude that "effective business leaders in any country are expected by their subordinates to provide a powerful and proactive vision to guide the company into the future, strong motivational skills to stimulate all employees to fulfill the vision, and excellent planning skills to assist in implementing the vision."[57] Some people suggest that the universal appeal of these transformational leader characteristics is due to the pressures toward common technologies and management practices, as a result of global competitiveness and multinational influences.

HOW DOES EMOTIONAL INTELLIGENCE AFFECT LEADERSHIP?   We visit the topic of emotional intelligence (EI) here because of recent studies indicating that EI—more than IQ, expertise, or any other single factor—is the best predictor of who will emerge as a leader.[58]

As we said in our earlier discussion of trait research, leaders need basic intelligence and job-relevant knowledge. But IQ and technical skills are "threshold capabilities." They're necessary but not sufficient requirements for leadership. It's the possession of the five components of emotional intelligence—self-awareness, self-management, self-motivation, empathy, and social skills—that allows an individual to become a star performer. Without EI, a person can have outstanding training, a highly analytical mind, a long-term vision, and an endless supply of terrific ideas but still not make a great leader, especially as individuals move up in an organization. The evidence indicates that the higher the rank of a person considered to be a star performer, the more that EI capabilities surface as the reason for his or her effectiveness. Specifically, when star performers were compared with average ones in senior management positions, nearly 90 percent of the difference in their effectiveness was attributable to EI factors rather than basic intelligence.

Interestingly, it's been pointed out that the maturing of Rudolph Giuliani's leadership effectiveness closely followed the development of his emotional intelligence. For the better part of the eight years he was mayor of New York, Giuliani ruled with an iron fist. He talked tough, picked fights, and demanded results. The result was a city that was cleaner, safer, and better governed—but also more polarized. Critics called Giuliani a tin-eared tyrant. In the eyes of many, something important was missing from his leadership. That something, his critics acknowledged, emerged as the World Trade Center collapsed. It was a newfound compassion to complement his command: a mix of resolve, empathy, and inspiration that brought comfort to millions.[59] It's likely that Giuliani's emotional capacities and compassion for others were stimulated by a series of personal hardships—including prostate cancer and the highly visible breakup of his marriage—both of which had taken place less than a year before the terrorist attacks on the World Trade Center.[60]

EI has been shown to be positively related to job performance at all levels. But it appears to be especially

Indra Nooyi, chief executive officer of PepsiCo, is a leader with high emotional intelligence. Nooyi possesses the five components of EI—self-awareness, self-management, self-motivation, empathy, and social skills—that have helped her emerge as a star performer in a job that demands a high degree of social interaction with employees, customers, and business and political leaders throughout the world. EI has contributed to Nooyi's high job performance and career success since she joined the company in 1994 as a senior vice president of strategy and development. Nooyi is shown here welcoming guests attending an annual PepsiCo shareholders meeting.

Newscom

relevant in jobs that demand a high degree of social interaction. And of course, that's what leadership is all about. Great leaders demonstrate their EI by exhibiting all five of its key components—self-awareness, self-management, self-motivation, empathy, and social skills.

Although there has been some controversy about the role of EI in leadership,[61] most of the research makes a case for concluding that EI is an essential element in leadership effectiveness.[62] As such, it could be added to the list of traits associated with leadership that we described earlier in the chapter.

WHY IS TRUST THE ESSENCE OF LEADERSHIP?

Discuss trust as the essence of leadership.

5

Trust, or lack of trust, is an increasingly important issue in today's organizations.[63] In today's uncertain environment, leaders need to build, or even rebuild, trust and credibility. Before we can discuss ways leaders can do that, we have to know what trust and credibility are and why they're so important.

The main component of credibility is honesty. Surveys show that honesty is consistently singled out as the number one characteristic of admired leaders. "Honesty is absolutely essential to leadership. If people are going to follow someone willingly, whether it be into battle or into the boardroom, they first want to assure themselves that the person is worthy of their trust."[64] In addition to being honest, credible leaders are competent and inspiring. They are personally able to effectively communicate their confidence and enthusiasm. Thus, followers judge a leader's credibility in terms of his or her honesty, competence, and ability to inspire.

Trust is closely entwined with the concept of credibility, and, in fact, the terms are often used interchangeably. Trust is defined as the belief in the integrity, character, and ability of a leader. Followers who trust a leader are willing to be vulnerable to the leader's actions because they are confident that their rights and interests will not be abused.[65] Research has identified five dimensions that make up the concept of trust:

- *Integrity:* honesty and truthfulness
- *Competence:* technical and interpersonal knowledge and skills
- *Consistency:* reliability, predictability, and good judgment in handling situations
- *Loyalty:* willingness to protect a person, physically and emotionally
- *Openness:* willingness to share ideas and information freely[66]

Of these five dimensions, integrity seems to be the most critical when someone assesses another's trustworthiness.[67] Both integrity and competence were seen in our earlier discussion of leadership traits found to be consistently associated with leadership.

Workplace changes have reinforced why such leadership qualities are important. For instance, trends of employee empowerment and self-managed work teams have reduced many of the traditional control mechanisms used to monitor employees. If a work team is free to schedule its own work, evaluate its own performance, and even make its own hiring decisions, trust becomes critical. Employees have to trust managers to treat them fairly, and managers have to trust employees to conscientiously fulfill their responsibilities.

Also, leaders have to increasingly lead others who may not be in their immediate work group or even may be physically separated—members of cross-functional or virtual teams, individuals who work for suppliers or customers, and perhaps even people who represent other organizations through strategic alliances. These situations don't allow leaders the luxury of falling back on their formal positions for influence. Many of these relationships,

credibility
The degree to which followers perceive someone as honest, competent, and able to inspire

trust
The belief in the integrity, character, and ability of a leader

EXHIBIT 7   Suggestions for Building Trust

1. **Practice openness.** Mistrust comes as much from what people don't know as from what they do know. Openness leads to confidence and trust. So keep people informed; make clear the criteria on how decisions are made; explain the rationale for your decisions; be candid about problems; and fully disclose relevant information.

2. **Be fair.** Before making decisions or taking actions, consider how others will perceive them in terms of objectivity and fairness. Give credit where credit is due; be objective and impartial in performance appraisals; and pay attention to equity perceptions in reward distributions.

3. **Speak your feelings.** Leaders who convey only hard facts come across as cold and distant. When you share your feelings, others will see you as real and human. They will know who you are and their respect for you will increase.

4. **Tell the truth.** If honesty is critical to credibility, you must be perceived as someone who tells the truth. Followers are more tolerant of being told something they "don't want to hear" than of finding out that their leader lied to them.

5. **Be consistent.** People want predictability. Mistrust comes from not knowing what to expect. Take the time to think about your values and beliefs. Then let them consistently guide your decisions. When you know your central purpose, your actions will follow accordingly, and you will project a consistency that earns trust.

6. **Fulfill your promises.** Trust requires that people believe that you're dependable. So you need to keep your word. Promises made must be promises kept.

7. **Maintain confidences.** You trust those whom you believe to be discrete and whom you can rely on. If people make themselves vulnerable by telling you something in confidence, they need to feel assured that you won't discuss it with others or betray that confidence. If people perceive you as someone who leaks personal confidences or someone who can't be depended on, you won't be perceived as trustworthy.

8. **Demonstrate confidence.** Develop the admiration and respect of others by demonstrating technical and professional ability. Pay particular attention to developing and displaying your communication, negotiating, and other interpersonal skills.

Sources: Based on P. S. Shockley-Zalabak and S. P Morreale, "Building High-Trust Organizations," *Leader to Leader*, Spring 2011, pp. 39–45; J. K. Butler Jr., "Toward Understanding and Measuring Conditions of Trust: Evolution of a Condition of Trust Inventory," *Journal of Management* (September 1991), pp. 643–663; and F. Bartolome, "Nobody Trusts the Boss Completely—Now What?" *Harvard Business Review*, March–April 1989, pp. 135–142.

in fact, are fluid and fleeting. So the ability to quickly develop trust and sustain that trust is crucial to the success of the relationship.

Why is it important that followers trust their leaders? Research has shown that trust in leadership is significantly related to positive job outcomes including job performance, organizational citizenship behavior, job satisfaction, and organizational commitment.[68] Given the importance of trust to effective leadership, leaders need to build trust with their followers. Some suggestions are shown in Exhibit 7.

Now, more than ever, managerial and leadership effectiveness depends on the ability to gain the trust of followers.[69] Downsizing, corporate financial misrepresentations, and the increased use of temporary employees have undermined employees' trust in their leaders and shaken the confidence of investors, suppliers, and customers. A survey found that only 39 percent of U.S. employees and 51 percent of Canadian employees trusted their executive leaders.[70] Today's leaders are faced with the challenge of rebuilding and restoring trust with employees and with other important organizational stakeholders.

A Final Thought Regarding Leadership

Despite the belief that some leadership style will always be effective regardless of the situation, leadership may not always be important! Research indicates that, in some situations, any behaviors a leader exhibits are irrelevant. In other words, certain individual, job, and organizational variables can act as "substitutes for leadership," negating the influence of the leader.[71]

For instance, follower characteristics such as experience, training, professional orientation, or need for independence can neutralize the effect of leadership. These characteristics can replace the employee's need for a leader's support or ability to create structure and reduce task ambiguity. Similarly, jobs that are inherently unambiguous and routine or that are intrinsically satisfying may place fewer demands on the leadership variable. Finally, such organizational characteristics as explicit formalized goals, rigid rules and procedures, or cohesive work groups can substitute for formal leadership.

Review

1. **Define *leader* and *leadership*.** A leader is someone who can influence others and who has managerial authority. Leadership is a process of leading a group and influencing that group to achieve its goals. Managers should be leaders because leading is one of the four management functions.

2. **Compare and contrast the early leadership theories.** Early attempts to define leader traits were unsuccessful although later attempts found seven traits associated with leadership.

   The University of Iowa studies explored three leadership styles. The only conclusion was that group members were more satisfied under a democratic leader than under an autocratic one. The Ohio State studies identified two dimensions of leader behavior—initiating structure and consideration. A leader high in both those dimensions at times achieved high group task performance and high group member satisfaction, but not always. The University of Michigan studies looked at employee-oriented leaders and production-oriented leaders. They concluded that leaders who were employee oriented could get high group productivity and high group member satisfaction. The Managerial Grid looked at leaders' concern for production and concern for people and identified five leader styles. Although it suggested that a leader who was high in concern for production and high in concern for people was the best, there was no substantive evidence for that conclusion.

   As the behavioral studies showed, a leader's behavior has a dual nature: a focus on the task and a focus on the people.

3. **Describe the four major contingency leadership theories.** Fiedler's model attempted to define the best style to use in particular situations. He measured leader style—relationship oriented or task oriented—using the least-preferred co-worker questionnaire. Fiedler also assumed a leader's style was fixed. He measured three contingency dimensions: leader-member relations, task structure, and position power. The model suggests that task-oriented leaders performed best in very favorable and very unfavorable situations, and relationship-oriented leaders performed best in moderately favorable situations.

   Hersey and Blanchard's situational leadership theory focused on followers' readiness. They identified four leadership styles: telling (high task–low relationship), selling (high task–high relationship), participating (low task–high relationship), and delegating (low task–low relationship). They also identified four stages of readiness: unable and unwilling (use telling style); unable but willing (use selling style); able but unwilling (use participative style); and able and willing (use delegating style).

   The leader-participation model relates leadership behavior and participation to decision making. It uses a decision tree format with seven contingencies and five alternative leadership styles.

   The path-goal model developed by Robert House identified four leadership behaviors: directive, supportive, participative, and achievement-oriented. He assumes that a leader can and should be able to use any of these styles. The two situational contingency variables were found in the environment and in the follower. Essentially the path-goal model says that a leader should provide direction and support as needed; that is, structure the path so the followers can achieve goals.

4. **Describe modern views of leadership and the issues facing today's leaders.** Leader-member exchange (LMX) theory says that leaders create in-groups and out-groups and those in the in-group will have higher performance ratings, less turnover, and greater job satisfaction.

   A transactional leader exchanges rewards for productivity where a transformational leader stimulates and inspires followers to achieve goals.

   A charismatic leader is an enthusiastic and self-confident leader whose personality and actions influence people to behave in certain ways. People can learn to be charismatic. A visionary leader is able to create and articulate a realistic, credible, and attractive vision of the future.

   A team leader has two priorities: manage the team's external boundary and facilitate the team process. Four leader roles are involved: liaison with external constituencies, troubleshooter, conflict manager, and coach.

   The issues facing leaders today include employee empowerment, national culture, and emotional intelligence. As employees are empowered, the leader's role tends to be one of not leading. As leaders adjust their style to the situation, one of the most important situational characteristics is national culture. Finally, EI is proving to be an essential element in leadership effectiveness.

5 **Discuss trust as the essence of leadership.** The five dimensions of trust include integrity, competence, consistency, loyalty, and truthfulness. Integrity refers to one's honesty and truthfulness. Competence involves an individual's technical and interpersonal knowledge and skills. Consistency relates to an individual's reliability, predictability, and good judgment in handling situations. Loyalty is an individual's willingness to protect and save face for another person. Openness means that you can rely on the individual to give you the whole truth.

UNDERSTANDING THE CHAPTER

1. Define *leader* and *leadership* and why managers should be leaders.

2. Discuss the strengths and weaknesses of the trait theory.

3. What does each of the behavioral leadership theories say about leadership?

4. What would a manager need to know to use Fiedler's contingency model? Be specific.

5. Do you think that most managers in real life use a contingency approach to increase their leadership effectiveness? Discuss.

6. "All managers should be leaders, but not all leaders should be managers." Do you agree or disagree with this statement? Support your position.

7. Do you think trust evolves out of an individual's personal characteristics or out of specific situations? Explain.

8. Do followers make a difference in whether a leader is effective? Discuss.

9. How can organizations develop effective leaders?

10. When might leaders be irrelevant?

Endnotes

1. "Inbox," *Time,* April 5, 2010, p. 7; M. Thompson, "The Sea Witch," *Time,* March 22, 2010, pp. 30–33; B. H. Johnsen, J. Eid, S. Pallesen, P. T. Bartone, and O. A. Nissestad, "Predicting Transformational Leadership in Naval Cadets: Effects of Personality Hardiness and Training," *Journal of Applied Social Psychology* (September 2009), pp. 2213–2235; and P. Thunholm, "Military Leaders and Followers: Do They Have Different Decision Styles?" *Scandinavian Journal of Psychology* (August 2009), pp. 317–324.

2. Most leadership research has focused on the actions and responsibilities of managers and extrapolated the results to leaders and leadership in general.

3. See D. S. Derue, J. D. Nahrgang, N. Wellman, and S. E. Humphrey, "Trait and Behavioral Theories of Leadership: An Integration and Meta-Analytic Test of Their Relative Validity," *Personnel Psychology,* Spring 2011, pp. 7–52; T. A. Judge, J. E. Bono, R. Ilies, and M. W. Gerhardt, "Personality and Leadership: A Qualitative and Quantitative Review," *Journal of Applied Psychology* (August 2002), pp. 765–780; and S. A. Kirkpatrick and E. A. Locke, "Leadership: Do Traits Matter?" *Academy of Management Executive*, May 1991, pp. 48–60.

4. K. Lewin and R. Lippitt, "An Experimental Approach to the Study of Autocracy and Democracy: A Preliminary Note," *Sociometry* 1 (1938), pp. 292–300; K. Lewin, "Field Theory and Experiment in Social Psychology: Concepts and Methods," *American Journal of Sociology* 44 (1939), pp. 868–896; K. Lewin, R. Lippitt, and R. K. White, "Patterns of Aggressive Behavior in Experimentally Created Social Climates," *Journal of Social Psychology* 10 (1939), pp. 271–301; and R. Lippitt, "An Experimental Study of the Effect of Democratic and Authoritarian Group Atmospheres," *University of Iowa Studies in Child Welfare* 16 (1940), pp. 43–95.

5. B. M. Bass, *Stodgill's Handbook of Leadership* (New York: Free Press, 1981), pp. 298–299.

6. R. Tannenbaum and W. H. Schmidt, "How to Choose a Leadership Pattern," *Harvard Business Review,* May–June 1973, pp. 162–180.

7. R. M. Stodgill and A. E. Coons, eds., *Leader Behavior: Its Description and Measurement*, Research Monograph No. 88 (Columbus: Ohio State University, Bureau of Business Research, 1951). See also S. Kerr, C. A. Schriesheim, C. J. Murphy, and R. M. Stodgill, "Toward a Contingency

Theory of Leadership Based upon the Consideration and Initiating Structure Literature," *Organizational Behavior and Human Performance* (August 1974), pp. 62–82; and B. M. Fisher, "Consideration and Initiating Structure and Their Relationships with Leader Effectiveness: A Meta Analysis," in F. Hoy, ed., *Proceedings of the 48th Annual Academy of Management Conference* (Anaheim, CA, 1988), pp. 201–205.

8. R. Kahn and D. Katz, "Leadership Practices in Relation to Productivity and Morale," in D. Cartwright and A. Zander, eds., *Group Dynamics: Research and Theory*, 2nd ed. (Elmsford, NY: Pow, Paterson, 1960).

9. From the Past to the Present box based on D. S. Derue, J. D. Nahrgang, N. Wellman, and S. E. Humphrey, "Trait and Behavioral Theories of Leadership: An Integration and Meta-Analytic Test of Their Relative Validity," *Personnel Psychology,* Spring 2011, pp. 7–52; and D. A. Wren and A. G. Bedeian, *The Evolution of Management Thought*, 6th ed. (Hoboken, NJ: John Wiley & Sons, 2009), pp. 345–346.

10. R. R. Blake and J. S. Mouton, *The Managerial Grid III* (Houston: Gulf Publishing, 1984).

11. P. C. Nystrom, "Managers and the Hi-Hi Leader Myth," *Academy of Management Journal* (June 1978), pp. 325–331; and L. L. Larson, J. G. Hunt, and R. N. Osborn, "The Great Hi-Hi Leader Behavior Myth: A Lesson from Occam's Razor," *Academy of Management Journal* (December 1976), pp. 628–641.

12. W. G. Bennis, "The Seven Ages of the Leader," *Harvard Business Review,* January 2004, p. 52.

13. F. E. Fiedler, *A Theory of Leadership Effectiveness* (New York: McGraw-Hill, 1967).

14. R. Ayman, M. M. Chemers, and F. Fiedler, "The Contingency Model of Leadership Effectiveness: Its Levels of Analysis," *Leadership Quarterly,* Summer 1995, pp. 147–167; C. A. Schriesheim, B. J. Tepper, and L. A. Tetrault, "Lease Preferred Co-Worker Score, Situational Control, and Leadership Effectiveness: A Meta-Analysis of Contingency Model Performance Predictions," *Journal of Applied Psychology* (August 1994), pp. 561–573; and L. H. Peters, D. D. Hartke, and J. T. Pholmann, "Fiedler's Contingency Theory of Leadership: An Application of the Meta-Analysis Procedures of Schmidt and Hunter," *Psychological Bulletin*, March 1985, pp. 274–285.

15. See B. Kabanoff, "A Critique of Leader Match and Its Implications for Leadership Research," *Personnel Psychology,* Winter 1981, pp. 749–764; and E. H. Schein, *Organizational Psychology*, 3rd ed. (Upper Saddle River, NJ: Prentice Hall, 1980), pp. 116–117.

16. P. Hersey and K. H. Blanchard, *Management of Organizational Behavior: Leading Human Resources*, 8th ed. (Englewood Cliffs, NJ: Prentice Hall, 2001); and P. Hersey and K. Blanchard, "So You Want to Know Your Leadership Style?" *Training and Development Journal* (February 1974), pp. 1–15.

17. See, for instance, E. G. Ralph, "Developing Managers' Effectiveness: A Model with Potential," *Journal of Management Inquiry* (June 2004), pp. 152–163; C. L. Graeff, "Evolution of Situational Leadership Theory: A Critical Review," *Leadership Quarterly* 8, no. 2 (1997), pp. 153–170; and C. F. Fernandez and R. P. Vecchio, "Situational Leadership Theory Revisited: A Test of an Across-Jobs Perspective," *Leadership Quarterly* 8, no. 1 (1997), pp. 67–84.

18. And the Survey Says box based on J. Yang and P. Trap, "I'm Concerned Most About My Manager," *USA Today,* April 25, 2011, p. 1B; "The New Employment Deal: Insights from the 2010 Global Workforce Study," *Towers Watson,* 2010, p. 7; "Key Global Findings from the Hay Group 2010 Best Companies for Leadership Study," *Hay Group,* www.haygroup.com (2010); "Selected Results from Best Companies for Leadership Survey," *Bloomberg BusinessWeek Online,* February 16, 2010; and "Still Haven't Closed the Gap," *Training* (March–April 2009), p. 9.

19. V. H. Vroom and P. W. Yetton, *Leadership and Decision Making* (Pittsburgh: University of Pittsburgh Press, 1973).

20. V. H. Vroom and A. G. Jago, *The New Leadership: Managing Participation in Organizations* (Upper Saddle River, NJ: Prentice Hall, 1988). See especially Chapter 8.

21. See, for example, R. H. G. Field and R. J. House, "A Test of the Vroom Yetton Model Using Manager and Subordinate Reports," *Journal of Applied Psychology* (June 1990), pp. 362–366; J. T. Ettling and A. G. Jago, "Participation Under Conditions of Conflict: More on the Validity of the Vroom Yetton Model," *Journal of Management Studies* (January 1988), pp. 73–83; C. R. Leana, "Power Relinquishment versus Power Sharing: Theoretical Clarification and Empirical Comparison of Delegation and Participation," *Journal of Applied Psychology* (May 1987), pp. 228–233; and R. H. G. Field, "A Test of the Vroom Yetton Normative Model of Leadership," *Journal of Applied Psychology* (October 1982), pp. 523–532.

22. For additional information about the exchanges that occur between the leader and the follower, see A. S. Phillips and A. G. Bedeian, "Leader Follower Exchange Quality: The Role of Personal and Interpersonal Attributes," *Academy of Management Journal* 37, no. 4 (1994), pp. 990–1001; and T. A. Scandura and C. A. Schriesheim, "Leader Member Exchange and Supervisor Career Mentoring as Complementary Constructs in Leadership Research," *Academy of Management Journal* 37, no. 6 (1994), pp. 1588–1602.

23. R. J. House, "Path-Goal Theory of Leadership: Lessons, Legacy, and a Reformulated Theory," *Leadership Quarterly,* Fall 1996, pp. 323–352; R. J. House and T. R. Mitchell, "Path-Goal Theory of Leadership," *Journal of Contemporary Business* (Autumn 1974), p. 86; and R. J. House, "A Path-Goal Theory of Leader Effectiveness," *Administrative Science Quarterly*, September 1971, pp. 321–338.

24. A. Sagie and M. Koslowsky, "Organizational Attitudes and Behaviors as a Function of Participation in Strategic and Tactical Change Decisions: An Application of Path-Goal Theory," *Journal of Organizational Behavior* (January 1994), pp. 37–47; and J. C. Wofford and L. Z. Liska, "Path-Goal Theories of Leadership: A Meta-Analysis," *Journal of Management* (Winter 1993), pp. 857–876.

25. L. Ma and Q. Qu, "Differentiation in Leader-Member Exchange: A Hierarchical Linear Modeling Approach," *Leadership Quarterly,* October 2010, pp. 733–744; C. P. Schriesheim, S. L. Castro, X. Zhou, and F. J. Yamarinno, "The Folly of Theorizing 'A' but Testing 'B': A Selective Level-of-Analysis Review of the Field and a Detailed Leader-Member Exchange Illustration," *Leadership Quarterly,* Winter 2001, pp. 515–551; R. C. Liden, R. T. Sparrowe, and S. J. Wayne, "Leader-Member Exchange Theory: The Past and Potential for the Future," in G. R. Ferris (ed.), *Research in Personnel and Human Resource Management*, vol. 15 (Greenwich, CT: JAI Press, 1997), pp. 47–119; G. B. Graen and M. Uhl-Bien, "Relationship-Based Approach to Leadership: Development of Leader-Member Exchange (LMX) Theory of Leadership Over 25 Years: Applying a Multi-Domain Perspective," *Leadership Quarterly,* Summer 1995, pp. 219–247; and R. M. Dienesch and

R. C. Liden, "Leader-Member Exchange Model of Leadership: A Critique and Further Development," *Academy of Management Review,* July 1986, pp. 618–634.

26. J. B. Wu, A. S. Tsui, and A. J. Kinicki, "Consequences of Differentiated Leadership in Groups," *Academy of Management Journal* (February 2010), pp. 90–106; S. S. Masterson, K. Lewis, and B. M. Goldman, "Integrating Justice and Social Exchange: The Differing Effects of Fair Procedures and Treatment on Work Relationships," *Academy of Management Journal* (August 2000), pp. 738–748; S. J. Wayne, L. J. Shore, W. H. Bommer, and L. E. Tetrick, "The Role of Fair Treatment and Rewards in Perceptions of Organizational Support and Leader-Member Exchange," *Journal of Applied Psychology* (June 2002), pp. 590–598; R. C. Liden, S. J. Wayne, and D. Stilwell, "A Longitudinal Study of the Early Development of Leader-Member Exchanges," *Journal of Applied Psychology* (August 1993), pp. 662–674; and R. C. Liden and G. Graen, "Generalizability of the Vertical Dyad Linkage Model of Leadership," *Academy of Management Journal* (September 1980), pp. 451–465.

27. V. L. Goodwin, W. M. Bowler, and J. L. Whittington, "A Social Network Perspective on LMX Relationships: Accounting for the Instrumental Value of Leader and Follower Networks," *Journal of Management* (August 2009), pp. 954–980; R. Vecchio and D. M. Brazil, "Leadership and Sex-Similarity: A Comparison in a Military Setting," *Personnel Psychology,* vol. 60 (2007), pp. 303–335; M. Uhl-Bien, "Relationship Development as a Key Ingredient for Leadership Development," in S. E. Murphy and R. E. Riggio (eds.), *Future of Leadership Development* (Mahwah, NJ: Lawrence Erlbaum, 2003), pp. 129–147; R. C. Liden, S. J. Wayne, and D. Stilwell, "A Longitudinal Study of the Early Development of Leader-Member Exchanges"; and D. Duchon, S. G. Green, and T. D. Taber, "Vertical Dyad Linkage: A Longitudinal Assessment of Antecedents, Measures, and Consequences," *Journal of Applied Psychology* (February 1986), pp. 56–60.

28. See, for instance, F. O. Walumbwa, D. M. Mayer, P. Wang, H. Wang, K. Workman, and A. L. Christensen, "Linking Ethical Leadership to Employee Performance: The Roles of Leader-Member Exchange Theory, Self-Efficacy, and Organizational Identification," *Organizational Behavior & Human Decision Processes,* July 2011, pp. 204–213; K. J. Harris, A. R. Wheeler, and K. M. Kacmar, "The Mediating Role of Organizational Embeddedness in the LMX-Outcomes Relationship," *Leadership Quarterly,* April 2011, pp. 271–281; W. M. Bowler, J. R. B. Halbesleben, J. R. B. Paul, "If You're Close with the Leader, You Must Be a Brownnose: The Role of Leader-Member Relationships in Follower, Leader, and Coworker Attributions of Organizational Citizenship Behavior Motives," *Human Resource Management Review,* December 2010, pp. 309–316; G. Sears and C. Holmvall, "The Joint Influence of Supervisor and Subordinate Emotional Intelligence on Leader-Member Exchange," *Journal of Business & Psychology* (December 2010), pp. 593–605; V. Venkataramani, S. G. Green, and D. J. Schleicher, "Well-Connected Leaders' Social Network Ties on LMX and Members' Work Attitudes," *Journal of Applied Psychology* (November 2010), pp. 1071–1084; Z. Chen, W. Lam, and J. A. Zhong, "Leader-Member Exchange and Member Performance: A New Look at Individual-Level Negative Feedback-Seeking Behavior and Team-Level Empowerment Culture," *Journal of Applied Psychology* (January 2007), pp. 202–212; R. Ilies, J. D. Nahrgang, and F. P. Morgeson,

"Leader-Member Exchange and Citizenship Behaviors: A Meta-Analysis," *Journal of Applied Psychology* (January 2007), pp. 269–277; and C. R. Gerstner and D. V. Day, "Meta-analytic Review of Leader-Member Exchange Theory: Correlates and Construct Issues," *Journal of Applied Psychology* (December 1997), pp. 827–844.

29. B. M. Bass and R. E. Riggio, *Transformational Leadership,* 2d ed. (Mahwah, NJ: Lawrence Erlbaum Associates, Inc., 2006), p. 3.

30. J. Seltzer and B. M. Bass, "Transformational Leadership: Beyond Initiation and Consideration," *Journal of Management* (December 1990), pp. 693–703; and B. M. Bass, "Leadership: Good, Better, Best," *Organizational Dynamics,* Winter 1985, pp. 26–40.

31. B. J. Avolio and B. M. Bass, "Transformational Leadership, Charisma, and Beyond." Working paper, School of Management, State University of New York, Binghamton, 1985, p. 14.

32. R. S. Rubin, D. C. Munz, and W. H. Bommer, "Leading from Within: The Effects of Emotion Recognition and Personality on Transformational Leadership Behavior," *Academy of Management Journal* (October 2005), pp. 845–858; T. A. Judge and J. E. Bono, "Five-Factor Model of Personality and Transformational Leadership," *Journal of Applied Psychology* (October 2000), pp. 751–765; B. M. Bass and B. J. Avolio, "Developing Transformational Leadership: 1992 and Beyond," *Journal of European Industrial Training* (January 1990), p. 23; and J. J. Hater and B. M. Bass, "Supervisors' Evaluation and Subordinates' Perceptions of Transformational and Transactional Leadership," *Journal of Applied Psychology* (November 1988), pp. 695–702.

33. M. Tims, A. B. Bakker, and D. Xanthopoulou, "Do Transformational Leaders Enhance Their Followers' Daily Work Engagement?" *Leadership Quarterly,* February 2011, pp. 121–131; X.-H. (Frank) Wang, and J. M. Howell, "Exploring the Dual-Level Effects of Transformational Leadership on Followers," *Journal of Applied Psychology* (November 2010), pp. 1134–1144; A. E. Colbert, A. L. Kristof-Brown, B. H. Bradley, and M. R. Barrick, "CEO Transformational Leadership: The Role of Goal Importance Congruence in Top Management Teams," *Academy of Management Journal* (February 2008), pp. 81–96; R. F. Piccolo and J. A. Colquitt, "Transformational Leadership and Job Behaviors: The Mediating Role of Core Job Characteristics," *Academy of Management Journal* (April 2006), pp. 327–340; O. Epitropaki and R. Martin, "From Ideal to Real: A Longitudinal Study of the Role of Implicit Leadership Theories on Leader-Member Exchanges and Employee Outcomes," *Journal of Applied Psychology* (July 2005), pp. 659–676; J. E. Bono and T. A. Judge, "Self-Concordance at Work: Toward Understanding the Motivational Effects of Transformational Leaders," *Academy of Management Journal* (October 2003), pp. 554–571; T. Dvir, D. Eden, B. J. Avolio, and B. Shamir, "Impact of Transformational Leadership on Follower Development and Performance: A Field Experiment," *Academy of Management Journal* (August 2002), pp. 735–744; N. Sivasubramaniam, W. D. Murry, B. J. Avolio, and D. I. Jung, "A Longitudinal Model of the Effects of Team Leadership and Group Potency on Group Performance," *Group and Organization Management* (March 2002), pp. 66–96; J. M. Howell and B. J. Avolio, "Transformational Leadership, Transactional Leadership, Locus of Control, and Support for Innovation: Key Predictors of Consolidated-Business-Unit Performance," *Journal of Applied Psychology* (December 1993), pp. 891–911; R. T. Keller,

"Transformational Leadership and the Performance of Research and Development Project Groups," *Journal of Management* (September 1992), pp. 489–501; and Bass and Avolio, "Developing Transformational Leadership."

34. M. Thompson and B. Tracy, "Building a Great Organization," *Leader to Leader,* Fall 2010, pp. 45–49; and F. Vogelstein, "Mighty Amazon," *Fortune,* May 26, 2003, pp. 60–74.

35. J. M. Crant and T. S. Bateman, "Charismatic Leadership Viewed from Above: The Impact of Proactive Personality," *Journal of Organizational Behavior* (February 2000), pp. 63–75; G. Yukl and J. M. Howell, "Organizational and Contextual Influences on the Emergence and Effectiveness of Charismatic Leadership," *Leadership Quarterly,* Summer 1999, pp. 257–283; and J. A. Conger and R. N. Kanungo, "Behavioral Dimensions of Charismatic Leadership," in J. A. Conger, R. N. Kanungo and Associates, *Charismatic Leadership* (San Francisco: Jossey-Bass, 1988), pp. 78–97.

36. J. A. Conger and R. N. Kanungo, *Charismatic Leadership in Organizations* (Thousand Oaks, CA: Sage, 1998).

37. F. Walter and H. Bruch, "An Affective Events Model of Charismatic Leadership Behavior: A Review, Theoretical Investigation, and Research Agenda," *Journal of Management* (December 2009), pp. 1428–1452; K. S. Groves, "Linking Leader Skills, Follower Attitudes, and Contextual Variables via an Integrated Model of Charismatic Leadership," *Journal of Management* (April 2005), pp. 255–277; J. J. Sosik, "The Role of Personal Values in the Charismatic Leadership of Corporate Managers: A Model and Preliminary Field Study," *Leadership Quarterly,* April 2005, pp. 221–244; A. H. B. deHoogh, D. N. den Hartog, P. L. Koopman, H. Thierry, P. T. van den Berg, J. G. van der Weide, and C. P. M. Wilderom, "Leader Motives, Charismatic Leadership, and Subordinates' Work Attitudes in The Profit and Voluntary Sector," *Leadership Quarterly,* February 2005, pp. 17–38; J. M. Howell and B. Shamir, "The Role of Followers in the Charismatic Leadership Process: Relationships and Their Consequences," *Academy of Management Review,* January 2005, pp. 96–112; J. Paul, D. L. Costley, J. P. Howell, P. W. Dorfman, and D. Trafimow, "The Effects of Charismatic Leadership on Followers' Self-Concept Accessibility," *Journal of Applied Social Psychology* (September 2001), pp. 1821–1844; J. A. Conger, R. N. Kanungo, and S. T. Menon, "Charismatic Leadership and Follower Effects," *Journal of Organizational Behavior,* vol. 21 (2000), pp. 747–767; R. W. Rowden, "The Relationship Between Charismatic Leadership Behaviors and Organizational Commitment," *Leadership & Organization Development Journal* (January 2000), pp. 30–35; G. P. Shea and C. M. Howell, "Charismatic Leadership and Task Feedback: A Laboratory Study of Their Effects on Self-Efficacy," *Leadership Quarterly,* Fall 1999, pp. 375–396; S. A. Kirkpatrick and E. A. Locke, "Direct and Indirect Effects of Three Core Charismatic Leadership Components on Performance and Attitudes," *Journal of Applied Psychology* (February 1996), pp. 36–51; D. A. Waldman, B. M. Bass, and F. J. Yammarino, "Adding to Contingent-Reward Behavior: The Augmenting Effect of Charismatic Leadership," *Group & Organization Studies,* December 1990, pp. 381–394; and R. J. House, J. Woycke, and E. M. Fodor, "Charismatic and Noncharismatic Leaders: Differences in Behavior and Effectiveness," in Conger and Kanungo, *Charismatic Leadership,* pp. 103–104.

38. B. R. Agle, N J. Nagarajan, J. A. Sonnenfeld, and D. Srinivasan, "Does CEO Charisma Matter? An Empirical Analysis of the Relationships Among Organizational Performance, Environmental Uncertainty, and Top Management Team Perceptions of CEO Charisma," *Academy of Management Journal* (February 2006), pp. 161–174.

39. R. Birchfield, "Creating Charismatic Leaders," *Management,* June 2000, pp. 30–31; S. Caudron, "Growing Charisma," *Industry Week,* May 4, 1998, pp. 54–55; and J. A. Conger and R. N. Kanungo, "Training Charismatic Leadership: A Risky and Critical Task," in Conger and Kanungo, *Charismatic Leadership,* pp. 309–323.

40. J. G. Hunt, K. B. Boal, and G. E. Dodge, "The Effects of Visionary and Crisis-Responsive Charisma on Followers: An Experimental Examination," *Leadership Quarterly,* Fall 1999, pp. 423–448; R. J. House and R. N. Aditya, "The Social Scientific Study of Leadership: Quo Vadis?" *Journal of Management,* 23, no. 3 (1997), pp. 316–323; and R. J. House, "A 1976 Theory of Charismatic Leadership."

41. This definition is based on M. Sashkin, "The Visionary Leader," in Conger and Kanungo et al., *Charismatic Leadership,* pp. 124–125; B. Nanus, *Visionary Leadership* (New York: Free Press, 1992), p. 8; N.H. Snyder and M. Graves, "Leadership and Vision," *Business Horizons,* January–February 1994, p. 1; and J. R. Lucas, "Anatomy of a Vision Statement," *Management Review,* February 1998, pp. 22–26.

42. Nanus, *Visionary Leadership,* p. 8.

43. S. Caminiti, "What Team Leaders Need to Know," *Fortune,* February 20, 1995, pp. 93–100.

44. Ibid., p. 93.

45. Ibid., p. 100.

46. D. S. DeRue, C. M. Barnes, and F. M. Morgeson, "Understanding the Motivational Contingencies of Team Leadership," *Small Group Research,* October 2010, pp. 621–651; B. Meredith, "Leader Characteristics: Is There a Shift in Requirements?" *Leadership Excellence,* September 2010, p. 19; B. Neal, "Heroes and Sidekicks: Ensuring Proper Followership," *T&D,* September 2010, pp. 76–77; R. D. Ramsey, "Preparing to Be Tomorrow's Leader Today," *Supervision,* January 2010, p. 79; N. Steckler and N. Fondas, "Building Team Leader Effectiveness: A Diagnostic Tool," *Organizational Dynamics,* Winter 1995, p. 20.

47. R. S. Wellins, W. C. Byham, and G. R. Dixon, *Inside Teams* (San Francisco: Jossey-Bass, 1994), p. 318.

48. Steckler and Fondas, "Building Team Leader Effectiveness," p. 21.

49. "The 100 Most Creative People in Business 2010," *Fast Company,* June 2010, pp. 70–119; and G. Colvin, "The FedEx Edge," *Fortune,* April 3, 2006, pp. 77–84.

50. J. Fabre, "The Importance of Empowering Front-Line Staff," *Supervision,* December 2010, pp. 6–7; S. Raub and C. Robert, "Differential Effects of Empowering Leadership on In-Role and Extra-Role Employee Behaviors: Exploring the Role of Psychological Empowerment and Power Values," *Human Relations,* November 2010, pp. 1743–1770; N. D. Cakar and A. Erturk, "Comparing Innovation Capability of Small and Medium-Sized Enterprises: Examining the Effects of Organizational Culture and Empowerment," *Journal of Small Business Management* (July 2010), pp. 325–359; A. Srivastava, K. M. Bartol, and E. A. Locke, "Empowering Leadership in Management Teams: Effects on Knowledge Sharing, Efficacy, and Performance," *Academy of Management Journal* (December 2006), pp. 1239–1251; P. K. Mills and G. R. Ungson, "Reassessing the Limits of Structural Empowerment:

Organizational Constitution and Trust as Controls," *Academy of Management Review,* January 2003, pp. 143–153; W. A. Rudolph and M. Sashkin, "Can Organizational Empowerment Work in Multinational Settings?" *Academy of Management Executive,* February 2002, pp. 102–115; C. Gomez and B. Rosen, "The Leader-Member Link Between Managerial Trust and Employee Empowerment," *Group & Organization Management,* March 2001, pp. 53–69; C. Robert and T. M. Probst, "Empowerment and Continuous Improvement in the United States, Mexico, Poland, and India," *Journal of Applied Psychology* (October 2000), pp. 643–658; R. C. Herrenkohl, G. T. Judson, and J. A. Heffner, "Defining and Measuring Employee Empowerment," *Journal of Applied Behavioral Science* (September 1999), p. 373; R. C. Ford and M. D. Fottler, "Empowerment: A Matter of Degree," *Academy of Management Executive*, August 1995, pp. 21–31; and W. A. Rudolph, "Navigating the Journey to Empowerment," *Organizational Dynamics*, Spring 1995, pp. 19–32.

51. T. A. Stewart, "Just Think: No Permission Needed," *Fortune,* January 8, 2001, pp. 190–192.

52. Technology and the Manager's Job box based on K. D. Strang, "Leadership Substitutes and Personality Impact on Time and Quality in Virtual New Product Development Projects," *Project Management Journal* (February 2011), pp. 73–90; A. Rapp, M. Ahearne, J. Mathieu, and T. Rapp, "Managing Sales Teams in a Virtual Environment," *International Journal of Research in Marketing* (September 2010), pp. 213–224; M. Muethel and M. Hoegl, "Cultural and Societal Influences on Shared Leadership in Globally Dispersed Teams," *Journal of International Management* (September 2010), pp. 234–256; J. Grenny, "Virtual Teams," *Leadership Excellence,* May 2010, p. 20; L. A. Hambley, T. A. O'Neill, and T. J. B. Kline, "Virtual Team Leadership: The Effects of Leadership Style and Communication Medium on Team Interaction Styles and Outcomes," *Organizational Behavior and Human Decision Processes,* May 2007, pp. 1–20; and B. J. Avolio and S. S. Kahai, "Adding the 'E' to E-Leadership: How It May Impact Your Leadership," *Organizational Dynamics,* January 2003, pp. 325–338.

53. F. W. Swierczek, "Leadership and Culture: Comparing Asian Managers," *Leadership & Organization Development Journal* (December 1991), pp. 3–10.

54. I. Wanasika, J. P. Howell, R. Littrell, and P. Dorfman, "Managerial Leadership and Culture in Sub-Saharan Africa," *Journal of World Business* (April 2011), pp. 234–241.

55. House, "Leadership in the Twenty-First Century," p. 443; M. F. Peterson and J. G. Hunt, "International Perspectives on International Leadership," *Leadership Quarterly*, Fall 1997, pp. 203–231; and J. R. Schermerhorn and M. H. Bond, "Cross-Cultural Leadership in Collectivism and High Power Distance Settings," *Leadership & Organization Development Journal* 18, no. 4/5 (1997), pp. 187–193.

56. Wanasika, Howell, Littrell, and Dorfman, "Managerial Leadership and Culture in Sub-Saharan Africa"; R. J. House, P. J. Hanges, S. A. Ruiz-Quintanilla, P. W. Dorfman, and Associates, "Culture Specific and Cross-Culturally Generalizable Implicit Leadership Theories: Are the Attributes of Charismatic/Transformational Leadership Universally Endorsed?" *Leadership Quarterly,* Summer 1999, pp. 219–256; and D. E. Carl and M. Javidan, "Universality of Charismatic Leadership: A Multi-Nation Study," paper presented at the National Academy of Management Conference, Washington, DC, August 2001.

57. D. E. Carl and M. Javidan, "Universality of Charismatic Leadership," p. 29.

58. This section is based on D. Goleman, R. E. Boyatzis, and A. McKee, *Primal Leadership: Realizing the Power of Emotional Intelligence* (Boston: Harvard Business School Press, 2002); D. R. Caruso, J. D. Mayer, and P. Salovey, "Emotional Intelligence and Emotional Leadership," in R. E. Riggio, S. E. Murphy, and F. J. Pirozzolo (eds.), *Multiple Intelligences and Leadership* (Mahwah, NJ: Lawrence Erlbaum, 2002), pp. 55–74; J. M. George, "Emotions and Leadership: The Role of Emotional Intelligence," *Human Relations,* August 2000, pp. 1027–1055; D. Goleman, "What Makes a Leader?" *Harvard Business Review,* November–December 1998, pp. 93–102; and D. Goleman, *Working with Emotional Intelligence* (New York: Bantam, 1998).

59. "The Secret Skill of Leaders," *U.S. News & World Report* (January 14, 2002), p. 8. See, also, L. Gardner and C. Stough, "Examining the Relationship Between Leadership and Emotional Intelligence in Senior Level Managers," *Leadership and Organization Development Journal,* January–February 2002, pp. 68–79.

60. Ibid.

61. F. Walter, M. S. Cole, and R. H. Humphrey, "Emotional Intelligence: Sine Qua Non of Leadership or Folderol?" *Academy of Management Perspectives,* February 2011, pp. 45–59.

62. See Walter, Cole, and Humphrey, "Emotional Intelligence: Sine Qua Non of Leadership or Folderol"; L. A. Zampetakis and V. Moustakis, "Managers' Trait Emotional Intelligence and Group Outcomes: The Case of Group Job Satisfaction," *Small Group Research,* February 2011, pp. 77–102; H.-W. Vivian Tang, M.-S. Yin, and D. B. Nelson, "The Relationship Between Emotional Intelligence and Leadership Practices," *Journal of Managerial Psychology,* 25, no. 8 (2010), pp. 899–926; P. K. Chopra and G. K. Kanji, "Emotional Intelligence: A Catalyst for Inspirational Leadership and Management Excellence," *Total Quality Management & Business Excellence,* October 2010, pp. 971–1004; R. Boyatzis and A. McKee, "Intentional Change," *Journal of Organizational Excellence* (Summer 2006), pp. 49–60, and R. Kerr; J. Garvin, N. Heaton, and E. Boyle, "Emotional Intelligence and Leadership Effectiveness," *Leadership and Organizational Development Journal* (April 2006), pp. 265–279.

63. S. Simsarian, "Leadership and Trust Facilitating Cross-Functional Team Success," *Journal of Management Development* (March–April 2002), pp. 201–215.

64. J. M. Kouzes and B. Z. Posner, *Credibility: How Leaders Gain and Lose It, and Why People Demand It* (San Francisco: Jossey-Bass, 1993), p. 14.

65. Based on F. D. Schoorman, R. C. Mayer, and J. H. Davis, "An Integrative Model of Organizational Trust: Past, Present, and Future," *Academy of Management Review,* April 2007, pp. 344–354; G. M. Spreitzer and A. K. Mishra, "Giving Up Control Without Losing Control," *Group & Organization Management*, June 1999, pp. 155–187; R. C. Mayer, J. H. Davis, and F. D. Schoorman, "An Integrative Model of Organizational Trust," *Academy of Management Review*, July 1995, p. 712; and L. T. Hosmer, "Trust: The Connecting Link Between Organizational Theory and Philosophical Ethics," *Academy of Management Review*, April 1995, p. 393.

66. P. L. Schindler and C. C. Thomas, "The Structure of Interpersonal Trust in the Workplace," *Psychological Reports*, October 1993, pp. 563–573.

67. H. H. Tan and C. S. F. Tan, "Toward the Differentiation of Trust in Supervisor and Trust in Organization," *Genetic, Social, and General Psychology Monographs,* May 2000, pp. 241–260.

68. J. H. Cho and E. J. Ringquist, "Managerial Trustworthiness and Organizational Outcomes," *Journal of Public Administration Research and Theory* (January 2011), pp. 53–86; R. C. Mayer and M. B. Gavin, "Trust in Management and Performance: Who Minds the Shop While the Employees Watch the Boss?" *Academy of Management Journal* (October 2005), pp. 874–888; and K. T. Dirks and D. L. Ferrin, "Trust in Leadership: Meta-Analytic Findings and Implications for Research and Practice," *Journal of Applied Psychology* (August 2002), pp. 611–628.

69. R. Zemke, "The Confidence Crisis," *Training* (June 2004), pp. 22–30; J. A. Byrne, "Restoring Trust in Corporate America," *BusinessWeek,* June 24, 2002, pp. 30–35; S. Armour, "Employees' New Motto: Trust No One," *USA Today,* February 5, 2002, p. 1B; J. Scott, "Once Bitten, Twice Shy: A World of Eroding Trust," *New York Times,* April 21, 2002, p. WK5; J. Brockner, P. A. Siegel, J. P. Daly, T. Tyler, and C. Martin, "When Trust Matters: The Moderating Effect of Outcome Favorability," *Administrative Science Quarterly,* September 1997, p. 558; and J. Brockner, P. A. Siegel, J. P. Daly, T. Tyler, and C. Martin, "When Trust Matters: The Moderating Effect of Outcome Favorability," *Administrative Science Quarterly,* September 1997, p. 558.

70. "Weathering the Storm: A Study of Employee Attitudes and Opinions," *WorkUSA 2002 Study,* Watson Wyatt, www.watsonwyatt.com.

71. S. Kerr and J. M. Jermier, "Substitutes for Leadership: Their Meaning and Measurement," *Organizational Behavior and Human Performance*, December 1978, pp. 375–403; J. P. Howell, P. W. Dorfman, and S. Kerr, "Leadership and Substitutes for Leadership," *Journal of Applied Behavioral Science* 22, no. 1 (1986), pp. 29–246; J. P. Howell, D. E. Bowen, P. W. Dorfman, S. Kerr, and P. M. Podsakoff, "Substitutes for Leadership: Effective Alternatives to Ineffective Leadership," *Organizational Dynamics*, Summer 1990, pp. 21–38; and P. M. Podsakoff, B. P. Niehoff, S. B. MacKenzie, and M. L. Williams, "Do Substitutes for Leadership Really Substitute for Leadership? An Empirical Examination of Kerr and Jermier's Situational Leadership Model," *Organizational Behavior and Human Decision Processes*, February 1993, pp. 1–44.

YOUR TURN TO BE A MANAGER

Leadership and Trust

Skill Development: Choosing a Leadership Style

The terms *management* and *leadership* are frequently used interchangeably. That's a misnomer. The two aren't the same but they are related. Although you don't need to hold a management position to be a leader, you're unlikely to be an effective manager if you can't be an effective leader.

Personal Insights: What Kind of Leader Am I?

The following items describe aspects of leadership behavior. Circle the number on the scale that best describes you. Use this scale for your responses:

1 = Strongly disagree

2 = Disagree

3 = Neither agree or disagree

4 = Agree

5 = Strongly agree

1. I like to stand out from the crowd. | 1 2 3 4 5

2. I feel proud and satisfied when I influence others to do things my way.   1 2 3 4 5

3. I enjoy doing things as part of a group rather than achieving results on my own.   1 2 3 4 5

4. I have a history of becoming an officer or captain in clubs and/or organized sports.   1 2 3 4 5

5. I try to be the one who is most influential in task groups at school or work.   1 2 3 4 5

6. In groups, I care most about good relationships.   1 2 3 4 5

7. In groups, I most want to achieve task goals.   1 2 3 4 5

8. In groups, I always show consideration for the feelings and needs of others.   1 2 3 4 5

9. In groups, I always structure activities and assignments to help get the job done.   1 2 3 4 5

Source: Based on S. P. Robbins and P. L. Hunsaker, *Training in Interpersonal Skills: TIPS for Managing People at Work*, 6th ed. (Upper Saddle River, NJ: Prentice Hall, 2011), pp. 220–221.

Analysis and Interpretation

This leadership instrument taps your readiness to be a leader and your leadership style. To calculate your readiness score, add the scale values you circled for items 1 through 5. Your leadership style score is composed of two subsets—a task-oriented score and a people-oriented score. Add your circled values for items 7 and 9; that's your task-oriented score. Add your circled values for items 6 and 8; that's your people-oriented score. Subtract your lower score from your higher score to calculate the difference and determine whether you are more task- or people-oriented.

If your readiness score is 20 or more, you are likely to enjoy being a leader. If your total score is 10 or less, at this time in your life, you are likely more interested in personal achievement than being a leader. If you score in the middle range, your leadership potential could go either direction, depending on events.

Your leadership style preference is indicated by whether your task-orientation or people-orientation score is higher. The difference between these scores indicates how strong this preference is.

The best leaders are ones who can balance their task/people orientation to various situations. If you're too task-oriented, you tend to be autocratic. You get the job done, but at a high emotional cost. If you're too people-oriented, your leadership style may be overly laissez-faire. People are likely to be happy in their work but sometimes at the expense of productivity.

Skill Basics

Simply put, leadership style can be categorized as task- or people-oriented. Neither one is right for all situations. Although a number of situational variables influence the choice of an effective leadership style, four variables seem most relevant:

1. *Task structure.* Structured tasks have procedures and rules that minimize ambiguity. The more structured a job is, the less need there is for a leader to provide task structure.

2. *Level of stress.* Situations differ in terms of time and performance stress. High-stress situations favor leaders with experience. Low stress favors a leader's intelligence.

3. *Level of group support.* Members of close-knit and supportive groups help each other out. They can provide both task support and relationship support. Supportive groups make fewer demands on a leader.

4. *Follower characteristics.* Personal characteristics of followers—such as experience, ability, and motivation—influence which leadership style will be most effective. Employees with extensive experience, strong abilities, and high motivation don't require much task behavior. They will be more effective with a people-oriented style. Conversely, employees with little experience, marginal abilities, and low motivation will perform better when leaders exhibit task-oriented behavior.

Based on R. J. House and R. N. Aditya, "The Social Scientific Study of Leadership: Quo Vadis?" *Journal of Management* (June 1997), pp. 409–473; and G. A. Yukl, *Leadership in Organizations*, 7th ed. (Upper Saddle River, NJ: Prentice Hall, 2010).

Skill Application

You recently graduated from college with your degree in business administration. You've spent the past two summers working at Connecticut Mutual Insurance (CMI), filling in as an intern on a number of different jobs while employees took their vacations. You have received and accepted an offer to join CMI full time as supervisor of the policy renewal department.

CMI is a large insurance company. In the headquarters office alone, where you'll be working, there are more than 1,500 employees. The company believes strongly in the personal development of its employees. This belief translates into a philosophy, emanating from the top executive offices, of trust and respect for all CMI employees. The company is also regularly atop most lists of "best companies to work for," largely due to its progressive work/life programs and strong commitment to minimizing layoffs.

In your new job, you'll direct the activities of 18 policy-renewal clerks. Their jobs require little training and are highly routine. A clerk's responsibility is to ensure that renewal notices are sent on current policies, to tabulate any changes in premiums, to advise the sales division if a policy is to be canceled as a result of nonresponse to renewal notices, and to answer questions and solve problems related to renewals.

The people in your work group range in age from 19 to 62, with a median age of 25. For the most part they are high school graduates with little prior working experience. They earn between $2,350 and $3,200 a month. You will be replacing a long-time CMI employee, Jan Allison. Jan is retiring after 37 years with CMI, the past 14 spent as a policy-renewal supervisor. Because you spent a few weeks in Jan's group last summer, you're familiar with Jan's style and are acquainted with most of the department members. But people don't know you very well and are suspicious of the fact that you're fresh out of college and have little experience in the department. The reality is that you got this job because management wanted someone with a college degree to oversee the department. Your most vocal critic is Lillian Lantz. Lillian is well into her 50s, has been a policy renewal clerk for over a dozen years, and—as the "grand old lady" of the department—carries a lot of weight with group members.

You know that it'll be very hard to lead this department without Lillian's support.

Using your knowledge of leadership concepts, which leadership style would you choose? And why?

Skill Practice

1. Think of a group or team to which you currently belong or of which you have been a part. What type of leadership style did the leader of this group appear to exhibit? Give some specific examples of the types of leadership behaviors he or she used. Evaluate the leadership style. Was it appropriate for the group? Why or why not? What would you have done differently? Why?

2. Observe two sports team (either college or professional—one that you consider successful and the other unsuccessful). What leadership styles appear to be used in these team situations? Give some specific examples of the types of leadership behaviors you observe. How would you evaluate the leadership style? Was it appropriate for the team? Why or why not? To what degree do you think leadership style influenced the team's outcomes?

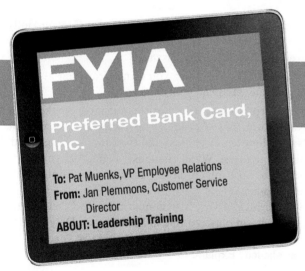

For Your Immediate Action

To: Pat Muenks, VP Employee Relations
From: Jan Plemmons, Customer Service Director
ABOUT: Leadership Training

I agree completely with your recommendation that we need a leadership training program for our customer service team leaders. These leaders struggle with keeping our customer service reps focused on our goal of providing timely, accurate, and friendly service to our bank card holders who call in with questions or complaints.

Put together a one-page proposal that describes the leadership topics you think should be covered. Also, give me some suggestions for how we might present the information in a way that would be interesting. We need to get started on this immediately, so please get this report to me by early next week.

This fictionalized company and message were created for educational purposes only, and not meant to reflect positively or negatively on management practices by any company that may share this name.

Case Application:
Master and Commander: Part 2

Go back and reread the chapter opener. As described there, it's easy to see that Commander Graf was quickly losing the trust of her crew and thus her ability to lead. Then, one eventful night began the unraveling of Graf's career.

On the eve of the Iraq war in 2003, the *Churchill* was steaming out of a Sicilian port when, without warning, all 9,000 tons of the vessel shuddered as it cleared the harbor's breakwater. It wasn't long before the 511-foot-long ship was adrift. "Commander Graf grabbed the cowering navigator and pulled him aside screaming, 'Did you run my #### ship aground?'" But amid all the chaos and shouting, the Navy chaplain aboard said that "the sound heard next was more startling. Sailors on the *Churchill's* stern, suspecting that their ship had run aground—meaning Graf's career would be instantly over—broke gleefully into song: "Ding Dong, the witch is dead!" He couldn't believe what he was hearing. Even today, the chaplain can't fathom which was worse, that U.S. sailors were openly berating a captain or that the captain seemed to deserve it. But that incident didn't end her career.

However, Graf's next command as captain of the guided missile-cruiser U.S.S. *Cowpens* would be her last. She was relieved of duty in January 2010, after nearly two years, for "cruelty and maltreatment" of her crew. The Navy Inspector General's report stated, "Persons in authority are forbidden to injure their subordinates by tyrannical or capricious conduct, or by abusive language." But Graf did so "by demeaning, humiliating, publicly belittling and verbally assaulting . . . subordinates while in command of *Cowpens* with harsh language and profanity . . . rarely followed by any instruction."

DISCUSSION QUESTIONS

1. What do you think of this description of Captain Holly Graf's leader style? Do you think that Captain Graf could even be called a leader? Discuss.

2. What kinds of power do you think Graf used as a ship commander? Explain your choices.

3. Not surprisingly, this whole scenario rocked the Navy to its core, because it reflected on the way the Navy chooses, promotes, and then monitors its hand-picked leaders. What changes, if any, do you think need to take place in its leadership training and development?

4. Some critics of Graf's treatment have said that institutional sexism played a role in her removal. Do you think that could be possible? Discuss. Would that "excuse" the way she led? Explain.

Managing Communication and Information

Managing Communication and Information

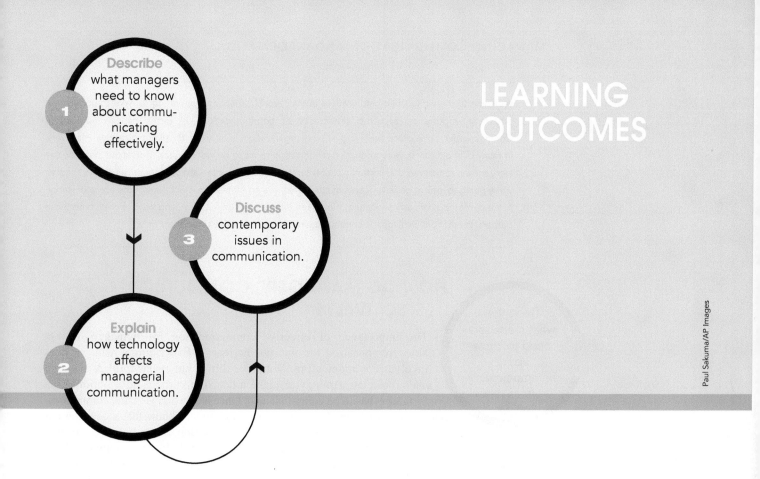

Describe
what managers
need to know
about commu-
nicating
effectively.

1

Discuss
contemporary
issues in
communication.

3

Explain
how technology
affects
managerial
communication.

2

Paul Sakuma/AP Images

Social Benefit or Social Disaster?

Tweets. Twittering. Six years ago, the only definition we would have
known for these words would have involved birds and the sounds they
make.[1] Now, practically everyone knows that Twitter is also an Internet
content service used by millions of people to trade short messages of
140 characters or less via the Web, cell phones, and other devices. And
large companies are beginning to recognize the power of social media.
At Best Buy, CEO Brian Dunn was encouraged by his chief marketing
officer a few years ago to try out social media. With some 180,000
employees—and most of those 24 years old or younger and heavily
involved with social media—Dunn realized that it would be a great way to
engage them *and* customers. He was soon "talking" to employees and
customers every night at 10 o'clock, tweeting on a variety of subjects
including his experiences in Best Buy stores, his kids, and even the
Minnesota Twins. However, at one point, Dunn's Twitter account was
hacked and an offensive tweet put out there for everyone to see. Overseas
on business at the time, Dunn first received a panicked call from his VP of
operations at 4 A.M. and then many other calls. The entire executive team
went into "crisis" mode to control the potential damage.

Welcome to the world of communication! In this "world," managers are going to have to understand both the importance and the drawbacks of communication—all forms of communication. Communication takes place every day in every organization. In all areas. By all organizational members. In many different forms. Most of that communication tends to be work-related. But as the Dunn Twitter story shows, sometimes that communication can cause some unintended consequences. In this chapter, we're going to look at basic concepts of interpersonal communication. We'll explain the communication process, methods of communicating, barriers to effective communication, and ways to overcome those barriers. In addition, we'll look at communication issues that today's managers face.

HOW DO MANAGERS COMMUNICATE EFFECTIVELY?

Describe what managers need to know about communicating effectively.

1

The importance of effective communication for managers cannot be overemphasized for one specific reason: Everything a manager does involves communicating. Not *some* things but *everything*! A manager can't formulate strategy or make a decision without information. That information has to be communicated. Once a decision is made, communication must again take place. Otherwise, no one will know that a decision has been made. The best idea, the most creative suggestion, or the finest plan cannot take form without communication. Managers, therefore, need effective communication skills. We're not suggesting, of course, that good communication skills alone make a successful manager. We can say, however, that ineffective communication skills can lead to a continuous stream of problems for a manager.

How Does the Communication Process Work?

Communication can be thought of as a process or flow. Communication problems occur when deviations or blockages disrupt that flow. Before communication can take place, a purpose, expressed as a message to be conveyed, is needed. It passes between a source (the sender) and a receiver. The message is encoded (converted to symbolic form) and is passed by way of some medium (channel) to the receiver, who retranslates (decodes) the message initiated by the sender. The result is communication, which is a transfer of understanding and meaning from one person to another.[2]

Exhibit 1 depicts the communication process. This model has seven parts: (1) the communication source or sender, (2) encoding, (3) the message, (4) the channel, (5) decoding, (6) the receiver, and (7) feedback.

EXHIBIT 1   The Communication Process

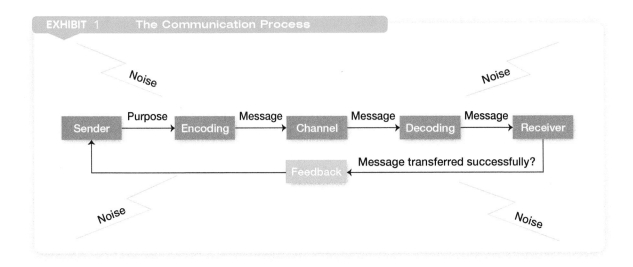

The source initiates a message by **encoding** a thought. Four conditions affect the encoded message: skill, attitudes, knowledge, and the social cultural system. Our message in our communication to you in this text depends on our writing *skills*; if we don't have the requisite writing skills, our message will not reach you in the form desired. Keep in mind that a person's total communicative success includes speaking, reading, listening, and reasoning skills as well. Our attitudes influence our behavior. We hold predisposed ideas on numerous topics, and our communications are affected by these *attitudes*. Furthermore, we're restricted in our communicative activity by the extent of our *knowledge* of the particular topic. We can't communicate what we don't know, and should our knowledge be too extensive, it's possible that our receiver will not understand our message. Clearly, the amount of knowledge the source holds about his or her subject will affect the message he or she seeks to transfer. And, finally, just as attitudes influence our behavior, so does our *position in the social cultural system* in which we exist. Your beliefs and values, all part of your culture, act to influence you as a communicative source.

The **message** is the actual physical product from the source that conveys some purpose. When we speak, the words spoken are the message. When we write, the writing is the message. When we paint, the picture is the message. When we gesture, the movements of our arms, the expressions on our faces are the message.[3] Our message is affected by the code or group of symbols we use to transfer meaning, the content of the message itself, and the decisions that we make in selecting and arranging both codes and content.[4]

The **channel** is the medium through which the message travels. It's selected by the source, who must determine whether to use a formal or an informal channel. Formal channels are established by the organization and transmit messages that pertain to the job-related activities of members. They traditionally follow the authority network within the organization. Other forms of messages, such as personal or social, follow the informal channels in the organization.

The receiver is the person to whom the message is directed. However, before the message can be received, the symbols in it must be translated into a form that can be understood by the receiver—the **decoding** of the message. Just as the encoder was limited by his or her skills, attitudes, knowledge, and social cultural system, the receiver is equally restricted. Accordingly, the source must be skillful in writing or speaking; the receiver must be skillful in reading or listening, and both must be able to reason. A person's knowledge, attitudes, and cultural background influence his or her ability to receive, just as they do the ability to send.

The final link in the communication process is a feedback loop. "If a communication source decodes the message that he encodes, if the message is put back into his system, we have feedback."[5] **Feedback** is the check on how successful we have been in transferring our messages as originally intended. It determines whether understanding has been achieved. Given the cultural diversity that exists in our workforce today, the importance of effective feedback to ensure proper communications cannot be overstated.[6]

Asako Hoshino, corporate vice president of Japan's Nissan Motor Company, chooses to use oral communication by holding a meeting in her Tokyo office with company managers and executives. For Hoshino, communicating verbally gives her and her coworkers the opportunity to share information, discuss what they hear, and ask questions and receive answers to ensure that what is said has been received and understood. In addition to a built-in feedback mechanism, oral communication has the advantage of conveying more information in less time than written communication.

Newscom

---

communication
A transfer of understanding and meaning from one person to another

communication process
The seven-part process of transferring and understanding of meaning

encoding
Converting a message into symbolic form

message
A purpose for communicating that's to be conveyed

channel
The medium by which a message travels

decoding
Translating a received message

feedback
Checking to see how successfully a message has been transferred

Are Written Communications More Effective Than Verbal Ones?

Written communications include memos, letters, e-mail and other forms of digital communication, organizational periodicals, bulletin boards, or any other device that transmits written words or symbols. Why would a sender choose to use written communications? Because they're tangible, verifiable, and more permanent than the oral variety. Typically, both sender and receiver have a record of the communication. The message can be stored for an indefinite period of time. If questions arise about the content of the message, it's physically available for later reference. This feature is particularly important for complex or lengthy communications. For example, the marketing plan for a new product is likely to contain a number of tasks spread out over several months. By putting it in writing, those who have to carry out the plan can readily refer to the document over the life of the plan. A final benefit of written communication comes from the process itself. Except in rare instances, such as when presenting a formal speech, more care is taken with the written word than with the spoken word. Having to put something in writing forces a person to think more carefully about what he or she wants to convey. Therefore, written communications are more likely to be well thought out, logical, and clear.

Of course, written messages have their drawbacks. Writing may be more precise, but it also consumes a great deal of time. You could convey far more information to your college instructor in a one-hour oral exam than in a one-hour written exam. In fact, you could probably say in 10 to 15 minutes what it takes you an hour to write. The other major disadvantage is feedback or, rather, lack of it. Oral communications allow receivers to respond rapidly to what they think they hear. However, written communications don't have a built-in feedback mechanism. Sending a memo is no assurance that it will be received and, if it is received, no guarantee that the recipient will interpret it as the sender meant. The latter point is also relevant in oral communication, but it's easier in such cases merely to ask the receiver to summarize what you have said. An accurate summary presents feedback evidence that the message has been received and understood.

Is the Grapevine an Effective Way to Communicate?

The grapevine is the unofficial way that communications take place in an organization. It's neither authorized nor supported by the organization. Rather, information is spread by word of mouth—and even through electronic means. Ironically, good information passes among us rapidly, but bad information travels even faster.[7] The grapevine gets information out to organizational members as quickly as possible.

The biggest question raised about grapevines, however, focuses on the accuracy of the rumors. Research on this topic has found somewhat mixed results. In an organization characterized by openness, the grapevine may be extremely accurate. In an authoritative culture, the rumor mill may not be accurate. But even then, although the information flowing is inaccurate, it still contains some element of truth. Rumors about major layoffs, plant closings, and the like may be filled with inaccurate information regarding who will be affected or when it may occur. Nonetheless, the reports that something is about to happen are probably on target.

How Do Nonverbal Cues Affect Communication?

Some of the most meaningful communications are neither spoken nor written. They are nonverbal communications. A loud siren or a red light at an intersection tells you something without words. A college instructor doesn't need words to know that students are bored; their eyes get glassy or they begin to read the school newspaper during class. Similarly, when papers start to rustle and notebooks begin to close, the message is clear: Class time is about over. The size of a person's office and desk or the clothes he or she wears also convey messages to others. However, the best-known areas of nonverbal communication are body language and verbal intonation.

Body language refers to gestures, facial configurations, and other movements of the body.[8] A snarl, for example, says something different from a smile. Hand motions, facial

From the Past to the Present

One of the most famous studies of the grapevine was conducted by management researcher Keith Davis who investigated the communication patterns among 67 managerial personnel.[9] The approach he used was to learn from each communication recipient how he or she first received a given piece of information and then trace it back to its source. It was found that, while the grapevine was an important source of information, only 10 percent of the executives acted as liaison individuals (that is, passed the information on to more than one other person). For example, when one executive decided to resign to enter the insurance business, 81 percent of the executives knew about it, but only 11 percent transmitted this information to others. At the time, this study was interesting both because of what it found, but more importantly because of what it showed about how the communication network worked.

Recent research by IBM and the Massachusetts Institute of Technology using a similar type of analysis focused more on people's social networks of contacts at work rather than on how information flowed through the organizational grapevine. However, what was noticeably interesting about this study was that it found that employees who have strong communication ties with their managers tend to bring in more money than those who steer clear of the boss.

What managers can learn from both these studies is that it's important to understand the social and communication networks that employees use as they do their work. Know who the key contact points are so that if you ever need to find out or relay information, you know who to go to.

Think About:

- Why is it important for managers to understand social and communication networks employees use?

- What have been your experiences with the "grapevine"?

- What did you learn from those experiences about dealing with the grapevine as a source of communication?

---

expressions, and other gestures can communicate emotions or temperaments such as aggression, fear, shyness, arrogance, joy, and anger.[10]

Verbal intonation refers to the emphasis someone gives to words or phrases. To illustrate how intonations can change the meaning of a message, consider the student who asks the instructor a question. The instructor replies, "What do you mean by that?" The student's reaction will vary, depending on the tone of the instructor's response. A soft, smooth tone creates a different meaning from one that is abrasive with a strong emphasis on the last word. Most of us would view the first intonation as coming from someone who sincerely sought clarification, whereas the second suggests that the person is aggressive or defensive. The adage, "it's not what you say but how you say it," is something managers should remember as they communicate.

The fact that every oral communication also has a nonverbal message cannot be overemphasized.[11] Why? Because the nonverbal component is likely to carry the greatest impact. Research indicates that from 65 to 90 percent of the message of every face-to-face conversation is interpreted through body language. Without complete agreement between the spoken words and the body language that accompanies it, receivers are more likely to react to body language as the "true meaning."[12]

What Barriers Keep Communication from Being Effective?

A number of interpersonal and intrapersonal barriers affect why the message decoded by a receiver is often different from what the sender intended. We summarize the more prominent barriers to effective communication in Exhibit 2 and briefly describe them here.

HOW DOES FILTERING AFFECT COMMUNICATION? Filtering refers to the way that a sender manipulates information so that it will be seen more favorably by the receiver. For example, when a manager tells his boss what he feels that boss wants to hear, he is filtering

---

grapevine
An unofficial channel of communication

body language
Nonverbal communication cues such as facial expressions, gestures, and other body movements

verbal intonation
An emphasis given to words or phrases that conveys meaning

filtering
Deliberately manipulating information to make it appear more favorable to the receiver

EXHIBIT 2	Barriers to Effective Communication
BARRIER	**DESCRIPTION**
Filtering	The deliberate manipulation of information to make it appear more favorable to the receiver.
Selective Perception	Receiving communications on the basis of what one selectively sees and hears depending on his or her needs, motivation, experience, background, and other personal characteristics.
Information Overload	When the amount of information one has to work with exceeds one's processing capacity.
Emotions	How the receiver feels when a message is received.
Language	Words have different meanings to different people. Receivers will use their definition of words being communicated.
Gender	How males and females react to communication may be different, and they each have a different communication style.
National Culture	Communication differences arising from the different languages that individuals use to communicate and the national culture of which they are a part.

information. Does filtering happen much in organizations? Sure it does. As information is passed up to senior executives, it has to be condensed and synthesized by subordinates so upper management doesn't become overloaded with information. Those doing the condensing filter communications through their own personal interests and perceptions of what's important.

The extent of filtering tends to be the function of the organization's culture and number of vertical levels in the organization. More vertical levels in an organization mean more opportunities for filtering. As organizations become less dependent on strict hierarchical arrangements and instead use more collaborative, cooperative work arrangements, information filtering may become less of a problem. In addition, the ever-increasing use of e-mail to communicate in organizations reduces filtering because communication is more direct as intermediaries are bypassed. Finally, the organizational culture encourages or discourages filtering by the type of behavior it rewards. The more that organizational rewards emphasize style and appearance, the more managers will be motivated to filter communications in their favor.

HOW DOES SELECTIVE PERCEPTION AFFECT COMMUNICATION? The second barrier is selective perception. We discuss it here because the receivers in the communication process selectively see and hear based on their needs, motivations, experience, background, and other personal characteristics. Receivers also project their interests and expectations into communications as they decode them. The employment interviewer who expects a female job applicant to put her family ahead of her career is likely to see that tendency in female applicants, regardless of whether the applicants would do so or not. We don't see reality; rather, we interpret what we see and call it reality.

HOW DOES INFORMATION OVERLOAD AFFECT COMMUNICATION? Individuals have a finite capacity for processing data. For instance, consider the international sales representative who returns home to find that she has more than 600 e-mails waiting for her. It's not possible to fully read and respond to each one of those messages without facing information overload. Today's typical executive frequently complains of information overload.[13] The demands of keeping up with e-mail, phone calls, faxes, meetings, and professional reading create an onslaught of data that is nearly impossible to process and assimilate. What happens when you have more information than you can sort out and use? You're likely to select out, ignore, pass over, or forget information. Or you may put off further processing until the overload situation is over. In any case, the result is lost information and less effective communication.

HOW DO EMOTIONS AFFECT COMMUNICATION?   How a receiver feels when a message is received influences how he or she interprets it. You'll often interpret the same message differently, depending on whether you're happy or distressed. Extreme emotions are most likely to hinder effective communications. In such instances, we often disregard our rational and objective thinking processes and substitute emotional judgments. It's best to avoid reacting to a message when you're upset because you're not likely to be thinking clearly.

HOW DOES LANGUAGE AFFECT COMMUNICATION?   Words mean different things to different people. "The meanings of words are not in the words; they are in us."[14] Age, education, and cultural background are three of the more obvious variables that influence the language a person uses and the definitions he or she applies to words. Columnist George F. Will and rapper Missy Elliott both speak English. But the language one uses is vastly different from how the other speaks.

In an organization, employees usually come from diverse backgrounds and, therefore, have different patterns of speech. Additionally, the grouping of employees into departments creates specialists who develop their own jargon or technical language.[15] In large organizations, members are also frequently widely dispersed geographically—even operating in different countries—and individuals in each locale will use terms and phrases that are unique to their area.[16] And the existence of vertical levels can also cause language problems. The language of senior executives, for instance, can be mystifying to regular employees not familiar with management jargon. Keep in mind that while we may speak the same language, our use of that language is far from uniform. Senders tend to assume that the words and phrases they use mean the same to the receiver as they do to them. This assumption, of course, is incorrect and creates communication barriers. Knowing how each of us modifies the language would help minimize those barriers.

HOW DOES GENDER AFFECT COMMUNICATION?   Effective communication between the sexes is important in all organizations if they are to meet organizational goals. But how can we manage the various differences in communication styles? To keep gender differences from becoming persistent barriers to effective communication, individuals must strive for acceptance, understanding, and a commitment to communicate adaptively with each other. Both men and women need to acknowledge differences are present in communication styles, that one style isn't better than the other, and that it takes real effort to talk successfully with each other.[17]

HOW DOES NATIONAL CULTURE AFFECT COMMUNICATION?   Finally, communication differences can also arise from the different languages that individuals use to communicate and the national culture of which they're a part.[18] For example, let's compare countries that place a high value on individualism (such as the United States) with countries where the emphasis is on collectivism (such as Japan).[19]

In the United States, communication patterns tend to be oriented to the individual and clearly spelled out. Managers in the United States rely heavily on memoranda, announcements, position papers, and other formal forms of communication to state their positions on issues. Supervisors here may hoard information in an attempt to make themselves look good (filtering) and as a way of persuading their employees to accept decisions and plans. And for their own protection, lower-level employees also engage in this practice.

Convergys Corporation provides customer service and sales support for clients in more than 70 countries speaking nearly 35 languages. Even though the call-center employees shown here at the company's facility in Gurgaon, India, and their clients speak the common language of English, communication barriers exist because of differences among country cultures, language accents, and different patterns of speech. To overcome these barriers, Convergys employees receive multicultural skills-based training and accent-neutralization training so they can be more easily understood by their calling clients.

Gurinder Osan/AP Images

---

selective perception
Selectively perceiving or hearing a communication based on your own needs, motivations, experiences, or other personal characteristics

information overload
What results when information exceeds processing capacity

jargon
Technical language, specific to a discipline or industry

In collectivist countries, such as Japan, there's more interaction for its own sake and a more informal manner of interpersonal contact. The Japanese manager, in contrast to the U.S. manager, engages in extensive verbal consultation with employees over an issue first and draws up a formal document later to outline the agreement that was made. The Japanese value decisions by consensus, and open communication is an inherent part of the work setting. Also, face-to-face communication is encouraged.[20]

Cultural differences can affect the way a manager chooses to communicate.[21] And these differences undoubtedly can be a barrier to effective communication if not recognized and taken into consideration.

How Can Managers Overcome Communication Barriers?

Given these barriers to communication, what can managers do to overcome them? The following suggestions should help make communication more effective (see also Exhibit 3).

WHY USE FEEDBACK?   Many communication problems are directly attributed to misunderstanding and inaccuracies. These problems are less likely to occur if the manager gets feedback, both verbal and nonverbal.

A manager can ask questions about a message to determine whether it was received and understood as intended. Or the manager can ask the receiver to restate the message in his or her own words. If the manager hears what was intended, understanding and accuracy should improve. Feedback can also be more subtle as general comments can give a manager a sense of the receiver's reaction to a message.

Feedback doesn't have to be verbal. If a sales manager e-mails information about a new monthly sales report that all sales representatives will need to complete and some of them don't turn it in, the sales manager has received feedback. This feedback suggests that the sales manager needs to clarify the initial communication. Similarly, managers can look for nonverbal cues to tell whether someone's getting the message.

WHY SHOULD SIMPLIFIED LANGUAGE BE USED?   Because language can be a barrier, managers should consider the audience to whom the message is directed and tailor the language to them. Remember, effective communication is achieved when a message is both received and *understood*. For example, a hospital administrator should always try to communicate in clear, easily understood terms and to use language tailored to different employee groups. Messages to the surgical staff should be purposefully different from those directed to the marketing team or office employees. Jargon can facilitate understanding if it's used within a group that knows what it means, but can cause problems when used outside that group.

WHY MUST WE LISTEN ACTIVELY?   When someone talks, we hear. But too often we don't listen. Listening is an active search for meaning, whereas hearing is passive. In listening, the receiver is also putting effort into the communication.

EXHIBIT 3	Overcoming Barriers to Effective Communication
Use Feedback	Check the accuracy of what has been communicated—or what you think you heard.
Simplify Language	Use words that the intended audience understands.
Listen Actively	Listen for the full meaning of the message without making premature judgment or interpretation—or thinking about what you are going to say in response.
Constrain Emotions	Recognize when your emotions are running high. When they are, don't communicate until you have calmed down.
Watch Nonverbal Cues	Be aware that your actions speak louder than your words. Keep the two consistent.

Many of us are poor listeners. Why? Because it's difficult, and most of us would rather do the talking. Listening, in fact, is often more tiring than talking. Unlike hearing, **active listening**, which is listening for full meaning without making premature judgments or interpretations, demands total concentration. The average person normally speaks at a rate of about 125 to 200 words per minute. However, the average listener can comprehend up to 400 words per minute.[22] The difference leaves lots of idle brain time and opportunities for the mind to wander.

Active listening is enhanced by developing empathy with the sender—that is, by putting yourself in the sender's position. Because senders differ in attitudes, interests, needs, and expectations, empathy makes it easier to understand the actual content of a message. An empathetic listener reserves judgment on the message's content and carefully listens to what is being said. The goal is to improve one's ability to get the full meaning of a communication without distorting it by premature judgments or interpretations. Other specific behaviors that active listeners use include making eye contact, exhibiting affirmative nods and appropriate facial expressions, avoiding distracting actions or gestures that suggest boredom, asking questions, paraphrasing using your own words, avoiding interrupting the speaker, not talking too much, and making smooth transitions between being a speaker and a listener.

WHY MUST WE CONSTRAIN EMOTIONS? It would be naïve to assume that managers always communicate in a rational manner. We know that emotions can cloud and distort communication. A manager who's upset over an issue is more likely to misconstrue incoming messages and fail to communicate his or her outgoing messages clearly and accurately. What to do? The simplest answer is to calm down and get emotions under control before communicating. The following is a good example of why it's important to be aware of your emotions before communicating.

Neal L. Patterson, CEO of Cerner Corporation, a health care software development company based in Kansas City, was upset with the fact that employees didn't seem to be putting in enough hours. So he sent an angry and emotional e-mail to about 400 company managers that said, in part:

> We are getting less than 40 hours of work from a large number of our K.C.-based EMPLOYEES. The parking lot is sparsely used at 8 a.m.; likewise at 5 p.m. As managers, you either do not know what your EMPLOYEES are doing, or you do not CARE. You have created expectations on the work effort which allowed this to happen inside Cerner, creating a very unhealthy environment. In either case, you have a problem and you will fix it or I will replace you . . . I will hold you accountable. You have allowed things to get to this state. You have two weeks. Tick, tock."[23]

Although the e-mail was meant only for the company's managers, it was leaked and posted on an Internet discussion site. The tone of the e-mail surprised industry analysts, investors, and of course, Cerner's managers and employees. The company's stock price dropped 22 percent over the next three days. Patterson apologized to his employees and acknowledged, "I lit a match and started a firestorm."

RIGHT or WRONG?

Sixty percent. That's the percentage of respondents in an employee survey who said that gossip was their biggest pet peeve about their jobs.[24] Although office gossip can benefit individuals and organizations, it often consists of hearsay, half-truths, and innuendo. It also can absorb large amounts of employees' time.

Think About:

- What do you think? Is office gossip beneficial for individuals? Organizations?

- What ethical dilemmas might arise because of office gossip?

- As a manager, how will you handle office gossip?

Anna Bryukhanova/iStockphoto.com

active listening
Listening for full meaning without making premature judgments or interpretations

WHY THE EMPHASIS ON NONVERBAL CUES? If actions speak louder than words, then it's important to make sure your actions align with and reinforce the words that go along with them. An effective communicator watches his or her nonverbal cues to ensure that they convey the desired message.

HOW IS TECHNOLOGY AFFECTING MANAGERIAL COMMUNICATION?

Explain how technology affects managerial communication.

2

Information technology has radically changed the way organizational members communicate. For example, it has significantly improved a manager's ability to monitor individual and team performance, it has allowed employees to have more complete information to make faster decisions, and it has provided employees more opportunities to collaborate and share information. In addition, information technology has made it possible for people in organizations to be fully accessible 24 hours a day, 7 days a week, regardless of where they are. Employees don't have to be at their desks with their computers on in order to communicate with others in the organization. Three developments in information technology appear to have had a significant effect on current managerial communication: networked computer systems, wireless capabilities, and knowledge management systems.

What Are Networked Communication Capabilities?

In a networked computer system, an organization links its computers together through compatible hardware and software, creating an integrated organizational network. Organization members can then communicate with each other and tap into information whether they're down the hall, across town, or anywhere on the globe. Although the mechanics of how networked systems work are beyond the scope of this text, we'll address some of the communication applications.

E-mail is the instantaneous transmission of messages on computers that are linked together. Messages wait at a receiver's computer and are read at the receiver's convenience. E-mail is fast and cheap and can be used to send the same message to many people at the same time. It's a quick and convenient way for organization members to share information and communicate. Files can also be attached to e-mail messages, which enables the receiver to print a hard copy of a document.

Some organization members who find e-mail slow and cumbersome are using *instant messaging (IM)*. This interactive, real-time communication takes place among computer users who are logged on to the computer network at the same time. Instant messaging was first popular among teens and preteens who wanted to communicate with their friends online. Now it's moved to the workplace. With IM, information that needs to be communicated can be done so instantaneously without waiting for colleagues to read e-mail messages. However, instant messaging is not without its drawbacks. It requires users to be logged on to the organization's computer network at the same time, which potentially leaves the network open to security breaches.

A *voice-mail* system digitizes a spoken message, transmits it over the network, and stores the message on a disk for the receiver to retrieve later.[25] This capability allows information to be transmitted even though a receiver may not be physically present to take the information. Receivers can choose to save the message for future use, delete it, or route it to other parties.

Fax machines can transmit documents containing both text and graphics over ordinary telephone lines. A sending fax machine scans and digitizes the document, and a receiving fax machine reads the scanned information and reproduces it in hard-copy form. Information that's best viewed in printed form can be easily and quickly shared by organization members.

Electronic data interchange (EDI) is a way for organizations to exchange business transaction documents such as invoices or purchase orders, using direct computer-to-computer networks. Organizations often use EDI with vendors, suppliers, and customers because it saves time and money. How? Information on transactions is transmitted from one organization's computer system to another through an interorganizational telecommunications network. The printing and handling of paper documents at one organization are eliminated as is the inputting of data at the other organization.

Meetings—one-on-one, team, divisional, or organization-wide—have always been one way to share information. The limitations of technology used to dictate that meetings take place among people in the same physical location. But that's no longer the case. Teleconferencing allows a group of people to confer simultaneously using telephone or e-mail group communications software. If meeting participants can see each other over video screens, the simultaneous conference is called videoconferencing. Work groups, large and small, which might be in different locations, can use these communication network tools to collaborate and share information. Doing so is often much less expensive than incurring travel costs for bringing members together from several locations.

Networked computer systems allow for organizational *intranets* and *extranets*. An intranet is an organizational communication network that uses Internet technology but is accessible only to organizational employees. Many organizations are using intranets as ways for employees to share information and collaborate on documents and projects—as well as access company policy manuals and employee-specific materials, such as employee benefits—from different locations.[26] An extranet is an organizational communication network that uses Internet technology and allows authorized users inside the organization to communicate with certain outsiders such as customers or vendors. Most of the large auto manufacturers, for example, have extranets that allow faster and more convenient communication with dealers.

Finally, organizations are using *Internet-based voice communication*. Popular Web sites such as Skype, Vonage, and Yahoo!, among others, let users chat with each other. A number of companies are making these services available for employees to use in conference calls or for instant messaging.

How Have Wireless Capabilities Affected Communication?

At Seattle-based Starbucks Corporation, district managers use mobile technology, giving them more time to spend in the company's stores. A company executive says, "These are the most important people in the company. Each has between 8 to 10 stores that he or she services. And while their primary job is outside of the office—and in those stores—they still need to be connected."[27] As this example shows, wireless communication technology has the ability to improve work for managers and employees.

TECHNOLOGY AND THE MANAGER'S JOB — FYEO: DECODING COMMUNICATION JARGON

Okay . . . how well do you know the Net lingo?[28] If you received an e-mail or text message with GFTD written in it, would you know what that meant? What about NSFW or BIL? When an employee received an e-mail at work from a friend with an attached slideshow entitled "Awkward Family Photos," she clicked through it and saw some pretty unusual—yes, awkward—photos. Looking back at the e-mail, that's when she also saw the abbreviation "NSFW" written at the bottom. Not knowing what that was, she looked the abbreviation up on netlingo.com (one of several Web sites that translate Internet and texting abbreviations). Come to find out, she should have paid more attention to the abbreviation: NSFW stands for "not safe for work."

As text-messaging shorthand becomes increasingly widespread in e-mails, text messages, and tweets, people need to be aware of what it means. At many workplaces, a working knowledge of Net lingo is becoming necessary. As employees use social media sites such as Twitter and Facebook and even text messaging to communicate with colleagues and customers, the shorthand abbreviations are often necessary to stay within message length limits. However, as the NSFW example showed, not knowing or even misunderstanding the lingo can lead to surprises, inappropriate responses, or miscommunications.

(BTW—which is Net lingo for "by the way": FYEO means "for your eyes only"; GFTD stands for "gone for the day"; and BIL is "boss is listening.")

Think About:

· What benefits does jargon or lingo have? What are the drawbacks?

· Go to www.netlingo.com and pick three phrases you were not familiar with. Were you surprised at the number of Net lingo phrases?

While networked computer systems require organizations and organizational members to be connected by wires, wireless communication doesn't. Smartphones, tablet computers, notebook computers, and mobile pocket communication devices have spawned a whole new way for managers to "keep in touch." Globally, millions of users use wireless technology to send and receive information from anywhere. One result: Employees no longer have to be at their desks with their computers plugged in and turned on in order to communicate with others in the organization. As technology continues to advance in this area, we'll see more and more organization members using wireless communication as a way to collaborate and share information.[29]

IBM cultivates a learning culture by using an internal social networking site called Beehive that enables employees to gather knowledge and share it with coworkers. Employees shown here with computer monitors displaying the Beehive portal can describe their expertise, promote their innovative ideas directly to other employees, generate feedback, and post pictures, videos, and updates about themselves. Beehive is helping to break down communication barriers by rank, location, and social groups within IBM and allowing employees to learn about projects and initiatives throughout the company. It also aids team building and trust among employees and allows IBM's management to get involved with employees and join their conversations.

How Does Knowledge Management Affect Communication?

Part of a manager's responsibility in fostering an environment conducive to learning and effective communications is to create learning capabilities throughout the organization. These opportunities should extend from the lowest to the highest levels in all areas. How can managers create such an environment? An important step is recognizing the value of knowledge as a major resource, just like cash, raw materials, or office equipment. To illustrate the value of knowledge, think about how you register for your college classes. Do you talk to others who have had a certain professor? Do you listen to their experiences with this individual and make your decision based on what they have to say (their knowledge about the situation)? If you do, you're tapping into the value of knowledge. But in an organization, just recognizing the value of accumulated knowledge or wisdom isn't enough. Managers must deliberately manage that base of knowledge. **Knowledge management** involves cultivating a learning culture in which organizational members systematically gather knowledge and share it with others in the organization so as to achieve better performance.[30] For instance, accountants and consultants at Ernst & Young document best practices that they've developed, unusual problems they've dealt with, and other work information. This "knowledge" is then shared with all employees through computer-based applications and through community of interest teams that meet regularly throughout the company. Many other organizations, including General Electric, Toyota, and Hewlett-Packard, have recognized the importance of knowledge management within a learning organization. Today's technologies are helping improve knowledge management and facilitating organizational communications and decision making.

WHAT COMMUNICATION ISSUES DO MANAGERS FACE TODAY?

3 Discuss contemporary issues in communication.

"Pulse lunches." That's what managers at Citibank's offices throughout Malaysia used to address pressing problems of declining customer loyalty and staff morale and increased employee turnover. By connecting with employees and listening to their concerns—that is, taking their "pulse"—during informal lunch settings, managers were able to make changes that boosted both customer loyalty and employee morale by more than 50 percent and reduced employee turnover to nearly zero.[31]

Being an effective communicator in today's organizations means being connected—most importantly to employees and customers, but in reality, to any of the organization's stakeholders. In this section, we examine five communication issues of particular significance to today's managers: managing communication in an Internet world, managing the organization's knowledge resources, communicating with customers, getting employee input, and communicating ethically.

Managing Communication in an Internet World

Lars Dalgaard, founder and chief executive of SuccessFactors, a human resource management software company, recently sent an e-mail to his employees banning in-house e-mail for a week. His goal? Getting employees to "authentically address issues amongst each other."[32] And he's not alone. Other companies have tried the same thing. As we discussed earlier, e-mail can consume employees, but it's not always easy for them to let go of it, even when they know it can be "intexticating." But e-mail is only one communication challenge in this Internet world. A recent survey found that 20 percent of employees at large companies say they contribute regularly to blogs, social networks, wikis, and other Web services.[33] Managers are learning, the hard way sometimes, that all this new technology has created special communication challenges. The two main ones are (1) legal and security issues, and (2) lack of personal interaction.

LEGAL AND SECURITY ISSUES.   Chevron paid $2.2 million to settle a sexual harassment lawsuit stemming from inappropriate jokes being sent by employees over company e-mail. U.K. firm Norwich Union had to pay £450,000 in an out-of-court settlement after an employee sent an e-mail stating that its competitor, Western Provident Association, was in financial difficulties. Whole Foods Market was investigated by federal regulators and its board after CEO John P. Mackey used a pseudonym to post comments on a blog attacking the company's rival Wild Oats Markets.[34]

Although e-mail, blogs, tweets, and other forms of online communication are quick and easy ways to communicate, managers need to be aware of potential legal problems from inappropriate usage. Electronic information is potentially admissible in court. For instance, during the Enron trial, prosecutors entered into evidence e-mails and other documents they say showed that the defendants defrauded investors. Says one expert, "Today, e-mail and instant messaging are the electronic equivalent of DNA evidence."[35] But legal problems aren't the only issue, security concerns are as well.

A survey addressing outbound e-mail and content security found that 26 percent of the companies surveyed saw their businesses affected by the exposure of sensitive or embarrassing information.[36] Managers need to ensure that confidential information is kept confidential. Employee e-mails and blogs should not communicate—inadvertently or purposely—proprietary information. Corporate computer and e-mail systems should be protected against hackers (people who try to gain unauthorized access to computer systems) and spam (electronic junk mail). These serious issues must be addressed if the benefits of communication technology are to be realized.

PERSONAL INTERACTION.   It may be called social media, but another communication challenge posed by the Internet age we live and work in is the lack of personal interaction.[37] Even when two people are communicating face-to-face, understanding is not always achieved. However, it can be especially challenging to achieve understanding and collaborate on getting work done when communication takes place in a virtual environment. In response, some companies have banned e-mail on certain days, as we saw earlier. Others have simply encouraged employees to collaborate more in-person. Yet, sometimes and in some situations, personal interaction isn't physically possible—your colleagues work

AND THE SURVEY SAYS...[38]

25 percent of employees say they withhold feedback on routine problems to avoid wasting their time.

47 percent of Wi-Fi users say they can wait one hour or less before getting "antsy" about checking e-mail, instant messaging, and social networking sites.

64 seconds is how long it takes to retrieve your train of thought after an e-mail interruption.

69 percent of executives say they're sending out more messages than ever to employees.

37 percent of employees say they're receiving more messages from executives.

54 percent of employees say their company prohibits employees from visiting social networking sites while at work.

42 percent of employees who have received employer-provided wireless devices feel they are expected to always be available.

28 percent of a day is how much the average worker loses to interruptions

knowledge management
Cultivating a learning culture in which organizational members systematically gather knowledge and share it with others

across the continent or even across the globe. In those instances, real-time collaboration software (such as private workplace wikis, blogs, instant messengers, and other types of groupware) may be a better communication choice than sending an e-mail and waiting for a response.[39] Instead of fighting it, some companies are encouraging employees to utilize the power of social networks to collaborate on work and to build strong connections. This trend is especially appealing to younger workers who are comfortable with this communication medium. Some companies have gone as far as to create their own in-house social networks. For instance, employees at Starcom MediaVest Group tap into SMG Connected to find colleague profiles that outline their jobs, list the brands they admire, and describe their values. A company vice president says, "Giving our employees a way to connect over the Internet around the world made sense because they were doing it anyway."[40]

Managing the Organization's Knowledge Resources

Kara Johnson is a materials expert at product design firm IDEO. To make finding the right materials easier, she built a master library of samples linked to a database that explains their properties and manufacturing processes.[41] What Johnson is doing is managing knowledge and making it easier for others at IDEO to learn and benefit from her knowledge. That's what today's managers need to do with the organization's knowledge resources—make it easy for employees to communicate and share their knowledge so they can learn from each other ways to do their jobs more effectively and efficiently. One way organizations can do this is to build online information databases that employees can access. For example, William Wrigley Jr. Co. launched an interactive Web site that allows sales agents to access marketing data and other product information. The sales agents can question company experts about products or search an online knowledge bank. In its first year, Wrigley estimates that the site cut research time of the sales force by 15,000 hours, making them more efficient and effective.[42] This one example, among many others, shows how managers can use communication tools to manage this valuable organizational resource called knowledge.

In addition to online information databases for sharing knowledge, companies can create communities of practice, which are groups of people who share a concern, a set of problems, or a passion about a topic, and who deepen their knowledge and expertise in that area by interacting on an ongoing basis. To make these communities of practice work, however, it's important to maintain strong human interactions through communication using such essential tools as interactive Web sites, e-mail, and videoconferencing. In addition, these groups face the same communication problems that individuals face—filtering, emotions, defensiveness, overdocumentation, and so forth. However, groups can resolve these issues by focusing on the same suggestions we discussed earlier.

The Role of Communication in Customer Service

You've been a customer many times; in fact, you probably find yourself in a customer service encounter several times a day. So what does a customer service encounter have to do with communication? As it turns out, a lot! *What* communication takes place and *how* it takes place can have a significant impact on a customer's satisfaction with the service and the likelihood of being a repeat customer. Managers in service organizations need to make sure that employees who interact with customers are communicating appropriately and effectively with those customers. How? By first recognizing the three components in any service delivery process: the customer, the service organization, and the individual service provider.[43] Each plays a role in whether communication is working. Obviously, managers don't have a lot of control over what or how the customer communicates, but they can influence the other two.

An organization with a strong service culture already values taking care of customers—finding out what their

Communication is an important part of the customer service strategy at the Four Seasons, a Toronto, Canada-based global luxury chain of hotels and resorts. Recognizing that *how* communication takes place has a significant impact on customer satisfaction, the company expects all employees to greet guests with a friendly hello and teaches them how to treat guests with warmth, courtesy, and respect. As front-line workers involved with critical service encounters, the concierge desk employees shown here are trained to listen actively and communicate efficiently and effectively in delivering exceptional service that sustains the Four Seasons' competitive advantage in service excellence.

Mark Peterson/Redux Pictures

needs are, meeting those needs, and following up to make sure that their needs were met satisfactorily. Each of these activities involves communication, whether face-to-face, by phone or e-mail, or through other channels. In addition, communication is part of the specific customer service strategies the organization pursues. One strategy that many service organizations use is personalization. For instance, at Ritz-Carlton Hotels, customers are provided with more than a clean bed and room. Customers who have stayed at a location previously and indicated that certain items are important to them—such as extra pillows, hot chocolate, or a certain brand of shampoo—will find those items waiting in their room at arrival. The hotel's database allows service to be personalized to customers' expectations. In addition, all employees are asked to communicate information related to service provision. For instance, if a room attendant overhears guests talking about celebrating an anniversary, he or she is supposed to relay the information so something special can be done.[44] Communication plays an important role in the hotel's customer personalization strategy.

Communication also is important to the individual service provider or contact employee. The quality of the interpersonal interaction between the customer and that contact employee does influence customer satisfaction, especially when the service encounter isn't up to expectations.[45] People on the front line involved with those "critical service encounters" are often the first to hear about or notice service failures or breakdowns. They must decide *how* and *what* to communicate during these instances. Their ability to listen actively and communicate appropriately with the customer goes a long way in whether the situation is resolved to the customer's satisfaction or spirals out of control. Another important communication concern for the individual service provider is making sure that he or she has the information needed to deal with customers efficiently and effectively. If the service provider doesn't personally have the information, there should be some way to get the information easily and promptly.[46]

Getting Employee Input

Nokia recently set up an intranet soapbox known as Blog-Hub, opening it up to employee bloggers around the world. There, employees have griped about their employer, but rather than shutting it down, Nokia managers want them to "fire away." They feel that Nokia's growth and success can be attributed to a "history of encouraging employees to say whatever's on their minds, with faith that smarter ideas will result."[47]

In today's challenging environment, companies need to get input from their employees. Have you ever worked somewhere that had an employee suggestion box? When an employee had an idea about a new way of doing something—such as reducing costs, improving delivery time, and so forth—it went into the suggestion box where it usually sat until someone decided to empty the box. Businesspeople frequently joked about the suggestion box and cartoonists lambasted the futility of putting ideas in the employee suggestion box. Unfortunately, this attitude about suggestion boxes still persists in many organizations, but it shouldn't. Managers do business in a world today where you can't afford to ignore such potentially valuable information. Exhibit 4 lists some suggestions for letting employees know that their opinions matter.

EXHIBIT 4	How to Let Employees Know Their Input Matters

- *Hold town-hall meetings* where information is shared and input solicited.
- *Provide information* about what's going on, good and bad.
- *Invest in training* so that employees see how they impact the customer experience.
- *Analyze problems together*—managers and employees.
- *Make it easy* for employees to give input by setting up different ways for them to do so (online, suggestion box, preprinted cards, and so forth).

communities of practice
Groups of people who share a concern, a set of
problems, or a passion about a topic, and who
deepen their knowledge and expertise in that area
by interacting on an ongoing basis

Maurice Moreno/Newscom

Following the merger of United and Continental airlines, Jeff Smisek, CEO of the new airline, established clear guidelines for ethical communications. Smisek and his management team began building a culture for the new carrier based on being honest and direct with employees and customers. In holding CEO exchanges with employees throughout Europe, Asia, Latin America, and the United States, Smisek answered employee questions honestly. In response to the question "When are you going to snap me back to the wages I had in the year 2000?" Smisek truthfully answered, "Never. That was a different time. We are in a different business now." Smisek believes that people respect you when you give them honest answers, and he expects employees to communicate ethically with the new airline's customers.

Communicating Ethically

It's particularly important today that a company's communication efforts be ethical. **Ethical communication** "includes all relevant information, is true in every sense, and is not deceptive in any way."[48] On the other hand, unethical communication often distorts the truth or manipulates audiences. What are some ways that companies communicate unethically? It could be by omitting essential information. For instance, not telling employees that an impending merger is going to mean some of them will lose their jobs is unethical. It's also unethical to plagiarize, which is "presenting someone else's words or other creative product as your own."[49] It would also be unethical communication to selectively misquote, misrepresent numbers, distort visuals, and fail to respect privacy or information security needs. For instance, although British Petroleum attempted to communicate openly and truthfully about the Gulf Coast oil spill, the public felt that much of the company's communication had some unethical elements to it.

So how can managers encourage ethical communications? One thing is to "establish clear guidelines for ethical behavior, including ethical business communication."[50] In a global survey by the International Association of Business Communicators, 70 percent of communication professionals said their companies clearly define what is considered ethical and unethical behavior.[51] If no clear guidelines exist, it's important to answer the following questions:

- Has the situation been defined fairly and accurately?
- Why is the message being communicated?
- How will the people who may be affected by the message or who receive the message be impacted?
- Does the message help achieve the greatest possible good while minimizing possible harm?
- Will this decision that appears to be ethical now seem so in the future?
- How comfortable are you with your communication effort? What would a person you admire think of it?[52]

Remember that as a manager, you have a responsibility to think through your communication choices and the consequences of those choices. If you always remember that, you're likely to have ethical communication.

ethical communication
Presented material that contains all relevant information, is true in every sense, and is not deceptive in any way.

Review

CHAPTER SUMMARY

1 Describe what managers need to know about communicating effectively. Communication is the transfer and understanding of meaning. The communication process consists of seven elements: First, a *sender* or source has a message. A *message* is a purpose to be conveyed. *Encoding* converts a message into symbols. A *channel* provides the medium along which a message travels. *Decoding* happens when the *receiver* retranslates a sender's message. Finally, *feedback* lets the sender know whether the communication was successful. The barriers to effective communication include filtering, emotions, information overload, defensiveness, language, and national culture. Managers can overcome these barriers by using feedback, simplifying language, listening actively, constraining emotions, and watching for nonverbal clues.

2 Explain how technology affects managerial communication. Technology has radically changed the way organizational members communicate. It improves a manager's ability to monitor performance; it gives employees more complete information to make faster decisions; it provides employees more opportunities to collaborate and share information; and it makes it possible for people to be fully accessible, anytime anywhere. IT has affected managerial communication through the use of networked computer systems, wireless capabilities, and knowledge management systems.

3 Discuss contemporary issues in communication. The two main challenges of managing communication in an Internet world are the legal and security issues and the lack of personal interaction.

Organizations can manage knowledge by making it easy for employees to communicate and share their knowledge so they can learn from each other ways to do their jobs more effectively and efficiently. One way is through online information databases, and another way is through creating communities of practice.

Communicating with customers is an important managerial issue because *what* communication takes place and *how* it takes place can significantly affect a customer's satisfaction with the service and the likelihood of being a repeat customer.

It's important for organizations to get input from their employees. Such potentially valuable information should not be ignored.

Finally, it's important that a company's communication efforts be ethical. Ethical communication can be encouraged through clear guidelines and through answering questions that force a communicator to think through the communication choices made and the consequences of those choices.

MyManagementLab   For more resources, please visit www.mymanagementlab.com

---

UNDERSTANDING THE CHAPTER

1. Which type of communication do you think is most effective in a work setting? Why?

2. Why isn't effective communication synonymous with *agreement?*

3. Which do you think is more important for a manager: speaking accurately or listening actively? Why?

4. "Ineffective communication is the fault of the sender." Do you agree or disagree with this statement? Discuss.

5. Is information technology helping managers be more efficient and effective? Explain your answer.

6. How might a manager use the grapevine to his or her advantage? Support your response.

7. Research the characteristics of a good communicator. Write up your findings in a bulleted list report. Be sure to cite your sources.

8. Discuss the five contemporary communication issues facing managers.

9. For one day, track nonverbal communication that you notice in others. What types did you observe? Was the nonverbal communication always consistent with the verbal communication taking place? Describe.

Endnotes

1. B. J. Dunn, "Best Buy's CEO on Learning to Love Social Media," *Harvard Business Review,* December 2010, pp. 43–48; D. Brady, "Brian Dunn," *Bloomberg BusinessWeek,* December 6, 2010, p. 104; J. Castaldo, "Are You Sure You Really Want to Tweet That, Boss?" *Canadian Business,* November 22, 2010, p. 79; A. Scardillo, "Old Spice Guy's Lessons in Crisis Management," *Marketing Magazine,* August 30, 2010, p. 27; and J. Bernoff and T. Schadler, "Empowered," *Harvard Business Review,* July–August 2010, pp. 95–101.

2. D. K. Berlo, *The Process of Communication* (New York: Holt, Rinehart & Winston, 1960), pp. 30–32.

3. Ibid., p. 54.

4. See, for instance, "Get the Message: Communication Is Key in Managing Change Within Organizations—Yet Ensuring Its Effectiveness at Times of High Concerns Can Be Tricky," *Employee Benefits,* February 2002, pp. 58–60.

5. Ibid., p. 103.

6. L. R. Birkner and R. K. Birkner, "Communication Feedback: Putting It All Together," *Occupational Hazards,* August 2001, p. 9.

7. L. Hilton, "They Heard It Through the Grapevine," *South Florida Business Journal,* August 18, 2000, p. 53.

8. L. Talley, "Body Language: Read It or Weep," *HR Magazine,* July 2010, pp. 64–65; and M. Fulfer, "Nonverbal Communication: How to Read What's Plain as the Nose . . . Or Eyelid . . . Or Chin . . . On Their Faces," *Journal of Occupational Excellence* (Spring 2001), pp. 19–38.

9. From the Past to the Present box based on S. Baker, "Putting a Price on Social Connections," *BusinessWeek Online,* April 8, 2009; and K. Davis, "Management Communication and the Grapevine," *Harvard Business Review,* September–October 1953, pp. 43–49.

10. Ibid; and T. Fernsler, "The Secrets and Science of Body Language," *Nonprofit World,* p. 25.

11. P. Mornell, "The Sounds of Silence," *Inc.,* February 2001, p. 117.

12. A. Warfield, "Do You Speak Body Language?" *Training and Development* (April 2001), p. 60.

13. S. Begley, "I Can't Think," *Newsweek,* March 7, 2011, pp. 28–33; D. Dean and C. Webb, "Recovering from Information Overload," *McKinsey Quarterly,* Issue 1, 2011, pp. 80–88; and "Information Overload," *Australian Business Intelligence,* April 16, 2002.

14. S. I. Hayakawa, *Language in Thought and Action* (New York: Harcourt Brace Jovanovich, 1949), p. 292.

15. "Jargon Leaves Us Lost for Words," *Australian Business Intelligence,* August 23, 2002; and W. S. Mossberg, "A Guide to the Lingo You'll Want to Learn for Wireless Technology," *Wall Street Journal,* March 28, 2002, p. B1.

16. "Gobbledygook Begone," *Workforce,* February 2002, p. 12; and "Business-Speak," *Training and Development* (January 2002), pp. 50–52.

17. J. Langdon, "Differences Between Males and Females at Work," *USA Today,* www.usatoday.com (February 5, 2001); J. Manion, "He Said, She Said," *Materials Management in Health Care*, November 1998, pp. 52–62; G. Franzwa and C. Lockhart, "The Social Origins and Maintenance of Gender Communication Styles, Personality Types, and Grid-Group Theory," *Sociological Perspectives*, 41, no. 1 (1998), pp. 185–208; and D. Tannen, *Talking From 9 to 5: Women and Men in the Workplace* (New York: Avon Books, 1995).

18. See, for example, M. K. Kozan, "Subcultures and Conflict Management Styles," *Management International Review,* January 2002, pp. 89–106.

19. A. Mehrabian, "Communication Without Words," *Psychology Today,* September 1968, pp. 53–55.

20. See also W. L. Adair, T. Okumura, and J. M. Brett, "Negotiation Behavior when Cultures Collide: The United States and Japan," *Journal of Applied Psychology* (June 2001), p. 371.

21. C. H. Tinsley, "How Negotiators Get to Yes: Predicting the Constellation of Strategies Used Across Cultures to Negotiate Conflict," *Journal of Applied Psychology* (August 2001), p. 583.

22. See, for instance, S. P. Robbins and P. L. Hunsaker, *Training in Interpersonal Skills*, 4e (Upper Saddle River, NJ: Prentice Hall, 2006); M. Young and J. E. Post, "Managing to Communicate, Communicating to Manage: How Leading Companies Communicate with Employees," *Organizational Dynamics*, Summer 1993, pp. 31–43; J. A. DeVito, *The Interpersonal Communication Book*, 6th ed. (New York: HarperCollins, 1992); and A. G. Athos and J. J. Gabarro, *Interpersonal Behavior* (Upper Saddle River, NJ: Prentice Hall, 1978).

23. "Electronic Invective Backfires," *Workforce,* June 2001, p. 20; and E. Wong, "A Stinging Office Memo Boomerangs," *New York Times,* April 5, 2001, pp. C1+.

24. Right or Wrong box based on "Office Gossip Ban," *HR Professional,* November–December 2010, p. 15; "It's Not 'Unprofessional' to Gossip at Work," *Harvard Business Review,* September 2010, pp. 28–29; J. Grunert, "When Gossip Strikes," *OfficePro,* January–February 2010, pp. 16–18; B. Weissenberger, "Gossip in the Workplace," *Bloomberg BusinessWeek Online,* November 3, 2009; and B. Nefer, "Neutralizing the Power of Workplace Gossip," *Supervision,* April 2009, pp. 14–16.

25. See, for example, R. R. Panko, *Business Data Networks and Communications*, 4th ed. (Upper Saddle River, NJ: Prentice Hall, 2003).

26. "Virtual Paper Cuts," *Workforce,* July 2000, pp. 16–18.

27. J. Karaian, "Where Wireless Works," *CFO,* May 2003, pp. 81–83.

28. Technology and the Manager's Job box based on S. Raposo, "Quick! Tell Us What KUTGW Means," *Wall Street Journal,* August 5, 2009, pp. D1+; and C. Tuna, "Corporate Blogs and

Tweets Must Keep SEC in Mind," *Wall Street Journal,* April 27, 2009, p. B4.

29. See, for instance, A. Cohen, "Wireless Summer," *Time,* May 29, 2000, pp. 58–65; and K. Hafner, "For the Well Connected, All the World's an Office," *New York Times,* March 30, 2000, p. D1.

30. J. S. Brown and P. Duguid, "Balancing Act: How to Capture Knowledge Without Killing It," *Harvard Business Review,* May–June 2000, pp. 73–80; and J. Torsilieri and C. Lucier, "How to Change the World," *Strategy and Business,* October 2000, pp. 17–20.

31. S. Luh, "Pulse Lunches at Asian Citibanks Feed Workers' Morale, Lower Job Turnover," *Wall Street Journal,* May 22, 2001, p. B11.

32. S. Shellenbager, "Backlash Against Email Builds," *Wall Street Journal,* April 29, 2010, p. D6.

33. H. Green, "The Water Cooler Is Now on the Web," *BusinessWeek,* October 1, 2007, pp. 78–79.

34. The Associated Press, "Whole Foods Chief Apologizes for Posts," *New York Times Online,* July 18, 2007; E. White, J. S. Lublin, and D. Kesmodel, "Executives Get the Blogging Bug," *Wall Street Journal,* July 13, 2007, pp. B1+; C. Alldred, "U.K. Libel Case Slows E-Mail Delivery," *Business Insurance,* August 4, 1997, pp. 51–53; and T. Lewin, "Chevron Settles Sexual Harassment Charges," *New York Times Online,* February 22, 1995.

35. J. Eckberg, "E-mail: Messages Are Evidence," *Cincinnati Enquirer,* www.enquirer.com (July 27, 2004).

36. M. Scott, "Worker E-Mail and Blog Misuse Seen as Growing Risk for Companies," *Workforce Management,* www.workforce.com (July 20, 2007).

37. K. Byron, "Carrying Too Heavy a Load? The Communication and Miscommunication of Emotion by Email," *Academy of Management Review,* April 2008, pp. 309–327.

38. And the Survey Says box based on J. R. Detert, E. R. Burris, and D. A. Harrison, "Debunking Four Myths About Employee Silence," *Harvard Business Review,* June 2010, p. 26; A. R. Carey and S. Ward, "Are You Fretting About Messages?" *USA Today,* May 28, 2009, p. 1A; T. Jackson, "Did You Know?" *O Magazine,* December 2008, p. 172; J. Yang and A. Gonzalez, "Can You Hear Me Now?" *USA Today,* November 23, 2009,

p. 1B; J. Yang and J Snider, "No Facebooking for Me," *USA Today,* October 22, 2009, p. 1B; J. Marquez, "Employer-Provided Wireless Devices: Benefit of Electronic Leashes?" *Workforce Management Online,* April 8, 2009; and M. Jackson, "May We Have Your Attention Please?" *BusinessWeek,* June 23, 2008, p. 56.

39. J. Marquez, "Virtual Work Spaces Ease Collaboration, Debate Among Scattered Employees," *Workforce Management,* May 22, 2006, p. 38; and M. Conlin, "E-Mail Is So Five Minutes Ago," *BusinessWeek,* November 28, 2005, pp. 111–112.

40. H. Green, "The Water Cooler Is Now on the Web"; E. Frauenheim, "Starbucks Employees Carve Out Own 'Space,'" *Workforce Management,* October 22, 2007, p. 32; and S. H. Wildstrom, "Harnessing Social Networks," *BusinessWeek,* April 23, 2007, p. 20.

41. J. Scanlon, "Woman of Substance," *Wired,* July 2002, p. 027.

42. H. Dolezalek, "Collaborating in Cyberspace," *Training* (April 2003), p. 33.

43. B. A. Gutek, M. Groth, and B. Cherry, "Achieving Service Success Through Relationship and Enhanced Encounters," *Academy of Management Executive,* November 2002, pp. 132–144.

44. R. C. Ford and C. P. Heaton, "Lessons from Hospitality That Can Serve Anyone," *Organizational Dynamics,* Summer 2001, pp. 30–47.

45. M. J. Bitner, B. H. Booms, and L. A. Mohr, "Critical Service Encounters: The Employee's Viewpoint," *Journal of Marketing* (October 1994), pp. 95–106.

46. S. D. Pugh, J. Dietz, J. W. Wiley, and S. M. Brooks, "Driving Service Effectiveness Through Employee-Customer Linkages," *Academy of Management Executive,* November 2002, pp. 73–84.

47. J. Ewing, "Nokia: Bring on the Employee Rants," *BusinessWeek,* June 22, 2009, p. 50.

48. J. V. Thill and C. L. Bovee, *Excellence in Business Communication,* 9th ed. (Upper Saddle River, NJ: Prentice Hall, 2011), pp. 24–25.

49. Ibid.

50. Ibid.

51. Ibid.

52. Ibid.

Skill Development: Applying Listening Skills

Most of us like to talk more than we like to listen. In fact, it's been facetiously said that listening is just the price we have to pay to get people to allow us to talk. Managers must be effective communicators if they are to do their job well. Part of effective communication is conveying clear and understandable messages. But it's also using active listening skills to accurately decipher others' messages.

Personal Insights: How Good Are My Listening Skills?

Respond to each of the 15 statements using the following scale:

1 = Strongly agree

2 = Agree

3 = Neither agree or disagree

4 = Disagree

5 = Strongly disagree

1. I frequently attempt to listen to several conversations at the same time.	1 2 3 4 5
2. I like people to give me only the facts and then let me make my own interpretation.	1 2 3 4 5
3. I sometimes pretend to pay attention to people.	1 2 3 4 5
4. I consider myself a good judge of nonverbal communications.	1 2 3 4 5
5. I usually know what another person is going to say before he or she says it.	1 2 3 4 5
6. I usually end conversations that don't interest me by diverting my attention from the speaker.	1 2 3 4 5
7. I frequently nod, frown, or provide other nonverbal cues to let the speaker know how I feel about what he or she is saying.	1 2 3 4 5
8. I usually respond immediately when someone has finished talking.	1 2 3 4 5
9. I evaluate what is being said while it is being said.	1 2 3 4 5
10. I usually formulate a response while the other person is still talking.	1 2 3 4 5
11. The speaker's "delivery" style frequently keeps me from listening to content.	1 2 3 4 5
12. I usually ask people to clarify what they have said rather than guess at the meaning.	1 2 3 4 5
13. I make a concerted effort to understand other people's points of view.	1 2 3 4 5
14. I frequently hear what I expect to hear rather than what is said.	1 2 3 4 5
15. Most people feel that I have understood their point of view when we disagree.	1 2 3 4 5

Source: Adapted from E. C. Glenn and E. A. Pood, "Listening Self-Inventory," *Supervisory Management*, January 1989, pp. 12–15. Used with permission of publisher; ©1989 American Management Association, New York.

Analysis and Interpretation

Effective communicators have developed good listening skills. This instrument is designed to provide you with some insights into your listening skills.

To calculate your score, sum up your responses for all items; however, you need to reverse your scores (5 becomes 1, 4 becomes 2, etc.) for statements 4, 12, 13, and 15.

Scores range from 15 to 75. The higher your score, the better listener you are. Although any cutoffs are essentially arbitrary, if you score 60 or above, your listening skills are fairly well honed. Scores of 40 or less indicate you need to make a serious effort at improving your listening skills.

Skill Basics

Too many people take listening skills for granted. They confuse hearing with listening. Hearing is merely picking up sound vibrations. Listening is making sense out of what we hear; and it requires paying attention, interpreting, and remembering. Active listening is hard work and requires you to "get inside" the speaker's head in order to understand the communication from his or her point of view.

Eight specific behaviors are associated with active listening. You can be more effective at active listening if you use these behaviors.

1. *Make eye contact.* We may listen with our ears, but others tend to judge whether we're really listening by looking at our eyes.

2. *Exhibit affirmative nods and appropriate facial expressions.* The effective active listener shows interest in what's being said through nonverbal signals.

3. *Avoid distracting actions or gestures.* When listening, don't look at your watch, shuffle papers, play with your pencil, or engage in similar distractions. They make the speaker feel that you're bored or uninterested.

4. *Ask questions.* The critical listener analyzes what he or she hears and asks questions. This behavior provides clarification, ensures understanding, and assures the speaker that you're really listening.

5. *Paraphrase.* Restate *in your own words* what the speaker has said. The effective active listener uses phrases such as "What I hear you saying is . . ." or "Do you mean . . .?" Paraphrasing is an excellent control device to check whether you're listening carefully and is also a control for accuracy of understanding.

6. *Avoid interrupting the speaker.* Let the speaker complete his or her thoughts before you try to respond. Don't try to second-guess where the speaker's thoughts are going.

7. *Don't overtalk.* Most of us would rather speak our own ideas than listen to what others say. Although talking might be more fun and silence might be uncomfortable, you can't talk and listen at the same time. The good active listener recognizes this fact and doesn't overtalk.

8. *Make smooth transitions between the roles of speaker and listener.* In most work situations, you're continually shifting back and forth between the roles of speaker and listener. The effective active listener makes transitions smoothly from speaker to listener and back to speaker.

Based on K. J. Murphy, *Effective Listening* (New York: Bantam Books, 1987); and T. Drollinger, L. B. Comer, and P. T. Warrington, "Development and Validation of the Active Empathetic Listing Scale," *Psychology & Marketing*, February 2006, pp. 161–180.

Skill Application

Break into groups of two. This exercise is a debate. Person A can choose any contemporary issue. Some examples include business ethics, value of unions, stiffer college grading policies, gun control, and money as a motivator. Person B then selects a position on this issue. Person A must automatically take the counterposition. The debate is to proceed for 8–10 minutes, with only one catch. Before each speaks, he or she must first summarize, in his or her own words and without notes, what the other has said. If the summary doesn't satisfy the speaker, it must be corrected until it does.

Skill Practice

1. In another class—preferably one with a lecture format— practice active listening. Ask questions, paraphrase, exhibit affirming nonverbal behaviors. Then ask yourself: Was this harder for me than a normal lecture? Did it affect my note taking? Did I ask more questions? Did it improve my understanding of the lecture's content? What was the instructor's response?

2. Spend an entire day fighting your urge to talk. Listen as carefully as you can to everyone you interact with and respond as appropriately as possible to understand, not to make your own point. What, if anything, did you learn from this exercise?

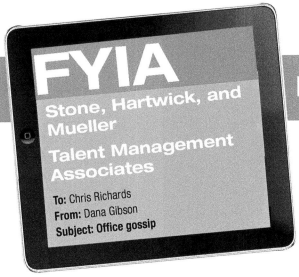

Stone, Hartwick, and Mueller

Talent Management Associates

To: Chris Richards
From: Dana Gibson
Subject: Office gossip

I need some advice, Chris. As you know, my department and all its employees are being transferred from Los Angeles to Dallas. We've had to keep the information "under wraps" for competitive reasons. However, one of my employees asked me point blank yesterday about a rumor she's heard that this move is in the works. I didn't answer her question directly. But I'm afraid that the office grapevine is going to start spreading inaccurate information and then affect morale and productivity. What should I do now? Send me your written response soon (confidential, please!) about what you would do.

This fictionalized company and message were created for educational purposes only, and not meant to reflect positively or negatively on management practices by any company that may share this name.

Bringing the Real World to Life

Case Application:
Social Benefit or Social
Disaster? Part 2

As the biggest electronics consumer store in the United States, Best Buy sells a lot of electronic gadgets (and other merchandise, also). With selling all the latest gadgets and devices and with all their young employees, it's not surprising that the company has been an early user of social media. But as investor Warren Buffet once said, "It takes 20 years to build a reputation and five minutes to ruin it." That's something to think about (for all of us). When CEO Brian Dunn's Twitter account was hacked, he recalls that "it was embarrassing and irritating. I felt violated." So what happened next?

After the initial "shock" over what had happened, Best Buy's IT team advised Dunn to change his password. Like many of us are guilty of, Dunn had been using a password that was easy to remember because it was based on something in his life. Now he changes his password every three weeks and it's a "well-constructed, tortured password." For companies that want to use every communication tool available, being security-minded isn't a maybe, it's a

must. But the most important part of the company's response was that they continued doing what they had been doing . . . using social media. "Despite the headaches they can cause, sites like Twitter, Facebook, and YouTube are powerful tools for spotting trends and communicating with employees and customers."

One interesting and successful social media strategy that Best Buy developed is its "Twelpforce." It's a system in which employees see Best Buy–related problems that customers have aired on Twitter. More than 2,500 employees have signed up including customer service staff, in-store sales associates (the Blue Shirts), and the Geek Squad. Any of the Twelpforce can respond to a customer's complaint, concern, or comment. For example, when a customer recently tweeted about his dissatisfaction over how his iPhone problem was resolved, a customer service rep responded quickly on Twitter. She was able to take care of the problem and the customer then tweeted about how great Best Buy's service was. Funny thing . . . the customer's wife, who has more than 3,000 Twitter followers, also tweeted about the great service.

As far as CEO Dunn, he continues to be a heavy user of Twitter and Facebook. He also has a large monitor in his office that shows all the activity where Best Buy is mentioned. He says that he learns a lot from the time he spends on those platforms. Such direct interactions provide him with information, trends, and news he would probably miss otherwise.

DISCUSSION QUESTIONS

1. What are the advantages and drawbacks of companies using social media to communicate with employees? How about with customers?

2. Do you think there would be more or fewer communication barriers when using social media? Discuss.

3. What should managers do to be sure they communicate effectively when using social media?

4. What type of rules should organizations have for employees using social media? Try to be as specific as possible.

5. What have been your experiences—both positive and negative—with social media? From your experiences, what guidelines could you suggest for managers and organizations?

Foundations of Control

Foundations
of Control

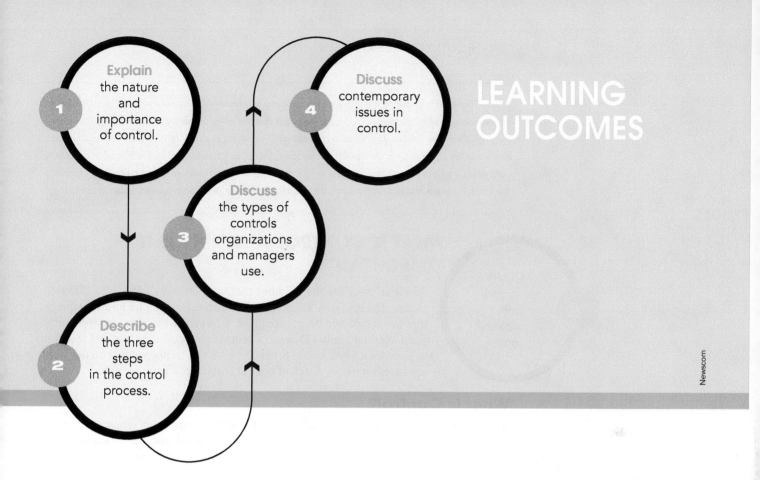

LEARNING OUTCOMES

1 Explain the nature and importance of control.

2 Describe the three steps in the control process.

3 Discuss the types of controls organizations and managers use.

4 Discuss contemporary issues in control.

Newscom

Deepwater in Deep Trouble

When all is said and done, which may not be for many years, it's likely to be one of the worst environmental disasters, if not the worst, in U.S. history.[1] British Petroleum's (BP) Deepwater Horizon offshore rig in the Gulf of Mexico exploded in a ball of flames on April 20, 2010, killing 11 employees. This initial tragedy set in motion frantic efforts to stop the flow of oil, followed by a long and arduous cleanup process. Although the impacts of the explosion and oil spill were felt most intensely by businesses and residents along the coast and by coastal wildlife, those of us inland who watched the disaster unfold were also stunned and dismayed by what we saw happening. What led to this disaster, and what should BP do to minimize the likelihood of it ever happening again?

Controlling is the final step in the management process. Managers must monitor whether goals that were established as part of the planning process are being accomplished efficiently and effectively. That's what they do when they control. Appropriate controls can help managers look for specific performance gaps and areas for improvement. As the BP story shows, things don't always go as planned. But that's why controlling is so important! In this chapter, we'll look at the fundamental elements of controlling, including the control process, the types of controls that managers can use, and contemporary issues in control.

WHAT IS CONTROL AND WHY IS IT IMPORTANT?

1 Explain the nature and importance of control.

"Bailout" was the magic word that cost Domino's Pizza 11,000 free pizzas. The company had prepared an Internet coupon for an ad campaign that was considered but not approved. However, when someone apparently typed "bailout" into a Domino's promotional code window and found it was good for a free medium pizza, the word spread like wildfire on the Web. Somewhere, somehow, a lack of control cost the company big time.[2]

What Is Control?

Control is the management function that involves monitoring activities to ensure that they're being accomplished as planned and correcting any significant deviations. Managers can't really know whether their units are performing properly until they've evaluated what activities have been done and have compared the actual performance with the desired standard. An effective control system ensures that activities are completed in ways that lead to the attainment of the organization's goals. The effectiveness of a control system is determined by how well it facilitates goal achievement. The more a control system helps managers achieve their organization's goals, the better it is.

Why Is Control Important?

A press operator at the Denver Mint noticed a flaw—an extra up leaf or an extra down leaf—on Wisconsin state quarters being pressed at one of his five press machines. He stopped the machine and left for a meal break. When he returned, he saw the machine running and assumed that someone had changed the die in the machine. However, after a routine inspection, the machine operator realized the die had not been changed. The faulty press had likely been running for over an hour and thousands of the flawed coins were now "co-mingled" with unblemished quarters. As many as 50,000 of the faulty coins entered circulation, setting off a coin collector buying frenzy.[4]

Can you see now why controlling is such an important managerial function? Planning can be done, an organizational structure created to facilitate efficient achievement of goals, and employees motivated through effective leadership. But there's no assurance that activities are going as planned and that the goals employees and managers are working toward are, in fact, being attained. Control is important, therefore, because it's the only way that managers know whether organizational goals are being met and if not, the reasons why. The value of the control function can be seen in three specific areas: planning, empowering employees, and protecting the workplace.

RIGHT ? WRONG

The practice is called "sweethearting."[3] It's when cashiers use subtle tricks to pass free goods to friends, doing things such as concealing the bar code, slipping an item behind the scanner, passing two items at a time but only charging for one. It's impossible for even the most watchful human eyes to keep it from happening. So retailers are using technology to block it. Surveillance cameras are used to record and study cashiers staffing checkout lines.

Think About:

- What do you think? Is surveillance less invasive when it's a computer watching instead of a human?

- How could organizations make sure it's being ethical in monitoring employees?

Steve Krongard/Getty Images USA, Inc.

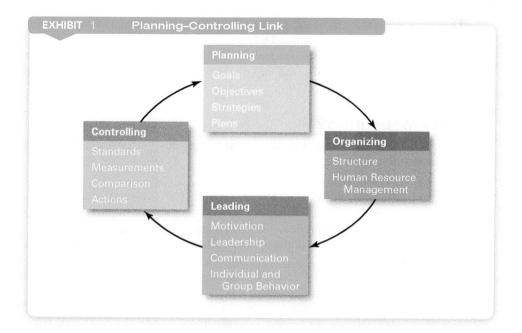

EXHIBIT 1   Planning–Controlling Link

Planning
Goals
Objectives
Strategies
Plans

Organizing
Structure
Human Resource
  Management

Controlling
Standards
Measurements
Comparison
Actions

Leading
Motivation
Leadership
Communication
Individual and
  Group Behavior

Just stating goals or having employees accept goals doesn't guarantee that the necessary actions to accomplish those goals have been taken. As the old saying goes, "The best-laid plans often go awry." The effective manager follows up to ensure that what employees are supposed to do is, in fact, being done and goals are being achieved. As the final step in the management process, controlling provides the critical link back to planning. (See Exhibit 1.) If managers didn't control, they'd have no way of knowing whether their goals and plans were being achieved and what future actions to take.

The second reason controlling is important is because of employee empowerment. Many managers are reluctant to empower their employees because they fear something will go wrong for which they would be held responsible. But an effective control system can provide information and feedback on employee performance and minimize the chance of potential problems.

The final reason that managers control is to protect the organization and its assets.[5] Organizations face threats from natural disasters, financial pressures and scandals, workplace violence, supply chain disruptions, security breaches, and even possible terrorist attacks. Managers must protect organizational assets in the event that any of these should happen. Comprehensive controls and backup plans will help minimize work disruptions.

WHAT TAKES PLACE AS MANAGERS CONTROL?

Describe the three steps in the control process.

2

When Maggine Fuentes joined Core Systems in Painesville, Ohio, as HR manager, she knew that her top priority was reducing employee injuries. The number of injuries was "through the roof; above the industry average." The high frequency and severity of the company's injury rates not only affected employee morale but also resulted in lost workdays and affected the bottom line.[6] Fuentes relied on the control process to turn this situation around.

control
Management function that involves monitoring
activities to ensure that they're being accomplished
as planned and correcting any significant deviations

The **control process** is a three-step process of measuring actual performance, comparing actual performance against a standard, and taking managerial action to correct deviations or to address inadequate standards. (See Exhibit 2.) The control process assumes that performance standards already exist, and they do. They're the specific goals created during the planning process.

What Is Measuring?

To determine actual performance, a manager must first get information about it. Thus, the first step in control is measuring.

HOW DO MANAGERS MEASURE?   Four common sources of information frequently used to measure actual performance are personal observation, statistical reports, oral reports, and written reports. Each has particular strengths and weaknesses; however, use of a combination of them increases both the number of input sources and the probability of receiving reliable information.

Personal observation provides firsthand, intimate knowledge of the actual activity—information that is not filtered through others. It permits intensive coverage because minor as well as major performance activities can be observed, and it provides opportunities for the manager to read between the lines. **Management by walking around (MBWA)** is a phrase used to describe when a manager is out in the work area, interacting directly with employees, and exchanging information about what's going on. Management by walking around can pick up factual omissions, facial expressions, and tones of voice that may be missed by other sources. Unfortunately, in a time when quantitative information suggests objectivity, personal observation is often considered an inferior information source. It is subject to perceptual biases; what one manager sees, another might not. Personal

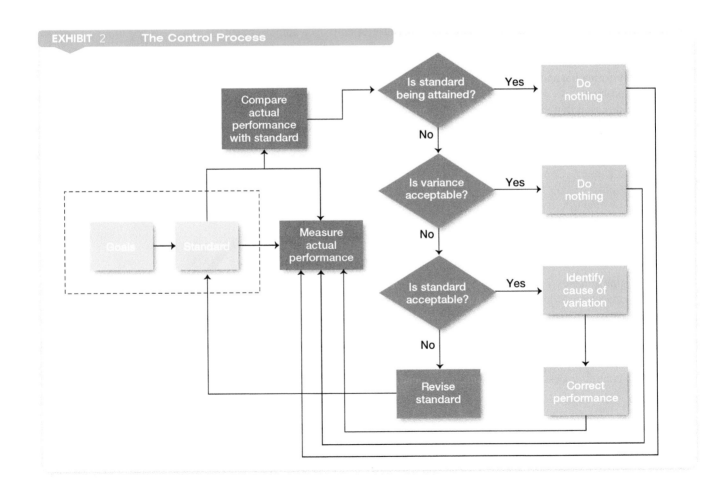

EXHIBIT 2   **The Control Process**

observation also consumes a good deal of time. Finally, this method suffers from obtrusiveness. Employees might interpret a manager's overt observation as a lack of confidence or a sign of mistrust.

The widespread use of computers has led managers to rely increasingly on *statistical reports* for measuring actual performance. This measuring device, however, isn't limited to computer outputs. It also includes graphs, bar charts, and numerical displays of any form that managers can use for assessing performance. Although statistical information is easy to visualize and effective for showing relationships, it provides limited information about an activity. Statistics report on only a few key areas and may often ignore other important, often subjective, factors.

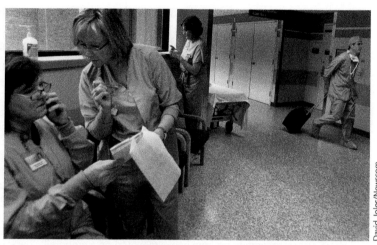

Information can also be acquired through *oral reports*—that is, through conferences, meetings, one-to-one conversations, or telephone calls. In employee-oriented organizations where employees work closely together, this approach may be the best way to keep tabs on work performance. For instance, at the Ken Blanchard Companies in Escondido, California, managers are expected to hold one-on-one meetings with each of their employees at least once every two weeks.[7] The advantages and disadvantages of this method of measuring performance are similar to those of personal observation. Although the information is filtered, it is fast, allows for feedback, and permits expression and tone of voice as well as words themselves to convey meaning. Historically, one of the major drawbacks of oral reports has been the problem of documenting information for later reference. However, our technological capabilities have progressed in the past couple of decades to the point where oral reports can be efficiently taped and become as permanent as if they were written.

Actual performance may also be measured by *written reports*. Like statistical reports, they are slower yet more formal than firsthand or secondhand oral measures. This formality also often gives them greater comprehensiveness and conciseness than found in oral reports. In addition, written reports are usually easy to catalog and reference.

Given the varied advantages and disadvantages of each of these four measurement techniques, managers should use all four for comprehensive control efforts.

In controlling the quality and efficiency of its medical services, Mayo Clinic measures performance indicators that include outcomes achieved, such as readmission rates and safety records. The clinic also measures compliance with specific processes that enhance patient care, including giving the right consultations and therapies, the right medication at the right time, and the right diagnostic studies for specific problems. Through surveys, Mayo measures consumer satisfaction to ensure that every patient is treated with respect, dignity, and kindness by all members of the Mayo team, including the nurses and staff shown here working at Saint Marys Hospital, which is part of the clinic's medical center in Rochester, Minnesota.

WHAT DO MANAGERS MEASURE? What managers measure is probably more critical to the control process than how they measure. Why? The selection of the wrong criteria can result in serious dysfunctional consequences. Besides, what we measure determines, to a great extent, what people in the organization will attempt to excel at.[8] For example, assume that your instructor has required a total of 10 writing assignments from the exercises at the end of each textbook chapter. But in the grade computation section of the syllabus, you notice that these assignments are not scored. In fact, when you ask your professor about this, she replies that these writing assignments are for your own enlightenment and do not affect your grade for the course; grades are solely a function of how well you perform on the three exams. We predict that you would, not surprisingly, exert most, if not all, of your effort toward doing well on the three exams.

Some control criteria are applicable to any management situation. For instance, because all managers, by definition, direct the activities of others, criteria such as employee satisfaction or turnover and absenteeism rates can be measured. Most managers have budgets for their area of responsibility set in monetary units (dollars, pounds, francs,

---

control process
A three-step process of measuring actual performance, comparing actual performance against a standard, and taking managerial action to correct deviations

management by walking around (MBWA)
When a manager is out in the work area interacting with employees

Since planning and controlling are so closely linked, it also has implications for control. Benchmarking has been a highly utilized management tool. Although Xerox is often credited with the first widespread benchmarking effort in the United States, the practice can actually be traced back much further.

The benefits of benchmarking have long been recognized in the manufacturing industry. At the Midvale Steel Company plant where he was employed, Frederick W. Taylor (of scientific management fame) used concepts of benchmarking to find the "one best way" to perform a job and to find the best worker to perform the job. Even Henry Ford recognized the benefits. Based on the techniques used at Chicago slaughterhouses where carcasses were hung from hooks mounted on a monorail, with each man performing his job and then pushing the carcass to the next work station, Ford's assembly line used the same concept for producing cars, beginning in 1913. "The idea that revolutionized manufacturing was imported from another industry."

Today, managers in diverse industries such as health care, education, and financial services are discovering what manufacturers have long recognized—the benefits of benchmarking. For instance, the American Medical Association developed more than 100 standard measures of performance to improve medical care. Carlos Ghosn, CEO of Nissan, benchmarked Walmart's operations in purchasing, transportation, and logistics. At its most basic, benchmarking means learning from others. However, as a tool for monitoring and measuring organizational and work performance, benchmarking can be used to identify specific performance gaps and potential areas of improvement.

Think About:

• What are the benefits of benchmarking? The challenges in doing it?

• Could the concept of benchmarking apply in your personal life? Discuss.

lire, and so on). Keeping costs within budget is, therefore, a fairly common control measure. However, any comprehensive control system needs to recognize the diversity of activities among managers. For example, a production manager in a paper tablet manufacturing plant might use measures of the quantity of tablets produced per day, tablets produced per labor hour, scrap tablet rate, or percentage of rejects returned by customers. On the other hand, the manager of an administrative unit in a government agency might use number of document pages produced per day, number of orders processed per hour, or average time required to process service calls. Marketing managers often use measures such as percent of market held, number of customer visits per salesperson, or number of customer impressions per advertising medium.

As you might imagine, some activities are more difficult to measure in quantifiable terms. It is more difficult, for instance, for a manager to measure the performance of a medical researcher or a middle school counselor than of a person who sells life insurance. But most activities can be broken down into objective segments that allow for measurement. The manager needs to determine what value a person, department, or unit contributes to the organization and then convert the contribution into standards.

Most jobs and activities can be expressed in tangible and measurable terms. When a performance indicator cannot be stated in quantifiable terms, managers should look for and use subjective measures. Certainly, subjective measures have significant limitations. Still, they are better than having no standards at all and ignoring the control function. If an activity is important, the excuse that it's difficult to measure is inadequate. In such cases, managers should use subjective performance criteria. Of course, any analysis or decisions made on the basis of subjective criteria should recognize the limitations of the data.

How Do Managers Compare Actual Performance to Planned Goals?

The comparing step determines the variation between actual performance and the standard. Although some variation in performance can be expected in all activities, it's critical to determine an acceptable range of variation (see Exhibit 3). Deviations outside this range need attention. Let's work through an example.

Chris Tanner is a sales manager for Green Earth Gardening Supply, a distributor of specialty plants and seeds in the Pacific Northwest. Chris prepares a report during the first week of each month that describes sales for the previous month, classified by product line.

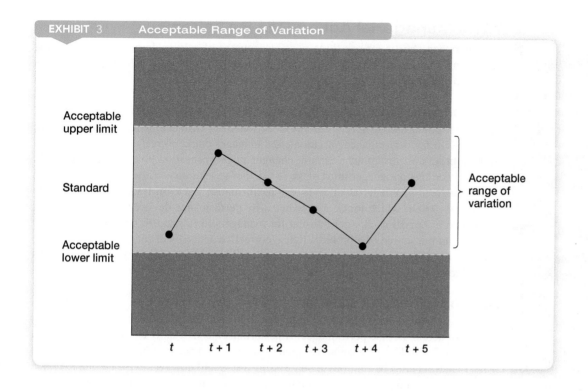

EXHIBIT 3   Acceptable Range of Variation

Exhibit 4 displays both the sales goals (standard) and actual sales figures for the month of June. After looking at the numbers, should Chris be concerned? Sales were a bit higher than originally targeted, but does that mean there were no significant deviations? That depends on what Chris thinks is *significant*; that is, outside the acceptable range of variation. Even though overall performance was generally quite favorable, some product lines need closer scrutiny. For instance, if sales of heirloom seeds, flowering bulbs, and annual flowers continue to be over what was expected, Chris might need to order more product from nurseries to meet customer demand. Because sales of vegetable plants were 15 percent below goal, Chris may need to run a special on them. As this example shows, both overvariance and undervariance may require managerial attention, which is the third step in the control process.

EXHIBIT 4   Example of Determining Significant Variation: Green Earth Gardening Supply—June Sales

PRODUCT	STANDARD	ACTUAL	OVER (UNDER)
Vegetable plants	1,075	913	(612)
Perennial flowers	630	634	4
Annual flowers	800	912	112
Herbs	160	140	(20)
Flowering bulbs	170	286	116
Flowering bushes	225	220	(5)
Heirloom seeds	540	672	132
Total	3,600	3,777	177

range of variation
The acceptable parameters of variance between actual performance and a standard

What Managerial Action Can Be Taken?

Managers can choose among three possible courses of action: do nothing, correct the actual performance, or revise the standards. Because "do nothing" is self-explanatory, let's look at the other two.

HOW DO YOU CORRECT ACTUAL PERFORMANCE?   Depending on what the problem is, a manager could take different corrective actions. For instance, if unsatisfactory work is the reason for performance variations, the manager could correct it by things such as training programs, disciplinary action, changes in compensation practices, and so forth. One decision that a manager must make is whether to take immediate corrective action, which corrects problems at once to get performance back on track or to use basic corrective action, which looks at how and why performance deviated before correcting the source of deviation. It's not unusual for managers to rationalize that they don't have time to find the source of a problem (basic corrective action) and continue to perpetually "put out fires" with immediate corrective action. Effective managers analyze deviations and if the benefits justify it, take the time to pinpoint and correct the causes of variance.

HOW DO YOU REVISE THE STANDARD?   It's possible that the variance was a result of an unrealistic standard—too low or too high a goal. In such cases, it's the standard that needs corrective action, not the performance. If performance consistently exceeds the goal, then a manager should look at whether the goal is too easy and needs to be raised. On the other hand, managers must be cautious about revising a standard downward. It's natural to blame the goal when an employee or a team falls short. For instance, students who get a low score on a test often attack the grade cutoff standards as too high. Rather than accept the fact that their performance was inadequate, they will argue that the standards are unreasonable. Likewise, salespeople who don't meet their monthly quota often want to blame what they think is an unrealistic quota. The point is that when performance isn't up to par, don't immediately blame the goal or standard. If you believe the standard is realistic, fair, and achievable, tell employees that you expect future work to improve, and then take the necessary corrective action to help make that happen.

WHAT SHOULD MANAGERS CONTROL?

Discuss the types of controls organizations and managers use. **3**

Cost efficiency. The length of time customers are kept on hold. Customers being satisfied with the service provided. These are just a few of the important performance indicators that executives in the intensely competitive call-center service industry measure. To make good decisions, managers in this industry want and need this type of information so they can control work performance.

How do managers know what to control? In this section, we're first going to look at the decision of *what* to control in terms of when control takes place. Then, we're going to discuss some different areas in which managers might choose to establish controls.

When Does Control Take Place?

Management can implement controls before an activity commences, while the activity is going on, or after the activity has been completed. The first type is called feedforward control, the second is concurrent control, and the last is feedback control (see Exhibit 5).

WHAT IS FEEDFORWARD CONTROL?   The most desirable type of control—feedforward control—prevents problems because it takes place before the actual activity.[11] For instance, when McDonald's opened its first restaurant in Moscow, it sent company quality control experts to help Russian farmers learn techniques for growing high-quality potatoes and to help bakers learn processes for baking high-quality breads. Why? McDonald's demands consistent product quality no matter the geographical location. They want french fries in Moscow to taste

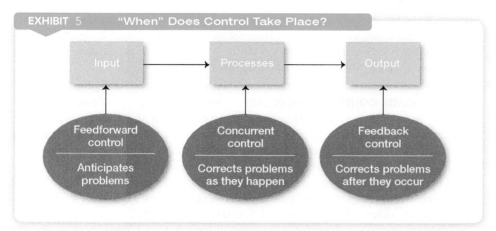

EXHIBIT 5   "When" Does Control Take Place?

Input → Processes → Output

Feedforward control
___
Anticipates problems

Concurrent control
___
Corrects problems as they happen

Feedback control
___
Corrects problems after they occur

like those in Omaha. Still another example of feedforward control is the scheduled preventive maintenance programs on aircraft done by the major airlines. These schedules are designed to detect and hopefully to prevent structural damage that might lead to an accident.

The key to feedforward controls is taking managerial action *before* a problem occurs. That way, problems can be prevented rather than having to correct them after any damage—poor-quality products, lost customers, lost revenue, etc.—has already been done. However, these controls require timely and accurate information that isn't always easy to get. Thus, managers frequently end up using the other two types of control.

WHEN IS CONCURRENT CONTROL USED?   Concurrent control, as its name implies, takes place while a work activity is in progress. For instance, the director of business product management at Google and his team keep a watchful eye on one of Google's most profitable businesses—online ads. They watch "the number of searches and clicks, the rate at which users click on ads, the revenue this generates—everything is tracked hour by hour, compared with the data from a week earlier and charted."[12] If they see something that's not working particularly well, they fine-tune it.

Technical equipment (such as computers and computerized machine controls) can be designed to include concurrent controls. For example, you've probably experienced this with word-processing software that alerts you to a misspelled word or incorrect grammatical usage. Also, many organizational quality programs rely on concurrent controls to inform workers whether their work output is of sufficient quality to meet standards.

The best-known form of concurrent control, however, is direct supervision. For example, Nvidia's CEO Jen-Hsun Huang had his office cubicle torn down and replaced with a conference table so he's now available to employees at all times to discuss what's going on.[13] Even GE's CEO Jeff Immelt spends 60 percent of

Nissan North America used feedback control to correct defects in vehicles produced at its Canton, Mississippi, assembly plant. In this photo, a Nissan production technician at the plant explains how a defect-analysis and problem-solving team of technicians and engineers identified quality problems that occurred during vehicle design and production processes. Team members worked with suppliers to reengineer parts and formed cross-functional quality teams to correct problems reported on quality surveys or in warranty data. They studied each part of the assembly line to detect and fix problems that resulted in squeaks, rattles, and other defects. Feedback control gave Nissan managers information they needed to make new plans for preventing problems before the production phase.

Rogelio Solis/AP Images

---

immediate corrective action
Corrective action that addresses problems at once to get performance back on track

basic corrective action
Corrective action that looks at how and why performance deviated before correcting the source of deviation

feedforward control
Control that takes place before a work activity is done

concurrent control
Control that takes place while a work activity is in progress

his workweek on the road talking to employees and visiting the company's numerous locations.[14] All managers can benefit from using concurrent control because they can correct problems before they become too costly. MBWA, which we described earlier in this chapter, is a great way for managers to do this.

WHY IS FEEDBACK CONTROL SO POPULAR?　The most popular type of control relies on feedback. In feedback control, the control takes place *after* the activity is done. For instance, remember our earlier Denver Mint example. The flawed Wisconsin quarters were discovered with feedback control. The damage had already occurred even though the organization corrected the problem once it was discovered. And that's the major problem with this type of control. By the time a manager has the information, the problems have already occurred, leading to waste or damage. However, in many work areas, the financial area being one example, feedback is the only viable type of control.

Feedback controls do have two advantages.[15] First, feedback gives managers meaningful information on how effective their planning efforts were. Feedback that shows little variance between standard and actual performance indicates that the planning was generally on target. If the deviation is significant, a manager can use that information to formulate new plans. Second, feedback can enhance motivation. People want to know how well they're doing, and feedback provides that information.

In What Areas Might Managers Need Controls?

Most organizations consist of countless activities taking place in different locations and functional areas of the organization. So *what* gets controlled? We need to look at some of the specific areas and control tools that managers can use.

HOW DO MANAGERS KEEP TRACK OF FINANCES?　Every business wants to earn a profit. To achieve this goal, managers need financial controls. For instance, they might analyze quarterly income statements for excessive expenses. They might calculate financial ratios to ensure that sufficient cash is available to pay ongoing expenses, that debt levels haven't become too high, or that assets are being used productively.

Traditional financial measures managers might use include ratio analysis and budget analysis. Exhibit 6 summarizes some of the most popular financial ratios that managers

EXHIBIT 6	**Popular Financial Ratios**		
OBJECTIVE	RATIO	CALCULATION	MEANING
Liquidity	Current ratio	$\dfrac{\text{Current assets}}{\text{Current liabilities}}$	Tests the organization's ability to meet short-term obligations
	Acid test	$\dfrac{\text{Current assets} - \text{Inventories}}{\text{Current liabilities}}$	Tests liquidity more accurately when inventories turn over slowly or are difficult to sell
Leverage	Debt to assets	$\dfrac{\text{Total debt}}{\text{Total assets}}$	The higher the ratio, the more leveraged the organization
	Times interest earned	$\dfrac{\text{Profits before interest and taxes}}{\text{Total interest charges}}$	Measures how many times the organization is able to cover its interest expenses
Activity	Inventory turnover	$\dfrac{\text{Sales}}{\text{Inventory}}$	The higher the ratio, the more efficiently inventory assets are being used
	Total asset turnover	$\dfrac{\text{Sales}}{\text{Total assets}}$	The fewer assets used to achieve a given level of sales, the more efficiently management is using the organization's total assets
Profitability	Profit margin on sales	$\dfrac{\text{Net profit after taxes}}{\text{Total sales}}$	Identifies the profits that are being generated
	Return on investment	$\dfrac{\text{Net profit after taxes}}{\text{Total assets}}$	Measures the efficiency of assets to generate profits

will analyze. Liquidity ratios measure an organization's ability to meet its current debt obligations. Leverage ratios examine the organization's use of debt to finance its assets and whether it's able to meet the interest payments on the debt. Activity ratios assess how efficiently a company is using its assets. Finally, profitability ratios measure how efficiently and effectively the company is using its assets to generate profits. These ratios are calculated using selected information from the organization's two primary financial statements (the balance sheet and the income statement) and are sometimes expressed as a percentage. Because you've probably studied these ratios in other accounting or finance courses, or will in the near future, we won't elaborate on how they're calculated. We mention them here to remind you that managers use such ratios as internal control tools.

Budgets are another type of financial control tool that are used for planning and controlling. When a budget is formulated, it's a planning tool because it indicates which work activities are important and what and how much resources should be allocated to those activities. Budgets are also used for controlling because they provide managers with quantitative standards against which to measure and compare resource consumption. If deviations are significant enough to require action, the manager examines what has happened and tries to uncover why. With this information, necessary action can be taken. For example, if you use a personal budget for monitoring and controlling your monthly expenses, you might find that one month your miscellaneous expenses were higher than you had budgeted for. At that point, you might cut back spending in another area or work extra hours to get more income.

HOW IS AN ORGANIZATION'S INFORMATION CONTROLLED?   Some 77 million accounts on Sony's PlayStation network were hacked, exposing those users to years of identity-theft risk. A computer with personal information (Social Security numbers, birth dates, etc.) on some 26.5 million military veterans stored on it was stolen from the residence of a Department of Veteran Affairs employee who had taken the computer home without authorization. Although the computer was eventually recovered with no loss of personal information, the situation could have been damaging to a large number of people. And these are just a few of the attacks on companies' information resources.[16] Talk about the need for information controls! Managers deal with information controls in two ways: (1) as a tool to help them control other organizational activities, and (2) as an organizational area they need to control.

Managers need the right information at the right time and in the right amount to help them *monitor and measure organizational activities*. In measuring actual performance, managers need information about what is happening within their area of responsibility and about the standards in order to be able to compare actual performance with the standard. They also rely on information to help them determine if deviations are acceptable. Finally, they rely on information to help them develop appropriate courses of action. Information *is* important! Most of the information tools that managers use come from the organization's management information system.

A **management information system (MIS)** is a system used to provide managers with needed information on a regular basis. In theory, this system can be manual or computer-based, although most organizations have moved to computer-supported applications. The term *system* in MIS implies order, arrangement, and purpose. Further, an MIS focuses specifically on providing managers with *information* (processed and analyzed data), not merely *data* (raw, unanalyzed facts). A library provides a good analogy. Although it can contain millions of volumes, a library doesn't do you any good if you can't find what you want quickly. That's why librarians spend a great deal of time cataloging a library's collections and ensuring that materials are returned to their proper locations. Organizations today are like well-stocked libraries with an abundance of data. What is lacking, however, is an ability to process that data so that the right information is available to the right person when he or she

feedback control	management information system (MIS)
Control that takes place after a work activity is done	A system used to provide management with needed information on a regular basis

Valery Sharifulin/Newscom

Cisco Systems, the global leader in networking equipment, uses a Balanced Scorecard approach in evaluating its performance. In addition to measuring performance in the financial, internal processes, and people/innovation/growth areas, Cisco developed a scorecard to address its commitment to customer satisfaction, a core value that drives the company's success. Each year Cisco sets goals for customer satisfaction and uses a customer loyalty measurement system to track its success with customers, such as Russia's mobile operator SkyLink shown here. Managers use the information they receive from annual customer satisfaction surveys to establish goals for each of Cisco's functional areas and for hiring and resource allocation decisions.

needs it. An MIS collects data and turns them into relevant information for managers to use.

It seems that every week, there's another news story about information security breaches. A recent survey found that 85 percent of privacy and security professionals acknowledged a reportable data breach occurred within their organizations within the last year alone.[17] Because information is critically important to everything an organization does, managers must have comprehensive and secure controls in place to *protect that information*. Such controls can range from data encryption to system firewalls to data backups, and other techniques as well.[18] Problems can lurk in places that an organization might not even have considered, like search engines. Sensitive, defamatory, confidential, or embarrassing organizational information has found its way into search engine results. For instance, detailed monthly expenses and employee salaries on the National Speleological Society's Web site turned up in a Google search.[19] Equipment such as laptop computers and even RFID (radio-frequency identification) tags are vulnerable to viruses and hacking. Needless to say, information controls should be monitored regularly to ensure that all possible precautions are in place to protect important information.

WHAT IS THE BALANCED SCORECARD APPROACH TO CONTROL? The balanced scorecard approach is a way to evaluate organizational performance from more than just the financial perspective.[20] A balanced scorecard typically looks at four areas that contribute to a company's performance: financial, customer, internal processes, and people/innovation/growth assets. According to this approach, managers should develop goals in each of the four areas and then measure whether the goals are being met.

Although a balanced scorecard makes sense, managers will tend to focus on areas that drive their organization's success and use scorecards that reflect those strategies.[21] For example, if strategies are customer-centered, then the customer area is likely to get more attention than the other three areas. Yet, you can't focus on measuring only one performance area because others are affected as well. For instance, at IBM Global Services in Houston, managers developed a scorecard around an overriding strategy of customer satisfaction. However, the other areas (financial, internal processes, and people/innovation/growth) support that central strategy. The division manager described it as follows, "The internal processes part of our business is directly related to responding to our customers in a timely manner, and the learning and innovation aspect is critical for us since what we're selling our customers above all is our expertise. Of course, how successful we are with those things will affect our financial component."[22]

WHAT CONTEMPORARY CONTROL ISSUES DO MANAGERS CONFRONT?

4 Discuss contemporary issues in control.

The employees of Integrated Information Systems Inc. didn't think twice about exchanging digital music over a dedicated office server they had set up. Like office betting on college and pro sports, it was technically illegal, but harmless, or so they thought. But after the company had to pay a $1 million settlement to the Recording Industry Association of America, managers wished they had controlled the situation better.[23] Control is an important managerial function. We're going to look at two control issues that managers face today: cross-cultural differences and workplace concerns.

Do Controls Need to Be Adjusted for Cultural Differences?

The concepts of control that we've discussed are appropriate for organizational units that aren't geographically distant or culturally distinct. But what about global organizations? Would control systems be different, and what should managers know about adjusting controls for national differences?

Methods of controlling employee behavior and operations can be quite different in different countries. In fact, the differences in organizational control systems of global organizations are primarily in the measurement and corrective action steps of the control process. In a global corporation, for instance, managers of foreign operations tend not to be closely controlled by the home office if for no other reason than that distance keeps managers from being able to observe work directly. Because distance creates a tendency for formalized controls, the home office of a global company often relies on extensive, formal reports for control. The global company may also use information technology to control work activities. For instance, Seven and i Holdings (Japan's biggest retail conglomerate and parent company of the 7-Eleven convenience store chain in the United States) uses automated cash registers not only to record sales and monitor inventory but also to schedule tasks for store managers and to track their use of the built-in analytical graphs and forecasts. If managers don't use them enough, they're told to increase their activities.[24]

Technology's impact on control is most evident in comparisons of technologically advanced nations with more primitive countries. Organizations in technologically advanced nations such as the United States, Japan, Canada, Great Britain, Germany, and Australia use indirect control devices—particularly computer-related reports and analyses—in addition to standardized rules and direct supervision to ensure that activities are going as planned. In less technologically advanced countries, direct supervision and highly centralized decision making are the basic means of control.

TECHNOLOGY
AND THE MANAGER'S JOB — MONITORING EMPLOYEES

Technological advances have made the process of managing an organization much easier.[25] But technological advancements have also provided employers a means of sophisticated employee monitoring. Although most of this monitoring is designed to enhance worker productivity, it could, and has been, a source of concern over worker privacy. These advantages bring with them difficult questions regarding what managers have the right to know about employees and how far they can go in controlling employee behavior, both on and off the job. Consider the following:

· The mayor of Colorado Springs, Colorado, reads the e-mail messages that city council members send to each other from their homes. He defended his actions by saying he was making sure that e-mails to each other were not being used to circumvent the state's "open meeting" law that requires most council business to be conducted publicly.

· The U.S. Internal Revenue Service's internal audit group monitors a computer log that shows employee access to taxpayers' accounts. This monitoring activity allows management to check and see what employees are doing on their computers.

· American Express has an elaborate system for monitoring telephone calls. Daily reports provided to supervisors detail the frequency and length of calls made by employees, as well as how quickly incoming calls are answered.

· Employers in several organizations require employees to wear badges at all times while on company premises. These badges contain a variety of data that allow employees to enter certain locations in the organization. Smart badges, too, can transmit where the employee is at all times!

Just how much control a company should have over the private lives of its employees also becomes an issue. Where should an employer's rules and controls end? Does the boss have the right to dictate what you do on your free time and in your own home? Could your boss keep you from engaging in riding a motorcycle, skydiving, smoking, drinking alcohol, or eating junk food? Again, the answers may surprise you. Today many organizations, in their quest to control safety and health insurance costs, are delving into their employees' private lives.

Although controlling employees' behaviors on and off the job may appear unjust or unfair, nothing in our legal system prevents employers from engaging in these practices. Rather, the law is based on the premise that if employees don't like the rules, they have the option of quitting. Managers, too, typically defend their actions in terms of ensuring quality, productivity, and proper employee behavior. For instance, an IRS audit of its southeastern regional offices found that 166 employees took unauthorized looks at the tax returns of friends, neighbors, and celebrities.

Think About:

· When does management's need for information about employee performance cross over the line and interfere with a worker's right to privacy?

· Is technology being misused?

· Is any action by management acceptable as long as employees are notified ahead of time that they will be monitored? What's your opinion?

---

balanced scorecard
A performance measurement tool that looks at more than just the financial perspective

Also, constraints on what corrective action managers can take may affect managers in foreign countries because laws in some countries do not allow managers the option of closing facilities, laying off employees, or bringing in a new management team from outside the country. Finally, another challenge for global companies in collecting data is comparability. For instance, a company's manufacturing facility in Mexico might produce the same products as a facility in Scotland. However, the Mexican facility might be much more labor intensive than its Scottish counterpart (to take advantage of lower labor costs in Mexico). If top-level executives were to control costs by, for example, calculating labor costs per unit or output per worker, the figures would not be comparable. Managers in global companies must address these types of global control challenges.

What Challenges Do Managers Face in Controlling the Workplace?

Today's workplaces present considerable control challenges for managers. From monitoring employees' computer usage at work to protecting the workplace against disgruntled employees intent on doing harm, managers need controls to ensure that work can be done efficiently and effectively as planned.

IS MY WORK COMPUTER REALLY MINE?   If you work, do you think you have a right to privacy at your job? What can your employer find out about you and your work? You might be surprised at the answers! Employers can (and do), among other things, read your e-mail (even those marked "personal or confidential"), tap your telephone, monitor your work by computer, store and review computer files, monitor you in an employee bathroom or dressing room, and track your whereabouts in a company vehicle. And these actions aren't that uncommon. In fact, some 30 percent of companies have fired workers for misusing the Internet and another 28 percent have terminated workers for e-mail misuse.[26]

Why do managers feel they need to monitor what employees are doing? A big reason is that employees are hired to work, not to surf the Web checking stock prices, watching online videos, playing fantasy baseball, or shopping for presents for family or friends. Recreational on-the-job Web surfing is thought to cost billions of dollars in lost work productivity annually. In fact, a survey of U.S. employers said that 87 percent of employees look at non-work-related Web sites while at work and more than half engage in personal Web site surfing every day.[27] Watching online video has become an increasingly serious problem not only because of the time being wasted by employees but because it clogs already-strained corporate computer networks.[28] If you had to guess the video site viewed most often at work, what would you guess? If you said YouTube, you'd be absolutely correct![29] However, as innocent as it may seem (after all, it may be just a 30-second video), all this nonwork adds up to significant costs to businesses.

Another reason that managers monitor employee e-mail and computer usage is that they don't want to risk being sued for creating a hostile workplace environment because of offensive messages or an inappropriate image displayed on a coworker's computer screen. Concerns about racial or sexual harassment are one reason companies might want to monitor or keep backup copies of all e-mail. Electronic records can help establish what actually happened so managers can react quickly.[30]

Finally, managers want to ensure that company secrets aren't being leaked.[31] In addition to typical e-mail and computer usage, companies are monitoring instant messaging, blogs, and other social media outlets, and banning phone cameras in the office. Managers need to be certain that employees are not, even inadvertently, passing information on to others who could use that information to harm the company.

Because of the potentially serious costs and given the fact that many jobs now entail computers, many companies have workplace monitoring policies. Such policies should control employee behavior in a nondemeaning way and employees should be informed about those policies.

IS EMPLOYEE THEFT ON THE RISE?   Would you be surprised to find that up to 85 percent of all organizational theft and fraud is committed by employees, not outsiders?[32] And it's a costly problem—estimated to be about $4,500 per worker per year.[33] In a recent survey of U.S. companies, 20 percent said that workplace theft has become a moderate to very big problem.[34]

Employee theft is defined as any unauthorized taking of company property by employees for their personal use.[35] It can range from embezzlement to fraudulent filing of expense reports to removing equipment, parts, software, or office supplies from company premises. Although retail businesses have long faced serious potential losses from employee theft, loose financial controls at start-ups and small companies and the ready availability of information technology have made employee stealing an escalating problem in all kinds and sizes of organizations. It's a control issue that managers need to educate themselves about and be prepared to deal with it.[36]

Why do employees steal? The answer depends on whom you ask.[37] Experts in various fields—industrial security, criminology, clinical psychology—have different perspectives. The industrial security people propose that people steal because the opportunity presents itself through lax controls and favorable circumstances. Criminologists say that it's because people have financial-based pressures (such as personal financial problems) or vice-based pressures (such as gambling debts). And the clinical psychologists suggest that people steal because they can rationalize whatever they're doing as being correct and appropriate behavior ("everyone does it," "they had it coming," "this company makes enough money and they'll never miss anything this small," "I deserve this for all that I put up with," and so forth).[38] Although each approach provides compelling insights into employee theft and has been instrumental in attempts to deter it, unfortunately, employees continue to steal. What can managers do?

The concept of feedforward, concurrent, and feedback control is useful for identifying measures to deter or reduce employee theft.[39] Exhibit 7 summarizes several possible managerial actions.

Autumn Cruz/Newscom

A growing number of employee thieves sell their stolen property on auction sites like eBay. For example, a former purchasing agent for California's state Department of Child Support Services was charged with embezzlement, grand theft, and possession of stolen property for stealing $320,000 in taxpayer money with a state-issued credit card that had no spending limit and no pre-approval required for purchases. The employee bought household items shown here for her own use or resold them on eBay and used the money to buy expensive items like the Lexus sports car. After filing an unusually large number of expenses, the employee's activity triggered a state audit that led to her arrest. To deter and reduce theft, the child services agency now requires pre-approval for employee purchases and has hired two internal auditors.

WHAT CAN MANAGERS DO ABOUT WORKPLACE VIOLENCE? A truck driver for a beer and wine distributor facing dismissal fatally shot eight coworkers outside Hartford, Connecticut, on August 3, 2010. On July 12, 2010, a man opened fire at his former company in Albuquerque, killing two people and wounding four others before fatally shooting himself. On November 5, 2009, at Fort Hood, Texas, an Army psychiatrist fatally shot 13 people and injured 32. On June 25, 2008, in Henderson, Kentucky, an employee at a plastics plant returned hours after arguing with his supervisor over his not wearing safety goggles and for using his cell phone while working on the assembly line. He shot and killed the supervisor, four other coworkers, and himself. In April 2007, the same month in which the Virginia Tech shootings occurred, a gunman at his former workplace in Troy, Michigan, and one at NASA in Houston shot and killed a person. On January 30, 2006, a former employee who was once removed from a Santa Barbara, California, postal facility because of "strange behavior" came back and shot five workers to death, critically wounded another, and killed herself. On January 26, 2005, an autoworker at a Jeep plant in Toledo, Ohio, who had met the day before with plant managers about a problem with his work, came in and killed a supervisor and wounded two other employees before killing himself.[40] Is workplace violence really an issue for managers? Yes. The latest data

---

employee theft
Any unauthorized taking of company property by employees for their personal use

EXHIBIT 7   Controlling Employee Theft

FEEDFORWARD	CONCURRENT	FEEDBACK
Engage in careful prehiring screening.	Treat employees with respect and dignity.	Make sure employees know when theft or fraud has occurred—not naming names but letting people know that these incidents are not acceptable.
Establish specific policies defining theft, fraud, and discipline procedures.	Openly communicate the costs of stealing.	Use the services of professional investigators.
Involve employees in writing policies.	Let employees know on a regular basis about their successes in preventing theft and fraud.	Redesign control measures.
Educate and train employees about the policies.	Use video surveillance equipment if conditions warrant.	Evaluate your organization's culture and the relationships of managers and employees.
Have professionals review your internal security controls.	Install "lock out" options on computers, telephones, and e-mail.	
	Use corporate hotlines for reporting incidences.	
	Set a good example.	

Sources: Based on A. H. Bell and D. M. Smith, "Protecting the Company Against Theft and Fraud," *Workforce Online,* www.workforce.com (December 3, 2000); J. D. Hansen, "To Catch a Thief," *Journal of Accountancy* (March 2000), pp. 43–46; and J. Greenberg, "The Cognitive Geometry of Employee Theft," in *Dysfunctional Behavior in Organizations: Nonviolent and Deviant Behavior* (Stamford, CT: JAI Press, 1998), pp. 147–193.

available (2009) showed that 12 percent of work-related deaths in the United States were workplace homicides.[41] But workplace violence doesn't just include homicides. The U.S. National Institute of Occupational Safety and Health says that each year, some 2 million American workers are victims of some form of workplace violence such as verbal abuse, yelling at coworkers, purposeful damage of machines or furniture, or assaulting coworkers. In an average week, one employee is killed and at least 25 are seriously injured in violent assaults by current or former coworkers. According to a Department of Labor survey, 58 percent of firms reported that managers received verbal threats from workers.[42] Anger, rage, and violence in the workplace are intimidating to coworkers and adversely affect their productivity. The annual cost to U.S. businesses is estimated to be between $20 and $35 billion.[43] And office rage isn't a uniquely American problem. A survey of aggressive behaviors in Europe's workplaces found that between 5 percent and 20 percent of European workers are affected by workplace violence.[44]

What factors are believed to contribute to workplace violence? Undoubtedly, employee stress caused by job uncertainties, declining value of retirement accounts, long hours, information overload, other daily interruptions, unrealistic deadlines, and uncaring managers play a role. Even office layout designs with small cubicles where employees work amidst the noise and commotion from those around them have been cited as contributing to the problem.[45] Other experts have described dangerously dysfunctional work environments characterized by the following as primary contributors to the problem:[46]

- Employee work driven by TNC (time, numbers, and crises)
- Rapid and unpredictable change where instability and uncertainty plague employees
- Destructive communication style where managers communicate in excessively aggressive, condescending, explosive, or passive-aggressive styles; excessive workplace teasing or scapegoating
- Authoritarian leadership with a rigid, militaristic mind-set of managers versus employees; employees not allowed to challenge ideas, participate in decision making, or engage in team-building efforts

Swedish furniture retailer IKEA has raised its security level at all of its stores throughout Europe following explosions caused by bombs at stores in Germany, France, Belgium, and the Netherlands. Store managers evacuated the stores after the explosions, and bomb-sniffing dogs searched the stores. The explosions intimidated employees and customers, although they did not seriously injure anyone. As a safety precaution to make employees and shoppers feel safer, IKEA put extra security guards in its stores, established other security measures not divulged, and closely monitored police investigations to determine a motive for the violence.

Ilvy Njiokiktjien/Newscom

EXHIBIT 8	Controlling Workplace Violence	
FEEDFORWARD	**CONCURRENT**	**FEEDBACK**
Ensure management's commitment to functional, not dysfunctional, work environments.	Use MBWA (managing by walking around) to identify potential problems; observe how employees treat and interact with each other.	Communicate openly about violent incidents and what's being done.
Provide employee assistance programs (EAPs) to help employees with behavioral problems.	Allow employees or work groups to "grieve" during periods of major organizational change.	Investigate incidents and take appropriate action.
Enforce organizational policy that any workplace rage, aggression, or violence will not be tolerated.	Be a good role model in how you treat others.	Review company policies and change, if necessary.
Use careful prehiring screening.	Use corporate hotlines or some other mechanism for reporting and investigating incidents.	
Never ignore threats.	Use quick and decisive intervention.	
Train employees about how to avoid danger if a situation arises.	Get expert professional assistance if violence erupts.	
Clearly communicate policies to employees.	Provide necessary equipment or procedures for dealing with violent situations (cell phones, alarm system, code names or phrases, and so forth).	

Sources: Based on M. Gorkin, "Five Strategies and Structures for Reducing Workplace Violence," *Workforce Management Online,* December 3, 2000; "Investigating Workplace Violence: Where Do You Start?" *Workforce Management Online,* December 3, 2000; "Ten Tips on Recognizing and Minimizing Violence," *Workforce Management Online,* December 3, 2000; and "Points to Cover in a Workplace Violence Policy," *Workforce Management Online,* December 3, 2000.

- Defensive attitude with little or no performance feedback given; only numbers count; and yelling, intimidation, or avoidance as the preferred ways of handling conflict
- Double standards in terms of policies, procedures, and training opportunities for managers and employees
- Unresolved grievances due to an absence of mechanisms or only adversarial ones in place for resolving them; dysfunctional individuals protected or ignored because of long-standing rules, union contract provisions, or reluctance to take care of problems
- Emotionally troubled employees and no attempt by managers to get help for these people
- Repetitive, boring work and little chance for doing something else or for new people coming in
- Faulty or unsafe equipment or deficient training, which keeps employees from being able to work efficiently or effectively
- Hazardous work environment in terms of temperature, air quality, repetitive motions, overcrowded spaces, noise levels, excessive overtime, and so forth; to minimize costs, a failure to hire additional employees when workload becomes excessive leading to potentially dangerous work expectations and conditions
- Culture of violence perpetuated by a history of individual violence or abuse, violent or explosive role models, or tolerance of on-the-job alcohol or drug abuse

Reading through this list, you surely hope that workplaces where you'll spend your professional life won't be like this. However, the competitive demands of succeeding in a 24/7 global economy put pressure on organizations and employees in many ways.

What can managers do to deter or reduce possible workplace violence? Once again, the concept of feedforward, concurrent, and feedback control can help identify actions that managers can take.[47] Exhibit 8 summarizes several suggestions.

Review

1 **Explain the nature and importance of control.** Control is the management function that involves monitoring activities to ensure that they're being accomplished as planned and correcting any significant deviations.

As the final step in the management process, controlling provides the link back to planning. If managers didn't control, they'd have no way of knowing whether goals were being met.

Control is important because (1) it's the only way to know whether goals are being met and, if not, why; (2) it provides information and feedback so managers feel comfortable empowering employees; and (3) it helps protect an organization and its assets.

2 **Describe the three steps in the control process.** The three steps in the control process are measuring, comparing, and taking action. Measuring involves deciding how to measure actual performance and what to measure. Comparing involves looking at the variation between actual performance and the standard (goal). Deviations outside an acceptable range of variation need attention.

Taking action can involve doing nothing, correcting the actual performance, or revising the standards. Doing nothing is self-explanatory. Correcting the actual performance can involve different corrective actions, which can either be immediate or basic. Standards can be revised by either raising or lowering them.

3 **Discuss the types of controls organizations and managers use.** Feedforward controls take place before a work activity is done. Concurrent controls take place while a work activity is being done. Feedback controls take place after a work activity is done.

Financial controls that managers can use include financial ratios (liquidity, leverage, activity, and profitability) and budgets. One information control managers can use is an MIS, which provides managers with needed information on a regular basis. Others include comprehensive and secure controls, such as data encryption, system firewalls, data backups, and so forth, that protect the organization's information. Also, balanced scorecards provide a way to evaluate an organization's performance in four different areas rather than just from the financial perspective.

4 **Discuss contemporary issues in control.** Adjusting controls for cross-cultural differences may be needed primarily in the areas of measuring and taking corrective actions.

Workplace concerns include workplace privacy, employee theft, and workplace violence. For each of these, managers need to have policies in place to control inappropriate actions and ensure that work is getting done efficiently and effectively.

MyManagementLab   For more resources, please visit www.mymanagementlab.com

---

UNDERSTANDING THE CHAPTER

1. What is the role of control in management?
2. Describe four methods managers can use to acquire information about actual work performance.
3. How are planning and control linked? Is the control function linked to the organizing and leading functions of management? Explain.
4. Contrast feedforward, concurrent, and feedback controls.
5. Why do you think feedback control is the most popular type of control? Justify your response.
6. Consider the "white-water rapids" view of change. Do you think it's possible to establish and maintain effective standards and controls in this type of environment? Discuss.
7. Why is it that what is measured is more critical to the control process than how it is measured?
8. "Every individual employee in an organization plays a role in controlling work activities." Do you agree with this statement, or do you think control is something that only managers are responsible for? Explain.

9. What are some work activities in which the acceptable range of variation might be higher than average? What about lower than average? (Hint: Think in terms of the output from the work activities, who it might affect, and how it might affect them.)

10. How could you use the concept of control in your personal life? Be specific. (Think in terms of feedforward, concurrent, and feedback controls as well as specific controls for the different aspects of your life—school, work, family relationships, friends, hobbies, etc.)

Endnotes

1. P. Elkind and D. Whitford, "An Accident Waiting to Happen," *Fortune,* February 7, 2011, pp. 105–132; G. Chazan, "BP's Safety Drive Faces Rough Road," *Wall Street Journal,* February 1, 2011, pp. A1+; C. Hausman, "Report Says Lack of Oversight Contributed to the Gulf Spill Disaster," *Ethics Newsline Online,* January 11, 2011; B. Casselman, "Supervisor Says Flaw Was Found in Key Safety Device," *Wall Street Journal,* July 21, 2010, pp. A6; R. Gold, "Rig's Final Hours Probed," *Wall Street Journal,* July 19, 2010, pp. A1+; S. Lyall, "In BP's Record, a History of Boldness and Costly Blunders," *New York Times Online,* July 12, 2010; B. Casselman and R. Gold, "Unusual Decisions Set Stage for BP Disaster," *Wall Street Journal,* May 27, 2010, pp. A1+; H. Fountain and T. Zeller, Jr., "Panel Suggests Signs of Trouble Before Rig Explosion," *New York Times Online,* May 25, 2010; and R. Gold and N. King Jr., "The Gulf Oil Spill: Red Flags Were Ignored Aboard Doomed Rig," *Wall Street Journal,* May 13, 2010, p. A6.

2. "Domino's Delivered Free Pizzas," *Springfield, Missouri News-Leader,* April 3, 2009, p. 3B.

3. Right or Wrong box based on T. Harbert, "When IT Is Asked to Spy," *Computerworld,* October 11, 2010, pp. 14–20; D. M. Amato-McCoy, "The, 'Not-So-Sweet' Side of Retail Loss," *Chain Store Age,* July 2009, pp. 38–39; A. Vanacore, "Cameras Scan Store Lines for 'Sweethearting,'" Associated Press, *Springfield, Missouri News-Leader,* May 11, 2009, p. 9A; L. Lewis, "Adios, Sweetheart," *Stores Magazine,* January 2009, pp. 72–74; and J. Tarnowski, "Good Night, Sweethearting," *Progressive Grocer,* May 1, 2008, p. 126.

4. B. Hagenbaugh, "State Quarter's Extra Leaf Grew Out of Lunch Break," *USA Today,* January 20, 2006, p. 1B.

5. J. F. Van Niekerk and R. Von Solms, "Information Security Culture: A Management Perspective," *Computers & Security,* June 2010, pp. 476–486; T. Vinas and J. Jusko "5 Threats That Could Sink Your Company," *Industry Week,* September 2004, pp. 52–61; "Workplace Security: How Vulnerable Are You?" Special section in *Wall Street Journal,* September 29, 2003, pp. R1–R8; P. Magnusson, "Your Jitters Are Their Lifeblood," *Business Week,* April 14, 2003, p. 41; and T. Purdum, "Preparing for the Worst," *Industry Week,* January 2003, pp. 53–55.

6. A. Dalton, "Rapid Recovery," *Industry Week,* March 2005, pp. 70–71.

7. B. Nelson, "Long-Distance Recognition," *Workforce,* August 2000, pp. 50–52.

8. S. Kerr, "On the Folly of Rewarding A, While Hoping for B," *Academy of Management Journal* (December 1975), pp. 769–783; and N. F. Piercy, D. W. Cravens, N. Lane, and D. W. Vorhies, "Driving Organizational Citizenship Behaviors and Salesperson In-Role Behavior Performance: The Role of Management Control and Perceived Organizational Support," *Journal of the Academy of Marketing Science* (Spring 2006), pp. 244–262.

9. From the Past to the Present box based on H. Min and H. Min, "Benchmarking the Service Quality of Fast-Food Restaurant Franchises in the USA," *Benchmarking: An International Journal* (April 2011), pp. 282–300; R. Pear, "A.M.A. to Develop Measure of Quality of Medical Care," *New York Times Online,* February 21, 2006; and A. Taylor III, "Double Duty," *Fortune,* March 7, 2005, pp. 104–110; C. Bogan and D. Callahan, "Benchmarking in Rapid Time," *Industrial Management,* March–April 2001, pp. 28–33; and L. D. McNary, "Thinking About Excellence and Benchmarking," *Journal for Quality and Participation* (July–August 1994).

10. And the Survey Says box based on J. Yang and P. Trap, "Participating in Office Pools," *USA Today,* April 5, 2010, p. 1B; J. Yang and S. Parker, "Unproductive Work Hours Cost Billions," *USA Today,* September 29, 2009, p. 1B; M. Leone, "Something Wicked This Way Comes," *CFO,* June 2010, pp. 14–15; "Light–Fingered Employees Lift Laptops, Hardware," *Workforce Management Online,* July 22, 2008; J. Casale, "Data Breach Threats from Within Growing," *Workforce Management Online,* April 2009; M. Conlin, "To Catch a Corporate Thief," *BusinessWeek,* February 16, 2009, p. 52; A. R. Carey and S. Ward, "Have a Boss Who Plays Games at Work?" *USA Today,* May 6, 2009, p. 1A; and S. L. Mintz, "The Gauge of Innocence," *CFO,* April 2009, pp. 52–57.

11. H. Koontz and R. W. Bradspies, "Managing Through Feedforward Control," *Business Horizons,* June 1972, pp. 25–36.

12. M. Helft, "The Human Hands Behind the Google Money Machine," *New York Times Online,* June 2, 2008.

13. B. Caulfield, "Shoot to Kill," *Forbes,* January 7, 2008, pp. 92–96.

14. T. Laseter and L. Laseter, "See for Yourself," *Strategy+Business,* www.strategy-business.com (November 29, 2007).

15. W. H. Newman, *Constructive Control: Design and Use of Control Systems* (Upper Saddle River, NJ: Prentice Hall, 1975), p. 33.

16. B. Molina and M. Snider, "PlayStation Breach Called One of the Largest Ever," *USA Today,* April 28, 2011, p. 2B; and D. Stout and T. Zeller Jr., "Vast Data Cache About Veterans Has Been Stolen," *New York Times Online,* May 23, 2006.

17. Deloitte & Touche and the Ponemon Institute, "Research Report: Reportable and Multiple Privacy Breaches Rising at Alarming Rate," *Ethics Newsline,* http://ethicsnewsline.wordpress.com (January 1, 2008).

18. B. Grow, K. Epstein, and C-C. Tschang, "The New E-Spionage Threat," *Business Week,* April 21, 2008, pp. 32–41; S. Leibs, "Firewall of Silence," *CFO,* April 2008, pp. 31–35; J. Pereira, "How Credit-Card Data Went Out Wireless Door," *Wall Street Journal,* May 4, 2007, pp. A1+; and B. Stone, "Firms Fret as Office E-Mail Jumps Security Walls," *New York Times Online,* January 11, 2007.

19. D. Whelan, "Google Me Not," *Forbes,* August 16, 2004, pp. 102–104.

20. E. R. Iselin, J. Sands, and L. Mia, "Multi-Perspective Performance Reporting Systems, Continuous Improvement Systems, and Organizational Performance," *Journal of General Management* (Spring 2011), pp. 19–36; L. Elmore, "The Balanced Business," *Women in Business,* Spring 2011, pp. 14–16; D. Agostino and M. Arnaboldi, "How the BSC Implementation Process Shapes Its Outcome," *International Journal of Productivity & Performance Management* (January 2011), pp. 99–114; R. S. Kaplan and D. P. Norton, "How to Implement a New Strategy Without Disrupting Your Organization," *Harvard Business Review,* March 2006, pp. 100–109; L. Bassi and D. McMurrer, "Developing Measurement Systems for Managers in the Knowledge Era," *Organizational Dynamics,* May 2005, pp. 185–196; G. M. J. DeKoning, "Making the Balanced Scorecard Work (Part 1)," *Gallup Brain,* www.brain.gallup.com (July 8, 2004); G. M. J. DeKoning, "Making the Balanced Scorecard Work (Part 2)," *Gallup Brain,* www.brain.gallup.com (August 12, 2004); K. Graham, "Balanced Scorecard," *New Zealand Management,* March 2003, pp. 32–34; K. Ellis, "A Ticket to Ride: Balanced Scorecard," *Training* (April 2001), p. 50; and T. Leahy, "Tailoring the Balanced Scorecard," *Business Finance,* August 2000, pp. 53–56.

21. J. B. Butler, S. C. Henderson, and C. Raiborn, "Sustainability and the Balanced Scorecard: Integrating Green Measures into Business Reporting," *Management Accounting Quarterly,* Winter 2011, pp. 1–10; T. L. Gonzalez-Padron, B. R. Chabowski, G. T. M. Hult, and D. J. Ketchen, "Knowledge Management and Balanced Scorecard Outcomes: Exploring the Importance of Interpretation, Learning, and Internationality," *British Journal of Management* (December 2010), pp. 967–982; and T. Leahy, "Tailoring the Balanced Scorecard."

22. T. Leahy, "Tailoring the Balanced Scorecard."

23. J. Yaukey and C. L. Romero, "Arizona Firm Pays Big for Workers' Digital Downloads," Associated Press, *Springfield, Missouri, News-Leader,* May 6, 2002, p. 6B.

24. Information on Hoovers Online, www.hoovers.com (June 17, 2011); and N. Shirouzu and J. Bigness, "7-Eleven Operators Resist System to Monitor Managers," *Wall Street Journal,* June 16, 1997, p. B1.

25. Technology and the Manager's Job box based on C. A. Ciocchetti, "The Eavesdropping Employer: A Twenty-First-Framework for Employee Monitoring," *American Business Law Journal* (Summer 2011), pp. 285–369;

G. M. Amsler, H. M. Findley, and E. Ingram, "Performance Monitoring: Guidance for the Modern Workplace," *Supervision,* January 2011, pp. 16–22; T. Harbert, "When IT Is Asked to Spy"; D. Searcey, "Employers Watching Workers Online Spurs Privacy Debate," *Wall Street Journal,* April 23, 2009, p. A13; D. Darlin, "Software That Monitors Your Work, Wherever You Are," *New York Times Online,* April 12, 2009; S. Boehle, "They're Watching You," *Training* (September 2008), pp. 23+; S. Shellenbarger, "Work at Home? Your Employer May Be Watching You," *Wall Street Journal,* July 30, 2008, p. D1+; J. Jusko, "A Watchful Eye," *Industry Week,* May 7, 2001, p. 9; "Big Brother Boss," *U.S. News and World Report,* April 30, 2001, p. 12; and L. Guernsey, "You've Got Inappropriate E-Mail," *New York Times,* April 5, 2000, pp. C1+.

26. "2007 Electronic Monitoring & Surveillance Survey," *American Management Association,* www.amanet.org.

27. S. Armour, "Companies Keep an Eye on Workers' Internet Use," *USA Today,* February 21, 2006, p. 2B.

28. B. White, "The New Workplace Rules: No Video-Watching," *Wall Street Journal,* March 4, 2008, pp. B1+.

29. Ibid.

30. N. Lugaresi, "Electronic Privacy in the Workplace: Transparency and Responsibility," *International Review of Law, Computers, & Technology,* July 2010, pp. 163–173; P-W Tam, E. White, N. Wingfield, and K. Maher, "Snooping E-Mail by Software Is Now a Workplace Norm," *Wall Street Journal,* March 9, 2005, pp. B1+; D. Hawkins, "Lawsuits Spur Rise in Employee Monitoring," *U.S. News & World Report,* August 13, 2001, p. 53; and L. Guernsey, "You've Got Inappropriate Mail," *New York Times,* April 5, 2000, pp. C1+.

31. S. Armour, "More Companies Keep Track of Workers' E-Mail," *USA Today,* June 13, 2005, p. 4B; and E. Bott, "Are You Safe? Privacy Special Report," *PC Computing,* March 2000, pp. 87–88.

32. A. M. Bell and D. M. Smith, "Theft and Fraud May Be an Inside Job," *Workforce Online,* www.workforce.com (December 3, 2000).

33. C. C. Verschoor, "New Evidence of Benefits from Effective Ethics Systems," *Strategic Finance,* May 2003, pp. 20–21; and E. Krell, "Will Forensic Accounting Go Mainstream?" *Business Finance,* October 2002, pp. 30–34.

34. B. Mirza, "Combat Costly Discrimination, Employee Fraud, Theft," *HR Magazine,* February 2011, p. 14; and S. E. Needleman, "Businesses Say Theft by Their Workers Is Up," *Wall Street Journal,* December 11, 2008, p. B8.

35. J. Greenberg, "The STEAL Motive: Managing the Social Determinants of Employee Theft," in R. Giacalone and J. Greenberg (eds.), *Antisocial Behavior in Organizations* (Newbury Park, CA: Sage, 1997), pp. 85–108.

36. M. S. Hershcovis, "Incivility, Social Undermining, Bullying . . . Oh My! A Call to Reconcile Constructs Within Workplace Aggression Research," *Journal of Organizational Behavior* (April 2011), pp. 499–519; B. E. Litzky, K. A. Eddleston, and D. L. Kidder, "The Good, the Bad, and the Misguided: How Managers Inadvertently Encourage Deviant Behaviors," *Academy of Management Perspective,* February 2006, pp. 91–103; "Crime Spree," *BusinessWeek,* September 9, 2002, p. 8; B. P. Niehoff and R. J. Paul, "Causes of Employee Theft and Strategies That HR Managers Can Use for Prevention," *Human Resource Management,* Spring 2000, pp. 51–64; and G. Winter, "Taking at the Office Reaches New Heights: Employee Larceny Is Bigger and Bolder," *New York Times,* July 12, 2000, pp. C1+.

37. This section is based on J. Greenberg, *Behavior in Organizations,* 10th ed. (Upper Saddle River, NJ: Prentice Hall, 2011).

38. A. H. Bell and D. M. Smith, "Why Some Employees Bite the Hand That Feeds Them," *Workforce Online,* www.workforce.com (December 3, 2000).

39. B. E. Litzky et al., "The Good, the Bad, and the Misguided"; A. H. Bell and D. M. Smith, "Protecting the Company Against Theft and Fraud"; J. D. Hansen, "To Catch a Thief," *Journal of Accountancy* (March 2000), pp. 43–46; and J. Greenberg, "The Cognitive Geometry of Employee Theft," in *Dysfunctional Behavior in Organizations: Nonviolent and Deviant Behavior* (Stamford, CT: JAI Press, 1998), pp. 147–193.

40. L. Waldman and T. El-Ghobashy, "Work Shooting Kills Nine," *Wall Street Journal,* August 4, 2010, p. A3; D. Leinwand, "Shooter Kills Two, Then Self at N.M. Plant," *USA Today,* July 13, 2010, p. 3A; R. Lenz, "Gunman Kills Five, Himself at Plant," *Associated Press, Springfield, Missouri, News-Leader,* June 26, 2008, p. 6A; S. Oppermann, "Violence in the Workplace: Is Your Agency Prepared?" *FedSmith,* www.fedsmith.com (May 30, 2007); CBS News, "Former Postal Worker Kills 5, Herself," www.cbsnews.com/stories (January 31, 2006); CBS News, and "Autoworker's Grudge Turns Deadly," www.cbsnews.com/stories (January 27, 2005).

41. L. D. Lieber, "HR's Role in Preventing Workplace Violence," *Employment Relations Today (Wiley),* Winter 2011, pp. 83–88.

42. J. McCafferty, "Verbal Chills," *CFO,* June 2005, p. 17; S. Armour, "Managers Not Prepared for Workplace Violence," July 15, 2004, pp. 1B+; and "Workplace Violence," OSHA Fact Sheet, U.S. Department of Labor, Occupational Safety and Health Administration, 2002.

43. "Ten Tips on Recognizing and Minimizing Violence," *Workforce Online,* www.workforce.com (December 3, 2000).

44. "Research News Round-Up," *Occupational Health,* April 2011, p. 12.

45. C. Cosh, "Keep a Close Eye Out for the Signs," *Macleans,* December 27, 2010, p. 24; and R. McNatt, "Desk Rage," *BusinessWeek,* November 27, 2000, p. 12.

46. M. Gorkin, "Key Components of a Dangerously Dysfunctional Work Environment," *Workforce Online,* www.workforce.com (December 3, 2000).

47. L. D. Lieber, "HR's Role in Preventing Workplace Violence"; C. Cosh, "Keep a Close Eye Out for the Signs"; "Ten Tips on Recognizing and Minimizing Violence"; A. C. Klotz and M. R. Buckley, "Where Everybody Knows Your Name: Lessons from Small Business About Preventing Workplace Violence," *Business Horizons,* November 2010, pp. 571–579; M. Gorkin, "Five Strategies and Structures for Reducing Workplace Violence"; "Investigating Workplace Violence: Where Do You Start?"; and "Points to Cover in a Workplace Violence Policy," all of these are articles from *Workforce Online,* www.workforce.com (December 3, 2000).

YOUR TURN TO BE A MANAGER

Foundations of Control

Skill Development: Dealing with Difficult People

Almost all managers will, at one time or another, have to deal with people who are difficult. There is no shortage of characteristics that can make someone difficult to work with. Some examples include short-tempered, demanding, abusive, angry, defensive, complaining, intimidating, aggressive, narcissistic, arrogant, and rigid. Successful managers have learned how to cope with difficult people.

Personal Insights: How Good Am I at Disciplining Others?

This instrument contains eight disciplining practices. For each statement, select the answer that best describes you. Remember to respond as you *have* behaved or *would* behave, not as you think you *should* behave. If you have no managerial experience, answer the statements assuming you are a manager. Use the following scale to express your response:

> **1** = Usually
> **2** = Sometimes
> **3** = Seldom

When disciplining an employee:

1. I provide ample warning before taking formal action.	1 2 3
2. I wait for a pattern of infractions before calling it to the employee's attention.	1 2 3
3. Even after repeated offenses, I prefer informal discussion about correcting the problem rather than formal disciplinary action.	1 2 3
4. I delay confronting the employee about an infraction until his or her performance-appraisal review.	1 2 3
5. In discussing an infraction with the employee, my style and tone are serious.	1 2 3
6. I explicitly seek to allow the employee to explain his or her position.	1 2 3
7. I remain impartial in allocating punishment.	1 2 3
8. I allocate stronger penalties for repeated offenses.	1 2 3

Source: S. P. Robbins, *Training in Interpersonal Skills: TIPS for Managing People at Work* (Upper Saddle River, NJ: Prentice Hall, 1989), pp. 104–105.

Analysis and Interpretation

This instrument is based on the literature defining preferred discipline techniques. It is not a precise tool but it will give you some insights into how effective you might be in practicing discipline in the workplace.

To calculate your score, add up the points for questions 2, 3, and 4. For the other 5 questions (1, 5, 6, 7 and 8), reverse score them by giving a "1" response 3 points and a "3" response 1 point.

Your score on this test will range from 8 to 24. A score of 22 or higher indicates excellent skills at disciplining. You understand that effective discipline recognizes the need to provide ample warning, act in a timely fashion, use a calm and serious tone, be specific about the problem, keep the process impersonal, and that disciplinary action should be progressive and consider mitigating circumstances. Scores in the 19 to 21 range suggest some deficiencies. Scores below 19 indicate considerable room for improvement.

Skill Basics

No single approach is always effective in dealing with difficult people. However, we can offer several suggestions that are likely to lessen the angst these people create in your life and may have some influence in reducing their difficult behavior.

Don't let your emotions rule. Our first response to a difficult person is often emotional. We get angry. We show frustration. We want to lash out at them or "get even" when we think they've insulted or demeaned us. This response is not likely to reduce your angst and may escalate the other person's negative behavior. So fight your natural tendencies and keep your cool. Stay rational and thoughtful. At worst, while this approach may not improve the situation, it is also unlikely to encourage and escalate the undesirable behavior.

Attempt to limit contact. If possible, try to limit your contact with the difficult person. Avoid places where they hang out and limit nonrequired interactions. Also, use communication channels—like e-mail and text messaging—that minimize face-to-face contact and verbal intonations.

Try polite confrontation. If you can't avoid the difficult person, consider standing up to them in a civil but firm manner. Let them know that you're aware of their behavior, that you find it unacceptable, and that you won't tolerate it. For people who are unaware of the effect their actions have on you, confrontation might awaken them to altering their behavior. For those who are acting purposefully, taking a clear stand might make them think twice about the consequences of their actions.

Practice positive reinforcement. We know that positive reinforcement is a powerful tool for changing behavior. Rather than criticizing undesirable behavior, try reinforcing desirable behaviors with compliments or other positive comments. This focus will tend to weaken and reduce the exhibiting of the undesirable behaviors.

Recruit fellow victims and witnesses. Finally, we know strength lies in numbers. If you can get others who are also offended by the difficult person to support your case, several positive things can happen. First, it's likely to lessen your frustrations because others will be confirming your perception and can offer support. Second, people in the organization with authority to reprimand are more likely to act when complaints are coming from multiple sources. And third, the difficult person is more likely to feel pressure to change when a group is speaking out against his or her specific behaviors than if the complaint is coming from a single source.

Based on N. Pelusi, "Dealing with Difficult People," *Psychology Today,* September–October 2006, pp. 68–69; and R. I. Sutton, *The No Asshole Rule: Building a Civilized Workplace and Surviving One That Isn't* (New York: Business Plus, 2007).

Skill Application

Your career has progressed even faster than you thought possible. After graduating from college with an accounting degree, you passed your CPA exam and worked three years for a major accounting firm. Then you joined General Electric in their finance department. Two employers and four jobs later, you have just been hired by a *Fortune* 100 mining company as their vice president for finance. What you didn't expect in the new job was having to deal with Mark Hundley.

Mark is the vice president of company operations. He has been with the company for eight years. Your first impression of Mark was that he was a "know-it-all." He was quick to put you down and acted as if he was your superior rather than an equal. Based on comments you've heard around the offices, it seems you are not alone. Other executives all seemed to agree that Mark is a brilliant engineer and operations manager but very difficult to work with. Specific comments you've heard include "an abrasive attitude"; "talks down to people"; "arrogant"; "thinks everyone is stupid"; and "poor listener."

In your short time in the new job, you've already had several run-ins with Mark. You've even talked to your boss, the company president, about him. The president's response wasn't surprising: "Mark isn't easy to deal with. But no one knows this company's operations like he does. If he ever leaves, I don't know how we'd replace him. But, that said, he gives me a lot of grief. Sometimes he makes me feel like I work for him rather than the other way around."

What could you do to improve your ability to work with Mark?

Skill Practice

1. Talk with a manager at three different organizations. Ask each what guidance, if any, they've received from their organizations in terms of dealing with difficult colleagues. Have them describe specific problems they've faced and how they've handled them.

2. Think of a recent experience you've had with a person who is difficult to work or interact with. How did you handle the situation? How effective was your approach? What could you have done differently to improve the outcome?

Skill Development: Providing Feedback

A part of every manager's job is providing performance feedback. Although this often takes place once or twice a year, during an employee's performance review, good managers provide performance feedback to employees on a continuing basis.

Personal Insights: How Good Am I at Giving Performance Feedback?

For each of the following pairs, identify the statement that most closely matches what you *normally* do when you give feedback to someone else on their job performance.

1. a. Describe the behavior
   b. Evaluate the behavior

2. a. Focus on the feelings that the behavior evokes
   b. Tell the person what they should be doing differently

3. a. Give specific instances of the behavior
   b. Generalize

4. a. Deal only with behavior that the person can control
   b. Sometimes focus on something the person can do nothing about

5. a. Tell the person as soon as possible after the behavior
   b. Sometimes wait too long

6. a. Focus on the effect the behavior has on me
   b. Try to figure out why the individual did what he or she did

7. a. Balance negative feedback with positive feedback
   b. Sometimes focus only on the negative

8. a. Do some soul searching to make sure that the reason I am giving the feedback is to help the other person or to strengthen our relationship
   b. Sometimes give feedback to punish, win against, or dominate the other person

Source: Adapted from L. A. Mainiero and C. L. Tromley, *Developing Managerial Skills in Organizational Behavior*, 2nd ed. (Englewood Cliffs, NJ: Prentice Hall, 1994), pp. 125–126. With permission.

Analysis and Interpretation

This instrument is designed to assess how good you are at providing performance feedback. To calculate your score, add up how many "a" responses you totaled. Do the same for "b" responses.

The "a" responses are your self-perceived strengths and the "b" responses are your self-perceived weaknesses. By looking at the proportion of your "a" and "b" responses, you will be able to see how effective you feel you are when giving performance feedback and determine where your strengths and weaknesses lie. For instance, an a:b ratio of 8:0, 7:1, or 6:2 suggests relatively strong feedback skills. In contrast, ratios of 3:5, 2:6, 1:7, or 0:8 indicate significant self-perceived weaknesses that can be improved upon.

Skill Basics

Many managers are derelict in providing performance feedback, especially when it's negative. Like most of us, managers don't particularly enjoy communicating bad news. They fear offending the other person or having to deal with the recipient's defensiveness. Nevertheless, providing performance feedback is an important part of effective employee communication.

You can be more effective at providing feedback if you use the following six specific suggestions.

1. *Focus on specific behaviors.* Feedback should be specific rather than general. Avoid such statements as "You have a bad attitude" or "I'm really impressed with the good job you did." They're vague and although they provide information, they don't tell the recipient enough to correct the "bad attitude" or on what basis you concluded that a "good job" had been done so the person knows what behaviors to repeat or to avoid.

2. *Keep feedback impersonal.* Feedback, particularly the negative kind, should be descriptive rather than judgmental or evaluative. No matter how upset you are, keep the feedback focused on job-related behaviors and never criticize someone personally because of an inappropriate action.

3. *Keep feedback goal oriented.* Feedback should not be given primarily to "blow off steam" or "unload" on another person. If you have to say something negative, make sure it's directed toward the recipient's goals. Ask yourself whom the feedback is supposed to help. If the answer is *you*, bite your tongue and hold the comment. Such feedback undermines your credibility and lessens the meaning and influence of future feedback.

4. *Make feedback well timed.* Feedback is most meaningful to a recipient when there's a very short interval between his or her behavior and the receipt of feedback about that behavior. Moreover, if you're particularly concerned with changing behavior, delays in providing feedback on the undesirable actions lessen the likelihood that the feedback will be effective in bringing about the desired change. Of course, making feedback prompt merely for the sake of promptness can backfire if you have insufficient information, if you're angry, or if you're otherwise emotionally upset. In such instances, "well timed" could mean "somewhat delayed."

5. *Ensure understanding.* Make sure your feedback is concise and complete so that the recipient clearly and fully understands the communication. It may help to have the recipient rephrase the content of your feedback to find out whether it fully captured the meaning you intended.

6. *Direct negative feedback toward behavior that the recipient can control.* There's little value in reminding a person of some shortcoming over which he or she has no control. Negative feedback should be directed at behavior that the recipient can do something about. In addition, when negative feedback is given concerning something that the recipient can control, it might be a good idea to indicate specifically what can be done to improve the situation.

Based on C. R. Mill, "Feedback: The Art of Giving and Receiving Help," in L. Porter and C. R. Mill (eds.), *The Reading Book for Human Relations Training* (Bethel, ME: NTL Institute for Applied Behavioral Science, 1976), pp. 18–19; and S. Bishop, *The Complete Feedback Skills Training Book* (Aldershot, UK: Gower Publishing, 2000).

Skill Application

Craig is an excellent employee whose expertise and productivity have always met or exceeded your expectations. But recently he's been making work difficult for other members of your advertising team. Like his coworkers, Craig researches and computes the costs of media coverage for your advertising agency's clients. The work requires laboriously leafing through several large reference books to find the correct base price and add-on charges for each radio or television station and time slot, calculating each actual cost, and compiling the results in a computerized spreadsheet. To make things more efficient and convenient, you've always allowed your team members to bring the reference books they're using to their desks while they're using them. Lately, however, Craig has been piling books around him for days and sometimes weeks at a time. The books interfere with the flow of traffic past his desk and other people have to go out of their way to retrieve the books from Craig's pile. It's time for you to have a talk with Craig.

Skill Practice

1. Think of three things that a friend or family member did well recently. Did you praise the person at the time? If not, why? The next time someone close to you does something well, give him or her positive feedback.

2. You have a good friend who has a mannerism (for instance, speech, body movement, or style of dress) that you think is inappropriate and detracts from the overall impression that he or she makes. Come up with a plan for talking with this person. What will you say? How will you handle his or her reaction?

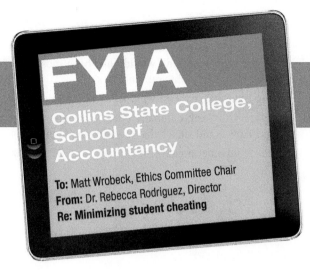

FYIA

Collins State College, School of Accountancy

To: Matt Wrobeck, Ethics Committee Chair
From: Dr. Rebecca Rodriguez, Director
Re: Minimizing student cheating

For Your Immediate Action

exams. As the ethics committee chair, I'd like you to work with them on developing some suggestions. As you look at this topic, please think in terms of ways to control cheating (1) before it happens, (2) while in-class exams or assignments are being completed, and (3) after it has happened.

Keep your list brief (around a page) and send it to me by the end of the week. I'd like to get this out to our entire faculty at our next scheduled monthly meeting.

Matt, you've probably heard that several of our faculty members want to develop some specific controls to minimize opportunities for our students to cheat on homework assignments and

This fictionalized company and message were created for educational purposes only, and not meant to reflect positively or negatively on management practices by any company that may share this name.

Bringing the Real World to Life

Case Application:
Deepwater in Deep Trouble: Part 2

One thing that has come to light in the disaster investigation is that it's no surprise that something like this happened. After Hurricane Dennis blew through in July 2005, a passing ship was shocked to see BP's new massive $1 billion Thunder Horse oil platform "listing precariously to one side, looking for all the world as if it were about to sink." Thunder Horse "was meant to be the company's crowning glory, the embodiment of its bold gamble to outpace its competitors in finding and exploiting the vast reserves of oil beneath the waters of the gulf." But the problems with this rig soon became evident. A valve installed backwards caused it to flood during the hurricane even before any oil had been pumped. Other problems included a welding job so shoddy that it left underwater pipelines brittle and full of cracks. "The problems at Thunder Horse were not an anomaly, but a warning that BP was taking too many risks and cutting corners in pursuit of growth and profits."

Then came the tragic explosion on the Deepwater Horizon. Before the rig exploded, there were strong warning signs that something was terribly wrong with the oil well. Among the red flags were several equipment readings suggesting that gas was bubbling into the well, a potential sign of an

impending blowout. Those red flags were ignored. Other decisions made in the 24 hours before the explosion included a critical decision to replace heavy mud in the pipe rising from the seabed with seawater, again possibly increasing the risk of an explosion. Internal BP documents also show evidence of serious problems and safety concerns with Deepwater. Those problems involved the well casing and blowout preventer. One BP senior drilling engineer warned, "This would certainly be a worst-case scenario."

The federal panel charged with investigating the spill examined 20 "anomalies in the well's behavior and the crew's response." The panel is also investigating in particular why "rig workers missed telltale signs that the well was close to an uncontrolled blowout." The panel's final report blamed both BP and its contractors for the failures that led to the explosion on the Deepwater Horizon. Many of those failings stemmed from shortcuts to save time and money. However, the report also faulted the government for lax oversight of the companies.

DISCUSSION QUESTIONS

1. What type(s) of control—feedforward, concurrent, or feedback—do you think would have been most useful in this situation? Explain your choice(s).

2. Using Exhibit 2, explain what BP could have done better.

3. Why do you think company employees ignored the red flags? How could such behavior be changed in the future?

4. What could other organizations learn from BP's mistakes?

Managing Communication and Information

Operations Management

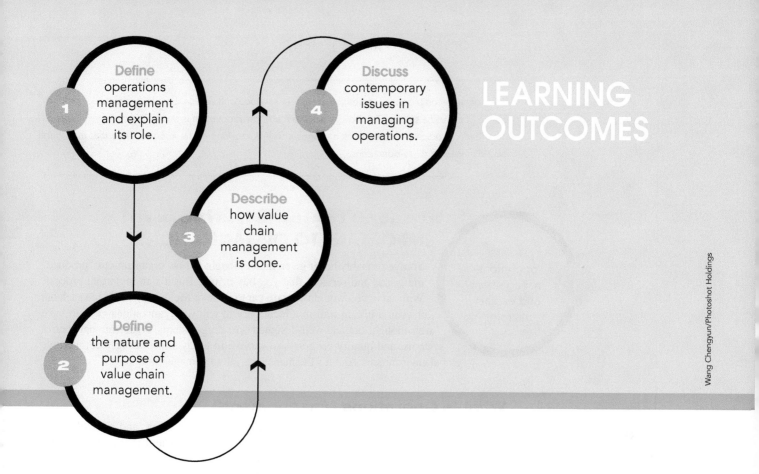

1 Define operations management and explain its role.

4 Discuss contemporary issues in managing operations.

3 Describe how value chain management is done.

2 Define the nature and purpose of value chain management.

Wang Chengyun/Photoshot Holdings

Stirring Things Up

The steaming cup of coffee placed in a customer's hand at any Starbucks store location starts as coffee beans (berries) plucked from fields of coffee plants.[1] From harvest to storage to roasting to retail to cup, Starbucks understands the important role each value chain participant plays.

Starbucks offers a selection of coffees from around the world, and its coffee buyers personally travel to the coffee-growing regions of Latin America, Africa/Arabia, and Asia/Pacific to select and purchase the highest-quality *arabica* beans. Once the beans arrive at any one of its five roasting facilities (in Washington, Pennsylvania, Nevada, South Carolina, or Amsterdam), Starbucks' master professional roasters do their "magic" in creating the company's rich signature roast coffees, a process that's the "cumulative result of expert roasters knowing coffee and bringing balance to all of its flavor attributes." There are many potential challenges in "transforming" the raw material into the quality product and experience that customers expect at Starbucks—weather, shipping and logistics, technology, political instability, and so forth. All could potentially affect the company. Although those operations management challenges are significant, the most challenging issue facing Starbucks today is balancing its vision of the uniquely Starbucks' coffee experience with the realities of selling a $4 latte in today's world.

Every organization produces something, whether it's a good or a service. Some, like Starbucks, produce both a good and a service. Technology has changed how production is done. This chapter focuses on organizations' process of operations management. We also look at the important role that managers play in managing those operations.

① **Define** operations management and explain its role.

WHY IS OPERATIONS MANAGEMENT IMPORTANT TO ORGANIZATIONS?

You've probably never given much thought to how organizations "produce" the goods and services that you buy or use. But it's an important process. Without it, you wouldn't have a car to drive or McDonald's fries to snack on, or even a hiking trail in a local park to enjoy. Organizations need to have well-thought-out and well-designed operating systems, organizational control systems, and quality programs to survive in today's increasingly competitive global environment. And it's the manager's job to manage those things.

What Is Operations Management?

The term **operations management** refers to the design, operation, and control of the transformation process that converts such resources as labor and raw materials into goods and services that are sold to customers. Exhibit 1 portrays a simplified overview of the transformation process of creating value by converting inputs into outputs. The system takes inputs—people, technology, capital, equipment, materials, and information—and transforms them through various processes, procedures, and work activities into finished goods and services. These processes, procedures, and work activities are found throughout the organization. For example, department members in marketing, finance, research and development, human resources, and accounting convert inputs into outputs such as sales, increased market share, high rates of return on investments, new and innovative products, motivated and committed employees, and accounting reports. As a manager, you'll need to be familiar with operations management concepts, regardless of the area in which you're managing, in order to achieve your goals more effectively and efficiently.

Why is operations management so important to organizations and managers? First, it encompasses processes in all organizations—services as well as manufacturing. Second, it's important in effectively and efficiently managing productivity. And third, it plays a strategic role in an organization's competitive success. Let's look more closely at each of these factors.

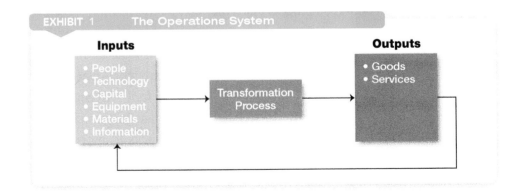

EXHIBIT 1   The Operations System

Inputs
- People
- Technology
- Capital
- Equipment
- Materials
- Information

Transformation Process

Outputs
- Goods
- Services

How Do Service and Manufacturing Firms Differ?

With a menu that offers more than 200 items made fresh each day, The Cheesecake Factory restaurants rely on a finely tuned production system. One food-service consultant says, "They've evolved with this highly complex menu combined with a highly efficient kitchen."[2]

All organizations produce goods or services through the transformation process. Simply stated, every organization has an operations system that creates value by transforming inputs into finished goods and services outputs. For manufacturers, the products are obvious: cars, cell phones, or food products. After all, manufacturing organizations produce physical goods. It's easy to see the operations management (transformation) process at work in these types of organizations because raw materials are turned into recognizable physical products. But that transformation process isn't as readily evident in service organizations because they produce nonphysical outputs in the form of services. For instance, hospitals provide medical and health care services that help people manage their personal health; taxi companies provide transportation services that move people from one location to another; cruise lines provide vacation and entertainment services; and residential plumbers and electricians ensure that we have electricity and running water where we live. All of these service organizations transform inputs into outputs. For example, look at your college. College administrators bring together inputs—instructors, books, academic journals, multimedia classrooms, and similar resources—to transform "unenlightened" students into educated and skilled individuals.

The reason we're making this point is that the U.S. economy, and to a large extent the global economy, is dominated by the creation and sale of services. Most of the world's developed countries are predominantly service economies. In the United States, for instance, almost 77 percent of all economic activity is services and in the European Union, it's nearly 73 percent.[3] In lesser-developed countries, the services sector is less important. For instance, in Nigeria, it accounts for only 33 percent of economic activity; in Laos, only 37 percent; and in Vietnam, 38 percent.[4]

Tyler Anderson/Newscom

The transformation process of creating value by converting inputs into outputs applies to both manufacturing and service organizations. While manufacturing firms produce physical goods, Netflix and other service organizations use inputs such as labor and technology to produce nonphysical outputs. Shown here is Netflix founder and CEO Reed Hastings, who created value for consumers by originally offering a DVD rental-by-mail service and then by introducing a streaming media service for viewing movies and television shows. After attempting to change what consumers valued about its service, Netflix had to do an about-face. As a result of the changes, Netflix saw its number of members drop significantly although it hopes to lure them back.

How Do Businesses Improve Productivity?

One jetliner has some 4 million parts. Efficiently assembling such a finely engineered product requires intense focus. Boeing and Airbus, the two major global manufacturers have copied techniques from Toyota. However, not every technique can be copied because airlines demand more customization than do car buyers and there are significantly more rigid safety regulations for jetliners than for cars.[5] At the Evans Findings Company in East Providence, Rhode Island, which makes the tiny cutting devices on dental-floss containers, one production shift each day is run without people.[6] The company's goal is to do as much as possible with no labor. And it's not because they don't care about their employees. Instead, like many U.S. manufacturers, Evans needed to improve productivity in order to survive, especially against low-cost competitors. So they turned to "lights-out" manufacturing where machines are designed to be so reliable that they make flawless parts on their own, without people operating them.

operations management
The study and application of the transformation process

transformation process
The process that converts resources into finished goods and services

manufacturing organizations
Organizations that produce physical goods

service organizations
Organizations that produce nonphysical products in the form of services

Although most organizations don't make products that have 4 million parts and most organizations can't function without people, improving productivity has become a major goal in virtually every organization. For countries, high productivity can lead to economic growth and development. Employees can receive higher wages and company profits can increase without causing inflation. For individual organizations, increased productivity gives them a more competitive cost structure and the ability to offer more competitive prices.

Over the past decade, U.S. businesses have made dramatic improvements to increase their efficiency. For example, at Latex Foam International's state-of-the-art digital facility in Shelton, Connecticut, engineers monitor all of the factory's operations. The facility boosted capacity by 50 percent in a smaller space and achieved a 30 percent efficiency gain.[7] And it's not just in manufacturing that companies are pursuing productivity gains. Pella Corporation's purchasing office improved productivity by reducing purchase order entry times anywhere from 50 percent to 86 percent, decreasing voucher processing by 27 percent, and eliminating 14 financial systems. Its information technology department slashed e-mail traffic in half and implemented work design improvements for heavy PC users such as call center users. The human resources department cut the time to process benefit enrollment by 156.5 days. And the finance department now takes 2 days, instead of 6 to do its end-of-month closeout.[8]

Organizations that hope to succeed globally are looking for ways to improve productivity. For example, McDonald's Corporation drastically reduced the time it takes to cook its french fries—65 seconds as compared to the 210 seconds it once took, saving time and other resources.[9] The Canadian Imperial Bank of Commerce, based in Toronto, automated its purchasing function, saving several million dollars annually.[10] And Skoda, the Czech car company owned by Germany's Volkswagen AG, improved its productivity through an intensive restructuring of its manufacturing process.[11]

From the Past to the Present

William Edwards Deming was an American statistician, professor, author, lecturer, and consultant.[12] He is widely credited with improving production in the United States during World War II, although he's probably best known for his work in Japan. From 1950 onward, he taught Japanese top managers how to improve product design and product quality, testing, and sales, primarily through applying statistical methods. His philosophy has been summarized as follows: "Dr. W. Edwards Deming taught that by adopting appropriate principles of management, organizations can increase quality and simultaneously reduce costs (by reducing waste, rework, staff attrition and litigation while increasing customer loyalty). The key is to practice continual improvement and think of manufacturing as a system, not as bits and pieces."

Putting that philosophy into practice required following Deming's 14 points for improving management's productivity. These suggestions are as follows:

- Plan for the long-term future.
- Never be complacent concerning the quality of your product.
- Establish statistical control over your production processes and require your suppliers to do so as well.
- Deal with the best and fewest number of suppliers.
- Find out whether your problems are confined to particular parts of the production process or stem from the overall process itself.

- Train workers for the job that you are asking them to perform.
- Raise the quality of your line supervisors.
- Drive out fear.
- Encourage departments to work closely together rather than to concentrate on departmental or divisional distinctions.
- Do not adopt strictly numerical goals.
- Require your workers to do quality work.
- Train your employees to understand statistical methods.
- Train your employees in new skills as the need arises.
- Make top managers responsible for implementing these principles.

These principles have withstood the test of time and are still applicable for managers looking to improve productivity.

Think About:

- Take each of Deming's 14 points for improving management's productivity and write a short explanation of what you think it means.
- Which one of these 14 points would you choose as the most important? Why?
- Given what you've learned in reading this textbook, do you think these principles are still appropriate today? Explain.

Productivity is a composite of people and operations variables. To improve productivity, managers must focus on both. The late W. Edwards Deming, a renowned quality expert, believed that managers, not workers, were the primary source of increased productivity. He outlined 14 points for improving management's productivity (see the From the Past to the Present box for more information). A close look at these suggestions reveals Deming's understanding of the interplay between people and operations. High productivity can't come solely from good "people management." The truly effective organization will maximize productivity by successfully integrating people into the overall operations system. For instance, at Simplex Nails Manufacturing in Americus, Georgia, employees were an integral part of the company's much-needed turnaround effort.[13] Some production workers were redeployed on a plantwide cleanup and organization effort, which freed up floor space. The company's sales force was retrained and refocused to sell what customers wanted rather than what was in inventory. The results were dramatic. Inventory was reduced by more than 50 percent, the plant had 20 percent more floor space, orders were more consistent, and employee morale improved. Here's a company that understood the important interplay between people and the operations system.

What Role Does Operations Management Play in a Company's Strategy?

Modern manufacturing originated more than 100 years ago in the United States, primarily in Detroit's automobile factories. The success that U.S. manufacturers experienced during World War II led manufacturing executives to believe that troublesome production problems had been conquered. These executives focused, instead, on improving other functional areas such as finance and marketing and paid little attention to manufacturing.

However, as U.S. executives neglected production, managers in Japan, Germany, and other countries took the opportunity to develop modern, technologically advanced facilities that fully integrated manufacturing operations into strategic planning decisions. The competition's success realigned world manufacturing leadership. U.S. manufacturers soon discovered that foreign goods were being made not only less expensively but also with better quality. Finally, by the late 1970s, U.S. executives recognized that they were facing a true crisis and responded. They invested heavily in improving manufacturing technology, increased the corporate authority and visibility of manufacturing executives, and began incorporating existing and future production requirements into the organization's overall strategic plan. Today, successful organizations recognize the crucial role that operations management plays as part of the overall organizational strategy to establish and maintain global leadership.[14]

The strategic role that operations management plays in successful organizational performance can be seen clearly as more organizations move toward managing their operations from a value chain perspective, which we're going to discuss next.

WHAT IS VALUE CHAIN MANAGEMENT AND WHY IS IT IMPORTANT?

It's 11 P.M., and you're reading a text message from your parents saying they want to buy you a laptop for your birthday this year and to order it. You log on to Dell's Web site and configure your dream machine. You hit the order button and within 3 or 4 days, your dream computer is delivered to your front door, built to your exact specifications, ready to set up and use immediately to type that management assignment due tomorrow. Or consider Siemens

Define the nature and purpose of value chain management.

2

453

AG's Computed Tomography manufacturing plant in Forchheim, Germany, which has established partnerships with about 30 suppliers. These suppliers are partners in the truest sense as they share responsibility with the plant for overall process performance. This arrangement has allowed Siemens to eliminate all inventory warehousing and streamlined the number of times paper changes hands to order parts from 18 to one. At the Timken's plant in Canton, Ohio, electronic purchase orders are sent across the street to an adjacent "Supplier City" where many of its key suppliers have set up shop. The process takes milliseconds and costs less than 50 cents per purchase order. And when Black & Decker extended its line of handheld tools to include a glue gun, it totally outsourced the entire design and production to the leading glue gun manufacturer. Why? Because they understood that glue guns don't require motors, which was what Black & Decker did best.[15]

As these examples show, closely integrated work activities among many different players are possible. How? The answer lies in value chain management. The concepts of value chain management have transformed operations management strategies and turned organizations around the world into finely tuned models of efficiency and effectiveness strategically positioned to exploit competitive opportunities.

What Is Value Chain Management?

Every organization needs customers if it's going to survive and prosper. Even a not-for-profit organization must have "customers" who use its services or purchase its products. Customers want some type of value from the goods and services they purchase or use, and these customers decide what has value. Organizations must provide that value to attract and keep customers. **Value** is defined as the performance characteristics, features and attributes, and any other aspects of goods and services for which customers are willing to give up resources (usually money). For example, when you download Katy Perry's new single on iTunes, buy a new pair of Australian sheepskin Ugg boots online at the company's Web site, purchase a Wendy's bacon cheeseburger at the drive-through location on campus, or get a haircut from your local hair salon, you're exchanging (giving up) money in return for the value you need or desire from these products— providing music during your evening study time, keeping your feet warm *and* fashionable during winter's cold weather, alleviating the lunchtime hunger pangs quickly since your next class starts in 15 minutes, or looking professionally groomed for the job interview you've got next week.

How *is* value provided to customers? Through transforming raw materials and other resources into some product or service that end users need or desire when, where, and how they want it. However, that seemingly simple act of turning varied resources into something that customers value and are willing to pay for involves a vast array of interrelated work activities performed by different participants (suppliers, manufacturers, and even customers)—that is, it involves the value chain. The **value chain** is the entire series of organizational work activities that add value at each step from raw materials to finished product. In its entirety, the value chain can encompass the supplier's suppliers to the customer's customer.[16]

Value chain management is the process of managing the sequence of activities and information along the entire value chain. In contrast to supply chain management, which is *internally* oriented and focuses on efficient flow of incoming materials (resources) to the organization, value chain management is *externally* oriented and focuses on both incoming materials and outgoing products and services. Although supply chain management is efficiency oriented (its goal is to reduce costs and make the organization more productive), value chain management is effectiveness oriented and aims to create the highest value for customers.[17]

At the BMW motorcycle plant in Berlin, Germany, production workers add value as they build motorcycles that are guided by a conveyor system through the entire assembly process according to individual orders. The flexibility, quality, and productivity of BMW's manufacturing plant are important aspects of the company's value chain. With state-of-the-art production technology, highly trained production workers, and process controls, BMW has mastered the complexity of tailoring products to individual customer specifications. By allowing every bike rider to order a custom-built motorcycle from anywhere in the world, BMW's production process provides value that attracts and keeps customers and differentiates the company from competitors.

Durand Florence/Newscom

What Are the Goals of Value Chain Management?

Who has the power in the value chain? Is it the supplier providing needed resources and materials? After all, suppliers have the ability to dictate prices and quality. Is it the manufacturer that assembles those resources into a valuable product or service? A manufacturer's contribution in creating a product or service is quite obvious. Is it the distributor that makes sure the product or service is available where and when the customer needs it? Actually, it's none of these. In value chain management, ultimately customers are the ones with the power.[18] They're the ones who define what value is and how it's created and provided. Using value chain management, managers seek to find that unique combination in which customers are offered solutions that truly meet their needs and at a price that can't be matched by competitors.[19] For example, in an effort to better anticipate customer demand and replenish customer stocks, Shell Chemical Company developed a supplier inventory management order network. The software used in this network allows managers to track shipment status, calculate safety stock levels, and prepare resupply schedules.[20] With this capability Shell Chemical enables its customers to purchase goods when desired and to receive them immediately.

A good value chain is one in which a sequence of participants works together as a team, each adding some component of value—such as faster assembly, more accurate information, or better customer response and service—to the overall process.[21] The better the collaboration among the various chain participants, the better the customer solutions. When value is created for customers and their needs and desires are satisfied, everyone along the chain benefits. For example, at Iomega Corporation, a manufacturer of personal computer storage devices, managing the value chain started first with improved relationships with internal suppliers, then expanded out to external suppliers and customers. As the company's experience with value chain management intensified and improved, so did its connection to customers, which ultimately paid off for all its value chain partners.[22]

How Does Value Chain Management Benefit Businesses?

Collaborating with external and internal partners in creating and managing a successful value chain strategy requires significant investments in time, energy, and other resources, and a serious commitment by all chain partners. Given this, why would managers ever choose to implement value chain management? A survey of manufacturers noted four primary benefits of value chain management: improved procurement, improved logistics, improved product development, and enhanced customer order management.[23]

RIGHT ?OR WRONG

Okay...so here's an "unusual" ethics dilemma for you and it's a fitting conclusion in the last chapter of the textbook. Why? Because it illustrates that questions of ethics can pop up in the most ordinary of places. Suppose that you went to a popular shopping area where parking was extremely limited and the store owner had instituted "customers only" parking and you were lucky enough to find an open space. Then suppose that once you finished your business at that store—having spent a fair amount of money—you had other shopping to do in the same vicinity so you left your car in that same "customers only" parking space. You believed that what you did was okay since you "paid" for that spot with your purchase. But your significant other disagreed saying that since you had finished your business at that store, your car should be moved.[24]

Think About:

- What do you think? Is this ethical? Why or why not? *Does* the fact that you spent a fair amount of money at the store mean that you "paid" for that spot with your purchase? Did that give you the right to continue to use that parking space once your business was done at that store?

- What about the other stakeholders in this situation (for instance, the store where you shopped, other customers, other businesses in the area)? How might this one seemingly simple decision affect them?

rosesmith/Shutterstock.com

---

value
The performance characteristics, features, attributes, and other aspects of goods and services, for which customers are willing to give up resources

value chain
The entire series of work activities that add value at each step from raw materials to finished product

value chain management
The process of managing the sequence of activities and information along the entire value chain

HOW IS VALUE CHAIN MANAGEMENT DONE?

3 Describe how value chain management is done.

The dynamic, competitive environment facing contemporary global organizations demands new solutions.[25] Understanding how and why value is determined by the marketplace has led some organizations to experiment with a new **business model**—that is, a strategic design for how a company intends to profit from its broad array of strategies, processes, and activities. For example, IKEA, the home furnishings manufacturer, transformed itself from a small, Swedish mail-order furniture operation into the world's largest retailer of home furnishings by reinventing the value chain in the home furnishings industry. The company offers customers well-designed products at substantially lower prices in return for the customers' willingness to take on certain key tasks traditionally done by manufacturers and retailers—such as getting the furniture home and assembling it.[26] The company's adoption of a unique business model and willingness to abandon old methods and processes have worked well. It also helped that IKEA recognized the importance of managing its value chain.

What Are the Requirements for Successful Value Chain Management?

So what does successful value chain management require? Exhibit 2 summarizes the six main requirements: coordination and collaboration, technology investment, organizational processes, leadership, employees/human resources, and organizational culture and attitudes. Let's look at each of these elements more closely.

COORDINATION AND COLLABORATION. For the value chain to achieve its goal of meeting and exceeding customers' needs and desires, comprehensive and seamless integration among all members of the chain is absolutely necessary. All partners in the value chain must identify things that they may not value but that customers do. Sharing information and being flexible as far as who in the value chain does what are important steps in building coordination and collaboration. This sharing of information and analysis requires open communication among the various value chain partners. For example, Furon Company, a manufacturer of specialty polymer products, believes that better communication with customers and with suppliers has facilitated timely delivery of goods and services and opened up additional business opportunities for all its value chain partners.[27]

TECHNOLOGY INVESTMENT. Successful value chain management isn't possible without a significant investment in information technology. The payoff from this investment is that

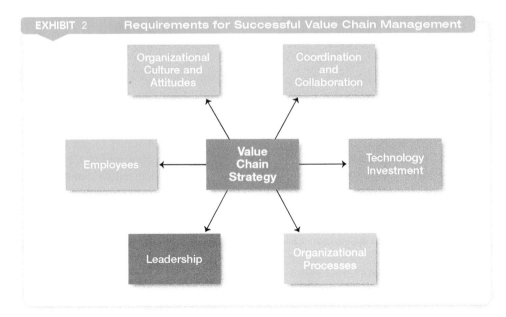

EXHIBIT 2 Requirements for Successful Value Chain Management

Organizational Culture and Attitudes

Coordination and Collaboration

Employees

Value Chain Strategy

Technology Investment

Leadership

Organizational Processes

information technology can be used to restructure the value chain to better serve end users.[28] For example, Rollerblade, Inc., invested heavily in developing a Web site and used it to educate customers about its products. Although the company has chosen not to sell its products over the Web for fear of antagonizing its dealer network, managers remain flexible about the issue and would reconsider if they felt that value could be better delivered to customers by doing so.[29]

What types of technology are important? According to experts, the key tools include a supporting enterprise resource planning software (ERP) system that links all of an organization's activities, sophisticated work planning and scheduling software, customer relationship management systems, business intelligence capabilities, and e-business connections with trading network partners.[30] For instance, Dell Inc. manages its supplier relationships almost exclusively online. The company has one Web site for customers and one for suppliers. The supplier Web site is the primary mode of communication between Dell and 33 of its largest suppliers. The company's investment in this type of information technology allows it to meet customers' needs in a way that competitors haven't been able to match.[31]

ORGANIZATIONAL PROCESSES. Value chain management radically changes organizational processes—that is, the way organizational work is done.[32] Managers must critically evaluate all organizational processes from beginning to end by looking at core competencies—the organization's unique skills, capabilities, and resources—to determine where value is being added. Non-value-adding activities are eliminated. Questions such as "Where can internal knowledge be leveraged to improve flow of material and information?" "How can we better configure our product to satisfy both customers and suppliers?" "How can the flow of material and information be improved?" and "How can we improve customer service?" should be asked for each process. For example, when managers at Deere & Company implemented value chain management in its Worldwide Commercial and Consumer Equipment Division, a thorough process evaluation revealed that work activities needed to be better synchronized and interrelationships between multiple links in the value chain better managed. They changed numerous work processes division-wide in order to improve these relationships.[33]

Three important conclusions can be made about how organizational processes must change. First, better demand forecasting is necessary and possible because of closer ties with customers and suppliers. For example, in an effort to make sure that Listerine was on the store shelves when customers wanted it, Walmart collaborated with product manufacturer Pfizer Consumer Healthcare on improving product demand forecast information. Through their mutual efforts, the partners boosted Walmart's sales of Listerine by $6.5 million. Customers also benefited because they were able to purchase the product when and where they wanted it.

Second, selected functions may need to be done collaboratively with other partners in the value chain. This collaboration may even extend to sharing employees. For instance, Saint-Gobain Performance Plastics, headquartered in Northboro, Massachusetts, places its own employees in customer sites and brings employees of suppliers and customers to work on its premises. Saint-Gobain's CEO says this type of collaboration is essential if an organization wants to "go from being a mere component supplier to being a solutions provider."[34]

Finally, new measures are needed for evaluating the performance of various activities along the value chain. Because the goal in value chain management is meeting and exceeding customers' needs and desires, managers need a better picture of how well value is being created and delivered to customers. For instance, when Nestlé USA implemented a value chain management approach, it redesigned its measurement system to focus on one consistent set of factors, including accuracy of demand forecasts and production plans, on-time delivery, and customer service levels. This redesign allowed management to more quickly identify problems and take actions to resolve them.[35]

AND THE SURVEY SAYS... [36]

22 percent of manufacturers introduced product innovations during a recent three-year time span.

58 percent of companies are looking to connect better with their suppliers.

56 percent of those companies hope to reduce procurement costs.

16 percent of employers prefer using employee referrals to locate quality employees.

12 percent of companies say that sustainability is among their top three supply chain priorities.

63 percent of those companies see sustainability as an opportunity for revenue growth.

64 percent of manufacturers say that they currently have wireless networks or intend to have them.

---

business model
A strategic design for how a company intends to profit from its broad array of strategies, processes, and activities

organizational processes
The way organizational work is done

LEADERSHIP. The importance of leadership to value chain management is plain and simple—successful value chain management isn't possible without strong and committed leadership.[37] From top organizational levels to lower levels, managers must support, facilitate, and promote the implementation and ongoing practice of value chain management. J. Michael Hagan, CEO of Furon Company, describes his role as follows: "Value is a mindset that not only has to be driven from the top down, but also from the bottom up. Everyone has to be asking whether a given task adds value, and if it doesn't, why do it."[38] Managers must make a serious commitment to identifying what value is, how that value can best be provided, and how successful those efforts have been. That type of organizational atmosphere or culture in which all efforts are focused on delivering superb customer value isn't possible without a serious commitment on the part of the organization's leaders.

Also, it's important that leaders outline expectations for what's involved in the organization's pursuit of value chain management. Ideally, articulating expectations should start with a vision or mission statement that expresses the organization's commitment to identifying, capturing, and providing the highest possible value to customers. For example, when American Standard Companies began its pursuit of value chain management, the CEO attended dozens of meetings across the country explaining the changing competitive environment and why the company needed to create better working relationships with its value chain partners.[39] Throughout the organization, then, managers should clarify expectations regarding each employee's role in the value chain. Being clear about expectations also extends to partners. For example, managers at American Standard identified clear requirements for suppliers and were prepared to drop any that couldn't meet them. The company was so serious about its expectations that it did cut hundreds of suppliers from air conditioning, bath and kitchen, and vehicle control systems businesses. The upside, though, was that those suppliers that met the expectations benefited from more business and American Standard had partners that could deliver better value to customers.

Employees such as the team leaders of the Bing search engine shown here play a significant role in Microsoft's value chain. The software developer's mission is "to enable people and businesses throughout the world to realize their full potential." To achieve this mission, Microsoft needs people who are smart, creative, flexible, and energetic and who have a passion for customers, technology, and creating quality products. The company uses an unstructured interview approach during the hiring process to identify employees who will help customers, possess qualities such as the willingness to take on big challenges and see them through, and are hard-working, self-critical, questioning, and committed to personal excellence and self-improvement.

EMPLOYEES/HUMAN RESOURCES. We know from our discussions of management theories and approaches throughout this textbook that employees are the organization's most important resource. So, not surprisingly, employees play an important part in value chain management. Three main human resources requirements for value chain management are flexible approaches to job design, an effective hiring process, and ongoing training.

Flexibility is the key description of job design in a value chain management organization. Traditional functional job roles—such as marketing, sales, accounts payable, customer service representative, and so forth—are inadequate in a value chain management environment. Instead, jobs need to be designed around work processes that link all functions involved in creating and providing value to customers. This type of flexible job design supports the company's commitment to providing superb customer value.[40] In designing jobs for a value chain approach, the focus needs to be on how each activity performed by an employee can best contribute to the creation and delivery of customer value, which requires flexibility in what employees do and how they do it.

The fact that jobs in a value chain management organization must be flexible contributes to the second requirement: Flexible jobs require employees who are flexible. In a value chain organization, employees may be assigned to work teams that tackle a given process and are often asked to do different things on different days, depending on need. In an environment focusing on collaborative relationships that may change as customer needs change, employees' ability to be flexible is critical. Accordingly, the organization's hiring process must be designed to identify those employees who have the ability to quickly learn and adapt.

Finally, the need for flexibility also requires a significant investment in ongoing employee training. Whether

the training involves learning how to use information technology software, how to improve the flow of materials throughout the chain, how to identify activities that add value, how to make better decisions faster, or how to improve any number of other potential work activities, managers must see to it that employees have the knowledge and tools they need to do their jobs. For example, at defense and electronics contractor Alenia Marconi Systems, based in Portsmouth, England, ongoing training is part of the company's commitment to efficiently and effectively meeting the needs of customers. Employees continually receive technical training as well as training in strategic issues including the importance of emphasizing people and customers, not just sales and profits.[41]

ORGANIZATIONAL CULTURE AND ATTITUDES. The last requirement for value chain management is having a supportive organizational culture and attitudes. Those cultural attitudes include sharing, collaborating, openness, flexibility, mutual respect, and trust. And these attitudes encompass not only the internal partners in the value chain but external partners as well. For instance, American Standard has chosen to practice these attitudes the old-fashioned way—with lots of face time and telephone calls. One of the company's suppliers, St. Louis–based White Rogers, described their relationship as follows: "Their goals are our goals, because both companies focus on growth. The keys to the relationship are mutual respect and open communications at all levels. No one has to go through a liaison. If our engineers need to talk to theirs, we just go right to the source."[42] However, as we mentioned earlier, Dell has taken a completely different approach, as it works with its value chain partners almost exclusively through cyberspace.[43] Both approaches, however, reflect each company's commitment to developing long-lasting, mutually beneficial, and trusting relationships that best meet customers' needs.

What Are the Obstacles to Value Chain Management?

As desirable as value chain management may be, managers must tackle several obstacles in managing the value chain including organizational barriers, cultural attitudes, required capabilities, and people (see Exhibit 3).

ORGANIZATIONAL BARRIERS. Organizational barriers are among the most difficult obstacles to handle. These barriers include refusal or reluctance to share information, reluctance to shake up the status quo, and security issues. Without shared information, close coordination and collaboration is impossible. And the reluctance or refusal of employees to shake up the status quo can impede efforts toward value chain management and prevent its successful implementation. Finally, because value chain management relies heavily on a substantial information technology infrastructure, system security and Internet security breaches are issues that need to be addressed.

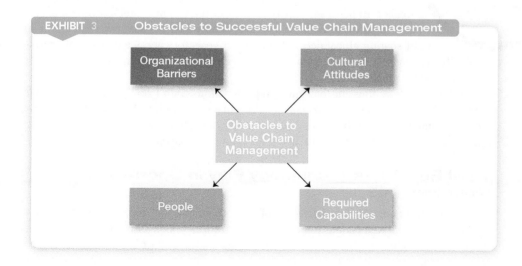

EXHIBIT 3   Obstacles to Successful Value Chain Management

CULTURAL ATTITUDES.   Unsupportive cultural attitudes—especially trust and control—also can be obstacles to value chain management. The trust issue is a critical one, both lack of trust and too much trust. To be effective, partners in a value chain must trust each other. There must be a mutual respect for, and honesty about, each partner's activities all along the chain. When that trust doesn't exist, the partners will be reluctant to share information, capabilities, and processes. But too much trust also can be a problem. Just about any organization is vulnerable to theft of intellectual property—that is, proprietary information that's critical to an organization's efficient and effective functioning and competitiveness. You need to be able to trust your value chain partners so your organization's valuable assets aren't compromised.[44] Another cultural attitude that can be an obstacle is the belief that when an organization collaborates with external and internal partners, it no longer controls its own destiny. However, this just isn't the case. Even with the intense collaboration that's important to value chain management, organizations still control critical decisions such as what customers value, how much value they desire, and what distribution channels are important.[45]

REQUIRED CAPABILITIES.   We know from our earlier discussion of requirements for the successful implementation of value chain management that value chain partners need numerous capabilities. Several of these—coordination and collaboration, the ability to configure products to satisfy customers and suppliers, and the ability to educate internal and external partners—aren't easy. But they're essential to capturing and exploiting the value chain. Many of the companies we've described throughout this section endured critical, and oftentimes difficult, self-evaluations of their capabilities and processes in order to become more effective and efficient at managing their value chains.

PEOPLE.   The final obstacles to successful value chain management can be an organization's people. Without their unwavering commitment to do whatever it takes, value chain management won't be successful. If employees refuse to be flexible in their work—how and with whom they work—collaboration and cooperation throughout the value chain will be hard to achieve. In addition, value chain management takes an incredible amount of time and energy on the part of an organization's employees. Managers must motivate those high levels of effort from employees, which isn't an easy thing to do.

Discuss contemporary issues in managing operations.

WHAT CONTEMPORARY ISSUES DO MANAGERS FACE IN MANAGING OPERATIONS?

Redesigned milk jugs that have been adopted by Walmart and Costco are cheaper to ship, better for the environment, cost less, and keep the milk fresher. Experts say this type of redesign is "an example of the changes likely to play out in the American economy over the next two decades. In an era of soaring global demand and higher costs for energy and materials, virtually every aspect of the economy needs to be re-examined and many products must be redesigned for greater efficiency."[46]

If you somehow thought that managing operations didn't really matter in today's online 24/7 global economy, think again. It does matter . . . a lot. We're going to look at three contemporary issues that managers face in managing operations: technology's role in operations management, quality initiatives, and project management.

What Role Does Technology Play in Operations Management?

As we know from our previous discussion of value chain management, today's competitive marketplace has put tremendous pressure on organizations to deliver products and services that customers value in a timely manner. Smart companies are looking at ways to harness technology to improve operations management. Many fast-food companies are competing to see who can provide faster and better service to drive-through customers. With drive-through now representing a huge portion of sales, faster and better delivery can be a significant competitive edge. For instance, Wendy's added awnings to some of its menu boards and replaced some of the text with pictures. Others use confirmation screens, a technology that helped McDonald's boost accuracy by more than 11 percent. And technology used by two national chains tells managers how much food they need to prepare by counting vehicles in the drive-through line and factoring in demand for current promotional and popular staple items.[47]

Although an organization's production activities are driven by the recognition that the customer is king, managers still need to be more responsive. For instance, operations managers need systems that can reveal available capacity, status of orders, and product quality while products are in the process of being manufactured, not just after the fact. To connect more closely with customers, production must be synchronized across the enterprise. To avoid bottlenecks and slowdowns, the production function must be a full partner in the entire business system.

Roland Weihrauch/Newscom

Amazon.com's fulfillment center shown here in Werne, Germany, is one of 40 the online retailer operates throughout the world. These centers stock millions of different items to meet Amazon's goal of carrying anything a customer wants to buy. To stock, retrieve, and ship its vast inventory, Amazon has developed sophisticated technology that tells the company what to order, where to store it, and what to charge for it. Amazon uses software and logistics technology to locate inventory and find the fastest way to get it to the customer. Technology increases Amazon's operating efficiency by reducing inventory costs and delivery times as well as providing online shoppers with the best customer service.

What's making such extensive collaboration possible is technology. Technology is also allowing organizations to control costs particularly in the areas of predictive maintenance, remote diagnostics, and utility cost savings. For instance, Internet-compatible equipment contains embedded Web servers that can communicate proactively—that is, if a piece of equipment breaks or reaches certain preset parameters indicating that it's about to break, it asks for help. But technology can do more than sound an alarm or light up an indicator button. For instance, some devices have the ability to initiate e-mail or signal a pager at a supplier, the maintenance department, or contractor describing the specific problem and requesting parts and service. How much is such e-enabled maintenance control worth? It can be worth quite a lot if it prevents equipment breakdowns and subsequent production downtime.

Managers who understand the power of technology to contribute to more effective and efficient performance know that managing operations is more than the traditional view of simply producing the product. Instead, the emphasis is on working together with all the organization's business functions to find solutions to customers' business problems. (See the Technology and the Manager's Job box for more information on technology's role in the factory of the future.)

TECHNOLOGY AND THE MANAGER'S JOB — WELCOME TO THE FACTORY OF THE FUTURE!

What would the ideal factory of the future look like?[48] Experts at Georgia Tech's Manufacturing Research Center say that three important trends are driving what tomorrow's factories will look like. One trend is *globalization of the supply chain*. In the factories of the future, design and business processes will be performed where it's most efficient and effective to do so. For example, parts for Boeing's 787 Dreamliner are produced around the world and then come together in Boeing's U.S. facilities. The second trend is *technology that simultaneously dematerializes the product while vastly increasing complexity*. The challenge for managing

operations is that despite simplicity in products, the production process is becoming more complex. The third trend is *demographics and the impact on demand patterns*. Products will have shorter life cycles and more variety and choices. "The challenge is for the future factory to be both adaptable over many different product life cycles and flexible with regard to the number of different products being produced in the same time frame." And it will be particularly important that these factories be efficient and effective.

Given these trends, it's clear that technology will continue to play a key role in transformation processes

that need to be collaborative, adaptive, flexible, and responsive. But keep in mind that technology is simply a tool. Future factories will also require a talented and skilled workforce and a clear understanding of managing operations processes. Those are the challenges facing managers who want their organizations to survive and thrive.

Think About:

· How will technology contribute to the operations management process?

· What are the downsides to using technology in the operations management process?

· In the factory of the future, what role does a manager play?

How Do Managers Control Quality?

Quality problems are expensive. For example, even though Apple has had phenomenal success with its iPod, the batteries in the first three versions died after 4 hours instead of lasting up to 12 hours, as buyers expected. Apple's settlement with consumers cost close to $100 million. At Schering-Plough, problems with inhalers and other pharmaceuticals were traced to chronic quality control shortcomings, for which the company eventually paid a $500 million fine. And the auto industry paid $14.5 billion to cover the cost of warranty and repair work in one year.[49]

Many experts believe that organizations unable to produce high-quality products won't be able to compete successfully in the global marketplace. What is quality? When you consider a product or service to have quality, what does that mean? Does it mean that the product doesn't break or quit working—that is, is it reliable? Does it mean that the service is delivered in a way that you intended? Does it mean that the product does what it's supposed to do? Or does quality mean something else? Exhibit 4 provides a description of several quality dimensions. We're going to define quality as the ability of a product or service to reliably do what it's supposed to do and to satisfy customer expectations.

HOW IS QUALITY ACHIEVED? How quality is achieved is an issue managers must address. A good way to look at quality initiatives is with the management functions—planning, organizing and leading, and controlling—that need to take place.

When *planning for quality,* managers must have quality improvement goals and strategies and plans to achieve those goals. Goals can help focus everyone's attention toward some objective quality standard. For instance, Caterpillar's goal is to apply quality improvement techniques to help cut costs.[50] Although this goal is specific and challenging, managers and employees are partnering together to pursue well-designed strategies to achieve the goals, and are confident they can do so.

When *organizing and leading for quality,* it's important for managers to look to their employees. For instance, at the Moosejaw, Saskatchewan, plant of General Cable Corporation, every employee participates in continual quality assurance training. In

---

EXHIBIT 4   What Is Quality?

PRODUCT QUALITY DIMENSIONS

1. Performance—Operating characteristics
2. Features—Important special characteristics
3. Flexibility—Meeting operating specifications over some period of time
4. Durability—Amount of use before performance deteriorates
5. Conformance—Match with preestablished standards
6. Serviceability—Ease and speed of repair or normal service
7. Aesthetics—How a product looks and feels
8. Perceived quality—Subjective assessment of characteristics (product image)

SERVICE QUALITY DIMENSIONS

1. Timeliness—Performed in promised period of time
2. Courtesy—Performed cheerfully
3. Consistency—Giving all customers similar experiences each time
4. Convenience—Accessibility to customers
5. Completeness—Full service, as required
6. Accuracy—Performed correctly each time

Sources: Based on J. W. Dean and J. R. Evans, *Total Quality: Management, Organization, and Society* (St. Paul, MN: West Publishing Company, 1994); H. V. Roberts and B. F. Sergesketter, *Quality Is Personal* (New York: The Free Press, 1993); D. Garvin, *Managed Quality: The Strategic and Competitive Edge* (New York: The Free Press, 1988); and M. A. Hitt, R. D. Ireland, and R. E. Hoskisson, *Strategic Management,* 4th ed. (Cincinnati: South-Western Publishing, 2001), p. 121.

addition, the plant manager believes wholeheartedly in giving employees the information they need to do their jobs better. He says, "Giving people who are running the machines the information is just paramount. You can set up your cellular structure, you can cross-train your people, you can use lean tools, but if you don't give people information to drive improvement, there's no enthusiasm." Needless to say, this company shares production data and financial performance measures with all employees.[51]

Organizations with extensive and successful quality improvement programs tend to rely on two important people approaches: cross-functional work teams and self-directed or empowered work teams. Because achieving product quality is something that all employees from upper to lower levels must participate in, it's not surprising that quality-driven organizations rely on well-trained, flexible, and empowered employees.

Finally, managers must recognize when *controlling for quality* that quality improvement initiatives aren't possible without having some way to monitor and evaluate their progress. Whether it involves standards for inventory control, defect rate, raw materials procurement, or other operations management areas, controlling for quality is important. For instance, at the Northrup Grumman Corporation plant in Rolling Meadows, Illinois, several quality controls have been implemented, such as automated testing and IT that integrates product design and manufacturing and tracks process quality improvements. Also, employees are empowered to make accept/reject decisions about products throughout the manufacturing process. The plant manager explains, "This approach helps build quality into the product rather than trying to inspect quality into the product." But one of the most important things they do is "go to war" with their customers—soldiers preparing for war or live combat situations. Again, the plant manager says, "What discriminates us is that we believe if we can understand our customer's mission as well as they do, we can help them be more effective. We don't wait for our customer to ask us to do something. We find out what our customer is trying to do and then we develop solutions."[52]

Quality improvement success stories can be found globally. For example, at a Delphi assembly plant in Matamoros, Mexico, employees worked hard to improve quality and made significant strides. For instance, the customer reject rate on shipped products is now 10 ppm (parts per million), down from 3,000 ppm—an improvement of almost 300 percent.[53] Quality initiatives at several Australian companies including Alcoa of Australia, Wormald Security, and Carlton and United Breweries have led to significant quality improvements.[54] At Valeo Klimasystemme GmbH of Bad Rodach, Germany, assembly teams build different climate-control systems for high-end German cars including Mercedes and BMW. Quality initiatives by those teams have led to significant improvements.[55]

WHAT QUALITY GOALS MIGHT ORGANIZATIONS PURSUE? To publicly demonstrate their commitment to quality, many organizations worldwide have pursued challenging quality goals. The two best-known are ISO 9000 and Six Sigma.

ISO 9000 is a series of international quality management standards established by the International Organization for Standardization (www.iso.org), which set uniform guidelines for processes to ensure that products conform to customer requirements. These standards cover everything from contract review to product design to product delivery. The ISO 9000 standards have become the internationally recognized standard for evaluating and

In this photo, the hands of Portuguese football player Cristiano Ronaldo holds a Nike Mercurial Vapor Superfly II football boot during a Nike press conference in London. High-quality products like the Mercurial Vapor that are used and endorsed by world-class athletes have helped Nike earn the top spot as global designer, marketer, and distributor of athletic footwear, apparel, and equipment. For Nike, quality means designing and developing innovative products that help athletes of every level of ability reach their potential. The quality of Nike footwear products that satisfy customer expectations includes the dimensions of product performance, features, flexibility, durability, and aesthetics.

Ben Stansall/Newscom

ISO 9000
A series of international quality standards that set uniform guidelines for processes to ensure that products conform to customer requirements

comparing companies in the global marketplace. In fact, this type of certification can be a prerequisite for doing business globally. Achieving ISO 9000 certification provides proof that a quality operations system is in place. As of 2009, more than 1 million certifications had been awarded to organizations in 175 countries. Almost 40,000 U.S. businesses are ISO 9000 certified. More than 200,000 Chinese firms have received certification.[56]

More than 30 years ago, Motorola popularized the use of stringent quality standards more through a trademarked quality improvement program called Six Sigma.[57] Very simply, Six Sigma is a quality standard that establishes a goal of no more than 3.4 defects per million units or procedures. What does the name mean? Sigma is the Greek letter that statisticians use to define a standard deviation from a bell curve. The higher the sigma, the fewer the deviations from the norm—that is, the fewer the defects. At One Sigma, two-thirds of whatever is being measured falls within the curve. Two Sigma covers about 95 percent. At Six Sigma, you're about as close to defect-free as you can get.[58] It's an ambitious quality goal! Although it's an extremely high standard to achieve, many quality-driven businesses are using it and benefiting from it. For instance, General Electric estimates that it has saved billions since 1995, according to company executives.[59] Other examples of companies pursuing Six Sigma include ITT Industries, Dow Chemical, 3M Company, American Express, Sony Corporation, Nokia Corporation, and Johnson & Johnson. Although manufacturers seem to make up the bulk of Six Sigma users, service companies such as financial institutions, retailers, and health care organizations are beginning to apply it. What impact can Six Sigma have? Let's look at an example.

It used to take Wellmark Blue Cross and Blue Shield, a managed-care health care company, 65 days or more to add a new doctor to its medical plans. Now, thanks to Six Sigma, the company discovered that half the processes they used were redundant. With those unnecessary steps gone, the job now gets done in 30 days or less and with reduced staff. The company also has been able to reduce its administrative expenses by $3 million per year, an amount passed on to consumers through lower health premiums.[60]

Although it's important for managers to recognize that many positive benefits come from obtaining ISO 9000 certification or Six Sigma, the key benefit comes from the quality improvement journey itself. In other words, the goal of quality certification should be having work processes and an operations system in place that enable organizations to meet customers' needs and employees to perform their jobs in a consistently high-quality way.

How Are Projects Managed?

Many organizations are structured around projects. A project is a one-time-only set of activities with a definite beginning and ending point.[61] Projects vary in size and scope, from a NASA space shuttle launch to a wedding. Project management is the task of getting the activities done on time, within budget, and according to specifications.

Project management has actually been around for a long time in industries such as construction and movie making, but now it has expanded into almost every type of business. What explains the growing popularity of project management? It fits well with a dynamic environment and the need for flexibility and rapid response. Organizations are increasingly undertaking projects that are somewhat unusual or unique, have specific deadlines, contain complex interrelated tasks requiring specialized skills, and are temporary in nature. These types of projects don't lend themselves well to the standardized operating procedures that guide routine and continuous organizational activities.[62]

In the typical project, team members are temporarily assigned to and report to a project manager who coordinates the project's activities with other departments and reports directly to a senior executive. The project is temporary: It exists only long enough to complete its specific objectives. Then it's wound down and closed up; members move on to other projects, return to their permanent departments, or leave the organization.

If you were to observe a group of supervisors or department managers for a few days, you would see them regularly detailing what activities have to be done, the order in which they are to be done, who is to do each, and when they are to be completed. The managers are doing what we call scheduling. The following discussion reviews some useful scheduling devices.

HOW DO YOU USE A GANTT CHART?   The Gantt chart is a planning tool developed around the turn of the century by Henry Gantt. The idea behind the Gantt chart is relatively simple. It's essentially a bar graph, with time on the horizontal axis and the activities to be scheduled on the vertical axis. The bars show output, both planned and actual, over a period of time. The Gantt chart visually shows when tasks are supposed to be done and compares the assigned date with the actual progress on each. This simple but important device allows managers to detail easily what has yet to be done to complete a job or project and to assess whether it's ahead of, behind, or on schedule.

Exhibit 5 shows a Gantt chart that was developed for book production by a manager in a publishing firm. Time is expressed in months across the top of the chart. Major activities are listed down the left side. The planning comes in deciding what activities need to be done to get the book finished, the order in which those activities need to be done, and the time that should be allocated to each activity. The blue shading represents actual progress made in completing each activity.

A Gantt chart, then, actually becomes a managerial control device as the manager looks for deviations from the plan. In this case, most activities were completed on time. However, if you look at the "review first pages" activity, you will notice that it's actually almost two and a half weeks behind schedule. Given this information, the manager might want to take some corrective action to make up the lost time and to ensure that no further delays will occur. At this point, the manager can expect that the book will be published at least two weeks late if no corrective action is taken.

A modified version of the Gantt chart is a load chart. Instead of listing activities on the vertical axis, load charts list either whole departments or specific resources. This information allows managers to plan and control for capacity utilization. In other words, load charts schedule capacity by workstations. For example, Exhibit 6 shows a load chart for six production editors at the same publishing firm. Each editor supervises the design and production of several books. By reviewing the load chart, the executive editor who supervises the six production editors can see who is free to take on a new book. If everyone is fully scheduled, the executive editor might decide not to accept any new projects, to accept some new projects and delay others, to ask the editors to work overtime, or to employ more production editors.

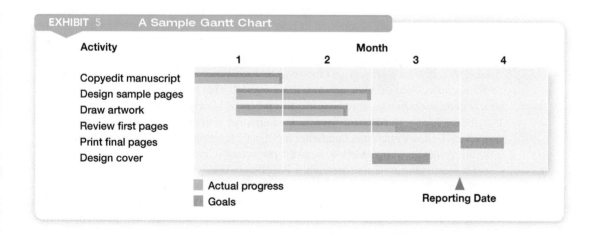

EXHIBIT 5   **A Sample Gantt Chart**

Activity	Month
	1 2 3 4
Copyedit manuscript	
Design sample pages	
Draw artwork	
Review first pages	
Print final pages	
Design cover	

▮ Actual progress
▮ Goals

▲ Reporting Date

Six Sigma
A quality standard that establishes a goal of no more than 3.4 defects per million units or procedures

project
A one-time-only set of activities with a definite beginning and ending point

project management
The task of getting project activities done on time, within budget, and according to specifications

gantt chart
A planning tool that shows in bar graph form when tasks are supposed to be done and compares that with the actual progress on each

load chart
A modified version of a Gantt chart that lists either whole departments or specific resources

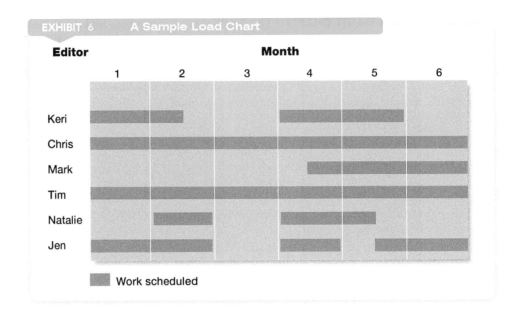

EXHIBIT 6   A Sample Load Chart

WHAT IS A PERT NETWORK ANALYSIS?   Gantt and load charts are helpful as long as the activities or projects being scheduled are few and independent of each other. But what if a manager had to plan a large project—such as a complex reorganization, the launching of a major cost-reduction campaign, or the development of a new product—that required coordinating inputs from marketing, production, and product design personnel? Such projects require coordinating hundreds or thousands of activities, some of which must be done simultaneously and some of which cannot begin until earlier activities have been completed. If you are constructing a shopping mall, you obviously cannot start erecting walls until the foundation has been laid. How, then, can you schedule such a complex project? You could use the program evaluation and review technique.

The program evaluation and review technique—usually just called PERT, or the **PERT network analysis**—was originally developed in the late 1950s for coordinating the more than 3,000 contractors and agencies working on the Polaris submarine weapon system. This project was incredibly complicated, with hundreds of thousands of activities that had to be coordinated. PERT is reported to have cut two years off the completion date for the Polaris project.

A PERT network is a flowchart-like diagram that depicts the sequence of activities needed to complete a project and the time or costs associated with each activity. With a PERT network, a project manager must think through what has to be done, determine which events depend on one another, and identify potential trouble spots (see Exhibit 7). PERT also makes it easy to compare the effects alternative actions will have on scheduling and costs. PERT allows managers to monitor a project's progress, identify possible bottlenecks, and shift resources as necessary to keep the project on schedule.

To understand how to construct a PERT network, you need to know three terms: *events, activities*, and *critical path*. Let us define these terms, outline the steps in the PERT process, and then develop an example. **Events** are end points that represent the completion of major activities. Sometimes called milestones, events indicate that something significant has happened (such as receipt of purchased items) or an important component is finished. In PERT, events represent a point in time. **Activities**, on the other hand, are the actions that take place. Each activity consumes time, as determined on the basis of the time or resources required to progress from one event to another. The **critical path** is the longest or most time-consuming sequence of events and activities required to complete the project in the shortest amount of time.[63] Let's apply PERT to a construction manager's task of building a 6,500-square-foot custom home.

As a construction manager, you recognize that time really is money in your business. Delays can turn a profitable job into a money loser. Accordingly, you must determine how long it will take to complete the house. You have carefully dissected the entire project into

Developing a PERT network requires the manager to identify all key activities needed to complete a project, rank them in order of dependence, and estimate each activity's completion time. This procedure can be translated into five specific steps:

1. Identify every significant activity that must be achieved for a project to be completed. The accomplishment of each activity results in a set of events or outcomes.

2. Ascertain the order in which these events must be completed.

3. Diagram the flow of activities from start to finish, identifying each activity and its relationship to all other activities. Use circles to indicate events and arrows to represent activities. The result is a flowchart diagram that we call the PERT network.

4. Compute a time estimate for completing each activity, using a weighted average that employs an optimistic time estimate (t_o) of how long the activity would take under ideal conditions, a most-likely estimate (t_m) of the time the activity normally should take, and a pessimistic estimate (t_p) that represents the time that an activity should take under the worst possible conditions. The formula for calculating the expected time (t_e) is then

$$t_e = \frac{t_o + 4t_m + t_p}{6}$$

5. Finally, using a network diagram that contains time estimates for each activity, the manager can determine a schedule for the start and finish dates of each activity and for the entire project. Any delays that occur along the critical path require the most attention because they delay the entire project. That is, the critical path has no slack in it; therefore, any delay along that path immediately translates into a delay in the final deadline for the completed project.

activities and events. Exhibit 8 outlines the major events in the construction project and your estimate of the expected time required to complete each activity. Exhibit 9 depicts the PERT network based on the data in Exhibit 8.

HOW DOES PERT OPERATE?   Your PERT network tells you that if everything goes as planned, it will take just over 32 weeks to build the house. This time is calculated by tracing the network's critical path: A B C D E I J K L M N P Q. Any delay in completing the events along this path will delay the completion of the entire project. For example, if it took six weeks instead of four to frame the house (event E), the entire project would be delayed by two weeks (or the time beyond that expected). But a one-week delay for installing the brick (event H) would have little effect because that event is not on the critical path. By using PERT, the construction manager would know that no corrective action would be needed. Further delays in installing the brick, however, could present problems—for such delays may, in actuality, result in a new critical path. Now back to our original critical path dilemma.

Notice that the critical path passes through N, P, and Q. Our PERT chart (Exhibit 9) tells us that these three activities take four weeks. Wouldn't path N O Q be faster? Yes. The PERT network shows that it takes only 3.5 weeks to complete that path. So why isn't N O Q on the critical path? Because activity Q cannot begin until both activities O and P are completed. Although activity O takes half a week, activity P takes one full week. So, the earliest we can begin Q is after one week. What happens to the difference between the critical activity (activity P) time and the noncritical activity (activity O) time? The difference, in this case half a week, becomes slack time. Slack time is the time difference between

---

PERT network analysis
A flowchart-like diagram that depicts the sequence of activities needed to complete a project and the time or costs associated with each activity

events
End points that represent the completion of major activities

activities
Actions that take place

critical path
The longest or most time-consuming sequence of events and activities required to complete a project in the shortest amount of time

slack time
The time difference between the critical path and all other paths

EXHIBIT 8   Major Activities in Building a Custom Home

EVENT	DESCRIPTION	TIME (WEEKS)	PRECEDING ACTIVITY
A	Approve design and get permits	3	None
B	Perform excavation/lot clearing	1	A
C	Pour footers	1	B
D	Erect foundation walls	2	C
E	Frame house	4	D
F	Install windows	0.5	E
G	Shingle roof	0.5	E
H	Install brick front and siding	4	F, G
I	Install electrical, plumbing, and heating and A/C rough-ins	6	E
J	Install insulation	0.25	I
K	Install sheetrock	2	J
L	Finish and sand sheetrock	7	K
M	Install interior trim	2	L
N	Paint house (interior and exterior)	2	H, M
O	Install all cabinets	0.5	N
P	Install flooring	1	N
Q	Final touch-up and turn over house to home owner	1	O, P

the critical path and all other paths. What use is there for slack? If the project manager notices some slippage on a critical activity, perhaps slack time from a noncritical activity can be borrowed and temporarily assigned to work on the critical one.

As you can see, PERT is both a planning and a control tool. Not only does PERT help us estimate the times associated with scheduling a project, but it also gives us clues about where our controls should be placed. Because any event on the critical path that is delayed will delay the overall project (making us not only late but also probably over budget), our attention needs to be focused on the critical activities at all times. For example, if activity F (installing windows) is delayed by a week because supplies have not arrived, that is not a major issue. It's not on the critical path. But if activity P (installing flooring) is delayed from one week to two weeks, the entire project will be delayed by one week. Consequently, anything that has the immediate potential for delaying a project (critical activities) must be monitored closely.

As we said in the beginning of this chapter, it's the manager's job to manage the organization's operating systems, organizational control systems, and quality programs. That's the only way organizations will survive in today's increasingly competitive global economy.

EXHIBIT 9   A PERT Network for Building a Custom Home

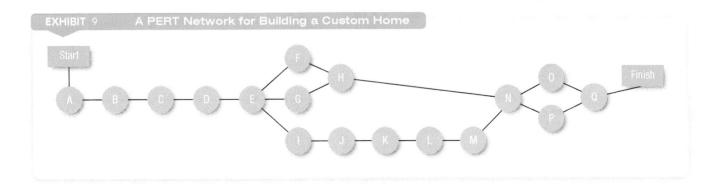

Review

1 **Define operations management and explain its role.** Operations management is the transformation process that converts resources into finished goods and services. Manufacturing organizations produce physical goods. Service organizations produce nonphysical outputs in the form of services. Productivity is a composite of people and operations variables. A manager should look for ways to successfully integrate people into the overall operations systems. Organizations must recognize the crucial role that operations management plays as part of their overall strategy in achieving successful performance.

2 **Define the nature and purpose of value chain management.** The value chain is the sequence of organizational work activities that add value at each step from raw materials to finished product. Value chain management is the process of managing the sequence of activities and information along the entire product chain.

The goal of value chain management is to create a value chain strategy that meets and exceeds customers' needs and desires and allows for full and seamless integration among all members of the chain.

Four benefits from value chain management include improved procurement, improved logistics, improved product development, and enhanced customer order management.

3 **Describe how value chain management is done.** The six main requirements for successful value chain management include coordination and collaboration, investment in technology, organizational processes, leadership, employees or human resources, and organizational culture and attitudes.

The obstacles to value chain management include organizational barriers (refusal to share information, reluctance to shake up the status quo, or security issues), unsupportive cultural attitudes, lack of required capabilities, and employees unwilling or unable to do it.

4 **Discuss contemporary issues in managing operations.** Companies are looking at ways to harness technology to improve their operations management by extensive collaboration and cost control.

ISO 9000 is a series of international quality management standards that set uniform guidelines for processes to ensure that products conform to customer requirements. Six Sigma is a quality standard that establishes a goal of no more than 3.4 defects per million units or procedures.

Project management involves getting a project's activities done on time, within budget, and accomplished to specifications. A project is a one-time-only set of activities that has a definite beginning and ending point in time. Popular project scheduling tools include Gantt charts, load charts, and PERT network analysis.

MyManagementLab   For more resources, please visit **www.mymanagementlab.com**

---

1. What is operations management and how is it used in both manufacturing and service organizations?

2. What strategic role does operations management play?

3. How might operations management apply to other managerial functions besides control?

4. Do you think that manufacturing or service organizations have greater need of operations management? Explain.

5. What is a value chain? What is value chain management? What is the goal of value chain management?

6. What types of organizational benefits does value chain management provide? What obstacles stand in the way of successful value chain management?

7. Explain why managing productivity is important in operations management.

8. Who has the power in the value chain? Explain your response.

9. Choose two tasks that you do every week (for example, shop for groceries, host a poker party, clean your house/apartment, do laundry). For each one, identify how you could (a) be more productive in doing that task, and (b) have higher-quality output from that task.

10. Select a company with which you're familiar. Describe its value chain. Be as specific as possible in your description. Evaluate how it "uses" the value chain to create value.

Endnotes

1. "Starbucks' Quest for Healthy Growth: An Interview with Howard Schultz," *McKinsey Quarterly,* no. 2 (2001), pp. 34–43; "Return to Glory," *Retail Traffic,* May/June 2011, p. 38; J. Jannarone, "Grounds for Concern at Starbucks," *Wall Street Journal,* May 3, 2011, p. C10; M. Morrison, "Bang for Its Starbucks: Hits No. 3 Despite Limited Ad Spending," *Advertising Age,* May 2, 2011, pp. 1+; W. Kendall, "A Long, Hard Grind," *Management Today,* May 2011, p. 27; "Howard Schultz, On Getting a Second Shot," *Inc.,* April 2011, pp. 52–54; "Starbucks Corp. Plans Retail Push," *Nation's Restaurant News,* April 4, 2011, p. 6; "Starbucks Marks 40th Anniversary," *Beverage Industry,* April 2011, p. 8; R. Lowenstein, "When Latte Lost Its Luster," *Wall Street Journal,* March 29, 2011, p. A17; H. Schultz, "How Starbucks Got Its Mojo Back," *Newsweek,* March 21, 2011, pp. 50–55; G. Charles, "Change Brewing at Starbucks," *Marketing,* January 2011, pp. 14–15; "Starbucks Outlines Strategies for Growth," *Beverage Industry,* January 2011, p. 14; and H. Edwards, "Howard Schultz's Tall Order," *Marketing,* January 2011, p. 19; and S. Berfield, "Starbucks: Howard Schultz vs. Howard Schultz," *BusinessWeek Online,* August 6, 2009; J. Jargon, "Latest Starbucks Buzzword: 'Lean' Japanese Techniques," *Wall Street Journal,* August 4, 2009, p. A1.

2. D. Eng, "Cheesecake Factory's Winning Formula," *Fortune,* May 2, 2011, pp. 19–20; and D. McGinn, "Faster Food," *Newsweek,* April 19, 2004, pp. E20–E22.

3. *World Factbook 2011,* http://www.cia.gov/library/publications/the-world-factbook/.

4. Ibid.

5. D. Michaels and J. L. Lunsford, "Streamlined Plane Making," *Wall Street Journal,* April 1, 2005, pp. B1+.

6. T. Aeppel, "Workers Not Included," *Wall Street Journal,* November 19, 2002, pp. B1+.

7. A. Aston and M. Arndt, "The Flexible Factory," *BusinessWeek,* May 5, 2003, pp. 90–91.

8. P. Panchak, "Pella Drives Lean Throughout the Enterprise," *IndustryWeek,* June 2003, pp. 74–77.

9. J. Ordonez, "McDonald's to Cut the Cooking Time of Its French Fries," *Wall Street Journal,* May 19, 2000, p. B2.

10. C. Fredman, "The Devil in the Details," *Executive Edge,* April–May, 1999, pp. 36–39.

11. http://new.skoda-auto.com/Documents/AnnualReports/skoda_auto_annual_report_2007_%20EN_FINAL.pdf (July 8, 2008); and T. Mudd, "The Last Laugh," *IndustryWeek,* September 18, 2000, pp. 38–44.

12. From the Past to the Present box based on "Honorary Members Form Impressive Lineup of Quality Thinkers," *Quality Progress,* March 2011, p. 17; "W. Edwards Deming," *Quality Progress,* November 2010, p. 17; R. Aguayo, *Dr. Deming: The American Who Taught the Japanese About Quality* (New York: Fireside Press, 1991); M. Walton, *The Deming Management Method* (New York: Penguin Group, 1986); and W. E. Deming, "Improvement of Quality and Productivity Through Action by Management," *National Productivity Review*, Winter 1981–1982, pp. 12–22.

13. T. Vinas, "Little Things Mean a Lot," *IndustryWeek,* November 2002, p. 55.

14. P. Panchak, "Shaping the Future of Manufacturing," *IndustryWeek,* January 2005, pp. 38–44; M. Hammer, "Deep Change: How Operational Innovation Can Transform Your Company," *Harvard Business Review,* April 2004, pp. 84–94; S. Levy, "The Connected Company," *Newsweek,* April 28, 2003, pp. 40–48; and J. Teresko, "Plant Floor Strategy," *IndustryWeek,* July 2002, pp. 26–32.

15. T. Laseter, K. Ramdas, and D. Swerdlow, "The Supply Side of Design and Development," *Strategy & Business,* Summer 2003, p. 23; J. Jusko, "Not All Dollars and Cents," *IndustryWeek,* April 2002, p. 58; and D. Drickhamer, "Medical Marvel," *IndustryWeek,* March 2002, pp. 47–49.

16. Q. H. Soon and Z. M. Udin, "Supply Chain Management from the Perspective of Value Chain Flexibility: An Exploratory Study," *Journal of Manufacturing Technology Management* (May 2011), pp. 506–526; G. Soni and R. Kodali, "A Critical Analysis of Supply Chain Management Content in Empirical Research," *Business Process Management,* April 2011, pp. 238–256; and J. H. Sheridan, "Managing the Value Chain," *IndustryWeek,* September 6, 1999, pp. 1–4, available online in archives at www.industryweek.com.

17. "Supply Chain Management: A New Narrative," *Strategic Direction,* March 2011, pp. 18–21; and J. H. Sheridan, "Managing the Value Chain."

18. S. Leibs, "Getting Ready: Your Suppliers," *IndustryWeek,* www. industryweek.com (September 6, 1999).

19. See, for example, J. Jusko, "Procurement—Not All Dollars and Cents," *IndustryWeek,* www.industryweek.com (April 4, 2002).

20. See "News Item Future Challenges for the Aromatics Supply Chain," speech given by Nancy Sullivan, Vice President Aromatics & Phenol, to the First European Aromatics and Derivatives Conference, London, UK (May 29, 2002). Available online at http://www.shellchemicals.com/newstroom/1,1098.71.00.html.

21. D. Bartholomew, "The Infrastructure," *IndustryWeek,* September 6, 1999, p. 1.

22. G. Taninecz, "Forging the Chain," *IndustryWeek,* May 15, 2000, pp. 40–46.

23. T. Vinas, "A Map of the World: IW Value-Chain Survey," *IndustryWeek,* September 2005, pp. 27–34.

24. Right or Wrong box based on C. Hausman, "Ethics of Using Store's Parking Lot Fuels Lively Debate in Newspaper Series,"

Ethics Newsline Online, April 25, 2011; J. Rose, "Ethics of Customer Parking in Portland: Circling the Block One More Time," *Oregonian Online,* April 21, 2011; and J. Rose, "The Ethics of 'Customer Only' Parking in the Pearl—and Beyond," *Oregonian Online,* April 16, 2011.

25. See J. H. Sheridan, "Now It's a Job for the CEO," *IndustryWeek,* March 20, 2000, pp. 22–30.

26. R. Norman and R. Ramirez, "From Value Chain to Value Constellation," *Harvard Business Review on Managing the Value Chain* (Boston: Harvard Business School Press, 2000), pp. 185–219.

27. S. Leibs, "Getting Ready: Your Customers," *IndustryWeek,* September 6, 1999, p. 4.

28. See, for example, C. Lunan, "Workers Doing More in Less Time," *Charlotte Observer,* June 1, 2002, p. D1.

29. S. Leibs, "Getting Ready: Your Customers," p. 3.

30. See, for instance, L. Harrington, "The Accelerated Value Chain: Supply Chain Management Just Got Smarter, Faster, and More Cost-Effective, Thanks to a Groundbreaking Alliance Between Intel and Technologies," *IndustryWeek,* April 2002, pp. 45–51.

31. Ibid.

32. Ibid.; and J. H. Sheridan, "Managing the Value Chain."

33. J. H. Sheriden, "Managing the Value Chain," p. 3.

34. S. Leibs, "Getting Ready: Your Customers," p. 4.

35. J. H. Sheriden, "Managing the Value Chain," pp. 2–3; S. Leibs, "Getting Ready: Your Customers," pp. 1, 4; and D. Bartholomew, "The Infrastructure," p. 6.

36. And the Survey Says box based on "Innovation Nation," *Industry Week,* November 2010, p. 15; "First-Hand Accounts," *Industry Week,* July 2008, p. 28; "State of the Workforce Report," *IndustryWeek,* November 2008, p. 18; "Sustainable Supply Chains," *IndustryWeek,* December 2008, p. 57; "Taking Charge of Mobile Workforce Costs," *IndustryWeek,* August 2009, p. 47; and "The Future of Manufacturing," *IndustryWeek,* November 2008, pp. 51–57.

37. G. Taninecz, "Forging the Chain."

38. S. Leibs, "Getting Ready: Your Customers," p. 1.

39. Ibid.

40. Ibid.

41. D. Drickhamer, "On Target," *IndustryWeek,* October 16, 2000, pp. 111–112.

42. S. Leibs, "Getting Ready: Your Customers," p. 2.

43. Ibid.

44. "Top Security Threats and Management Issues Facing Corporate America: 2003 Survey of *Fortune* 1000 Companies," ASIS International and Pinkerton, www.asisonline.org.

45. J. H. Sheridan, "Managing the Value Chain," p. 4.

46. S. Rosenbloom, "Solution, or Mess? A Milk Jug for a Green Earth," *New York Times Online,* June 30, 2008.

47. K. T. Greenfeld, "Taco Bell and the Golden Age of Drive-Thru," *Bloomberg BusinessWeek Online,* May 5, 2011;

and S. Anderson, Associated Press, "Restaurants Gear Up for Window Wars," *Springfield, Missouri, News-Leader,* January 27, 2006, p. 5B.

48. Technology and the Manager's Job box based on S. Minter, "What Is Advanced Manufacturing?" *IndustryWeek,* August 2009, p. 7; J. Bush, "Russia's Factories Shift Gears," *BusinessWeek,* May 18, 2009, pp. 50–51; D. Blanchard, "A Manufacturer for All Seasons," *IndustryWeek,* December 2008, p. 7; J. Teresko, "Planning the Factory of the Future," *IndustryWeek,* December 2008, pp. 22–24; and J. Teresko, "Winning with Digital Manufacturing," *IndustryWeek,* July 2008, pp. 45–47.

49. D. Bartholomew, "Quality Takes a Beating," *IndustryWeek,* March 2006, pp. 46–54; J. Carey and M. Arndt, "Making Pills the Smart Way," *BusinessWeek,* May 3, 2004, pp. 102–103; and A. Barrett, "Schering's Dr. Feelbetter?" *BusinessWeek,* June 23, 2003, pp. 55–56.

50. T. Vinas, "Six Sigma Rescue," *IndustryWeek,* March 2004, p. 12.

51. J. S. McClenahen, "Prairie Home Companion," *IndustryWeek,* October 2005, pp. 45–46.

52. T. Vinas, "Zeroing In on the Customer," *IndustryWeek,* October 2004, pp. 61–62.

53. W. Royal, "Spotlight Shines on Maquiladora," *IndustryWeek,* October 16, 2000, pp. 91–92.

54. See B. Whitford and R. Andrew (eds.), *The Pursuit of Quality* (Perth: Beaumont Publishing, 1994).

55. D. Drickhamer, "Road to Excellence," *IndustryWeek,* October 16, 2000, pp. 117–118.

56. J. Heizer and B. Render, *Operations Management,* 10th ed. (Upper Saddle River, NJ: Prentice Hall, 2011), p. 193.

57. G. Hasek, "Merger Marries Quality Efforts," *IndustryWeek,* August 21, 2000, pp. 89–92.

58. J. Jusko, "An Elite Crew," *IndustryWeek,* March 2011, pp. 17–18; and M. Arndt, "Quality Isn't Just for Widgets," *BusinessWeek,* July 22, 2002, pp. 72–73.

59. E. White, "Rethinking the Quality Improvement Program," *Wall Street Journal,* September 19, 2005, p. B3.

60. M. Arndt, "Quality Isn't Just for Widgets."

61. For a thorough overview of project management, see S. Berkun, *The Art of Project Management* (Upper Saddle River, NJ: Prentice Hall, 2005); or J. K. Pinto, *Project Management: Achieving Competitive Advantage and MS Project* (Upper Saddle River, NJ: Prentice Hall, 2007).

62. H. Maylor, "Beyond the Gantt Chart: Project Management Moving On," *European Management Journal* (February 2001), pp. 92–101.

63. For additional information on CPM, see W. A. Haga and K. A. Marold, "A Simulation Approach to the PERT/CPM Time-Cost Trade-Off Problem," *Project Management Journal* (June 2004), pp. 31–37.

Skill Development: Project Management Skills

Managing any project will require good negotiation skills. You'll typically have to work across vertical and horizontal levels in the organization, deal with people over whom you have no formal authority, and have to negotiate schedules, deadlines, work assignments, and the like with people possibly both inside and outside the organization.

Personal Insights: What's My Negotiation Style?

Listed here are seven characteristics related to a person's negotiating style. Each characteristic demonstrates a range of variation. Indicate your own preference by selecting a point along the 1-to-5 continuum for each characteristic.

1. Approach	Confrontational	1	2	3	4	5	Collaborative
2. Personality	Emotional	1	2	3	4	5	Rational
3. Formality	High	1	2	3	4	5	Low
4. Communication	Indirect	1	2	3	4	5	Direct
5. Candidness	Closed	1	2	3	4	5	Open
6. Search for options	Limited	1	2	3	4	5	Many
7. Willingness to use power	Low	1	2	3	4	5	High

Source: Based on R. Fisher and W. Ury, *Getting to Yes* (New York: Penguin, 1981); and J. W. Salacuse, "Ten Ways That Culture Affects Negotiating Style: Some Survey Results," *Negotiation Journal* (July 1998), pp. 221–239.

Analysis and Interpretation

People differ in the way they handle negotiations. This instrument attempts to tap the key dimensions that differentiate preferences in negotiation style.

Add up the scores for the seven items. Your score on this test will range between 7 and 35. Research indicates that negotiation style is influenced by a number of factors—including the situation, your cultural background, and your work occupation. Nevertheless, experts in negotiation generally recommend individuals use a style that will result in a high score on this test. That is, they favor collaboration, rationality, a direct communication style, and so on. We think it best to consider your total score in a situational context. For instance, while a high total score may generally be favorable, the use of an informal style may be a handicap for North Americans or Europeans when negotiating with Nigerians, who favor high formality. Similarly, Latin Americans tend to show their emotions in negotiation. So if you're negotiating with Brazilians or Costa Ricans, a more emotional approach on your part may be appropriate or even expected.

Skill Basics

You can be more effective at negotiating if you use the following five recommended behaviors.

1. *Begin with a positive overture.* Studies on negotiation show that concessions tend to be reciprocated and lead to agreements. As a result, begin bargaining with a positive overture—perhaps a small concession—and then reciprocate the other party's concessions.

2. *Address problems, not personalities.* Concentrate on the negotiation issues, not on the personal characteristics of the individual with whom you're negotiating. When negotiations get tough, avoid the tendency to attack this person. Remember it's that person's ideas or position that you disagree with, not him or her personally. Separate the people from the problem, and don't personalize differences.

3. *Pay little attention to initial offers.* Treat an initial offer as merely a point of departure. Everyone must have an initial position. These initial offers tend to be extreme and idealistic. Treat them as such.

4. *Emphasize win–win solutions.* Inexperienced negotiators often assume that their gain must come at the expense of the other party. That needn't be the case. Assuming a zero-sum game means missed opportunities for trade-offs that could benefit both sides. So if conditions are supportive, look for an integrative solution. Frame options in terms of the other party's interests and look for solutions that can allow this person, as well as yourself, to declare a victory.

5. *Create an open and trusting climate.* Skilled negotiators are better listeners, ask more questions, focus their arguments more directly, are less defensive, and have learned to avoid words or phrases that can irritate the person with whom they're negotiating (such as "generous offer," "fair price," or "reasonable arrangement"). In other words, they're better at creating the open and trusting climate that is necessary for reaching a win–win settlement.

Based on R. Fisher and W. Ury, *Getting to Yes: Negotiating Agreement Without Giving In* (New York: Penguin Books, 1986); J. A. Wall, Jr. and M. W. Blum, "Negotiations," *Journal of Management* (June 1991), pp. 273–303; and M. E. Roloff, L. L. Putnam, and L. Anastasiou, "Negotiation Skills," in J. O. Greene and B. R. Burleson (eds.), *Handbook of Communication and Social Interaction Skills* (Mahwah, NJ: Lawrence Erlbaum, 2003), pp. 801–833.

Skill Application

As marketing director for Done Right, a regional home-repair chain, you've come up with a plan you believe has significant potential for future sales. Your plan involves a customer information service designed to help people make their homes more environmentally sensitive. Then based on homeowners' assessments of their homes' environmental impact, your firm will be prepared to help them deal with problems or concerns they may uncover. You're really excited about the competitive potential of this new service. You envision pamphlets, in-store appearances by environmental experts, as well as contests for consumers and school kids. After several weeks of preparations, you make your pitch to your boss, Nick Castro. You point out how the market for environmentally sensitive products is growing and how this growing demand represents the perfect opportunity for Done Right. Nick seems impressed by your presentation, but he's expressed one major concern. He thinks your workload is already too heavy. He doesn't see how you're going to have enough time to start this new service *and* still be able to look after all of your other assigned marketing duties.

People in the class should form pairs. One will play the marketing director; the other will play the role of Nick Castro. Nick seems convinced you can't handle your present responsibilities and start the new service. Negotiate a solution.

Skill Practice

1. Negotiate with a course instructor to raise the grade on an exam or paper on which you think you should have received a higher grade.

2. The next time you purchase a relatively expensive item (e.g., automobile, apartment lease, appliance, jewelry), negotiate a better price and gain some concessions such as an extended warranty, smaller down payment, maintenance services, or the like.

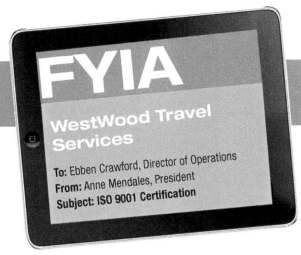

FYIA

WestWood Travel Services

To: Ebben Crawford, Director of Operations
From: Anne Mendales, President
Subject: ISO 9001 Certification

For Your Immediate Action

I've been doing a lot of reading on total quality management and I think we need to look at using TQM principles. Since our business has grown from one office to five offices with nearly 50 employees, I want to ensure that we're doing everything we can to meet our clients' needs, especially since we've lost some clients to competitors. Could you do an analysis describing how we might apply the concepts of customer focus, continuous process improvement, benchmarking, training, teamwork, and empowerment to our travel business to make us more competitive? Write up your analysis in a bulleted list format (no more than two pages please) and get it to me by the end of the week.

This fictionalized company and message were created for educational purposes only, and not meant to reflect positively or negatively on management practices by any company that may share this name.

Bringing the Real World to Life

Case Application:
Stirring Things Up: Part 2

Starbucks products have become an unaffordable luxury for many. As revenues and profits declined during the economic downturn, CEO Howard Schultz realized that "the company needed to change almost everything about how it operates." Although it built its business as "the anti-fast-food joint," the recession and growing competition forced Starbucks to become more streamlined. Under one new initiative put into effect at its U.S. stores, employee time wasters such as bending over to scoop coffee from below the counter, idly standing by waiting for expired coffee to drain, or dawdling at the pastry case were discouraged. Instead, employees were to keep busy doing something, such as helping customers or cleaning. At one of the first stores to implement the "lean" techniques, the store manager looked for ways for her employees to be more efficient with simple things like keeping items in the same place, moving drink toppings closer to where drinks are handed to customers, and altering the order of assembly. After two months under the new

methods, her store experienced a 10 percent increase in transactions.

Another thing that Schultz did that was quite unprecedented was to close every one of its stores for three hours on one Tuesday evening to train ALL of their some 135,000 baristas (a barista is a person who prepares and serves espresso-based coffee drinks). During that training, baristas were reminded that "pouring espresso is an art. If poured too fast from the spout into a shot glass, the espresso's flavor will be weak and the body will be thin. A shot poured too slow means the grind is too fine, and the flavor will be bitter. The perfect shot looks like honey pouring from a spoon. It is dense and tastes caramely sweet." Despite warnings that closing the stores would be a public relations nightmare and a financial mistake, the decision seemed to be a sound one. In the weeks following the retraining, quality scores for the company's beverages went up and stayed there.

DISCUSSION QUESTIONS

1. Would you describe production/operations technology in Starbucks retail stores as unit, mass, or process? Explain your choice. How does its production/operations technology approach affect the way products are produced?

2. What uncertainties does Starbucks face in its value chain? Can Starbucks manage those uncertainties? If so, how? If not, why not?

3. Go the company's Web site at www.starbucks.com and find the information on the company's environmental activities from bean to cup. Select one of the steps in the chain (or your professor may assign one). Describe what environmental actions it's taking. How might these affect the way Starbucks "produces" its products?

4. Research the concept of *lean organizations*. What benefits does "lean" offer? How might a business like Starbucks further utilize the concepts of being lean?

5. What lessons could other organizations learn from Starbucks' actions?

Entrepreneurship Module:
MANAGING ENTREPRENEURIAL VENTURES

MANAGING ENTREPRENEURIAL VENTURES

Russell Simmons is an entrepreneur. He cofounded Def Jam Records because the emerging group of New York hip-hop artists needed a record company, and the big record companies refused to take a chance on unknown artists. Def Jam was just one piece of Simmons's corporation, Rush Communications, which also included a management company; a clothing company called Phat Farm; a movie production house; television shows; a magazine; and an advertising agency. In 1999, Simmons sold his stake in Def Jam to Universal Music Group, and in 2004, he sold Phat Farm. Today, Simmons is involved in UniRush, a Cincinnati company that sells a prepaid Visa debit card and Russell Simmons Argyle Culture, a clothing line aimed at older men. *USA Today* named Simmons one of the top 25 Influential People while *Inc.* magazine named him one of America's 25 Most Fascinating Entrepreneurs.

In this appendix, we're going to look at the activities engaged in by entrepreneurs like Russell Simmons. We'll start by looking at the context of entrepreneurship and then examining entrepreneurship from the perspective of the four managerial functions: planning, organizing, leading, and controlling.

What Is Entrepreneurship?

Entrepreneurship is the process of starting new businesses, generally in response to opportunities. For instance, Fred Carl, founder of the Viking Range Corporation, saw an opportunity to create an appliance that combined the best features of commercial and residential ranges.

Many people think that entrepreneurial ventures and small businesses are the same, but they're not. Entrepreneurs create **entrepreneurial ventures**—organizations that pursue opportunities, are characterized by innovative practices, and have growth and profitability as their main goals. On the other hand, a **small business** is an independent business having fewer than 500 employees that doesn't necessarily engage in any new or innovative practices and that has relatively little impact on its industry. A small business isn't necessarily entrepreneurial because it's small. To be entrepreneurial means that the business is innovative and seeking out new opportunities. Even though entrepreneurial ventures may start small, they pursue growth. Some new small firms may grow, but many remain small businesses, by choice or by default.

Who's Starting Entrepreneurial Ventures?

"Call them accidental entrepreneurs, unintended entrepreneurs, or forced entrepreneurs." As the unemployment rate hovers around double digits, many corporate "refugees" are becoming entrepreneurs. These individuals are looking to entrepreneurship, not because they sense some great opportunity, but because there are no jobs. The Index of Entrepreneurial Activity by the Kauffman Foundation showed the rate at which new businesses formed in 2010 remained high, representing the "highest level of entrepreneurship over the past decade and a half." The report found that "the patterns provided some early evidence that 'necessity' entrepreneurship is increasing and 'opportunity' entrepreneurship is decreasing." But "accidental or by design," entrepreneurship is on the rise again.

As many entrepreneurs (successful and not-so-successful) would attest, being an entrepreneur isn't easy. According to the Small Business Administration, only two-thirds of new businesses survive at least two years. The survival rate falls to 44 percent at four years, and to 31 percent at seven. But the interesting thing is that entrepreneurial venture survival rates are about the same in economic expansions and recessions.

What Do Entrepreneurs Do?

Describing what entrepreneurs do isn't an easy or simple task! No two entrepreneurs' work activities are exactly alike. In a general sense, entrepreneurs create something new, something different. They search for change, respond to it, and exploit it.

Initially, an entrepreneur is engaged in assessing the potential for the entrepreneurial venture and then dealing with start-up issues. In exploring the entrepreneurial context, entrepreneurs gather information, identify potential opportunities, and pinpoint possible competitive advantage(s). Then, armed with this information, an entrepreneur researches the venture's feasibility—uncovering business ideas, looking at competitors, and exploring financing options.

After looking at the potential of the proposed venture and assessing the likelihood of pursuing it successfully, an entrepreneur proceeds to plan the venture. This process includes such activities as developing a viable organizational mission, exploring organizational culture issues, and creating a well-thought-out business plan. Once these planning issues have been resolved, the entrepreneur must look at organizing the venture, which involves choosing a legal form of business organization, addressing other legal issues such as patent or copyright searches, and coming up with an appropriate organizational design for structuring how work is going to be done.

Only after these start-up activities have been completed is the entrepreneur ready to actually launch the venture. A launch involves setting goals and strategies, and establishing the technology-operations methods, marketing plans, information systems, financial-accounting systems, and cash flow management systems.

Once the entrepreneurial venture is up and running, the entrepreneur's attention switches to managing it. What's involved with actually managing the entrepreneurial venture? An important activity is managing the various processes that are part of every business: making decisions, establishing action plans, analyzing external and internal environments, measuring and evaluating performance, and making needed changes. Also, the entrepreneur must perform activities associated with managing people including selecting and hiring, appraising and training, motivating, managing conflict, delegating tasks, and being an effective leader. Finally, the entrepreneur must manage the venture's growth including such activities as developing and designing growth strategies, dealing with crises, exploring various avenues for financing growth, placing a value on the venture, and perhaps even eventually exiting the venture.

What Planning Do Entrepreneurs Need to Do?

Planning is important to entrepreneurial ventures. Once a venture's feasibility has been thoroughly researched, an entrepreneur then must look at planning the venture. The most important thing that an entrepreneur does in planning the venture is developing a business plan—a written document that summarizes a business opportunity and defines and articulates how the identified opportunity is to be seized and exploited. A written business plan can range from basic to thorough. The most basic type of business plan would simply include an *executive summary,* sort of a mini-business plan that's no

---

entrepreneurship
The process of starting new businesses, generally in response to opportunities

entrepreneurial ventures
Organizations that pursue opportunities, are characterized by innovative practices, and have growth and profitability as their main goals

small business
An independent business having fewer than 500 employees that doesn't necessarily engage in any new or innovative practices and that has relatively little impact on its industry

business plan
A written document that summarizes a business opportunity and defines and articulates how the identified opportunity is to be seized and exploited

longer than two pages. A *synopsis* type plan is a little more involved. It's been described as an "executive summary on steroids." In addition to the executive summary, it includes a business proposal that explains why the idea is relevant to potential investors. A *summary business plan* includes an executive summary and a page or so of explanation of each of the key components of a business plan. A *full business plan* is the traditional business plan, which we describe fully next. Finally, an *operational business plan* is the most detailed (50 or more pages) that is used by ventures already operating with an existing strategy. It's often used to "plan the business" but also can be used to raise additional money or to attract potential acquirers. It's important for entrepreneurs to know which type of business plan they need for their purposes.

What's in a Full Business Plan?

For many would-be entrepreneurs, developing and writing a business plan seems like a daunting task. However, a good business plan is valuable. It pulls together all of the elements of the entrepreneur's vision into a single coherent document. The business plan requires careful planning and creative thinking. But if done well, it can be a convincing document that serves many functions. It serves as a blueprint and road map for operating the business. And the business plan is a "living" document, guiding organizational decisions and actions throughout the life of the business, not just in the start-up stage.

If an entrepreneur has completed a feasibility study, much of the information included in it becomes the basis for the business plan. A good business plan covers six major areas: executive summary, analysis of opportunity, analysis of the context, description of the business, financial data and projections, and supporting documentation.

> *Executive summary.* The executive summary summarizes the key points that the entrepreneur wants to make about the proposed entrepreneurial venture. These might include a brief mission statement; primary goals; brief history of the entrepreneurial venture, maybe in the form of a timeline; key people involved in the venture; nature of the business; concise product or service descriptions; brief explanations of market niche, competitors, and competitive advantage; proposed strategies; and selected key financial information.

> *Analysis of opportunity.* In this section of the business plan, an entrepreneur presents the details of the perceived opportunity, which essentially includes (1) sizing up the market by describing the demographics of the target market; (2) describing and evaluating industry trends; and (3) identifying and evaluating competitors.

> *Analysis of the context.* Whereas the opportunity analysis focuses on the opportunity in a specific industry and market, the context analysis takes a much broader perspective. Here, the entrepreneur describes the broad external changes and trends taking place in the economic, political-legal, technological, and global environments.

> *Description of the business.* In this section, an entrepreneur describes how the entrepreneurial venture is going to be organized, launched, and managed. It includes a thorough description of the mission statement; a description of the desired organizational culture; marketing plans including overall marketing strategy, pricing, sales tactics, service-warranty policies, and advertising and promotion tactics; product development plans such as an explanation of development status, tasks, difficulties and risks, and anticipated costs; operational plans, including a description of proposed geographic location, facilities and needed improvements, equipment, and work flow; human resource plans, including a description of key management persons, composition of board of directors including their background experience and skills, current and future staffing needs, compensation and benefits, and training needs; and an overall schedule and timetable of events.

> *Financial data and projections.* Every effective business plan contains financial data and projections. Although the calculations and interpretation may be

difficult, they are absolutely critical. No business plan is complete without financial information. Financial plans should cover at least three years and contain projected income statements, pro forma cash flow analysis (monthly for the first year and quarterly for the next two), pro forma balance sheets, breakeven analysis, and cost controls. If major equipment or other capital purchases are expected, the items, costs, and available collateral should be listed. All financial projections and analyses should include explanatory notes, especially where the data seem contradictory or questionable.

Supporting documentation. This *is* an important component of an effective business plan. The entrepreneur should back up his or her descriptions with charts, graphs, tables, photographs, or other visual tools. In addition, it might be important to include information (personal and work-related) about the key participants in the entrepreneurial venture.

Just as the idea for an entrepreneurial venture takes time to germinate, so does the writing of a good business plan. It's important for an entrepreneur to put serious thought and consideration into the plan. It's not an easy thing to do. However, the resulting document should be valuable in current and future planning efforts.

What Issues Are Involved in Organizing an Entrepreneurial Venture?

Once the start-up and planning issues for the entrepreneurial venture have been addressed, the entrepreneur is ready to begin organizing the entrepreneurial venture. The main organizing issues an entrepreneur must address include the legal forms of organization, organizational design and structure, and human resource management.

What Are the Legal Forms of Organization for Entrepreneurial Ventures?

The first organizing decision that an entrepreneur must make is a critical one. It's the form of legal ownership for the venture. The two primary factors affecting this decision are taxes and legal liability. An entrepreneur wants to minimize the impact of both of these factors. The right choice can protect the entrepreneur from legal liability as well as save tax dollars, in both the short run and the long run.

The three basic ways to organize an entrepreneurial venture are sole proprietorship, partnership, and corporation. However, when you include the variations of these basic organizational alternatives, you end up with six possible choices, each with its own tax consequences, liability issues, and pros and cons. These six choices are sole proprietorship, general partnership, limited liability partnership (LLP), C corporation, S corporation, and limited liability company (LLC).

The decision regarding the legal form of organization is important because it has significant tax and liability consequences. Although the legal form of organization can be changed, it's not easy to do. An entrepreneur needs to think carefully about what's important, especially in the areas of flexibility, taxes, and amount of personal liability in choosing the best form of organization.

What Type of Organizational Structure Should Entrepreneurial Ventures Use?

The choice of an appropriate organizational structure is also an important decision when organizing an entrepreneurial venture. At some point, successful entrepreneurs find that they can't do everything. They need people. The entrepreneur must then decide on the most appropriate structural arrangement for effectively and efficiently carrying out the organization's activities. Without a suitable type of organizational structure, an entrepreneurial venture may soon find itself in a chaotic situation.

In many small firms, the organizational structure tends to evolve with very little intentional and deliberate planning by the entrepreneur. For the most part, the structure may be very simple—one person does whatever is needed. As an entrepreneurial venture grows and the entrepreneur finds it increasingly difficult to go it alone, employees are brought on board to perform certain functions or duties that the entrepreneur can't handle. As the company continues to grow, these individuals tend to perform those same functions. Soon, each functional area may require managers and employees.

As the venture evolves to a more deliberate structure, an entrepreneur faces a whole new set of challenges. All of a sudden, he or she must share decision making and operating responsibilities, which are typically the most difficult things for an entrepreneur to do—letting go and allowing someone else to make decisions. *After all*, he or she reasons, *how can anyone know this business as well as I do?* Also, what might have been a fairly informal, loose, and flexible atmosphere that worked well when the organization was small may no longer be effective. Many entrepreneurs are greatly concerned about keeping that "small company" atmosphere alive even as the venture grows and evolves into a more structured arrangement. But having a structured organization doesn't necessarily mean giving up flexibility, adaptability, and freedom. In fact, the structural design may be as fluid as the entrepreneur feels comfortable with and yet still have the rigidity it needs to operate efficiently.

Organizational design decisions in entrepreneurial ventures also revolve around the six elements of organizational structure: work specialization, departmentalization, chain of command, span of control, amount of centralization-decentralization, and amount of formalization. Decisions about these six elements will determine whether an entrepreneur designs a more mechanistic or organic organizational structure. When would each be preferable? A mechanistic structure would be preferable when cost efficiencies are critical to the venture's competitive advantage; when more control over employees' work activities is important; if the venture produces standardized products in a routine fashion; and when the external environment is relatively stable and certain. An organic structure would be most appropriate when innovation is critical to the organization's competitive advantage; for smaller organizations where rigid approaches to dividing and coordinating work aren't necessary; if the organization produces customized products in a flexible setting; and where the external environment is dynamic, complex, and uncertain.

What Human Resource Management (HRM) Issues Do Entrepreneurs Face?

As an entrepreneurial venture grows, additional employees must be hired to perform the increased workload. As employees are brought on board, two HRM issues of particular importance are employee recruitment and employee retention.

An entrepreneur wants to ensure that the venture has the people to do the required work. Recruiting new employees is one of the biggest challenges that entrepreneurs face. In fact, the ability of small firms to successfully recruit appropriate employees is consistently rated as one of the most important factors influencing organizational success.

Entrepreneurs, particularly, look for high-potential people who can perform multiple roles during various stages of venture growth. They look for individuals who "buy into" the venture's entrepreneurial culture—individuals who have a passion for the business. Unlike their corporate counterparts who often focus on filling a job by matching a person to the job requirements, entrepreneurs look to fill in critical skills gaps. They're looking for people who are exceptionally capable and self-motivated, flexible, multi-skilled, and who can help grow the entrepreneurial venture. While corporate managers tend to focus on using traditional HRM practices and techniques, entrepreneurs are more concerned with matching characteristics of the person to the values and culture of the organization; that is, they focus on matching the person to the organization.

Getting competent and qualified people into the venture is just the first step in effectively managing the human resources. An entrepreneur wants to keep the people he or she has hired and trained. A unique and important employee retention issue entrepreneurs must deal with is compensation. Whereas traditional organizations are more likely to view compensation from the perspective of monetary rewards (base pay, benefits, and incentives), smaller entrepreneurial firms are more likely to view compensation from a total rewards perspective. For these firms, compensation encompasses psychological rewards, learning opportunities, and recognition in addition to monetary rewards (base pay and incentives).

What Issues Do Entrepreneurs Face in Leading an Entrepreneurial Venture?

Leading is an important function of entrepreneurs. As an entrepreneurial venture grows and people are brought on board, an entrepreneur takes on a new role—that of a leader. In this section, we want to look at what's involved with that. First, we're going to look at the unique personality characteristics of entrepreneurs. Then we're going to discuss the important role entrepreneurs play in motivating employees through empowerment and leading the venture and employee teams.

What Type of Personality Do Entrepreneurs Have?

Think of someone you know who is an entrepreneur. Maybe it's someone you personally know or maybe it's someone you've read about, like Bill Gates of Microsoft. How would you describe this person's personality? One of the most researched areas of entrepreneurship has been the search to determine what—if any—psychological characteristics entrepreneurs have in common; what types of personality traits entrepreneurs have that might distinguish them from non-entrepreneurs; and what traits entrepreneurs have that might predict who will be a successful entrepreneur.

Is there a classic "entrepreneurial personality"? Although trying to pinpoint specific personality characteristics that all entrepreneurs share has the same problem as identifying the trait theories of leadership—that is, being able to identify specific personality traits that *all* entrepreneurs share—this hasn't stopped entrepreneurship researchers from listing common traits. For instance, one list of personality characteristics included the following: high level of motivation, abundance of self-confidence, ability to be involved for the long term, high energy level, persistent problem solver, high degree of initiative, ability to set goals, and moderate risk-taker. Another list of characteristics of "successful" entrepreneurs included high energy level, great persistence, resourcefulness, the desire and ability to be self-directed, and relatively high need for autonomy.

Another development in defining entrepreneurial personality characteristics was the proactive personality scale to predict an individual's likelihood of pursuing entrepreneurial ventures. The **proactive personality** is a personality trait describing those individuals who are more prone to take actions to influence their environment—that is, they're more proactive. Obviously, an entrepreneur is likely to exhibit proactivity as he or she searches for opportunities and acts to take advantage of those opportunities. Various items on the proactive personality scale were found to be good indicators of a person's likelihood of becoming an entrepreneur, including gender, education, having an entrepreneurial parent, and possessing a proactive personality. In addition, studies have shown that entrepreneurs have greater risk propensity than do managers. However, this propensity is moderated by the entrepreneur's primary goal. Risk propensity is greater for entrepreneurs whose primary goal is growth versus those whose focus is on producing family income.

proactive personality
A personality trait describing those individuals who are more prone to take actions to influence their environment

How Can Entrepreneurs Motivate Employees?

When you're motivated to do something, don't you find yourself energized and willing to work hard at doing whatever it is you're excited about? Wouldn't it be great if all of a venture's employees were energized, excited, and willing to work hard at their jobs? Having motivated employees is an important goal for any entrepreneur, and employee empowerment is an important motivational tool entrepreneurs can use.

Although it's not easy for entrepreneurs to do, employee empowerment—giving employees the power to make decisions and take actions on their own—is an important motivational approach. Why? Because successful entrepreneurial ventures must be quick and nimble, ready to pursue opportunities and go off in new directions. Empowered employees can provide that flexibility and speed. When employees are empowered, they often display stronger work motivation, better work quality, higher job satisfaction, and lower turnover.

Empowerment is a philosophical concept that entrepreneurs have to "buy into." It doesn't come easily. In fact, it's hard for many entrepreneurs to do. Their life is tied up in the business. They've built it from the ground up. But continuing to grow the entrepreneurial venture is eventually going to require handing over more responsibilities to employees. How can entrepreneurs empower employees? For many entrepreneurs, it's a gradual process.

Entrepreneurs can begin by using participative decision making in which employees provide input into decisions. Although getting employees to participate in decisions isn't quite taking the full plunge into employee empowerment, at least it's a way to begin tapping into the collective array of employees' talents, skills, knowledge, and abilities.

Another way to empower employees is through delegation—the process of assigning certain decisions or specific job duties to employees. By delegating decisions and duties, the entrepreneur is turning over the responsibility for carrying them out.

When an entrepreneur is finally comfortable with the idea of employee empowerment, fully empowering employees means redesigning their jobs so they have discretion over the way they do their work. It's allowing employees to do their work effectively and efficiently by using their creativity, imagination, knowledge, and skills.

If an entrepreneur implements employee empowerment properly—that is, with complete and total commitment to the program and with appropriate employee training—results can be impressive for the entrepreneurial venture and for the empowered employees. The business can enjoy significant productivity gains, quality improvements, more satisfied customers, increased employee motivation, and improved morale. Employees can enjoy the opportunities to do a greater variety of work that is more interesting and challenging.

How Can Entrepreneurs Be Leaders?

The last topic we want to discuss in this section is the role of an entrepreneur as a leader. In this role, the entrepreneur has certain leadership responsibilities in leading the venture and in leading employee work teams.

Today's successful entrepreneur must be like the leader of a jazz ensemble known for its improvisation, innovation, and creativity. Max DePree, former head of Herman Miller, Inc., a leading office furniture manufacturer known for its innovative leadership approaches, said it best in his book, *Leadership Jazz*, "Jazz band leaders must choose the music, find the right musicians, and perform—in public. But the effect of the performance depends on so many things—the environment, the volunteers playing the band, the need for everybody to perform as individuals and as a group, the absolute dependence of the leader on the members of the band, the need for the followers to play well. . . . The leader of the jazz band has the beautiful opportunity to draw the best out of the other musicians. We have much to learn from jazz band leaders, for jazz, like leadership, combines the unpredictability of the future with the gifts of individuals."

The way an entrepreneur leads the venture should be much like the jazz leader—drawing the best out of other individuals, even given the unpredictability of the situation. One way an entrepreneur does this is through the vision he or she creates for the organization.

In fact, the driving force through the early stages of the entrepreneurial venture is often the visionary leadership of the entrepreneur. The entrepreneur's ability to articulate a coherent, inspiring, and attractive vision of the future is a key test of his or her leadership. But if an entrepreneur can do this, the results can be worthwhile. A study contrasting visionary and nonvisionary companies showed that visionary companies outperformed the nonvisionary ones by six times on standard financial criteria, and their stocks outperformed the general market by 15 times.

Many organizations—entrepreneurial and otherwise—are using employee work teams to perform organizational tasks, create new ideas, and resolve problems. The three most common types of employee work teams in entrepreneurial ventures are empowered teams (teams that have the authority to plan and implement process improvements), self-directed teams (teams that are nearly autonomous and responsible for many managerial activities), and cross-functional teams (work teams composed of individuals from various specialties who work together on various tasks).

Developing and using teams is necessary because technology and market demands are forcing entrepreneurial ventures to make products faster, cheaper, and better. Tapping into the collective wisdom of a venture's employees and empowering them to make decisions just may be one of the best ways to adapt to change. In addition, a team culture can improve the overall workplace environment and morale. For team efforts to work, however, entrepreneurs must shift from the traditional command-and-control style to a coach-and-collaboration style.

What Controlling Issues Do Entrepreneurs Face?

Entrepreneurs must look at controlling their venture's operations in order to survive and prosper in both the short run and long run. The unique control issues that face entrepreneurs include managing growth, managing downturns, exiting the venture, and managing personal life choices and challenges.

How Is Growth Managed?

Growth is a natural and desirable outcome for entrepreneurial ventures. Growth is what distinguishes an entrepreneurial venture. Entrepreneurial ventures pursue growth. Growing slowly can be successful, but so can rapid growth.

Growing successfully doesn't occur randomly or by luck. Successfully pursuing growth typically requires an entrepreneur to manage all the challenges associated with growing, which entails planning, organizing, and controlling for growth.

How Are Downturns Managed?

Although organizational growth is a desirable and important goal for entrepreneurial ventures, what happens when things don't go as planned—when the growth strategies don't result in the intended outcomes and, in fact, result in a decline in performance? There are challenges, as well, in managing the downturns.

Nobody likes to fail, especially entrepreneurs. However, when an entrepreneurial venture faces times of trouble, what can be done? How can downturns be managed successfully? The first step is recognizing that a crisis is brewing. An entrepreneur should be alert to the warning signs of a business in trouble. Some signals of potential performance decline include inadequate or negative cash flow, excess number of employees, unnecessary and cumbersome administrative procedures, fear of conflict and taking risks, tolerance of work incompetence, lack of a clear mission or goals, and ineffective or poor communication within the organization.

Although an entrepreneur hopes to never have to deal with organizational downturns, declines, or crises, these situations do occur. After all, nobody likes to think about things going bad or taking a turn for the worse. But that's exactly what the entrepreneur should do—think about it *before* it happens. It's important to have an up-to-date plan for covering crises. It's like mapping exit routes from your home in case of a fire. An entrepreneur wants to be prepared before an emergency hits. This plan should focus on providing specific details for controlling the most fundamental and critical aspects of running the venture—cash flow, accounts receivable, costs, and debt. Beyond having a plan for controlling the venture's critical inflows and outflows, other actions would involve identifying specific strategies for cutting costs and restructuring the venture.

What's Involved with Exiting the Venture?

Getting out of an entrepreneurial venture may seem to be a strange thing for entrepreneurs to do. However, the entrepreneur may come to a point at which he or she decides it's time to move on. That decision may be based on the fact that the entrepreneur hopes to capitalize financially on the investment in the venture—called harvesting—or that the entrepreneur is facing serious organizational performance problems and wants to get out, or even on the entrepreneur's desire to focus on other pursuits (personal or business). The issues involved with exiting the venture include choosing a proper business valuation method and knowing what's involved in the process of selling a business.

Although the hardest part of preparing to exit a venture may involve valuing it, other factors are also important. These include being prepared, deciding who will sell the business, considering the tax implications, screening potential buyers, and deciding whether to tell employees before or after the sale. The process of exiting the entrepreneurial venture should be approached as carefully as the process of launching it. If the entrepreneur is selling the venture on a positive note, he or she wants to realize the value built up in the business. If the venture is being exited because of declining performance, the entrepreneur wants to maximize the potential return.

Why Is It Important to Think About Managing Personal Challenges as an Entrepreneur?

Being an entrepreneur is extremely exciting and fulfilling, yet extremely demanding. It involves long hours, difficult demands, and high stress. Yet, many rewards can come with being an entrepreneur as well. In this section, we want to look at how entrepreneurs can make it work—that is, how can they be successful and effectively balance the demands of their work and personal lives?

Entrepreneurs are a special group. They're focused, persistent, hardworking, and intelligent. Because they put so much of themselves into launching and growing their entrepreneurial ventures, many may neglect their personal lives. Entrepreneurs often have to make sacrifices to pursue their entrepreneurial dreams. However, they can make it work. They can balance their work and personal lives. But how?

One of the most important things an entrepreneur can do is *become a good time manager*. Prioritize what needs to be done. Use a planner (daily, weekly, monthly) to help schedule priorities. Some entrepreneurs don't like taking the time to plan or prioritize, or they think it's a ridiculous waste of time. Yet identifying the important duties and distinguishing them from those that aren't so important actually makes an entrepreneur more efficient and effective. In addition, part of being a good time manager is delegating those decisions and actions the entrepreneur doesn't have to be personally involved in to trusted employees. Although it may be hard to let go of some of the things they've always done, entrepreneurs who delegate effectively will see their personal productivity levels rise.

Another suggestion for finding that balance is to *seek professional advice* in those areas of business where it's needed. Although entrepreneurs may be reluctant to spend scarce cash, the time, energy, and potential problems saved in the long run are well worth the investment. Competent professional advisers can provide entrepreneurs with information to make more intelligent decisions. Also, it's important to *deal with conflicts* as they arise—both workplace and family conflicts. If an entrepreneur doesn't deal with conflicts, negative feelings are likely to crop up and lead to communication breakdowns. When communication falls apart, vital information may get lost, and people (employees *and* family members) may start to assume the worst. It can turn into a nightmare situation that feeds upon itself. The best strategy is to deal with conflicts as they come up. Talk, discuss, argue (if you must), but an entrepreneur shouldn't avoid the conflict or pretend it doesn't exist.

Another suggestion for achieving that balance between work and personal life is to *develop a network of trusted friends and peers.* Having a group of people to talk with is a good way for an entrepreneur to think through problems and issues. The support and encouragement offered by these people can be an invaluable source of strength for an entrepreneur.

Finally, *recognize when your stress levels are too high.* Entrepreneurs *are* achievers. They like to make things happen. They thrive on working hard. Yet, too much stress can lead to significant physical and emotional problems. Entrepreneurs have to learn when stress is overwhelming them and to do something about it. After all, what's the point of growing and building a thriving entrepreneurial venture if you're not around to enjoy it?

Sources: Entrepreneurship Module based on T. Padgett, "Russell Simmons: Getting Rich Is So Simple," *CNNMoney.com,* April 29, 2011; R. Schmidt and P. O'Connor, "Def Jam's Founder Out-Lobbies Big Banks," *Bloomberg BusinessWeek,* June 28, 2010, pp. 21–22; R. A. Smith, "From Phat to Skinny," *Wall Street Journal,* May 1, 2010, p. W7; J. Dean, "The Endless Flow of Russell Simmons," *Entrepreneur,* September 2009, pp. 24–28; S. Page, "Top 25 Influential People," *USA Today,* September 4, 2007, p. A10; S. Berfield, "Hip-Hop Nation," *BusinessWeek,* June 13, 2005, p. 12; R. Kurtz, "Russell Simmons, Rush Communications," *Inc.,* April 2004, p. 137; J. Reingold, "Rush Hour," *Fast Company,* November 2003, pp. 68–80; S. Berfield, "The CEO of Hip Hop," *BusinessWeek,* October 27, 2003, pp. 90–98; J. L. Roberts, "Beyond Definition," *Newsweek,* July 28, 2003, pp. 40–43; C. Dugas, "Hip-Hop Legend Far Surpassed Financial Goals," *USA Today,* May 15, 2003, p. 6B; "Jobless Entrepreneurship Tarnishes Steady Rate of U.S. Startup Activity, Kauffman Study Shows," www.kauffman.org/newsroom/ (March 7, 2011); "Frequently Asked Questions," *U.S. Small Business Administration,* www.sba.gov/advo (September 2008); D. E. Gumpert, "The Right Business Plan for the Job," *BusinessWeek Online,* January 7, 2008; W. H. Stewart, "Risk Propensity Differences Between Entrepreneurs and Managers: A Meta-Analytic Review," *Journal of Applied Psychology* (February 2001), pp. 145–153; I. O. Williamson, "Employer Legitimacy and Recruitment Success in Small Businesses," *Entrepreneurship Theory and Practice,* Fall 2000, pp. 27–42; R. L. Heneman, J. W. Tansky, and S. M. Camp, "Human Resource Management Practices in Small and Medium-Sized Enterprises: Unanswered Questions and Future Research Perspectives," *Entrepreneurship Theory and Practice,* Fall 2000, pp. 11–26; T. L. Hatten, *Small Business: Entrepreneurship and Beyond* (Upper Saddle River, NJ: Prentice Hall, 1997), p. 5; L. W. Busenitz, "Research on Entrepreneurial Alertness," *Journal of Small Business Management* (October 1996), pp. 35–44; J. M. Crant, "The Proactive Personality Scale as Predictor of Entrepreneurial Intentions," *Journal of Small Business Management* (July 1996), pp. 42–49; J. C. Collins and J. I. Porras, *Built to Last: Successful Habits of Visionary Companies* (New York: Harper Business, 1994); M. Depree, *Leadership Jazz* (New York: Currency Doubleday, 1992), pp. 8–9; P. B. Robinson, D. V. Simpson, J. C. Huefner, and H. K. Hunt, "An Attitude Approach to the Prediction of Entrepreneurship," *Entrepreneurship Theory and Practice,* Summer 1991, pp. 13–31; P. F. Drucker, *Innovation and Entrepreneurship: Practice and Principles* (New York: Harper & Row, 1985); and J. W. Carland, F. Hoy, W. R. Boulton, and J. C. Carland, "Differentiating Entrepreneurs from Small Business Owners: A Conceptualization," *Academy of Management Review,* 9, no. 2 (1984), pp. 354–359.

harvesting
Exiting a venture when an entrepreneur hopes to capitalize financially on the investment in the venture

Glossary

A

Absenteeism The failure to show up for work

Active listening Listening for full meaning without making premature judgments or interpretations

Activities Actions that take place

Adjourning The final stage of group development for temporary groups during which group members are concerned with wrapping up activities rather than task performance

Affective component That part of an attitude that's the emotional or feeling part

Affirmative action programs Programs that ensure that decisions and practices enhance the employment, upgrading, and retention of members of protected groups

Assumed similarity The assumption that others are like oneself

Attitudes Evaluative statements, either favorable or unfavorable, concerning objects, people, or events

Attribution theory A theory used to explain how we judge people differently depending on what meaning we attribute to a given behavior

Authority The rights inherent in a managerial position to give orders and expect the orders to be obeyed

Autocratic style A leader who dictates work methods, makes unilateral decisions, and limits employee participation

B

Balanced scorecard A performance measurement tool that looks at more than just the financial perspective

Basic corrective action Corrective action that looks at how and why performance deviated before correcting the source of deviation

Behavior The actions of people

Behavioral component That part of an attitude that refers to an intention to behave in a certain way toward someone or something

Behavioral theories Leadership theories that identify behaviors that differentiated effective leaders from ineffective leaders

Benchmarking The search for the best practices among competitors or noncompetitors that lead to their superior performance

Big Five Model Personality trait model that includes extraversion, agreeableness, conscientiousness, emotional stability, and openness to experience

Board representatives Employees who sit on a company's board of directors and represent the interest of employees

Body language Gestures, facial configurations, and other body movements that convey meaning

Boundaryless career When an individual takes personal responsibility for his or her own career

Boundaryless organization An organization whose design is not defined by, or limited to, boundaries imposed by a predefined structure

Bounded rationality Making decisions that are rational within the limits of a manager's ability to process information

Brainstorming An idea-generating process that encourages alternatives while withholding criticism

Break-even analysis A technique for identifying the point at which total revenue is just sufficient to cover total costs

Business plan A written document that summarizes a business opportunity and defines and articulates how the identified opportunity is to be seized and exploited

C

"Calm waters" metaphor A description of organizational change that likens that change to a large ship making a predictable trip across a calm sea and experiencing an occasional storm

Capabilities An organization's skills and abilities in doing the work activities needed in its business

Career The sequence of work positions held by a person during his or her lifetime development, then and now

Centralization The degree to which decision making takes place at upper levels of the organization

Certainty A situation in which a decision maker can make accurate decisions because all outcomes are known

Chain of command The line of authority extending from upper organizational levels to lower levels, which clarifies who reports to whom

Change agents People who act as change catalysts and assume the responsibility for managing the change process

Channel The medium a message travels along

Charismatic leader An enthusiastic, self-confident leader whose personality and actions influence people to behave in certain ways

Code of ethics A formal document that states an organization's primary values and the ethical rules it expects managers and nonmanagerial employees to follow

Cognitive component That part of an attitude that's made up of the beliefs, opinions, knowledge, or information held by a person

Cognitive dissonance Any incompatibility or inconsistency between attitudes or between behavior and attitudes

Commitment concept The idea that plans should extend far enough to meet those commitments made when the plans were developed

Communication The transfer and understanding of meaning

Communication process The seven elements involved in transferring meaning from one person to another

Communities of practice Groups of people who share a concern, a set of problems, or a passion about a topic, and who deepen their knowledge and expertise in that area by interacting on an ongoing basis

Compensation administration The process of determining a cost-effective pay structure that will attract and retain employees, provide an incentive for them to work hard, and ensure that pay levels will be perceived as fair

Competitive advantage What sets an organization apart; its distinctive edge

Competitive intelligence A type of environmental scanning that gives managers accurate information about competitors

Competitive strategy An organizational strategy for how an organization will compete in its business(es)

Compressed workweek A workweek in which employees work longer hours per day but fewer days per week

Conceptual skills A manager's ability to analyze and diagnose complex situations

Concurrent control Control that takes place while a work activity is in progress

Consideration The extent to which a leader has work relationships characterized by mutual trust and respect for group members' ideas and feelings

Contingency approach (or situational approach) An approach to management that says that organizations, employees, and situations are different and require different ways of managing

Contingent workers Temporary, freelance, or contract workers whose employment is contingent upon demand for their services

Contingent workforce Part-time, temporary, and contract workers who are available for hire on an as-needed basis

Control The management function that involves monitoring activities to ensure that they're being accomplished as planned and correcting any significant deviations

Controlling The process of monitoring performance, comparing it with goals, and correcting any significant deviations

Control process A three-step process of measuring actual performance, comparing actual performance against a standard, and taking managerial action to correct deviations or inadequate standards

Core competencies The major value-creating capabilities of an organization

Corporate social responsibility (or CSR) A business firm's intention, beyond its legal and economic obligations, to do the right things and act in ways that are good for society

Corporate strategies An organizational strategy that specifies what businesses a company is in or wants to be in and what it wants to do with those businesses

Cost leadership strategy When an organization competes on the basis of having the lowest costs in its industry

Creativity The ability to produce novel and useful ideas

Credibility The degree to which followers perceive someone as honest, competent, and able to inspire

Critical path The longest or most time-consuming sequence of events and activities required to complete a project in the shortest amount of time

Cross-functional team A work team composed of individuals from various functional specialties

Customer departmentalization Grouping activities by customer

D

Decentralization The degree to which lower-level managers provide input or actually make decisions

Decisional roles Entail making decisions or choices

Decision criteria Factors that are relevant in a decision

Decision implementation Putting a decision into action

Decision-making process A set of eight steps that includes identifying a problem, selecting a solution, and evaluating the effectiveness of the solution

Decision trees A diagram used to analyze a progression of decisions. When diagrammed, a decision tree looks like a tree with branches

Decoding Retranslating a sender's message

Demographics The characteristics of a population used for purposes of social studies

Departmentalization How jobs are grouped together

Differentiation strategy When an organization competes on the basis of having unique products that are widely valued by customers

Directional plans Plans that are flexible and set general guidelines

Discipline Actions taken by a manager to enforce an organization's standards and regulations

Distributive justice Perceived fairness of the amount and allocation of rewards among individuals

Divisional structure An organizational structure made up of separate business units or divisions

Division of labor (or job specialization) The breakdown of jobs into narrow, repetitive tasks

Downsizing The planned elimination of jobs in an organization

E

Economic order quantity (EOQ) A model that seeks to balance the costs involved in ordering and carrying inventory, thus minimizing total costs associated with carrying and ordering costs

Effectiveness Doing the right things, or completing activities so that organizational goals are attained

Efficiency Doing things right, or getting the most output from the least amount of inputs

Electronic meeting A type of nominal group technique in which participants are linked by computer

Emotional intelligence (EI) The ability to notice and to manage emotional cues and information

Employee assistance programs (EAPs) Programs offered by organizations to help employees overcome personal and health-related problems

Employee benefits Nonfinancial rewards designed to enrich employees' lives

Employee counseling A process designed to help employees overcome performance-related problems

Employee engagement When employees are connected to, satisfied with, and enthusiastic about their jobs

Employee oriented leader A leader who emphasizes the people aspects

Employee productivity A performance measure of both efficiency and effectiveness

Employee recognition programs Personal attention and expressing interest, approval, and appreciation for a job well done

Employee theft Any unauthorized taking of company property by employees for their personal use

Employee training A learning experience that seeks a relatively permanent change in employees by improving their ability to perform on the job

Employment planning The process by which managers ensure they have the right numbers and kinds of people in the right places at the right time

Empowerment The act of increasing the decision-making discretion of workers

Encoding Converting a message into symbols

Entrepreneurial ventures Organizations that are pursuing opportunities, are characterized by innovative practices, and have growth and profitability as their mai goals

Entrepreneurship The process of starting new businesses, generally in response to opportunities

Environmental complexity The number of components in an organization's environment and the extent of knowledge that the organization has about those components

Environmental scanning An analysis of the external environment that involves screening large amounts of information to detect emerging trends

Environmental uncertainty The degree of change and complexity in an organization's environment

Equity theory The theory that an employee compares his or her job's input–outcomes ratio with that of relevant others and then corrects any inequity

Escalation of commitment An increased commitment to a previous decision despite evidence that it may have been a poor decision

Ethical communication Communication that includes all relevant information, is true in every sense, and is not deceptive in any way

Ethics A set of rules or principles that defines right and wrong conduct

Ethnicity Social traits, such as one's cultural background or allegiance, that are shared by a human population

Events End points that represent the completion of major activities

Expectancy theory The theory that an individual tends to act in a certain way based on the expectation that the act will be followed by a given outcome and on the attractiveness of that outcome to the individual

Exporting Making products domestically and selling them abroad

External environment Factors, forces, situations, and events outside the organization that affect its performance

F

Family-friendly benefits Benefits that provide a wide range of scheduling options that allow employees more flexibility at work, accommodating their needs for work/life balance

Feedback Checking to see how successfully a message has been transferred

Feedback control Control that takes place after a work activity is done

Feedforward control Control that takes place before a work activity is done

Fiedler contingency model A leadership theory proposing that effective group performance depends upon the proper match between a leader's style and the degree to which the situation allows the leader to control and influence

Filtering The deliberate manipulation of information to make it appear more favorable to the receiver

First-line managers Supervisors responsible for directing the day-to-day activities of non-managerial employees

Fixed-point reordering system A method for a system to "flag" the need to reorder inventory at some pre-established point in the process

Flexible work hours A scheduling system in which employees are required to work a certain number of hours per week but are free, within limits, to vary the hours of work

Flextime A scheduling system in which employees are required to work a certain number of hours per week but are free, within limits, to vary the hours of work

Focus strategy When an organization competes in a narrow segment or niche with either a cost focus or a differentiation focus

Foreign subsidiary A direct investment in a foreign country that involves setting up a separate and independent facility or office

Formal planning department A group of planning specialists whose sole responsibility is to help write the various organizational plans

Forming stage The first stage of group development in which people join the group and then define the group's purpose, structure, and leadership

Franchising An agreement primarily used by service businesses in which an organization gives another organization the right, for a fee, to use its name and operating methods

Functional departmentalization Grouping activities by functions performed

Functional strategies The strategies used in an organization's various functional departments to support the competitive strategy

Functional structure An organizational design that groups similar or related occupational specialties together

Fundamental attribution error The tendency to underestimate the influence of external factors and overestimate the influence of internal factors when making judgments about the behavior of others

G

Gantt chart A planning tool that shows in bar graph form when tasks are supposed to be done and compares that with the actual progress on each

General administrative theorists Writers who developed general theories of what managers do and what constitutes good management practice

Geographic departmentalization Grouping activities on the basis of geography or territory

Global corporation An MNC that centralizes management and other decisions in the home country

Global Leadership and Organizational Behavior Effectiveness (GLOBE) A program that studies cross-cultural leadership behaviors

Global sourcing Purchasing materials or labor from around the world wherever it is cheapest

Global strategic alliance A partnership between an organization and a foreign company partner(s) in which resources and knowledge are shared in developing new products or building production facilities

Global village Refers to the concept of a boundaryless world where goods and services are produced and marketed worldwide

Goals (objectives) Desired outcomes or targets

Goal-setting theory The proposition that specific goals increase performance and that difficult goals, when accepted, result in higher performance than do easy goals

Grapevine The informal organizational communication network

Group Two or more interacting and interdependent individuals who come together to achieve specific goals

Group cohesiveness The degree to which group members are attracted to one another and share the group's goals

Groupthink When a group exerts extensive pressure on an individual to withhold his or her different views in order to appear to be in agreement

Growth strategy A corporate strategy in which an organization expands the number of markets served or products offered either through its current business(es) or through new business(es)

H

Halo effect A general impression of an individual based on a single characteristic

Harvesting Exiting a venture when an entrepreneur hopes to capitalize financially on the investment in the venture

Hawthorne studies Research done in the late 1920s and early 1930s devised by Western Electric industrial engineers to examine the effect of different work environment changes on worker productivity, which led to a new emphasis on the human factor in the functioning of organizations and the attainment of their goals

Heuristics Judgmental shortcuts or "rules of thumb" used to simplify decision making

Hierarchy of needs theory Maslow's theory that human needs—physiological, safety, social, esteem, and self-actualization—form a sort of hierarchy

Human resource inventory A report listing important information about employees such as name, education, training, skills, languages spoken, and so forth

Human resource management (HRM) The management function concerned with getting, training, motivating, and keeping competent employees

Hygiene factors Factors that eliminate job dissatisfaction, but don't motivate

I

Idea champions Individuals who actively and enthusiastically support new ideas, build support for, overcome resistance to, and ensure that innovations are implemented

Immediate corrective action Corrective action that corrects problems at once to get performance back on track

Importing Acquiring products made abroad and selling them domestically

Industrial Revolution The advent of machine power, mass production, and efficient transportation begun in the late eighteenth century in Great Britain

Informational roles Involve collecting, receiving, and disseminating information

Information overload When information exceeds our processing capacity

Initiating structure The extent to which a leader defines his or her role and the roles of group members in attaining goals

Innovation The process of taking a creative idea and turning it into a useful product, service, or method of operation

Intergroup development Activities that attempt to make several work groups more cohesive

Interpersonal roles Involve people (subordinates and persons outside the organization) and other duties that are ceremonial and symbolic in nature

Interpersonal skills A manager's ability to work with, understand, mentor, and motivate others, both individually and in groups

Intuitive decision making Making decisions on the basis of experience, feelings, and accumulated judgment

ISO 9000 A series of international quality standards that set uniform guidelines for processes to ensure that products conform to customer requirements

J

Jargon Specialized terminology or technical language that members of a group use to communicate among themselves

Job analysis An assessment that defines jobs and the behaviors necessary to perform them

Job characteristics model (JCM) A framework for analyzing and designing jobs that identifies five primary core job dimensions, their interrelationships, and their impact on outcomes

Job description A written statement that describes a job

Job design The way tasks are combined to form complete jobs

Job enrichment The vertical expansion of a job by adding planning and evaluating responsibilities

Job involvement The degree to which an employee identifies with his or her job, actively participates in it, and considers his or her job performance to be important to self-worth

Job satisfaction An employee's general attitude toward his or her job

Job sharing When two or more people split (share) a full-time job

Job specialization (or division of labor) The breakdown of jobs into narrow, repetitive tasks

Job specification A written statement of the minimum qualifications that a person must possess to perform a given job successfully

Joint venture A specific type of strategic alliance in which the partners agree to form a separate, independent organization for some business purpose

K

Karoshi A Japanese term that refers to a sudden death caused by overworking

Knowledge management Cultivating a learning culture in which organizational members systematically gather knowledge and share it with others

L

Laissez-faire style A leader who lets the group make decisions and complete the work in whatever way it sees fit

Layoff-survivor sickness A set of attitudes, perceptions, and behaviors of employees who survive layoffs

Leader Someone who can influence others and who has managerial authority

Leader-member exchange theory (LMX) The leadership theory that says leaders create in-groups and out-groups and those in the in-group will have higher performance ratings, less turnover, and greater job satisfaction

Leader-participation model A leadership contingency theory that's based on a sequential set of rules for determining how much participation a leader uses in decision making according to different types of situations

Leadership A process of influencing a group to achieve goals

Leading Includes motivating employees, directing the activities of others, selecting the most effective communication channel, and resolving conflicts

Learning Any relatively permanent change in behavior that occurs as a result of experience

Learning organization An organization that has developed the capacity to continuously learn, adapt, and change

Least-preferred coworker (LPC) questionnaire A questionnaire that measures whether a leader is task or relationship oriented

Licensing An agreement primarily used by manufacturing businesses in which an organization gives another the right, for a fee, to make or sell its products, using its technology or product specification

Linear programming A mathematical technique that solves resource allocation problems

Line authority Authority that entitles a manager to direct the work of an employee

Load chart A modified version of a Gantt chart that lists either whole departments or specific resources

Locus of control The degree to which people believe they are masters of their own fate

Long-term plans Plans with a time frame beyond three years

M

Machiavellianism A measure of the degree to which people are pragmatic, maintain emotional distance, and believe that ends justify means

Management The process of getting things done, effectively and efficiently, through and with other people

Management by objectives (MBO) A process of setting mutually agreed-upon goals and using those goals to evaluate employee performance

Management by walking around A term used to describe when a manager is out in the work area interacting directly with employees

Management information system (MIS) A system used to provide management with needed information on a regular basis

Managerial grid A two-dimensional grid for appraising leadership styles

Managerial roles Specific categories of managerial behavior; often grouped under three primary headings: interpersonal relationships, transfer of information, and decision making

Managers Individuals in an organization who direct the activities of others

Mass production Large-batch manufacturing

Matrix structure A structure in which specialists from different functional departments are assigned to work on projects led by a project manager

Means-ends chain An integrated network of goals in which higher-level goals are linked to lower-level goals, which serve as the means for their accomplishment

Mechanistic organization A bureaucratic organization; a structure that's high in specialization, formalization, and centralization

Message A purpose to be conveyed

Middle managers Individuals who are typically responsible for translating goals set by top managers into specific details that lower-level managers will see get done

Mission A statement of an organization's purpose

Motivation The process by which a person's efforts are energized, directed, and sustained toward attaining a goal

Motivators Factors that increase job satisfaction and motivation

Multidomestic corporation An MNC that decentralizes management and other decisions to the local country where it's doing business

Multinational corporation (MNC) Any type of international company that maintains operations in multiple countries

Myers-Briggs Type Indicator (MBTI®) A personality assessment that uses four dimensions of personality to identify different personality types

N

Need for achievement (nAch) The drive to succeed and excel in relation to a set of standards

Need for affiliation (nAff) The desire for friendly and close interpersonal relationships

Need for power (nPow) The need to make others behave in a way that they would not have behaved otherwise

Network organization An organization that uses its own employees to do some work activities and networks of outside suppliers to provide other needed product components or work processes

Nominal group technique A decision-making technique in which group members are physically present but operate independently

Nonmanagerial employees People who work directly on a job or task and have no responsibility for overseeing the work of others

Nonprogrammed decision A unique and nonrecurring decision that requires a custom-made solution

Norming stage The third stage of group development, characterized by close relationships and cohesiveness

Norms Standards or expectations that are accepted and shared by a group's members

O

Omnipotent view of management The view that managers are directly responsible for an organization's success or failure

Open-book management A motivational approach in which an organization's financial statements (the "books") are shared with all employees

Open systems Systems that dynamically interact with its environment

Operant conditioning A theory of learning that says behavior is a function of its consequences

Operations management The transformation process that converts resources into finished goods and services

Opportunities Positive trends in the external environment

Organic organization A structure that's low in specialization, formalization, and centralization

Organization A systematic arrangement of people brought together to accomplish some specific purpose

Organizational behavior (OB) The field of study that researches the actions (behaviors) of people at work

Organizational change Any alteration of an organization's people, structure, or technology

Organizational citizenship behavior (OCB) Discretionary behavior that is not part of an employee's formal job requirements, but which promotes the effective functioning of the organization

Organizational commitment The degree to which an employee identifies with a particular organization and its goals and wishes to maintain membership in that organization

Organizational culture The shared values, principles, traditions, and ways of doing things that influence the way organizational members act

Organizational design When managers develop or change the organization's structure

Organization development (OD) Efforts that assist organizational members with a planned change by focusing on their attitudes and values

Organizing Includes determining what tasks are to be done, who is to do them, how the tasks are to be grouped, who reports to whom, and where decisions are to be made

Orientation Introducing a new employee to the job and the organization

P

Parochialism A narrow focus in which managers see things only through their own eyes and from their own perspective

Path-goal theory A leadership theory that says the leader's job is to assist followers in attaining their goals and to provide direction or support needed to ensure that their goals are compatible with the goals of the group or organization

Pay-for-performance programs Variable compensation plans that pay employees on the basis of some performance measure

Perception A process by which we give meaning to our environment by organizing and interpreting sensory impressions

Performance management system A system that establishes performance standards that are used to evaluate employee performance

Performance-simulation tests Selection devices based on actual job behaviors

Performing stage The fourth stage of group development when the group is fully functional and works on the group task

Personality A unique combination of emotional, thought, and behavioral patterns that affect how a person reacts to situations and interacts with others

PERT network analysis A flowchart-like diagram that depicts the sequence of activities needed to complete a project and the time or costs associated with each activity

Planning Includes defining goals, establishing strategy, and developing plans to coordinate activities

Plans Documents that outline how goals are going to be met

Policy A guideline for making decisions

Political skills A manager's ability to build a power base and establish the right connections

Power An individual's capacity to influence decisions

Principles of management Fayol's fundamental or universal principles of management practice

Proactive personality, A personality trait describing those individuals who are more prone to take actions to influence their environment

Problem A discrepancy between an existing and a desired state of affairs

Problem-solving team A team from the same department or functional area that's involved in efforts to improve work activities or to solve specific problems

Procedural justice Perceived fairness of the process used to determine the distribution of rewards

Procedure A series of interrelated, sequential steps used to respond to a structured problem

Process consultation Using outside consultants to assess organizational processes such as workflow, informal intra-unit relationships, and formal communication channels

Process departmentalization Grouping activities on the basis of work or customer flow

Process production Continuous flow of products being produced

Product departmentalization Grouping activities by major product areas

Production oriented leader A leader who emphasizes the technical or task aspects

Programmed decision A repetitive decision that can be handled using a routine approach

Project A one-time-only set of activities with a definite beginning and ending point

Project management The task of getting project activities done on time, within budget, and according to specifications

Project structure A structure in which employees continuously work on projects

Q

Quantitative approach The use of quantitative techniques to improve decision making

Queuing theory Also known as waiting line theory, it is a way of balancing the cost of having a waiting line versus the cost of maintaining the line.

R

Race The biological heritage (including physical characteristics, such as one's skin color and associated traits) that people use to identify themselves

Range of variation The acceptable parameters of variance between actual performance and the standard

Rational decision making Describes choices that are consistent and value-maximizing within specified constraints

Readiness The extent to which people have the ability and willingness to accomplish a specific task

Real goals Those goals an organization actually pursues as shown by what the organization's members are doing

Realistic job preview (RJP) A preview of a job that provides both positive and negative information about the job and the company

Recruitment Locating, identifying, and attracting capable applicants

Referent The persons, systems, or selves against which individuals compare themselves to assess equity

Reliability The degree to which a selection device measures the same thing consistently

Renewal strategies A corporate strategy that addresses declining organizational performance

Resources An organization's assets that it uses to develop, manufacture, and deliver products to its customers

Responsibility An obligation to perform assigned duties

Rights view of ethics View that says ethical decisions are made in order to respect and protect individual liberties and privileges

Ringisei Japanese consensus-forming group decisions

Risk A situation in which a decision maker is able to estimate the likelihood of certain outcomes

Role Behavior patterns expected of someone who occupies a given position in a social unit

Rule An explicit statement that tells employees what can or cannot be done

S

Satisfice Accepting solutions that are "good enough"

Scientific management The use of scientific methods to define the "one best way" for a job to be done

Selection process Screening job applicants to ensure that the most appropriate candidates are hired

Selective perception Selectively perceiving or hearing a communication based on your own needs, motivations, experiences, or other personal characteristics

Self-efficacy An individual's belief that he or she is capable of performing a task

Self-esteem (SE) An individual's degree of like or dislike for himself or herself

Self-managed work team A type of work team that operates without a manager and is responsible for a complete work process or segment

Self-monitoring A personality trait that measures the ability to adjust behavior to external situational factors

Self-serving bias The tendency for individuals to attribute their own successes to internal factors while putting the blame for failures on external factors

Sexual harassment Any unwanted action or activity of a sexual nature that explicitly or implicitly affects an individual's employment, performance, or work environment

Shaping behavior The process of guiding learning in graduated steps using reinforcement or lack of reinforcement

Short-term plans Plans with a time frame of one year or less

Simple structure An organizational design with low departmentalization, wide spans of control, authority centralized in a single person, and little formalization

Single-use plan A one-time plan specifically designed to meet the needs of a unique situation

Situational approach (or contingency approach) An approach to management that says that organizations, employees, and situations are different and require different ways of managing

Situational leadership theory (SLT) A leadership contingency theory that focuses on followers' readiness

Six Sigma A quality standard that establishes a goal of no more than 3.4 defects per million units or procedures

Skill-based pay A pay system that rewards employees for the job skills they demonstrate

Slack time The time difference between the critical path and all other paths

Small business An organization that is independently owned, operated, and financed; has fewer than 100 employees; doesn't necessarily engage in any new or innovative practices, and has relatively little impact on its industry

Social learning theory A theory of learning that says people can learn through observation and direct experience

Social loafing The tendency for individuals to expend less effort when working collectively than when working individually

Social obligation When a business firm engages in social actions because of its obligation to meet certain economic and legal responsibilities

Social responsibility A business firm's intention, beyond its legal and economic obligations, to do the right things and act in ways that are good for society

Social responsiveness When a business firm engages in social actions in response to some popular social need

Span of control The number of employees a manager can efficiently and effectively supervise

Specific plans Plans that are clearly defined and leave no room for interpretation

Stability strategy A corporate strategy in which an organization continues to do what it is currently doing

Staff authority Positions with some authority that have been created to support, assist, and advise those holding line authority

Stakeholders Any constituencies in an organization's environment that are affected by that organization's decisions actions

Standing plans Plans that are ongoing and provide guidance for activities performed repeatedly

Stated goals Official statements of what an organization says, and wants its stakeholders to believe, its goals are

Status A prestige grading, position, or rank within a group

Stereotyping Judging a person on the basis of one's perception of a group to which he or she belongs

Storming stage The second stage of group development, characterized by intragroup conflict

Strategic business units (SBUs) An organization's single businesses that are independent and formulate their own competitive strategies

Strategic management What managers do to develop an organization's strategies

Strategic management process A six-step process that encompasses strategy planning, implementation, and evaluation

Strategic plans Plans that apply to the entire organization and encompass the organization's overall goals

Strategies Plans for how the organization will do what it's in business to do, how it will compete successfully, and how it will attract its customers in order to achieve its goals

Strengths Any activities the organization does well or any unique resources that it has

Stress The adverse reaction people have to excessive pressure placed on them from extraordinary demands, constraints, or opportunities

Stressors Factors that cause stress

Strong culture Cultures in which the key values are deeply held and widely shared

493

Structured problem A straightforward, familiar, and easily defined problem

Survey feedback A method of assessing employees' attitudes toward and perceptions of a change

Sustainability A company's ability to achieve its business goals and increase long-term shareholder value by integrating economic, environmental, and social opportunities into its business strategies

SWOT analysis The combined external and internal analyses

Symbolic view of management The view that much of an organization's success or failure is due to external forces outside managers' control

Systems approach An approach to management that views an organization as a system, which is a set of interrelated and interdependent parts arranged in a manner that produces a unified whole

T

Tactical plans Plans that specify the details of how the overall goals are to be achieved

Team building Using activities to help work groups set goals, develop positive interpersonal relationships, and clarify the roles and responsibilities of each team member

Team structure A structure in which the entire organization is made up of work teams

Technical skills Job-specific knowledge and techniques needed to perform work tasks

Technology Any equipment, tools, or operating methods that are designed to make work more efficient

Telecommuting A job approach in which employees work at home but are linked by technology to the workplace

Theory of justice view of ethics View that says ethical decisions are made in order to enforce rules fairly and impartially

Theory X The assumption that employees dislike work, are lazy, avoid responsibility, and must be coerced to perform

Theory Y The assumption that employees are creative, enjoy work, seek responsibility, and can exercise self-direction

Threats Negative trends in the external environment

Three needs theory The motivation theory that says three acquired (not innate) needs—achievement, power, and affiliation—are major motives in work

360-degree appraisal An appraisal device that seeks feedback from a variety of sources for the person being rated

Top managers Individuals who are responsible for making decisions about the direction of the organization and establishing policies that affect all organizational member

Total quality management (TQM) A management philosophy devoted to continual improvement and responding to customer needs and expectations

Traditional goal setting Goals set by top managers flow down through the organization and become subgoals for each organizational area

Trait theories of leadership Theories that isolate characteristics (traits) that differentiate leaders from nonleaders

Transactional leaders Leaders who lead primarily by using social exchanges (or transactions)

Transformational leaders Leaders who stimulate and inspire (transform) followers to achieve extraordinary outcomes

Transnational (borderless) organization A structural arrangement for global organizations that eliminates artificial geographical barriers

Trust The belief in the integrity, character, and ability of a leader

Turnover The voluntary and involuntary permanent withdrawal from an organization

Two-factor theory The motivation theory that intrinsic factors are related to job satisfaction and motivation, whereas extrinsic factors are associated with job dissatisfaction

Type A personality People who have a chronic sense of urgency and an excessive competitive drive

Type B personality People who are relaxed and easygoing and accept change easily

U

Uncertainty A situation in which a decision maker has neither certainty nor reasonable probability estimates available

Unit production The production of items in units or small batches

Unity of command The management principle that no person should report to more than one boss

Unstructured problem A problem that is new or unusual for which information is ambiguous or incomplete

Utilitarian view of ethics View that says ethical decisions are made solely on the basis of their outcomes or consequences

V

Validity The proven relationship between a selection device and some relevant criterion

Value The performance characteristics, features, and attributes, and any other aspects of goods and services for which customers are willing to give up resources

Value chain The entire series of organizational work activities that add value at each step from raw materials to finished product

Value chain management The process of managing the sequence of activities and information along the entire value chain

Variable pay A pay system in which an individual's compensation is contingent on performance

Verbal intonation An emphasis given to words or phrases that conveys meaning

Virtual organization An organization that consists of a small core of full-time employees and outside specialists temporarily hired as needed to work on projects

Virtual team A type of work team that uses technology to link physically dispersed members in order to achieve a common goal

Visionary leadership The ability to create and articulate a realistic, credible, and attractive vision of the future that improves upon the present situation

W

Weaknesses Activities the organization doesn't do well or resources it needs but doesn't possess

Wellness programs Programs offered by organizations to help employees prevent health problems

"White-water rapids" metaphor of change A description of organizational change that likens that change to a large ship making a predictable trip across a calm sea and experiencing an occasional storm

Work councils Groups of nominated or elected employees who must be consulted when management makes decisions involving personnel

Workforce diversity Ways in which people in a workforce are similar and different from one another in terms of gender, age, race, sexual orientation, ethnicity, cultural background, and physical abilities and disabilities

Workplace misbehavior Any intentional employee behavior that is potentially damaging to the organization or to individuals within the organization

Workplace spirituality A spiritual culture where organizational values promote a sense of purpose through meaningful work that takes place in the context of community

Work specialization Dividing work activities into separate job tasks; also called division of labor

Work teams Groups whose members work intensely on a specific, common goal using their positive synergy, individual and mutual accountability, and complementary skills

Index